Universal Usability

Designing Computer Interfaces for
Diverse User Populations

Universal Usability

Designing Computer Interfaces for
Diverse User Populations

Edited by Jonathan Lazar

John Wiley & Sons, Ltd

Copyright © 2007   John Wiley & Sons Ltd, The Atrium, Southern Gate, Chichester,
West Sussex PO19 8SQ, England

Telephone   (+44) 1243 779777

Email (for orders and customer service enquiries): cs-books@wiley.co.uk
Visit our Home Page on www.wiley.com

Other Wiley Editorial Offices

John Wiley & Sons Inc., 111 River Street, Hoboken, NJ 07030, USA

Jossey-Bass, 989 Market Street, San Francisco, CA 94103-1741, USA

Wiley-VCH Verlag GmbH, Boschstr. 12, D-69469 Weinheim, Germany

John Wiley & Sons Australia Ltd, 42 McDougall Street, Milton, Queensland 4064, Australia

John Wiley & Sons (Asia) Pte Ltd, 2 Clementi Loop #02-01, Jin Xing Distripark, Singapore 129809

John Wiley & Sons Canada Ltd, 6045 Freemont Blvd, Mississauga, ONT, L5R 4J3

Wiley also publishes its books in a variety of electronic formats. Some content that appears in print
may not be available in electronic books.

Anniversary Logo Design: Richard J. Pacifico

British Library Cataloguing in Publication Data

A catalogue record for this book is available from the British Library

ISBN 978-0-470-02727-1

Typeset in 10/13 pt Sabon by Thomson Digital
Printed and bound in Great Britain by Bell & Bain, Glasgow
This book is printed on acid-free paper responsibly manufactured from sustainable forestry
in which at least two trees are planted for each one used for paper production.

Contents

Editor's Note

It is important to note that there is not one agreed-upon standard for how to properly refer to individuals with disabilities. Different communities (academic, government, industrial) have different terms that they prefer to use. Different geographic continents have different terms that are considered appropriate. In addition, some communities of people with disabilities (such as the blind and the deaf) oppose the use of the terms 'with disabilities' or 'with impairments' and prefer to be known as blind people or deaf people. Since there is no agreed-upon standard, each team of authors was encouraged to use the terminology that was most respectful and appropriate within the communities that they work.

Preface

Universal usability (UU) is more than a noble pursuit that benefits special communities; it clarifies thinking about advanced interfaces that benefit all information and computer systems users. The breakthroughs needed to enable diverse users to succeed, will often accelerate progress on current technology priorities such as trusted voting, medical error reduction, and emergency response.

Research on universal usability focuses on user experiences and stretches the bounds of current thinking in several ways. It makes explicit the need to accommodate users with different skills, knowledge, age, gender, disabilities, literacy, culture, income, etc. Design for diverse users can take extra effort, but there is growing evidence that accommodating the needs of diverse users can improve designs for all users. Another growing success story are the improved designs for diverse technologies such as small and large displays as well as slow and fast networks.

The business case for universal usability is increasingly clear: advanced designs expand the audience and enable greater levels of success for all users. For e-commerce the payoff is clear: larger markets and increased sales. For government service and information providers the benefits can be measured in web log statistics which show more unique visitors and page views.

There is a good lesson from civic infrastructure design. Sidewalk curbcuts were required to facilitate movement by users with wheelchairs but they also benefit parents with children in strollers, delivery workers with large loads, and users of skateboards, scooters, and Segway transporters. Similarly, electronic curbcuts could benefit many users, for example, control over color palettes for users with color vision deficiencies also helps when lighting conditions change, projection devices distort color, and monochrome display devices must be used (Shneiderman, 2000; Shneiderman and Hochheiser, 2001).

Another highly successful example of specialized needs benefiting many users was the addition of closed captioning systems to enable users with hearing disabilities to follow television news and other programs. The requirement for rapid and low-cost closed captioning increased demand for higher quality speech recognition software. Then when the textual transcripts were available they could be searched and automatically translated our technology, advance basic research, and bring the greatest benefits to the greatest number.

1 History of Universal Usability

Universal usability is still a young discipline but some lessons are already apparent by looking back at what has been accomplished (Edwards, 1995). Thirty years ago information and computing technologies were used by only a small fraction of the population, but design improvements have made word processing and email common in developed nations, while cell phones have become remarkably ubiquitous in developing nations. The growing sophistication of users means that newer technologies can be readily disseminated, such as digital cameras, personal calendars, and the Apple iPod or other MP3 music players. This paves the way for future developments such as personal medical devices, improved healthcare recordkeeping, and expanded government services. Educational technologies are already raising the expectations of teachers of what they can accomplish, and even more dramatically enabling administrators to change the curriculum.

Early research in universal usability, such as Gregg Vanderheiden's efforts, was often tied to needs of users with disabilities. Vanderheiden's inspiring story starts with his undergraduate efforts to build communications technologies for a young boy with cerebral palsy (Vanderheiden *et al.,* 1973; Vanderheiden, 1980, 1981). His work grew, supported by sympathetic administrators at the University of Wisconsin and the US National Science Foundation. Vanderheiden's many recognitions include being the first recipient of the ACM SIGCHI Social Impact Award in 2004 for his work in influencing operating system developers to include support for users with disabilities. The University of Wisconsin Trace Research and Development Center remains a world leader in technologies that promote universal usability (Vanderheiden, 1990, 2001, 2004).

Constantine Stephanidis also understood the importance of helping individuals with disabilities and expanded his scope to include other users and broader applications (Stephanidis, 1995; Stephanidis *et al.,* 1998, 1999), leading to the concept of User Interfaces for All, rooted in the principles of Universal Access and Design for All (Stephanidis, 2001). His tireless organizing efforts in the European Community produced a series of workshops, conferences, books, and a new scientific journal. The Working Group 'User Interfaces for All' (UI4All) of the European Consortium for Informatics and Mathematics (ERCIM), active from 1995 to 2006, created a lively community of researchers and has had influence at the policy level in Europe. Research and development efforts toward universal usability are continuing through the into other languages. Furthermore, closed captioning became useful to viewers in noisy environments such as bars, trains, gyms, or airports, or in quiet places such as hospitals and libraries. Closed captioning also benefited those who were learning a new language.

Another payoff from research on universal usability is the support for greater technology variety (Keates and Clarkson, 2003). Modern systems have enhanced support for a broader range of hardware, software, and networking situations. A key success story is to enable access to the web by users with slow and fast network connections, small and large displays, new and older hardware, and diverse software platforms. There is strong progress in web access design for small mobile devices, but many breakthroughs are needed, such as improved designs for zoomable user interfaces. Compression algorithms have made widespread dissemination possible for music, photos, animations, and videos, but there are many further opportunities.

Yet another payoff from universal usability is that it focuses attention on designs that bridge the gap between what users know and what they need to know. No matter what level of computer experience and domain knowledge users have, they often have a need to learn something more when using desktop applications, web services, or mobile devices. Rapid, flexible, user-controlled strategies to enable users to acquire new knowledge are still needed. Current online help strategies are largely ineffective, especially in challenging situations, such as life-critical information provision, voting, and e-commerce, where users may be under stress and high success rates are required. Multilayer interfaces that enable users to start simply and gracefully evolve to more complexity are one solution that is beginning to be applied in medical applications, drawing tools, and advanced video editing applications (Shneiderman, 2003; Christiernin et al., 2004). An increasingly popular and successful method for learning about applications is the use of animated narrated demonstrations. These 1–3 minute screen captures, stored more compactly than video, show the application in use for meaningful tasks while the narration explains each step (Plaisant and Shneiderman, 2005).

Fundamental technology research breakthroughs are needed to ensure that every user can derive the full benefits of information access, social support through communication, and fulfilling self-expression. Designers need improved software tools, and evaluators need better ways to log and analyze usage patterns. Cognitive theories can be expanded from ones that deal with error-free performance by expert users to those that make predictions for diverse users who need help in recovering from common errors.

We have the opportunity to promote creative contributions from young children and older adults, from struggling novices to proficient experts, and from low literacy to multilingual users. Human diversity is a strength, and accommodating this diversity is a grand challenge that we should enthusiastically embrace. It will enrich

ERCIM Working Group Smart Environments and Systems for Ambient Intelligence (SESAMI).

Other pioneers include Alan Newell, a professor at the University of Dundee, Scotland, whose work to help users with disabilities and older adults, led to his championing the idea of access for all users (Newell, 1993, 1996; Newell and Gregor, 2002; Dickinson *et al.*, 2005). Similarly, Vicki Hanson began with research for deaf users but has expanded her role as the manager of the Accessibility Research group at IBM's T.J. Watson Research Center (Hanson and Richards, 2005). She also chairs the ACM Special Interest Group on Accessible Computing (SIGACCESS) whose annual conference, ASSETS, is a forum for researchers and practitioners working on accessible technology.

Some researchers have been motivated to work on universal usability in order to facilitate use of computers by all users. Jack Carroll, now a professor at Penn State University, recognized the problems that users had in mastering new user interfaces and developed principles for the design of minimal manuals (Carroll, 1990). They were designed to be short, pushing users to learn by being active in using their software. Tom Tullis's early work on screen design metrics served him well in developing a deep understanding of web design for Fidelity, a major investment firm managing the savings of millions of users (Chadwick-Dias *et al.*, 2003).

Many other universal usability researchers, authors, and practitioners have played major roles in stimulating early interest, making the payoffs clear, and guiding practitioners (Paciello, 2000; Horton, 2005). An important shift in research has been the expansion from early work on addressing motor and perceptual impairments to more recent efforts that also deal with cognitive impairments, aging, language diversity, and technology diversity.

2 Contributions of this Volume

This volume contains reports from a diverse set of researchers, each working hard to satisfy the needs of one or more special communities. Their insights bring immediate benefits to their users, as well as broader spin-offs and payoffs in the form of design breakthroughs, innovative research methods, and more sophisticated theories. These research contributions are applicable in future projects that will improve life for many users.

The design breakthroughs contribute to our growing understanding of how to make successful web pages, online communities, and educational resources. It is wonderful to learn that blind users' success with screen readers is steadily improving and that even highly visual materials, such as maps, can be sonified. It is encouraging to know that improved text entry methods help users with motor impairments and that the right kind of screen-based avatars are engaging to children with autism.

The innovative research methods stem from the need to study diverse users in which it is difficult to ensure uniformity in subject background, especially when dealing with small numbers of subjects. Controlled studies can be effective when small variations in independent variables produce clear differences in the dependent variables such as performance speed, but ethnographic and longitudinal case studies are valuable in gaining insights that might later be tested in controlled studies. The educational resources include more well-designed web sites for children's skill learning, public health information, and older adults coping with loss of memory and cognitive skills.

The touching stories of benefits to users with severe injuries are matched by the inspiring reports of successes by poor or low literacy users. Every reader will smile at the story of the older adult who opposed learning about computers to get personal medical information, but after a few weeks she commented enthusiastically that 'This computer is better than all my medication combined.' Readers will also gain hope for the future by reading how government services and digital libraries are being redesigned to make them more usable for diverse users.

The chapters give a good taste of the breadth of research being done: not only for the diversity of users and their special needs, but for the research methods and outcomes. I liked the common framework in which authors closed by describing the implications for users, researchers, practitioners, and policymakers. The breadth of these implications highlights why universal usability research is so important. There is progress and hope, but there are many minds to be changed and much work to be done.

Ben Shneiderman
University of Maryland
College Park, Maryland USA

References

Carroll, J.M. (1990) *The Nurnberg Funnel: Designing Minimalist Instruction for Practical Computer Skill*. MIT Press, Cambridge, MA.

Chadwick-Dias, A., McNulty, M. and Tullis, T. (2003) Web usability and age: how design changes can improve performance. *Proceedings of the ACM Conferences on Universal Usability*, ACM Press, New York, 30–37.

Christiernin, L.G., Lindahl, F. and Torgersson, O. (2004) Designing a multi-layered image viewer. *Proceedings of the 3rd Nordic Conference on Human-Computer Interaction (NordCHI 2004)*, ACM Press, New York, 181–184.

Dickinson, A., Newell, A.F., Smith, M.J. and Hill, R. (2005) Introducing the Internet to the over-60s: developing an email system for older novice computer users. *Interacting Computers,* 17, 621–642.

Edwards, A. (1995) *Extra-Ordinary Human–Computer Interaction: Interfaces for Users With Disabilities.* Cambridge University Press, Cambridge.

Hanson, V. and Richards, J.T. (2005) Achieving a more usable World Wide Web. *Behavioral Information Technology,* 24(3), 231–246.

Hochheiser, H. and Shneiderman, B. (2001) Universal usability statements: marking the trail for all users. *ACM Interactive,* 8(2), 16–18.

Horton, S. (2005) *Access by Design: A Guide to Universal Usability for Web Designers.* New Riders Press, Indianapolis, IN.

Keates, S. and Clarkson, P.J. (2003) Countering design exclusion through inclusive design. *Proceedings of the ACM Conferences on Universal Usability,* ACM Press, New York, 69–76.

Newell, A.F. (1993) Interfaces for the ordinary and beyond. *IEEE Software,* 10(5), 76–78.

Newell, A.F. (1996) Technology and the disabled. *Technology Innovation in Society,* 12(1), 21–23.

Newell, A.F. and Gregor, P. (2002) Design for older and disabled people – where do we go from here? *Universal Access in the Information Society,* 2(1), 3–7.

Paciello, M.G. (2000) *Web Accessibility for People With Disabilities.* CMP Books, Gilroy, CA.

Plaisant, C. and Shneiderman, B. (2005) Show Me! Guidelines for producing recorded demonstrations. *Procedings of the Conference on Visual Languages/Human-Centric Computing,* IEEE Press, Piscataway, NJ, 171–178.

Shneiderman, B. (2000) Universal Usability: Pushing human–computer interaction research to empower every citizen. *Communications of the ACM,* 43(5), 84–91.

Shneiderman, B. (2003) Promoting universal usability with multi-layer interface design. *ACM Conference on Universal Usability,* ACM Press, New York, 1–8.

Shneiderman, B. and Hochheiser, H. (2001) Universal usability as a stimulus to advanced interface design. *Behavioral Information Technology,* 20(5), 367–376.

Stephanidis, C. (2001) *User Interfaces for All – Concepts, Methods, and Tools.* Lawrence Erlbaum Associates, Mahwah, NJ.

Stephanidis, C. *et al.,* (1998) Toward an information society for all: an international R&D agenda. *International Journal of Human–Computer Interaction,* **10**(2), 107–134.

IR `http://www.ics.forth.gr/hci/files/white_paper_1998.pdf`

Stephanidis, C. *et al.,* (1999) Toward an information society for all: HCI challenges and R&D recommendations. *International Journal of Human–Computer Interaction,* **11**(1), 1–28.

IR `http://www.ics.forth.gr/hci/files/white_paper_1999.pdf`

Vanderheiden, G.C. (1980) Microcomputer aids for individuals with severe or multiple handicaps . . . barriers and approaches. *Proceedings of the IEEE Computer Society Workshop on the Application of Personal Computing to Aid the Handicapped,* April, pp. 72–74.

Vanderheiden, G. (1981) Practical applications of microcomputers to aid the handicapped. *IEEE Computing,* **14**(1), 54–61.

Vanderheiden, G.C. (1990) Thirty-something million: should they be exceptions? *Human Factors,* **32**(4), 383–396.

Vanderheiden, G. (2001) Everyone interfaces. In Stephanidis C. (Ed.), *User Interfaces for All: Concepts, Methods, and Tools,* Lawrence Erlbaum Associates, Mahwah, NJ, 115–133.

Vanderheiden, G.C. Using extended and enhanced usability (EEU) to provide access to mainstream electronic voting machines. *Information Technology and Disabilities,* Vol. X, No. 2 (December 2004). Retrieved April 28, 2005 from `http://www.rit.edu/~easi/itd/itdv10n2/vanderhe.htm`.

Vanderheiden, G., Volk, A.M. and Geisler, C.D. (1973) The Auto-monitoring technique and its application in the auto-monitoring communication board (Autocom). A new communication aid for the severely handicapped. *Proceedings of the 1973 Carnahan Conference on Electronic Prosthetics,* Lexington, KY, 47–51.

Further Reading

Selected Web Resources

Defining Universal Usability `http://instone.org/universalusability`
`http://instone.org/node/40?PHPSESSID=d785b97f1d3c4f9c749c0d4`
`05a5ff4df`

Universal Usability in Practice: principles and strategies for practitioners designing universally usable sites. Resources website `http://www.otal.umd.edu/uupractice/`

ACM Conferences on Universal Usability 2003: `http://www.acm.org/sigchi/cuu2003/2000: http://sigchi.org/cuu/`

ACM SIGCHI: `http://www.acm.org/sigchi/`

ACM SIGCHI on Accessibility: `http://www.hcibib.org/accessibility/`

ACM SIGACCESS: `http://www.acm.org/sigaccess/index.php`

Accessible Design in the Digital World Conference: `http://www.accessinthedigitalworld.org/2005/`

Universal Access in Human–Computer Interaction (UAHCI) `http://www.hcii2007.org/ta/ua.html`

Held every two years in conjunction with the HCI International Conference series.

User Interfaces for All Conferences (UI4ALL): `http://ui4all.ics.forth.gr/`

TRACE Center: `http://trace.wisc.edu/`

European Research Consortium for Informatics and Mathematics. Workshops: User Interfaces For All, founded by Professor Constantine Stephanidis in 1995 (`http://www.ui4all.gr/`)

2004: `http://ui4all.ics.forth.gr/workshop2004/`

2002: `http://ui4all.ics.forth.gr/workshop2002/`

Springer Journal: Universal Access in the Information Society (UAIS): `http://www.springeronline.com/east/journal/10209/`

California State University, Northridge Center on Disabilities' 22nd Annual International Technology and Persons with Disabilities Conference. `http://www.csun.edu/cod/conf/http://www.csun.edu/cod/conf/proceedings_index.htm`

Rehabilitation Engineering & Assistive Technology Society of North America `http://www.resna.org/`

The National Institute on Disability and Rehabilitation Research (NIDRR) `http://www.ed.gov/about/offices/list/osers/nidrr/index.html`

Introduction to Universal Usability

1

Jonathan Lazar

Department of Computer and Information Sciences and Universal Usability Laboratory, Towson University, USA

The phrase 'universal usability' was first coined by Shneiderman in his landmark article in 2000, which appeared in the *Communications of the ACM* (Shneiderman, 2000). Universal usability is focused on three areas – user diversity, technology diversity, and bridging the gap between what users know and what they need to know. User diversity includes novice and expert users, younger and older users, users with perceptual, cognitive, and motor impairments, users with learning disabilities, low-income users, and illiterate users. Technology diversity includes desktop computers, laptop computers, portable devices and PDAs, mobile phones, and various screen sizes and connection speeds. There is often a gap between what users know and what they need to know, and there are many ways to bridge this gap. Some 'gap fillers' include help menus, tutorials, and natural-language assistance systems (e.g. 'clippy'). This is a very large area of study, and realistically, it is too broad a topic to be covered in one book. So this book focuses on the user diversity area of universal usability. Other books in the future will need to address technology diversity and bridging gaps in user knowledge.

Conceptually, universal access means something different from universal usability. Universal access means ensuring that all people have access to technology. For instance, many individuals in the United States pay a fee on their telecommunications bill, and that fee goes to a central fund which helps connect schools, libraries, and rural health care facilities to the Internet. Access means simply having the equipment, the technology, and the opportunity to access a system. User diversity does not come into play, and ease of use is not an issue. In reality, the term 'universal access' is often used to mean the exact definition of universal usability, and many of the conferences in this area are called universal access while featuring work on usability (see Shneiderman's Preface for more information on the history of universal usability).

Some say that universal usability is an elusive, impossible goal. Others say that while it is theoretically possible, the amount of work required to make interfaces universally usable makes it impractical. I disagree with both statements. First of all, there is no problem in interface design that cannot be solved, or at least improved. To deal with these challenges, we may need to choose different design strategies, we may need an increased amount of user involvement in development, or we may need to design adaptive interfaces. I'm not saying that this goal is easy. But in life, the most important goals, the ones that you care about in your gut, generally are not easy. They are challenging, and are indeed the ones most worth working toward.

1.1 How Does It Happen?

There are really two types of universal interface design strategies, and it depends on the usage of the software application being designed. There are some types of applications that potentially will be used by all users. For instance, government and news web sites, digital libraries, and online communities can benefit all users, regardless of disability or age. Everyone can benefit from these resources, and therefore, they should work properly for all users, regardless of age, experience, or disability. On the other hand, there will be some applications that will be designed for a specific population. In this book, the chapters on Alzheimer's, autism, and dementia, showcase applications that were built for a specific population. The applications built for children with autism may not be usable by other populations, regardless of how good the interfaces are. Those applications designed for children with autism will not serve a useful goal for blind users, regardless of how good the interface is. The goals of these types of applications were not universal, they were only meant to meet the needs of a specific user population. These applications can then be maximized to meet the needs of that user population. So some application interfaces will be designed for all, while others will be designed for a specific population, because other populations do not need to use the application at all.

For applications or web sites that are built to serve multiple user populations, we like to minimize the use of a different interface for each population. Realistically, multiple interfaces can add to development time and costs. And if there are multiple different interfaces, not all of them are supported or updated as frequently as they should be. For instance, the Web Content Accessibility Guidelines (http://www.w3.org/wai) state that if a web page cannot be made accessible, then an alternate web page should be set up with equivalent content that is fully accessible. However, this is not encouraged, as it is likely that a second interface which is accessible would have more out-of-date content than the main web site, because it might not be properly maintained. There are some circumstances where it actually might be appropriate to have multiple separate interfaces and content, but those situations are limited. For instance, most people would agree that it is acceptable to have two separate web sites for NASA (the National Aeronautics and Space Agency), one primary web site and a second web site focused on children. The goal of the children's NASA web site is to get children interested in space and astronomy. Sounds good, right? However, what about the National Cancer Institute's web site, where information was presented separately for doctors, researchers, patients, and family members? Many users felt that they wanted to get the same information as their physicians, and felt very uncomfortable having separate web information for the different groups. Their feelings were really strong, despite the reality that the terminology used will probably need to be different for medical personnel and patients (Lazar, 2006).

Despite all of this, a well-designed interface can appeal to multiple populations, even when it wasn't originally designed for multiple populations. For instance, while the chapter from Matthew Meyers highlights the development of training modules for users with Down Syndrome, their 'Web Fun Central' is actually used by many librarians to teach web skills to patrons without any disabilities. While this was unexpected, it demonstrates that good design generally benefits not only those it is designed for, but also many others.

1.2 Universal Usability in the Real World

Universal usability is simply good design. And there are precedents in the physical world around us. For years, the argument has been made that 'curb cuts' in streets are the equivalent of universal usability. These curb cuts were designed for people in wheelchairs, to get from the sidewalk level to the street level. These curb cuts not only help individuals in wheelchairs but also bikers, parents with strollers, and people with wheeled luggage. I want to extend this argument to other examples of universal usability in noncomputer design. A curb cut is something that is necessary, but also expensive, and most people couldn't create a curb cut themselves. However, there are many other things that can be done to improve universal usability of physical spaces, which are inexpensive and easy to do. Similarly, there are many things to improve the universal usability of computer interfaces, which are quick and easy, and simply aren't being done due to the perceived large cost in time required. Some examples follow that help illustrate the point.

For instance, EMCO Windows and Doors offer a feature on their screen doors that greatly increases the ease of use for many populations. Most screen doors have one arm, up high, where a small metal hinge can be pushed into place to help the door stay open

Figure 1.1 A traditional screen door hinge, too high for most people to reach.

for an extended period of time (see Figure 1.1). The hinge is hard to reach, and stretching up high to reach the hinge could possibly make someone lose their balance and fall. The EMCO screen door has two arms, one high and one low. The low arm has a small button that can be pressed with the foot (see Figure 1.2). This makes it much easier to reach, and therefore increases the number of people who can use the feature.

There are numerous people who benefit from the ability to more easily keep a screen door open, similarly to the curb cut: individuals carrying groceries, pushing strollers, or using luggage. But at least two other populations benefit. For individuals who are shorter, they could not normally reach the hinge on the high arm, and now they can. In addition, there are many individuals (especially those with mobility impairments) who need more time going through the door, and the door needs to stay open for longer, rather than closing automatically. This button on the door arm, in a convenient place, benefits multiple user populations!

Another example can be seen by examining thermostats in a home or office setting. These thermostats control temperature (both heating and air conditioning) in a room, office, or house. Certain thermostats can be too simplistic. For instance, consider the thermostat in Figure 1.3. It doesn't provide enough information, and it is unclear which side of the dial the user should point in the direction that they want. It simply doesn't provide the functionality that users need.

Figure 1.2 An EMCO screen door hinge, lower, where more people can reach it.

Figure 1.3 An inadequate thermostat (picture courtesy of Evan Golub).

Figure 1.4 *A thermostat that offers the needed functionality, but is too small to read and accurately control.*

Now, if you consider a second thermostat (Figure 1.4), it seems to provide all of the control that the users need: you can program it for certain days or hours, you can make it the exact temperature that you want – it offers all of the functionality that users want. It seems like the ideal thermostat. However, it has problems related to usability. The buttons are too small, and the readout is so small that individuals with limited finger dexterity, or with minor visual impairments, or individuals who are older, and may have both limited finger dexterity and minor visual impairment, will find this readout hard to use. Now, consider a third thermostat. It has the same functionality as thermostat number 2, except that it has a bigger temperature readout, the buttons are larger, and it is less likely that the users will hit one button when they mean to hit another (see Figure 1.5). This thermostat is more usable. And while it might not offer voice output (for blind users) or speech recognition (for users with full motor impairment), it is a great improvement for older users with either limited finger dexterity or minor visual impairment.

1.3 **Making Small Strides**

It has sometimes been said that 'Perfection is the enemy of the good' (attributed to the French writer Flaubert). Sometimes, designers, web masters, project managers, or others worry about making their interface 100% accessible and perfect. And since

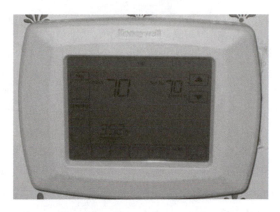

Figure 1.5 This thermostat offers larger controls and display, making it easier for older individuals.

they can't make it perfectly accessible, they feel that it is not worth the effort. But the goal shouldn't be perfection. Over time, our standards related to universal usability may change. Over time, we may learn more. However, we should implement as much knowledge as we currently have that we can use in a practical way. By making small improvements, it might make an interface usable for certain user populations, even if it is not fully usable for other populations.

Two related research projects examined accessibility levels of web sites, and web master perceptions of web accessibility. In the first study, accessibility levels were examined on 50 web sites, and only 1 out of 50 web sites were determined to be fully accessible (Lazar *et al.*, 2003). However, there was great diversity among the levels of inaccessibility. Many of the web sites were actually close to full accessibility. For instance, nearly 70% of the web sites had only violated one to three accessibility guidelines. And these tended to be the guidelines that, from a technical point of view, were easiest to fix. The most frequent violations were that (1) there was no alternative text for graphics and (2) there was no device-independent alternative text for scripting. Both of these are technically easy to solve. These web sites were not that far from being accessible. In another study, web masters were surveyed to determine their perceptions of web accessibility (Lazar *et al.*, 2004). Among the misperceptions cited by web masters was that an accessible site is text-only, with no graphics. At the time of the study, 20% of web masters did not even know that software tools existed that could help with accessibility. While web accessibility is just one aspect of universal usability, it shows how part of the challenge is 'selling the topic' as something that is do-able, that improves the user experience for all. Again, the perception of the work involved, and the misperception that only perfection is acceptable, can be stumbling blocks to moving toward improvements in usability for all.

In other words, don't worry about making the whole house or office 100% accessible yet. Start with the small things, like the screen door and the thermostat. Don't worry about making the computer interface 100% accessible yet. Start with the small things, like alternative text, better labels for tables and frames, adding appropriate labels for forms, and then go on from there. To paraphrase Flaubert, perfect accessibility is the enemy of good accessibility. Don't worry about making an interface 100% accessible. It may cause some people to avoid doing it, to be intimidated with the process, to say 'why bother?' Let's shoot for 95% accessible. And then once we're there, we'll see what new guidelines or tools exist at that time. And what we can do to take another step forward.

1.4 Connection between Universal Usability and Public Policy

Universal usability is not only good design, it's also good policy. In many countries (Australia, Canada, Portugal, Taiwan, USA, UK, and others), there are laws that require government technology (including web sites) to be accessible for individuals with disabilities (see Paris, 2006 or Lazar *et al.*, 2003 or Chen *et al.*, 2005 or http://www.w3.org/WAI/Policy/ for more information). Many countries also address language diversity as a universal usability issue, for instance, in Canada, government web sites must be available in both French and English. Even though laws generally don't address design for older or younger users, many government agencies have separate and appropriate information for different age groups. And while these laws cover only government computers and web sites, policy is increasing in scope: many private companies and organizations are now also required to make their web sites accessible. The rights of individuals with disabilities are well established in legal systems around the world. The rights of diverse users to access computers and online information are now starting to be recognized. The US Public Policy Group of ACM SIGCHI (which, in all openness, I currently chair) recently approved a policy statement, encouraging the passage of laws that clearly state the rights of individuals with disabilities to have fully accessible web sites, both for governmental information and nongovernmental information on company or organizational web sites (see www.sigchi.org/uspolicy for more information). By the time you read this book, it is certain that the policy situation for universal usability in a number of countries will have changed.

1.5 **About this Book**

The goal of this book is to highlight some of the current research projects that focus on practical outcomes in moving toward a goal of universal usability. These are not theoretical readings about what might happen in the future. These are hands-on readings about what we are capable of doing today.

Since Ben Shneiderman created the concept and coined the term 'universal usability,' he seemed like the natural choice to write the Preface. His historical overview provides useful information on where these concepts were created, who created them, and how they have grown over time. In addition, Shneiderman provides a comprehensive list of web sites and references related to the topic.

You are currently reading Chapter 1, so no summary is needed!

In Chapter 2, Hutchinson *et al.* describe design issues related to the development of an International Children's Digital Library (ICDL). Specifically, this chapter focuses on searching and browsing behaviors. A review of the literature provides information on how children look for information, and specifically, what has been done in the area of digital libraries. After describing the ICDL, the authors of this chapter describe the challenges of designing search tools for children, and how they were addressed in the ICDL.

In Chapter 3, O'Connell discusses web usability issues for older users. This is one of the great usability challenges of our time. As current users get older, they will want to continue using computers, and our interface design strategies need to improve to meet this great challenge. O'Connell provides guidelines and examples from a number of different web sites, in how to improve web usability for older users.

In Chapter 4, Evers and Hillen provide a description of their new approach for providing web navigation to blind users. They attempted to separate out the structural information on a web site from the content, to assist in navigation of a web site for blind users. Their application, called 'NavAccess,' allows users to listen to a high-level overview of the architecture of the web site, without having to listen concurrently to the content. The results of their evaluation are presented in the chapter.

In Chapter 5, Zhao *et al.* describe the interface they built called *iSonic*. The goal of iSonic was to allow users with low or no vision to listen to a map. iSonic adapts information visualization approaches to sonification, so that users can hear a high-level view of the data that is presented on a map, through the use of different non-textual sounds. Since tactile maps are prohibitively expensive, iSonic can provide a map experience for blind users utilizing only standard computer hardware.

In Chapter 6, Lazar and Allen present their project which investigated how to improve screen reading for blind users on the web. The frustrations of blind users browsing the web were investigated, and suggestions for both improved web site design and improved screen reader design are presented. In addition, the impact of the frustrations on user mood is discussed.

In Chapter 7, Kirijian *et al*. describe the web site that was built to help teenagers with Down Syndrome learn how to use the web. This web site, built in partnership with the National Down Syndrome Society, was the first known effort to include users with Down Syndrome into systems development. The learning modules have not only been used extensively in the Down Syndrome community, but they have also been used throughout public libraries in the United States to help teach web skills.

In Chapters 8 and 9, two sets of authors present different approaches for improving skills among children with autism. Autism is an epidemic, and there is no clear evidence as to the causes of autism or the most effective approaches for intervention. Tartaro and Cassell use animated virtual peers to interact with children and tell them stories. Whalen *et al*. use the scenario of a town to teach both social and learning skills.

In Chapter 10, Alm *et al*. present an application that they built for users with dementia. This system, which is touch screen based, assists the users with dementia in accessing long-term memories, through the use of pictures and music. This, in turn, helps spur communication between the users who have lost use of much of their short-term memory, and family members and/or caregivers.

In Chapter 11, Wu *et al*. address the needs of users with amnesia. The tool they developed, the OrientingTool, helps provide information about current activities and schedules, which can reduce confusion and disorientation for users with amnesia. As caregivers cannot be present at every moment, the OrientingTool can help those with amnesia to better manage their own daily schedules and events.

In Chapter 12, Cohene *et al*. address the topic of users with Alzheimer's disease (which is more specific than dementia, although related). They created computing applications that help users build a personal life history. This is not only a good activity for users and family members, but in the chapter, it was reported that the histories were repeatedly watched by the individuals with Alzheimer's disease. Compared with Chapter 10, these users took a more passive role and were more limited in their abilities.

In Chapter 13, Feng *et al*. examine speech recognition for users with spinal cord injuries (SCI). Although speech recognition is a natural choice for users with SCI, error rates are high, which discourages users from using speech. Feng *et al*. present and investigate new approaches for target-based and direction-based navigation using speech recognition.

In Chapter 14, Wobbrock and Myers discuss issues related to text input for users who have spinal cord injuries and are often limited to wheelchairs. Their work looks at turning pointing devices (such as joysticks and trackballs) into devices that can easily be used for text entry. Their chapter discusses EdgeWrite, which they created to allow joystick users to perform text entry faster and more successfully.

In Chapter 15, Pinkett discusses the Community Connections project, in which community-based software was built for the residents of the Camfield Estates community, in partnership with MIT. The goal of the system was to help with economic self-sufficiency for the residents of the community, who were economically disadvantaged. The chapter discusses the development and evaluation of the community networking project.

In Chapter 16, Maloney-Krischmar *et al.* investigate how to improve access to online health care information for economically disadvantaged African–American women. This population is often overlooked in the research community as it relates to interface design. Suggestions for improving access and interfaces are provided.

In Chapter 17, Murphy *et al.* discuss accessibility issues in US Census Bureau forms. Every 10 years, the US government takes a census of data, involving all individuals and residences. In 2000, there was a small test of an online option for filling out a census form. In 2010, it is expected that online census forms will be filled out by a large percentage of Americans. Ensuring the accessibility of these forms for all users is therefore paramount, and this chapter presents the multiyear effort that took place!

In Chapter 18, Nichols *et al.* discuss the creation of Greenstone, a tool for creating digital libraries. These digital libraries must address not only different user populations (such as librarians, readers, and anthologists), but also searches in one language for documents in another language. And the content can come in multiple forms – for instance, text, images, audio, and video. The chapter discusses the challenges and solutions in meeting the needs of so many.

In Chapter 19, Preece lays out the future for universal usability, talking about where we need to be going. She discusses universal usability in the context of social computing, which is a major trend right now in the online world. In this context, Preece presents her vision for how universally usable communities can help bring people together.

1.6 The Challenge!

I hope that you will find this book inspiring in your work. I often hear that 'we can't develop an interface for population X. It simply can't be done.' Even with very challenging user populations (e.g. users with autism, Alzheimer's, or dementia), appropriate interfaces and applications CAN be developed. In reality, developing interfaces for diverse and specialized user populations may be more challenging, it may take more time, and in all honesty, it may take more resources. However, it CAN be done. We are capable of making this happen. The skeptics who say it can't be done are wrong. Period. Don't listen to them. Prove the skeptics wrong.

Instead, go out and make the world a better place, by making the world of computing more inclusive.

References

Chen, Y., Chen, Y. and Shao, M. (2005) Accessibility diagnosis on the government web sites in Taiwan R.O.C. *Proceedings of the 2006 International Cross-Disciplinary Workshop on Web Accessibility* (W4A), 132–142.

Lazar, J. (2006) *Web Usability: A User-Centered Design Approach*. Addison-Wesley, Boston, MA.

Lazar, J., Beere, P., Greenidge, K. and Nagappa, Y. (2003) Web accessibility in the mid-Atlantic United States: a study of 50 web sites. *Universal Access in the Information Society* **2**(4), 331–341.

Lazar, J., Dudley-Sponaugle, A. and Greenidge, K. (2004) Improving web accessibility: a study of webmaster perceptions. *Computing and Human Behaviour* **20**(2), 269–288.

Paris, M. (2006) Website accessibility: a survey of local e-government web sites and legislation in Northern Ireland. *Universal Access in the Information Society* **4**(4), 292–299.

Shneiderman, B. (2000) Universal usability: pushing human–computer interaction research to empower every citizen. *Communications of the ACM* **43**(5), 84–91.

Designing Searching and Browsing Software for Elementary-Age Children

2

Hilary Hutchinson[a], Allison Druin[b], and Benjamin B. Bederson[b]

[a] Google, Inc., 1600 Amphitheatre Parkway, Mountain View, CA 94043, USA
[b] Human-Computer Interaction Lab, College of Information Studies and Department of Computer Science, University of Maryland, College Park, MD 20742, USA

2.1 Introduction

One of the largest groups of computer and Internet users is elementary-age children (aged 6 to 11). In both the EU and the USA, households with children are more likely to have computers and Internet access than households without children (Day *et al.*, 2005; Demunter, 2005). In 2003, 42% of U.S. children aged 5 to 9, and 67% of U.S. children aged 10 to 13, used the Internet (NTIA, 2004). One of the most common ways children use the Internet is for schoolwork (CPB, 2002; SAFT, 2006), and search engines and digital libraries are popular ways that children can search and browse for information for their assignments. Children spend time playing games and communicating with each other using computers as well (CPB, 2002; SAFT, 2006), and these activities often require searching and browsing. Children also use the Internet for shopping, where they search and browse for merchandise and have an enormous impact on the buying decisions of their parents (NIMF, 2000, 2002).

Web sites such as Yahoo! Kids (www.kids.yahoo.com) and Ask for Kids (www.askforkids.com) are examples of portals that children can use to find age-appropriate content for school projects. Project Gutenberg (www.promo.net/pg) and the Rosetta Project (www.childrensbookonline.org) are examples of digital libraries that provide access to scans of children's books from around the world. However, these and many other web sites for children have interfaces with one or more of three crucial problems. First, they do not take into account the information processing and motor skills of children, specifically their difficulties selecting small targets with a mouse (Hourcade *et al.*, 2004). Second, they do not consider children's searching and browsing skills, specifically their difficulties with spelling, typing, navigating, and composing queries (Druin, 2005). Third, they do not consider how children prefer to find things, presenting searching and browsing criteria appropriate for adults but not for children (Bilal, 2002). The ability to select content such as reading material on their own is a powerful motivator for children (Kragler and Nolley, 1996), and many of these web sites prevent children from doing so.

In this chapter, we discuss how these three issues affect children's searching and browsing and illustrate how they have been addressed in the International Children's Digital Library (ICDL, www.childrenslibrary.org) (Druin *et al.*, 2003). We consider browsing – also called exploratory searching (White *et al.*, 2006) – to be an open-ended exploration of an information space and searching to be a more task-driven activity. Browsing emphasizes rapid, progressive filtering of results on the fly, based on visual scanning of the current result set, while searching is a goal-oriented, methodical activity (Ahlberg and Shneiderman, 1994). Digital libraries and search engines must usually support both of these activities, and must be designed accordingly.

2.2 Why Children are Different
2.2.1 Differences in Information Processing and Motor Skills

Young children process information more slowly than adults, and this affects their motor skills. Information processing speed increases exponentially with age (Kail, 1991), and this has a direct effect on motor skills, because the slower speed with which children can process information affects how quickly they can adjust their movements (Thomas, 1980). For motor skills that involve moving a mouse, the total time is governed by Fitts' Law, which says that the time to move the mouse is directly proportional to the distance to the target and inversely proportional to the size of the target (Fitts, 1954). In other words, the farther away the target and the smaller it is, the harder it is to click.

For children, this means that large target sizes (e.g. buttons and other widgets) allow them to make selections more quickly while small targets slow them down and can lead to frustration. Hourcade *et al.* (2004) found that 64-pixel targets offered significant advantages over 32- and 16-pixel targets for children aged 4 to 5. Certain interaction styles can also frustrate children. Strommen (1994) found that children have difficulty holding down a mouse button for extended periods of time and coordinating dragging and clicking. Inkpen (2001) showed that children perform better and prefer interfaces with point-and-click interaction to those with drag-and-drop style interaction. Children also struggle with double clicking and multibutton mice (Bederson *et al.*, 1996), and with differentiating the left and right buttons found on some mice (Hourcade *et al.*, 2004).

Children, like adults, can also become frustrated with interfaces that fail to take advantage of human perceptual abilities. Relying on the recognition ability of the perceptual system through direct manipulation of objects on the screen is faster than recalling and typing information (Shneiderman, 1983). Ahlberg *et al.* (1992) expanded this idea to searching with dynamic queries, allowing users to control graphical widgets rather than typing queries to find information. Doan *et al.* (1996) introduced query previews to avoid getting too many results or none at all by presenting intermediate summary information about search results. Ahlberg and Shneiderman (1994) introduced tight coupling, where dynamic query controls and results are presented together on the same screen, and both are rapidly updated in sync to reflect the current state of the query. Schneider (1996) notes that such techniques can have additional benefits for children given their smaller memories and shorter attention spans, provided the interface is not overwhelmed with too many objects, colors, or motions.

2.2.2 Differences in Searching and Browsing Skills

Keyword Searching vs. Category Browsing

In many searching and browsing environments, two interfaces are commonly supported: keyword entry to support directed search and category selection to support browsing. Many studies have shown that children are capable of using both techniques, but generally prefer and are more successful with category browsing (e.g. Borgman *et al.*, 1995; Schacter *et al.*, 1998; Hirsh, 1999; Cooper, 2002). Borgman *et al.* (1995) explain this result as a combination of children's 'natural tendency to explore' and the ease of recognition of categories rather than recall or formulation of keywords. Researchers have also noted that young children tend not to plan out their searches, and simply react to the results they receive, making category browsers a more logical choice (Marchionini, 1989; Solomon, 1993).

The reasons for children's preference for and better performance with browsing interfaces are related to both their physical and cognitive development. While spelling and typing keywords are difficult for young children (Solomon, 1993; Borgman *et al.*, 1995), before they can get to this stage, they face two other obstacles. First, they must have sufficient domain knowledge to come up with useful keywords (Moore and St. George, 1991). At this point, many children, not understanding how keyword systems work, will enter a full natural language query (Marchionini, 1989; Solomon, 1993; Schacter *et al.*, 1998). For children who know they need to use keywords, the second step is to extract keywords from their query. Cognitively, this can be a difficult task for young children who don't yet think abstractly (Spavold, 1990). For those children who do extract appropriate keywords, the search engine may use different indexing terminology, resulting in no hits and the need to use synonyms, further complicating the process (Moore and St. George, 1991).

Structure and Presentation in Category Browsers

While elementary-age children often do better with category browsers, there are important differences to consider when designing both the structure and presentation of the categories. Three of the most common structures for classifying information in category browsers are hierarchies, trees, and facets (Kwasnik, 1999). Both hierarchies and trees subdivide a set of data using specific rules for distinction between and across levels, but hierarchies also enforce inheritance relationships between parents and children. Facets do not require any type of relationship across levels, but are used to classify a set of data in different, equally meaningful ways. For instance, a user searching in a census database might want to search according to age, location, or income, all unrelated but equally useful facets.

These categorization structures are often presented using either sequential or simultaneous menus (Hochheiser and Shneiderman, 2000). These two presentations differ according to whether users explore different branches or facets of a structure independently (sequential) or in parallel (simultaneous). A sequential presentation has the advantage of allowing users to contend with only a small amount of information at a time, at the expense of backtracking to explore other areas. A simultaneous presentation has the advantage of avoiding backtracking between branches or facets, at the expense of a more complex visual presentation and the possible need for scrolling or paging as more branches or facets are opened.

There are three possible combinations of structure and presentation (Figure 2.1). In a sequential presentation of a hierarchy, tree, or hierarchical facets (cell 1), users navigate down a single branch or facet at a time and then backtrack to explore other branches or facets. In a simultaneous presentation of a hierarchy, tree, or hierarchical facets (cell 2), multiple branches or facets can be explored in parallel. Finally, in

	Sequential Presentation	Simultaneous Presentation
Hierarchical Structure	1. Backtracking exploration, Multiple levels of data	2. Parallel exploration, Multiple levels of data
Flat Structure	3. Not Applicable	4. Parallel exploration, One level of data

Figure 2.1 *Combinations of structure and presentation in category browsers.*

a simultaneous presentation of flat facets (cell 4), all the facets are on the same level and can be explored in parallel. The other possible combination, sequential presentation of a flat structure (cell 3), isn't possible.

Hochheiser and Shneiderman (2000) compared sequential and simultaneous menus for presenting hierarchical category facets for adults (cell 1 vs. cell 2). They found that for simple tasks that did not require backtracking in the sequential interface, users were faster with sequential menus. For more complex tasks that did require backtracking in the sequential interface, they were faster with simultaneous menus. Neither interface was found to be subjectively easier to use overall than the other. Hutchinson *et al.* (2005) compared a sequential presentation of hierarchical facets with a simultaneous presentation of flat facets with children aged 6 to 11 (cell 1 vs. cell 4). They found that for simple tasks that only involved selecting a single category, there was no difference overall in performance or preference. However, for complex tasks that required backtracking, children were faster with the flat, simultaneous interface, considered it easier to use, and preferred it to the hierarchical, sequential interface.

Hierarchical Structure in Category Browsers

If a hierarchical structure is used in a category browser for children, care must be taken when considering the depth/breadth trade-off in the structure, the intended audiences' familiarity with the search domain, and their ability to think abstractly about the domain. Beginning with Miller (1981), many studies have been conducted with adults to understand the optimal depth/breadth ratio in a hierarchy, and all are in agreement that broad, shallow presentations are better than deep, narrow ones. This is also true for children, who are less efficient in navigating hierarchical contexts (Marchionini and Teague, 1987) and may not explore different branches unless prompted in a directed searching task (Reuter and Druin, 2004).

A number of studies indicate that hierarchical organization is not the initial way young children group objects (Piaget and Inhelder, 1969). Researchers have demonstrated that children aged 3 to 4 are more likely to group objects by perceptual features, such as shape and color, than by functional or taxonomic features (Tversky, 1985; Gentner and Namy, 1999; Nazzi and Gopnik, 2000). However, given some additional scaffolding, such as multiple examples of a given category, researchers have found that young children can use simple hierarchies (Gentner and Namy, 1999; Nazzi and Gopnik, 2000; Hayes and Younger, 2004). Research also indicates that localized domain expertise can improve children's hierarchical categorization skills. For instance, children with expertise about dinosaurs will categorize them using hierarchical information in the same way as adults (Chi *et al.*, 1989; Johnson and Eilers, 1998).

While it is thus possible for young children to categorize hierarchically, some difficulties still arise if the category domains are too abstract. Rosch *et al.* (1976) found that children aged 4 to 6 could sort basic-level categories (e.g. cats and cars) more than 90% correctly but could only sort super ordinate-level categories (e.g. animals and vehicles) correctly less than 60% of the time. Gelman and O'Reilly (1988) found that both preschoolers and second graders could draw inferences about objects in basic-level categories, but that the older children drew more inferences about super ordinate-level categories. Hutchinson *et al.* (2005) found that children could infer what topics would be found under hierarchical categories such as color and age, but had difficulty inferring what topics would be found under more abstract categories like genre and format.

Boolean Search in Category Browsers

It has long been known that people have difficulty with Boolean logic, which is the use of the connectives AND, OR, and NOT to determine whether statements are true or false (e.g. Tversky and Kahneman, 1974). With the advent of computer databases, this problem showed up in query languages for databases (Zloof, 1975), and later in digital library catalogs (Hildreth, 1983), where people frequently misused this feature or didn't use it at all (Borgman, 1986). The crux of the issue is that in conversational language, AND is an inclusive term, while in logic, it is exclusive, and vice versa for OR (Johansson and Sjolin, 1975). Despite these difficulties, researchers continue to look for ways to support Boolean search because when used conjunctively, it allows users to narrow down a large set of data quickly.

Children also have difficulty with Boolean logic, particularly disjunction, though they are still capable of using it. Children as young as 2 years old use and understand conjunction in conversational language (Bloom *et al.*, 1980), and by age 4 use and understand disjunction (Johansson and Sjolin, 1975). However, Neimark and Slotnick (1970) found that children didn't understand the use of Boolean conjunction until the fourth grade and Boolean disjunction until high school. In keyword-based interfaces, children have as many or more problems as adults. By high school, children still struggle with using keyword-based interfaces to create both conjunctive and disjunctive Boolean searches in digital libraries (Nahl and Harada, 1996).

Many attempts have been made to simplify the specification of Boolean queries in adult computer interfaces using graphical methods (e.g. Zloof, 1975; Spoerri, 1993; Young and Shneiderman, 1993; Fishkin and Stone, 1995; Furnas and Rauch, 1998). However, Druin *et al.* (2001) noted that many of these interfaces are too complex for children to use. For children, confusion between AND and OR, exacerbated by difficulties with spelling and typing, leads to the creation of simpler, automated, graphic-based Boolean search tools. The first example of such a tool was the QueryKids interface (Druin *et al.*, 2001). In this interface, children could search for animals with a hierarchical category browser. Boolean searches were created automatically with conjunctions between selected categories and disjunctions within them. Using this interface, children aged 7–9 were able to successfully construct both single category and multiple category Boolean queries when asked 85% of the time (Revelle *et al.*, 2002). However, Hutchinson *et al.* (2005) found that while children aged 6–11 were able to create Boolean searches using similar interfaces, only about half of younger children (age 6–9) actually understood what they were doing. As a result, more research is needed into whether comprehension can be improved with alternative interfaces.

2.2.3 Differences in Selection Criteria

The final issue to consider when designing a searching and browsing interface is how children like to look for information. For example, the QueryKids project found that children like to look for information about animals based on where they live and what they eat, as opposed to more common adult preferences such as biological taxonomies (Druin *et al.*, 2001). In this section, we consider how users like to look for books as another example of how children and adults can differ in their searching and browsing preferences.

While adults have become accustomed to searching for books using bibliographic information such as title or author, elementary-age children use different methods. Preschool and early elementary children choose based on the appearance of the cover and illustrations (Moore and St. George, 1991; Kragler and Nolley, 1996; Fleener *et al.*, 1997). Older children focus on textual summary information in jackets, covers, and indices (Wendelin and Zinck, 1983). Younger children tend not to make a distinction between fiction and nonfiction books, and prefer books about genres like fantasy to fiction or learning books (Kuhlthau, 1988; Fleener *et al.*, 1997; Cooper, 2002). Older children focus on particular genres that interest them, such as sports and animals (Wendelin and Zinck, 1983; Kuhlthau, 1988). Children of all ages enjoy rereading books (Wendelin and Zinck, 1983; Fleener *et al.*, 1997), and recommendations by peers and teachers are also important (Kragler and Nolley, 1996; Fleener *et al.*, 1997). Most of these criteria do not fit into typical physical library organizations, making finding books a frustrating experience for children (Edmonds *et al.*, 1990).

Later studies of digital libraries reflect the same general patterns found in physical libraries. Reuter and Druin (2004) found that when choosing books in the ICDL, younger elementary children tended to open books more frequently so they could see the illustrations, whereas older children relied on textual information in the book summary. Younger children like to search by physical attributes such as color (Busey and Doerr, 1993), while older children search using genres such as animals (Reuter and Druin, 2004). In the areas of repetition and recommendation, the digital also reflects the physical. In both search engines and digital libraries, children return to previous searches rather than running new ones (Bilal, 2002; Reuter and Druin, 2004). The top five books in the ICDL accounted for 20% of all book selections (Reuter and Druin, 2004), and the 100 most frequently used search terms accounted for 51% of all search terms used in Solomon's study of an online catalog (Solomon, 1993).

2.3 Solutions from Past and Present Children's Digital Libraries

A number of researchers have built digital libraries to address children's searching and browsing skills. Pejtersen (1989) created the BookHouse interface with category icons for different facets of the book classification scheme and tools to find previously read or similar books. Borgman *et al.* (1995) used a bookshelf metaphor with category icons in the Dewey Decimal hierarchy for the Science Library Catalog. Busey and Doerr (1993) worked with children to create the Kids Catalog, which provided multiple modes of access. Both Borgman *et al.* and Busey and Doerr found that the Dewey system didn't capture the search needs of children well. Both renamed the categories with more child-appropriate terminology, and Busey and Doerr added categories like animals and fairy tales. Külper *et al.* (1997) designed Bücherschatz with a category hierarchy and designed the interaction to avoid getting no hits. Druin *et al.* (2001) designed the QueryKids interface for finding information about animals.

While all of these systems provided improvements over adult-oriented libraries, none was a publicly accessible library containing scans of entire books. Some provided access to bibliographic records, and others were small collections of specialized media. In 2002, this changed with the launch of the ICDL, which provides free access to children's books from all over the world using interfaces designed for and with children (Druin, 2005). The ICDL now provides the largest collection of children's books with an age-appropriate interface.

A number of other projects also provide large numbers of children's books on the Internet, but use adult-oriented interfaces. Project Gutenberg (www.promo.net/pg) and the Rosetta Project (www.childrensbooksonline.org) both provide access to scans of out-of-copyright books from around the world, but both have text-only interfaces. Other projects pay more attention to providing a child-appropriate interface, but have limited content in a single language. Children's Story Books Online (www.magickeys.com/books) provides access to about 30 English books created specifically for the web environment and published only online. Stories from the Web (www.storiesfromtheweb.org) provides access to published English books and book excerpts for children, with interfaces for three different age groups.

2.4 The International Children's Digital Library

2.4.1 Background

The ICDL (Figure 2.2) was initiated in 2002 with funding by the National Science Foundation and the Institute for Museum and Library Services. The University of Maryland runs the library and the Internet Archive was a founding partner. The goals of the project include creating a collection of 10 000 children's books in 100 languages,

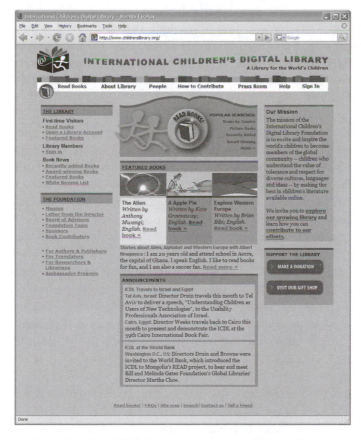

Figure 2.2 *The ICDL home page at www.childrenslibrary.org.*

collaborating with children to develop new interfaces for searching, browsing, reading, and sharing books, and evaluating the impact of access to multicultural materials on children, schools, and libraries. The project has two main audiences: children aged 3 to 13 and adults such as teachers and librarians who work with them, as well as international scholars who study children's literature.

2.4.2 **System overview**

The ICDL currently allows both children and adults to explore and read books in a collection of over 1000 books written in more than 35 languages. Books are scanned at a high resolution and presented in an HTML interface that works on any standard web browser with an Internet connection. The interface is currently translated into 13 different languages, and allows users to create personalized accounts where they can set preferences and save their favorite books on a personal bookshelf. The ICDL was originally implemented as a Java application that could be downloaded and run over the Internet using the freely available Java Web Start plug-in. However, the project quickly discovered that many users were unable to install plug-ins and/or didn't have broadband access, so the decision was made to create a more accessible HTML version, released in May 2003.

Users can search for books in the ICDL in three different ways. They can use the Location search to spin a globe using a large, easily clickable arrow and then select a continent to see books from, about, or set in that continent (Figure 2.3). This tool is popular with the youngest users of the library due to its simplicity and large, easily clickable graphics. Older users can use the Keyword search to find books with matching metadata in book title, author, summary, and publication information (Figure 2.4). Finally, users can use the Simple or Advanced search category browsers to create searches by selecting categories from various facets that describe the book (e.g., color, shape, language) (Figures 2.5 and 2.6). The Advanced browser is targeted toward older children and adults, while the Simple browser was designed for use by elementary-age children. A broad, two-level faceted category hierarchy of over 100 categories is presented in textual format in the Advanced browser. A smaller, single-level set of the most popular, child-appropriate categories is presented in graphical format in the Simple browser. In both browsers, conjunctive Boolean searches, such as 'Red Covers AND Happy Books,' are automatically created by selecting multiple categories.

These search tools all return a list of matching books, presented with thumbnail images of their covers. In the Simple and Advanced searches, the books appear on the same page with the category browser (Figures 2.5 and 2.6). In the Keyword and

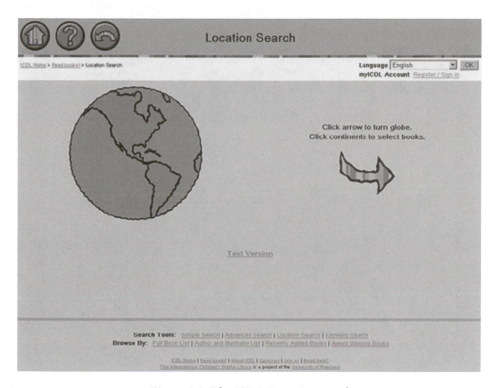

Figure 2.3 The ICDL Location search.

Location searches, users are taken to a new page with the results (Figure 2.7). Users can then select a book and get more information about it on a preview page, such as a summary and a list of the authors (Figure 2.8). Finally, users can choose to read the book using one of three book readers – the Standard reader that presents pages one at a time (Figure 2.9), the Comic reader that presents an overview of all the pages using Java Web Start (Figure 2.10), or the Spiral reader that presents the pages in a spiral using Java Web Start (Figure 2.11).

2.4.3 Research Team and Methods

The ICDL draws together an interdisciplinary team of 10 to 15 adult researchers from computer science, library and information science, education, and art backgrounds. These include university faculty, research staff, and graduate and undergraduate students. The research team is also intergenerational, including a 'kids team'

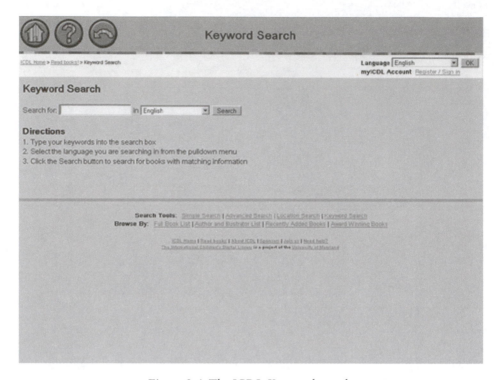

Figure 2.4 *The ICDL Keyword search.*

of six to eight children aged 7 to 11, who work with the adult members of the team twice a week after school to design the software for the ICDL and other projects in our university laboratory. The adults and children on the team work together in a process known as cooperative inquiry (Druin, 1999).

Cooperative inquiry adapts the idea of contextual inquiry (Beyer and Holtzblatt, 1998) from adults observing adults in the workplace to kids observing each other using technology. Children take notes or draw pictures with Post It notes about what they observe rather than writing extensively (Figure 2.12). From participatory design (Schuler and Namioka, 1993), cooperative inquiry adapts the idea of low-tech prototyping to brainstorm about new technologies by building them first with art supplies like pipe cleaners, toilet paper tubes, and socks (Figure 2.13). Finally, cooperative inquiry makes use of technology immersion by observing what children do with technologies of the future. The advantages of working with children as design partners are that the children are equals in the process from the beginning, giving them

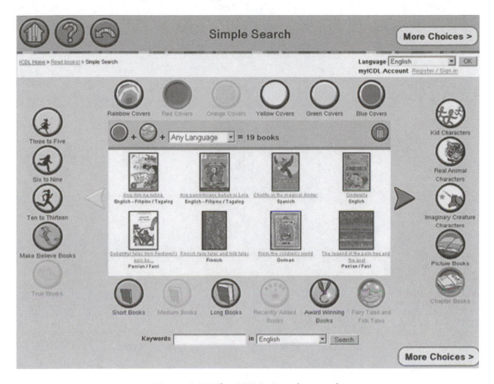

Figure 2.5 The ICDL Simple search.

more influence on the technology developed and a huge sense of empowerment. The downsides are that children and adults must learn to work together as a team, which can take many months, and researchers must work around the limits of children's schedules and attention spans.

In the ICDL project, child design partners have participated in the development from the very beginning of the project. In the early stages, they visited local public libraries to interview children about their book selection choices, helped develop and design the categories for the category browser, and traveled to the Library of Congress in Washington, DC to select some of the books included in the library. Later, they were part of the iterative prototyping process, creating and critiquing low- and high-fidelity prototypes for both the searching and reading tools in the software. Today, they continue to help in brainstorming about new features to include in the library and in designing and critiquing the prototypes we develop for these features.

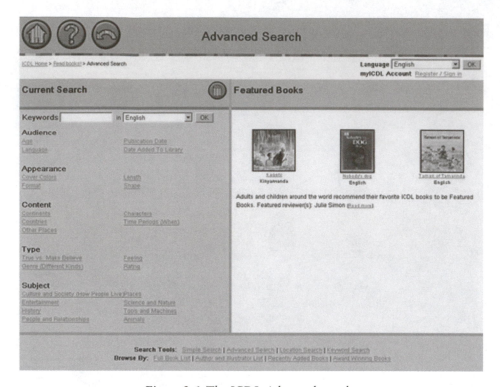

Figure 2.6 *The ICDL Advanced search.*

In addition to working with children on the team, the ICDL project also employs a number of other research methods to learn about users. The team conducts usability tests with small groups of children both in a laboratory and offsite in places like public libraries. The team designs and conducts formal user studies with large numbers of children in partnership with schools and after-school programs (e.g. Reuter and Druin, 2004; Hutchinson *et al.*, 2005). The team also has two ongoing, multiyear projects with children in different countries to learn more about cultural similarities and differences. The ICDL Communities project works with children in Hungary, Mexico, and the United States to develop tools to support intercultural communication and understanding through sharing books in the library (Alburo *et al.*, 2005). The International Research with Children project works with children in New Zealand, Honduras, Germany, and the United States to learn more about children's perceptions of books, libraries, and technology (Massey *et al.*, 2005; in press).

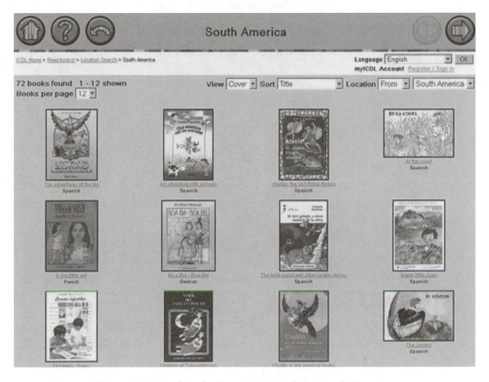

Figure 2.7 *Results of a Location search in South America.*

2.4.4 **Supporting Children's Searching and Browsing Skills**

Information Processing and Motor Skills

The ICDL interface draws heavily from previous research about children's perceptual skills and adeptness at handling a mouse. Important interface tools are implemented with pictorial icons to accommodate children who cannot yet read. The icons are at least 64 pixels in diameter to allow for easy selection and are accompanied by descriptive text for those users who can read. Important functions are executed using direct manipulation of these buttons via a single point-and-click action and require the use of only a single mouse button. In the Simple category browser, a simple form of query preview is created by enabling category buttons that have matching results in the current search and disabling buttons that don't (Figure 2.14). This method allows users to see the extent of category coverage in their search and prevents the creation of no-hit queries. The category browser is also tightly coupled with matching search results,

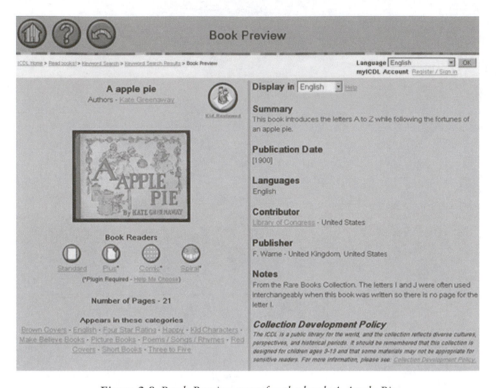

Figure 2.8 *Book Preview page for the book A Apple Pie.*

which are presented on the same page and updated as the search is refined. For instance, in Figure 2.14, books matching the categories 'Red Covers' and 'Fairy Tales' are shown.

Searching and Browsing Skills

To accommodate the skills and needs of both children and adults who use the library, the ICDL supports a number of different tools for searching and browsing. The Location search consists of a simple globe that users can spin to select books. The Keyword search allows adults and older children to type in keywords that match different types of book metadata. In the first version of the ICDL, a hierarchical category browser allowed children to navigate and select category icons to find books. The team's research indicated that young children preferred the simplicity and concreteness of spinning the globe in the world interface, while older children preferred the category interface (Reuter and Druin, 2004).

In the first version of the ICDL, the category browser allowed users to create Boolean searches by selecting more than one category in the hierarchy. However, Reuter and Druin (2004) found that while elementary-age children were able to navigate this hierarchy when asked, they did not make use of the Boolean capability on their own when browsing. As a result, the team decided to redesign the category browser, creating the Simple browser for young children and the Advanced browser for older children and adults. For children, the hierarchy was flattened so that leaf-level category icons are presented as buttons arranged around the perimeter of a box showing matching books (Figure 2.5). The selected categories are only joined conjunctively because children have an easier time with conjunction than with disjunction. In addition, unlike disjunction, conjunction facilitates narrowing down the results so that children can easily select from a few books. Hutchinson *et al.* (2005) found that this flattened structure combined with simultaneous presentation was faster, easier, and preferred to a hierarchical, sequential design similar to the original category browser.

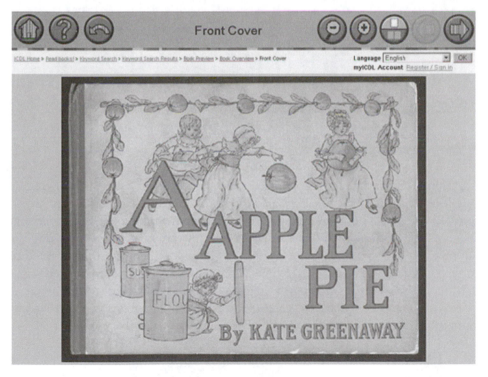

Figure 2.9 The ICDL Standard Book Reader.

Figure 2.10 *The ICDL Comic Book Reader.*

Selection Criteria

To facilitate easy selection of books in the ICDL, the team spent a great deal of time researching, organizing, and designing the categories for the category browser. The team looked at previous research on how children search for books in physical libraries, visited physical libraries to observe children looking for books, sketched icons, and sorted them into a hierarchy. The final hierarchy included some traditional library categories, such as genre and subject, plus several more child-oriented categories, such as color, shape, and feeling. When the category browser was redesigned, the team analyzed a year's worth of web log data from the first category browser and researched the most popular categories for younger children to select a smaller, more manageable subset of categories to include in the Simple search.

2.4.5 **Current Status and Future Directions**

The ICDL enters its fifth year with plans to expand and improve its searching and browsing tools in every area, from interface design to collection development to

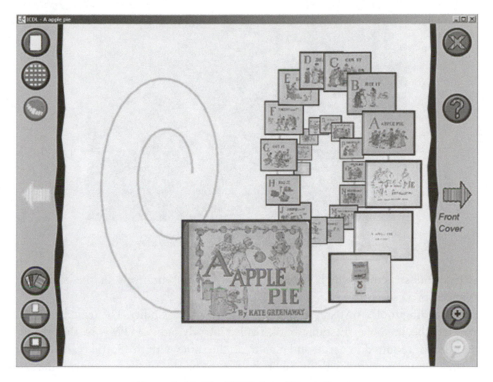

Figure 2.11 *The ICDL Spiral Book Reader.*

international research. The team is also working toward making the reading tools in the library more accessible. In addition, the project has formed the nonprofit *Children's Digital Library Foundation* to develop partnerships with other organizations, companies, and individuals to sustain the digital library for many more years to come.

Interface Design Research

The ICDL team continues to focus on research questions concerning the design of searching and reading interfaces. For the Simple searching interface, usability analysis from a recent study indicates that some of the categories may be over-specified (e.g. Make Believe Books and Fairy Tales are very similar), some of the categories need to be renamed with simpler vocabulary (e.g. Characters), and the meaning of some categories is unclear (e.g. Rating). As the library has expanded to include books on an ever-increasing number of topics, the original categorization structure has become insufficient. The team is currently developing a more easily extensible faceted

Figure 2.12 Sketching ideas with the kids team.

classification structure which will have different presentations in the Simple and Advanced browsers.

For reading tools, the team is focusing on better accessibility. The team has already converted the Java-based Comic book reader into dynamic HTML so that the Java plug-in is not required to use it, and plan to do the same with the Spiral reader. In addition, the team is working with the rights holders of books and volunteer translators to

Figure 2.13 Low-tech prototyping materials for working with the kids team.

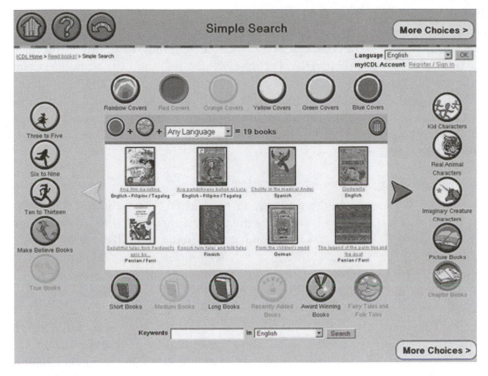

Figure 2.14 *The ICDL Simple search with 'Red Covers' and 'Fairy Tales' selected. Categories for which there are no matching books are grayed out to prevent no-hit searches.*

get the text of books transcribed and translated so that this information can be presented together with the book scans. Having this text available will greatly improve the readability of the books in their native language, as many scans are difficult to read on small computer monitors. Translating this text to different languages will make books more accessible to users who can't read the native language of the book. In addition, having the text separated from the scans will allow users with visual impairments to use screen-reading technologies to read the books. Currently, users with visual impairments are unable to enjoy the books in the ICDL unless someone else reads the text from the scans to them.

Collection Development

The project continues to collect books from libraries, publishers, and individuals from around the world to move toward the goal of 10 000 books in 100 languages.

This is a challenging process, as different countries have different laws about rights, and often there are multiple rights-holders (authors and publishers) who must provide permission before a book can be included. In addition, the library is also growing to host a number of special collections of literature, and the team is currently designing interface mechanisms that will enable users to include and exclude these collections in their searching and browsing activities. Many of these collections will contain large numbers of books on narrow topics in a single language, so providing children with an easy way to focus on or not get lost in these collections is an important usability challenge.

International Research

The team's work with children outside of the United States continues to inform our research. Over the past three years the team has worked with 12 elementary-age children, their parents, teachers, and school media specialists in: (1) Munich, Germany; (2) La Ceiba, Honduras; (3) Wellington, New Zealand; and (4) Chicago, IL, USA (Massey *et al.*, in press). During this time, the children read digital books from the ICDL and reviewed them. Each year, the children were interviewed during site visits, along with their parents, teachers, librarians, and principals. The team also asked the children to be 'ICDL researchers' keeping 'Observation Journals' to take notes about other children using the ICDL. They also took pictures of their 'favorite places' as well as sketching what they believed the 'computer of the future' and the 'library of the future' would look like. While the team continues to synthesize the enormous amount of data, a short summary of findings includes:

- The way children catalogued the ICDL books differed by country, particularly in the way children catalogued books by emotions (e.g. 'I think this is a happy book.' 'I think this is a sad book.'). The US children catalogued more 'sad' books than children in the other countries. This suggests that there may be cultural differences in children's expectations of where books should be found. For future ICDL development, the team will need to consider what this means for the searching and browsing tools.
- When the children in each country were asked what they would change about their physical school libraries, they uniformly spoke about the places they read, not the places they searched. Across all countries, the children were concerned with the 'floor' of the library. This suggests that while the team continues to make progress in new search interfaces, future ICDL enhancements will also have to be focused on the book-reading experience.

- In all countries, children accepted the integration of digital materials in their library experiences. There was no question if digital materials should live side-by-side with traditional books. This finding suggests that we may look to a future when the ICDL or digital collections like it will be a common part of every child's school library.

2.5 Conclusions

2.5.1 Implications for Users

The good news for elementary-age children is that more and more companies are realizing that children are frequent and savvy users of computer and Internet technology. Portals, libraries, and search engines with searching and browsing tools are all targeting younger and younger users. As companies gain more experience in developing these tools for children, usability will improve. In addition, more academic researchers are tackling issues in children's interface design, evidenced by the growth of the ACM-sponsored Interaction Design and Children conference over the last 5 years. However, as is the case for the adult population, the usability of searching and browsing tools for children with various disabilities is still largely unsupported and under-researched.

2.5.2 Implications for Designers

Designers of searching and browsing software for elementary-age children have a small but growing body of literature to rely on now. This literature suggests that designers should consider the following guidelines when creating searching and browsing tools for children:

- Support large, easily clickable icons rather than text-based links for accessing information.
- Use textual keywords for directed searching if necessary for older children, but support icon-based category browsing otherwise.
- Use flat category structures where possible since hierarchical category structures can be difficult for children to understand and navigate, particularly for Boolean queries.
- Support Boolean queries to help narrow down search results, but realize that some children will not fully understand this functionality.
- Design a search category structure based on how children like to look for things in the information space using age-appropriate vocabulary.

2.5.3 **Implications for Researchers**

Although a body of research for designing searching and browsing software for elementary-age children now exists, there are still two major areas that need more research. First, the structure and presentation of category browsers for children has not been explored completely. Hutchinson *et al.* (2005) looked at flat structures presented simultaneously and hierarchical structures presented sequentially. They found a number of advantages for the former, particularly for Boolean searches, but it is not clear whether structure or presentation played more of a role. They did not explore the third possible combination, hierarchical structures presented simultaneously, which may help determine the relative importance of structure vs. presentation.

Second, the use and understanding of Boolean search has been limited in most children's applications. While it is clear that keyword-based Boolean search is too difficult, icon-based Boolean search has shown promise. The original ICDL category browser and the QueryKids interface both supported disjunctive Boolean search within a particular top-level category and conjunctive Boolean search between top-level categories. The new ICDL category browser only supports conjunction. While a number of studies indicate that children have an easier time with conjunction than with disjunction, and conjunction helps narrow down the list of items to choose from, it would be useful to explore other logical combinations, particularly negation.

2.5.4 **Implications for Policymakers**

As children continue to use the Internet in growing numbers, at younger ages, and for a greater variety of activities, it is imperative that interfaces be designed to support their skills and needs. Just like their adult user counterparts, children become frustrated when they can't use a computer interface, and may be turned off from the experience as a result. Digital libraries, search engines, and other online information tools can provide vast quantities of information for children that may not be available to them at home or school, but only if they are able to access it. There is now a sizable body of research on how children search for certain types of information, and a growing body of research about how children search and browse using computers. Just as policymakers at the World Wide Web Consortium have created the Web Accessibility Initiative (www.w3.org/WAI) and the US government has created Section 508 (www.section508.gov) for supporting people with disabilities, these and other groups can and should create guidelines for designing usable software for children, including children with various disabilities.

References

Ahlberg, C. and Shneiderman, B. (1994) Visual information seeking: tight coupling of dynamic query filters with starfield displays, *Proceedings of Human Factors in Computing (CHI '94)*, pp. 313–317.

Ahlberg, C., Williamson, C. and Shneiderman, B. (1992) Dynamic queries for information exploration: an implementation and evaluation, *Proceedings of Human Factors in Computing (CHI '92)*, pp. 619–626.

Alburo, J., Komlodi, A., Preece, J. *et al.* (2005) Evaluating a cross-cultural children's online book community: sociability, usability, and cultural exchange. *Human–Computer Interaction Lab Technical Report*, HCIL-2005-18.

Bederson, B.B., Hollan, J., Druin, A. *et al.* (1996) Local tools: an alternative to tool palettes, *Proceedings of User Interface Software and Technology (UIST '96)*, pp. 169–170.

Beyer, H. and Holtzblatt, K. (1998) *Contextual Design: Defining Customer-Centered Systems*, Morgan Kaufmann, San Francisco, CA.

Bilal, D. (2002) Children's use of the Yahooligans! web search engine. III. Cognitive and physical behaviors on fully self-generated tasks. *Journal of the American Society of Information Science and Technology*, 53(2), 1170–1183.

Bloom, L., Lahey, M., Hood, L. *et al.* (1980) Complex sentences: acquisition of syntactic connectives and the semantic relations they encode. *Journal of Child Language*, 7, 235–261.

Borgman, C. (1986) The user's mental model of an information retrieval system: an experiment on a prototype online catalog, *International Journal of Man–Machine Studies*, 24, 47–64.

Borgman, C., Hirsh, S., Walter, A. and Gallagher, A. (1995) Children's searching behavior on browsing and keyword online catalogs: the science library catalog project. *Journal of the American Society of Information Science and Technology*, 46(9), 663–684.

Busey, P. and Doerr, T. (1993) Kid's catalog: an information retrieval system for children. *Youth Services Libraries*, 7(1), 77–84.

Chi, M., Hutchinson, J. and Robin A. (1989) How inferences about novel domain-related concepts can be constrained by structural knowledge. *Merrill-Palmer Quarterly*, 35(1), 27–62.

Cooper, L. (2002) Methodology for a project examining cognitive categories for library information in young children. *Journal of the American Society of Information Science and Technology*, 53(14), 1223–1231.

Corporation for Public Broadcasting (CPB) (2002) Connected to the future: a report on children's Internet use. `http://www.cpb.org/stations/reports/connected/connected_report.pdf` [accessed 27 March 2006].

Day, J., Janus, A. and Davis, J. (2005) Computer and Internet Use in the United States: 2003, US Census Bureau.

Demunter, C. (2005) The digital divide in Europe. *Eurostat 38/2005*, ISSN 1561–4840.

Doan, K., Plaisant, C. and Shneiderman, B. (1996) Query previews in networked information systems, *Proceedings of Research and Technology Advances in Digital Libraries,* pp. 120–129.

Druin, A. (1999) Cooperative inquiry: developing new technologies for children with children, *Proceedings of Human Factors in Computing (CHI '99)*, pp. 592–599.

Druin, A. (2005) What children can teach us: developing digital libraries for children. *Library Quarterly*, 75(1), 20–41.

Druin, A., Bederson, B.B., Hourcade, J. *et al.* (2001) Designing a digital library for young children: an intergenerational partnership, *Proceedings of the Joint Conference on Digital Libraries (JCDL '01)*, pp. 398–405.

Druin, A., Bederson, B.B., Weeks, A. *et al.* (2003) The international children's digital library: description and analysis of first use. *First Monday* 8(5), `http://firstmonday.org/issues/issue8_5/druin/index.html` [accessed 27 March 2006].

Edmonds, L., Moore, P. and Balcom, K. (1990) The effectiveness of an online catalog. *School Library Journal*, 36(10), 28–33.

Fishkin, K. and Stone, M. (1995) Enhanced dynamic queries via moveable filters, *Proceedings of Human Factors in Computing (CHI '95)*, pp. 415–420.

Fitts, P.M. (1954) The information capacity of the human motor system in controlling the amplitude of movement. *Journal of Experimental Psychology*, **47**, 381–391.

Fleener, C., Morrison S., Linek, W. and Rasinski, T. (1997) Recreational reading choices: how do children select books? in: Exploring Literacy: The 19th Annual Yearbook of the College Reading Association, (eds. W. Linek and E. Sturtevant) University of Wisconsin, Platteville, WI, 75–84.

Furnas, G. and Rauch S. (1998) Considerations for information environments and the NaviQue workspace, *Proceedings of Digital Libraries*, pp. 79–88.

Gelman, S. and O'Reilly, A. (1988) Children's inductive inferences within superordinate categories: the role of language and category structure.*Child Development*, **59**, 876–887.

Gentner, D. and Namy, L. (1999) Comparison in the development of categories. *Cognitive Development*, **14**, 487–513.

Hayes, B. and Younger, K. (2004) Category-use effects in children. *Child Development*, **75**(6), 1719–1732.

Hildreth, C. (1983) To Boolean or not to Boolean? *Information Technology Libraries*, 235–237.

Hirsh, S. (1999) Children's relevance criteria and information seeking on electronic resources. *Journal of the American Society of Information Science and Technology*, **50**(14), 1265–1283.

Hochheiser, H. and Shneiderman, B. (2000) Performance benefits of simultaneous over sequential menus as task complexity increases. *International Journal of Human–Computer Interaction*, **12**(2), 173–192.

Hourcade, J., Bederson, B.B., Druin A. and Guimbretiere F. (2004) Differences in pointing task performance between preschool children and adults using mice. *ACM Transactions on Computer–Human Interaction*, **11**(4), 357–386.

Hutchinson, H., Bederson, B.B. and Druin, A. (2005) Interface design for children's searching and browsing. *University of Maryland Human–Computer Interaction Lab Technical Report*, HCIL-2005-24.

Inkpen, K. (2001) Drag-and-drop versus point-and-click mouse interaction styles for children. *ACM Transactions on Computer–Human Interaction*, **8**(1), 1–33.

Johansson, B. and Sjolin, B. (1975) Preschool children's understanding of the coordinators 'and' and 'or'. *Journal of Experimental Child Psychology*, **19**, 233–240.

Johnson, K. and Eilers, A. (1998) Effects of knowledge and development on subordinate level categorization. *Cognitive Development*, **13**(4), 515–545.

Kail, R. (1991) Developmental change in speed of processing during childhood and adolescence. *Psychology Bulletin*, **109**(3), 490–501.

Kragler, S., and Nolley, C. (1996) Student choices: book selection strategies of fourth graders. *Reading Horizons*, **36**(4), 354–365.

Kuhlthau, C. (1988) Meeting the information needs of children and young adults: basing library media programs on developmental states. *Journal of Youth Services Libraries,* 51–57.

Külper, U., Schulz, U. and Will, G. (1997) Bücherschatz – a prototype of a children's OPAC. *Information Services Use,* **17**, 201–214.

Kwasnik, B. (1999) The role of classification in knowledge representation and discovery. *Library Trends,* **48**(1), 22–47.

Marchionini, G. (1989) Information-seeking strategies of novices using a full-text electronic encyclopedia. *Journal of the American Society of Information Science,* **40**(1) 54–66.

Marchionini, G. and Teague, J. (1987) Elementary students' use of electronic information services: an exploratory study. *Journal of Research on Computers in Education,* **20**(2), 139–155.

Massey, S., Weeks, A. and Druin, A. (2005) Initial findings from a three-year international case study exploring children's responses to literature in a digital library. *Library Trends,* **54**(2).

Massey, S., Weeks, A. and Druin, A. (in press) When children are digital librarians: reader response to books in the International Children's Digital Library (ICDL). In *Information and Emotions*, (ed. D. Nahle) ASIST Monograph Series, Medford, NJ.

Miller, D. (1981) The depth/breadth tradeoff in hierarchical computer menus, *Proceedings of the Human Factors Society,* pp. 296–300.

Moore, P. and St. George, A. (1991) Children as information seekers: the cognitive demands of books and library systems. *School Library Media Quarterly,* **19**, 161–168.

Nahl, D. and Harada, V. (1996). Composing Boolean search statements: self-confidence, concept analysis, search logic, and errors. *School Library Media Quarterly,* **24**(4), 199–207.

National Institute on Media and the Family (2000) Fact sheet: Internet advertising and children. `www.mediafamily.org/facts/facts_internetads.shtml` [accessed 27 March 2006].

National Institute on Media and the Family (2002) Fact sheet: Children and advertising. `www.mediafamily.org/facts/facts_childadv.shtml` [accessed 27 March 2006].

National Telecommunications and Information Administration (NTIA) (2004) A nation online: entering the broadband age. `www.ntia.doc.gov/reports/anol/index.html` [accessed 27 March 2006].

Nazzi, T. and Gopnik, A. (2000) A shift in children's use of perceptual and causal cues to categorization. *Device Science,* **3**(4), 389–396.

Neimark, E. and Slotnick, N. (1970) Development of the understanding of logical connectives. *Journal of Educational Psychology,* **61**(6), 451–460.

Pejtersen, A. (1989) A library system for information retrieval based on a cognitive task analysis and supported by an icon-based interface. *ACM Conference on Information Retrieval,* 40–47.

Piaget, J. and Inhelder, B. (1969) *The Psychology of the Child,* Basic Books, New York

Reuter, K. and Druin, A. (2004) Bringing together children and books: an initial descriptive study of children's book searching and selection behavior in a digital library, *Proceedings of the 67th Annual Meeting of the American Society for Information Science and Technology,* pp. 339–348.

Revelle, G., Druin, A., Platner, M. *et al.* (2002) A visual search tool for early elementary science students. *Journal of Science Education and Technology,* **11**(1), 49–57.

Rosch, E., Mervis, C., Gray, W. *et al.* (1976) Basic objects in natural categories. *Cognitive Psychology,* **8**, 382–439.

SAFT (2006) Summary – The SAFT Survey 2006. `http://www.saftonline.org/PressReleases/2881/` [accessed March 3, 2007].

Schacter, J., Chung G. and Dorr A. (1998) Children's Internet searching on complex problems: performance and process analysis. *Journal of the American Society of Information Science,* **49**, 840–849.

Schneider, K. (1996) Children and information visualization technologies. *Interactions,* 68–74.

Schuler, D. and Namioka, A. (Eds.) (1993) *Participatory Design: Principles and Practice,* Lawrence Erlbaum, New Jersey.

Shneiderman, B. (1983) Direct manipulation: a step beyond programming languages. *IEEE Computer,* **16**(8), 57–68.

Solomon, P. (1993) Children's information retrieval behavior: a case analysis of an OPAC. *Journal of the American Society of Information Science and Technology,* **44**(5), 245–264.

Spavold, J. (1990) The child as naïve user: a study of database use with young children. *International Journal of Man–Machine Studies,* **32**, 603–625.

Spoerri, A. (1993) InfoCrystal: a visual tool for information retrieval and management. *Proceedings of Information Knowledge and Management,* pp. 11–20.

Strommen, E. (1994) Children's use of mouse-based interfaces to control virtual travel, *Proceedings of Human Factors in Computing (CHI '94)*, pp. 405–410.

Thomas, J. (1980) Acquisition of motor skills: information processing differences between children and adults. *Research Quarterly on Exercise and Sport*, **51**(1), 158–173.

Tversky, B. (1985) Development of taxonomic organization of named and pictured categories. *Device Psychology*, **21**(6), 1111–1119.

Tversky, A. and Kahneman, D. (1974) Judgements under uncertainty: heuristics and biases. *Science*, **185**, 1124–1131.

Wendelin, K. and Zinck, R. (1983) How students make book choices. *Reading Horizons*, **23**, 84–88.

White, R.W., Kules, B., Drucker, S.M. and Schraefel, M.C. (2006) Supporting exploratory search. *Communications of the ACM*, **49**(4).

Yee, P., Swearingen, K., Li, K. and Hearst, M. (2003) Faceted metadata for image search and browsing, *Proceedings of Human Factors in Computing Systems (CHI '03)*, pp. 401–408.

Young, D. and Shneiderman, B. (1993) A graphical filter/flow representation of Boolean queries: a prototype implementation and evaluation. *Journal of the American Society of Information Science*, **44**(6), 327–339.

Zloof, M. (1975) Query-By-Example: a data base language, *Proceedings of AFIPS Conference*, **44**, pp. 324–343.

The Why and How of Senior-Focused Design

3

Theresa A. O'Connell[a,b]

[a] *Humans & Computers, Inc., 14322 Old Marlboro Pike, Upper Marlboro, MD 20772, USA*
[b] *US National Institute of Standards and Technology, 100 Bureau Drive, Gaithersburg, MD 20899, USA*

Summary

As the world population ages, so does the need for meeting the computing needs of older users. Aging does not equate with an inability or disinclination to use computers. People over the age of 65 constitute a fast-growing user group who are increasingly embracing the Internet. Empowering seniors to compute is largely a usability engineering issue. It pertains to designing human–computer interfaces that promote user success and satisfaction by accommodating the characteristics of older users. This group has characteristics that overlap with those of users in general and users with disabilities, but also adds a unique set of characteristics that impact human–computer interaction design strategies. Key to meeting the needs of this important user group is to accommodate expectations and work styles rooted in the twentieth century by applying twenty-first century technologies and design strategies.

3.1 Introduction

The fastest growing computer user group is one we all hope to join one day. It is the group we call senior citizens. The range of issues that impact on designing for an aging population is immense. Within this chapter, the scope includes only software interface design. There is no intention to downplay the importance of hardware issues. Exciting developments in intelligent wheelchairs, monitoring devices, even mobile phones bode well for the future of senior citizens. However, space limitations oblige a limited scope.

This chapter talks about who seniors are. It explores the reality and potential of senior computing. It presents a set of guidelines for designing for this unique user group based on a definition of usability where user success and satisfaction are equal components.

Because there is such a focus on and migration to web-based applications, this chapter concentrates on senior-focused web design. However, many of the guidelines apply to other software as well. The guidelines derive from the author's experience in usability engineering for senior citizens. They draw on widely accepted usability principles. They are backed up with references to start interested readers on the road to learning more about how to empower seniors to interact with home and office software and the web.

3.1.1 A Changing World

The world is changing. Computing technology is a primary motivation behind that change. It has impacted virtually every aspect of our daily lives, from using kitchen appliances in the morning to watching a movie in the evening. Computing has changed the way we organize our time, establishing new expectations for productivity. It has changed the way we speak, introducing new terms into the general vocabulary – *snail mail, brick and mortar store.*

Most importantly, computing technology has empowered us to exchange amounts of information unimaginable in prior ages. Where information-seeking was once labor-intensive, information now pursues us ubiquitously. Information is the great equalizer, the ticket to full participation in the society of the twenty-first century. It is this aspect that impacts most upon senior citizens.

For seniors, computing technology is a two-edged sword. It bears the highest potential to improve their lives, but also raises the unacceptable fact that people who are not plugged into the massive information exchange can be left behind, unable to reap the benefits that can make their quality of life superior to that of prior generations of senior citizens.

Today, computing is pervasive. Even the TV requires computing – how are seniors to cope? Computing has an image associated with youth and technical expertise. The first quality, by definition, does not characterize the senior user group. The second requires a background in topics that were not even invented when seniors were children in school.

Computer education is certainly part of the answer and younger generations are responding to the need, for example, by introducing grandparents to email. But there is a larger issue. Computer screens that should welcome and encourage seniors to interact with technology too often have the opposite effect. This chapter focuses on empowering those seniors who decide to give computing a try. At the same time, it offers strategies to engage and empower those seniors who have not yet embraced computing. It is all about designing usable interfaces for seniors – interfaces that empower senior success and satisfaction with computing.

3.2 **Senior Users**

In this chapter, as in the real world, seniors include active people in the workplace, active retired people, and people with disabilities both in and out of the workplace. While our concept of senior computer users may include gray hair and advanced years, the fact is that the effects of aging that impact on computing behaviors start to appear at around age 40. However, the age span of this user class, for purposes of this chapter, starts at age 50, and focuses on users 65 years of age and older.

The 2000 US Census showed that 12.4% of the US population, or 35 million people, were aged 65 and over (US Census Bureau, 2001). In 2006, one-quarter of the population of the United States was 50 years old or older (AARP, 2006b). The United Nations (2004) found that 20% of the world's population is 60 or over and predicts that by 2050 this figure will grow to 32%. Worldwide, by 2050, there will be two seniors for every one child.

The facts that this trend is global and is expected to continue are well documented (e.g. US Census Bureau, 2001; Chadwick-Dias *et al.*, 2003; United Nations, 2004; US Department of Commerce, 2004). The growth is fueled by people living longer. The United Nations (2004) predicts that global life expectancy will continue to rise with an average lifespan expectancy of 75 years by 2045–2050.

Aging is characterized by a variety of declines, for example: sensory impairments such as vision or hearing loss; physical or motor deficiencies such as decreased manual dexterity; and cognitive deterioration such as diminished short-term memory. Aging is not a static condition; the sensory, motor, and cognitive declines are incremental and ongoing. A counterbalance to this decline is a rising need for tending to the needs of seniors through usable interfaces. The more we age, the more we need design that fosters senior-focused usability.

Approximately 72% of people 65 and over suffer some degree of disability (Forrester, 2004b). Because of this, there is an overlap between accessibility design strategies and design strategies for older users. Sometimes, the combined effect of several age-related disabilities makes computing uniquely difficult for seniors. Kurniawan and Zaphiris (2005) cite the example of a senior devoting so much cognitive effort to taking in sensory information that there is a detrimental effect on the ability to achieve cognitive interpretation.

There are factors beyond health that build barriers to senior computing. Some of them have to do with preferences derived from historical or social sources. For example, this group includes people who never learned to type or who grew up learning that typing was not an appropriate activity for them.

We still don't know all the ways that senior computing differs from the way that younger people use computers. We can start by working with what we do know. So, we'll examine the known goals that seniors bring to computing. Then, we'll apply standard usability principles to suggest design tactics to improve senior–computer interaction. We do know that the declines discussed in this section each impact on senior interaction. For example, seniors tend to type slowly, sometimes because of cognitive declines, sometimes because of motor declines, sometimes because of a concern to 'do it right.'

In the United States, aging baby boomers are beginning to swell the ranks of older computer users. While this influx of expert computer users may one day decrease the need to design for novice senior users, the impacts of aging on people's ability to compute still raise the need for senior-focused design.

The sum total of the effects of aging is not an inability or disinclination to use computers. The fact that seniors are taking to computing in increasing numbers indicates just the opposite. The Pew Internet and American Life Project (Fox, 2004) found that once seniors take the leap into computing, they dig in with a degree of enthusiasm that at least equals that of younger users.

Accommodating the effects of aging does not dictate a purely negative design approach limited to addressing shortcomings and disabilities. While our approach must accommodate expectations and work styles developed in the twentieth century, it must also encompass the positive aspects of being a senior citizen in the twenty-first century, for example a longer life span with more time to pursue interests and interact with other people. We need to design to accommodate the particular needs of twenty-first century seniors from a broad range of perspectives that respects the diversity inevitably inherent in such a large user group.

3.2.1 **Senior Computing at Home and in Society**

Eighty percent of people 65 and over own their own residences (He *et al.*, 2005). For many seniors, a desire to live self-sufficient, independent lives in their own homes is a driving force toward computing. For seniors, quality of life 'is largely determined by their ability to maintain autonomy and independence' (WHO, 2002, p. 13). The benefits that seniors can reap by online shopping or online banking illustrate this point.

In the early years of the twenty-first century, an increase in web use by adults has been driven by an increase in users over 55 years old, including new users over 75 years old (International Demographics, 2004; McGann, 2004). Twenty-two percent of Americans 65 and over use the Internet (Fox, 2004). Seniors are not only coming to the web in increasing numbers, once they start to surf, they are likely to do so daily.

Seniors bring a variety of goals to the Internet. They send greeting cards, research family histories, and participate in virtual book clubs; they satisfy curiosity about religion, health, travel, hobbies, and history (Haffner, 2004; Fox, 2004). In the United States, more than half of online seniors visit US Government web sites (Fox, 2005). For seniors, surfing the web can be a trip down memory lane, a visit to places that are now only recollections. Or, it can open doors to new worlds of information, community, and entertainment unimaginable in their childhood.

The social isolation of home-bound seniors can have its roots in physical or cognitive disabilities. Isolation increases with age as their circle of friends diminishes due to infirmity and death. Computing can alleviate this disconnectivity. The web harbors the potential of widening a circle of friends and maintaining connections between people who can no longer physically visit others.

Younger family members are often the impetus that brings seniors to the web; a common lure is the ability to exchange email with family. Ninety-four percent of online American seniors use email – 2% more than the rest of connected Americans (Fox, 2005). Computer card games are popular and often a senior's first foray into computing. There's even growing evidence of seniors playing complex computer games (Hahn, 2005). Computing has unique potential to improve the quality of life for this aging population.

In a population where at least one out of every eight people is 65 or older (US Census Bureau, 2001), by sheer numbers, seniors become an e-economy force. Seniors are increasingly shopping online. In the United States, by the end of 2003, 47% of online seniors had made an online purchase.

Maguire (2005a,b) has studied this trend and notes that almost 60% of seniors who go online, shop online. The older they are, the more inclined they are to buy, preferring online merchants they already know from the brick and mortar shopping world (Maguire, 2005a).

By 2015, 76 million American 'baby boomers,' a $20 trillion market, will have entered the ranks of senior citizenhood (Amend, 2005). The baby boomers are used to shopping online and present an attractive customer base for e-retailers (Fox, 2005; Maguire, 2005b). As the boomers age and experience the declines that aging brings, the e-commerce sites that they are accustomed to using will have to adapt to accommodate these e-customers' new needs.

Despite the rise in computer use among seniors, there remains a segment that has not embraced computing. Resistance to change is natural. With seniors it is sometimes exacerbated by not being prepared for that change. What is often perceived as technophobia may really be more a feeling of being overwhelmed by what appears to be a large body of technical expertise, shared by everyone in the younger generation, yet *terra incognita* to people who grew up at a time when *computing* meant adding numbers.

People over 60 are less likely to use computers in public places, with the likelihood decreasing even more for those with disabilities. The US Department of Commerce (2002) has shown that the special needs population uses computers and the Internet less than people without special needs. Despite this, computer clubs are popping up in community centers and nursing homes. Something is changing. A generation that was taught to study independently (sharing answers was cheating) is congregating around computer screens and collaborating to find information. Seniors even report peer-group pressure to go online (Haffner, 2004). Traditional behaviors are giving way to an interest in computing. These adventurous souls are entitled to empowerment, not barriers. What they need is senior-focused design.

3.2.2 **Seniors in the Workplace**

The Bureau of Labor Statistics (2005b) reported that in 2005, 15% of the US population was people 65 and over who held jobs. Many of these were part-time workers. By 2020, 20% of office workers will be at least 55 years old (Forrester, 2004b).

Retirement is no longer a one-step milestone for older Americans. Increasingly, seniors are seeking part-time employment, volunteering or starting their own part-time businesses. The older the worker, the more likely that the motivation for employment is not a need for income; these people enjoy feeling useful. And in today's high-tech information-rich society, being employed is synonymous with usefulness. Seniors who are gainfully employed report fewer health problems, are usually better educated and generally have higher incomes than their retired contemporaries (He *et al.*, 2005).

The US Department of Commerce (2000) has uncovered what they call a 'critical connection' between computer use at home and at the office. The more people use computers at work, the more likely they are to use a computer at home. The more they use the Internet at work, the more likely they are to use the Internet at home. However, people 60 years old and older are less likely to have a computer at home.

Overall, older workers are less likely to use computers in the workplace than their younger coworkers. The difference is more marked for men than women. At age 55, approximately 55% of men and approximately 63% of women use computers in their workplaces. By the time these workers reach the age of 65, the percentages drop to approximately 37% of men and 47% of women. By 75 years of age, 23% of men and 30% of women use computers at work (US Department of Commerce, 2002).

Overall, 33.6% of employed people aged 65 and over used a computer at work in 2001; by 2003, the percentage had risen to 41.7% (US Bureau of Labor Statistics, 2005a). Increasingly, employed seniors need to be computer literate to participate in the modern workplace.

The fact that seniors are less likely to use a computer at work than younger workers is partially explained by the fact that some of these workers are in upper management positions that do not require computing. Another part of the explanation is the fact that the senior population is not as computer literate as other segments of the population. People between the ages of 55 and 64 are more likely to use computers at work than the elderly did at that age (Forrester, 2004a). As these computer-literate workers age, their computer use will continue. At the same time, the trend of seniors adapting to computing will also rise. Combine these trends with the trend toward seniors remaining in the workplace, and the result will be larger numbers of people bringing age-related needs to workplace software.

In this fast-paced era, performance is the driving force in worker evaluations. In order to excel at their jobs, seniors not only need to embrace technology, they need to harness its potential to improve their performance. The sensory, cognitive, and motor declines that mark aging can lead to longer times to complete tasks and lower success rates. Research is beginning to disclose a direct relationship between design that addresses the effects of aging and improved performance (e.g. Chadwick-Dias *et al.*, 2003). Seniors in the workplace need workplace applications and intranets that do not discriminate against them. They need software that accommodates age-related factors.

3.3 Wide Benefits of Senior-Focused Design

Universal accessibility (UA) is that branch of usability engineering that promotes the design of interfaces that can be used by everyone, regardless of factors such as locale, work styles, or disabilities. While its scope is universal, UA methodology addresses individual factors such as the impact of specific disabilities on human–computer interaction.

One outcome of UA design has been the discovery that accommodating the particular needs of a specific user group such as senior users has the broader benefit of improving the experience of other users too (Berger *et al.*, 2005; Chiswell *et al.*, 2006). For example, Forrester Research (2004a) estimates that 57% of computer users under the age of 65 can benefit from designing for special needs access. Therefore, many of this chapter's recommendations can benefit users outside of the senior user group.

3.4 **Addressing the Needs of Older Users in a Software Development Life Cycle**

Although this chapter focuses on designing for senior users, it must be noted that design is only one part of a larger software development life cycle. In order to achieve usability for seniors, it is important to address the needs of older users throughout this life cycle, from the earliest discussions of product functionality, through planning, iterative usability testing, and finally through postinsertion satisfaction surveys. It has been demonstrated that early awareness and consistent attention to users' needs throughout the software development life cycle empowers addressing usability and accessibility (Addelston and O'Connell, 2004, 2005; O'Connell and Murphy, 2006). The same applies for software intended for senior citizens.

A senior-focused software development life cycle involves seniors. Listen to this population and observe them in their homes, in society, and in their workplaces to understand their computing needs. Then apply usability principles to meet those needs. It is especially important to involve seniors during usability testing. This can mean taking extra steps to accommodate senior users with special needs or planning to test in a nursing home (Hix and O'Connell, 2005). The goal is to produce software that empowers senior users in their own environments and on their own terms. Please read the box below for an example of this.

Ellis and Kurniawan (2000) demonstrated that involving seniors in design results in web sites that meet their unique needs. In their study, developers partnered with seniors in their late 60s and 70s throughout a redesign life cycle, taking into account seniors' recommendations, observing seniors interacting with prototypes, and iteratively improving the site. Developers also considered feedback from more than 300 senior survey respondents averaging 77.4 years of age with varying levels of computer literacy. They backed up their findings and redesign strategies with a literature search, benefiting from usability principles developed by others who had worked with seniors.

The seniors taught the developers that their highest concerns were for easy-to-use menus and windows controls; icons and links that are easy to click on; readability and legibility; and graphics size. The collaboration resulted in a new color scheme, new page architecture, additional content, and larger more noticeable clickable areas. Ellis and Kurniawan found that changes the seniors said they needed reflected those recommended by the literature. The result was a site with higher usability for seniors.

3.5 **Designing for a Better Future**

In this chapter, we apply commonly accepted usability principles to designing for older users. Usability principles are a set of research-based and proven rules, guidelines and standards, drawn from many disciplines, to promote user success and satisfaction with software. They are the foundation of all usability engineering activities, continuously updated and widely discussed in usability engineering literature (e.g. Koyani *et al.*, 2003; Theofanos and Redish, 2003; Zaphiris *et al.*, 2005; Caldwell *et al.*, 2006). Each of the sections below starts with bullet points stating the usability principles it discusses.

The most basic usability principle is to know your users. Most people who design and develop web sites are not senior citizens. An important goal of this chapter is to help these designers and developers understand the unique characteristics of senior citizens to empower them to design and develop for this unique and important user group. This chapter aims to help twenty-first century designers and developers empower users whose twentieth century experiences drive the way they interact with each other, the world around them, and technology.

To general usability principal-based design approaches, designing for seniors adds strategies to accommodate novice users and users with special needs. It must address concerns that are important to seniors. There are a variety of ways to address seniors' needs in software design:

- Design special versions for seniors. This is not always economically feasible.
- Design software that empowers customization, for example web pages that show seniors how to enlarge font size.
- Design software that can adapt to meet seniors' needs, for example web pages hospitable to assistive technologies such as screen readers.
- Design the interface to accommodate a large range of senior users, for example those suffering cognitive declines and others with hearing loss.
- Design for seniors as a cultural group. Just as we would internationalize or localize an interface to serve a specific user group, we can design to address the cultural characteristics of the senior user group, for example the need for companionship at the same time that the number of companions is decreasing.

The strategies this chapter puts forward draw on all of these approaches, except the first.

Designing for any user group is a series of trade-offs. Designing for seniors is no exception – it may even be more difficult. For example, older users tend to read everything on the page, so you need to keep content to a minimum. But they can't click on small areas, so clickable elements must be large, claiming the giant's share of the screen. There's no one set of answers, but senior-focused design offers viable options.

The goal is to achieve usability for seniors, that is, to promote successful and satisfactory computing experiences. It is not just about ease of use. It is about the entire senior user experience, from the time the senior user opens a web page or a new application, through learning, while getting up to speed, while exercising the software, all the way to the time when the senior exits the web site or closes the application. Senior-focused design has to do with the interface's look and feel and every interaction the senior user experiences.

The focus is on empowering seniors within the confines of decreased cognitive, perceptual, and physical capabilities. We want to put them at ease and in control of their computing experiences. To demonstrate how this can be done, this chapter organizes some of the most important usability principles that pertain to senior computing into seven categories:

- Engaging seniors.
- Building seniors' trust.
- Placing seniors in control.
- Emphasizing discernibility for seniors.
- Respecting seniors' work styles.
- Empowering senior computer literacy.
- Building seniors' confidence.

3.6 **Engaging Seniors**

- Give seniors a personalized welcome.
- Encourage senior participation.
- Don't discriminate against seniors.

Within the context of three usability principles, we discuss design strategies that say welcome and encourage seniors to use the software or web site. The biggest challenge is to convince seniors that computing can be worthwhile for them personally. It is about engaging seniors to transition from watching someone else use a computer to actually giving computing a try for themselves. From their first moments at a web site or using new software, seniors must be able to discern that the site intends to engage them in a beneficial way.

The goal is to engage seniors by demonstrating that the software was designed with them in mind. Make it a badge of honor that an interface treats seniors not as less-valued users, but welcomes them.

3.6.1 **Give Seniors a Personalized Welcome**

Web sites have a unique opportunity to invite senior users to explore their pages. Leverage the power of graphics to say welcome; show seniors in photos. Build on this by making sure that when a site has content of value to seniors, this content is immediately noticeable for them.

3.6.2 **Encourage Senior Participation**

There are many possibilities for encouraging senior participation by engaging seniors. It is just a matter of considering the senior culture from the beginning of the design process. For example, when designing a game, offer an option for an avatar who looks like a senior citizen. If you are designing a web site that sells medications, when designing the site's information architecture, consider having a special section for the products that seniors use most often. Add content that showcases the value of a web site for seniors. Invite senior comments to generate senior dialogue and community.

3.6.3 **Don't Discriminate Against Seniors**

What better way is there to engage this segment of the population than to show respect? Avoid content that disparages seniors. Even sites that present senior humor can do so respectfully.

When referring to that segment of the senior population with disabilities, use American Psychological Association (APA) guidelines when referring to people with disabilities (American Psychological Association, 2001). A significant portion of senior users fall into this category. The rule of thumb is to consider the disability an attribute, not the defining characteristic of an older user. For example, on a web site that provides information about hearing aids, never refer to a deaf senior; talk about a senior with a hearing disability.

3.7 **Building Seniors' Trust**

- Show respect through ease of use.
- Respect seniors' right to privacy.
- Demonstrate credibility.

- Prove reliability consistently.
- Show helpfulness.
- Make security evident.

Whatever the application, building trust starts at the user interface, not only on the first screen the senior user encounters, but on every screen until the senior user closes the site or application. Demonstrate trustworthiness immediately upon welcoming seniors to the site.

Much of what we know about building trust of an application or web site derives from research into building trust for e-commerce (e.g. Kim and Ahn, 2005). Building trust is especially important for senior users because their comfort level with online purchasing may be low. The trusting relationship built with familiar vendors is often absent; ordering groceries at megafoodstore.com after years of dealing at a corner grocery store can be daunting.

Designing for this audience bears the burden of convincing senior users that they are in a safe, trustworthy environment. Kim and Ahn (2005) cite usability and security as two of the most important determining factors that build trust in an e-commerce site. Add respect, credibility, reliability, and willingness to help, and you have a formula for building trustworthy applications within and beyond the e-commerce domain.

3.7.1 Show Respect Through Ease of Use

It may seem counter-intuitive that bad design can generate an impression of disrespect, but studies (e.g. Araujo and Araujo, 2003) have demonstrated that users will equate design that promotes ease of use with a sign of respect. This is one reason why seniors will reject software with confusing navigation paths, needlessly complex interactions, and dense displays that obscure important content.

3.7.2 Respect Seniors' Right to Privacy

Respect seniors' right to privacy with clear and obvious access to a web site's privacy policy. The goal is to reassure seniors that personal information such as credit card numbers will not be exploited. This reassurance is vital to senior user trust. Present the privacy notice before asking the senior to divulge personal information and make it available the whole time seniors are at the site.

3.7.3 Demonstrate Credibility

Another usability principle for instilling trust is to demonstrate credibility. Putting your software's best foot forward by having an appealing interface has a strong impact in this department (Fogg *et al.*, 2002). An information architecture that meets users' expectations contributes to credibility. Make sure that information in a web site is credible and accurate. Stating a reliable source for information establishes a site's trustworthiness.

Communicating a site or application's identity contributes to building trust by demonstrating credibility. Consistently communicate identity at least once on every screen or page. If a web page requires a great deal of vertical scrolling, identify the site several times within a page, for example in the upper left corner, in a set of anchor links at the bottom of the page, and perhaps even in a navigation sidebar when the contents of that sidebar go 'below the fold' of the page. Designers have many tools that, if used consistently, can communicate identity. These tools include a software provider's logo, tag line, and name. Because a consistent look and feel is the motivation behind these tools, a distinctive and consistent color palette and a page layout template are important.

3.7.4 Prove Reliability Consistently

For the senior user, especially one who has a low level of confidence in his or her computing abilities, encountering bugs can build an impression of an untrustworthy web site, and ultimately, an untrustworthy software provider or e-vendor. Whether the perception is correct or not, the bad impressions persist and can ultimately bring the e-shopping to an unsuccessful end. This is an argument for reliability.

The World Wide Web Consortium (W3C) has identified four basic usability principles for accessibility. One of these specifies operability and another robustness (Caldwell *et al.*, 2006). It is significant that both of these principles point to reliability. Software that is not in good working order threatens seniors' sense of control over their experience. Broken links, links that lead to unadvertised destinations, inoperable controls and inconsistent system response to input contradict seniors' expectations. Such glitches also deprive seniors of their ability to control the system.

Consistency builds a sense of reliability. Senior users who can depend on an action producing the expected result will find software to be reliable and trustworthy. Reinforce this sense of reliability with consistent information about products and informative labels that deliver what they promise.

If, for any reason, there is going to be a gap in reliable delivery of functionality or information, prepare the senior audience. For example, if you know ahead of time that a web page will be down, inform your regular users with a notice (Figure 3.1).

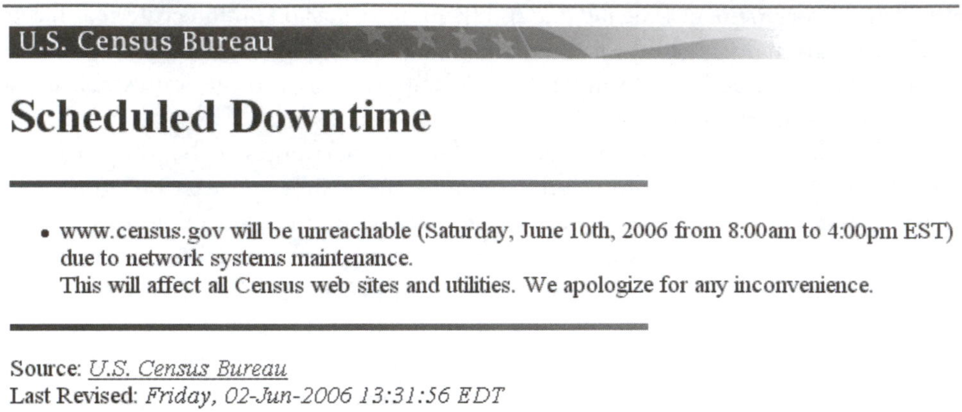

U.S. Census Bureau

Scheduled Downtime

- www.census.gov will be unreachable (Saturday, June 10th, 2006 from 8:00am to 4:00pm EST) due to network systems maintenance.
  This will affect all Census web sites and utilities. We apologize for any inconvenience.

Source: *U.S. Census Bureau*
Last Revised: *Friday, 02-Jun-2006 13:31:56 EDT*

Figure 3.1 *Users follow a first page link titled 'Scheduled Downtime' to learn when a web site will be out of service (US Census Bureau, 2006b).*

3.7.5 **Show Helpfulness**

Show a willingness to help. Again, we draw a lesson from e-commerce. Araujo and Araujo (2003) have demonstrated that providing clear notice of customer support helps build trust. Remember that the senior user group includes many people new to the Internet. They are phasing into the twenty-first century paradigm of interacting with technology instead of with people after a long lifetime of human-to-human commerce. They need more help not only because of problems with technology; they need help because they are used to human help. It is the way they have always made purchases. The feelings of frustration at an unsuccessful attempt to purchase online will only be exacerbated by the inability to find human help.

Quick and informative customer service, whether it be human or electronic, not only alleviates the frustration, it builds trust and, ultimately, it builds a senior customer base. Obvious links to customer service and contact information say loudly and clearly that a web site's providers want their users to be successful and satisfied. If possible, give senior users something beyond an email link. If you can't provide a phone number, give a snail mail address.

Remember to speak the seniors' language when offering to help. If you want to direct seniors to a FAQ, call it Frequently Asked Questions – FAQ is techno-jargon that new senior users may not understand.

3.7.6 **Make Security Evident**

The relationship between trust and security notices has been well documented, especially for e-commerce (e.g. Araujo and Araujo, 2003; Kim and Ahn, 2005). Security is just as important to seniors as it is to other segments of the web market. A site that wants seniors to supply their credit card numbers must clearly and obviously reassure them that they are working in a safe environment. E-vendors can't rely on this user group to notice or understand the significance of a tiny padlock in the periphery of the screen. Make access to security information available at all points during the buying experience, for example through an obvious and easily understood icon or text links that lead to a page that explains why and to what degree the site is secure.

3.8 Placing Seniors in Control

- Relieve cognitive load.
- Put seniors in control of navigation.
  - Provide obvious pathways to content.
  - Help seniors return from pop-ups to their starting point.
  - Don't force seniors to explore.
- Empower successful searches.
- Eliminate barriers to information or functionality.
- Never depend solely on visual signals.
- Give notice of what the system is doing.

This section derives from a fundamental usability principle that users must feel that they, not the computer, are in control. Doubt about control leads to a loss of confidence and at worst, a loss of self-esteem that will have serious negative impacts on satisfaction. A key strategy to building a sense of control is to prevent situations where seniors' characteristics put them at risk of losing control.

3.8.1 Relieve Cognitive load

There are several tactics to relieve cognitive load for senior users. They revolve around letting the system do the remembering for the senior. For example, have the system remember a password, use remembered information to prepopulate forms, change the look of visited links, and store search queries for reuse.

It is easier for seniors to recognize than to recall, so provide information rather than asking senior users to recall it. For example, let seniors select from a static list or a set of easy-to-recognize icons. Don't force seniors to remember what buttons are for. Give those buttons clear labels.

Don't force seniors to figure out what icons stand for. Lopes (2001) illustrates the problem of having to learn the meaning of icons with a discussion of seniors playing onscreen games where each player's moves are identified by an individual icon. Instead of requiring seniors to learn what each abstract symbol signifies, Lopes suggests using a photo of the player himself. If incorporating a photo is not an option for you, consider giving the senior a variety of photos of seniors to choose among, against the possibility of finding one that resembles the player himself.

There are opportunities for the interface to relieve seniors of cognitive burdens by showing them what actions they have taken with the system. Seniors need clearly discernible signals that they have successfully performed an operation. For example, mouseovers must sharply contrast with the look of the premouseover state. An email notice reinforces the expectation that an e-purchase has been successful. Distinguishing visited links by changing their color to strongly contrast with the color of nonvisited links relieves seniors of having to remember which link they have followed (Figure 3.2).

Lengthy bodies of text place heavy demands on working memory, forcing seniors to keep track of what they've read throughout a long dense paragraph. Couple this with seniors' tendency to read all of a page's text. There emerges a need to write concisely.

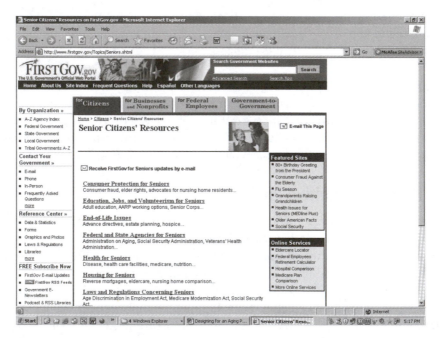

Figure 3.2 *This page briefly sets out content of interest to senior users. The left column remains visible on lower-level pages (US General Services Administration, 2006).*

3.8.2 **Put Seniors in Control of Navigation**

Simplify navigation so seniors won't have to remember a complicated site structure. A horizontal, shallow architecture keeps page-to-page navigation to the lowest number of levels possible, even if it means more clicks within a page. If this is not possible, make sure to provide shortcuts to and from lower levels, for example direct links from a table of contents can provide one-click access to several levels of a site. At most, limit the number of clicks to a destination to five (Chisnell *et al.*, 2006).

Provide Obvious Pathways to Content

Diminished working memory can cause seniors to have problems recognizing a navigation path that they've traversed only moments earlier. An interface that requires its users to remember complex navigation paths within and among screens builds navigation barriers for seniors. So, give them landmarks, street signs, and directions along the way. Provide navigation aids on every web page in addition to the browser buttons. Make these aids easy to identify; their purpose easy to understand. Seniors need pathways, not barriers. Pave the pathways with understandable icons, titles, labels, lists, and links located where seniors are sure to find them. In a broader sense, this is a clear argument for ease of use. Don't force seniors to take extra steps that may lead them to fear they have made a navigation error. Don't force them to exert great effort trying to find controls (Figure 3.3).

Remember, the goal is to empower senior users to find information and functionality. So, make navigation aids obvious. Give them a consistent look and placement. When seniors use the aids, ensure that they reliably and consistently deliver them to the advertised location. Avoid disorientation and dissatisfaction. Remove dead links. And let seniors know that they've navigated to their intended destination with large page titles or section headings that match the titles of the links that they've followed.

Short-term memory problems may contribute to a sense of confusion about where a senior user is in a navigation scheme. Give the senior users clues. For example, if there is a list of links to pages that remains visible in its entirety no matter which page the senior user is on, change the look of the link that led to the page in focus. This strategy reminds the senior user which page is the current page and can reduce errors of clicking on a link to the current page. And make sure that seniors always have access to a browser back button that reliably returns them to their previous page.

To help seniors navigate within a page or screen, show them that screen elements are related by grouping them. For example, group

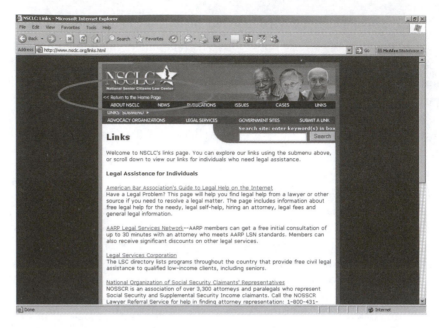

Figure 3.3 *An obvious navigation aid shows seniors how to return to the home page. Web-savvy seniors can also take the customary route home of clicking on the site logo (NSCLC, 2006).*

- related options within the same menu;
- related links in the same list;
- related icons in the same toolbar;
- related information within the same area of a web page.

Empower seniors who use screen readers to navigate directly to the content they need. Give them a 'Skip to main content' link so they don't have to listen to the names of links that appear at the top of every page. Empower them to scan lists of links by giving each link a unique informative name, preferably one that corresponds to common keywords (Theofanos and Redish, 2003).

As seniors become more web literate, they will discover site maps. To help them, provide links to the site map on every site page. Make sure that the site map presents the site's entire contents. And make sure that it presents them in a way that helps seniors to find what they seek. Alphabetical order is an easy solution (Figure 3.4).

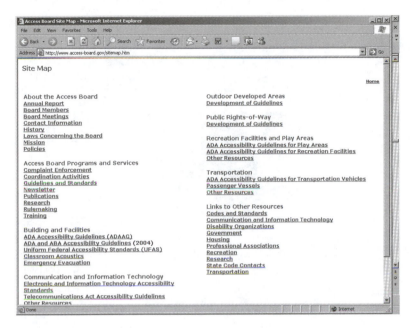

Figure 3.4 This site map alphabetizes names of sections and section contents, building on what users already know (i.e. the alphabet) to help them find what they need (US Access Board, 2006).

Help Seniors Return from Pop-ups to Their Starting Point

If you must launch an additional browser instance, let the senior users know. Remember, this is a group with many novices who rely on the back button. They may not realize that they are suddenly working in a new window, especially if the new window has obscured the window they have navigated from. The discovery that, for reasons unknown, they can no longer use that back button will certainly diminish their sense of being in control. If you cannot avoid using pop-ups, launch them as smaller windows than the window immediately previously in focus. This will empower the seniors to see the page they have just left and, when desired, easily navigate back to it (Figure 3.5).

The modal windows that are only an annoyance for seasoned computer users can be show-stoppers for novice seniors. If modal windows are necessary, for example to prevent a fatal error, make sure to clearly communicate their purpose and to give clear instructions on what must be done to close the window.

Don't Force Seniors to Explore

This usability principle takes on special significance in an e-commerce scenario. Don't oblige seniors to wander through a page to find the shopping cart link. Remember

Figure 3.5 *When it is necessary to launch an additional browser window, launch it as a smaller window so seniors can still see the page they were working on (Sunrise Senior Living, 2006).*

that, yes, this is an audience with spending money, but it also includes people on fixed incomes. Don't take them all the way to the end of the shopping experience to bombard them with the news that shipping costs are higher than the cost of the item they want to purchase. Inform them as they go along of how you are going to calculate extra charges to keep them in control of the experience.

An information architecture that requires senior users to understand its structure builds barriers. Consider the senior who wants to order vitamins from a site that requires knowing, before browsing, which products are natural or synthetic, or who the manufacturer is. Or consider a large portal that requires the senior to know which of its providers sells shoes before letting the senior search for shoes. Don't force them to explore; empower them to navigate.

If seniors don't perceive that functionality or information is available to them, then, in effect, that content is behind a barrier. Hiding functionality in right-click menus or presenting available links and active icons in light gray are examples of building barriers.

3.8.3 **Empower Successful Searches**

A successful search is one that brings the senior all and only the information sought. The movement toward natural language searches favors seniors. However, sometimes, building a more complex query is necessary. If it is, don't require seniors to learn or remember the mechanics of building a Boolean query. Lead them through the process with clearly marked fields to enter their terms.

Hands with tremors make typos. Novice users depend on search boxes. These two factors combined create a need for search engines that include misspellings among their synonyms. And make those search boxes large so that they will be easy targets for positioning a cursor.

3.8.4 **Eliminate Barriers to Information or Functionality**

In the twenty-first century, access to information is perhaps the most exciting benefit of computing. In an age where information is power, seniors more than ever need information to function within society and the workplace. New functionality that computing delivers, for example the ability to shop online, can uniquely empower seniors, in some cases even empowering self-sufficiency. Twenty-first century access to this information and functionality is beyond the paradigms taught to people who were educated in the early twentieth century. For this reason, we need to do everything we can to facilitate computer access to information and functionality. At the least, design must prevent barriers to information and functionality.

Any screen element or design approach that requires seniors to exert unneeded effort is a barrier. Forcing seniors to navigate through unnecessary content places a barrier between them and the content they seek. Build a pathway that reflects the senior's logical workflow, for example don't ask them to go through the trouble of providing personal information before they have made a decision to register or buy.

3.8.5 **Never Depend Solely on Visual Signals**

Onscreen directions such as *click here* require senior users to be able to see where they must click and have the ability to click there. The users have no option other than responding to the visual signal. An informative text label for a hypertext link is screen-reader accessible and concisely directs the user, eliminating the unnecessary *click here* barrier. Make sure that seniors who use screen readers or who have difficulty discerning or activating screen elements can use the keyboard as alternative access to every interface element.

3.8.6 **Give Notice of What the System is Doing**

The goal of giving notice is to keep seniors confidently in control by communicating about the state of the system as seniors perceive that system. Seniors don't always need to understand what is going on 'under the hood,' but they do need to know that the system is churning, why the system is churning, and how much longer it is going to be churning. Tell them there is a process in progress and let them know if this means they must suspend work for a while.

An hour glass or status bar doesn't actually put the senior in control of the experience, but knowing that something is happening contributes to a feeling of control over that experience. So, if you use a progress bar, be sure to also give an estimate of how much time remains or what percentage of the process has completed – the concept of a bar gradually turning blue does not always translate into a message of time elapsing or a process completing.

If a web site offers downloads, explain that how long a download will take depends on bandwidth and explain what bandwidth means in nontechnical terms. Let novice seniors know if the system is going to launch a plug-in. Novice seniors who unknowingly launch a. pdf reader may lose their sense of control when the. pdf document appears with a look and feel that is not consistent with what they were viewing moments earlier.

3.9 **Emphasizing Discernibility**

- Help seniors discern graphics.
- Promote legibility.
  - Empower seniors to have large text.
  - Use strong color contrasts to support legibility.
  - Keep text presentation simple.
  - Use upper and lower case.
  - Don't animate text.
- Draw contrasts among screen elements.
- Apply color as a supporting signal.

Visual and auditory impairments are at the root of many barriers to senior–computer interaction. For example, age brings declines in our abilities to perceive colors and discern contrasts. The goal of the designer is to empower the senior to discern interface elements whether they be objects on a screen or sounds. The W3C (Caldwell *et al.*, 2006) states this usability principle succinctly, 'Content must be perceivable.'

3.9.1 **Help Seniors Discern Graphics**

Color distinctions that succeed on paper can lose their oomph with the lower resolution of a computer screen. Highly detailed graphics do not scale down. Both these issues are exacerbated by an age-related decline in ability to perceive colors, depth, or small details. Simple graphics with strong color distinctions are more easily discernible for seniors.

And while you're at it, remember that some seniors will discern your graphics through sound, not sight; they will depend on a screen reader to tell them the content of graphics. Prepare for them with alternative text (alt tags) for all graphics, images, and image maps. When there is text within a graphic, make sure the alt tag contains that same text to provide an equivalent experience for users with screen readers. For icons, for example a 'home' icon, include the name of the icon in the alt text. When a graphic contains no information, for example, if it is only used to insert space, use alt =". The screen reader will pass over the graphic, saving the senior user time (Figure 3.6).

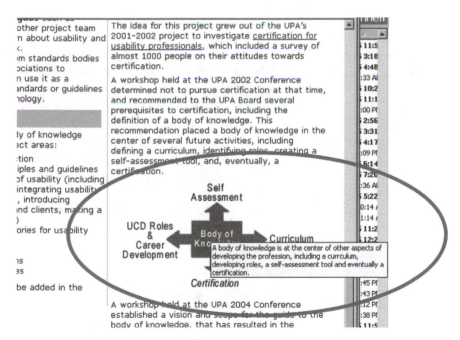

Figure 3.6 This alt tag that tells the whole story (UPA, 2005).

3.9.2 **Promote Legibility**

Legibility becomes more important for older users because they tend to read screen content more than younger users who tend to scan. The first factor that comes to mind when discussing legibility is text size. Text should never be smaller than 12 points (Nahm *et al.*, 2004).

Empower Seniors to Have Large Text

The text size factor has almost entered the realm of urban myth as a driving factor in improving seniors' onscreen experiences. There is surprising evidence that enlarging text size does not improve the reading experience for seniors, but seniors do prefer it (Chadwick-Dias *et al.*, 2003). So, because satisfaction is an important component of usability, there is an argument for continuing to accommodate seniors' preference for large text size. This introduces a potential to demonstrate the fact that a web site welcomes seniors by using adjustable fonts and showing seniors on the home page how to adjust font size (Figure 3.7).

If you can't use adjustable fonts, design for the lowest resolution that senior users will use. Remember that many seniors do not know how to change display resolution. The out-of-the-box resolution is the one they retain.

Use Strong Color Contrasts to Support Legibility

Color contrasts and brightness impact legibility. For example, it is difficult for the senior eye to focus on pastel type against a light background because there is not enough contrast between text and background. Not so long ago, the rule of thumb was 'Never use white type against a black background.' In fact, for senior citizens reading titles onscreen, white font on a black background is more legible than black on white (Arditi, 2006a). Aim for strong color contrasts with screen background colors, not only for bodies of text, but also for headlines and subtitles (Figure 3.8).

Keep Text Presentation Simple

As with so many other aspects of onscreen design, 'keep it simple' is a basic usability principle for legibility. Distorting text reduces legibility; it adds information for the

Figure 3.7 *These controls empower novice seniors to enlarge the font on their site without having to use the browser controls (ASHA, 2006).*

Figure 3.8 The left column provides sharp contrast between link titles and background in the left column. The variety in letter sizes with initial capital letters and lower case letters promotes legibility (US Census Bureau, 2006a).

brain to process. Stretching text builds a barrier between the senior user and the message you are trying to send in the interface. Avoid fancy font effects such as handwriting, italics, or condensed effects. Kurniawan and Zaphiris (2005) recommend a sans serif 12–14 point font.

Spaces between characters, words, or lines of text play important roles in legibility for seniors. Don't crowd characters or words together. Senior readers will have difficulty distinguishing among the words if they appear to be one long word. Don't fully justify text on a page that you intend to present to seniors. Gordon (2005) shows that the variations in spaces between words in fully justified text cause confusion during visual processing. It is also important to leave sufficient space between lines. Arditi (2006b) recommends that the height of the space between lines be 25% to 30% of the height of the type.

Use Upper and Lower Case

Because reading speed can decrease with age, make sure the interface does nothing to add to the trend. Trying to read text that only contains upper case letters can slow users down by 14% to 20% (Black, 2002). The human eye perceives words presented in upper case as solid visual blocks because every letter is the same height. Initial capital letters provide an appreciable difference between the first letter and the rest of the word. When a user is reading, the eye perceives whole words, especially the tops of words. There is variety among the heights of lower case letters and the contrast of an initial capital followed by lower case letters. This variety in height makes the whole word easier to discern. No matter if it's a label, a title, a headline, or a body of text, don't present text entirely in capital letters.

Don't Animate Text

Seniors who read slowly are not going to get your message if it cycles off the page. Those with short-term memory reductions may need to revisit the text, which is impossible to do if the text has disappeared. If you must animate, move the text slowly. Gordon (2005) shows that presenting information to a senior too quickly can cause reading problems.

3.9.3 Draw Contrasts Among Screen Elements

Not only do people tend to react quickly to strong contrasts in brightness, many seniors need those strong contrasts to help them discern important screen elements. For example, to make sure that critical warning messages catch the senior user's attention, maximize the brightness contrast between the message and other elements on the screen. One strategy is to present the warning message in a very dark font against a very light background. If there is no way to get around using a graphic with small details, for example a company logo, make sure that the brightness of these details contrasts strongly with the brightness of nearby elements in the display (Figure 3.9).

If there is too much brightness, some seniors cannot discern screen elements, for example when the background is white. Lopes (2001) suggests giving these senior users a gray background with a density not brighter than 30% of white intensity.

3.9.4 Apply Color as a Supporting Signal

Because our ability to discern colors decreases with age, never depend on color alone to distinguish screen content. As our eyes age, they lose some of their ability to distinguish between colors in certain combinations.

Relegate color to the role of a supporting signal. Never rely on color alone to distinguish screen elements. When applying color to a screen element, view the element in black and white to make sure that color doesn't have to work alone to distinguish that element. In this age of mobile computing, consider the senior with a color deficiency who is looking at a small screen in bright sunshine. Color distinctions can be nonexistent to this senior user. Provide redundant signals; for example, in addition to changing colors to signal system status, change the shape of the icon when the status changes.

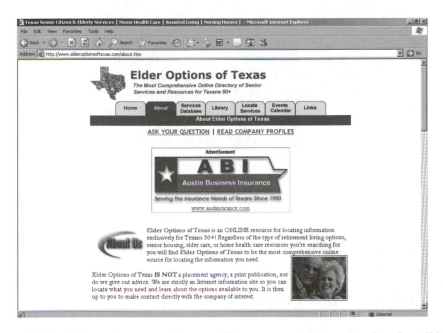

Figure 3.9 Outlining tabs assures that, even if a user turns off the color, the tabs will be discernible. Strong color contrasts denote the current page. They also build trust by identifying the advertisement so that users won't be led to think that it is part of the site's offerings. Note the use of the verbs, ask and read (Elder Options of Texas, 2006).

Think twice before deciding to use color coding to distinguish among modules of a complex application or groups of pages on a web site. Forcing the senior user to keep track of many different color distinctions can cause confusion. On the other hand, using the same color scheme throughout a web site or application can help seniors reinforce seniors' observation that they have not arrived at an unintended destination.

3.10 Accommodating Seniors' Work Styles

- Make software configurable.
- Provide large clickable areas.
- Offer alternative access to information.
- Meet seniors' expectations.
- Assure multimodal interaction.
- Give seniors time to complete tasks.

Seniors' work styles are sometimes influenced by cognitive and physical disabilities. They may read or work more slowly than other users. Some seniors with limited manual dexterity use a track ball instead of a mouse. To reduce seniors' input effort, screen elements need to be located together in a sequence that conforms with the seniors' logical workflow. Others, who must slowly sweep and click, for example because arthritis inhibits dragging and dropping, benefit from this design strategy too.

Just as importantly, seniors are influenced by a lifetime of workplace paradigms that have changed radically in the last decades. Chief among these is the independent work style which contrasts so sharply with the collaborative work style of younger workers. Chadwick-Dias *et al.* (2004) have shown that this lack of collaboration while learning to use the web leads to seniors experiencing more usability problems than younger users do, regardless of how frequently the seniors use the web. This argues for design that makes software easy to learn and easy to use by accommodating seniors' work styles.

3.10.1 **Make Software Configurable**

An important strategy is to make the software configurable. For example, certain disabilities may cause a senior to unintentionally click repeatedly when she only wants to click once. Software that accommodates these unintentional extra clicks empowers that senior to use a mouse or other clicking device. Sticky keys empower seniors who have difficulty pressing more than one key at a time.

3.10.2 **Provide Large Clickable Areas**

Diminished manual dexterity and tremors characterize the senior user group. In comparison with younger users, seniors can take twice as long to position the cursor over a small icon and make five times as many positioning errors in the process (Worden *et al.*, 1997). Kurniawan and Zaphiris (2005) point out that seniors should not be required to double click for the simple reason that they may not be able to.

When the interface requires them to click on a screen element, seniors need that element to be large. Chisnell, Redish, and Lee (2006) discovered in their work for the American Association of Retired People (AARP) that buttons should be at least 180 × 22 pixels (Figure 3.10).

Consider seniors who have difficulty locating the cursor over even a large clickable area by providing clickable white space around the area and separating the clickable elements so that they don't unintentionally click on one element when intending to click on another (Figure 3.11).

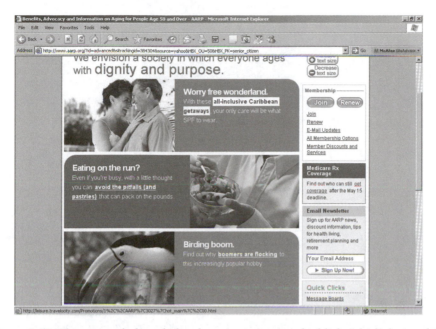

Figure 3.10 *This site underlines links, then, on mouseover, highlights the links in white, displaying a large clickable area with strong color contrast (AARP, 2006a).*

3.10.3 **Offer Alternative Access to Information and Functionality**

One of the principal means of accommodating senior work styles is to provide alternative interaction mechanisms. Make sure that interfaces support input devices beyond the traditional keyboard and mouse, such as trackballs, typing sticks, and speech commands. Give seniors options, for example:

- Keyboard alternatives.
- Icons that repeat menu options.
- Repeated links at strategic points on web pages.
- The choice between mousing from field to field or using the tab key.

Most importantly, remember that this group includes many novices, so make the options obvious. Don't require the seniors to discover the options. If the only alternative is through a secret right mouse button, in fact, there's no redundancy at all for the novice senior (Figure 3.12).

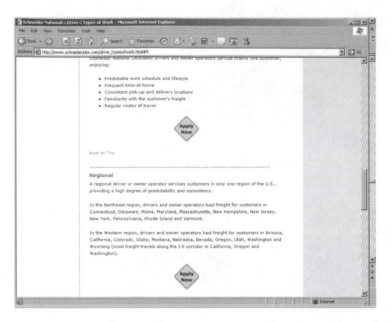

Figure 3.11 *A company that actively recruits senior workers leaves plenty of white space around buttons (Schneider National, 2006).*

Drop-down and fly-out menus can be unattainable targets for hands that have trouble controlling a pointer. For a hand with tremors, locating a pointer over a pull-down or fly-out menu, then clicking and dragging to a selection can be problematic. When an interface features such devices, make sure it also offers a stationary alternative, for example the option to locate the cursor over large icons or a list of links. Lists of links, especially if arranged hierarchically with indentations, take up more room, but are accessible to these users. Plus, with the whole list visible, there is no need to remember the options. Holding the pointer over a scroll bar falls into the same category. Seniors do better with screens that curtail the need to scroll by offering within-page links (Figure 3.13).

3.10.4 **Meet Seniors' Expectations**

User-centered design arises from understanding not only users' needs, but also their expectations. Sometimes twenty-first century designers' expectations don't align with the expectations that seniors bring to the web. For example, the days of underlined links are quickly falling behind us. Today, designers expect users to identify links by

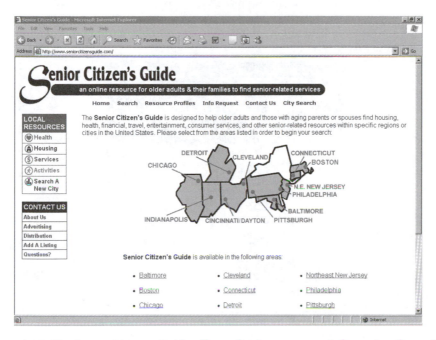

Figure 3.12 *The Senior Citizens Guide offers redundant access to information, large titles so that users don't have to click on small points on a map, plus an alphabetized list of links. In the bar on the left, while the icons are clickable, so are their text labels; the combination results in large clickable areas (Spindle, 2006).*

mouseovers. Novice senior users don't have the same expectations for the look of links as younger users do. If a title looks like the answer to their information need, senior users are likely to click on the title expecting transport to relevant information. Accommodate seniors' expectations. When text, for example a title, looks to seniors like a link, make it a link.

3.10.5 **Assure Multimodal Interaction**

We are in the midst of a migration away from WIMP (windows, icons, menus, and pointers) interfaces toward multimodal interfaces. This is a good trend for seniors. Like fire engines with sirens and flashing lights, an application or a web site needs to send redundant signals to its senior users. For example, a sound can accompany a text signal in a warning message box. The goal is to accommodate seniors with different capabilities, expertise, or expectations.

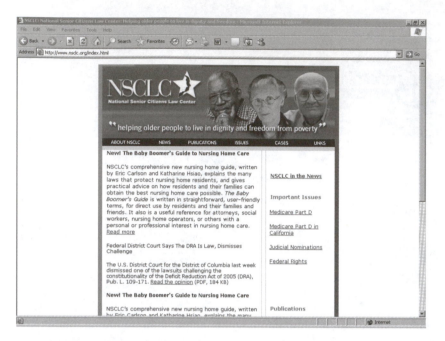

Figure 3.13 *This page welcomes seniors with photos that show the site is for them. It presents its contents in easy-to-navigate lists with plenty of white space around list items. Underlining identifies links. Strong contrast between font and background promote legibility (NSCLC, 2006).*

If the web site or application is designed strictly for seniors, consider providing an entire text page and make sure to give quick notice that you've done so. As soon as the screen reader comes to the page, the first element it should encounter is notice of the text version. Don't burden seniors using screen readers with the need to listen to nonintegral information on the entire page to learn at the bottom that there was a text version available.

While sound can be an empowering mechanism for senior users with visual disabilities, don't depend on sound alone. The senior user group has many users with hearing deficiencies. So, if there's a video on the site or in the tutorial, make sure there are text captions or subtitles.

3.10.6 Give Seniors Time to Complete Tasks

No one would deny that helping users work more efficiently makes good sense in a call center. It also makes sense when designing for seniors. Gordon (2005) shows that when information processing speed is impaired, so is response time. Seniors may not work as quickly as their younger colleagues. Windows that expire quickly are not appropriate for senior users who think or move slowly. When seniors are filling out forms, tactics such as word prediction, prepopulating fields with defaults, importing data from other forms, all combine to reduce the workload. An added benefit to each of these tactics is reduced input errors.

Even though seniors tend to read rather than scan a web page, there is still a strong argument for providing short salient pieces of information rather than long paragraphs. Gordon (2005) points out that these brief information presentations are easier to process when there is impaired attention span.

3.11 **Empowering Senior Computer Literacy**

- Direct seniors through design.
- Leverage the power of metaphors.
- Be sure that titles and labels inform.
- Be consistent.
- Speak the seniors' language.
- Provide a workplace without distractions.
- Teach through tutorials and wizards.

A notable, and possibly unique attribute of the senior user group is the fact that computing experience, at least using the web, does not necessarily translate into expertise (Chadwick-Dias *et al.*, 2004). It may take seniors longer to learn how to use software. Even seniors who use the web frequently may persist in displaying naïve user behaviors long after younger novices have moved to expert levels. Seniors may encounter learning obstacles that younger users do not, for example eye and hand coordination (Lopes, 2001). For example, it may be difficult for a senior to learn which direction to move a mouse to scroll to the top of a document.

Empowering computer literacy starts with respecting the fact that when there is cognitive degeneration, seniors' learning styles may be slow and require lots of repetition (Gordon, 2005). Empowering seniors to be computer literate requires building reasonable expectations about computing and meeting those expectations, for example by providing a consistent interface to facilitate learning and remembering. Minimizing cognitive load is a powerful tool for empowering senior computer literacy.

3.11.1 **Direct Seniors Through Design**

The usability principle of directing through design is about providing content that shows users where to go next or what to do next. Examples include wizards, forms that lead senior users from field to field, and navigation schemes that lead senior users through tasks, pages, or web sites. Not only do seniors require more navigation cues than other users, but those cues must be more noticeable (Kurniawan and Zaphiris, 2005). Directing senior users through design relieves some of the learning burden.

Directive design can relieve cognitive burden. For example, if senior users always perform certain actions in predictable sequences, lead them through the familiar sequence without asking them to remember what they need to do next. Group related content to accommodate the usability principle of meeting users' expectations (Figure 3.14).

Directive design can reduce user errors. To help seniors stay on course when navigating onscreen tables, distinguish table rows and columns with outlining, for example black or gray. Alternate row colors, for example with gray and white fill. But don't get too fancy – plaid patterns or textured effects present too much visual information.

Directive design can even help seniors work faster. Many usability engineers who have worked with seniors have noticed a slow, careful approach characterized

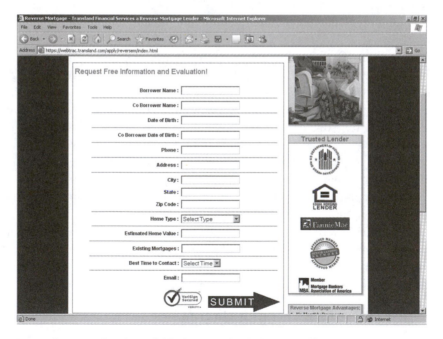

Figure 3.14 *This site offers large fields for users to click in as well as a large submit icon. It also leads seniors from top to bottom through a simple form (Transland Financial Services, 2006).*

by pausing before clicking. To help seniors work faster despite what he calls 'cautious clicking,' Tullis recommends using action words in links (Sharton, 2005). In Figure 3.14 above, this approach provides a verb in the title, *Request Free Information and Evaluation!*

3.11.2 **Leverage the Power of Metaphors**

In a human–computer interface, metaphor is the use of a familiar graphic or word to represent something other than the meaning usually associated with that graphic or word, for example a technical concept. Metaphors make it easier for people to understand and learn. The desktop metaphor that employs nested folders to represent directory structures is commonplace in graphical user interfaces. Photographs and graphics can introduce design themes through metaphor. For senior users, well-chosen metaphors reduce the need for cognitive effort and improve learnability (Yousef, 2001).

Lopes (2001) points out a problem that seniors often encounter with onscreen metaphors; they expect to apply problem-solving strategies that derive from using technologies that they know about, such as TV or radio. You can turn this expectation into a design opportunity. The usability principle is to build on what the seniors know to provide metaphors that empower them to do new things with computers (Figure 3.15).

Figure 3.15 Drawing on the metaphor of a mailman, seniors are invited to sign up for an online newsletter (SeniorMag, 2006).

Reduce the need for cognition by not forcing seniors to learn something new. Give seniors metaphors that build on the world where they've lived most of their lives, not the world of twenty-first century technology. Instead of asking them to drag names from one column to another to build a list, empower them to build that list by clicking in large check boxes or simply clicking on items as if they were checking off items on a shopping list. In this case, there's the added benefit of eliminating the need to drag and drop, a difficult or impossible maneuver for some seniors with manual dexterity deficiencies.

3.11.3 Be Sure That Titles and Labels Inform

Informative titles and labels give seniors a preview of an application or a site's content. The information they convey empowers seniors to confidently, quickly, and accurately navigate past unwanted content.

Much web design focuses on concise presentations, one-word links, and pithy sound bites for titles. Remember, seniors not only don't mind reading, they need navigation guidance. Within the boundaries of balancing white space and screen clutter, consider adding some action words to those short links. Let the seniors know what's going to happen when they click. Instead of having a link that simply says *more ¨* say *see more dresses*. The value added is that informative titles and labels decrease navigation errors for all user groups.

Teach seniors about the interface with content links 7–12 words long. These short explanations help novice seniors learn about screen elements and help other novice users learn about infrequently used screen elements.

3.11.4 Be Consistent

The cumulative effect of consistent use of color, graphics style, and fonts and consistent location of screen elements is a sense of familiarity that promotes learning. When the look and feel consistently meet their expectations, seniors' sense of control over the system grows.

Start by meeting expectations seniors have developed from prior web visits. When conventions already exist, for example providing a link to the home page in the upper left corner of a web page, empower seniors to reuse what they've already learned by incorporating the convention. Then, be sure to be consistent within the site, for example, if unvisited links are blue and visited links are red on the home page, make sure this is the scheme throughout the site.

Make sure that the effect of any action is consistent throughout an application, and as far as possible, among applications. Make sure that the meaning of an icon does not change within a web site or an application suite. This consistency builds confidence that a specific action will produce an expected result.

Locate screen elements consistently. If the OK button is located in the center bottom of one screen, don't move it to the right bottom on the next. Name items consistently too. If you call the search button *Search* on one page, don't change its name to *Go* on another.

If you're going to use bullets, always make them large. If those bullets look like links, either make them links or change their look so that novice seniors won't think they are supposed to click on the bullets.

Filling in forms is a common activity in office applications and on the web, for example registering for restricted sites or creating a customer profile. Consistent form design helps to build a set of met expectations that empower seniors to work confidently.

3.11.5 Speak the Seniors' Language

Simply put, techno-jargon is anything the senior without a technical background will not understand. People who have tried to troubleshoot for novice senior users often run into a communication barrier. The seniors may not know the names of screen elements. They may not even be able to describe what they're doing in language that makes sense to a young techie. Have every screen of the site or application reviewed by typical senior users to find remnants of jargon. Then replace that jargon with words the senior reviewers use.

The interface and any documentation that may accompany it need to speak the seniors' language, not the developers' or designers' language. For example, directions such as 'Download now' tell novice seniors little and threaten their sense of control over their experience. If you're trying to sell this customer base downloadable software, explain what *download* means. If you're concerned that the definition will be a distraction for more computer-sophisticated users, include the definition in instructions for new users. Provide an obvious link to those instructions on the home page.

Speech interfaces have special obligations to courteously speak the seniors' language. Again, it's a matter of respect. Whether they're interacting with voice prompts or personal autonomous intelligent agents, seniors, like other user groups, can be expected to respond positively to courtesy.

Speaking the seniors' language includes spell-checking and using correct grammar. Not only does this make a better impression, it facilitates machine translation – producing better translations for those seniors who must translate a web page into another language.

3.11.6 **Provide a Workplace Without Distractions**

Just like the fashion industry, web design has its design trends and fads. Over time, they rotate between clean design with lots of white space and then densely populated pages that crowd content into one-glance presentations. Aging often brings on reduced ability to find important details in a complex screen presentation. Instead of quick paths, there is distraction. Simple design reduces distractions and expedites access to a screen's offerings. Simplicity is a common usability principle to accommodate senior users, especially novices (e.g. O'Connell *et al.*, 2003).

At first glance, a Web page appears to be a pattern. The pattern is established by the arrangement of screen elements into areas, for example areas of color, areas of text, or areas devoted to graphics. A page with too many areas, each competing for the seniors' attention, defeats the goal of delivering content to them. A page with too many variations within areas, for example many type fonts or colors within an area, also barrages seniors with too much information.

Start by focusing on the site or application's goals to make sure that only needed content contributes to the pattern. For example, in an informational web site, eliminate distracting off-topic content and eliminate screen elements that compete with important content for seniors' attention. Next, group content elements of similar function or topic into page areas to empower seniors to focus on the aspects of their chosen tasks. The goal is to present the senior with a simple but engaging visual pattern with no competition among the parts of that pattern.

While aesthetics are important, clean design is more important. Wallpaper may fill an aesthetic purpose for web pages, but for seniors, wallpaper can turn into clutter competing with a page's principal content or diminishing legibility.

Don't distract seniors with invitations to use unavailable content. If there is information or functionality that is off-limits to unauthorized users, don't display links to that content in public parts of a site or on application screens that can be accessed by all users.

While animated text can be a distraction, some seniors require a degree of animation to help them discern difficult-to-notice screen elements such as a pointer. In this case, it also helps to make the pointer very large (Lopes, 2001).

It's a fact of life that web sites have ads and that the site providers want the users to see the ads. This doesn't mean that the ads need to distract the users. Distinguish ads from other content so that users can discern that ads are ads, and view the ads, but not to the detriment of performing other tasks at the site. For example, use a different color background in the area that contains the ads. When the content of the ads strongly contrasts with the content of the site, label the ads so that seniors don't think they've arrived at the wrong site.

3.11.7 **Teach Through Tutorials and Wizards**

There's evidence that seniors learn computing better if they have a teacher (Billipp, 2001). Young people are responding to this need. In many countries, there are programs partnering computer-savvy youngsters with seniors (e.g. Aphek, 2001). However, sometimes there's no human teacher available and the senior must depend on onscreen tutorials or wizards. If the application or site offers this functionality, put the seniors in control of the experience. Give them the ability to go back and review at any point. Provide plenty of screen shots to demonstrate various states of the system, illustrating the effects of user actions. In tutorials and wizards, it is especially important to make sure that language doesn't resort to techno-jargon.

3.12   **Building Seniors' Confidence**

• Manage errors.
  ○ Prevent errors.
  ○ Help seniors recover from errors.
• Make sure help really helps.

Chisnell *et al.* (2006) remind us that when designing for seniors we need to consider not only age, ability, and aptitude, but also attitude. Building seniors' confidence is key to helping them develop a positive attitude toward computing.

Like other novice users, novice seniors worry about clicking on something that's not a link, or worse, clicking on something that takes them someplace unexpected; not being able to find their way back on a web site; being unable to compose or send an email; losing their work; or causing the computer to crash. The best way to overcome this lack of confidence is to put seniors firmly in control of their computing experiences by empowering them to manage errors. A basic usability principle is to make sure that adequate help is always available.

3.12.1 **Manage Errors**

The classic purposes of error messages are to

• Prevent errors.
• Notify users when errors have been made.
• Explain what the error is.

- Provide remedies.
- Empower users to employ these remedies.

Designing for seniors brings to light additional purposes.

- Put users at their ease.
- Build confidence in the seniors' own sense of control over the system.

Prevent Errors

If an application doesn't help seniors avoid errors, there is a high potential that their success and satisfaction will suffer. Where there is a known high potential for senior users to make errors, the system must guide senior users to avoid those errors. For example, in forms, it is helpful to show what format is required for entering dates. On an e-commerce site, seniors benefit from clear instructions that walk them through shopping and purchasing (Figure 3.16).

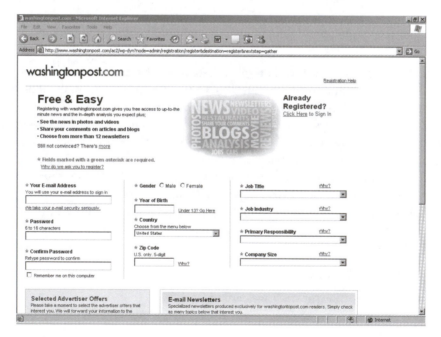

Figure 3.16 *To prevent errors, this form gives directions for correct input and courteously offers links to the reasons it requests information. It explains the significance of the required field asterisks for novices.*

Sometimes a warning message is the only way to prevent an error. Make the message polite, not threatening. There's no need to intimidate the senior user; the goal is to empower him or her to avoid making an error. To that end, inform the senior user of what the impending error is, what its possible consequences are, and how to avoid making it. And don't forget to emphasize the brightness contrast between the message and other screen content to bring this important information to the seniors' immediate attention.

Don't invite seniors to make errors by trying to activate unavailable functionality. Eliminate or change the look of controls for unavailable functionality. For example, gray out the element or position an X over it.

Help Seniors Recover from Errors

Seniors grew up in a world where error recovery simply was not part of the technology they knew. In their youth and early adulthood, technology was kitchen appliances, electric clocks, radios, cars. Either the interface was so simple that mistakes were unlikely (e.g. turning the radio on or off) or the mistakes were disasters (failing to step on the break at a stop sign). Build a bridge from seniors' knowledge of earlier technologies to the age of twenty-first century senior users in control of computing experiences by showing seniors that they can recover from errors.

By empowering recovery from errors, a system reinforces senior users' sense of control and helps them build confidence in their ability to succeed. Start by putting senior users at ease. Error messages that scream in bold capital letters against red backgrounds can intimidate when the goal should be to empower. Use a less threatening background color, for example light yellow, and use everyday upper and lower case sentences. Clear, nonthreatening, informative language is essential. Phrase the message to inform seniors why there is an error situation, not to blame them or threaten them with dire consequences.

Cryptic messages such as 'Error #123456' are meaningless to someone other than the developer and can be perplexing or intimidating to the novice senior. Explain what the error was and set out steps to remedy it. Whenever possible, let the system lead the senior users through error recovery. For example, at the end of form filling, the system can take senior users to blank fields that require an answer.

3.12.2 **Make Sure Help Really Helps**

Most importantly, make sure that help really does help. Lead seniors through the help experience with easy to understand, legible, step-by-step instructions illustrated by screen shots.

Informative and easy-to-use help is essential to seniors' success and satisfaction. Make help visible to seniors when and where they are trying to solve a problem. Don't burden people who have memory deficiencies with the problem of having to remember what they've seen in the help screen when they return to the application screen. Make both visible simultaneously.

Focus groups are an important prerequisite to identifying the terms seniors will use to name help topics. In a focus group, each senior has the opportunity to nominate terms. Then they work together to decide on the best choices. Once the names of the help topics are identified, provide access to help through as many of these terms as you can.

Present help topic terms in alphabetical order, not according to the designers' or developers' expectations of how people will use the site. Ordering links to help topics according to a representation of the structure of a site or application places a cognitive burden on the senior who does not know that structure. This approach does not provide help for seniors who are under stress because they have a problem. They come to the web site or application already knowing alphabetical order. Take advantage of what they already know to lead them to what they need to find.

Finally, don't limit helpfulness to help screens. Clear instructions within an application or web site, presented at the point when seniors need them most, are the best kind of help because they prevent problems. And make sure to test those instructions with seniors before publishing.

3.13 **Imagine the Future**

Consider the potential benefits of twenty-first century senior computing. Anyone who has ever sat at their grandparents' knees and listened to stories of their lives knows the power of those stories. Imagine empowering seniors to easily record those stories to share them with future generations, even with people outside the family circle. Imagine seniors who have trouble hearing over the telephone swapping emails with grandchildren away at college. Imagine empowering home-bound seniors with the independence of ordering their own groceries and medications from within the comfort and safety of their own homes. Imagine unlocking the joy of visiting the world's museums, having history and the latest breaking news at their beck and call.

Technology promises an empowered world for twenty-first century seniors. Intelligent agents will fill their information needs. Smart houses will monitor their well-being. Smart robots will tend to their needs. The web will connect them to each other and to the world, perhaps empowering them to live at home longer, perhaps enabling them to live more productive lives. Computing technology's potential to improve twenty-first century senior living depends on our ability to provide senior-focused user interfaces.

Imagine a better world for seniors and because of that, a better world for us all. It all comes down to being 'compassionate and aware computer scientists' (Hix and O'Connell, 2005), and bringing that compassion and awareness to life through senior-focused design.

Imagine a twenty-first century world that's better for all of us because it empowers senior computing. Then do something about it. The next time you're involved in user interface design, focus on the seniors.

3.13.1 Implications for Users

The implications of senior-centered design can be as minor as making it easier to click on a button or as major as opening the world of computing to people whose backgrounds have not prepared them for it. Perhaps the most exciting aspect is an improved quality of life embodied in the ability to connect with other people even when confined to one's home or to realize a life-time dream of running one's own small business even though times have changed and business now requires computer literacy. Senior-focused design implies empowerment to choose one's own groceries and clothing even though an outing to a shopping center is a problem; to partake of the twenty-first century information feast; to enjoy electronic games; and to relax with onscreen reading. It's all about thinking in the future tense, empowering twenty-first century senior citizenhood enriched by the power of computing.

But the power of senior-focused design isn't limited to senior citizens. Because it addresses so many special-needs issues, it also benefits users with disabilities. Finally, as this chapter has noted above, the benefits will extend to other users. Improved legibility, improved discernibility, improved navigation, in short, improved design benefits a wide range of users.

3.13.2 Implications for Designers

Senior-focused design means a new approach for designers. It means a refocusing on those usability principles that address senior computing. For some designers, senior-focused design implies a change of mindset. It implies a stronger consideration of older users' needs and a willingness to address those needs in design. It presents a challenge to achieve engaging designs that work for a web site's wide user base, but also accommodate the unique needs that occur incrementally as we age. At some point, any computer user, even twenty-first century designers, will need and benefit from senior-centered design.

Throughout the development life cycle, all design activities need to involve seniors and to address their needs. This concern starts during product conceptualization and requirements definition. It continues all the way through site launch or product release. It means including seniors in all testing that focuses on user interaction. If designers are involved in testing, the fact is that senior-focused design can mean more work, for example, adding extra test cycles for senior-related interface issues. It can mean more effort, perhaps recruiting users at a senior center or moving testing activities to a senior living facility; perhaps providing a test environment that is accessible for seniors with disabilities. It can take more time. For example, instead of scheduling five user observations, you may have to schedule 10 sessions for seniors, each half as long as sessions for younger users who do not tire as quickly as seniors. Senior-focused design may require the designer to become its advocate, selling the idea to managers who keep their eyes on the bottom line and resist this extra time, effort, and expense.

3.13.3 Implications for Researchers

The implications of senior-centered design for researchers are exciting and brimming with questions to answer and possibilities to make unique contributions. The base question is simple: what do we need to do to empower seniors to compute? However, the implications of the simple question are wide-ranging. Much remains to be learned about how seniors interact with computing. What are the best design strategies to accommodate those behaviors? How can we best assuage the reluctance of some seniors to embrace computing? We've just begun to understand how web use can improve seniors' lives. What technologies, services, and information should we add to the web to help them enjoy a better twenty-first century senior citizenhood?

The senior-centered task list for researchers is long, interesting, and challenging. It is multidisciplinary, requiring participation of experts in fields such as aging, computer science, human factors, usability, psychology, all the disciplines that can shed light on senior computing issues. It will require collaboration across these disciplines. Just like senior-focused design, this research will require participation by seniors and special consideration of their uniqueness. Again, a mindset change may be in order. It's time to start thinking about senior research issues in the future tense. It's all about focusing on improving seniors' futures. It means understanding their twentieth century roots, their present unique needs, and their potential to include computing in a future they could hardly imagine in their early youth.

3.13.4 **Implications For Policymakers**

This chapter argues for recognition of the fact that senior citizens bring unique needs to computing. Policymakers have the opportunity to make sure that these needs are acknowledged and met. In organizations that commission software applications or web sites, policymakers are in a position to require that senior users' needs are met. Legislative policymakers have already implemented legislation requiring some software providers to meet the needs of users with special needs. This legislation needs to be expanded to include senior-specific needs by a wider range of providers. Academic policymakers have the opportunity to influence the thinking of twenty-first century designers by including senior needs in their course topics. And while we're at it, policies that promote computing education geared to seniors speak to another side of the issue.

Sadly, research funding for senior-centered computing often takes a back seat to other equally important topics. Policymakers have a need and an obligation to shine a spotlight on the needs of this important user group and fund the research that is needed to empower them to harness the potential of computing to improve their senior years.

References

Addelston, J.D. and O'Connell, T.A. (2004) Usability and the agile project management framework. *Cutter Consortium Agile Software Development and Project Management Executive Report*, 5(10).

Addelston, J.D. and O'Connell, T.A. (2005) Integrating accessibility into the spiral model of the software development life cycle. In *Universal Access in HCI* (ed. C., Stephanidis), Lawrence Erlbaum Associates, Mahway, NJ, [CD-ROM].

Amend, J.M. (2005) Retiring boomers represent next big windfall for fund industry. `http://www.financial-planning.com/pubs/fpi/20050411102.html` [accessed 5 August 2006].

American Association of Retired People (2006a) Home page. `http://www.aarp.org` [accessed 25 August 2006].

American Association of Retired People (2006b) Overview. `http://www.aarp.org/about_aarp/aarp_overview/a2003-01-13-aarphistory.html` [accessed 15 April 2006].

American Psychological Association (2001) *Publication Manual of the American Psychological Association*, 5th edn. Washington, D.C., American Psychological Association.

American Speech Language Hearing Association (ASHA) (2006) Home page. `http://www.asha.org/default.htm` [accessed 6 June 2006].

Aphek, E. (2001) Minimizing the digital divide and the inter-generation gap. In *Ubiquity* (2, 29), New York; ACM, p. 1.

Araujo, I. and Araujo I. (2003) Developing trust in internet commerce, Proceedings of the 2003 Conference of the Centre for Advanced Studies on Collaborative Research, Toronto, Canada, IBM Press 1–15.

Arditi, A. (2006a) Effective color contrast: designing for people with partial sight and color deficiencies. `http://www.lighthouse.org/color_contrast.htm` [accessed 21 April 2006].

Arditi, A. (2006b) Making text legible: designing for people with partial site. `http://www.lighthouse.org/print_leg.htm` [accessed 21 April 2006].

Berger, M., Chadwick-Dias, A. and Tullis, T. (2005) Leveraging universal design in a financial services company. `http://www.acm.org/sigaccess/newsletter/june05/june05_4.php` [accessed 6 June 2006].

Billipp, S.H. (2001) The psychosocial impact of interactive computer use within a vulnerable elderly population: a report on a randomized prospective trial in a home health care setting. *Public Health Nursing* 18: 138.

Black, J. (2002) Usability is next to profitability. `http://www.businessweek.com/technology/content/dec2002/tc2002124_2181.htm` [accessed 5 August 2006].

Caldwell, B., Chisholm, W., Slatin, J. and Vanderheiden, G. (eds) (2006) Web content accessibility guidelines 2.0. World Wide Web Consortium. `http://www.w3.org/TR/WCAG20` [accessed 20 May 2006].

Chadwick-Dias, A., McNulty, A.M. and Tullis, T. (2003) Web usability and age: how design changes can improve performance, *Proceedings of the 2003 Conference on Universal Usability,* 10–11 November, Vancouver, B.C., Canada. New York, ACM, pp. 30–37.

Chadwick-Dias, A., Tedesco, D. and Tullis, T. (2004) Older adults and web usability: is web experience the same as web expertise? *Proceedings of the Conference on Human Factors in Computing Systems,* Vienna, Austria. New York, ACM, pp. 1391–1394.

Chisnell, D.E., Redish, J.C. and Lee, A. (2006) New heuristics for understanding older adults as Web users. *Techniques in Communications* 53(1), 39–59.

Elder Options of Texas (2006) Home page. `http://www.elderoptionsoftexas.com/about.htm` [accessed 25 August 2006].

Ellis R.D. and Kurniawan S.H. (2000) Increasing the usability of online information for older users: a case study in participatory design. *International Journal of Human–Computer Interaction* 12(2), 263–276.

Fogg, B.J., Marable, L., Stanford, J. and Tauber, E.R. (2002) How do people evaluate a Web site's credibility? Results from a large study. `http://www.consumerwebwatch.org/news/report3_credibilityresearch/stanfordPTL_part1.htm` [accessed 13 May 2006].

Forrester Research (2004a) Accessible technology in computing – examining awareness, use, and future potential. `http://www.microsoft.com/enable/research/phase2.aspx` [accessed 20 May 2006].

Forrester Research (2004b) The wide range of abilities and its impact on computer technology. `http://www.microsoft.com/enable/research/phase2.aspx` [accessed 20 May 2006].

Fox, S. (2004) Older Americans and the Internet. Pew Internet & American Life Project, Washington, DC. `http://www.pewinternet.org/pdfs/PIP_Seniors_Online_2004.pdf` [accessed 25 March 2006].

Gordon, W.A. (2005) The interface between cognitive impairments and access to information technology. ACM SIGACCESS Accessibility and Computing (83). New York, ACM, pp. 3–6.

Haffner, K. (2004) The net's late bloomers. *New York Times.* `http://www.nytimes.com/2004/03/25/technology/circuits/25elde.html?th=andpagewanted=printandposition` [accessed 25 March 2004].

Hahn, C. (2005) Attack of the gaming grannies. `http://www.businessweek.com/innovate/content/oct2005/id20051018_173699.htm` [accessed 20 May 2006].

He, W., Sengupta, M., Velkhoff, V.A. and DeBarros, K.A. (2005) *65+ in the United States: 2005.* Washington, DC, US Census Bureau.

Hix, D. and O'Connell, T.A. (2005). Usability engineering as a critical process in designing for accessibility. In *Universal Access in HCI*, C. Stephanidis (ed.). Lawrence Erlbaum Associates, Mahway, NJ, [CD-ROM].

International Demographics (2004) The Media Audit: Internet use continues growing; most new use driven by older age groups. Houston, TX, International Demographics.

Kim, M. and Ahn, J. (2005) A model for buyer's trust in the e-marketplace, *Proceedings of the 7th International Conference on Electronic Commerce, USA,* pp. 195–200.

Koyani, S.J., Bailey, R.W., Nall J.R. *et al.* (2003) *Research-Based Web Design and Usability Guidelines,* Washington, DC, National Institutes of Health.

Kurniawan, S. and Zaphiris, P. (2005) Research-derived web design guidelines for older people Proceedings of the 7th International ACM SIGACCESS Conference on Computers and Accessibility, Baltimore, MD, New York, ACM, 129–135

Lopes, J.B. (2001) Designing user interfaces for severely handicapped persons. *Proceedings of the 2001 EC/NSF Workshop on Universal Accessibility of Ubiquitous Computing: Providing for the Elderly.* New York, ACM, pp. 100–106.

Maguire, J. (2005a) Seniors and e-commerce: selling to the older shopper. `http://www.ecommerce-guide.com/news/trends/article.php/3532196` [accessed 20 May 2006].

Maguire, J. (2005b) Seniors and e-commerce: selling to the older shopper. Part 2. `http://www.smallbusinesscomputing.com/emarketing/article.php /3550366%20` [accessed 20 May 2006].

McGann, R. (2004) People aged 55 and up drive U.S. Web growth. `http://www.clickz.com/stats/sectors/traffic_patterns/article.php/3446641` [accessed 3 May 2006].

Nahm, E.-S., Preece, J., Resnick, B., and Mills, M.E. (2004) Usability of health Web sites for older adults: a preliminary study. `http://www.nursingcenter.com/prodev/ce_article.asp?tid 5 532954` [accessed 5 August 2006].

National Senior Citizens Law Center (NSCLC) (2006) Home page. `http://www.nsclc.org/index.html` [accessed 25 August 2006].

O'Connell, T.A., Jonker, C., Burgett, J.L. and Silz K. (2003) Prospectives of the benefits of agent and semantic web based wireless applications for the elderly user in: Stephanidis C.(Ed.). *Universal Access in HCI: Inclusive Design in the Information Society,* Lawrence Erlbaum Associates, Mahway, NJ, 1025–1029.

O'Connell, T.A. and Murphy, E.D. (2006) The usability engineering behind user-centered processes for Web site development lifecycles in: Zaphiris P. Kuriniawan S.(Eds.), *Human Computer Interaction Research in Web Design and Evaluation,* Hershey, PA, Idea Group, 1–21

Schneider National (2006) Types of work. `http://www.schneiderjobs.com/drive_typesofwork.html#top` [accessed 23 September 2006].

SeniorMag (2006) Newsletter. `http://www.seniormag.com/business/newsletter.htm` [accessed 25 August 2006].

Sharton, E. (2005) Designing Web sites with senior citizens in mind. `http://www.boston.com/business/technology/articles/2005/04/03/designing_websites_with_senior_citizens_in_mind/` [accessed 5 August 2006].

Spindle Publishing Company (2006) Senior citizens' guide. `http://www.seniorcitizensguide.com/` [accessed 25 August 2006].

Sunrise Senior Living (2006) Home page. `http://www.sunriseseniorliving.com/Home.do` [accessed 23 September 2006].

Theofanos, M.F. and Redish, J.D. (2003) Guidelines for accessible and usable Web sites: observing users who work with screen readers. *Interactions* 10(6) 36–51.

Transland Financial Services (2006) Home page. `https://webtrac.transland.com/apply/reversem/index.html` [accessed 25 August 2006].

United Nations (2004) World population prospects: the 2004 revision: highlights. ESA/P/WP.193. 25 February 2004. New York, United Nations.

`http://www.un.org/esa/population/publications/WPP2004/2004Highlights_finalrevised.pdf` [accessed 20 May 2006].

US Access Board (2006) Site map. `http://www.access-board.gov/sitemap.htm` [accessed 23 September 2006].

US Bureau of Labor Statistics (2005a) Computer and Internet use at work summary. USDL 05-1457. `http://www.bls.gov/news.release/ciuaw.nr0.htm` [accessed 13 May 2006].

US Bureau of Labor Statistics (2005b) Household data annual averages: employment status of the civilian noninstitutional population by age, sex and race. `http://www.bls.gov/cps/cpsaat3.pdf` [accessed 13 May 2005].

US Census Bureau (2001) Census 2000 Brief: The 65 Years and Over Population: 2000 (C2KBR/01-10). `http://www.census.gov/prod/2001pubs/c2kbr01-10.pdf` [accessed 3 May 2006].

US Census Bureau (2006a) Home page. `http://www.census.gov/` [accessed 6 June 2006].

US Census Bureau (2006b) Scheduled downtime page. `http://www.census.gov/main/www/downtime.html` [accessed 6 June 2006].

US Department of Commerce (2002) A Nation online: How Americans are expanding their use of the Internet. Washington, DC, US Department of Commerce.

US Department of Commerce (2004) *A Nation Online: Entering the Broadband Age.* Washington, DC, US Department of Commerce.

US General Services Administration (2006) Senior citizens' resources. `http://www.firstgov.gov/Topics/Seniors.shtml` [accessed 1 October 2006].

Usability Professionals Association (UPA) (2005) Body of knowledge projects page. Accessed 1 July 2005.

Worden, A., Walker, N., Bharat, K. and Hudson, S. (1997) Making computers easier for older adults to use: area cursors and sticky icons *Proceedings of the SIGCHI Conference on Human Factors in Computing Systems* Atlanta, GA, New York, ACM, pp. 266–271.

World Health Organization (WHO) (2002) Active Aging: A Policy Framework. `http://www.euro.who.int/document/hea/eactagepolframe.pdf` [accessed 20 May 2006].

Yousef, M. (2001) Assessment of metaphor efficacy in user interfaces for the elderly: a tentative model for enhancing accessibility, *Proceedings of the 2001 EC/NSF Workshop on Universal Accessibility of Ubiquitous Computing: Providing for the Elderly,* New York, ACM, pp. 120–124.

Zaphiris, P., Ghiawadwala, M. and Mughal S. (2005) Age-centered research-based web design guidelines, *Conference on Human Factors in Computing Systems,* Portland, OR, New York, ACM, pp. 1897–1900.

Online Redesign of a Web Site's Information Architecture to Improve Accessibility for Users Who are Blind

4

Vanessa Evers and Hans Hillen

Human Computer Studies Laboratory, Institute for Informatics, University of Amsterdam, The Netherlands

Summary

This chapter addresses web site navigation for users who are blind. The chapter starts with a review of the relevant literature addressing Internet use by people who are blind, the problems they encounter while using the Internet, and the solutions that are currently available. The findings from this review offer an overview of requirements for the development of a prototype system that offers alternative navigation of the main content by audio output and keyboard input. The prototype system analyzes the pages of a web site to construct a main information architecture navigable by audio as well as extra functionality to provide context to aid the user in making decisions when navigating. This prototype is then tested in a small-scale qualitative study that assesses the ways in which users who are blind actually navigate web sites, the problems they encounter, and a usability evaluation of the prototype system. Ten users who are blind were involved in an in-depth user evaluation using interviews and observation techniques. The findings of the study show that users who are blind adopt a set of different reconnaissance strategies when navigating web sites. Results also show that successful navigation is mostly disrupted because of cognitive overload, lack of context when a decision needs to be made what direction to take on a web site, and inaccessible design elements. The user evaluation of the prototype system leads to further insights into the needs of users who are blind for navigating web sites and resulted in the identification of specific focus areas that need to be addressed to solve navigation problems for users who are blind.

4.1 Theoretical Background

In order to gain a better understanding of the way in which people who are blind use the Internet and the role that technology plays in their daily lives, the remainder of this section will evaluate literature relevant to Internet users who are blind, Internet accessibility for the blind, and assistive technology available to users who are blind.

4.1.1 **Internet Users Who are Blind**

It is important to distinguish between different types of blindness, as each type involves different problems which require different technological solutions (Paciello, 2000). This chapter will focus on Internet users who are considered blind as opposed to those who have low vision. According to the World Health Organization (WHO) there were 162 million visually impaired people world wide in 2002, of whom 124 million had low vision and 37 million were blind.[1]

The Internet can be seen as a possible environment where people who are blind should not be hampered by their visual impairment (Donker *et al.*, 2002). It allows users who are blind to directly access textual information without being dependent on third parties to convert text into Braille or speech. In other words, the barriers that visually impaired people encounter in the real world (such as reading mail or performing transactions) do not have to be present on the Internet. Because of this, people who are blind are theoretically able to access the same information as sighted users in the Internet. It is often assumed that people who are blind are also socially isolated. For example, the *compensation model* described by Guo *et al.* (2005) states that people who are socially inactive in the real world due to their impairment tend to compensate for this by being socially active on the Internet. However, a small-scale previous study on blind children's Internet use by Evers *et al.* (2005) shows that blind users were not found to be socially isolated. The children involved in the study were found to have strong social ties, only fewer than sighted children. The participants were not using the Internet to increase the number of ties but saw Internet communication and virtual communities as possible ways to maintain and extend existing ties.

4.1.2 **The Way in Which Blind Users Experience the Internet**

To assist users who are blind in accessing the Internet as well as their personal computer, hardware and software products called *assistive technology* have been developed (Paciello, 2000). The types of assistive technology which are mostly used are screen readers and refreshable Braille displays. *Screen readers* are operated through a keyboard-driven interface, and translate information displayed on the user's screen

---

[1]http://www.who.int/mediacentre/factsheets/fs282/en/.

(including text, but also navigation items such as form widgets and links) to synthetic speech. Screen readers can be used in combination with most common software applications, including mainstream browsers such as Internet Explorer or Mozilla Firefox. For web sites the screenreader provides structural navigation based on the web page's Document Object Model (DOM) structure, allowing the user to navigate a page by specific elements (e.g. headings, tables, and forms). Differences in voice patterns such as prosody and voice rate can be used to distinguish between different types of information. *Refreshable Braille displays* are rectangular rulers containing pins which can automatically protrude and retract to form Braille characters, depending on the textual content currently selected by the user. Braille displays offer a Braille representation of the text but are limited in the size of chunks they can process, making it a slow alternative except for very experienced users. Its output (which is silent) can provide a good addition to screen reader technology and can be useful when the screen reader pronounces text incorrectly (e.g. when text is written in a foreign language).

4.1.3 Accessibility Problems Related to Web site Navigation

The Web Accessibility Initiative, founded by the World Wide Web Consortium (W3C) has erected guidelines which should be followed by web content providers in order to create accessible web sites. However, several studies [e.g. by Sullivan and Matson, 2000; Stowers, 2002; and the UK Disability Rights Commission (Petrie, 2004)] show that these content providers are often not aware of these guidelines, or unwilling to invest time, money, and effort for such a relatively small user group (Lazar *et al.*, 2004). The remainder of this section will provide an overview of the common problems experienced by users who are blind on the Internet.

Internet users who are blind have to deal with problems inherent to the use of assistive technology in general. Research by Pitt and Edwards (1996) and Leporini *et al.* (2004) suggests that *converting large quantities of information into speech* can place a high demand on the user's recall ability, leading to cognitive overload. Also, because the output generated by assistive technology (i.e. speech and Braille) consists of linear information structures, only one specific element of a web page can be focused on at a given moment, as opposed to a regular monitor screen which provides an overview of the entire page to a user who is sighted. This makes it difficult for users to obtain a clear overview of the page's structure and appearance. Furthermore, because of the linear nature of this output, it is difficult to place a focused element in its wider context.

Based on the Web Content Accessibility Guidelines (WCAG) specified by the W3C (Chisholm *et al.*, 2001), Hillen (2006) deduced four problem categories specific to web site navigation. (1) The *lack or incorrect use of meaningful textual alternatives for visual content*, such as images or embedded objects, make visual elements invisible for assistive technology. If such elements are crucial for successful navigation of the page, the user will not be aware of their function. (2) *Inaccessible navigational content* relates to navigation structures such as menus or hyperlink structures not accessible by assistive technology. (3) The *use of mark-up and layout to convey relevant information*, such as color and size for headings rather than their intended tags or tables to structure information, causes such information to be lost. (4) *Content requiring interaction and embedded content* relates to multimedia objects such as applets, Flash animations and movie instances without textual or audio alternatives. The following section will discuss possible solutions to overcome these main problems.

4.1.4 **Overview of Solutions to Improve Internet Accessibility**

Several solutions have been provided to assist visually impaired users in accessing the World Wide Web. These solutions can roughly be divided into two categories: *manual solutions and automated solutions*.

Manual solutions: These solutions require human input, usually through annotation of web page elements, which provide extra information about the information located on a site. Asakawa and Hironobu (2000) propose an annotation-based transcoding proxy which provides visually impaired users with information about the relevance of page elements. Filepp *et al.* (2002) propose Table To Prose Mark-up Language (TTPML) to facilitate the generation of prose descriptions of tabular information, making audio-rendered tables easier to understand for users who are visually impaired. Huang and Sundaresan (2000) created a semantic transcoding system called Aurora, which transforms web sites into an accessible format based on semantic rather than syntactic constructs. The trade-off is scalability: categories and rules have to be manually specified per site, and are therefore time-consuming to prepare and update. Speroni *et al.* (2004) suggest that a user's web experience can be assimilated to a voice dialog between the user and the machine. Based on this idea a web site was developed which provides a navigation interface in the form of a dialog, asking questions about the user's preferences. This approach prevents cluttering of navigational controls, as the user only has to deal with one concept at a time. However, such a site would not be efficient for users who are sighted. Extensive research on accessible navigation of multidimensional HTML concepts such as frames, tables, and forms has been done by Pontelli *et al.* (2002). Their approach is based on explicit representations of the navigational semantics of the documents and uses a domain-specific language to query the semantic representation to derive navigation strategies.

Automated solutions: Automated solutions require no manual input, and can be used without intervention by others. Because no human input is required, such solutions are not always as effective as manual solutions. Early text-based browsers such as Lynx, developed in 1992,[2] allowed blind users to navigate through text-based sites using only a keyboard. However, such browsers did not provide support for anything other than text (Asakawa, 2005). Arons (1991) developed a system called 'hyperspeech.' This system's purpose was to allow a user to wander through a database of prerecorded interviews, using speech as input. Hyperspeech is mainly suitable for static, predefined hypermedia structures as opposed to the dynamic and unpredictable structures of web sites. However, it can serve as an example for audio-based navigation interfaces. Another early attempt to automatically modify HTML content is the 'Web Access for Blind users' (WAB) system developed at the University of Zürich (Kennel *et al.*, 1996). The system consisted of a proxy, which yielded a modified web page containing the original document with navigational links added, a list of all links on the page, and a nested list of titles on the page. Later, this functionality has been embedded into mainstream screen readers such as JAWS for Windows, and a proxy-based approach is no longer necessary. In 1998, Hermsdorf *et al.* (1998) developed a prototype called WebAdapter, which rearranged HTML pages to add additional accessibility features. Tables were converted to sequential structures, periods were added to list elements in order to let screen readers lower their voice at the end of a list item, and acronyms and abbreviations were replaced with more understandable terms. James (1998) aimed to create a framework for understanding how to represent document structure in audio, and developed an 'Auditory HTML Access' (AHA) system. This system allowed users to mimic visual skimming by enabling controls for jumping between page elements and used auditory icons to provide feedback. Petrie *et al.* (1997) developed DAHNI: Demonstrator of the Access Hypermedia Non-visual Interface. This system allowed blind users to navigate through hypermedia nodes using either a conventional keyboard, a touch tablet, or a joystick.

Fernandes *et al.* (2001) have developed the 'Audiobrowser' (AB), an automated transformation tool which provides different document views for a specific web site. Navigation is simplified by presenting a document's page hierarchy and by offering an abstract of the web page comprising key sentences. The approach by Ebina *et al.*

---

[2]http://lynx.isc.org/.

(2000) focused on compensating the significant decrease in speed that nonvisual browsing implies. A tool was developed that provided a faster web experience by implementing updated content detection and in-page bookmarking. Fast (known) content searches and new (unknown) content searches are trade-offs, as fast searching (e.g. as implemented in the Home Page Reader proposed by Asakawa and Itoh, 1998) can skip relevant information to provide a faster search process. The proposed tool compared the current state of a site with a buffered state that was recorded during a previous visit. Parente (2004) proposed an automated tool that facilitated audio enriched links. This approach is based on the 'Agile views' framework (Marchionini *et al.*, 2000) which recognizes different views for a document, namely *overview, preview, review, peripheral view, and shared view*. Parente's approach used the concept of preview to provide additional information about linked web pages to users with visual impairments. Petrucci *et al.* (1999) proposed a system called 'WebSound' which uses three-dimensional sound to create a spatial representation of the page layout. This approach is impractical for everyday use due to the large costs in hardware requirements and the high learning curve. However, it does provide an effective method for separating structure from content. A similar approach was followed by Donker *et al.* (2002) who created an environment where three-dimensional auditory objects were positioned in an 'auditory interaction realm' (AIR).

The manual solutions described in this section offer some very effective solutions for specific problems, but often lack efficiency. They require volunteers, who manually create and update meta-information. Providing these annotations can be a very time-consuming and tedious task, especially for larger sites that require updates often. The automated tools are efficient and can be used immediately when the web content becomes available. There is no need to wait for assistance from others to access information. The drawback is that these tools mostly provide a broad, general functionality, which lacks understanding of the actual meaning of web-based content. There appears to be a trade-off between efficient solutions and semantically rich solutions. The manual solutions give a visually impaired user a better understanding of a site's structure, while the automated solutions provide a more efficient navigation of the actual information content contained by the structure. Most solutions provided so far are limited to providing a better understanding of a specific web page, but few to none solutions found in current literature deal with the actual navigation between pages, or the web site's structure as a whole. This suggests a need for a web navigation tool that addresses the navigation of an entire web site rather than a single page. However, to be able to develop a tool that can aid users in navigating web sites, it must first be determined in what manner blind users navigate. This will be discussed in the next section.

4.1.5 **The Ways in which Blind Users Navigate the Internet**

An important concept for navigation is the *mental model* the user constructs of the environment that is navigated. A mental model is an internal, symbolic representation of some part of the external world (Slone, 2002). In the context of this research it can be described as a cognitive representation a user has of a web site, which can be seen as such an external world, including its navigational elements and the changes they produce when invoked. Mental models are important because they help users predict commands and interpret system actions. If a system is designed in such a fashion that it does not correspond with the mental model the user develops of the site, then interaction is more likely to be impeded.

A framework for navigation that explains how such models are constructed has been presented by Spence (1999). This framework can offer a foundation for the concept of navigation, whether it occurs in virtual, physical, or social environments. The framework is based on the idea that navigation is concerned with *learning* about an information space, as opposed to activities that deal with actually *using* that space. Spence defines navigation as '*the creation and interpretation of an internal model*' (Spence, 1999).

Spence's model consists of an iterative loop of activities and their results. In the *browsing* stage (also referred to as elicitation or assessment) the navigator attempts to find an answer to the 'what's there?' question. *Content* is registered which provides a rapid glance of the information environment. This newly acquired content is then available for integration in the navigator's internal representation of the environment, constituting the formation of an *internal model* or cognitive map. In the next step, the model is interpreted. One interpretation could be that no more browsing is needed for the specific task at hand, or it may be clear that the model is currently inadequate. In the latter case the manner in which the model is judged to be inadequate will influence the subsequent activity: the *formulation of the browsing strategy*. When this strategy has been determined, a new iteration starts with the execution of the updated browsing strategy. Spence notes that the modeling phase is affected by the manner in which the raw data is externalized. In other words, the formation of an internal model is influenced by the way in which the data is presented to the navigator.

In order to provide a basis for solving navigational issues, an attempt has been made at the University of Manchester to map the concepts related to blind user navigation in a real-world environment to navigation through hypertext. Based on a '*travel metaphor*' Goble *et al.* (2000) have developed a travel mobility framework which likens the concept of physical travel to hypermedia navigation. In this context, 'travel' is defined as '*The whole experience of moving from one place to another regardless of whether the destination is known at the start of the journey or whether the journey is initially aimless*' (Harper and Green, 2000). Travel contains two key aspects: *orientation*, that is knowledge of the basic spatial relationships between objects within the environment and *navigation*, that is the ability to move within the local environment, either by preplanning or 'on the fly.' Goble *et al.* suggest that each blind journey consists of a continuous series of interrelated orientation and navigation tasks.

The relevant components of the travel/mobility framework as described by Harper *et al.* (2001) can be divided into three categories: *mobility objects, mobility principles, and mobility techniques*. The components will be further explained below.

- *Mobility objects* are the components of an environment which a blind traveler can use as a landmark for navigation and orientation. Landmarks can be either cues or obstacles. A *cue* is an object that travelers actively use to facilitate their onward journey. Cues can either be *navigational* (providing an answer to the question 'where can I go?') or *orientational* (providing an answer to the question 'where am I?'). An *obstacle* is an object that either directly or indirectly inhibits the traveler in his onward journey. All detectable landmarks and memory objects are potential cues, and even specific obstacles can be used as cues for orientation. Whether or not an object is a cue or an obstacle is influenced by the travel purpose (e.g. an object can be a cue in an information search but an obstacle in an orientation task) and the user's experience with and knowledge of the information environment. '*Out of view*' objects relate to preview information about objects, which lie ahead, and can be used for obstacle detection and avoidance. Navigational and orientational memories, such as maps or travel aids, contain external knowledge, which can help the traveler to decide whether an object is a cue or an obstacle.
- *Mobility principles* describe the differences in strategies performed by blind travelers as compared with sighted travelers. People who are sighted can adapt more easily to unpredictable environments, while the blind require environments with a high level of consistency and predictability in order to travel without assistance from others (*regularity*). They have to rely on an increased use of cognitive or mental maps (*memory*), which help them store route and survey knowledge about the local environment. Travelers who are blind use simple information more frequently than complex information (*information flow*). They describe routes using more temporal and ego-centered terminology whereas sighted users make more use of spatial and environmental terms. Sighted travelers tend to ignore details while blind

travelers constantly probe the environment to reassure themselves of their location within it. Their cognitive maps therefore tend to be more exact and have a higher level of granularity: routes are divided into smaller steps to identify more landmarks, which are needed to compensate for the limited preview of coming objects (*granularity*).

- *Mobility techniques* are the methods a traveler who is blind can use to travel within an environment. Preview information about the environment ahead can be obtained by *probing* (acquiring information about a location without actually moving to it). In a web environment probing can occur by obtaining information about a hyperlink's target without actually following it. *Obstacle detection and avoidance* is based on knowledge of the environment acquired either through *planning* (using external memory) or probing, and navigating oneself around obstacles based on encounters with those obstacles within the environment. *External memory* provides knowledge about the environment and can take form as sitemaps, document overviews, or help systems. Since travelers who are blind require orientational updates more often than sighted travelers, the environment must be updated regularly in order to provide explicit landmarks, which give the traveler an idea of 'whereness.'

Research by Otter and Jonson (2000) suggests that to successfully navigate through web sites, users who are blind must have a clear understanding of their position within the current site, have access to a history of their actions, be aware of the available paths leading from the current position, and have knowledge of the site's structure in order to know which path to choose from in order to reach a specific goal.

Besides the more general concepts of navigation by the blind described in this section so far, more knowledge is needed which provides a better understanding of blind navigation specifically to virtual environments such as web sites. In discussion groups with experienced blind Internet users described by Donker *et al.* (2002), participants mentioned that navigating through a web site was primarily goal-oriented; the participants seldom surfed the Internet purely for pleasure. They also mentioned that although they did not want to know what a web page looks like exactly, they did want to understand its object structure.

The solutions in Section 4.1.4 mainly focused on the sensory translation of visual textual content rather than enhancing web navigation. Research seems to focus more on navigation of a single page rather than navigation of a whole web site as an information space. In the following section, requirements will be determined from existing literature for a tool that functions as such a solution.

4.1.6 **Requirements for a Successful Navigation Tool for the Blind**

Before developing a web site navigation tool for the blind and before involving actual blind users, current literature will be analyzed to determine a set of basic requirements for such a tool. In this section a basic set of such requirements will be described, which will be used in the following section to develop a crude prototype of a navigation tool for users who are blind.

The W3C User Agent Accessibility Guidelines (UAAG) provide rules of thumb that can be applied in the design of a navigation tool for the blind. Since most of these guidelines are already being followed by mainstream web browsers such as MS Internet Explorer, this paragraph will only discuss the guidelines which are applicable for a navigation tool that functions as an extension to a browser. The tool should be *customizable*, as well as *configurable* to be used with multiple input and output devices. The agent should allow the user to *skip* past certain elements, which may cause disorientation and therefore reduce accessibility. The agent should be able to *communicate with other software* such as the user's web browser and assistive technology. The agent should allow for different navigation mechanisms, and provide information, which helps the user understand the browsing context.

When applying the travel metaphor described by Harper and Green (2000) (as mentioned in Section 4.1.5) to web site navigation by blind users, it can be determined that successful navigation is dependent on the *maximization of cues* and the *minimization of obstacles*. The granularity level of the navigational actions must be as high as possible, and the navigational interface must be *consistent, easy to learn*, and *predictable*. Users must have as many as possible opportunities to request orientational information, and should be allowed to obtain *preview information* about a navigational target in order to decide whether it will take the users closer to their navigational goal. *External memories* such as help systems and document overviews must be present to provide the user with knowledge about the information environment.

Some of the solutions mentioned earlier have yielded certain requirements that can be used as a base for the tool discussed in this research: based on the development of his 'Hyperspeech' system, Arons (1991) states that streamlining the interactions between the user and the system is one of the highest priorities. Because time has such a high value in speech-based applications, every effort must be made to keep these interactions as simple as possible. However, a balance must be found between simplicity and understandability; if the interface is kept too simple it can fall apart due to the lack of identifiable landmarks. Arons further recommends to keep system feedback concise, or allow the user to choose between various degrees of feedback (i.e. through configurability). The user must also be able to easily *interrupt* any system action, and the system should provide immediate feedback to confirm this interruption.

Other requirements are proposed by Barnicle (2000), in the form of four key aspects which should be taken into account when designing software compatible with screen readers. First of all, efficient search strategies are needed to prevent users having to sequentially read content one item at a time in order to achieve a goal. Furthermore, contextual information regarding graphical user interface controls should be provided, changes on screen must be detected, and the user must be notified of them. Finally, as mentioned earlier: software interfaces should be consistent. Hermsdorf *et al.* (1998) state that a 'user interface for all' should support dual use (i.e. allow blind and sighted users to collaborate using the same interface), and be modality independent, that is able to present information using different sensory channels (e.g. Braille, speech, and visual output).

The solutions mentioned so far mostly focus on issues relating to one specific web page, while problems caused by disorientation and inefficiency also exist on the level of an entire site. In other words, a successful navigation tool should provide a way for blind users to navigate through a web site's structure more efficiently, effectively, and comfortably, besides only providing support for page-related issues.

4.2 Problem Statement

It is plausible that blind users would benefit from an overview of the content of an entire web site to support their navigation. An *overview* of the structure and content of the site would prevent the one-step-at-a-time approach and offer a way to point the user in the right direction from the start. *Preview information* describing a navigation element should be offered to assist the user in realizing what will happen when the element is followed, or what to do with the object (e.g. when filling in a form field or selecting a hyperlinked image). The context, in which an information element is placed, should be made available upon request in order to clarify its function. Finally, possible ways to *decrease the amount of page content* (e.g. through filtering) should be explored, in order to reduce the user's level of cognitive overload.

Because navigation and content are not separated on web sites, blind users have to work through a lot of information before finding the actual navigation components. The lack of persistent information due to dependency on sequential audio input places a high demand on the user's memory load, and can easily lead to memory overloading. Based on these findings, a tool is proposed that provides an alternative audio interface to a web site's *navigational structure that is not embedded in the web site content.*

The aim of this research is to gain better understanding of the problems that exist in blind navigation of web sites by developing a solution that improves blind user navigation. A study is carried out to address the following questions:

- *How do blind users navigate web sites on the Internet?* The literature described in the previous section provides a general overview of the problems users who are blind encounter when using the Internet. However, little information was found on the actual methods and techniques used by blind users to perform navigation tasks and respond to such problems. Also, more insight is needed into actual blind user behavior to ensure that the solution sought in this research will be compatible with the manner in which users who are blind navigate web sites.
- *Can an alternative audio-based interface to a web site's navigational structure offer a more efficient, effective, and pleasant form of web site navigation?* The literature offers basic requirements for the support of web site navigation by users who are blind. From the analysis of the literature it seems that apart from providing context for links and textual descriptions of nonvisual information elements, separating the web site's navigational structure from the content for users who are blind may solve problems related to page-by-page navigation and cognitive overload.

4.3 **Methodology**

The development of an initial prototype named 'NavAccess' was started to explore possibilities for an audio interface to a web site's navigational structure, as described in the previous section. Furthermore, a small-scale user study was carried out to investigate current navigation behavior and usability problems encountered by Internet users who are blind as well as an evaluation of the NavAccess prototype to establish whether separating navigation structure from content will improve navigation by blind users.

4.3.1 **The NavAccess Prototype**

A crude prototype of the NavAccess tool has been developed which aimed to assist users who are blind in navigating web sites. The prototype was based mainly on the premise that by providing access to a web site's information architecture through an audio-based interface which is not embedded in the web site's content, blind user navigation will improve. In this section the functionality of the initial NavAccess prototype will be described.

A NavAccess session is initiated by a server script which recursively crawls through a web site's infrastructure starting from its home page by following every hyperlink it encounters and collecting information about each linked page within the site's domain. This information is stored in an XML model, which eventually contains the entire infrastructure of the site (i.e. all pages that are reachable through hyperlinks). The XML model is then parsed by a NavAccess client script, which provides access to the site's information architecture through an audio interface. This interface can be accessed through a separated NavAccess client window, from which the user's browser can be controlled as well. By switching between the two windows (i.e. the browser window and the NavAccess window) the user also switches between two different types of navigation:

1. The *NavAccess navigation style* allows users to quickly navigate through a web site's structure without having to listen through the content of an entire page, thereby allowing the user to perform a macro analysis and construct a mental image of how the web site is structured. However, this form of navigation has a low level of detail: page content is skipped and only information regarding navigation items (i.e. linked content) and pages is included. Basically, this form of navigation functions as an enriched list of links for an entire site rather than a single page.
2. The second style is the *main browser style*, and can be accessed through the regular interface provided by the user's Internet browser. When the user has located a page of interest within the site via NavAccess navigation, he or she can have NavAccess open this specific page in the main web browser where the page can be read through in more detail. This way the user can perform a micro analysis of a specific page.

These two navigation styles complement each other in the following manner: the NavAccess interface allows for quick navigation with a relatively low level of detail, while the main browser navigation provides a slow form of navigation but with a high level of detail, as no information is skipped. By allowing the user to switch between these styles it is expected that users will be more successful in navigating web sites.

The NavAccess controls can be operated with one hand by using the right numeric keypad on a standard keyboard. Main control is based on the four arrow keys located on the right numeric pad. The 'left' and 'right' arrow keys are used to browse through available links on the currently selected page. The 'down' arrow key is used to follow a link to its target page, while the 'up' arrow key functions as a back button, returning the user to the previously selected page. Other controls were implemented to assist the user in the following ways:

Providing the context in which an information element is placed. Because NavAccess mainly functions as a list of links for an entire web site (as opposed to providing link lists per single page, as is done by major screen readers such as JAWS), it would suffer from the same problem a regular link list suffers from: links, which are part of a textual context, may lose their meaning. For instance, a page may contain multiple instances of links such as 'here' where the sentences to which these links refer are filtered out while creating the list. NavAccess attempts to compensate for this loss of context by offering the option to hear the link as part of its complete sentence use.

Providing link title alternatives. A common obstacle mentioned in the studied literature is the presence of unclear or meaningless link titles. NavAccess provides link title alternatives for each link title. These alternatives are based on information extracted from the link's target page, and consist in the current prototype of the target page's URL and title tag.

Providing link preview information. The travel model discussed earlier states that preview information is an important part in the process of maximizing cues and avoiding obstacles. NavAccess provides such information whenever a link is selected by the user. To minimize the possibility of speech overload, the NavAccess prototype uses nonspeech sounds to convey preview information for link targets. This information can be used by the user to determine whether a link should be followed or not. Currently, the prototype provides audio information about link conditions when the link is broken (sound of broken glass), the link leads to the web site's home page (a door closing), the link leads to a different domain (splashing sound), the link leads to document that is not HTML, such as a PDF file (a ping sound), or when the link doesn't lead to a HTTP protocol, such as links starting with ftp:// or mailto:// (a knocking sound).

Providing an alternative main information architecture of the web site to reduce cognitive overload. To provide a navigation structure for the main components of a web site and to compensate for large numbers of links on web pages, the NavAccess prototype categorizes links based on the number of times they appear within a web site. When the number of times a link occurs on a page is higher than 80% of the total number of pages in a web site, it is classified as a 'main link.' In the NavAccess interface main links form a separate category, which can be accessed using separate controls. Using these controls, the user can follow main links even when they are not actually present on the currently selected page. All occurrences of main links on pages within the web site are removed, leaving only regular links. This way a page selected in NavAccess will have less links for a user to work through.

Providing information on the current location in the web site and the path the user has taken to support backtracking. NavAccess was designed to offer feedback upon request on the depth a link is embedded in a site by a sequence of short beeps that indicate how many levels the user is distanced from the site's home page. NavAccess also offers feedback on request on the path taken in the navigation structure by reading out the links that were followed in a reverse order. However, both these functions were not tested in the study described in the next section.

In order to determine whether the main premise on which NavAccess is based is correct, and to determine what functionality of NavAccess should be modified, removed, or added, the prototype was evaluated during a user evaluation study with users who are blind, as described in the following section.

4.3.2 User Evaluation Study

This study was carried out to collect more detailed information regarding blind user navigation, to determine usability issues in blind user navigation, and to evaluate effectiveness of solutions to support web site navigation for users who are blind. The study was conducted through individual sessions with 10 Internet users who are blind. These sessions took about 45 minutes each, and consisted of:

- *A semi-structured interview*, during which participants were asked demographic questions and questions related to computer and Internet experience.
- *A user observation session*, during which participants were observed while performing a task on the Internet. These observations were followed by unstructured interviews to gain deeper understanding of the observed behavior.
- A structured user evaluation of the NavAccess tool followed by an unstructured exploration of the NavAccess tool.

Ten participants were involved in the study. Differences among the participants' age, expertise in computing, or level of blindness were controlled for. Participants were recruited through Dutch online forums for the visually impaired. An introduction by telephone was scheduled before making an appointment for a test session. The sessions took place at the participant's usual environment of Internet use, such as the participant's home, or at a different location of his or her preference. This course was taken to minimize the effort for the participant and to ensure their assistive technology was set up in a familiar way. A laptop was brought along by the researcher on which the NavAccess prototype was installed, as well as the most frequently used screen readers mentioned in literature and in the phone conversations.

At the start of the session, the researcher introduced himself and explained the purpose of the research. After participants were given the opportunity to ask further questions, short interviews were held to obtain information about the participants' age, visual impairment, experience with assistive devices, computers and the Internet, and his/her activities on the Internet. Participants were also asked about the web sites they visit and the main problems they encounter during these visits. After the interview, the observation session would start. The participants were asked to pick a web site they frequently visited and demonstrate a task they would normally carry out, such as online banking, reading the latest news, and so on. Allowing participants to navigate through a familiar web site was hoped to make them feel at ease and make it easier for them to describe difficulties they usually encounter. Participants were asked to 'talk out loud' to describe their actions and their thoughts. Because output was provided by the screen reader and the researcher did not have the expertise in listening to the screen reader that the participants had, the participants were asked to navigate slowly, and to provide further comments once the screen reader had stopped talking. In the case that participants had a monitor they were asked to turn it on so that the researcher could more easily observe. Afterwards, the researcher would start the NavAccess tool to analyze a sample web site. In a structured step-by-step approach the researcher first explained the main functionality of NavAccess and the participant provided feedback on each of the functions and interaction. Finally, the participants had the opportunity to explore the web site him/herself by using NavAccess. The sessions were concluded by thanking the participant for participating, noting any comments, and answering any other questions they might have.

4.4 Findings

This section will first offer a description of the participants involved in this study. Afterward, results for the interviews, web site navigation, and NavAccess evaluation will be reported.

4.4.1 Sample Description and Interview Results

The request was placed on several mailing lists targeted at blind users and yielded 11 responses, out of which 10 participants were chosen. The participants' ages ranged between 17 and 55. Nine of the participants were male, one was female. The reason for this gender imbalance was that only one female participant had responded to the online request. The one female participant was not found to give extremely different responses compared with the male participants in the sample. However, in order to determine whether gender is a determining factor in Internet navigation, a larger sample would be necessary in future studies. Four participants lived by themselves, while six of them shared a home with other people. Of these six, five lived together with their family or spouse, and one participant was part of a community apartment arranged by a Dutch school for the blind where he lived together with three other visually impaired inhabitants. Two participants were following regular education, one as a high school student and one as a university student. The other eight had varying occupations.

All participants were considered legally blind, although gradual differences existed from person to person. Five participants had 0% sight and five still possessed some residual sight, meaning that the participant was able to detect changes in brightness and contrast in the surroundings. This distinction was made based on the participant's own description and whether the participant generally used a monitor display while navigating. The participants who possessed residual sight were able to use contrast changes on the screen as a last resort in case their assistive technology failed them. The number of years for which participants had been blind ranged from 4 to 40 years. Four participants were blind since birth. All participants made use of Microsoft Internet Explorer as their main browser and a screen reader. Six participants used speech in combination with a Braille display. These six had all been blind for a period longer than 10 years, and included the four participants who had been blind since birth. A possible explanation could be that Braille is a difficult language which can take years to master, and is easier to learn at a relatively young age. This explanation was shared by the four participants who did not use Braille. They all found the language too difficult to learn to invest their time and effort in. All six Braille users mentioned they preferred Braille to speech and only turned on their screen reader when they had to work through large quantities of text or large web sites. Six participants used JAWS for Windows. This screen reader provides extensive support for web site navigation, which also makes it more expensive and heavier to run by the participant's computer. For this reason the four other participants used HAL, developed by Dolphin. This screen reader is cheaper compared with JAWS, and does not provide extra functionality such as header navigation or link lists. Two of the participants who used HAL also used a browser extension, Webformator[3] and Webwizard,[4] respectively. Both extensions convert a web page to textual form, allowing it to be navigated one line at a time.

[3]http://www.webformator.com.
[4]http://www.baum.ro/web_wizard.html.

To gain a better understanding of the methods used by blind people to obtain their day-to-day information, participants were asked to list their daily information sources. All participants mentioned the Internet as well as friends and/or relatives. The participants who lived together mentioned their spouse or family as an information source, while participants living by themselves mentioned friends. Two participants received professional assistance such as a homecare representative who would visit daily to help out with daily chores and reading mail. Four participants mentioned computer-related sources, two of which were scanning of physical mail in order to process it digitally using optical character recognition, and two used e-books, which could be read by assistive technology. Two participants mentioned the radio. There were no noticeable differences in information sources mentioned by participants who had been blind since birth and those who turned blind later in life. One participant made use of a dial-up connection; all others had access to a permanent high-speed broadband connection. This may be an important factor because people who have to dial in generally tend to minimize their time on line due to costs, while broadband users do not.

Internet Use

All participants had a high level of Internet experience, which can be explained by the fact that the sample was recruited through online communities. Participants were asked to list the activities they performed on the Internet. *Email* was the main form of communication for all participants. Participants also mentioned that one of the main problems of being blind was reading mail that was sent by surface post. Two participants used a scanner and optical character recognition in order to read their mail independently, the other eight had to rely on others to read their mail for them. This was thought unpleasant at times as a letter can contain personal information. Having email as a main form of communication allowed participants to communicate independently. For reasons to use the Internet, all participants mentioned *general information retrieval* such as looking up travel information or looking up information about a company. Three participants mentioned that they used the Internet to keep up with the news. Five participants used the Internet to assist them in their occupation, such as retrieving school or work-related information. All participants visited online blind communities regularly, such as weblogs, wikipedia sites, forums, and news groups. This finding may not be representative as the participants were recruited through online forums. Five participants also actively contributed to these communities, either by answering questions asked by other visitors or adding information to the content of a community. Of these five participants, four lived independently by themselves. *Chatting* was only mentioned by half of the participants. The participants who did not use it said they found chatting to be intrusive, and preferred to meet people in real life. Only two participants made use of voice chat, the other three only used text-based chat. A possible reason is that voice chat is a relatively new development and not yet familiar to the participants. There was no difference regarding the use of chat for participants living by themselves and those living with others. Five participants mentioned online shopping. One of them used the online grocery delivery service of a major supermarket, while the other four purchased electronic equipment or made travel reservations with an airline. All participants who purchased products online were 30 years or older. Four of the participants actively contributed web-based content by *developing web sites*. These sites had subjects ranging from regular topics such as fishing to topics more related to visual impairments, such as information sites on accessibility for the blind.

Problems in Web site Navigation

Participants were asked to list the problems they encountered while navigating web sites. The reported problems were consistent with those found in the literature. There was no noticeable difference between the problems mentioned by participants of different age groups. There were also no substantial differences found between the problems mentioned by participants who only used a screen reader compared with the participants who also made use of a Braille display. This was surprising because the tactile channel used by Braille has higher information bandwidth compared with speech. Braille users were therefore expected to identify efficiency-related problems less often. Also, there were no noticeable differences between problems identified by participants who had been blind since birth and those who had lost sight at a later age, or between participants who still had a certain level of residual sight and those who had 0% sight left. Additionally, there were no noticeable differences in the problems mentioned by the three participants who had used the Internet while they were still sighted and those who had never seen a web site before. This was surprising because the researchers expected these participants to have a better understanding of what a web site is supposed to look like, rather than perceiving it solely through speech or Braille.

The three problems mentioned most often relate to navigation between pages, while the other six relate to the sensory translation of content of individual pages. This corresponds with the findings from the literature that support is also needed for navigation at the level of the entire web site rather than page-specific navigation alone. Seven participants mentioned use of *images without the correct use of a textual alternative*. One participant even mentioned he would rather not know such images were there, as they served no purpose to him. More crucial problems arise when images are used as a part of the site's navigation structure in the form of hyperlinked images, since this makes it impossible for the user to be aware of where the image is leading. Six participants mentioned *unclear link titles*. The participants using screen reader software which provided link lists for a page mentioned that *context-dependent titles* were very annoying, because link lists take away a link's context. People using assistive technology which didn't provide these lists had fewer problems with contextless links, as they had to manually navigate to them anyway. However, links with unclear descriptions such as a number were a major usability problem, as the linked page then needs to be opened in order to understand its purpose. Five of these six participants mentioned they would like to have certain *preview information about a link's target*, so they would not have to follow it in order to find out it leads to an undesired location. Five participants mentioned *too much navigational content* on a page. They would often get frustrated by the large quantities of what one participant referred to as 'navigational junk' present on every single page on a web site. Such content is generally outputted first by assistive technology before the desired content can be read. Sites having 50 or more links were mentioned to be tedious to work with, as all links would have to be read again each time a page was loaded. Participants mentioned they would prefer to have a skip link to the main content at the beginning of the page, but an even better solution would be to first hear the content, with an optional skip link to the navigation menu following this content. Four participants mentioned the use of *unclear forms*. They mentioned the use of *inaccessible embedded objects* such as Flash menus or Java Applets. Three participants mentioned *inconsistencies in web sites*. Such inconsistencies could occur over time, for example a set of options available through a dropdown list at one point gets redesigned to a table-based list after a site upgrade.

4.4.2 Observation of Web site Navigation

The task observations were conducted as follows. Based on Internet activities mentioned earlier by the participants, a specific navigation task was chosen to be demonstrated by the participant. In the following sections each task that participants chose will be described, providing the main flow of actions performed by the participant and system responses to these actions. For each observation session the encountered user problems are listed, as well as the participant's navigation actions. This study was performed in week 44 of 2005, and the web sites described in the following sections reflect their state at that time.

The nature of this study is qualitative. To offer the readers the benefit of detailed insight into the experiences of blind participants, we have chosen to give a rather detailed account of each of the observation sessions followed by an overview of the problems encountered and the navigation styles observed.

Participant 1

Profile: A 55-year-old male who has been blind for 10 years and had no residual sight left. He used Supernova (a suite including the HAL screen reader) as assistive technology. The participant had been visually impaired since birth, and before turning fully blind he had been using screen-magnifying software as assistive technology.

Web site: http://www.aktiebenin.nl, a Dutch charity site for mothers and children in Benin, Africa.

Task description: Find the link leading to the participant's own home page.[5]

Duration of task: Approximately 10 minutes.

User actions and system responses: The participant selects the address box using his browser's CTRL + O shortcut. While typing in the URL address, each letter is repeated by the screen reader. This way the participant is able to detect a typographical error ('ww' instead of 'www') before the address is submitted. When the page has loaded, an extra pop-up window is opened without the participant being aware of this. Using the TAB key the participant attempts to browse through the available links on what he thinks is the web site's main page. For a minute the participant is confused, thinking that he opened the wrong page. After checking the URL of the document loaded in the current browser window, the participant realizes multiple windows have been opened and switches to the main page using the ALT + TAB shortcut.

The main content frame contains a 'latest news' link, which changes every 3 seconds using a JavaScript function call. Whenever the participant selects a link to listen to its name, it is replaced by a different link, causing the screen reader to reset to the beginning of the page. The participant assumes the screen reader is malfunctioning, and does not realize the different links are basically on the same location. The participant decides to ignore this problem and switches to the next frame in the frameset, which is a frame containing the site's main menu links in the form of a JavaScript dropdown menu. Using the TAB key the participant browses through these links, where only the ones which do not fold out into more submenu links are detected by the screen reader. Finally, the participant encounters a link called 'links' which he follows.

---

[5]The participant had developed a home page which contained information about a school for the blind project in Benin, and this website was referenced on the Benin site.

A new page containing 113 links is loaded. The participant skips to main content frame which contains 56 links. Because it would take too long to browse through the page one link at a time, the participant utilizes the browser's search function with the CTRL + F shortcut, providing his own name as search query. Result: the link is found.

Types of navigation: The participant's style was semi-explorative because even though he was familiar with the web site, he did not know the structure of the web site well. Frames were followed sequentially as was their content. However, when the participant reached the page on which he believed his task target (i.e. the link to his own home page) was located the participant switched to a different style. Because this page contained a relatively large quantity of links, the participant performed an in-page search where the search query (in this case the participant's own name) was utilized as a skip-function, which allowed the participant to directly jump to a certain location within the page. The participant commented that such a technique is only possible when one is familiar with a web site's contents (e.g. in this case the participant knew a link to his own web site would be present on the 'links' page). Had the participant been on this web site for the first time, each page would have to be read sequentially.

Participant 2

Profile: A 17-year-old male who has been blind since birth but still retained some residual sight. He used JAWS for Windows as a screen reader and a Voyager Braille display. It was interesting to note that the participant was able to listen to English content using a Dutch synthesizer. The participant mentioned that he was used to this set-up and that he did not mind the incorrect pronunciation by the Dutch voice.

Web site: http://www.asus.com, a site for a company which provides computer hardware-related products.

Task description: Find specifications for a motherboard.

Duration of task: Approximately 10 minutes.

User actions and system responses: The participant entered the URL address using the CTRL + O shortcut. The main page loaded, which consisted of a Flash animation depicting a world map, with buttons describing different sections of the world (e.g. 'global,' 'Europe region,' etc.). The participant's screen reader provides Flash support for text and menu items, but does not read out the world map image. The participant prefers to read the site either in Dutch or English, and selects 'global' as geographical category. This causes the world map to change: dots light up specific countries, which can be selected in this category using a pointing device. The participant is not aware of this result at all, and assumes the Flash animation is not working properly. He decides to leave the Flash object and listen through the rest of the page.

The Flash animation is followed by a list of images containing names of specific countries in which this company is active. Again, the participant wants to have either a Dutch or English site and starts searching for suitable country names. However, while the images contain country names they do not have textual alternatives. The participant's screen reader uses the image name as link titles instead, which is 'entry/interfaceXX,' where 'XX' is a different number for each country. Because it is not possible to identify the country links based on their link description, the participant decides to randomly try out one of the country links, which turns out to be a link to the company page of Serbia and Montenegro. Using the browser's back-function he goes back to try different links; after two other incorrect choices (Finland and China), the participant arrives on the Canadian page, which he finds acceptable.

The participant searches for a link labeled 'products,' using the link list option provided by his screen reader. Many links in this list contain unclear descriptions such as prog_footer/asus_under06. Using a first letter search the 'products' link is found and followed. On the products page the participant performs an in-page search using the browser's Ctrl + F shortcut with the query 'motherboards.' The first hit found is a link to the motherboards section, which is followed.

A page containing different motherboard categories is loaded. Again, the participant attempts to perform an in-page search, using the desired category name as search query. However, this search query does not yield any results because the category names are displayed as images, which do not contain a textual alternative in the form of an ALT attribute. By using the TAB key to browse through the page one link at a time, the participant discovers that the category links are still understandable because their target URLs contain the specific category name in their path. By sequentially listening to each link's URL the desired category is eventually found. The link on the right motherboard category is followed.

A new page is loaded containing the specific motherboards, which are part of the currently selected category. Again, the participant performs an in-page search using his motherboard's type and number as a query. The first result is a link to the specifications of the desired motherboard. The participant follows the link. Because the participant does not know precisely how this page is structured, he goes through the content sequentially until the main content (i.e. the product specifications) is reached.

Types of navigation: When confronted with a lack of meaningful link descriptions, the participant decided to randomly follow links in order to discover where they were leading. The participant mentioned this was a 'last resort' strategy, which he only followed if all else failed. The participant performed in-page jumps as often as possible, either by performing in-page searches or making use of the link lists provided by his screen reader. This style allowed the participant to compensate for the lack of skip links on a page, but is mostly effective when one is familiar with a site. In cases when this in-page jumping was not possible (either by lack of landmarks on a page, or lack of knowledge about them), the participant had to resort to a linear approach (i.e. sequentially reading through the page) until the desired content was encountered.

Participant 3

Profile: A 43-year-old male who has been blind for 11 years but still regained a small percentage residual sight. He used JAWS for Windows as screen reader and an Alfa Satellite Braille display. The participant mentioned he did not like having to search for information, and would rather have the information come to him. He also mentioned that he generally did not attempt to create a visual mental representation of what a web page looks like, because this often leads to incorrect assumptions. The participant explained that visiting a site can be difficult in the beginning, because a certain 'strategy' will have to be developed in order to navigate it successfully

Web site: http://www.connexxion.nl, a Dutch site providing timetables and travel information for a Dutch bus company.

Task description: Find out at which time the participant's bus arrives at the nearest bus stop.

Duration of task: Approximately 15 minutes.

User actions and system responses: The web site is opened through the participant's favorites, located in the browser's menu. On the starting page of the web site, the participant sequentially reads through the page until the word 'search' is found. The F key is a shortcut for the participant's screen reader, allowing him to jump to the first form element. In this case this is a textbox labeled 'edit.' Although this is an ambiguous label, the participant assumes it is a search field because it is the first form field after the word 'search.' The participant enters the bus number and city as a search query and submits it.

It is unclear to the participant what the result of this action is, since there is no clear way to be sure whether the screen reader has loaded a new page or not ('sometimes it starts reading the links on the page, but sometimes it doesn't'). The page did in fact load, but instead of search results, the page contains input fields for more specific search terms. Because the participant cannot find any results, he assumes the page did not load correctly and enters his search query again, this time using separate fields for the bus number and his city. For the second time a search page is opened, this time including a map of the country on which areas can be selected through image maps. The participant enters search data again.

Multiple bus lines were found, even though the participant had specified the name of his city. Using the screen reader's link list the participant tries to find the correct one. However, the link only contains the bus line number and not the area, causing all links in the list to be called '4.' The participant uses CTRL + M to select the first link in the list, and sequentially reads on from there. After the correct bus line number has been found, the participant follows its timetable link. This leads to a large list of bus stops, out of which the participant selects his stop using a first letter search in the link list provided by his screen reader. This leads to a news page containing the timetable for the current stop. However, this table is very complex and difficult to comprehend in a nonvisual way. After a few minutes the correct time is found.

Types of navigation: The participant manually read through the page until a term relevant for the participant's goal was encountered (in this case the term 'search'). On other pages, the participant either used the TAB key or the screen reader's link list to quickly browse through the available links on a page. When using a link list, a first letter search was performed to immediately select the right link. However, in some cases these link-oriented styles were not sufficient due to duplicate or context-dependent link titles. When this happened, the participant switched back to sequentially reading through the page.

Participant 4

Profile: A 21-year-old male who has been completely blind since birth. He used a HAL screen reader and a Voyager Braille display. The participant noted that the solution he would find most useful is a way to ignore navigation clutter which is present on every page within a web site. For instance, a solution which compares two consecutive pages and skips directly to the content which was not present on the previous page. When the participant started using the Internet he mainly used Bulletin Board Sites, which had little accessibility problems but also a limited choice of information. He also mentioned that while he could do most of the things he wanted on the World Wide Web, the biggest problem was efficiency: he wanted to be able to do them faster.

Web site: http://www.9292ov.nl, a Dutch site providing travel information for public transport within the Netherlands.

Task description: Get a route description from the participant's house to a friend's house.

Duration of task: Approximately 5 minutes.

User actions and system responses: The participant entered the web site's address using his browser's CTRL + O shortcut. When the page finished loading, the participant searched within the main page for the word 'street' because he knew that it is the first form element of the search form. The participant enters the search terms, which are the starting address and destination address. No problems occurred during this action and the form is submitted. There was no feedback on whether a new page has loaded or is still loading; the participant waited a few seconds and assumed it was done.

The results page loaded containing the route information, which is displayed in an HTML table. Each row depicts a step within the travel process, describing starting point, finishing point, duration, and method of travel. The participant's screen reader reads out the rows. However, it was difficult for the participant to remember which column each value belonged to. The screen reader does not specify whether the down arrow button causes the next line in the same cell, the next cell, or the next row to be read.

Types of navigation: The participant was an experienced user of the site, and used his knowledge by identifying specific landmarks (in this case the word 'street' which specified the start of the search form) on a page to jump to a certain location within that page. The participant explained that the first thing to do when visiting a new site was to locate such landmarks, in order to navigate more efficiently during subsequent visits.

Participant 5

Profile: A 43-year-old male who had been completely blind for 10 years. He used a HAL screen reader, assisted by a browser extension called Webformator. This extension converts HTML output to text, allowing the participant to read through it as if it was a regular text file. The participant mentioned that the ideal web site is one that is 'tranquil,' meaning a site with a high level of consistency, not too much content per page and a clear separation of navigation and content. The participant also mentioned that by visiting sites often he develops certain strategies, which help in speeding up navigation on subsequent visits. An interesting observation was that the participant adapted certain existing sites so that they would become more accessible. This way, the participant took control over a site's accessibility and discarded irrelevant information from a page, making navigation more effective and efficient.

Web site: http://www.postbank.nl, web site for a Dutch bank.

Task description: Go to the transaction page on his personal bank account page.

Duration of task: Approximately 5 minutes.

User actions and system responses: The participant opens the web site through his browser favorites. When the page has loaded the participant switches to the text version of the page generated by the Webformator extension (using the F12 key). Within this textual page a search is performed using the keywords [participant name]. This allows the participant to instantly locate the first form element of the page's login section. The participant then switches back to the actual site with the F12 key. The login field, which had been selected in the textual version, is now also selected. The participant enters the login data and submits it.

The account page opens, which is frame-based and therefore not possible to be read. Using F12 the participant switches back to the original browser window. The participant manually searches for the term 'new transaction,' which he eventually finds.

Types of navigation: Because the site was familiar to the participant, he knew exactly which search keywords to use in order to directly jump to a specific location on a page. The browser extension allowed him to switch between text and HTML versions of the page. For quick navigation the text view was used, where each line of text could be directly translated to the participant's Braille display. This text view allowed the participant to perform in-page searches (which did not function correctly using only a screen reader). For complex content the HTML view was selected, allowing the participant to enter data and browse through frames.

Participant 6

Profile: A 55-year-old male who had been completely blind for 33 years. He used JAWS for a Windows screen reader. The participant had learned to use the Internet in a DOS environment, mostly for activities such as email and visiting 'De Digitale Stad' (the digital city Amsterdam, DDS), a virtual community where people could navigate through a virtual representation of a city, communicate with other citizens and add local content. The participant mentioned that this community was ideal for a blind person because every visitor had to use their imagination, thereby removing the difference between blind and sighted users. The participant mentioned that he does not try to find out in what way a page's layout is designed, unless this information is necessary to reach a certain location on a page. In this case the participant asks help from a sighted person. The participant also mentioned that he encourages the use of frames (whereas frames are often mentioned as an accessibility obstacle) because they allow him to skip inaccessible content.

Web site: http://www.albert.nl, an online store which delivers groceries for major Dutch supermarkets.

Task description: Find out how much it costs to have groceries delivered next Tuesday 5 PM.

Duration of task: Approximately 15 minutes.

User actions and system responses: When the participant starts his task, his email client application, which was already running, is still selected. The participant listens through some of the content before realizing this and switches to the browser application. The participant has learned the necessary steps needed to log in to the site by heart, and knows that the login form on the site's home page does not work with his assistive technology (the input fields can be selected but are not described by the screen reader). The participant accidentally presses enter while a link was selected, and ends up on an unfamiliar page. To undo this error, he uses the browser's back-function to return to the starting page. However, the location he returns to cannot be read correctly by his screen reader. At this point, the participant starts over by re-entering the site's URL in the address field.

Because the login form on the starting page does not function correctly, the participant has to take a detour which he has discovered during an earlier visit: after following the link to 'special deals' he selects one of the products which are currently offered at a low price. This action generally places the product in the participant's shopping basket, but since he is not logged in yet he is rerouted to a login page containing a form, which can be read by assistive technology. By doing a page search for the term 'password' the form is found immediately and the participant can enter his login data.

After being logged in, the participant follows a link labeled 'delivery times.' On this page, the delivery times are displayed as a table, with days of the current week in columns, and the delivery hours in rows. Each cell contains the cost to have groceries delivered at that specific day and time. While the participant describes the table, the researcher notices that the participant's mental visualization of the table has the dimensions switched: the days in rows and the hours in columns.

The participant listens through the table using the down arrow key. It is difficult to remember which value belongs to which row and column combination, also because some cells are empty.

When the participant has identified the delivery cost for the day and time specified, it turns out he is mistaken by one day because he thought the table started at a different day. Since he used this incorrect information to navigate the table (counting the number of days starting from the first), he ended up at the wrong day.

Types of navigation: The participant navigated a predefined route during the task. By knowing which obstacles to avoid (the inaccessible login form) the participant took a detour to arrive at his destination, and by memorizing necessary steps (such as counting rows and columns) the participant knew exactly how to navigate within his predefined path. This approach is only possible when one has a lot of experience with a specific web site, and will most likely fail when a web site's content or structure is updated over time. The participant mentioned that when this happened a new 'orientation phase' was necessary.

Participant 7

Profile: A 55-year-old male who had been blind for 4 years. The participant used a JAWS screen reader.

Web site: http://www.challenge-media.nl, a site which provides news for people with a reading impairment.

Task description: Find a specific article about an Internet-related subject, which the participant has read before and found interesting.

Duration of task: Approximately 5 minutes.

User actions and system responses: The participant opens the web site using the browser's CTRL + O shortcut. When the page has loaded, the participant browses the available links with the TAB key. Finally, a link labeled 'challenge-news' is encountered. The participant knows that this was the main site category containing the article. The site uses heading tags correctly to specify document structure, and the participant uses his screen reader to jump from one heading to the next, until the start of the main content is reached. The main content starts with an in-page skip link which points to the page section behind the main textual content of the page, at the point where news categories can be chosen.

Using the TAB key, the participant browses through the news category, eventually following a link labeled 'Internet News' to a page which contains the news items contained by this category The participant knows that the title of each article on this page is marked up as a level 4 heading, and uses his screen reader to move through these headings using the '4' key repeatedly until the title is encountered. Using the TAB key the participant selects the first link, which in this case is the link leading to the actual article.

Types of navigation: The participant made extensive use of the site's accessible layout structure, mainly through the use of skip links and header navigation within a page. Because the participant was already aware how the page was structured he knew which heading levels were used to specify main items and sub-items on a page. This knowledge allowed him to navigate at a relatively high speed, comparable with the speed a sighted person would scan a page.

Participant 8

Profile: A 26-year-old male who had been blind for 18 years, but still had some residual sight in his left eye. He used a HAL screen reader and a Braille display. Web sites were generally read using a browser extension called Webwizard, which displays a web page as text. The participant mentioned that while it is convenient when a web designer adds skip links to a page, he does not like the fact that specific attention is focused on his visual impairment and would rather be treated similar to other users. The participant also mentioned that when visiting a news web site he usually performs a 'scouting mission' during which he remembers specific parts of a page which can be used as identifiable elements (landmarks) when navigating the page during a later visit.

Web site: www.telefoongids.nl, an online telephone book for the Netherlands.

Task description: Look up a specific phone number.

Duration of task: Approximately 5 minutes.

User actions and system responses: The site is opened using the browser's CTRL + O shortcut. When the page has loaded, the participant switches to the textualized version of the page, which is read one line at a time by the participant's Braille display. A search is performed in order to locate the specific input fields. By pressing the F12 key, the participant switches back to the normal HTML output of the page. The participant enters name and city in the HTML search field, which is now also selected.

After the search query has been submitted and the results page has been loaded, the participant switches back to the text version of the page using F12. The participant knows that the search results on this site are always preceded by a certain term (the term 'surroundings,' which is part of a link labeled 'search in this city's surroundings').

By doing an in-page search for this term, the participant arrives at the start of the results list, which has only 1 result.

Types of navigation: The participant was able to navigate efficiently by switching between a textualized and a HTML version of the web site. Because he had already identified specific landmarks during previous visits, he was able to use search queries as skip links.

Participant 9

Profile: A 40-year-old female who had been blind since birth, but still had some residual sight. She used JAWS for Windows and a Braille display. The participant mentioned that she mainly used the Google search engine to discover new web sites. She did not mind to sequentially listen through page content because she was patient and the reward of eventually finding the desired information was worth the time-consuming process. However, when encountering a problem, which does not seem to have a clear solution, she rather quits than trying to figure out how to get around the problem. The participant also mentioned that navigating was easier under DOS, because the Braille display would just read the 24 lines on the screen. Now that most interfaces are graphically oriented to make them easier to use for inexperienced people, she feels blind people have to suffer because others need visual aid. When visiting a web site for the first time she usually enters a 'learning phase' first, during which a better understanding can be created on what can be done on the site and how it can be done.

Web site: www.voedingscentrum.nl, a Dutch government site providing nutritional advice.

Task: Find a recipe, based on available ingredients.

Duration of task: Approximately 10 minutes.

User actions and system responses: The participant opens the page through a browser bookmark. Using the screen reader's link list a first letter search is performed for the link 'recipes,' which is followed. The participant knows that the resulting page contains a search form, which starts with the words 'search by title.' Using the browser's search function the participant jumps to this section of the page. The participant enters different available ingredients to use in the recipe, and submits the form. Sequentially reading the page from the beginning, the participant reaches a list of three resulting recipes of which the third one is chosen.

The recipe page contains a lot of information regarding the different categories the recipe belongs to. The participant skips this content by performing an in-page search for the term 'ingredients,' because she knows the recipe starts from there.

Navigation styles: The participant used page searches and link lists provided by the participant's screen reader. When these methods were not available the participant would switch to a more linear form of navigation, where a page was read through sequentially.

Participant 10

Profile: A 39-year-old male. Blind since birth, with some residual sight. He used a JAWS for Windows screen reader and a Braille display. The participant mentioned he prefers to try out 'hard URLs' to discover new web sites rather than using search engines such as Google. The reason for disliking search engines was that their output is too time-consuming to read through, and annoying to listen to through a screen reader. The participant also mentioned he had limited patience: his main focus was to navigate to the desired information as quickly as possible, avoiding irrelevant information encountered along the way. Encountered problems posed a challenge to solve them, rather than to avoid them.

Web site: www.klm.nl, a web site for a Dutch airline company.

Task description: Find available flights to Sydney, Australia.

Duration of task: Approximately 15 minutes, not completed.

User actions and system responses: The participant opens the page using his browser's CTRL + O shortcut. When the page has loaded the screen reader mentions 180 links are present. Instead of reading through the site sequentially the participant opens a link list and performs a first letter search to select the link 'make reservations.' The participant knows that each page consists of a frameset, which has logical names such as 'menu' and 'content,' which allow him to directly select this specific part of the page. The content frame is selected, which contains a search form.

The participant reads through the form sequentially. Because two form labels ('from' and 'to') are mentioned before the actual input elements, the participant makes a mistake by treating the first element (a combo box containing a list of departure locations) as a list containing destinations. Since the combo box only contains Dutch airports, the participant realizes this must belong to the 'from' label, even though it was read right after the 'to' label. A second form field is encountered after the first, labeled 'edit.' The participant assumes this second form element belongs to the 'to' label and enters the name of his destination. By pressing enter the form is submitted, even though it was not completed yet.

The resulting page gives a warning, saying that there are no available flights available on the selected date. A calendar with clickable dates allows the participant to select a different date of departure and return. However, this is not correctly read out loud by the screen reader and the participant decides to use the browser's back-function in order to return to the previous page where he can enter the correct data in the original form. The browser now provides a warning because the previous page is not available any more. The search form has to be resubmitted in order to reload the page. However, this warning is ignored by the participant's screen reader, making it unclear what happened to the search form, which the participant had already filled in. The participant decides to close the browser and start at the beginning again.

At this point the session is concluded because of lack of time.

Types of navigation: The participant knew that the web site's frames were consistently labeled on each page, allowing him to separate navigational page content from main page content. After having selected the correct frame the participant either used a linear approach where a page's content was traversed sequentially, or a link list approach where large quantities of links could be browsed more efficiently.

Summary of observations

Only one participant (no. 7) chose a web site which was compliant with W3C guidelines. The participant who performed a task on this site showed that such a site can be navigated both efficiently and effectively without any problems. The other nine participants had to find creative solutions to deal with large quantities of context. They all made use of search functions, link lists, and browsing a page one link at a time. The problems that were encountered were different for each site and task. Nine of the participants had to deal with an overload of navigational content, although this problem was only reported by five participants during the interviews. Three participants became disoriented because they encountered an unexpected situation. For participant 1 this situation was caused by a pop-up window. For participant 6 this was after accidentally following a link. Participants 3 and 10 became disoriented because the result of their search (request for more detailed query or a change of an incorrect query) did not match their expectations. This made them uncertain about whether the form had been submitted correctly. Two participants were unable to continue because they were not able to undo a certain action. Participant 6 accidentally followed a link and wanted to perform a back operation, only to arrive on a different page. Participant 10 wanted to resubmit a search form, which had not been completely entered, but was unable to reload the page.

4.4.3 **Evaluation of the NavAccess Prototype**

Participants were given a step-by-step demonstration of how the NavAccess interface worked. For each step they were asked to comment on that specific part of the interface, which has been discussed in more detail in Section 4.1. After these steps had been discussed, the participants spent 5 minutes exploring the web site with NavAccess. Because the system had no functional help system available, the researcher acted as a mock-up help system: the participant could ask questions about a specific key or function and the participant would read a standard response which would be given by the system itself.

Step 1: Separate navigation
The participants were told that NavAccess provides an audio-based interface to a web site's navigational structure, and that the aim is to improve blind user navigation by offering access to a navigation structure by separating it from the web site's content. Seven participants commented that they would consider such a form of separated navigation an improvement compared with having content and navigation mixed together. One participant said that his screen reader already provided enough navigational support, and two participants did not know whether or not they would appreciate such a separated navigation style. Five participants mentioned that their screen reader already supported the separation of navigation and content through the use of link lists for individual pages, and that it would be convenient to also have this functionality for the entire web site.

Step 2: One-hand control on numeric pad
Four of the participants mentioned that they would prefer an interface, which focused on the right numeric pad if it did not conflict with the controls of their screen reader (which is also based on the right numeric pad). The participants who made use of a refreshable Braille display ($N = 4$) mentioned that this control setup was convenient because it allowed them to interact with the application using only one hand, leaving the other hand available to interact with the Braille display.

Step 3: Use of the arrow keys
The prototype makes use of the four arrow keys located on the right numeric pad. The left and right arrow keys are used to browse through available links on the currently selected page, similar to the TAB and SHIFT + TAB shortcuts used by screen readers to browse through links within a page. The down arrow key is used to follow a link to its target page, while the up arrow key functions as a back button,

returning the user to the previously selected page. All of the participants commented that these controls were clear and easy to remember. Four participants also mentioned that they would prefer link browsing to also be available through the TAB and SHIFT keys, because they were already used to these controls due to experience with their screen reader.

Step 4: Use of sound
To minimize the possibility of speech overload, the NavAccess prototype utilizes non-speech sounds to convey information, which would normally be spoken out loud. Sounds that provided information about the current application state were low volume background sounds. Five participants commented that the use of a background sound was a convenient way to remember which application is currently selected, and five participants mentioned they considered the use of sound in general intrusive because it interfered with the speech output of their screen reader. All participants mentioned the function should be customizable and easy to turn off. Other sounds used in the prototype were sounds providing preview information of the currently selected link. Five participants said they would prefer it if sounds were used instead of textual notifications, while the other five commented that the sounds were distracting them from their screen reader's speech output. All participants agreed that the use of preview sounds should be customizable, allowing the user to choose between sound, text, or both.

Step 5: Providing preview information
Eight participants mentioned it would be convenient to have information on the target content of a link available, because it could tell in advance whether they should follow a link or not. Two participants did not know whether they thought such information useful.

Step 6: Use of title alternatives
Nine participants commented that such alternatives would be convenient to use, especially when dealing with linked images, which do not have textual alternatives. These participants also mentioned that the alternatives that were currently available in NavAccess would not be sufficient in many web sites where the page's URL and title are incomprehensible. The participants mentioned that in order to be truly useful, more advanced title alternatives such as providing a description of the target page's contents should be provided.

Step 7: Use of separate link categories
Eight participants commented that they would appreciate the separation of link categories, because they preferred the link browsing process to be as efficient as possible. The other two participants did not know whether they would prefer these categories.

Step 8: Availability of link context

Eight participants thought the availability of such a function would be convenient. These eight included participants who made use of a screen reader, which provides link lists. The two participants who used a browser extension mentioned they currently did not have any problems with retrieval of link context, because they were able to quickly read the previous and next line surrounding the link.

Exploration of a Web site with NavAccess

Afterward, participants were asked to try out the NavAccess interface themselves. The navigation structure of a web site (www.danbrown.com) had been prepared as a testing domain for the participants to navigate through. Because the laptop on which the NavAccess prototype was installed was not connected to the Internet, only the NavAccess side of the navigation was available. Because of this, NavAccess could not be used to open pages in the browser, in order to perform more detailed navigation tasks there.

While the participants worked with the NavAccess interface the researcher observed their actions. Participants quickly forgot how to use the keys of the numeric keypad. Because the participants had relatively little time to learn the NavAccess interface, each of them had problems remembering the meaning of the different keys used. Six participants were unsuccessful in locating the corresponding keys after their description was given. For instance, when the functionality of the page up and page down key was explained, participants had to be instructed on where to find these keys. Because of this, participants would use incorrect keys in order to perform a function (e.g. the 'home' key instead of the left arrow key, which is located beneath the home key). Because the prototype did not provide feedback about which key was pressed, the participants would get confused when NavAccess provided a different result. Four participants would switch the functionality of the left and right arrow key (browsing through links on a page) with that of the up and down arrow key ('go back' and 'follow a link'). They mentioned that they perceived web sites as having a vertical menu on the left, and therefore found it more logical to browse through these links using up and down arrow keys while submenus were entered using the right arrow key.

All participants found it difficult at times to understand the pronunciation of the synthetic voice used in the NavAccess speech output, which was the Microsoft Speech synthesizer. Because of this, participants were not sure what exactly they were listening to. For instance, one link on the Dan Brown web site was labeled 'secrets,' which one participant comprehended as 'sequence,' thinking it was a setting for the application's speech settings. The people who made use of a Braille display ($N = 6$) all mentioned they would prefer Braille output in order to provide a clearer understanding of the spoken text. None of the sounds used in NavAccess were intuitive in meaning for the participants and had to be explained by the researcher. Four participants asked questions about the meanings of the sounds, while six ignored them and mentioned that they interrupted their understanding of the speech.

When asked whether they would want to use the NavAccess tool in the future based on this experience, six participants mentioned they would appreciate its specific functions, that is preview information and link categorization, link title alternatives, and context extraction, to be a part of their current assistive technology. However, they would not want to use NavAccess as a separate application next to their current browser and assistive technology. Four participants mentioned they would not want to use NavAccess at all. Two because they were satisfied in using their own screen reader and two mentioned they would find it too confusing to learn new functionality.

Two participants mentioned that while they approved the separation of navigation and content, they would only prefer the NavAccess approach if it would allow the user to skip to the start of the main content when a page is opened in the user's browser. Currently the user has to navigate to a certain page using the NavAccess tool, which then opens the page in the user's browser to be read there in more detail. However, the user still has to listen to the navigational content on this page, whereas ideally the user would skip directly to the page's main content.

4.5 Discussion

Based on the observation sessions described in the previous chapter, it appears that blind users seem to go through a '*learning phase*' when visiting a web site for the first time. During this phase as many landmarks as possible are collected to achieve a certain goal (e.g. locating a form or a specific section of a page). Once these landmarks have been identified, they are used in subsequent visits to retrace their previous route in a more efficient manner.

In navigating web sites, participants were found to apply different techniques in order to achieve a specific goal. The most common technique was sequential reading through a page. Starting from the beginning, no information is skipped so that the user does not miss any possibly relevant information. This *sequential approach* is therefore most suitable for a learning phase, as it allows the user to identify relevant landmarks in an unfamiliar document structure. The second approach is performing a keyword search (using the browser's standard search function), which allows the user to avoid having to read sequentially through a page. Searching was performed either through the browser's search function or by performing a first letter search within a link list generated by the user's screen reader. For this strategy to work, the user's search query has to match the terms used on the web page. For this reason, the *keyword search approach* is not always effective in situations where the desired content is unknown, such as a news site where content changes each day or a page containing the results of a search action. In these situations (where the user does not know the actual search key) the user can memorize a specific textual landmark that is known to be located near the desired content (such as a sentence which always precedes the latest news section on a news site). Using this form of *landmark search approach* allows users to mimic functionality, which would ideally be implemented by the content provider in the form of skip links. In other words, the user can break out of the sequential document structure by memorizing landmarks denoting locations relevant for the user's goal. These landmarks can then be used to 'jump to' a desired page location, thus skipping whatever irrelevant content would normally have to be listened through first. Another approach is the memorization of the exact steps necessary to achieve a certain goal. In this approach landmarks are barely used. An example is counting the links that have to be traversed before the desired link is reached. This *recall approach* can be useful when a web site's content remains consistent over time.

Participants were found to switch between approaches. There was no superior style that a participant used exclusively. By successfully going through a learning phase on a specific web site and memorizing the relevant landmarks as well as the actions required to achieve a specific goal, the user is able to create alternative paths through the web site's content. This could suggest that the mental models that blind users create of a web site are limited to the paths leading them toward a specific goal, while all other goal-irrelevant information is discarded after such a path has been created. Instead of attempting to provide blind users with a complete and detailed description of what the site looks like, it might be more relevant to assist them in constructing and maintaining these alternative paths.

Apart from the above-mentioned navigation techniques, it seems that blind user navigation is based on a trial and error approach: blind people perform a specific navigation step, reorient using their senses (e.g. using touch to recognize a door in a wall or a certain type of wall), and make a decision based on whether the previous step brought them closer to their goal or not. Similarly, when trying to achieve a certain navigation goal on a web site, blind users have often to confirm whether their last step was the right one. If so, they can decide whether to move on in this direction. If not, they can backtrack to the last known location. They begin their exploration at the start page and listen carefully for something that sounds like it may have something to do with the goal they are trying to achieve. When they encounter a link that seems promising, they follow it and again listen for another clue to continue. Sighted users also take their web site navigation one page at a time but have the benefit that the main links on the page offer a constant external memory of what can be done and where one can go. Such an external memory is difficult to provide by audio, as auditory information is always spread out over time and does not have the possibility to present such information in a persistent way. Therefore audio may not be a suitable medium to communicate a complex structure such as a web site's navigational model to blind users.

From the literature it seemed preferable to offer blind users a representation of a web site's overall structure. However, the evaluation of the NavAccess prototype shows that a second interface to such a different 'view' of the web site actually leads to more confusion than improvement. Blind users already have to deal with issues related to each specific page, and prefer to only deal with the content relevant to their intended paths. When participants performed tasks in familiar domains, they seemed to retrace a familiar route, based on landmarks on each specific page rather than constructing a mental representation of the web site's overall structure over time. It seemed that once participants had found a way to do something on a web site, from that point on this was the main functionality of that web site for them, and they would never encounter any of the other options it may offer. Offering a site's entire navigational structure would therefore only increase the user's level of cognitive overload. However, it can still be useful to offer a site's main information architecture to the user through separated controls for 'main' site links (as used in the NavAccess prototype). Most participants found the separation of these main links and regular links useful. The main categories could be available through a specific shortcut or menu, allowing users to directly move from one main category to the other. It seems clear that blind users could benefit from a functionality that would specify upon entering the starting page what the web site is about, for who it is designed, and what the main things are one can do on the site, even if just to point them in the right direction.

The findings in this study also show that the audio channel for blind users is already heavily burdened and that channel overloading can occur easily. Half of the participants experienced the use of sounds other than speech as intrusive and distracting. The sounds used in NavAccess were purposefully included to decrease the quantity of speech the user had to cope with, as this is thought to cause cognitive overload. It appears that even when nonspeech sounds are used, cognitive overload can still occur and should therefore be avoided. A possible explanation is that speech itself requires a relatively high level of attention, making the user unable to process the meaning of the other sounds being played. The participants in this study all used a screen reader at relatively high speeds, and were used to listening to large quantities of speech when navigating web sites. A better solution may be to provide a link's meta-information using speech as well, even though this can still lead to cognitive overload. Another solution is to provide tactile feedback even though this would burden users with the costs of purchasing yet another assistive device. Participants who also used Braille mentioned that the possibility to interact with the NavAccess prototype using only one hand was convenient because it allowed them to use the other hand to detect feedback from their Braille output. Even though this could make it possible to receive output via one hand and provide input via another hand, it has to be assumed that a user needs to be highly trained to perform this type of coordination.

Finally, it appears that a fully accessible web site design, in combination with a successful learning phase, can allow blind users to navigate the site at similar speeds to a sighted user without any noticeable problems. However, both the results found in literature as well as the user sessions show that currently, content providers are often not interested in or aware of accessibility issues and that this is not likely to change soon. Until it does, accessibility solutions, which extend the user agent, rather than support the content provider (such as guidelines and evaluation tools), will still be useful. In the following section the findings from this study will be used to develop a framework of 'challenge focus areas' for such solutions, describing what types of support are still required as well as possible implementations of these types.

4.6 New Focus Areas for Accessible Navigation Issues

Based on the literature, interviews, and observations discussed in this chapter it is possible to identify specific *challenge focus areas* which can be treated as abstract containers for issues related to web site navigation by Internet users who are blind. This framework can be used to categorize problems as well as the possible solutions for those problems. For each focus area certain guidelines can be determined, either very specific or on a more abstract level. These focus areas do not contain guidelines for accessible web design, as the latter are targeted at content providers and are already covered in accessibility guidelines such as the W3C WCAG. Instead, these guidelines describe additional recommendations, which should be implemented for navigation tools. It should also be noted that navigation problems experienced by users who are blind are not always limited to one specific area, as they can easily overlap. The focus areas are listed below.

- *Providing guidance.* This focus area contains the guidelines that assist the user in obtaining a better understanding of the virtual surroundings (i.e. the web site), and helps the user to navigate through these surroundings. Providing guidance is especially of importance while the user is still in the learning phase of a particular web site, as the user will then be unfamiliar with the site's structure. Depending on which goal the user is trying to achieve, the user should be assisted in determining which path he or she should follow to reach this goal. Providing guidance in this context can be compared with a guide taking a blind person by the hand and showing him or her around a specific building. The guide can describe the purpose of the building, what the most important rooms are and how they can be reached. Instead of the blind person having to obtain information about specific rooms by trying out multiple paths in order to discover which one is the right one, the guide describes what is in a specific room so the person knows whether or not it is worth entering. The guide is also available to respond to questions about how a certain task can be performed or how a certain location can be reached.
- The comparison with a human guide described in the previous paragraph can be used to contemplate how a virtual guide for web site navigation should behave. Currently, a blind user manually explores a web site to achieve a certain goal, for example to find information about a specific subject. Using a trial and error approach the chances are that the user will eventually discover a specific 'path' to reach the desired goal, but this process can be inefficient because the user will have to navigate through large amounts of irrelevant information, which a sighted person would most likely overlook when scanning a page. Ideally, this process of exploring in order to find out how to get from A to B would be minimized through the use of an assistive agent, which guides the user in making navigation decisions.
- *Empowering users.* The current research has proved that blind Internet users can be very resourceful when it comes to dealing with complex sites. They identify landmarks which can be used to skip to content relevant to their goals, and are able to determine which steps are necessary to reach this goal. These different methods used by blind users need to be supported in assistive software in order to provide blind users with additional means which extend the specific techniques used for web site navigation.
- *Reducing cognitive overload.* A major problem regarding web site navigation by blind Internet users is having to deal with an overflow of information. Such an overload can cause both problems regarding the effectiveness (the user will lose track and become disoriented) and efficiency (navigation is time-consuming and

tedious to perform) of user navigation. While users who are sighted can ignore information by scanning, users who are blind must rely on different techniques to filter out the relevant from the irrelevant content. A navigation tool should therefore aid the user in reducing the amount of information that has to be read through.

4.7 **Conclusions**

Two research questions were asked in this study. First, how do blind users navigate web sites? The findings show that blind users adopt different approaches during navigation to compensate for lack of accessibility in web design. Successful blind user navigation depends mostly on the availability of clear landmarks to guide navigation. Blind users appear to experience a 'learning phase' when navigating through unfamiliar web sites, during which landmarks for later visits are determined using a mostly sequential approach. The users proved to be resourceful in their techniques to use these landmarks, thus providing compensation for lack of accessible web design. Using memorized search queries as shortcuts they are able to avoid having to read sequentially through page content. Blind users were hindered most by cognitive overload and incomprehensible textual descriptions for navigation items.

Second, a high level representation of a web site's overall navigation structure with audio navigation was expected to support blind users. The findings indicate that blind users do not become aware of the structure of entire web sites but focus on identifying page-specific landmarks. Once these landmarks have been identified, and the goal achieved, the mental image the user has constructed of the web site is limited to these landmarks to reach a particular goal. Having an alternative interface to the overall site structure lead to cognitive overload for the participants, and this approach would therefore only be successful in a limited form (e.g. by providing the user with access to only the main categories of the site structure).

It proved difficult to present an overview of a web site's entire information architecture by audio. Cognitive overload occurs when too much information has to be taken in by the user. The findings suggest that more research is needed in audio design to provide awareness of the virtual space in which a user navigates. Designers should keep in mind that blind users navigate by meaningful landmarks rather than sequential rendering of the content of a web site. However, this finding could also indicate that blind users may benefit from knowing more about the decisions made by other users before them, such as community-based tools that allow sharing of landmarks and predefined paths. Combined with the finding that blind user interaction could benefit from recommender or adaptive agent technology, this seems a promising focus for future research.

Based on the findings from this study, three 'focus areas' were identified: *providing guidance, empowering users and reducing cognitive overload*. Each focus area addresses blind user navigation-related problems and the solutions which will have to be found for these problems. The three focus areas have been used to start a new project in which a NavAccess prototype will be developed as part of a Mozilla Firefox extension. This prototype will include modules that provide support for problems in each area.

The results show clearly how time-consuming, laborious, and frustrating the experiences can be for blind Internet users and how small design choices can cause a user to abort tasks even though they are almost completed. The results also show the inventiveness of blind users and the way in which they find ways to get around limitations of the assistive technology as well as a web site's design.

4.7.1 Implications for Designers

This research clearly shows that many designers are still either not aware of accessibility guidelines, not able or not willing to invest in following them. Furthermore, it appears that sometimes, designers who *do* put effort into making their web sites accessible are only motivated to do so because they 'have to,' rather than actually understanding *why* the modifications are necessary. Such designers will make sure they pass the automated evaluation checks, but they do not manually evaluate the level of accessibility. In these cases, text alternatives are added but are not descriptive to the user. Web designers should always perform test runs with assistive technology themselves, or have it evaluated by people who have a visual impairment. This way, they will discover that a web site, though 'officially' accessible, might still be very unpleasant to use in a nonvisual manner. To summarize, designers should be more engaged in making web sites pleasant to use for visually impaired users. Solving accessibility problems not only addresses the needs of users who are impaired but also improves the user experience of users who are able-bodied, such as the users of mobile devices and car audio interfaces.

The three focus areas that are discussed in this chapter can be used by designers of user agent technology as well as assistive technology as a framework for the specific problems related to web site navigation by users who are blind, and the solutions which are needed for them. In other words, designers should make sure that users have tools that provide guidance, empower them, and reduce cognitive overload.

4.7.2 Implications for Researchers

The results of this study should be carefully interpreted and generalized because of its limitations and small-scale nature. The research focused on experienced users rather than novice users and the issues identified are those encountered by users who have learnt to use their assistive technology creatively to overcome many of the accessibility and usability problems that are encountered. It is most likely that novice users have much more difficulty in accessing web sites as they need to overcome the limitations of the assistive devices and learn to find creative solutions to common accessibility problems. Involving a small number of participants allowed for an in-depth exploration of the way blind users experience web site navigation. However, generalization of these findings should be done with caution. The participants involved were all Dutch citizens and the level of technology experience for blind people in the Netherlands may be higher or lower than in other countries. Future research should therefore focus on larger and more diverse user groups.

In this chapter we have mostly focused on navigation within the domain of a specific web site, while the use of search engines such a Google also requires more attention. More research is also needed to provide a better understanding of different types of web site navigation and interaction with interfaces by users who are blind. Findings from future research are also expected to inform human–computer interaction research into small-screen and nonvisual interfaces for mobile and wearable technology.

4.7.3 **Implications for Users**

The implications of the findings are hoped to impact accessibility of the Internet and the ongoing developments of tools to improve the user experience of the Internet. With an increasingly aging population of technology users and technological developments becoming increasingly less dependent on large monitors, such research will prove valuable to ensure effective and pleasant interaction in general. The Internet can be a world in which users who are blind are able to move unimpeded by physical obstacles and where they should experience no limitations due to their impairments in social and professional activities.

4.7.4 **Implications for Policymakers**

An important task for policymakers is to make accessibility awareness more common in society. Laws such as Section 508 of the Rehabilitation Act in the USA are a good example of the role governments can play by providing rules for content providers which are legally binding. Besides such coercive methods, policymakers should also stimulate accessibility awareness through campaigns, proper training, and subsidizing accessible web sites.

References

Arons, B. (1991) Hyperspeech: navigating in speech-only hypermedia, *Proceedings of the Third Annual ACM Conference on Hypertext,* ACM Press, San Antonio, TX, pp. 133–146.

Asakawa, C. (2005) What's the web like if you can't see it?, *Proceedings of the 2005 International Cross-Disciplinary Workshop on Web Accessibility (W4A),* ACM Press, Chiba, Japan.

Asakawa, C. and Hironobu, T. (2000) Annotation-based transcoding for nonvisual web access, *Proceedings of the Fourth International ACM Conference on Assistive Technologies,* ACM Press, Arlington, VA, pp. 172–179.

Asakawa, C. and Itoh, T. (1998). User interface of a home page reader, *Proceedings of the Third International ACM Conference on Assistive Technologies,* ACM Press, Marina del Rey, CA, pp. 149–156.

Barnicle, K. (2000) Usability testing with screen reading technology in a windows environment, *Proceedings on the 2000 Conference on Universal Usability,* ACM Press, Arlington, VA, pp. 102–109.

Chisholm, W., VanderHeiden, G. and Jacobs I. (2001) Web content accessibility guidelines 1.0. *Interactions* 8(4), 35–54.

Donker, H., Klante, P. and Gorny, P. (2002) The design of auditory user interfaces for blind users, *Paper Presented at the Proceedings of the Second Nordic Conference on Human-Computer Interaction,* ACM Press, Aarhus, Denmark, pp. 149–156.

Ebina, T., Igi, S. and Miyake, T. (2000) Fast web by using updated content extraction and a bookmark facility, *Proceedings of the Fourth International ACM Conference on Assistive Technologies,* ACM Press, Arlington, VA, pp. 64–71.

Evers, V., Luteyn, C., Damsma, P., and Norgaard, J. (2004) Beyond Physical and Cultural Barriers: The Development of an International Community Environment for Seeing and Visually Impaired Children. *International Conference on Virtual Communities,* the Hague, 10–12 June.

Fernandes, A.R., Martins, F.M., Parades, H. and Pereira J. (2001) A different approach to real web accessibility, *Paper Presented at the Proceedings of HCI International,* Lawrence Erlbaum Associates, pp. 723–727.

Filepp, R., Challenger, J. and Rosa D. (2002) Improving the accessibility of aurally rendered HTML tables, *Proceedings of the Fifth International ACM Conference on Assistive Technologies,* ACM Press, Edinburgh, Scotland, pp. 9–16.

Goble, C., Harper, S. and Stevens, R. (2000) The travails of visually impaired web travellers, *Proceedings of the Eleventh ACM on Hypertext and Hypermedia,* ACM Press, San Antonio, pp. TX, pp. 1–10.

Guo, B., Briscout, J.C. and Huang, J. (2005) A common open space or a digital divide? A social model perspective on the online disability community in China. *Disability Society* **20**(1), 49–66.

Harper, S. and Green, P. (2000) A travel flow and mobility framework for visually impaired travellers. *Paper presented at the ICCHP, Karlsruhe, Germany.*

Harper, S., Stevens, R. and Goble, C. (2001) Web mobility guidelines for visually impaired surfers. *Journal of Research Practice in Information Technology (Special Issue on HCI),* **33**(2).

Hermsdorf, D., Gappa, H. and Pieper, M. (1998) Webadapter: A prototype of a www-browser with special needs adaptations. *Paper presented at the ICCHP 98,* pp. 151–160.

Hillen, H. (2006) *Navaccess, Designing an Auditory Based Web-Navigation Tool for the Blind,* University of Amsterdam, Amsterdam.

Huang, A.W. and Sundaresan, N. (2000) A semantic transcoding system to adapt web services for users with disabilities, *Proceedings of the Fourth International ACM Conference on Assistive Technologies,* ACM Press, Arlington, VA.

James, F. (1998) *Presenting HTML Structure in Audio: User Satisfaction with Audio Hypertext,* Stanford University.

Kennel A., Perrochon L., & Darvishi A. (1996) WAB: World Wide Web access for blind and visually impaired computer users. *SIGCAPH Computers and Physical Handicaps,* **55**, 10–15.

Lazar, J., Dudley-Sponaugle, A. and Greenidge, K.-D. (2004) Improving web accessibility: a study of webmaster perceptions. *Computers and Human Behavior,* **20**(2), 268–288.

Leporini, B., Andronico, P. and Buzzi, M. (2004) Designing search engine user interfaces for the visually impaired, *Proceedings of the 2004 International Cross-Disciplinary Workshop on Web Accessibility (W4A),* ACM Press, New York, pp. 57–66.

Marchionini, G., Geisler G. and Brunk B. (2000) Agileviews: a human-centered framework for interfaces to information spaces, *Proceedings of the Annual Conference of the American Society for Information Science,* Chicago, IL, pp. 271–280.

Otter, M. and Jonson, H. (2000) Lost in hyperspace: metrics and mental models. *Interacting Computers,* **13**(1), 1–40.

Paciello, M.G. (2000) *Web Accessibility for People with Disabilities,* CMP Books, Lawrence.

Parente, P. (2004) *Audio Enriched Links: Web Page Previews for Blind Users,* ACM Press, Atlanta, GA.

Petrie, H. (2004) *The Web: Access and Inclusion for Disabled People: A Formal Investigation Conducted by the Disability Rights Commission,* Disability Rights Commission, London.

Petrie, H., Morley, S., McNally, P. et. al. (1997) Initial design and evaluation of an interface to hypermedia systems for blind users, *Proceedings of the Eighth ACM Conference on Hypertext,* ACM Press, Southampton, UK, pp. 48–56.

Petrucci, L., Roth, P., Assimacopoulos, A. and Pun, T. (1999) An audio browser for increasing access to World Wide Web sites for blind and visually impaired computer users, *Proceedings of HCI International '99 (the 8th International Conference on Human-Computer Interaction): Communication, Cooperation, and Application Design, 2,* Lawrence Erlbaum Associates, pp. 995–998.

Pitt, I.J. and Edwards, D.N.A. (1996) Improving the usability of speech-based interfaces for blind users, *Paper presented at the Proceedings of the Second Annual ACM Conference on Assistive Technologies,* Vancouver, BC, Canada, ACM Press, pp. 124–130.

Pontelli, E., Gillan, D. and Gupta, G. et. al. (2002) Intelligent non-visual navigation of complex HTML structures. *Information Society,* 2(1), 56–69.

Slone, D.J. (2002) The influence of mental models and goals on search patterns during web interaction. *Journal of the American Society on Information Science and Technology,* 53(13), 1152–1169.

Spence, R. (1999) A framework for navigation. *International Journal on Human-Computer Studies,* 51(5), 919–945.

Speroni, M., Di Blas, N. and Paolini, P. (2004) Listen to a web site. *Paper presented at the World Conference on Educational Multimedia,* Hypermedia and Telecommunications, AACE, Lugano, Switzerland, pp. 5224–5225.

Stowers, G.N.L. (2002) *The State of Federal Websites: The Pursuit of Excellence,* Public Administration Program, San Francisco State University.

Sullivan, T., and Matson, R. (2000) Barriers to use: usability and content accessibility on the web's most popular sites, *Proceedings on the 2000 Conference on Universal Usability,* ACM Press, Arlington, VA, pp. 139–144.

Listening to Choropleth Maps: Interactive Sonification of Geo-referenced Data for Users with Vision Impairment

5

Haixia Zhao, Ben Shneiderman, and Catherine Plaisant

Human-Computer Interaction Lab,
University of Maryland Institute of Advanced Computer Studies, University of Maryland, USA

5.1 Introduction

Information visualization has produced many innovative techniques/interfaces for people with normal vision to use their tremendous visual ability to explore and discover facts/trends in data, such as financial data, business information, and government census data. However, most visualizations are not usable for users with vision impairment.

One example is the current access to the enormous amounts of data accumulated by government agencies and to be made available to every citizen. These data are useful to senior citizens looking for a place to settle after retirement, business analysts, managers considering relocation, etc. Such data is often geography-related, such as population distribution by geographical regions, and often presented as choropleth maps that typically use colors to show the value for each map region. Several interactive map visualization tools have been developed for exploring such data (e.g. Andrienko and Andrienko, 1999; MacEachren *et al.*, 1999; Dang *et al.*, 2001), but none of them are accessible to users with visual impairments.

About 7.4 million people in the European Union (1.92% of the total population) are estimated to have vision impairments (European Blind Union, 2005). In the USA, there are about 1.3 million blind people (NFB, 2005). The visual disability is one of the main factors contributing to the 'digital gap' in accessing information resources provided by the global information revolution. To help bridge such gaps and promote the 'Universal Usability' (ACM, 2000) of information systems, many countries and organizations have taken initiatives to achieve information accessibility for blind users (eEurope; WWAI), or even made it a legal requirement (S508USRA).

For people with visual impairments, sound is an important alternative or supplemental information channel. While people with limited vision can use screen magnifiers (for instance, the magnifier available in the accessibility accessories from the Start menu of MS Windows), those with severe vision impairments have to rely on tactile or audio material. Reading tactile material, such as Braille, requires significant learning and was hard especially for people who acquired blindness later in life. A number of reports have estimated that Braille literacy is only between 10–20% and is still declining (`http://www.nfb.org/braille/chap1.htm`). The most widely used accommodation for users with vision impairment to access digital information is to rely on screen readers, such as JAWS (Freedom Scientific), to speak the textual content. To make nontextual elements accessible to screen readers, textual equivalences are needed. For static graphs or maps, it is a standard practice to provide textual labels during the system development (WCAG). For dynamic graphs or maps, tabular data presentations are used instead (e.g. Willuhn *et al.*, 2003), or textual summaries can be automatically generated from the data set (e.g. Sripada *et al.*, 2003).

Several problems exist in such text-based speech approaches. First, while a concise textual description is helpful, the data interaction that is a critical part of the data exploration process is lost. Second, a tabular presentation may be good for basic data browsing but is hard for in-depth data comprehension and analysis, especially in the geographical context. Third, although speech can accurately describe information, presenting information in speech tends to be longer in duration, and harder to realize complex information.

Sonification is the use of nonspeech sounds to present information (Kramer *et al.*, 1997). As reviewed in more detail in the next section, sonification has been used effectively for many application purposes, including data presentations. However, previous work on data sonification focused on data to sound mapping and lacked the support for task-oriented data interaction for the purpose of exploratory data analysis. Additionally, most previous data sonifications were not designed for blind users.

Other perceptual channels, especially tactile feedback, are often used together with auditory feedback to convey information. Such multimodal approaches were employed by many existing assistive technology projects for graph and map access. While tactile feedback is important, it relies heavily on the availability of special devices, such as tactile graphics embossers or refreshable tactile displays. These special devices are usually very expensive, not widely available, and generally not portable. Additionally, the displays are static and a limited amount of information can be presented. Computer synthesized sound, on the other hand, has become almost a standard resource on many computers. Considering the goal of universal usability (ACM, 2000), it is important to provide effective sound-only solutions, and limit the dependence on special devices.

After reviewing related work in Section 2, we describe in Section 3 the design and implementation of a highly interactive sonification tool, iSonic, for blind users to explore geo-referenced data for analytical purposes. iSonic can be used effectively with a keyboard only and standard computer speakers or headphones. In Section 4, we summarize the results and lessons from several iSonic evaluations with both blind and blindfolded sighted users. This chapter describes the current status of iSonic and discusses future directions.

5.2 **Related Work**

5.2.1 **Sonification**

Sonification is 'the use of nonspeech sound to convey information,' or more specially, 'the transformation of data relations into perceived relations in an acoustic signal for the purposes of facilitating communication or interpretation' (Kramer *et al.*, 1997). Research into sonification has developed rapidly in recent decades. It brought together interests from various fields, such as sound synthesis (e.g. Duda, 1993; Shinn-Cunningham, 2000), computer music (e.g. Moore, 1990), acoustic psychology, and human–computer interaction (e.g. Perlman, 2004). Sonification has been used for many application purposes, both as a supplementary information channel to enhance visual representation and as an alternative in the absence of visual feedback. Examples of application domains include data mining (e.g. Hermann *et al.*, 2000), GUI access/navigation (e.g. Gaver, 1986; Blattner *et al.*, 1989; Mynatt and Weber, 1994; Brewster, 1998), web access (e.g. James, 1998), information presentation and interaction on mobile devices (e.g. Leplâtre and Brewster, 2000; Walker *et al.*, 2001; Pirhonen *et al.*, 2002), graph and image presentation (e.g. Meijer, 1992; Kennel, 1996; Roth *et al.*, 2000), mathematics access (e.g. Stevens *et al.*, 1994), algorithm presentation and computer program debugging (e.g. Brown and Hershberger, 1992; Vickers, 1999), map exploration (e.g. Parente and Bishop, 2003), and collaborative environments (e.g. Müller-Tomfelde and Steiner, 2001).

5.2.2 **Nonspeech Sound**

Nonspeech sound can be categorized into two types: real-life natural sound, and musical sound. Gaver (1986) first described auditory icons, the use of real-life sound to present events in a computer. The concept has since been explored by many researchers (e.g. Mynatt and Weber, 1994). Real-life sounds have the ability to convey complex messages in a single sound, and do not require learning, provided that the sound is easy to identify and is a good conceptual mapping of the event or operation. Yet users report them to be annoying after prolonged use (Sikora *et al.*, 1995; Roberts and Sikora, 1997). Additionally, it will not work if there is no everyday equivalent to the event or operation. It can also be misleading if the users' interpretation of the sound is different from the designers (Bussemakers and Haan, 2000).

In recent years, researchers have also been exploring using the highly structured nature of musical sounds to convey information. Blattner *et al.* (1989) first developed earcons, the use of abstract, synthetic tones in structured combinations to create auditory messages that are used in the computer/user interface to provide information about some computer object, operation, or interaction. As icons are visually recognizable computer objects, earcons also target individual recognizable entities. Brewster and colleagues further studied the structures of earcons and extensively used earcons in various applications, such as to enhance GUI widgets (Brewster, 1994), menu hierarchy navigation (Brewster, 1998), mathematics access (Stevens *et al.*, 1994), information presentation or navigation on small devices (Leplâtre and Brewster, 2000; Walker *et al.*, 2001). Although earcons do not possess an intuitive mapping as auditory icons do, therefore they have to be learnt, they also do not have many disadvantages that auditory icons have. Users found earcons in general more appropriate for applications (Roberts and Sikora, 1997).

A musical sound is made up from three basic components: pitch, timbre, and loudness. Pitch is related to the frequency of the tone, and decides the order of sounds on a musical scale (ASA, 1960). Loudness is the perceived intensity of a sound, and is often referred to as the sound volume. Timbre is the 'quality' of a sound, through which a user can distinguish two sounds similarly presented and having the same loudness and pitch (ANSI, 1973). In other words, timbre is that which allows a listener to distinguish between a piano and a violin playing the same note.

Sounds arising from real-world sources carry spatial location information. Sounds available from a computer traditionally are mono or stereo. Recently, researchers have been able to simulate spatial localization cues for computer-synthesized sounds. Currently there are two ways to generate sounds that have spatial locations similar to sounds arising from real-world sources. Some systems vary the signals presented from two (or more) loudspeakers to simulate sources from different locations (e.g. Shinn-Cunningham *et al.*, 1996). Other systems are headphone-based in which sounds are processed using a Head Related Transfer Function (HRTF) to simulate the normal auditory localization cues (e.g. Carlile, 1996; Zotkin *et al.*, 2002a). The latter approach is often preferred because it allows precise stimulus control and retains good simulation effect regardless of listener movements. However, in order to achieve good source location perception, particularly the source elevation, individualized HRTFs need to be used (Wenzel *et al.*, 1993). In practice, individualized HRTFs can be measured directly using moving speakers and in-the-ear microphones. It is the most accurate but a very time-consuming process that requires precise measurement and careful calibration (Carlile, 1996). A number of studies have sought to perform simple HRTF personalization. For example, Middlebrooks (1999) used frequency scaling of nonindividualized HRTFs to improve localization. Zotkin *et al.* (2002b, 2003) showed that localization accuracy improved from matching the listener's unique anthropometric ear parameters with the HRTF database, and incorporation of a low-frequency 'head-and-torso' model.

5.2.3 **Nonvisual Map Access**

Current assistive technology research is exploring a number of techniques to help blind users benefit from the spatial awareness provided by maps. For navigation in the real world, GPS-based talking maps have been developed (Golledge, 1991; Golledge *et al.*, 1991). One example product is a talking nationwide digital map consisting of most addresses and street intersections (The Sendero Group, 2003). Users can navigate the map using the arrow keys and listen to speech-synthesized descriptions of the map and directions. Trekker (VGPSOS, 2003) is another GPS-based application that helps the blind to navigate. Maps are also important to learn an area beforehand and choose a route. Schneider and Strothotte (2000) have designed a tangible interface using physical building blocks that users manipulate to promote constructive exploration of the map.

When using maps to learn geo-referenced data, it is a standard accessibility practice to provide a 'd' link mark for image descriptions that visually impaired users are able to search for. OptiMaps (Corda Technologies Inc., 2003) employs such a mark below each choropleth map to provide a hyperlink to a textual version of the data, generated automatically with the dynamic map. Examples are available in AtlasPlus (NCI, 2003). New vector graphic file formats, such as SVG, permit embedding text descriptions with the graphic information and should simplify this process as a result. Unfortunately, reading the data values still does not give an adequate feeling for the spatial relationships between areas that only spatial techniques can provide. Tactile and haptic techniques (and strategies for signifying data haptically) have been devised (Griffin, 2002). Virtual Touch provides an example of map exploration using a tactile mouse. The mouse is equipped with two Braille character mechanical units, which can be used to indicate tactile patterns (using Braille and other alternatives), as shown in

Figure 5.1 *The VTPlayer is a mouse equipped with two Braille character units that can also be used to indicate patterns. For example, as users explore a map of the USA, patterns change over different states. © Virtouch Ltd. Used with permission.*

Figure 5.1. As users explore the map, the patterns change over different states or areas. One of the limitations of the mouse is that it is an input device providing only relative positioning, so absolute position on the map has to be provided by audio feedback.

Another example developed by TouchGraphics and their research colleagues (Landau and Gourgey, 2001) augments standard printed tactile maps. Maps are secured on top of a touchscreen that provides the location of each touch (Figure 5.2). The TouchGraphics Atlas has five operational modes. Users can simply explore by touching a physical tactile map and hear names of places touched. They select a destination from an index, and listen to directions that are updated as a user's

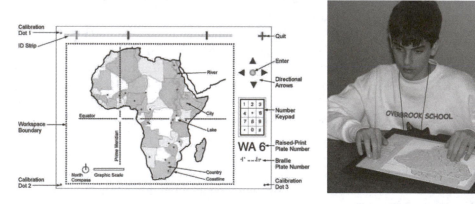

Figure 5.2 *An example of a tactile map augmented with an audio description when mounted on a touchscreen (Touch Graphics, undated). (a) Sample map plate; (b) the sample map plate in use with the talking tactile tablet (TTT). © Touch Graphics Inc. Used with permission.*

finger gets closer to the destination. Distance between two points can be calculated, and descriptions of the areas can be listened to. This work was inspired by Nomad (Parkes, 1994). 3D maps can benefit from the use of haptic devices. For example, the Phantom device provides 6 degrees of freedom input and 3 degrees of freedom output to explore the virtual sound space and augment it with haptic feedback providing the same sensation as moving a single finger over a physical 3D map. Tactile maps can be augmented with abstract audio output (Fisher, 1994; Krygier, 1994). For example, users can hear a series of graduated pitches proportional to elevations above sea level as they explore the map. Jeong (2001) compared the effectiveness of and preferences for using auditory feedback (volume of sound), haptic feedback (extent of vibration), or both in the tasks of identifying the highest or the middle-valued state on a static choropleth map of the USA. The experiment showed that overall performance is most successful when using haptic feedback alone, but users prefer having both haptic and audio feedback. This result may be attributed to the fact that haptic devices provided spatial cues while the standard sound output does not.

Unfortunately, tactile and haptic techniques require special hardware, from embossed maps to specialized input devices, and hardware is usually a limiting factor for wide dissemination, as users may not have access to the technology or the financial means to purchase it. Techniques relying solely on sonification have the potential to be used by a larger population as blind users, who often already rely on headphones when using screen readers.

The BATS project (Parente and Bishop, 2003) uses simple spatial audio (mostly stereo effects) to sonify maps as shown in Figure 5.3. Real-world auditory icons are played as the user moves the cursor over the map. For example, car noises are heard over cities and birds and crashing waves are heard over forests and beaches. The sound becomes louder as the user gets close to the source of the sound.

5.2.4 **Auditory Perception**

A rich history of research has provided valuable insight into the perceptual and cognitive aspects of general auditory perception. Examples regarding speech and relatively simple auditory tones include intensity (loudness), frequency (pitch), and temporal discrimination of static sounds (Moore, 1995), the determinants of pitch and loudness (Gulick *et al.*, 1989), and auditory localization abilities (Blauert, 1997). Investigations have also been done into the perception of more complex, dynamic auditory patterns in speech and music (Bregman, 1990). The perceptual interferences among sound properties and cross modalities have also been studied, such as the

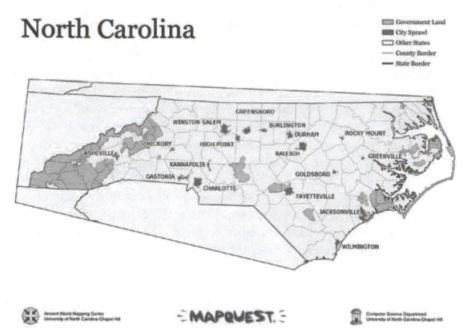

Figure 5.3 *The BATS sonic map helps those without sight to explore spatial information (Parente and Bishop, 2003). Real-world audio icons (car noises, wave crashing, etc.) are played as the user navigates the map and appear clearly as coming from your right or your left. Volume increases as users get closer to the source of the sound. © Blind Audio Tactile Mapping System (BATS) Project. Used with permission.*

interferences between pitch and localization (Roffler and Butler, 1968), pitch and loudness (Neuhoff *et al.*, 2000), and visual and auditory perceptions (Radeau, 1992). Much of the work is very relevant for designing data sonification.

Much research has shown that visually impaired people have better hearing and sound localization ability than normal sighted people. For example, visually impaired people show greater locomotion ability than blindfolded sighted people, using natural auditory cues for guidance (Strelow and Brabyn, 1982). They also displayed better sound localization ability than blindfolded sighted people (Roder *et al.*, 1999). While early visual experience benefits spatial hearing ability of people who became blind later on (Abel *et al.*, 2002), congenitally or early-blind people can replace vision with audiomotor feedback to calibrate their auditory space (Ashmead *et al.*, 1998). Studies have also shown evidence that early vision deprivation leads to cross-modal cerebral reorganization, enabling totally blind individuals to have better auditory ability than sighted people, in order to compensate for the loss of vision (Roder *et al.*, 1999).

There has been consistent evidence that congenitally totally blind people were able to construct and operate mental spatial imagery and pictorial imagery, but performed poorer than sighted people in demanding spatial tasks, such as mental rotation and scanning (e.g. Vecchi, 1998; Aleman *et al.*, 2002). Explanations in the literature of such deficits take two sides: representation explanation and processing explanation. Representation explanations emphasize that congenitally blind people and sighted people use different spatial representation formats (e.g. Zimler and Keenan, 1983). Processing explanations argue that the performance difference is due to processing deficiencies in the stages of constructing, integrating, and manipulating, since the serial processing of sound and touch is slower and more prone to error than the parallel processing of vision (e.g. Aleman *et al.*, 2002). Evidence has been presented suggesting that most blind visuo-spatial deficits are the result of processing differences between blind and normally sighted people. For example, Vecchi (1998) found that the blind users are equally able to remember spatial patterns when they are engaged in a task that does not require manipulation or elaboration through active processing.

5.2.5 Data Sonification

Scientific Data Sonification

Scientific data sonification is used to refer to sonification of scientific data, just as scientific visualization has been used by Card *et al.* (1999) to differentiate visualization of scientific data from abstract data. There have been numerous case studies of using sound to present scientific data, for revealing interesting patterns and helping understand underlying structures. For example, Blattner *et al.* (1990) sonified turbulence information. Axen and Choi (1996) described using audio to present structures of complex and large data sets such as flow patterns, turbulence of fluids, and complex topological representations. Fitch and Kramer (1994) sonified physiological data.

Abstract Data Sonification

There has also been research using sonification to present abstract data, both for monitoring purposes and for analytical purposes. Among the numerous examples are some pioneering work by Kramer and others in the early 1990s on sonifying high-dimensional data (Kramer, 1993).

Smith *et al.* (1990) described a method to sonically probe an iconographic display of high-dimensional data. The data is depicted as small icons on a 2D scatterplot representing two dimensions with the remaining dimension values visually represented as the shapes and colors of the icons. When users swept the display with mice, the iconographic pattern and the speeds and directions of the movements determine how many notes and different timbres sound simultaneously, thus producing various 'auditory textures' of the data display.

Hermann *et al.* (2000) showed that principle curve sonification can facilitate the detection of the 'main' structures in high-dimensional data. The principle curve (PC) of a data set is a trajectory that passes through the 'middle' of the data. While moving along the principle curve in the high-dimensional virtual space, the listener hears a changing auditory scene that presents the properties of the principle curve, the data points, and the locally averaged density of the data.

Some researchers have examined the ability of humans with normal sight to perceive facts in abstract data sets by listening to sonified graphs, such as line graphs, scatterplots, and diagrams. For example, Flowers and colleagues examined univariate line graphs (Flowers and Hauer, 1995) and bivariate scatterplots (Flowers *et al.*, 1997), showing that most people can understand trends, clustering, outliers, correlations, and other simple statistical features of a data set just as well by listening to it as they could by reading the visual graph. Bonebright *et al.* (2001) further studied sonified graph comprehension and found that most people can understand multivariate scatterplots except for those with widely dispersed data points and without an easily discernable 'envelope.' Brown and Brewster (2003) found that people can possibly interpret line graphs containing two data series. Franklin and Roberts (2003) evaluated five sonification designs of pie charts. From data sonification practices and user evaluations, some guidelines have also been extracted and summarized, such as the guidelines for sonifying line graphs and tables (Brown *et al.*, 2003).

For general data-to-sound mapping, various experimental assessments have been done to find effective or natural mappings from data attributes to sound attributes. For example, Kramer (1994) summarized some organization principles for representing data with sound. Walker conducted a series of experiments on the general psychophysical scaling, polarity, and magnitude estimation (Walker, 2002).

Sound is time-sensitive stimuli. Human auditory perception is far less synoptic than visual perception. It limits the number of individual data items that can be presented in parallel to the user. As a result, multiple data items need to be presented in a sequenced manner. For data that contains the time dimension (such as a time-series data collection), a sequencing order is already naturally implied. In fact, many sonification projects have used that implicit order. For data that does not imply any natural data to time dimension mapping, an appropriate data dimension needs to be picked for sequencing. Saue (2000) defined temporization as the process of mapping from a nontemporal to a temporal domain. The definition implies both sequencing during automatic sonification of the data items (automatic sequencing), and sequencing according to the order of the users' movements among the data items (manual sequencing).

The need for automatic sequencing has already been recognized by researchers in designing auditory information presentations. For example, Alty and Rigas (1998) used various scanning orders (top down, central scan, and ascending by object size) to present the layout of a set of simple 2D graphical objects. Franklin and Roberts (2004) proposed a tour-based model to unify various methods of sequencing that exist in previous research, and to create new sequencing designs in a 2D or 3D presentation space.

Various data sonification toolkits have been developed to help researchers experiment with different sonification designs. Examples of toolkits that accept general data sets in tabular form include Listen (Wilson and Lodha, 1996), MUSE (Lodha *et al.*, 1997), SonART (Ben-Tal *et al.*, 2002), Sandbox (Walker and Cothran, 2003), and Interactive Sonification Toolkit (Pauletto and Hunt, 2004). Ramloll and Brewster also described AudioCave, an environment for studying sonified graphs (Ramloll and Brewster, 2002).

Barrass (1996) recognized the importance of tasks in sonification design, and proposed a TaDa method for auditory information design that is 'Task-oriented and Data-sensitive.' The method includes a design process that integrates task analysis through scenario description and requirement analysis, a database of sound examples, a rule-based mapping design aid, and interactive sound design tools.

5.2.6 **Interaction with Data Sonification**

While there has been much research on data sonification design, the support for user interaction with the data set, that is moving around in the data set and examining various parts, is missing from most systems and toolkits. In those systems, the process of sonification is done through parameter mapping (Scaletti, 1994), which involves taking data attributes and converting them into sound. The user is allowed to control this mapping process (e.g. to change the scaling or mapping). After the user scales the data and specifies the parameter mapping, the entire data set is converted into a sound file, which is then listened to noninteractively, rather like a CD. The emphasis of those systems and toolkits is on creating sonification for experimenting with various sonification mappings. Although in some of these tools, the user can dynamically change the mapping during the playback of the sonification, such as adjusting the panning of individual channels, as in Pauletto and Hunt (2004), the interaction is done to the mapping function but not with the data. While such systems and toolkits may satisfy the needs for experimenting with different sonification mappings or monitoring tasks, they are not satisfactory for the purpose of exploratory data analysis.

Some researchers have recognized the importance of interaction with data in sonification, and provided some support for the users to move around in the auditory scene. For example, Smith *et al.* (1990) allow user-controlled mouse movements to 'sonic probe' the iconographic display (a 2D scatterplot) of high-dimensional data. Sounds associated with the icons (data items) on the iconographic display are activated when the icons are swept by the mouse movements. Similarly, Fernstrom and Brazil (2001) described a sonic browser in which users can use an 'active cursor' to move around in the starfield presentation of the data files (sonic objects). The objects closest to the cursor are activated and the associated sound files start to play. In the work by Ramloll *et al.* (2001) to use nonspeech sound to improve vision-impaired users' access to 2D tabular numerical information, users are allowed to use a keyboard to move up, down, left, and right among the 2D table cells. In the sonification of line graphs containing one or two data series, the user can use a numerical keypad to move along the *x*-axis to activate a note presenting the *y*-value of each individual data point visited (Brown *et al.*, 2002). In the Interactive Sonification Toolkit (Pauletto and Hunt, 2004), multiple data streams (in the form of a matrix where each column is a data series evolving over time) can be loaded and is presented in a rectangle interaction area (with time portrayed from left to right). The user can click and drag the mouse along the *x*-axis over the area to instantly listen to the sound of each data array visited (all data along the *y*-axis belongs to an array). However, most of these approaches did not consider whether the interaction can be effectively used without visual feedback, thus making them suitable for users with visual impairments. The interactions were all casually designed without systematically considering task needs.

In order to unify the design of interaction with data sonification, some modes have been proposed (Hermann and Ritter, 1999; Saue, 2000). But they assume the data set has natural physical presentations (like in scientific visualization), and thus may not be appropriate for abstract data. Additionally, some models emphasize using special devices to issue the interactions (Hermann *et al.*, 2002) to achieve real-world acoustic interaction effects (Hunt *et al.*, 2004). None of the models take into account user task needs, or the suitability for users with vision impairment. Similarly, none of the user-controlled activation of object sounds in virtual environments, such as sonic probes by mice (Smith *et al.*, 1990), virtual microphones (Grohn and Takala, 1995), control paths (Choi and Bargar, 1995), auditory cursor and radar interactor (Röber and Masuch, 2004), have considered the needs of data interaction without visual aids.

5.2.7 Discussion

Reviewing previous work shows that audio could be an effective means of presenting information. Sonification has been used in computer interfaces for many purposes, including conveying abstract data. However, previous data sonification applications typically lack support for users to interact with the data. Most sonification tools were developed for researchers to experiment with various sonification mappings, but not to support users in exploratory data analysis, especially for users with visual impairments. Previous work on making maps accessible focused on real-world geography learning, not for task-oriented analytical data exploration, such as for geo-referenced statistical data analysis. Many nonvisual map access systems were designed to depend on tactile material that limits the wide dissemination of the systems.

5.3 iSonic: Interactive Sonification for Geo-referenced Data Exploration for Users with Vision Impairments

The goal of the iSonic project is to improve blind users' access and comprehension of abstract data, especially geo-referenced data. It focuses on supporting data interactions that are helpful to analytical data exploration and suitable without any visual aids. To achieve universal usability, the project emphasizes designs that only utilize standard devices and resources, that is a keyboard plus a speaker or headphone, a standard hardware configuration of almost every computer.

5.3.1 Description of iSonic Features

The current iSonic design was based on the design space exploration of geo-referenced statistical data, guided by the Action-by-Design-Component (ADC) framework described in our earlier paper (Zhao *et al.*, 2005d). Two users without residual vision were involved in the iterative design process. Many iSonic design decisions were based on their suggestions, as well as results from the evaluation of some design choices with blindfolded sighted subjects (Zhao *et al.*, 2004, 2005a).

Guided by the ADC framework, iSonic currently supports exploratory data analysis tasks by providing the following Auditory Information Seeking Actions (AISA): *gist*, *navigate*, *situate*, *details-on-demand*, *select*, and *brush*. Each AISA consists of one or multiple interaction loops that involve four main design components. Users use an *input device* to issue a command and listen to the *auditory feedback*. The center of the loop is the *data view* that decides the appropriate *navigation structure* and allows the user to build a mental representation of the data space and correctly interpret the auditory feedback.

Data Views

iSonic provides two highly coordinated data views (Figure 5.7) – a region-by-variable table and a choropleth map. The table shows multiple statistical variables simultaneously. Each row corresponds to a geographical region and columns to variables. Table rows can be sorted by pressing 'O' while at the desired column, allowing quick locating of low or high values. The map view shows the value of each geographical region for one statistical variable, and can be used for geography-related tasks.

Input Devices and Navigation Structures

When choosing input devices, we considered both device availability and how effectively their physical properties match the navigational properties of the two data views.

iSonic works with a keyboard alone. A keyboard is available on most computers and blind users are very comfortable using it. We use the arrow keys as natural means for relative movements in the left, right, up, and down directions. We also transform the keyboard into a low resolution 2D absolute pointing device by recursively mapping the 3×3 layout of the numerical keypad on the keyboard to 2D map positions.

iSonic also works with other common devices such as a touchpad. A 14″ touchpad costs less than $150, provides high-resolution 2D absolute pointing and allows continuous movements by fingers. The kinesthetic feedback associated with arm and finger movements, combined with the tablet frame as the position reference, could help with users' position awareness on maps. Tactile maps placed on the touchpad could be helpful, but we chose not to use them because they need to be changed when the map changes and tactile printers are expensive and rarely available. When resources are available, a generic grid with subtle tactile dots may be used as a position and direction aid.

In iSonic, the table navigation follows the row and column table structure. It is discrete and relative because what matters is the relative row/column order, not the exact spatial location or size of each table cell. On the other hand, the map navigation follows the regions' positions and adjacencies. Both the relative region layout and the absolute region locations and sizes are useful.

Auditory Feedback

iSonic integrates the use of speech and musical sounds. Values are categorized into five ranges, as in many choropleth maps, and mapped to five musical pitches of a string instrument by default. The length of the sound for each value is configurable, and by default lasts for 150 ms. The sound duration could be used instead to present the value but would significantly prolong the feedback and is not appropriate when values of many regions need to be presented. The table view uses the same value to pitch mapping. Various musical instruments are used to indicate when users are outside the map or crossing a region border in the touchpad interface, or crossing a water body to reach a neighboring region in the keyboard interface. Stereo panning effects are used to indicate a region's azimuth position on the virtual auditory map. It is also used in the table to indicate the column order. Using the plus and minus keys, users can switch among four information levels for each region: region name only, musical sound only, name and sound, name and sound plus reading of the numerical value.

While we focus on MIDI stereo sound, we have also connected iSonic to a virtual spatial sound server (Zotkin *et al.*, 2002a) that uses Head Related Transfer Functions (HRTF) to synthesize virtual spatial sounds. In such configuration, the region locations are mapped to sound locations. Although the synthesized spatial sound, especially when a generic HRTF is used, does not provide satisfactory perceptual resolution in the elevation plane, it could potentially help to enhance the effect of a virtual half-cylinder shaped auditory map surrounding the user located at the center (Figure 5.4).

iSonic supports AISAs in both the table and the map views, including sequential brushing between the two views. Each interface function can be activated from a menu system that also gives the hotkey and a brief explanatory message.

Gist

A gist is a short auditory message that conveys the overall data trends. It guides further data exploration. In the table view, a gist is produced by automatically playing all values in a column or a row. The sequencing follows the values' order in the table, from top to bottom, or left to right. In the map view, there is no natural mapping from the geographical relation to the time relation. Research has shown that sequencing

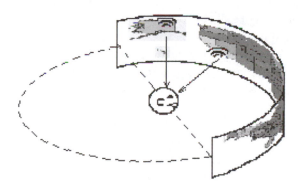

Figure 5.4 *Spatial sounds tied to the map create the effect of a virtual half-cylinder shaped auditory map surrounding the user located at the center. The illustration does not reflect the real spatial parameters.*

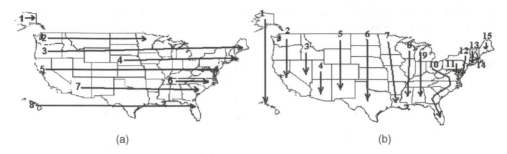

Figure 5.5 *Two spatial sweep orders on the map: (a) horizontal sweep; (b) vertical sweep.*

that preserves spatial relations helps users to construct a mental image of the 2D representation. Sequencing is done by spatially sweeping the map. In a horizontal sweep, the sweep goes horizontally from left to right then vertically, like in a typewriter (Figure 5.5(a)). When the end of the sweep row is reached, a tick mark sound is played and the stereo effect reinforces the change. A bell indicates the end of the sweep of the whole map. The same sweep order holds for sub-gists of parts of the map. Users can also choose to sweep horizontally (Figure 5.5(b)). For both views, the current information level controls the amount of details in the gist, thus controlling its duration. For example, when the information level is set to 'musical sound only,' a sweep of the entire US state map containing 51 regions lasts for 9 seconds.

Navigate

Table navigation is done by using arrow keys to move up, down, left, right, top, bottom, left, and right edges. Users can press 'U' to switch between two modes. In the cell mode, only the current cell is played. In the row/column mode, a sub-gist of the whole row or column is played.

In the map view, users can use four arrow keys to move between neighboring regions (Figure 5.6(a)). Because a map is not a perfect grid, it is a challenge to define a good adjacency navigation path. A movement may deviate from the direction users expect. Reversibility of movements can also be a problem in which a reversed keystroke may fail to take the user back to the original region. Many users reported only having weak location awareness by using this relative navigation method (Zhao *et al.*, 2004, 2005a).

To improve location awareness, iSonic also supports map navigation based on absolute pointing. The map is automatically divided into 3 × 3 ranges according to the regions' geometric centers (Figure 5.6(b)). Users can use a 3 × 3 numerical keypad to activate a spatial sweep of the regions in each of the nine map ranges. For example, hitting '1' plays all regions in the lower left of the map, using the same sweep scheme

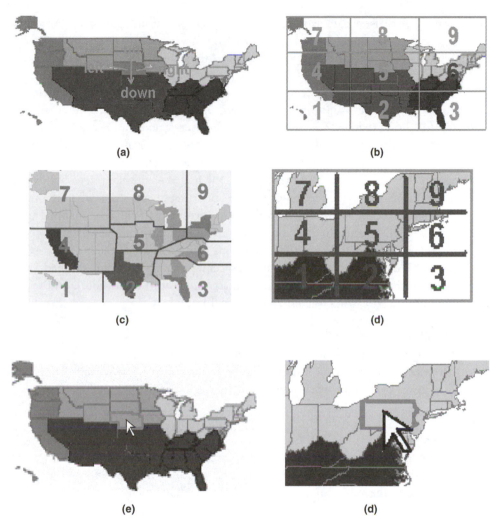

Figure 5.6 *Map navigation methods in iSonic: (a) relative navigation among adjacent regions using the four arrow keys; (b) automatically divide the map into 3 × 3 ranges and press each key to listen to a partial sweep of the corresponding map range; (c) predefined 3 × 3 map partitioning; (d) press CTRL + 6 to zoom into range 6 of the map in (b) and recursively explore the zoomed range in the 3 × 3 style; (e) use a touchpad to continuously explore the whole map. The whole touchpad surface is mapped to the whole map; (f) after zooming into range 6, only the zoomed range is mapped to the surface of the touchpad, resulting in a higher pointing resolution.*

as the overall gist. Users can also predefine a manual partition of the map. For example, the partition in Figure 5.6(c) is extended from a very common practice to group US states into New England (range 9), Middle Atlantic (range 6), and so on. iSonic uses predefined manual partitions whenever they are available in the input data set. Users can use CTRL + [number] to zoom into any of the ranges, within which they can recursively explore using the 3 × 3 pattern or use arrow keys to move around. Figure 5.6(d) shows the 3 × 3 exploration after the user zooms into range 6 of the map in Figure 5.6(b). Pressing '0' sweeps the current zoomed map range or the whole map.

With the touchpad, users press spots or drag their fingers on the smooth surface touchpad to activate the sound of the region at the finger position. Stereo sounds provide some complementary direction cues. The sound feedback stops when the finger lifts off. The touchpad is calibrated so that the current map range is mapped to its entire surface. This means that without any map zooming, the touchpad maps to the whole map (Figure 5.6(e)). When the user zooms into one part of the map, for example range 6 (Figure 5.6(d)), the touchpad is remapped to only the zoomed range (Figure 5.6(f)). Preliminary observations suggest that both the keyboard and touchpad navigations allow users to gain geographical knowledge.

Details on Demand

Pressing 'space' plays the details of the current region. Another way to get the details is to increase the information level to the maximum level in which all details of a region are given by default when users navigate to that region.

Situate

When users press 'I' (as for 'Information'), iSonic speaks the current interface operational status. In the table, it includes the row/column counts, headings of the current table position, navigation mode, sorting status, regions selected, and so on. In the map, it includes the name of the variable displayed, navigation position, regions selected, and so on.

Select

In both views, users can press 'L' (as for 'Lock') to select/unselect the current region and press 'A' to switch between 'all regions' and 'selected regions only.' In 'selected regions only,' AISAs only activate sounds of the selected regions.

Brush

Brushing is done by users switching back and forth between the two views. The views are tightly coupled so that action results in one view are always reflected in the other

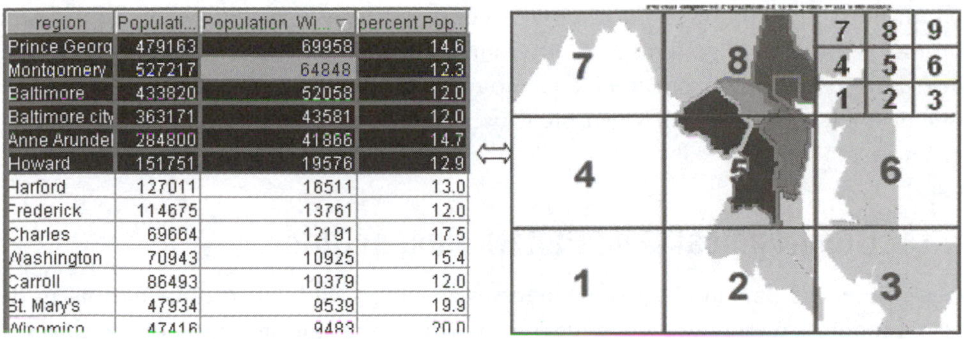

region	Populati...	Population Wi... ▽	percent Pop...
Prince Georg	479163	69958	14.6
Montgomery	527217	64848	12.3
Baltimore	433820	52058	12.0
Baltimore city	363171	43581	12.0
Anne Arundel	284800	41866	14.7
Howard	151751	19576	12.9
Harford	127011	16511	13.0
Frederick	114675	13761	12.0
Charles	69664	12191	17.5
Washington	70943	10925	15.4
Carroll	86493	10379	12.0
St. Mary's	47934	9539	19.9
Wicomico	47416	9483	20.0

Figure 5.7 *Highly coordinated table and map views in iSonic. The result of any action in one view is always reflected in another (e.g. select, zoom). The screenshots show a sample data set of Maryland counties.*

(e.g. selecting, zooming) (Figure 5.7). The example below shows how to find 'what and where are the 5 counties with the highest employment rate for disabled population,' given a data set on disabled population by counties. Users can first use arrow keys to find the column 'employment rate,' then use the sorting shortcut to sort the column in descending order. The top five rows are the 5 counties with the highest employment rate. To locate them on the map, users can select the 5 counties in the table, then switch to the map view and choose to only listen to the selected counties. The 3 × 3 keyboard exploration tells users that the 5 counties are all in the middle part of the map. By using arrow keys to move around, users can find they are next to each other.

5.4 Implementation

iSonic is implemented in Java. The GUI part is written in Java JFC/Swing and the stereo musical sounds are produced through the Java MIDI Sound technique. Speech is synthesized by an accompanying speech server built on Microsoft Speech SDK 5.1. Prerecorded sound files can also be loaded and played. iSonic gives real-time auditory response to every user action, with delays less than 100 ms. Through network datagrams, we have also connected iSonic to a sound server that simulates virtual spatial sounds using Head Related Transfer Functions (Zotkin *et al.*, 2002a).

5.5 Evaluations

User evaluation was carried out in various forms throughout the iterative design process of iSonic. Two users without any residual vision were involved as design partners. In the early stage, we also conducted two controlled experiments with blindfolded sighted users to qualitatively compare the effectiveness of various design options as well as to gain insights into humans' ability to perceive geographical data distribution patterns from interactive sounds. Extending from that, we conducted intensive case studies with seven blind users on iSonic usability and its support for general data analysis tasks.

5.5.1 **Geographical Data Pattern Recognition**

Geo-referenced data analysis often involves geographical context information. In the visual mode, a picture is often said to be worth a thousand words. A quick glance at the geographic distribution pattern of the data often gives users very valuable information. The geographic distribution pattern of geo-referenced data involves three dimensions, where the data points scatter on a 2D map plane with the values of the data points as the third dimension. Research has shown that users can interpret a quick sonified overview of 2D line graphs containing a single data series (Flowers and Hauer, 1995), and two data series (Bonebright *et al.*, 2001; Brown and Brewster, 2003), and bivariate scatterplots (Flowers *et al.*, 1997). Research has also shown that users can recognize 2D graphical shapes by listening to sounds tracing the border of the shapes (Alty and Rigas, 1998).

However, there have been few observations about the ability to recognize data distribution patterns with more than two dimensions in the auditory mode. Meijer's work (Meijer, 1992) translates an arbitrary image into a time-multiplexed sound representation that is the superposition of the sound of multiple image pixels. The effectiveness of this approach remains to be established. Wang and Ben-Arie (1996) found that people can recognize simple shapes on binary images of 9×13 resolutions where the pixels are raster-scanned slowly. Jeong (2001) shows that people can locate the minimum/maximum value on a simplified choropleth map with up to nine geographic regions, with the values presented as different sound volumes.

We conducted two controlled experiments investigating whether users could perceive geographic distribution patterns of five-category data on a 51-region US state map (not grids or simplified maps). The first experiment (Zhao *et al.*, 2004) investigated the effect of data views by comparing pattern recognition using a spatial choropleth map design and an enhanced table design. The second experiment (Zhao *et al.*, 2005a) compared the effectiveness of two navigation structures (state-by-state navigation vs. cell-by-cell navigation on a mosaic version of the map, see Figure 5.8) and two auditory feedback encoding schemes (with elevation position pitch vs. without) on choropleth maps. For each pattern recognition task, users first listened to the gist once and chose the general pattern type from five pattern types (horizontal strip,

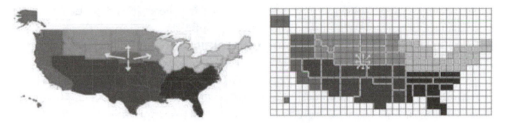

Figure 5.8 (a) State-by-state column navigation. (b) Cell-by-cell mosaic navigation.

vertical strip, diagonal strip, cluster, and no pattern). Then they used a keyboard to explore the pattern for up to 3 minutes and chose the matching visual pattern out of three other distracters. Third, they were told the correct answer and had the chance of exploring again for up to 1 minute.

Results

In the visual mode, such pattern recognition tasks would take only seconds. Our study results showed that it was much harder in auditory mode, but novice users were still able to do it with overall reasonable accuracy in a short time. For example, after listening to the gist once, subjects recognized the general pattern type with an overall accuracy of 56% in the first study, and 50.7% in the second study (chance accuracy 20% in both). After exploration, subjects in the first study were able to choose the correct pattern out of distracters with good accuracy (67% in table and 75% in map, while the chance accuracy was 25%). In the second study, the accuracy was 48.7% (chance accuracy 25%) due to the increased similarity among the correct pattern and distracters, and the lack of reward as an incentive for the subjects.

In the first study there was no statistically significant difference in pattern recognition between map (75%) and table (67%). Eight out of nine subjects strongly preferred the choropleth map-based design over the enhanced table-based design, because it was very helpful to be able to move west–east on the map to confirm and remember patterns. The results suggested that a map view was better than a table view for geographical pattern recognition tasks. The lack of a statistically significant difference may be due to the small numbers of subjects.

In the second study, the pattern recognition performance was significantly affected by three correlation factors. First, subjects' knowledge of US geography was positively correlated with the performance. Second, subjects with better pitch differentiation ability generally did better. Third, some strategies appeared to have been more effective than others. Subjects who reported listening for changes did particularly well after the exploration. Subjects who reported trying to visualize the map did particularly well identifying the general pattern type after the gist. Subjects who reported paying attention to the piano sound (which indicated the vertical position of the states) did significantly worse identifying specific patterns.

Although no statistically significant difference was found across the four interfaces in terms of pattern recognition performance or location awareness on the map, the vertical position sound seems to have been unhelpful at best, and subjects that reported paying attention to it did worse than those that did not. It also seems to have taken away from utilization of the stereo sound. Subjects reported tasks to be hard in all four conditions. But the column navigation interface was ranked significantly easier than the mosaic navigation interface. Possible explanations were because it was somewhat simpler to use, with fewer keystrokes necessary, and feedback given after every keystroke.

Summary of Lessons

Observations of the two blind design partners were consistent with the results from the two controlled experiments described above. The results led to the following lessons:

1. Recognizing geographical data distribution patterns on real maps with irregularly shaped and sized regions through audio is hard. But many people were able to do it.
2. It is important to choose the appropriate data view for a specific task. For tasks that involve geographical knowledge, a map view is helpful.
3. Using an extra sound to indicate the vertical position of a region is unhelpful at best. Designers need to find other ways to improve users' location awareness.
4. An auditory feedback should be provided as a response to each user action.
5. Training on map knowledge and map sweep order improves pattern recognition. Blind users would likely spend considerable amounts of time learning and using new systems, so more training time is reasonable.
6. It may be useful to suggest certain strategies to users during training, such as visualizing the map and trying to listen for changes, as these strategies were helpful for other users.

5.5.2 **Case Studies**

The findings from the two controlled experiments, together with the suggestions from the two blind design partners, have led to the current iSonic design, as described in Section 3. To evaluate the effectiveness of iSonic for general exploratory data analysis tasks besides geographical data distribution pattern recognition, we also conducted intensive case studies with seven local blind users, producing 42 hours of observation and interview data, with an average of 6 hours per user (Zhao *et al.*, 2005d). Subjects differed in age, gender, education background, and pre-test geographical knowledge (see Zhao *et al.*, 2005d for details). Some were born blind and some became blind after age 15. None of them had residual vision.

The studies used the basic iSonic configuration that is accessible to most computer users: stereo auditory feedback through a pair of speakers and a standard computer keyboard as the input device. Three data sets were used, one for training, one for testing, and one for post-test free exploration. The training data set contained eight variables and was about the 50 US states plus the District of Columbia. The test data set contained 12 variables and was about the 24 counties in the State of Maryland. The post-test data set was about the 44 counties in the State of Idaho (but subjects were not told what it was).

Seven tasks were designed for each data set. Three tasks required value comparison in the geographical context, and four did not need any geographical knowledge.

Subjects also performed a similar set of testing tasks in Microsoft Excel 2002 with their usual screen readers, and compared the task experience. The comparison was used as a method to solicit user comments on what interface features were helpful to each task.

Each case study was carried out in two sessions on consecutive days, at the subject's home or office. In the first session, the subject used a self-paced auditory step-by-step tutorial to learn iSonic and practiced seven sample tasks with the training data set. In the second session, they performed seven similar tasks in both Excel and iSonic, and compared the task experience. An interview was conducted after subjects performed all the testing tasks in both interfaces. Finally, they freely explored an unknown map and data (the post-test data set) for 5 minutes and reported things they found interesting. This allowed the experimenter to observe what users would do when they encountered a new map and data.

Results

After spending an average of 1 hour 49 minutes going through all the interface features by following the tutorial, subjects successfully completed 67% of the training tasks without referring to the sample solution or any other help. After the training, subjects were able to retain their newly acquired knowledge and successfully completed 90% of tasks on the next day in a different context without any help.

For tasks that did not require geographical knowledge, the average testing success rates were similar for iSonic and Excel, both at 86%, although subjects ranked iSonic easier than Excel. For geography-related tasks, the average testing success rate was 95% in iSonic. In Excel, the two subjects with excellent knowledge about Maryland geography achieved a success rate of 67%. Other subjects either skipped some tasks due to the lack of geographical knowledge or tried to make an educated guess but gave incorrect answers, resulting in an average success rate of 20%. iSonic was rated much easier than Excel. Examples of frequently reported reasons included: (1) the map was easy to use and very helpful (mentioned by all subjects in all three tasks); (2) it was great to be able to switch between the map and table, select things in one view then look at them in another; (3) the pitch was helpful in getting the value pattern and comparing values; (4) it was helpful to isolate a few regions from other interfering information by selecting; (5) it was flexible to adjust the information level during the task.

Summary of Lessons

The case studies showed that iSonic enabled subjects to find facts and discover data trends within geo-referenced data, even in unfamiliar geographical contexts. The design choices in iSonic were overall easy to use and allowed subjects to effectively explore data in the map and table views without special interaction devices. Cross-case analysis of task strategies and iSonic usage patterns validated the ADC framework and revealed the following design implications:

1. All subjects used the table for most value comparisons, and used the map when they needed to compare items in the geographical context or to acquire/confirm region locations. They were capable of choosing and switching between highly coordinated table and map auditory views.
2. Using musical pitches to present numerical data makes it easier to perceive data trends in data series and enhances close-up value pair comparison. The integrated use of musical sounds and speech allows users to listen to overall trends and to get details.
3. A single auditory feedback detail level is not sufficient. All the four levels in iSonic were used productively. While it is hard to understand a data element without the appropriate context, too much detail slows down the sequential presentation and can be overwhelming for gaining the big picture. Designers need to carefully select multiple information levels and let users adjust it to fit their tasks.
4. A rapid auditory gist is valuable in conveying overall data trends and guiding exploration. For maps, perceiving spatial relations from a sequence of sounds can be difficult, but sweeping the map as separate smaller ranges in a consistent order was effective.
5. Navigation structures should reflect the data relation presented by the data view. In the map, designers would do well to provide 3×3 exploration using the numeric keypad and adjacency navigation using arrow keys. Users benefited from absolute localization and relative movements. Even a coarse map partitioning mapped to the physical spatial layout.

6. Selecting was valuable for all subjects in focused data examination. They were able to operate selection within and across data views and accomplish brushing.

5.6 **Current Status and Future Directions**

Readers can try the current research prototype of iSonic by visiting the project web site at `http://www.cs.umd.edu/hcil/audiomap`.

Our research shows that it is possible to use only stereo sounds and a standard keyboard to convey geographical data patterns on real maps, and to significantly improve blind users' abilities to comprehend and answer sophisticated questions about geo-referenced data. We plan to conduct more user studies to further investigate its design space. A study that is currently underway is to investigate how geographical data pattern recognition is affected by the choice of input devices and the visual experience of different user groups (Zhao *et al.*, 2005c). Another study being planned is to examine the effect of using individual HRTF spatial sounds. It will also be very interesting to compare iSonic with tactile approaches.

Our studies also showed that the ADC framework, which is analogous to many interactions in visualizations, works for auditory interfaces when applied properly. We plan to extend this framework by applying it to the interactive sonification of graphs. By defining a programming paradigm and incorporating more data views into iSonic, we intend to develop a unified auditory workspace for general analytical data exploration.

References

Abel, S.M., Figueiredo, J.C., Consoli, A. et al. (2002) The effect of blindness on horizontal plane sound source identification, *International Journal of Audio*, **41**(5), 285–292.

ACM (2000) Conference on Universal Usability. `http://sigchi.org/cuu/`.

Aleman, A., van Lee, L. and Mantione, M.H. et. al. (2002) Visual imagery without visual experience: evidence from congenitally totally blind people. *Neuroreport*, **12**(11), 2601–2604.

Alty, J.L. and Rigas, D. (1998) Communicating graphical information to blind users using music: the role of context. *ACM SIGCHI*.

American National Standards Institute (ANSI) (1973) *American National Psychoacoustic Terminology* (No. S3.20). American National Standards Institute, New York.

American Standards Association (ASA) (1960) *Acoustical Terminology* (No. S1.1). American Standards Association, New York.

Andrienko, G. and Andrienko, N. (1999) Interactive maps for visual data exploration, *International Journal of Geographic Information Science*, **13**(4), 355–374.

Ashmead, D.H., Wall, R.S., and Ebinger, K.A. et al. (1998) Spatial hearing in children with visual disabilities, *Perception*, **27**(1), 105–122.

Axen, U. and Choi, I. (1996) Investigating geometric data with sound, *Proceedings of the International Conference on Auditory Display*, PC Palo Alto, November 4–6.

Barrass, S. (1996) TaDa! Demonstrations of auditory information design, *Proceedings of the International Conference on Auditory Display*.

Ben-Tal, O., Berger, J. and Cook, B. et al. (2002) SONART: the sonification application research toolbox, *Proceedings of the International Conference on Auditory Display*.

Blattner, M., Sumikawa, D. and Greenberg, R. (1989) Earcons and icons: their structure and common design principles. *Human Computer Interaction*, **4**(1), 11–44.

Blattner, M., Greenberg, R.M. and Kamegai, M. (1990) Listening to turbulence: an example of scientific audiolization. *Proceedings of the SIGCHI Workshop on Multimodia and Multimodal Interface Design*, 1990, pp. 1–8. ACM Press, New York.

Blauert, J. (1997) *Spatial Hearing: The Psychophysics of Human Sound Localization*, MIT Press, Cambridge, MA.

Bonebright, T.L., Nees, M.A., Connerley. T.T. and McCain, G.R. (2001) Testing the effectiveness of sonified graphs for education: a programmatic research project, *Proceedings of the International Conference on Auditory Display*, Espoo, Finland, pp. 62–66.

Bregman, A.S. (1990) *Auditory Scene Analysis*, MIT Press, PL Cambridge, MA.

Brewster, S.A. (1994) Providing a Structured Method for Integrating Non-Speech Audio into Human–Computer Interfaces. PhD Thesis, University of York.

Brewster, S.A. (1998) Using nonspeech sounds to provide navigation cues. *ACM Transactions CHI*, **5**(3), 224–259.

Brown, L., Brewster, S.A., Ramloll, R. et al. (2002) Browsing modes for exploring sonified line graphs, *Proceedings of BCS HCI*.

Brown, L. and Brewster, S.A. (2003) Drawing by ear: interpreting sonified line graphs, *Proceedings of the International Conference on Auditory Display*.

Brown, L., Brewster, S.A. and Ramloll R. et al. (2003) Design guidelines for audio presentation of graphs and tables, *Proceedings of the International Conference on Auditory Display*, Boston, July 6–9.

Brown, M.H. and Hershberger J. (1992) Color and sound in algorithm animation, *IEEE Computers*, **25**(12), 52–63.

Bussemakers, M.P. and Haan, A.de. (2000) When it sounds like a duck and it looks like a dog . . . Auditory icons vs. earcons in multimedia environments, *Proceedings of the International Conference on Auditory Display*.

Card, S., Mackinlay, J.D. and Shneiderman, B. (1999) *Readings in Information Visualization: Using Vision to Think*, Morgan-Kaufmann.

Carlile, S. (1996) *Virtual Auditory Space: Generation and Applications*, RG Landes, New York.

Choi, I. and Bargar, R. (1995) Interfacing sound synthesis to movement for exploring high-dimensional system in a virtual environment, *IEEE International Conference on Systems, Man Cybernetics*, **3**, 2772–2777.

Corda Technologies Inc. (2003) Corda Products Optimap 5. `http://www.corda.com/products/optimap/` (23/10/03).

Dang, G., North, C. and Shneiderman, B. (2001) Dynamic queries and brushing on choropleth maps, *Proceedings IEEE Information Visualization*, pp. 757–764.

Duda, R. (1993) Modeling head related transfer function, *Proceedings of Asilomar Conference on Signals, Systems and Computers*.

eEurope. eEurope Standards, `http://www.e-europestandards.org/`.

European Blind Union (2005) *Statistics*, `http://www.euroblind.org/fichiersGB/STAT.htm` (last accessed on 19 October 2005).

Fernstrom, M. and Brazil, E. (2001) Sonic browser: an auditory tool for multimedia asset management, *Proceedings of the International Conference on Auditory Display*.

Fisher, P. (1994) Hearing the reliability in classified remotely sensed images, *Cartography and Geographic Information Systems*, **21**(1), 31–36.

Fitch, T. and Kramer, G. (1994) Sonifying the body electric: superiority of an auditory over a visual display in a complex, multi-variate system. In *Auditory Display: Sonification, Audification and Auditory Interfaces*, G. Kramer (ed.). Santa Fe Institute, Studies in the Sciences of Complexity Proceedings (Vol. XVIII). Addison-Wesley, Reading, MA.

Flowers, J.H. and Hauer, T.A. (1995) Musical versus visual graphs: cross-modal equivalence in perception of time series data, *Human Factors*, 37(3), 553–569.

Flowers, J.H., Buhman, D.C. and Turnage K.D. (1997) Cross-modal equivalence of visual and auditory scatterplots for exploring bivariate data samples, *Human Factors*, 39(3), 340–350.

Franklin, K.M. and Roberts, J.C. (2003) Pie chart sonification. *Proceedings on Information Visualization*. IEEE Computer Society, pp. 4–9.

Franklin, K.M. and Roberts, J.C. (2004) A path based model for sonification. *Proceedings on Information Visualization*. IEEE Computer Society, pp. 865–870.

Freedom Scientific. JAWS for Windows. `http://www.freedomscientific.com/fs_products/software_jaws.asp`.

Gaver, W. (1986) Using sound in computer interfaces. *Human Computer Interactions*, 2(2), 167–177.

Golledge, R.G. (1991) Tactual strip maps as navigational aids. *Journal of Blindness and Vision Impairment*, 85(7), 296–301.

Golledge, R.G., Loomis, J.M., and Klatzky, R.L. et al. (1991) Designing a personal guidance system to aid navigation without sight: progress on the GIS component. *International Journal on Geographic Information Systems*, 5(4), 373–395.

Griffin, A. (2002) Feeling it out: the use of haptic visualization for exploratory geographic analysis. *Cartographic Perspectives*, 39, 12–29.

Grohn, M. and Takala, T. (1995) MagicMikes – methods for spatial sonification, *Proceedings of SPIE2410 (Visual Data Exploration and Analysis II)*, 294–301.

Gulick, W.L., Gescheider, G.A. and Frisina, R.D. (1989) *Hearing: Physiological Acoustics, Neural Coding, and Psychoacoustics*, Oxford University Press.

Hermann, T., Krause, J. and Ritter, H. (2002) Real-time control of sonification models with a haptic interface, *Proceedings of the International Conference on Auditory Display*, Kyoto, Japan, July 2–5.

Hermann, T., Meinicke, P. and Ritter, H. (2000) Principle curve sonification, *Proceedings of the International Conference on Auditory Display*.

Hermann, T. and Ritter, H. (1999) Listen to your data: model-based sonification for data analysis. In *Advances in Intelligent Computing and Multimedia Systems*, M.R. Syed (ed.). International Institute for Advanced Studies in System Research and Cybernetics.

Hunt, A., Hermann, T. and Pauletto, S. (2004) Interacting with sonification systems: closing the loop. *Proceedings on Information Visualization.* IEEE Computer Society.

James, J. (1998) Lessons from developing audio HTML interfaces, *Proceedings ASSETS*, ACM Press.

Jeong, W. (2001) Adding Haptic and Auditory Display to Visual Geographic Information. PhD Thesis, Florida State University.

Kennel, A. (1996) AudioGraf: diagram reader for the blind, *Proceedings ASSETS*, ACM Press.

Kramer, G. (1993) Sonification of financial data: an overview of spreadsheet and database sonification. *Proceedings of Virtual Reality Systems '93.* SIG Advanced Applications, New York.

Kramer, G. (1994) Some organizing principles for representing data with sound. In *Auditory Display: Sonification, Audification and Auditory Interfaces*, G. Kramer (ed.). SFI Studies in the Sciences of Complexity Proceedings (Vol. XVIII). Addison-Wesley, Reading, MA.

Kramer, G., Walker, B. and Bonebright T. et al. (1997) Sonification report: status of the field and research agenda, *International Community Audit Discussion.*

Krygier, J. (1994) Sound and geographic visualization, in MacEachren A.M., Taylor D.R.F., *Visualization in Modern Cartography*, Pergamon, Oxford, UK, 146–166.

Landau, S. and Gourgey, K. (2001) Development of a talking tactile tablet, *Information Techniques in Disability,* VII(2).

Leplâtre, G. and Brewster, S.A. (2000) Designing non-speech sounds to support navigation in mobile phone menus, *Proceedings of International Conference on Auditory Display.*

Lodha, S.K., Beahan, J. and Heppe, T. et al. (1997) MUSE: a musical data sonification toolkit, *Proceedings of International Conference on Auditory Display.*

MacEachren, A.M., Wachowicz, M. and Haug D. et al. (1999) Constructing knowledge from multivariate spatiotemporal data: integrating geographic visualization with knowledge discovery in database methods. *International Journal of Geographic Information Science*, 13(4), 311–334.

Meijer, P.B.L. (1992) An experimental system for auditory image representations. *IEEE Transactions on Biomedical Engineering*, 39(2), 112–121.

Middlebrooks, J.C. (1999) Virtual localization improved by scaling non-individualized external-ear transfer functions in frequency. *Journal of the Acoustic Society of America*, **106**(3), 1493–1510.

Moore, F.R. (1990) Elements of Computer Music, Prentice Hall.

Moore, B.C.J. (1995) *Handbook of Perception and Cognition: Hearing*, 6, Academic Press, New York.

Müller-Tomfelde, C. and Steiner, S. (2001) Audio-enhanced collaboration at an interactive electronic whiteboard, *Proceedings of the International Conference on Auditory Display*.

Mynatt, E.D. and Weber, G. (1994) Nonvisual presentation of graphical user interfaces: contrasting two approaches, *Proceedings of SIGCHI*, ACM Press.

National Cancer Institute (NCI) (2003) Cancer Mortality Maps and Graphs. `http://www3.cancer.gov/atlasplus/` (23/10/03).

National Federation of the Blind (NFB) (2005) Blindness Statistics. `http://www.nfb.org/stats.htm` (last accessed on 19 October 2005).

Neuhoff, J.G., Kramer, G. and Wayand, J. (2000) Sonification and the interaction of perceptual dimensions: can the data get lost in the map? *Proceedings of International Conference on Auditory Display*.

Parente, P. and Bishop G. BATS: The Blind Audio Tactile Mapping System, *ACMSE*.

Parkes, D. (1994) Audio tactile systems for designing and learning complex environments as a vision impaired person: static and dynamic spatial information access, Steele J., Hedberg J.G., *Learning Environment Technology: Selected Papers from LETA 94*, AJET Publications, Canberra, 219–223.

Pauletto, S. and Hunt, A. (2004) A toolkit for interactive sonification, *Proceedings of the International Conference on Auditory Display*.

Perlman, G. (2004) Human–computer interaction on-line bibliography. `http://www.hcibib.org` (last accessed September 2004).

Pirhonen, A., Brewster, S.A. and Holguin, C. (2002) Gestural and audio metaphors as a means of control for mobile devices, *Proceedings of SIGCHI*, ACM Press.

Radeau, M. (1992) Cognitive impenetrability in auditory-visual interaction, *Analytic Approaches to Human Cognition*, Elsevier Science, Amsterdam, 41–55.

Ramloll, R. and Brewster, S.A. (2002) An environment for studying the impact of spatialising sonified graphs on data comprehension, *Proceedings of the Sixth International Conference on Information Visualization*, July 10–12, London, UK.

Ramloll, R. Yu, W., Riedel, B. and Brewster, S.A. (2001) Using non-speech sounds to improve access to 2-D tabular numerical information for visually impaired users. *Proceedings of BCS IHM-HCI*, Lille, France, pp. 515–530.

Roberts, L.A. and Sikora, C.A. (1997) Optimising feedback signals for multimedia devices: earcons vs. auditory icons vs. speech. *Proceedings of IEA*, Tampere, Finland, pp. 224–226.

Röber, N. and Masuch, M. (2004) Interacting with sound: an interaction paradigm for virtual auditory worlds, *Proceedings of the International Conference on Auditory Display*.

Roder, B., Teder-Salejarvi, W. and Sterr, A. et al. (1999) Improved auditory spatial tuning in blind humans, *Nature*, **400**(6740), 162–166.

Roffler, S. and Butler, R. (1968) Localization of tonal stimuli in the vertical plane, *Journal of the Acoustic Society of America*, **43**, 1260–1266.

Roth, P., Petrucci, L. and Pun, T. (2000) From dots to shapes: an auditory haptic game platform for teaching geometry to blind pupils, *Proceedings of the International Conference on Auditory Display*.

Saue, S. (2000) A model for interaction in exploratory sonification displays, *Proceedings of the International Conference on Auditory Display*.

Scaletti, C. (1994) Sound synthesis algorithms for auditory data representations, in Kramer G., *Auditory Display*, Addison-Wesley.

Schneider, J. and Strothotte, T. (2000) Constructive exploration of spatial information by blind users, *Proceedings of ASSET*, ACM Press.

Section 508 of the US Rehabilitation Act. `http://www.section508.gov/`.

The Sendero Group (2003) Sendero Group Homepage – GPS for the blind. `http://www.senderogroup.com`.

Shinn-Cunningham, B.G. (2000) Distance cues for virtual auditory space, *IEEE-PCM*.

Shinn-Cunningham, B.G., Zurek, P.M., Stutman, E.R. and Berkovitz, R. (1996) Perception of azimuth for sources simulated using two loudspeakers in natural listening environments. *19th ARO Midwinter Meeting*, St. Petersburg Beach, FL.

Sikora, C.A., Roberts, L.A. and Murray L. (1995) Musical vs. real world feedback signals. *Proceedings of ACM SIGCHI' 95*, Denver, CO, pp. 220–221.

Smith, S., Grinstein, G.G. and Bergeron, R.D. (1990) Stereophonic and surface sound generation for exploratory data analysis, *Proceedings of SIGCHI*, ACM Press, pp. 125–132.

Sripada, S.G., Reiter, E., Hunter, J. and Yu J. (2003) Generating English summaries of time series data using the Gricean maxims, *Proceedings of KDD*, pp. 187–196.

Stevens, R.D., Brewster, S.A., Wright, P.C. and Edwards, A.D.N. (1994) Design and evaluation of an auditory glance at algebra for blind readers, in Kramer G., *Auditory Display: The Proceedings of the Second International Conference on Auditory Display*, Addison-Wesley.

Strelow, E.R. and Brabyn, J.A. (1982) Locomotion of the blind controlled by natural sound cues, *Perception*, **11**(6), 635–640.

Vecchi, T. (1998) Visuo-spatial imagery in congenitally totally blind people, *Memory*, **6**(1), 91–102.

Vickers, P. (1999) CAITLIN: implementation of the musical program auralisation system to study the effects on debugging tasks as performed by novice Pascal programmers. PhD Thesis, Loughborough University, UK.

VisuAide (2003). GPS Orientation Solutions – Trekker 2003. `http://www.visuaide.com/gpssol.html` (23/10/03).

W3C, Web Accessibility Initiative (WAI). `http://www.w3.org/WAI/`.

W3C, Web Content Accessibility Guidelines (WCAG). `http://www.w3.org/WAI/intro/wcag.php`.

Walker, B. (2002) Magnitude estimation of conceptual data dimensions for use in sonification, *Journal of Experimental Psychology*, April 8.

Walker, B.N. and Cothran, J.T. (2003) Sonification sandbox: a graphical toolkit for auditory graphs, *Proceedings of the International Conference on Auditory Display*.

Walker, A., Brewster, S.A., McGookin, D. and Ng, A. (2001) Diary in the sky: a spatial audio display for a mobile calendar. *Proceedings of BCS IHM-HCI*, Lille, France, pp. 531–540.

Wang, Z. and Ben-Arie, J. (1996) Conveying visual information with spatial auditory patterns, *IEEE Transactions on Speech and Auditory Processing*, **4**, 446–455.

Wenzel, E.M., Arruda, M., Kistler, D.J. and Wightman, F.L. (1993) Localization using nonindividualized head-related transfer functions, *Journal of the Acoustic Society of America*, **94**(1), 111–123.

Willuhn, D., Schulz, C., and Knoth-Weber, L. et al. (2003) Developing accessible software for data visualization, *IBM Systems Journal*, **42**(4).

IR `http://www.research.ibm.com/journal/sj/424/willuhn.html`.

Wilson, C.M. and Lodha, S.K. (1996) Listen: a data sonification toolkit, *Proceedings of the International Conference on Auditory Display*.

Zhao, H., Plaisant, C., Shneiderman, B. and Duraiswami, R. (2004) Sonification of geo-referenced data for auditory information seeking: design principle and pilot study, *Proceedings of the International Conference on Auditory Display*, Sydney, Australia, 6–10 July.

Zhao, H., Smith, B.K., Norman, K. et al. (April–June 2005a) Listening to maps: user evaluation of multiple designs of interactive geo-referenced data sonification, *IEEE Multimedia Special Issue on Interactive Sonification*.

Zhao, H., Plaisant, C. and Shneiderman, B. (2005b) I hear the pattern – interactive sonification of geographical data patterns, *(Poster) in ACM SIGCHI Extended Abstracts on Human Factors in Computer Systems*.

Zhao, H., Plaisant, C., Shneiderman, B. et al. (2005c) iSonic: interactive sonification for geo-referenced data exploration for the vision impaired (Demonstration), *Proceedings Interaction*.

Zhao, H., Plaisant, C., Shneiderman, B. and Lazar, J. (2005d) A framework for auditory data exploration and evaluation with geo-referenced data sonification. Tech Reports (No. HCIL-2005-28), Human Computer Interaction Laboratory, University of Maryland, College Park, MD.

Zimler, J. and Keenan, J.M. (1983) Imagery in the congenitally blind: how visual are visual images? *Journal of Experimental Psychology: Learning, Memory Cognition*, 9, 269–282.

Zotkin, D.N., Duraiswami, R. and Davis, L.S. (2002a) Customizable auditory displays, *Proceedings of the International Conference on Auditory Display*, PC Kyoto.

Zotkin, D.N., Duraiswami, R. and Davis, L.S. et al. (2002b) Virtual audio system customization using visual matching of ear parameters, *Proceedings of IEEE ICPR*, Quebec City, Canada, pp. 1003–1006.

Zotkin, D.N., Hwang, J., Duraiswami, R. and Davis, L.S. (2003) HRTF personalization using anthropometric measurements, *Proceedings of IEEE WASPAA*, Mohonk.

Improving the Screen Reading Experience for Blind Users on the Web

6

Jonathan Lazar and Aaron Allen

Department of Computer and Information Sciences, Universal Usability Laboratory, Towson University, USA

Summary

Screen readers, where the contents of the screen are provided as output using computer-synthesized speech, are among the most popular forms of assistive technology, and certainly the most popular assistive technology utilized by blind individuals. Previous research on how blind individuals utilize screen readers is limited. The goal of this study is to document the frustrations that blind users face when browsing the web using screen readers. One hundred blind individuals recorded their frustrations on the web using a diary study format. This chapter reports the most common causes of frustration, the actions taken by blind users, the time lost due to these frustrations, and the impact on user mood. Implications for users, designers, researchers, and policymakers are discussed.

6.1 Introduction

The screen reader is one of the most common forms of assistive technology used by the blind. Screen readers are software applications that provide computer-synthesized speech to represent and describe what is appearing on the monitor screen. They are typically used by persons with complete or partial visual impairment, who cannot see the text or graphics on the screen, and therefore must rely on other forms of output, such as sound and touch. While other forms of assistive technology do exist for blind users, such as refreshable Braille displays, screen readers are the most popular form of assistive technology.

Given that screen readers are so popular among the blind, it seems that there would be a wealth of research on how screen readers are used, however, this is not the case. It is undeniable that the Internet and World Wide Web (WWW) have changed how individuals use computers and even how they communicate with each other. However, much of the content on the web is graphical, and in many cases, equivalents are not provided, so the content is inaccessible to blind users. Blind users face the most challenges when attempting to access web content. Government policies and developer initiatives try to address some of these web shortcomings. However, since there are currently many obstacles, it is important to study, in depth, the problems of blind users. The objective is to provide better guidance to developers on how to improve both screen readers themselves, as well as web sites, to address the needs of blind users.

The goal of this study is to document the challenges that screen reader users face on the web. There are multiple data collection goals:

• To learn more about the specific interface causes of frustration.
• To learn more about how blind users respond to these frustrations.
• To learn how it impacts on their mood.
• To learn how much time is lost by these users in these situations

It is hoped that this data will provide important information for developers, policy-makers, users, and researchers, in improving the web experience for all users.

6.2 Research Literature

6.2.1 Screen Readers

As previously stated, screen readers are among the most popular forms of assistive technology. Screen readers, such as Window-Eyes and Job Access With Speech (JAWS), read the text that is on the screen, along with textual equivalents for graphics or dynamic content, and produce computer-synthesized speech output (Slatin and Rush, 2003). There are a number of reasons for the high level of screen reader usage. Other interfaces available may rely on Braille output (such as large refreshable Braille displays, Braille printers, and even portable Braille note-takers), however, these have limited success, due to both high costs, and low Braille literacy (National Federation of the Blind, 2005). Some estimates have placed Braille literacy among the blind in the United States at only 20%. Other assistive technologies, such as tactile maps, and special printing devices, such as printers that can print raised paper maps, are very expensive, and therefore are rarely used (Wall and Brewster, 2006). There are many benefits to screen readers: they require no special experience or education, they work using standard computer hardware (the speakers and sound card), and the only purchase required is a new software application. The screen reader application is usually inexpensive and, in many cases, will be provided by social services or governmental agencies at no cost. Furthermore, users with any level of visual impairment, who have been relying on their hearing for a number of years, are able to discern more detail than the typical user with vision, who would not notice the intricate details being produced by the computer speaker.

The two best-known screen readers on the market are JAWS (by Freedom Scientific) and Window-Eyes (by GW-Micro). While they are no means the only choices (HAL is another option), new approaches to presenting text have been presented in the literature. For instance, the BrookesTalk screen reader provided more navigational information to users (Zajicek *et al.*, 1998) and math markup languages improve the comprehension of math formulae through screen readers (Karshmer and Gillian, 2005). Modified screen users, using primarily musical tones, have been used to present map information using only audio, in a technique known as information sonification (Zhao *et al.*, submitted). While these new approaches may help specific users in specific types of applications, the large majority of blind computer users utilize either JAWS or Window-Eyes, and these standard screen readers will therefore be the focus of our study.

6.2.2 Accessibility Online

One of the challenges of using a screen reader is that many applications and web pages are not designed to be compatible with a screen reader. A screen reader attempts to ascertain as much textual information as possible, from the code of the application or web page. The challenge comes when there is information that is not strictly textual, and equivalents are not provided for the screen reader. For instance, contextual information (i.e. where information is located on the screen and how it relates to nearby information), color and size of text, graphics, and multimedia, are not all automatically explained on a display. The developer needs to encode the meaning of all of these details (context, color, images, video) into a textual equivalent that can easily be understood and interpreted by the screen reader (Lazar *et al.*, 2003).

While these equivalents for screen reader use seem at first to be very abstract, guidelines for making both desktop (e.g. Windows XP-based) applications and web pages compatible for users with disabilities do exist. These guidelines come from various sources, but the best-known guidelines are from the US Government (known as Section 508: http://www.section508.gov) and the Web Accessibility Initiative (http://www.w3.org/wai). These guidelines actually cover interface design for users with most perceptual or motor impairments, not only users with visual impairment.

These guidelines do not really address full usability, but only address functionality for users with disabilities, known as 'accessibility.' For instance, if a web page includes 'alt' text for an image, describing in text what the image represents, this would be an accessibility feature. However, if the alt text said 'picture here,' then this would not be usable (Theofanos and Redish, 2003). These guidelines have been around since 1999 (for the WAI) and 2001 (for Section 508). However, despite the availability of these guidelines, most web pages are inaccessible to those using screen readers. A number of previous studies have examined accessibility levels on the web, and depending on what types of web sites have been examined, only 2–20% of web sites were found to be fully compliant with every accessibility guideline (Sullivan and Matson, 2000; Stowers, 2002; Lazar *et al.*, 2003; Loiacono and McCoy, 2004).

6.2.3 **Why this Project is Important**

Visual impairment impacts on a large number of people throughout the world. There are many different estimates of the number of individuals with visual impairment, and while the exact number is unknown, various estimates from government sources all point to the large scope of the problem. In 2002, the US Census Bureau estimated that 7.8 million individuals age 15 or older had some form of visual impairment, and of those, 1.8 million people in the United States had no vision (US Census Bureau, 2002). This is very similar to the estimate from 1996 of 8.2 million individuals with some form of visual impairment in the United States (US Census Bureau, 1996). In addition, approximately 20% of Americans over age 70 have some form of visual impairment (US Centers for Disease Control and Prevention, 2006). Internationally, the statistics also show the large number of people who have visual impairment or blindness. In 2002, it was estimated that 37 million individuals were totally blind, and 124 million individuals had some form of visual impairment, for a total of 161 million people impacted by visual impairment in the world (World Health Organization, 2006).

Note: In this chapter, the terms 'blind user' and 'user with visual impairment' are used interchangeably. In other chapters, the term visual impairment is used to describe users with limited vision, while the term blind is used to describe users with no vision. In addition, some authors do not use the word 'blind.' However, it is the policy of the National Federation of the Blind that the term 'blind' applies to both individuals with partial and full visual impairment. Furthermore, in this chapter, the individuals that took part in the research study did not have residual vision, and did not utilize screen magnifiers.

This project was developed in conjunction with the National Federation of the Blind (NFB). The National Federation of the Blind is the oldest and largest organization of blind people in the United States, and is headquartered in Baltimore, MD. Frequently, when the NFB talks to various technology companies, the companies do not just want to hear stories from a few individuals. They want hard data. Users with disabilities are actually a large customer base in information technology. While large companies such as Microsoft might have a relatively small percentage of their user population with disabilities, that small percentage still translates into millions of users. For companies that focus solely on assistive technology, most of their customer base has at least one disability, and many have multiple disabilities. These companies work closely with the populations that they serve, and they are generally very interested in research in this area, and very open to improving their products. Suggestions to these companies often do translate into actual changes in their software and hardware products. Therefore, this research can help impact on screen reader design, and web page design, in the future.

The organized blind community complained that there were not many research studies focusing on blind users that have had a sufficient number of users taking part. And this is a valid concern. For most research studies that involve users with disabilities, 10 users is frequently considered sufficient. In most formal research in human–computer interaction, 10 users would never be considered sufficient. However, it is challenging enough to find representative users to take part in any type of human–computer interaction research (Lazar and Norcio, 2002). No question, it is a greater challenge to find large numbers of representative, workplace users that are blind, and would be willing to take part in research. However, there is a need for exactly that type of research. Furthermore, rather than building a new interface for the blind and evaluating it, there is a need to evaluate how blind users have been using existing screen readers. Chances are not good that a new interface method for blind users, developed in a research lab, would impact on the lives of many blind users. However, understanding more about how blind users use screen readers could lead to small changes in what the blind users already use – which would have a greater impact on the lives of blind users in a shorter time period.

While it is hoped that this research will be useful for the organized blind community, and the assistive technology community, another goal of this study is to provide ideas and guidance for researchers. There is not unlimited time, unlimited resources, or an unlimited supply of researchers focusing on assistive technology for blind users. Therefore, it is important to determine what areas are most problematic for users, and which areas of study might prove to be most fruitful in improving the web experience for blind users.

6.3 **Data Collection**

The data in this research study was collected using a time diary. A time diary is similar to a survey, in that there are questions, both open-ended and closed-ended, that users are asked to fill out (Fowler, 1993). However, what differentiates a time diary is that users must fill in responses as they occur, rather than from memory, after the fact. In a time diary, users record items such as mood, response, and time lost, as they occur, with the corresponding times, which lead to a more accurate response. This data could easily be overestimated or underestimated if users had to do this from memory, and time diaries have proven to be a more accurate method for collecting this type of data (Robinson and Godbey, 1997). With time diaries, the results are not biased by the user's recollection of events; instead they are captured in real time, and therefore have higher levels of validity than surveys (Czerwinski *et al.*, 2004). In addition, another advantage of a time diary is that users record actual times, which helps in determining the time impact of whatever occurred to them while they are on the computer.

The time diaries used in this study consisted of a series of forms to help measure frustration as the blind users in this study were using the web. The users were asked to record any frustrations that occurred over a minimum of 2 hours spent on the computer. Users could choose to work on any tasks that interested them, since, in reality, assigned tasks to users would mean that the tasks were not truly important to the users, and therefore, would not represent their true levels of frustration (Ceaparu *et al.*, 2004). The general process is as follows:

1. Before starting their session, the users would fill out demographic information and questions relating to pre-session mood.
2. Every time that the users felt frustrated, they would fill out a frustration experience form, noting the cause of the frustration, how they responded to the frustration, the time lost, and their mood. They could fill out as many or as few forms as they wanted.
3. At the end of the session, users would fill out a post-session form, noting their mood.
4. Throughout the process, users would note their start and stop times on a time log.

This is the data collection process that was used in two previous studies relating to user frustration on the computer in general. One study focused on students and their friends, with 111 subjects (Ceaparu *et al.*, 2004). Another study focused on 50 workplace users (Lazar *et al.*, 2006b). Before both of these studies were run, the data collection forms used in the time diary were pilot-tested. The same data collection forms used in those two studies were slightly modified for appropriateness to this study. Due to the desire to compare results, wording modifications were kept to a minimum, only wording was changed to reflect the fact the users were blind, and that screen readers were used. A few questions relating to perceptions of web accessibility were added. In terms of the wording of the time diaries, the forms for the current study and the previous studies are nearly identical.

Technical modifications were made to the forms to be used in this study. While the forms in the previous research study were primarily paper and data was recorded by hand, this would not be feasible for a population of blind users. Since handwriting is not a primary form of communication for blind users, handwriting is often messy and illegible. Furthermore, to send printed time diaries could require that users utilize some type of scanner or reader, which would only compound the frustrations that they feel. For the same reason, we felt that it was inappropriate to use web pages for data collection, as a web-based method of collection would create more frustration for a blind computer user if problems occurred in accessing the web. If for any reason the Internet connection went down, or the web browser crashed, there would be no way of recording a potential substantial source of frustration for the user. If the user could not connect, the online web-based form would be totally useless. When a user gets frustrated with the web, they should not be forced to record their frustrations by actually using the web, since that would create a multiplier effect, increasing the level of frustration. Therefore, it seemed that a non web-based electronic form would be the superior way to collect data for this study.

6.3.1 Pilot Testing

The data forms were tested by both blind users and experts in the field of assistive technology, to ensure the technical accessibility of the forms. Not only must the forms work with both JAWS and Window-Eyes, but with multiple versions of those screen readers, multiple operating systems, as well as multiple versions of text editing software. The original idea was to utilize the form features in MS-Word documents. However, during the testing, it was discovered that form features in MS-Word crashed both major screen readers a number of times, in specific combinations of screen reader/ operating system/word processor environments. The forms were then created in rich text format, and tested with the same group of users. While the RTF documents were not able to keep the form controls that exist in MS-Word, the RTF versions did work in both screen readers, multiple operating systems, and multiple text editors. Therefore, the RTF forms were considered appropriate for data collection. Details on the pilot study of these data collection forms are available (Lazar *et al.*, 2005).

Although the forms themselves were only available in an electronic version, supporting documentation for this research study was also made available upon request in Braille and large-print. While these options were not requested frequently, some users did want to be able to read Braille versions of the forms, and some did request large-print versions, primarily for their helpers to read to them. This is also standard policy for the National Federation of the Blind, that all documents must be available in large-print, Braille, and electronic formats. Public information is frequently offered in all three formats, for instance, Transport for London offers transportation information in large print, tactile, and electronic formats, as well as the standard-size print.

Note: A thorough statistical analysis of the data collected appears in two research papers: Lazar *et al.* (in press-a, in press-b). This chapter is a summary of the data collected, as well as a discussion of implications for the various user populations.

6.4 **Results**

6.4.1 **Demographics**

Between September 2004 and May 2005, data on user frustration was collected from 100 blind users. The users were recruited in partnership with the National Federation of the Blind, by using word-of-mouth, listservers, and booths set up at conferences to recruit users. All of the users that took part met three qualifications: they were blind, and used screen readers, to browse the web on a regular basis. Of the participants, there were 61 females and 39 males, with an average age of 43.37 years, and a range of 18–81 years old. The participants were generally very experienced with using computers: those who took part reported an average of 8.06 years on the web, 13.31 years of computer experience, and spent an average of 31.34 hours a week on the computer. Of the 100 participants, 75 reported having, at minimum, a bachelor's degree or higher degree. This is representative of the population of blind computer users. It is true that not all blind individuals use computers, however, of those who do use computers, they tend to be individuals with a high level of formal education. Computer usage is very closely correlated to employment and education for blind individuals. Of the participants, 84 reported using primarily the JAWS screen reader, 12 reported using primarily Window-Eyes, and four participants reported using other screen readers.

6.4.2 **Frustrations Reported**

During a minimum 2-hour session on the computer, participants were instructed to fill out a frustration experience form any time that they felt frustrated, regardless of the cause. There was no minimum or maximum number of frustrations. The 100 participants filled out a total of 308 frustrating experience forms (an average of 3.08 frustrations per person).

The data on causes of frustration are inherently qualitative, and therefore, a structured content analysis, with five researchers, was used to interpret the data. The data was examined multiple times to best determine the intent of the participants. Table 6.1 lists the causes of frustration, organized by category. The top five causes of frustration were:

Table 6.1 Causes of frustration

Causes of frustration	Number of occurrences
Alt text	
No alt text for pictures	18
No alt text for pictures-required registration	5
Nondescriptive alt text	10
Links	
Misleading links	15
Link not working	3
Couldn't find link	5
No skip navigation	3
Forms	
Poorly designed/unlabeled form	23
Plug-ins	
Inaccessible portable document format (PDF)	15
Inaccessible flash	12
Java applets causing problems	3
Active X not working	1
Windows media player/real audio not working	8
Navigation	
Auto-refresh causes SR to continually restart	5
Broken back button	4
No frame name	2
Timed out	1
Can't find info	2
Mouse required for navigation	1
Layout	
Page layout causing confusing screen reader feedback	36
Pop-up frustration	13
Table won't read linearly	1

(continued)

Table 6.1 Continued

Causes of frustration	Number of occurrences
Failures	
Screen reader crash	15
Couldn't connect to server	4
404-file not found	6
Computer freeze	4
Find feature (on page) not working	2
Conflict between screen reader and application	28
Email server down	2
Application/network conflict	1
Slow web site download	7
Other	49
Total	304

Note: In four frustrating situations, the user didn't record the cause of the frustration.

(1) page layout causing confusing SR feedback; (2) conflict between SR and application; (3) poorly designed/unlabeled form; (4) no alt text for pictures; and (5) three-way tie between misleading links, inaccessible PDF, and a screen reader crash. The other causes of frustration are available in Table 6.1. Table 6.2 lists how participants responded to the frustrations. While in 100 instances, the users were unable to solve the problem, the responses cited next most often were 'I knew how to solve it because it has happened before' (54), 'I ignored the problem or found an alternative solution' (48), 'I figured out a way to fix it myself without help' (39), all of which indicate a successful outcome.

Table 6.2 Summary of how often participants reported these frustration experiences occurring

How did participants respond to the frustrations?	
I was unable to solve it	110
I knew how to solve it because it has happened before	54
I ignored the problem or found an alternative solution	48
I figured out a way to fix it myself without help	39
I asked someone for help	32
I tried again	18
I rebooted	15
I restarted the program	7

Table 6.3 Summary of how these frustrating experiences made users feel

How did the frustrating experience make you feel?	
Angry at the computer	55
Angry at myself	19
Helpless	82
Determined to fix it	81
Neutral	36
Other	91

Table 6.3 lists how the frustrations made users feel. While in 82 instances, users reported feeling helpless, just as often (81 instances), users felt determined to fix the problem. Table 6.4 lists the level of frustration, reported by participants. The average level of frustration was 6.71, and the frustration scale went from 1 (not very frustrating) to 9 (very frustrating). An average frustration level of 5 could be interpreted as 'somewhat frustrated,' however, since the average frustration score was close to 7, this is a relatively high amount of frustration. More comprehensive data related to the causes of frustration is available (Lazar *et al.*, in press-a)

6.4.3 **Impact of Frustration on User Mood**

Since mood before and after the participant session was measured, as well as mood during a frustration incident, it is possible to understand how these frustrations impact on the mood of participants. Emotion is a growing research topic within human–computer interaction, and researchers have examined topics such as the relationship between online

Table 6.4 Level of frustration reported by users

Level of frustration in an experience (1 = low, 9 = high)	$n = 308$
1	3
2	9
3	17
4	20
5	38
6	33
7	52
8	53
9	83

use and depression (Kraut *et al.*, 1996), the relationship between computer frustration and physiological measures such as blood volume pressure and muscle tension (Riseberg *et al.*, 1998; Hazlett, 2003), and the relationship between computer usage and job satisfaction (Murrell and Sprinkle, 1993). However, users with visual impairment have not been included in the past research.

While the analysis in the previous section on cause of frustration was either qualitative, or quantitative but simple, the analysis on mood is statistically complex. The full statistical results of this work appear in Lazar *et al.* (in press-b) and are outside of the scope of this chapter. Only major findings will be reported in this chapter.

A multivariate hierarchical regression analysis was conducted, to help build a model that maximizes the variance in the dependent variable that can be explained by the independent variable(s) through a series of trial sessions (Kleinbaum *et al.*, 1997).

In the first regression analysis, the dependent variable is the change in mood, which was measured by the difference between the mood score reported in the pre-session form and the mood score reported in the post-session form. All independent variables were investigated. The results suggest that the change of mood before and after the sessions was significantly affected only by six factors. The impact of all other independent variables is not statistically significant. The six factors are:

1. The overall frustration score.
2. The impact of the frustration on the ability to get the work done.
3. Internet experience.
4. Anxiety.
5. Software or hardware sufficiency.
6. Whether the user continues thinking about the problem afterward.

A second hierarchical regression analysis was conducted to investigate the factors that impact the frustration score in a particular session. The dependent variable of the analysis is the frustration scores of the first and the last frustrating experiences. The independent variables were the same as in the first hierarchical regression analysis. Only one independent variable was found to significantly impact the frustration level: importance of work.

6.4.4 Time Lost

The data was examined to determine, on average, how much time was lost due to frustration experiences. Since time logs were recorded by participants, it was possible to measure the exact amount of time lost due to frustrating experiences. In the previous research on user frustration (Ceaparu *et al.*, 2004; Lazar *et al.*, 2006b), the method for measuring time lost was defined as follows: Percent Time Lost = (MS + MR)/MT, where MS is minutes spent to solve the problem, MR is minutes spent to recover lost work, and MT is total minutes spent on the computer. In this data collection, the same formula was used to calculate time lost, so as to provide one method for comparing blind users and visual users. In this data collection, participants lost an average of 30.4% of time on the computer.

6.5 Discussion

There are a number of fascinating findings from this research. The project helped to document the most frequent causes of frustration for blind users on the web. Some of the most frequent causes of frustration are, from a technical point of view, very easy to solve. For instance, the top five causes of frustration were: (1) page layout causing confusing SR feedback; (2) conflict between SR and application; (3) poorly designed/unlabeled form; (4) no alt text for pictures; and (5) three-way tie between misleading links, inaccessible PDF, and a screen reader crash. Pictures must have alternative text, and forms must have labels, and neither one of these issues are difficult to solve. If a form is poorly labeled, or a link name is misleading, again, these areas are easy to fix. These problems can be alleviated by user involvement in the original design, or usability testing, to get feedback on appropriate picture, form, and link labels (Lazar, 2006). In addition, inaccessible PDF files are also not a great challenge. Newer versions of PDF writers do incorporate accessibility features, so that a screen reader can interface with them correctly. Page layout causing confusing screen reader feedback is a bit more challenging, however, with more navigational information (skip navigation links, use of cascading style sheets rather than tables for layout), blind users will find the page layout to be less confusing. It is true, that other causes of frustration, including application/screen reader conflicts and screen reader crashes, have technical causes and will be much more challenging to solve.

It appears that blind users do respond to frustrating situations differently than visual users. For instance, while participants said most often (110 instances) that they were unable to solve the problem, very frequently, participants stated that they knew how to solve it because it had happened before (54), ignored the problem or found an alternative solution (48), or figured out how to fix it without any help (39). Compared to the visual users that took part in the previous research studies, blind users were much less likely to restart the program or reboot the entire computer. Not only did blind users respond with different actions, but it also had a different impact on their mood. While in 82 instances, the participants felt helpless, just as often (81 instances), the participants felt determined to fix the problem. Again, the blind users reported a different impact on mood than the visual users.

From the statistical analysis of impact on mood, it was again clear that blind users had a different response than the visual users in previous research. The 'impact on work' was the only factor that had an impact on mood in both statistical analyses. In previous research with visual users, the factors that impacted on mood were both the impact on work, and the time lost (Lazar *et al.*, 2006a). For the blind users that participated in this study, there was no relationship between mood and time lost. This is an interesting phenomenon: compared with the visual users in previous research on user frustration, the blind users seemed less likely to give up, more determined to fix problems, and less likely to have their mood impacted simply based on the amount of time lost (Lazar *et al.*, in press-a). Time lost is itself an interesting factor. In this study, participants reported losing an average of 30.4% of time spent on the computer due to frustrating situations. In the previous research studies with visual users, the student users reported losing 38.9% of time spent on the computer due to frustrating situations, and the workplace users reported losing 42.7% of time spent on the computer (*note*: to be as conservative as possible in data reporting, these are all figures that do not include the outlier data). While it is true that both of the studies with visual users included both web tasks and nonweb tasks (such as word processing and working with spreadsheets), the majority of tasks were web-based.

These data points all lead to an interesting story. It seems that blind users are actually more effective than visual users in responding to frustrating situations on the web. It is clear that blind users have different responses to frustrating situations than visual users do. How the blind users respond, the methods that they use, the time lost, and how it impacts on their mood are all different than visual users. The causes of this difference are only speculative, but it is possible that the challenges that blind individuals face in their daily lives train them to become good problem-solvers, and these skills transfer over to their ability to interact in the web environment.

6.5.1 **Implications of this Study**

Implications for Users

This study documents how blind users typically respond to frustrating experiences on the web. The keys to success for blind users were their positive attitudes and their coping strategies. These strategies, including standard work-arounds, looking for alternative solutions, and not rebooting the computer, helped users successfully respond to frustrating situations. Both training and years of experience can help in building these coping strategies. Until web sites become uniformly more accessible, the responsibility for ensuring a successful web browsing experience still falls on the shoulders of the user. The more experience that users have, the better they can cope with problems, the better their browsing experience will be. Furthermore, users are encouraged to email the web masters of certain sites that have interface problems, providing suggestions for improvement. Web masters sometimes misperceive that they have no users with disabilities using their site, and simply the knowledge that users with disabilities do use their site might help bring about some changes in accessibility (Lazar *et al.*, 2004).

Implications for Designers

The primary findings of this study relate directly to designers. The causes of frustration can be seen as a 'to-do' list for designers when initially designing or when redesigning a web site. Most of the top causes of frustration are usability-related, and many of these are relatively easy to solve. For instance, it takes almost no time to add labels to forms or add alt text for graphics. The challenge is to choose text labels that are useful and appropriate. Hopefully, designers will involve users in the design or redesign process, which will help the designers in ascertaining what text will be most appropriate. Choosing link labels that are more descriptive will also go a long way toward improving accessibility. It is also important to make sure that any older versions of PDF have been recreated as accessible versions of PDF files. Many of these most common frustrations, and some that are less common, will be discovered if designers include users with disabilities, especially blind users, in the development process. Designers must take the lead in building web sites that are accessible for all users.

Implications for Researchers

This study provides useful information to researchers, in two areas: research methods, and future research topics. Unfortunately, many research studies on blind users feature a small number of blind users participating. This is, in part, because many researchers have little access to large numbers of blind users in their geographic area. The current study offers a sound method for remotely collecting research data from blind users. While no research methods are perfect, this research method comes from previous research, was appropriately modified for use with blind users, and included multiple controls to ensure valid data collection. In addition, this research study can point to many appropriate future topics for research. Each section of data in this chapter could itself be a future research topic. For instance, new web interface design methods could be tested, to address some of the causes of frustration (e.g. different page layouts). New features in current screen readers could also be tested, to address some of the frustrations that occur (e.g. different methods for determining navigation on a page, more features to provide contextual information about links or graphics when no alt text is present). Controlled studies in a usability lab could examine how blind users respond, looking at their actions that they take when a frustration occurs. It would be fascinating to expand some of the research on physiological measurements of frustration (using EMG) to blind users, to determine if their bodies even respond differently to frustration. Any of these topics could provide a better window into the everyday experiences of blind computer users, and how to improve their interactions with computers.

Implications for Policymakers

The findings from this research should aid policymakers in developing new policies, or changes in existing policies, that foster the development of a more accessible web. This research can directly influence policy, because government policies specifically define what accessibility means. In the United States, accessibility is defined by the guidelines set out in Section 508 of the Rehabilitation Act (section 1194.22). If these guidelines are expanded by the results of research, these expanded guidelines can immediately impact on any government web sites or government-funded web sites. Other governments around the world (including the UK, Australia, and Canada) have similar laws. And these legal guidelines could be expanded to also cover nongovernment web content, such as those for transportation (airlines) and other travel sites, or companies selling products online.

6.6 **Conclusion**

While government efforts have helped bring attention to the topic of web accessibility for people with disabilities, it is clear that there is still a long way to go to make the web easy for all users. This study examined the frustrations of 100 blind users on the web, and determined that many of the most frequent causes of frustration are relatively easy to solve, if web designers take the time to involve blind users and address these problems. One of the most fascinating findings from this research is that blind users respond differently than visual users to frustrations, in a way that makes the blind users more effective in their responses. They have better response actions, less impact on mood, and are generally able to respond to frustrations more quickly on the web than visual users. This study provides many potential avenues for future research.

Acknowledgments

We would like to acknowledge Dr Betsy Zaborowski, Brad Hodges, and Chris Danielsen, all from the National Federation of the Blind, for their assistance in participant recruitment and data collection. We would also like to thank Jessica Lawrence, Jason Kleinman and Chris Malarkey, who were involved with data collection, and Jared Smulison and Ellen Libao, who ensured that participants were paid for their participation.

This material is based upon work supported by the National Science Foundation under Grant No. 0414704. Any opinions, findings, and conclusions or recommendations expressed in this material are those of the author(s) and do not necessarily reflect the views of the National Science Foundation.

References

Ceaparu, I., Lazar, J. and Bessiere, K. *et al.* (2004) Determining causes and severity of end-user frustration. *International Journal of Human–Computer Interaction*, 17(3), 333–356.

Czerwinski, M., Horvitz, E., Wilhite, S. (2004) A diary study of task switching and interruptions, *Proceedings of the ACM Conference on Human Factors in Computing Systems*, pp. 175–182.

Fowler, F. (1993) *Survey Research Methods*, 2nd edn. Sage Publications, Newbury Park, CA.

Hazlett, R. (2003) Measurement of user frustration: a biologic approach, *Proceedings of the ACM Conference on Human Factors in Computing Systems*, pp. 734–735.

Karshmer, A. and Gillian D. (2005) Math readers for blind students: errors, frustrations, and the need for a better technique, *Proceedings of the 2005 International Conference on Human–Computer Interaction (HCII)*, (on CD-ROM).

Kleinbaum, D., Kupper L., Muller K. and Nizam A. (1997) *Applied Regression Analysis and Multivariable Methods*, 3rd edn., Duxbury Press.

Kraut, R., Scherlis, W., and Mukhopadhyay, T. *et al.* (1996) The homenet field trial of residential internet services, *Communications of the ACM*, 39(12), 55–63.

Lazar, J. (2006) *Web Usability: A User-Centered Design Approach*, Addison-Wesley, Boston, MA.

Lazar, J. and Norcio A. (2002) Service-research: community service partnerships for experimental research. In Lazar J. (ed.), *Managing IT/Community Partnerships in the 21st Century*, Hershey, Idea Group Publishing, 271–283.

Lazar J., Beere P., Greenidge K. and Nagappa Y (2003) Web accessibility in the mid-Atlantic United States: a study of 50 web sites, *Universal Access in the Information Society*, 2(4), 331–341.

Lazar, J., Dudley-Sponaugle A. and Greenidge K. (2004) Improving web accessibility: a study of webmaster perceptions, *Computers and Human Behavior*, 20(2), 269–288.

Lazar, J., Allen, A., Kleinman, J. and Lawrence, J. (2005) Methodological issues in using time diaries to collect frustration data from blind computer users, *Proceedings of the 11th International Conference on Human–Computer Interaction (HCII),* (on CD-ROM).

Lazar, J., Jones, A., Hackley, M. and Shneiderman, B. (2006a) Severity and impact of computer user frustration: a comparison of student and workplace users, *Interactions in Computers*, 18(2), 187–207.

Lazar, J., Jones, A. and Shneiderman, B. (2006b) Workplace user frustration with computers: an exploratory investigation of the causes and severity, *Behavioral Information Technology*, 25(3), 239–251.

Lazar, J., Allen, A., Kleinman, J. and Malarkey, C. (2007) What frustrates screen reader users on the web: a study of 100 blind users. *International Journal of Human–Computer Interaction*, 22(3), 247–269.

Lazar, J., Feng, J. and Allen, A. (2006) Determining the impact of computer frustration on the mood of blind users browsing the web. *Proceedings of the ACM Conference on Assistive Technology (ASSETS)*, pp. 149–156.

Loiacono, E. and McCoy S. (2004) Web site accessibility: an online sector analysis, *Information Technology for People*, 17(1), 87–101.

Murrell, A. and Sprinkle J. (1993) The impact of negative attitudes towards computers on employees' satisfaction and commitment within a small company, *Computers and Human Behavior*, 9(1), 57–63.

National Federation of the Blind (2005) *Braille Usage: Perspectives of Legally Blind Adults and Policy Implications for School Administrators.* Available at: `http://www.nfb.org/brusage.htm`.

Riseberg, J., Klein, J., Fernandez, R. and Picard R. (1998) Frustrating the user on purpose: using biosignals in a pilot study to detect the user's emotional state, *Proceedings of the CHI 1998: ACM Conference on Human Factors in Computing Systems*, pp. 227–228.

Robinson J. and Godbey, (1997) *Time for Life: The Surprising Ways Americans Use Their Time,* University Park, PA, Pennsylvania State University Press.

Slatin J. and Rush S. (2003) *Maximum Accessibility,* Addison-Wesley, New York.

Stowers, G. (2002) The state of federal web sites: the pursuit of excellence. Available at: `http://endowment.pwcglobal.com/pdfs/StowersReport0802.pdf`.

Sullivan, T. and Matson, R. (2000) Barriers to use: usability and content accessibility on the web's most popular sites, *Proceedings of the ACM Conference on Universal Usability,* pp. 139–144.

Theofanos, M. and Redish, J. (2003) Bridging the gap: between accessibility and usability, *Interactions,* 10(6), 36–51.

US Census Bureau (1996). Prevalence of selected chronic conditions by age and sex: 1996. Available at: `http://www.census.gov/prod/2001pubs/statab/sec2003.pdf`.

US Census Bureau (2002). Americans with Disabilities: 2002. Available at: `http://www.census.gov/hhes/www/disability/sipp/disab02/ds02ta.html`.

US Centers for Disease Control and Prevention (2006). *Trends in Vision and Hearing Among Older Americans.* Available at: `http://www.cdc.gov/nchs/pressroom/01facts/olderame.htm`.

Wall, S. and Brewster, S. (2006) Feeling what you hear: tactile feedback for navigation of audio graphs, *Proceedings of the ACM Conference on Human Factors in Computing Systems (CHI),* pp. 1123–1132.

World Health Organization (2006). *Magnitude and Causes of Visual Impairment.* Available at: `http://www.who.int/mediacentre/factsheets/fs282/en/`.

Zajicek, M., Powell, C. and Reeves C. (1998) A web navigation tool for the blind, *Proceedings of the ACM Conference on Assistive Technology (ASSETS),* pp. 204–206.

Zhao, H., Plaisant, C., Shneiderman, B. and Lazar J. (submitted). *Interactive Auditory Data Exploration: A Framework and Evaluation with Geo-referenced Data Sonification.* Available at: `http://www.cs.umd.edu/hcil`.

Web Fun Central: Online Learning Tools for Individuals with Down Syndrome

7

Assadour Kirijian and Matthew Myers.
Contributing writer: Sylvie Charland

A.K.A. New Media Inc., Toronto, Canada

Summary

In the summer of 2001, A.K.A. New Media Inc. (A.K.A.) was commissioned by the National Down Syndrome Society (NDSS) in New York City to develop online learning modules and games for individuals with Down Syndrome, made possible with financial support provided by a grant from the Ericsson Inc. ERICA program. These online tools were created to help individuals with Down Syndrome learn and practice the basic skills required to use the Internet, allowing them to take better advantage of the entertainment and educational benefits that the Internet can provide.

As far as A.K.A. was able to ascertain at the time, an initiative of this nature had not been attempted before. In fact initially, A.K.A. was not even sure if such a thing was possible. The result was a year-long odyssey of intensive research, usability testing, and production, culminating with a suite of innovative online learning tools and games called Web Fun Central. The entire journey from conceptualization to testing to final production was a series of trial and error, surprises, failures, and successes. It is hoped that sharing these experiences will provide some insight, guidance, and encouragement to other researchers, educators, and designers interested in furthering this important work. Today, Web Fun Central is being used by individuals with Down Syndrome across North America and around the world and can be accessed at http://www.clubndss.org/clubndss.cfm?fuseaction=computercenter.

7.1 About A.K.A.

A.K.A. is an award-winning communication and technology company based in Toronto, Canada. For almost a decade, A.K.A. has developed solutions and products for a wide variety of companies and organizations in both the corporate and not-for-profit sectors. A.K.A.'s work encompasses branding and communication, online learning and training, as well as complete software application development. On the corporate side, A.K.A.'s clients range from major corporations such as Compaq, Ericsson, McDonald's, Royal & SunAlliance, Purolator, and Verizon Wireless to emerging mid-sized technology and manufacturing companies from across North America. A.K.A. also works with a number of established professional associations including the Insurance Broker Associations of Ontario, the Insurance Broker Association of Canada, The Canada Students Federation, and the Canadian Public Affairs Association, to name but a few. A.K.A. has also developed technical products and solutions for government at both municipal and provincial levels in Canada.

Since its inception, a primary mandate of A.K.A. has been to continually look for opportunities to take the skills and expertise gained from working with some of the most innovative and leading-edge corporations operating today and apply them to the not-for-profit sector. In keeping with this commitment, A.K.A. has had the privilege of working with organizations such as the Student Work Abroad Program (SWAP), Social and Enterprise Development Innovations (SEDI), Youth Challenge International, the National Down Syndrome Society (NDSS), The Princess Margaret Hospital Foundation, and The Campbell Family Institute for Breast Cancer Research.

7.2 **About the Team**

A.K.A. founding partners, Assadour Kirijian (Creative Director/Partner) and Matthew Myers (Account Director/Partner), played a direct hands-on role throughout the entire Web Fun Central project. Assadour's professional background in architecture and Matthew's background in psychology and entertainment helped shape and inform their approach to this ambitious initiative. A.K.A. had always prided itself on the usability of its design and online learning work, yet the learnings from this Down Syndrome project – what the team gleaned from dissecting usability to the most minute detail for users with a myriad of specific needs – has informed and enhanced the firm's work ever since.

The other highly talented and skilled members of the A.K.A. team who played an instrumental role in helping to develop the usability tests and learning modules included Blakely McAlister (Art Direction/Design), Eric Liphardt (Art Direction/Design/Flash Programming), John Kane (Director of Technology), and Paul Uchitel (Director of Technical Production). Without their tireless efforts and passion for this project, it would not have been the success that it was.

Although this chapter focuses on the usability testing session and the online tools developed by A.K.A., as is the case with most projects of this kind, Web Fund Central could not have been developed without the support, contribution, and guidance of several other individuals. Special contributors include Helen Simpson (ERICA Program Manager) of Ericsson and Jennifer Schell Podoll (Project Manager) of the NDSS.

During the usability testing session, A.K.A. received expert support, advice, and participation from Jo Mills and Barbara Bain of the Down Syndrome Research Foundation and Belinda Netley and Carolyn Steeles of the Centennial Infant & Child Center.

The people who contributed the most in helping A.K.A. develop this project were the six remarkable individuals with Down Syndrome who participated in the usability testing and who formed an integral part of the 'Design Team.' Without their collaboration and generous feedback, Web Fun Central simply could not have been developed. A.K.A. learned more in a couple of days with these individuals than it had from months of research. The 'Design Team' included Genevieve Gibbs, Nicholas Herd, Katy Hughes, Jordana Kerbel, Ryan Reid, and Lindsay Richards (Figure 7.1).

Figure 7.1 *'Design Team' member Genevieve Gibbs wearing her team hat and receiving her appreciation plaque from Belinda Netley of the Centennial Infant & Child Center.*

7.3 **About Down Syndrome**

Web Fun Central is so simple and user-friendly that it is being used by other segments of the general public wanting to learn basic Internet skills, like seniors for example, however it was designed expressly for individuals with Down Syndrome. The specific target group is middle-functioning (reading level grade three or four) young adults aged 14–20 with Down Syndrome. It was the learning and perception characteristics and styles of this target population that informed, shaped, and guided the development of Web Fun Central.

Down Syndrome is the most common chromosomal abnormality, with more than 350 000 people in the USA having Down Syndrome. One in every 800 to 1000 live births is a child with Down Syndrome, representing approximately 5000 births per year in the USA alone. Due to advances in medical technology, individuals with Down Syndrome are living longer than ever before. In 1910, children with Down Syndrome were expected to survive to age nine. With the discovery of antibiotics, the average survival age increased to 19 or 20. With today's new advancements in clinical treatment, as many as 80% of adults with Down Syndrome reach age 55, with many living longer. As the mortality rate decreases, the number of individuals with Down Syndrome will increase (NDSS.org).

The nature of this condition speaks to the need for specialized learning tools such as Web Fun Central. Individuals with Down Syndrome have an extra, critical portion of the number 21 chromosome present in all, or some, of their cells. This additional genetic material alters the course of development and causes the characteristics associated with the syndrome. This excess genetic material affects a person's physical and cognitive development. People with Down Syndrome will have some degree of mental retardation, usually in the mild to moderate range. Continuing to develop accessible learning tools designed specifically to these needs is critical to enabling individuals to reach their full potential.

7.4 **About Web Fun Central: Goals**

7.4.1 **Primary Goal: Teaching Basic Internet Skills**

The main purpose of the Web Fun Central modules and games is to help people with Down Syndrome learn and practice some of the basic skills required to use the Internet. Teaching these skills was deemed particularly important for people with Down Syndrome in their late teens who are likely to experience increased isolation as they leave high school and enter adulthood. In the course of this growing isolation, they also tend to lose some of their reading, writing, and communication skills. Web

Fun Central would provide a means for them to learn how to use the Internet for communication and entertainment, which in turn might help them maintain reading and writing skills. The interactive learning process itself lays the groundwork for the opportunity to introduce more advanced technological concepts and Internet functions in the future, and the game segments provide an enjoyable means for the user to practice the skills learned.

7.4.2 Overarching Goal

At the onset of this project, very little specific research had been done in this area and the undertaking involved many unknowns. In light of this, A.K.A. decided early on in the process that the overarching goal must be to ensure that Web Fun Central was at the very least as intuitive, fun, engaging, and empowering as possible for individuals with Down Syndrome, regardless of whether any real learning occurred.

7.5 How Web Fun Central Came To Be

The development of this project occurred in three distinct phases: Phase One – Research; Phase Two – Usability Testing; and Phase Three – Production and Development.

7.5.1 Phase One – Research

With guidance and support from the NDSS, A.K.A.'s first step was to survey the most recent related research that it could find in this area. A.K.A. was aware from the beginning that people with Down Syndrome were primarily visual learners and that this would be crucial to developing learning modules that might lead to providing increased connectivity and accessibility for this community. A.K.A. also knew that many of the same issues of usability that hamper the general population would apply to the Down Syndrome community, in various degrees. That being said, A.K.A. also knew that it needed to learn as much as possible about the specific learning styles of people with Down Syndrome and to draw on the important work others had done in terms of the teaching methodologies and processes that had proved effective. Some of the findings from this initial research included:

- Learning strategies based on real-world situations are beneficial. If reinforced in real-world situations, learning is likely to increase (Kumin, 1999).
- Inclusive learning in mainstream schools is more beneficial than in special schools (Wolpert, 1996).

- Many children with Down Syndrome learn to read effectively, which helps in further learning (Buckley and Bird, 1993). Shorter phrases are easier to understand (Kumin, 1998).
- Relatively slow presentation speed is more effective for learning than a faster presentation speed (Biederman *et al.*, 1999).
- Receptive language skills are usually much more advanced than expressive language skills in young people with Down Syndrome (Kumin, 1998).

Other research reviewed included:

- Lazar (2006)
- Nielsen (1994)
- Preece (2000)
- Schuler and Namioka (1993)
- Sears (2003)
- Newell *et al.* (2003)
- Shneiderman (2000)
- Slatin and Rush (2003)

The next step in A.K.A.'s research process was to conduct a series of direct interviews with experts and educators in order to introduce them to the project, ask a series of specific questions relating to the project, and garner any feedback or guidance that they cared to offer. This group of interview subjects provided A.K.A. with some important insights and a deeper understanding of how individuals with Down Syndrome learn, what teaching methodologies have been developed to date, and some important advice about how to develop and conduct the usability testing sessions. Some of the individuals who generously provided their guidance and input included:

Joan Green
Greenhouse Publications
Input: visual strategies

Joan Guthrie Medlen
Disability Solutions
Input: visual strategies, healthy lifestyles, dual diagnosis

Dr Libby Kumin
Department of Speech-Language Pathology, Loyola College
Input: language development, teaching methodologies

Dr Jonathan Lazar
Department of Computer and Information Sciences, Towson University
Input: web usability, usability testing

What became clear through these discussions was that although an immense amount of research existed, there was still so much more that remained unknown, particularly relating to the use of rich media as a teaching tool and the imparting of Internet skills to individuals with Down Syndrome. Many of the questions that A.K.A. posed to these experts were met with answers like 'I have no idea. You might want to test that first and make sure you document your findings as I doubt this has been attempted previously.' Although this reinforced the importance of the work that A.K.A. was undertaking, it also fostered a significant level of trepidation and uncertainty as to whether these modules would be successful. Given these knowledge gaps, A.K.A. needed to dramatically increase the scope of its usability testing in order to establish a foundation upon which the learning modules and games could be developed.

In tandem with the research phase, A.K.A. began analyzing, dissecting, and prioritizing the individual components, attributes, and activities involved in using the Internet. A.K.A. filtered these through its findings about how individuals with Down Syndrome learn, in order to determine what skills needed to be taught and how the teaching could occur. The often counter-intuitive nature of surfing the Internet (e.g. multilayered windows, 'Back' buttons, pull-down menus, etc.) made this a particularly daunting process and provided countless opportunities for what could be examined during the usability testing phase.

A.K.A. documented all of its research and sorted it according to its relevance to the project at hand, which created a roadmap of sorts for the team as it began to ponder ways to teach these specific skills and develop usability tests to determine whether these strategies would work. The following is an outline of what A.K.A. learned through the research phase and drew on to develop the usability tests. It is important to note that A.K.A.'s findings from the usability tests did not always conform to this research.

Approach for Usability Testing Sessions

- During the usability tests, don't make the participants feel like they are being tested. Socialize with them and present this as a collaborative effort rather than a testing exercise.
- Start with something they can easily do successfully. Lay a foundation of success then gradually start to challenge them.
- Personalization is effective.

- Unstructured activities with no defined goals are still effective. As long as they are entertaining, they will be liked.
- Expect concentration to last a maximum of 10–15 minutes.
- Use rewards and positive reinforcement to congratulate the user (e.g. 'Great you did it!') and be specific about the task accomplished (e.g. 'Great, you learned how to use the scrollbar!').
- Start with fun activities before getting into more arduous individual testing.
- Music, motion, and pop-culture will help keep this age group engaged and motivate them to learn.
- To test preferences, watch what the participants like and what they repeat. Avoid suggesting answers and keep questions open-ended.
- The use of characters or personalities to guide the learning should certainly be tested.

Target Population Profile
- Love of music.
- Love of pop-culture.
- Easily led.
- Easily frustrated.
- Enjoy accomplishing things.
- Adverse to change.
- Reward-oriented.

Visual Learning Strategies
- Use consistent and repetitive symbols.
- Subjects are not likely to have a preference between photographs and illustrations, however, literal is better than abstract.
- To test visual noise, find a clear starting point that users understand, and then gradually layer additional visual details in stages until problems occur.
- Use a visual schedule to show participants where they are in the overall process.

Text and Voice-over
- Text and voice-over should be short and simple.
- Voice-over is a helpful support but should not be used alone. Users need to see something on-screen.
- Avoid conditional phrasing (e.g. first you click on this, to be able to click on that) and break the directions down into steps.
- A Comics Sans Serif font will be most effective.

7.5.2 **Phase Two – Usability Testing**

The development of the content for the usability testing sessions was a major under-taking in itself, given the wide breadth of areas that A.K.A deemed necessary to examine in order to be able to even begin developing effective learning modules and games. A.K.A. developed material for two distinct and intensive usability sessions designed to test a range of functions, including: usability best practices (e.g. prefer-ence for fonts, link styles, colors, images, visual cues, rewards); specific iterative and visual learning techniques; and mini-learning modules to explore how specific Internet concepts might be taught and practiced. Equally important to A.K.A. was to observe the participants' general attitudes toward the technology and the specific tasks, including their attention span, their ability to move through the modules, and even the emotional state in which they responded to elements. In addition to testing modules that A.K.A. developed, A.K.A. had the users engage in a series of unstruc-tured tasks, activities, and games related to using computers and the Internet to learn more about their general interests and hobbies and their overall familiarity with the Internet. These particular sections helped to ensure that the content chosen for the modules would be compelling for this population and age group.

The usability testing sessions involved six participants with Down Syndrome, ages ranging from 16 to 23. The testing was divided into two distinct 4-hour sessions held 4 weeks apart at Ericsson Inc.'s computer laboratories in Mississauga, Ontario. A.K.A. opted for two distinct sessions for two main reasons. Firstly, if the teaching strategies that A.K.A. was proposing turned out to be an abject failure, the team would have some time to go back to the drawing board. Secondly, if on the contrary participants were able to make their way through the testing modules and the numer-ous elements that A.K.A. was testing for, a second session would allow the team to take the testing to the next step and either further confirm findings or test additional things.

Based on the advice collected from experts, A.K.A. adopted a very inclusive cele-bratory approach to these sessions, conveying to participants that they were an inte-gral member of a design team helping to create the best online learning tools and games possible. No mention of testing was ever made to the participants. To control for variation, a single person, in this case A.K.A.'s Assadour Kirijian, was assigned to be the main facilitator for the sessions, provide general instruction to the group, and help participants individually should they have a question or need assistance. The process was rigorously documented with the help of observers using standardized observation sheets. There was one observer for each participant plus several roamers. The observer remained very passive throughout the testing session, sitting behind the subject and capturing their observations. The observer simply notified the facilitator whenever a participant required assistance.

Most of the user's actions were dynamically tracked and the data saved to a database as they progressed through the modules, which greatly facilitated later review and analysis. Both usability testing sessions were videotaped in their entirety, from two separate angles: a back angle to get a general sense of what was occurring on the screen and to see the participant's hand and mouse movements, and a front angle to view the participant's face and emotional state as they progressed through the tasks.

Beyond the empirical tracking measures used in the testing sessions, A.K.A. found that observers' notes proved equally if not more informative than the data captured in the database when cross-referenced with each other. For instance, A.K.A. could learn from an observer that the reason the user was taking an inordinate amount of time to complete a certain task was that she was laughing and enjoying the images and sound. The observer's input was immensely important because without it, the assumption from the data might have been that the user was confused and having trouble completing the task. Post-session debriefing discussions with all the observers allowed the team to share insights and discoveries while these were still top of mind.

Although there were many factors present that could have affected the test results, every attempt was made to give users the freedom to make selections on their own. One of the challenges faced was that the users often appeared to be more focused on completing the task at hand rather than carefully considering their selections and not all questions were necessarily understood correctly. In spite of these obstacles and the fact that the team would have welcomed the opportunity to do considerably more usability testing, both the results and the process yielded a significant number of interesting findings that equipped A.K.A. with a foundation upon which it could begin developing the modules.

As to A.K.A.'s overarching goal of making the tools fun, engaging, and empowering, there was some apprehension in the first session. A.K.A. did not know what to expect – would the subjects be engaged by the modules or would they stare blankly at the screen? By the end of the first session, A.K.A. was elated to discover that the participants were engaged in the tasks for several hours and were clearly enjoying themselves. One of the participants had a parent present and he was delighted that his 18-year-old daughter, a withdrawn young person who had been unresponsive and had not spoken much in many months since her mother had died, was obviously engaged, responsive, and having fun throughout the usability testing session. This revelation and others like it proved to be a great relief and inspiration for A.K.A.'s team. The findings resulting from the first session provided A.K.A. with the data required to make a series of adjustments to the material in preparation for the second session, in order to further refine the findings.

Test Modules

A.K.A. developed a series of novel testing modules to test a variety of specific elements (e.g. font treatment) as well as teaching and game concepts (e.g. interactive art tools). The following describes some of these modules and the lessons learned from them.

'You Pick'

This module was designed to test user preferences, A.K.A.'s newly developed teaching methods, and the user's ability to follow those methods. Consisting of many screens and elements, this lengthy exercise gauged the users' preferences for visual elements, their interest level, their ability to remain focused, and their response to the rewards and feedback. The user was asked to select a favorite item from a sampling of items. A.K.A. tested preference on a wide variety of things, including preferences for fonts, colors, photographs, illustrations, animation, scale, and spatial perspective, among others. Figure 7.2 shows an example of where the user could note their preference for pictures of people.

All test subjects completed this module and did well with it. They quickly got accustomed to selecting and clicking the 'Next' button to proceed. When confronted with an anomaly, they paused and appeared confused at first, yet persisted in completing the task. They diligently read the instructions when it wasn't immediately obvious to them what they should do.

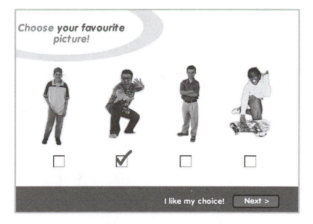

Figure 7.2 *People preference module.*

When difficulties were not encountered, most users rushed through without reading the on-screen instructions and did not always consider their selections carefully. In sections where the 'Next' button was available before an element had been completed (e.g. a reward page with sound and animation saying 'Great job, you found the link!'), users tended to automatically click 'Next' without waiting. A.K.A. corrected this anomaly in the second testing session.

'Pick and Click'

The goal of this module was to see how successfully users could complete increasingly difficult tasks with only simple initial instructions. They were asked to click on a specific object/item on screen. The same type of task was repeated several times across different screens. As the user progressed, more complexities were introduced to the task. A 'Help' feature was made available. Figure 7.3 shows an example of the pick and click.

This test proved to be relatively easy for the users. They grasped the concept immediately and were able to proceed quickly. When confronted with a complex task, several participants used the 'Help' function that showed them which button/item to click. Some observers noted that the participants were eager to begin before the teaching demonstration ended. In one instance for example, the subject did not follow the instructions and simply clicked on all the options until eventually falling on the correct one.

In the second session, this module was repeated with the addition of several more complex tasks requiring deductive logic. Instead of being told to 'Click on this' they were told what not to click on (see Figure 7.4). Most subjects did extremely well, but took more time to consider the question before selecting. As in the previous session, one user clicked on all the options randomly until the correct one was found.

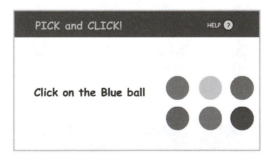

Figure 7.3 '*Pick and Click,*' level 2.

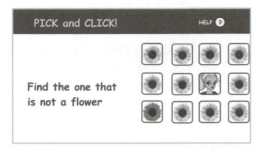

Figure 7.4 'Pick and Click,' session two.

'Art Maker'

This module introduced more advanced mouse control skills such as 'click, hold and drag,' with detailed step-by-step instructions in the form of tests and animation. Users were also taught some more advanced skills, building on previous teachings. This was also the first time that they were introduced to an open-ended game, allowing the test team to observe and evaluate the participants' ability to handle tasks with less guidance (see Figure 7.5).

All the subjects required encouragement to create/use the open-ended game at the end of the module. They instinctively wanted to drag all the items onto the pasteboard and complete the module, without giving much thought or emotion to what they were creating. No one used the extra controls to resize or rotate the items, unless they were expressly encouraged to do so. They were not particularly interested in the

Figure 7.5 'Art Maker,' instructions C.

space theme of the exercise, which may have accounted for their lack of desire to explore this tool further.

On average, users completed the tasks well, however they needed encouragement to play and explore. They were very goal-oriented. This was also true when surfing the Internet – users were fixated on finding and clicking buttons rather than focusing on the content. Where they couldn't find links on the site, they were at a loss as to what to do and wanted specific directions.

Surfing/Browsing the Internet

Participants were asked to apply what they had learned so far in modules 1 to 3 by randomly surfing the Internet. This was done in a guided fashion, with some basic instructions from test facilitators.

Users often typed the web address incorrectly, commonly adding unnecessary spaces. Two participants were able to use the 'Back' button, one was able to use search engines and a hotmail account, and some were able to use arrow keys to scroll down the page.

They loved game sites and did particularly well with games that were not timed and that used simple mouse and arrow controls (e.g. pick then click go). Users were fond of animated Flash introductions and were very excited by motion and sound. The downloading plug-ins confused them however – they were eager to enter their personal information but were perplexed by the download installation process.

Participants often asked, 'What do I do?' when visiting certain sites, focusing more on finding and clicking links rather than absorbing the content. They commonly chose to click on image/graphic links as opposed to text links.

'Rate It'

This module asked participants to rate their preferences for a series of images and sounds on a scale of 1 to 3. Each page featured two objects, which users were asked to rate individually (see Figure 7.6). Although A.K.A. consciously paired images that would yield polar results (one positive, one negative), users were not asked to rate comparatively. The images were chosen based on the preliminary findings from the previous test session and were intended to either confirm or refute some of the opinions formed.

Overall, the results provided a solid look at the wide range of personal preferences among the test subjects while at the same time identifying certain patterns and consistencies that would prove helpful in developing clear guidelines.

Some users had difficulty with the pull-down box at the beginning of the module, where they were asked to choose their name. Most selections were immediate and few

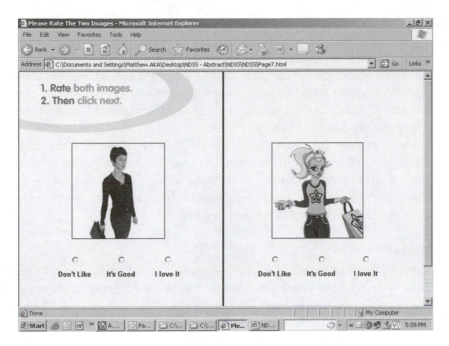

Figure 7.6 *'Rate It,' image vs. animation.*

users reconsidered their selection. After making a series of selections, some lost interest in the exercises and seemed to be clicking simply to complete the task. Some users were required to go through the module a second time due to technical errors whereby observers noted that selections were largely identical to the ones made the first time around. Technical difficulties prevented some users from completing the module altogether.

On the positive side, most users had little difficulty making selections using radio buttons. When faced with error messages, they quickly corrected the error and continued. Some users displayed great concentration and determination to complete this section and rated each image very carefully.

'Window Find'

This more advanced module dealt with some of the possible methods used to control windows in a web environment. The users were required to manipulate windows using the 'Close (x),' 'Drag,' and 'Window focus' functions. Teaching components in this section were presented in text only, without any help buttons or animated demonstrations.

Subjects did surprisingly well with this advanced module and often re-read instructions before proceeding. They found the 'Window focus' function the most challenging and were most comfortable with the 'Window close (x)' button. In the 'Drag the window' exercise, most users clicked on all the orange words. They needed to read the sentence twice to fully understand the instructions. Some were confused and asked, 'Where is the blue bar?,' yet eventually figured it out for themselves and dragged the window correctly.

The rate of success was much higher when users were able to see the contents of the window revealed underneath. They understood the task and completed it easily. Users were confused however by the word 'drag' and most had difficulty resting the mouse on the 'x' icon due to limited motor skills. In general, they were confused at first, began experimenting' and eventually succeeded.

'Web Maker'

This module allowed subjects to become 'web designers' by giving them the means to create their own customized web sites using a number of elements and options. They were able to choose site colors, fonts, imagery, and background texture. The first task was to enter their name, followed by a series of screens where they made various selections and were immediately able to see the results on screen (see Figure 7.7).

On every screen, users could either experiment with the different options or immediately continue with their first choice. Once they clicked on a selection, they were able to click 'Next' and proceed to a confirmation page (e.g. 'Are you happy with the color?'). At the end, subjects were rewarded for succeeding and were advised that they could go back to the selection pages to alter the look of their web pages as much as they wanted until they were happy with the final result.

Figure 7.7 *'Web Maker,' image choice.*

This module was very successful, with all participants completing the tasks and enjoying themselves tremendously in the process. Instructions were followed with ease when they were clear and simple, in other words, presented as one task at a time.

Subjects had some difficulty entering their name, possibly because this task consisted of a multistep series of instructions and no demonstration. The lesson learned for A.K.A. was to use step instructions for this type of task (e.g. 'Type your name, like this. Now you try.').

At the end of the module, when the guided exercises ended, subjects were reluctant to use the 'Now you can go back and explore' feature and needed encouragement to move from a linear scenario to an open-ended one. However, once they began exploring the options using the global navigation (four buttons at the top of the screen, one per design option), they enjoyed testing all the options. Interestingly, most participants reverted to their original selections and decided they were done.

Interim Adjustments between Sessions

Many adjustments were made to the testing elements during the 4 weeks between sessions one and two, and several completely new modules were developed. The team used some of the key learnings and pitfalls from session one to either fine-tune the testing elements for session two or create new ones, in order to solidify the research findings. Some benefits of spanning the testing over two sessions included:

- Where users selected a preference for a particular element among many (e.g. color palette), A.K.A. could take a smaller sampling of the most popular and re-test them for further preference in session two (see Figure 7.8).

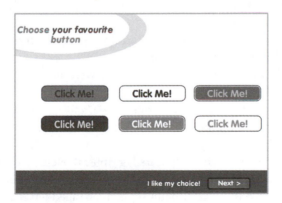

Figure 7.8 Link button style re-test.

- The second session allowed A.K.A. to further confirm findings by controlling other factors that might be affecting the user's preference (e.g. perhaps the user selected a particular image because it was closer to the 'Next' button and not necessarily because they liked it better).
- Where participants indicated a preference for individual items such as colors or fonts, A.K.A. was able to combine them together to see if there was an added preference for them or not.
- Having two sessions allowed A.K.A. to test learning over time. For example, in the first session participants went through an interactive learning process to teach an individual how to do a novel task, namely to click three buttons to play a movie. In the second session 4 weeks later, the user was presented the task again but without the instructions, to see if this novel learning held true.

General Lessons Learned

The results of the usability testing offered interesting findings and provided A.K.A. with the foundation upon which it could develop the learning modules and games for Web Fun Central. It is these findings that will hopefully provide other designers with some interesting insights.

Fonts

- Contrary to the research A.K.A. had completed, A.K.A. found no preference for the Comics Sans Serif style font (handwritten). The repeated use of this font in materials designed for people with Down Syndrome should perhaps be questioned.
- A.K.A. did find a preference for Italic Serif fonts, particularly at larger sizes in 'You Pick,' 'Rate It,' and 'Web Maker.'
- Font treatments with bright colors and outlines proved very popular. Treatments that added depth (extrusion) were popular.
- Large size words with a heavy bold treatment were popular (e.g. Futura Bold to emphasize a word).
- Accentuated words in a sentence, using color and scale worked. Most of the instructions in some of the modules were treated this way and no comments were made about reading difficulty.
- Stylized words treated with highlighted graphical elements (stars in the background, arrows, colored elements) scored very highly over plain text treatments.
- Font decoration made the text difficult to read (changed letter shape, obscured outlines, drop shadows).

Colors

- Color preference seemed relatively subjective, but some conclusions can be drawn from the patterns in the choices made. In general, darker colors were preferred, namely blues and purples (five out of six chose blue, purple, or gray).
- Users were not limited to liking just combinations of primary colors in high contrast of hue comparisons. Many selections were tints and tones of one particular color or split complementary colors (e.g. more sophisticated color combinations were interesting to them. Orange with two blue tones was popular).
- Dull colors were not popular.

Graphics/Images

- A strong preference for images that were clearly identifiable (objects at a distance that were shown in their entirety). Context for the object did not seem relevant or important.
- Naturally colored images scored better than those that were colorized or digitally manipulated.
- Images of people were popular. Images of young attractive females/males scored very well. Generally male participants showed more interest in images of women and female participants showed more interest in males. Observers noted a number of comments such as: 'I like boys,' 'He's sexy,' etc.
- Action images with people jumping, dancing, or gesturing scored well. Sports images scored high (e.g. girl playing soccer).
- Generally, photographic images scored better than illustrations, however fun and whimsical illustrations were popular.
- Images that users had trouble identifying were unpopular (e.g. a machine sprocket, a close-up of a phone), especially when compared with images that they could easily identify.
- There was more interest in images of people who were of a similar age group or older. Pictures of young children were rarely chosen.
- Illustrations of stars were very popular (e.g. wallpaper for 'Web Builder,' 'Rate It').

Animations

- Animations that combined bright colors with motion were preferred.
- When given the choice between animation of motion, size, and color, most picked the animating colors.
- When an animation was personalized, the response was very favorable. The user's name written on a bouncing ball was chosen more often than a star on a bouncing ball. The computer screen with 'NDSS Design Team' rated exceptionally well.

Music and Sounds
- Cartoon sounds (fun, exaggerated) scored best.
- Pop music (BackStreet Boys) did very well. Classical and Country (fun, yee-haw type) were not widely popular. Sentimental music (Elton John) was second in popularity to pop, although this could have been the result of familiarity with the song.

Buttons
- Favored clicking the largest button on the page.
- Interested in clicking more on buttons with a dark background color and light text on top (high contrast).
- Buttons that make it clear what the user is to do scored very well. When it was clear the object was a button and/or the clickable area was shown, the button was more popular.
- Buttons with a clear clickable area (an outline shape) were popular. Framed buttons were preferred to floating buttons (e.g. underlines).
- Buttons with an arrow pointing towards them were very popular.
- No clear findings on preference for button location (spatial preference).

Typing Name
Five out of six users completed this test successfully. They proved to be able to read the three-step instructions to enter their name or knew immediately what they had to do. One user was confused and proceeded without entering their name (left the field blank and confirmed the blank field when asked to verify name). None used the 'Help' feature.

Instructional Demonstrations
When shown a brief animation demonstrating how something works (e.g. a pull-down menu) participants often did not understand that they should wait until the demonstration was over before trying it. This despite the text instructing them to wait.

Summary of Findings
The beginning of the usability session generated great enthusiasm. However, after repeating the same type of task (picking favorites or rating images), some subjects were bored. Changing tasks and types of rewards is essential in keeping them engaged and interested.

When required to do tasks that are learning focused, it is important to make the rewards exciting and animated. Help them want to get to the reward as an incentive to keep focused, make it clear and add help to avoid frustration. Once they have learned a task, it helps to have them practice it by sending them to a game that is open-ended, so that they can practice it as long as they want. The learning module or game needs to generate rewards to keep them engaged. However, once engaged and enjoying themselves, individuals with Down Syndrome will continue progressing through the task for a much longer time stay than A.K.A.'s initial research suggested was likely.

7.5.3 **Phase Three – Development and Production**

Armed with the learnings from the usability sessions and after distilling a boundless array of possible Internet skills to teach, A.K.A. settled on three Internet concepts for the Web Fun Central learning modules and games. The selected topics were:

- How to use web links.
- How to use pull-down menus.
- How to use the browser 'Back' button.

The teaching components were developed in Flash in order to take advantage of the attributes that this technology affords in creating a rich learning experience, such as sound and animation and the ability to capture and utilize user information and behavior. Once launched, Flash offers consistency and control over the user experience, providing the user has the necessary plug-in. Conversely, A.K.A opted not to develop the modules in a different format such as HTML, where the user experience could not be controlled and would be affected by such things as web browser versions.

The Development Process

Once A.K.A. had identified the particular Internet skills that it wanted to teach in this initial set of three modules (with additional modules to be developed in the future), it developed the concepts for both the learning segments and their related games. These concepts were shared with the NDSS for feedback and guidance before proceeding.

The next step was to develop the script and storyboard for every screen of each module, to ensure that everything was accounted for and that the findings from the usability sessions were being maximized. For each module, A.K.A. developed the complete script (see Figure 7.9) then submitted it to the NDSS, who would in turn

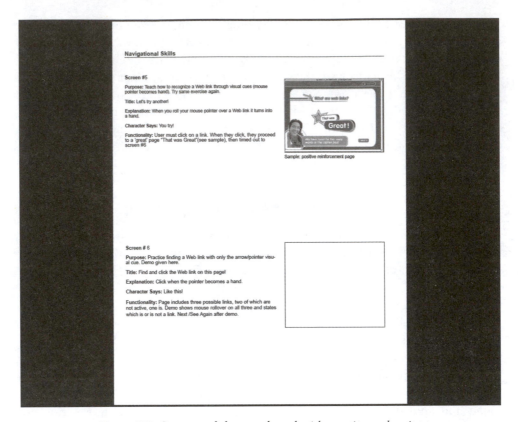

Figure 7.9 Game module, storyboard with creative and script.

verify that the appropriate level of grammar was being used and that the sentence structure and lexicon were optimized for this audience.

The next step was the development of creative mock-ups to visually express how elements would appear and how elements such as the 'Guide' would be introduced. Again, these would be vetted in advance by the NDSS for their perspective and input. Once all these building blocks were in place, A.K.A. could then enter the creative and technical production phase in full force.

A.K.A. developed all aspects of the production internally. This involved the creation and development of all the assets that made up the modules, including all creative design elements, original sound score and music production, photo sessions for the guides and other characters, creation sound effects and voice-over recording, and much more. As all of these components were being created, A.K.A. began the Flash programming that tied all of the elements together into a rich media learning tool and game. At every stage, from the beginning right through to the end, A.K.A. submitted each element to the NDSS for review and feedback to ensure that the project was optimized for the specific target population. Of course the final test was for the NDSS to have individuals with Down Syndrome walk through each module themselves and provide feedback. Once this had been completed and final adjustments were made, Web Fun Central was ready for launch!

End Result – Web Fun Central

The end result of all this work was a series of learning modules and games called Web Fun Central – an online tool that is interactive, graphically rich, and enhanced with animation and sound. These modules have been widely used by visitors of ClubNDSS.org and adopted by educators working with people with Down Syndrome in the USA and elsewhere as part of their regular curriculum. Before walking through the individual learning modules and games, the following will provide a general overview of the structure and some particular attributes that make Web Fun Central unique:

- First, the user enters through a main portal page (Figure 7.10). Although the user has the option to proceed to the games directly (e.g. primarily for repeat users who have completed the learning module), Web Fun Central is designed to direct the user to the learning modules first. The user has the option to choose between three modules with 'How to use web links' being the first as this one provides the main foundation for using the Internet. Once the user completes both the learning module and the associated game, they return to the portal page where they can either quit Web Fun Central or select another learning module and game.
- In order to further empower the user and increase the number of different scenarios in which an individual with Down Syndrome could use Web Fun Central (e.g. in a group setting as part of a computer lab group at school or at home alone), the team designed the modules to be as self-directed as possible. In other words, once the Web Fun Central portal page is launched, a facilitator would not be required to assist the user throughout the process. This was achieved by creating a character or personality, a human face, to guide the user through the modules and games, provide feedback and encouragement, and generally entertain. Since people with Down Syndrome do not typically see themselves reflected in popular culture, the media and the Internet, it was decided that these virtual guides and characters (including the voice-over actors) would be individuals with Down Syndrome (see Figure 7.11). There was one exception where the character in the game 'Wacky

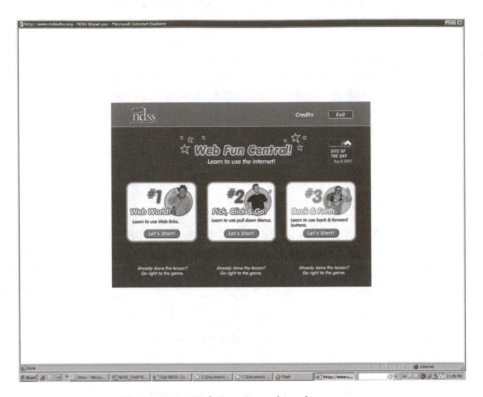

Figure 7.10 *'Web Fun Central,' welcome page.*

Pack' was played by Blake McAlister, A.K.A.'s Art Director. This added a level of familiarity and comfort for the user and made it clear that these modules were developed specifically for them, hopefully offsetting some of the reticence and frustration that they might have been feeling as a result of the poorly designed and confusing mainstream sites they had experienced up until now.

- Throughout the modules and games, users are gently eased into a series of tasks where a pattern of success is established before complexities are added in a supportive and iterative approach. There are positive reinforcements and rewards throughout (see Figure 7.12).
- When showing an instructional animation within the learning module, voiceover, animation, and visual language are employed to help the user clearly understand that they are expected to simply watch the presentation and not interact (see Figure 7.13).

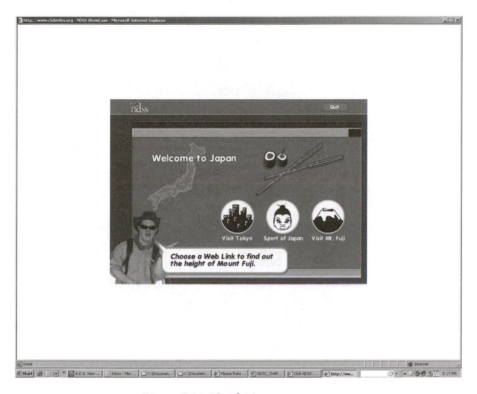

Figure 7.11 *'Guide' in game context.*

- Time delays are used to avoid the user's tendency to click the 'Next' button before reading the instructions. The instructions are presented and after a brief pause, the 'Next' button appears (Figure 7.14).

Web Fun Central Modules
Web World

The 'Web World' module focuses on how to use web links and has the user proceed through an iterative learning process of increasing complexity that teaches the various characteristics and behaviors inherent to web links.

Once the learning module is complete, the user plays a game called 'The Globe Trotter Game' to practice these newly acquired skills. The game requires the user to visit various web sites that represent countries from around the world (see Figure 7.15) and

Figure 7.12 *Positive reinforcement page.*

search for specific information about each country in order to collect passport stamps and eventually a '5 Star Web Traveler Certificate.' Each of the web sites adopts various web link treatments (e.g. text link, image link), information architecture, and navigational strategies that the user could potentially find when surfing the Internet and that they were introduced to in the learning module. This approach also introduces and reinforces the concept that the Internet is made up of web sites containing content on a particular topic and that these sites can be explored to find specific information of interest. The learning and skills involved in the 'Web World' module are considered to be the most important, since it covers the most fundamental principals on how the Internet works.

Pick, Click & Go

The 'Pick, Click & Go' module teaches the user how to use a pull-down menu by focusing on the three main actions involved, namely click, pick and go.

Figure 7.13 *'Instructional Animation,' user instruction.*

Once this process is learned and practiced, the user plays a game called 'Wacky Pack' that allows them to use pull-down menus to help a character pack for a trip to various exotic locations around the world (Figure 7.16). Some amusing scenarios result once the character is revealed wearing the clothes that were selected for him.

Back & Forth

This final module teaches the user how to use the browser 'Back' button (Figure 7.17). This skill was not initially considered one of the more important ones to teach, however A.K.A. reconsidered this position. Upon further reflection, A.K.A. felt that it was important to arm the user with a universal escape strategy in case they become confused or trapped when surfing the Internet. In other words, the 'Back' button always gives the user a means of returning to the last page they visited, regardless of how poorly designed or confusing the web site in question might be.

Figure 7.14 *Learning module instruction without user prompts and with user prompts.*

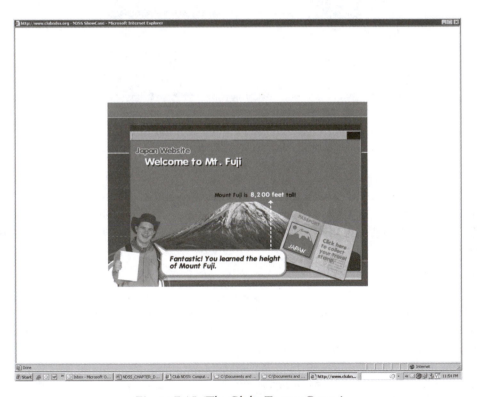

Figure 7.15 *'The Globe Trotter Game.'*

Figure 7.16 '*Pick, Click & Go,*' *pull-down menu component.*

After completing the back and forth activity, users played a game called 'Party Planner.' The premise of the game is a bus ride to a party with various stops along the way. After taking the bus ride, the user is then asked to return to previous stops along the way to pick up items for the party. The user has to use the browser 'Back' and 'Forward' buttons to collect supplies and make the party a success.

7.6 **Successes Today and Beyond**

Web Fun Central modules and games have been widely used by visitors at ClubNDSS.org and adopted by educators across the country as part of their regular curriculum. Web Fun Central was selected by Macromedia as 'Web site of the day' in August 2002 and enjoyed an increasingly larger audience as a result. In fact, its value as a learning tool now extends beyond the Down Syndrome community. For instance, personnel at the Toronto Public Library informed A.K.A. that they direct members of

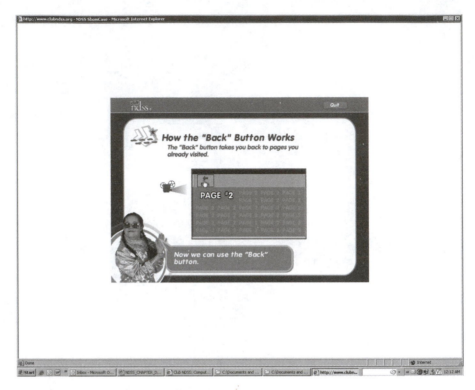

Figure 7.17 '*Back & Forth.*'

the general public to Web Fun Central, particularly seniors, to learn basic Internet skills. Given the overarching goal that A.K.A. had initially set for itself, perhaps the most rewarding evidence of the success of this project for A.K.A. has been watching individuals with Down Syndrome become thoroughly engaged and having fun as they proceed, generally unassisted, through these modules.

Although users are clearly enjoying these tools, it still begs the question: Is learning occurring beyond these learning modules and games, and are users indeed better able to use the Internet on their own afterwards? Although much more needs to be done to test this empirically, informal evidence suggests that the answer is yes. An educator in Florida who uses Web Fun Central as part of her regular computer lab curriculum for individuals with Down Syndrome reports that once these individuals complete Web Fun Central and return to their regular classes, their home class teachers report a marked increase in the student's ability to use the Internet.

Further testing, broader test groups, and a greater range of learning tools would generate that many more rich and meaningful learning experiences. With this in mind, A.K.A. is currently completing usability testing for the NDSS in an effort to determine best practices in web site design for individuals with Down Syndrome. The usability tests are also developed in Flash and involve the user surfing through a series of web sites looking for various pieces of information. The web sites differ in design (from simple text links to graphically rich navigation buttons), navigation strategy (simple top navigation to a dynamic rollover left navigation), and information architecture (pagination vs. relative links). The user's time as well as their click location behavior (correct link click link vs. close click vs. missed click) will provide insight as to which approach is user-friendliest. In other words, web site approaches that allow the user to find the information the fastest with the fewest amount of incorrect clicks would demonstrate better usability as opposed to approaches that take longer to get through and that yield a greater number of incorrect clicks.

The results of this project may have implications for designers, researchers, and policymakers well beyond the field of Down Syndrome.

7.6.1 **Implications for Users**

This project bears a number of interesting implications for users. Considering the benefits demonstrated through this project, and the fact that this is merely the first step in an untapped world of new media possibilities, there is reason to believe that further research and development in this area could yield unprecedented benefits for people with Down Syndrome.

Improved Testing Experiences

Evolving technologies and tools will continue to further our ability to develop more engaging, meaningful, and effective usability testing experiences for people with Down Syndrome. These experiences will become more refined as they mirror more closely the real-life perceptual and cognitive experiences that the users face each day. Not only will these usability tests become more enjoyable learning experiences in and of themselves, but they will also provide some key insights that would not easily have been identified through more traditional methods.

Positive Portrayals in the Media

Hopefully, this project will spur other media developers to portray people with Down Syndrome as role models, actors, and characters. This will go a long way in signifying to the user that this material is obviously intended for them, while also alleviating the sense of alienation from mainstream society that people with Down Syndrome typically feel by not seeing themselves reflected in the media. They will become better connected and integrated with the media and, by extension, with their community.

Technology Adapted to Their Own Learning Strengths

It is hoped that others will develop rich media content that is responsive to the Down Syndrome population, in other words geared to visual iterative learners who benefit greatly from auditory reinforcement, animation, immediate positive feedback, and support. This approach provides quality entertainment while at the same time empowering users to learn and practice vital communication and life skills.

A Safe Learning Environment Mirroring Real-Life Situations

Given that people with Down Syndrome benefit from repetitive iterative learning, it would follow that rich media learning environments where they could learn and practice skills in a safe and supportive setting would serve them well in the real world. These rich media environments are at the very least a major improvement on the more linear, single-dimensional approaches adopted in the past.

More Accessibility, Less Isolation

Any user with access to a computer and the Internet can access this content any time, from anywhere in the world. The social connectedness that this access provides is invaluable, particularly for people with Down Syndrome who have completed high school and who find themselves more isolated, with fewer opportunities to practice communication and life skills. As more rich media continues to be developed specifically for the Down Syndrome population, users may become more discriminating and demanding, which in turn may empower them to lay blame for poor content where it belongs: a lack on the designers' part.

Significant Potential for Personal Growth

Web Fun Central demonstrates that when developed properly, rich media succeeds in keeping users with Down Syndrome engaged and focused on the content for considerably longer periods of time, even longer than initial research suggested. Increased exposure to more comprehensive entertainment and learning environments holds interesting potential for significant personal development, growth, and learning.

Groundwork in Place for New Initiatives

As stated at the beginning of this chapter, a primary goal of the project (which was not assured at the onset) was to develop learning modules and games that individuals with Down Syndrome could not only complete, but that they would also enjoy on an ongoing basis while being entertained, empowered, and informed. This project certainly demonstrates that this is possible and will hopefully encourage other educators and designers to develop more rich media content for this and other populations with special needs.

7.6.2 **Implications for Designers**

In addition to the specific design considerations generated by A.K.A.'s aforementioned usability testing, there are a number of more general implications that A.K.A. deems important to flag with designers communicating to individuals with Down Syndrome and the general public. These include:

- *Provide clear guidance, feedback, and rewards*. Clearly tell the user what they will find and how to find it. Open-ended, ambiguous content will not be effective without support. Positive reinforcement is very important from both a learning perspective as well as simple enjoyment
- *Don't underestimate the impact of images*. Visual learning strategies clearly work best for this and other populations, but perhaps of equal importance is the treatment and quality of the design.
- *Remember that everything means something*. It is typical for individuals with Down Syndrome to methodically scan every piece of information on the page in an attempt to garner meaning and direction. Designers cannot be careless with what they choose to design for them because every single variation, from image treatments to font changes, will be interpreted in some way by the user, whether any meaning was intended or not.
- *You have the means to teach skills, empower, and support*. The advances of rich interactive media offer a host of new possibilities for developing learning tools and games that specifically meet the needs of populations with special needs.
- *Reach a whole new population of viewers*. A.K.A. saw firsthand how mainstream sites frustrated individuals with Down Syndrome. If these were treated in a slightly user-friendlier manner, without diminishing the overall design, they would have been considerably more accessible and the designers (and those who hire them) could reach whole new audiences.
- *It can be done*. Perhaps the single most important conclusion of this project is that in spite of the many unknowns and challenges in embarking on such an endeavor, if one takes the time to value and understand design from the user's perspective, one can chart unknown territory and yield transformational results.

And finally, educators who use Web Fun Central on a regular basis with individuals with Down Syndrome and as part of their regular curriculum report that users stay engaged with it for over an hour at a time and often have to be told to stop because the class time has ended. This might suggest that the research stating that individuals with Down Syndrome will only have an attention span of 10–15 minutes to stick to a task might say more about the quality of the tasks that are commonly developed for this population, rather than the users themselves.

7.6.3 Implications for Researchers

Given the scope and nature of this project, A.K.A. barely scraped the surface in terms of what could be tested and developed. Today's evolving design industry opens up limitless opportunities for creating meaningful experiences for individuals with special needs. The ongoing introduction and improvement of design tools like Flash have implications for researchers in terms of the new opportunities they afford in significantly enhancing usability testing experiences. They allow a deeper understanding of the learning strategies and preferences of individuals with Down Syndrome and other groups.

There are obvious improvements to be made to the testing methodology that A.K.A. undertook, such as testing a larger subject pool over more sessions and spanning more time, and putting tighter controls to ensure more certain results. However, this approach spawned countless research ideas and possibilities of new things to test related to individuals with Down Syndrome and beyond.

There is already encouraging anecdotal evidence that students with Down Syndrome who have used these tools are showing notable improvement in the classroom in their ability to use computers and the Internet. Imagine how much more empowered and independent these students would be with more tools like these? A.K.A. hopes that designers and researchers will continue to join forces along these lines to further this exciting, important, and rewarding work.

Much more could be done to Web Fun Central not only to confirm whether individuals are actually learning these Internet skills, but also to assess the more fundamental issues that this project was intended to address. Once the skills are learned, can the Internet indeed be used by young adults with Down Syndrome and others with special needs to alleviate isolation and maintain writing and communication skills during the transition between high school and adulthood? A great deal more research could and should be done in this area.

7.6.4 Implications for Policymakers

As individuals with Down Syndrome become increasingly integrated into society, more and more people will interact with them, thereby increasing the need for widespread public education and acceptance. Children with Down Syndrome have been included in typical academic classrooms in schools across the country. In some instances they are integrated into specialized courses, while in other situations students are fully included in the regular classroom for all subjects. The degree of mainstreaming is based on the abilities of the individual but the trend is for full inclusion in the social, educational, and employment life of the community.

It is becoming increasingly important to provide teaching tools that will allow this population to participate fully in all areas, including the use of computers and the Internet. This will require investment in additional usability testing and the development of learning approaches designed specifically for the unique needs of this population. Policies such as 'No Child Left Behind' should recognize the value of developing curricula specifically for individuals with Down Syndrome and the power of using interactive rich media for doing so. This project and others like it can help social advocates and government decision-makers build a stronger case for creating support systems for individuals with Down Syndrome.

The fact that organizations like the NDSS are looking for ways to reduce the isolation and waning skills that individuals with Down Syndrome experience after high school, coupled with the fact that these individuals are expected to have an increasingly longer life expectancy, simply magnifies the need for policy commitment and support.

7.7 Conclusion

Web Fun Central was created to help individuals with Down Syndrome learn and practice the basic skills required to use the Internet. The hope was that it would improve their quality of life by allowing them to take better advantage of the entertainment, educational, and social benefits that the Internet can provide. Since no known initiative of this kind had ever been attempted before, the process was rife with challenge, uncertainty, and new discoveries but ultimately, it exceeded the developers' expectations. After a year of intensive research, usability testing, and production, a series of innovative online learning tools and games were born. Web Fun Central itself is an exciting new development for the Down Syndrome community, but perhaps even more significant is the potential it holds for further development and opportunity. The groundwork has been laid for other researchers, educators, and designers to further this initiative, for the benefit of people with Down Syndrome as well as other populations with special needs. Web Fun Central can be accessed at http://www.clubndss.org/clubndss.cfm?fuseaction=computercenter.

References

Biederman *et al.* (1999) *Observational Learning in Children with Down Syndrome.* The Down Syndrome Education Trust, University of Toronto, Toronto.

Buckley, S. and Bird, G. (1993) Teaching children with Down's syndrome to read. In *Down's Syndrome: Research and Practice,* 1, 34–39.

Kumin, L. (1999) Comprehensive speech and language treatment for infants, toddlers, and children with Down syndrome. In Hassold, T. J. & Patterson, D., *Down syndrome: A promising future, together,* Wiley-Liss, New York, NY, pp. 145–153.

Lazar, J. (2006) *Web Usability: A User-Centered Design Approach,* Addison-Wesley, Boston, MA.

Nielsen, J. (1994) *Usability Engineering,* Academic Press, Boston, MA.

Preece, J. (2000) *Online Communities: Designing Usability, Supporting Sociability,* John Wiley & Sons, New York.

Schuler, D., Namioka A. (eds.), (1993) *Participatory Design: Principles and Practices,* Lawrence Erlbaum Associates, Hillsdale, NJ.

Sears, A. (2003) Universal usability and the web. In Ratner J. (ed.), *Human Factors and Web Development,* 2nd edn., Lawrence Erlbaum Associates, Mahwah, NJ, 21–46.

Newell, A., Carmichael, A., Gregor, P. and Alm, N. (2003). Information technology for cognitive support. In Jacko J., & Sears A. (ed.), *The Handbook of Human–Computer Interaction,* Lawrence Erlbaum Associates, Mahwah, NJ, 464–481.

Shneiderman, B. (2000) Universal Usability: Pushing Human–Computer Interaction Research to Empower Every Citizen, *Communications of the ACM,* 43(5), 84–91.

Slatin, J. and Rush, S. (2003) *Maximum Accessibility,* Addison-Wesley, New York.

Wolpert, G (1996) *The educational challenges inclusion study.* National Down Syndrome Society, New York, NY.

Using Virtual Peer Technology as an Intervention for Children with Autism

8

Andrea Tartaro and Justine Cassell

Center for Technology and Social Behavior, Northwestern University, Evanston, USA

Summary

In this chapter we discuss the motivation, design, and implementation of PAT (Play and Tell), an *authorable virtual peer* for children with autism spectrum disorder (ASD). Based on research on the triad of impairments that characterize ASD, and how these impairments may be linked to deficits in theory of mind, we lay out a set of key features that we believe to be important – and as yet undervalued – in technological interventions for children with autism: (1) a peer context, rather than a virtual parent or teacher, so that children can practice peer social interaction skills; (2) a personally meaningful storytelling task for practicing imagination and language; (3) a system that incorporates not just interaction with the technology, but also a control and author mode, to allow the child to build appropriate social skills from the ground up. These features are instantiated in an authorable, life-size, full-body virtual peer that tells collaborative stories and thereby gives children with ASD a space to play with social interaction, communication, and imaginative play behaviors. Pilot studies demonstrate that for at least some children with ASD and related diagnoses, the PAT system is intuitive, motivating, and capable of engaging children in the kind of tight reciprocal social interaction that is otherwise so difficult for them, and that is the basis for both play and learning among children.

Introduction

Instructional technologies increasingly integrate a social as well as a cognitive component to help scaffold learning. Thus, virtual peers (Ryokai *et al.*, 2003), affective pedagogical agents (Johnson and Carlisle, 1996; Lester *et al.*, 1997; Gratch, 2000), interactive pedagogical dramas (Si *et al.*, 2005), and peer-directed online learning communities (Cassell, 2002) are all leveraging the ability of the computer to create a social context for learning. However, the Universal Usability tradition in human–computer interaction research reminds us not to take for granted that new technologies are usable by all populations (Shneiderman, 2000), and on examination these social learning technologies may be least usable by a population that needs them most. The social and communication deficits of ASD make it difficult to engage in social interaction, and therefore access learning opportunities in these systems as well as in their classrooms and lives. And yet we know from the reports of parents, teachers, therapists, and researchers (cf. Hart, 2005), that many children with ASD show an affinity for computers. Instead of labeling these technologies as useless for children with ASD, in this chapter we propose to leverage the social context that is created in these systems to help develop social and communication skills. In particular, this chapter proposes a computer system called 'Play and Tell' (PAT) that allows children with ASD to tell stories with a life-size, indefatigable virtual peer, as well as to control and to author interactions for that virtual peer. PAT incorporates three features which we believe will be crucial to its success as an intervention for children with ASD: (1) a virtual peer context so that children can practice peer social interaction skills; (2) a personally meaningful storytelling task for practicing imagination and language; (3) a system that is controllable and authorable by the child to allow children with ASD to come to understand and scaffold their own communication and reciprocal social interaction in typical social settings. An additional goal of the system is to allow researchers to better understand the mechanisms underlying the communicative deficits of ASD by observing children with ASD interacting with the storytelling virtual peer, and authoring interactions for it.

In what follows we first describe autism spectrum disorder, provide a theoretical framework of ASD deficits in terms of theory of mind, give some estimates on the prevalence of ASD, and explain why social skills development is crucial for children with ASD. Next we summarize previous nontechnical and technical interventions for children with ASD, and examine the key features of the interventions that contribute to their success. We then introduce the three key features of our own intervention: virtual peers as partners in learning, storytelling as a developmental task, and a system for controlling and authoring social interactions. We describe PAT, our authorable virtual peer for children with ASD, and describe our methodology for designing and evaluating virtual peers. Finally, we offer some initial findings from our pilot studies, and conclude with the implications of our work for designers, researchers, and policymakers.

8.1 What is Autism Spectrum Disorder?

Autism is a pervasive developmental disorder that affects a person's ability to communicate and interact with others. People with ASD experience difficulty in three main areas, known as the triad of impairments: reciprocal social interaction (for example, they may appear indifferent to other people); social communication (such as not understanding common gestures, facial expressions, or affective responses); and imagination (difficulty developing interpersonal play and telling stories) (NAS, 2005).

These deficits manifest themselves in a variety of ways. For example, individuals with ASD may be echolalic (they repeat or echo what they overhear) and may speak in monotone. Individuals with ASD have difficulty understanding what others are feeling and may need to be explicitly taught social skills that typically developing children pick up incidentally. Their play may lack imagination (Brill, 2001). Level of functioning varies greatly in children with ASD. Some children lack any functional language, while others may be able to express more than they can understand (Brill, 2001).

Asperger syndrome, pervasive developmental disorder – not otherwise specified PDD-NOS, and nonverbal learning disorder (NLD) are all diagnoses related to autism. Of these, Asperger syndrome and PDD-NOS are characterized as disorders on the autism spectrum. Thus, people with Asperger syndrome have similar social difficulties, but have normal or above-average intelligence (Ghaziuddin and Mountain-Kimchi, 2004). Similarly, a diagnosis of PDD-NOS is given when children demonstrate autistic social and communicative disabilities, but do not fully meet the diagnostic criteria for other pervasive developmental disorders diagnoses (Paul *et al.*, 2004). For the most part, individuals with Asperger syndrome and PDD-NOS show higher verbal abilities than those with autism (Ghaziuddin and Mountain-Kimchi, 2004; Paul *et al.*, 2004).

Nonverbal learning disorder is a neurological syndrome (not on the autism spectrum) that many consider to be a mild form of autism (Little, 1999). Individuals with NLD have high verbal ability, and in fact may speak well and be verbose, but they have significant problems with social skills, academics, visual–spatial abilities, and motor coordination (Little, 2003). Similarly to children with autism, they often have difficulty deciphering the communicative intent of nonverbal behaviors such as tone of voice, gesture, facial expressions, nuances, and body language (Little, 2003). They may interrupt conversations and change the subject to unrelated and irrelevant issues. Integrating new information and applying learning from one situation to another is also problematic for children with NLD; it is therefore difficult for them to cope with new situations (Little, 1999).

The difficulties with communication and reciprocal social interaction seen in autism and related disorders have been interpreted by some as reflecting an underlying deficit in theory of mind (Baron-Cohen, 1995). Theory of mind is the ability to understand that others have beliefs, desires, and intentions that are different from one's own, and individuals with autism often demonstrate deficits in exactly this kind of understanding. This kind of lack of understanding can be illustrated by the following excerpt from *The Curious Incident of the Dog in the Night-time* (Haddon, 2003), a novel told from the point of view of a child with ASD:

> And one day Julie sat down at a desk next to me and put a tube of Smarties on the desk, and she said, 'Christopher, what do you think is in here?'
>
> And I said, 'Smarties.'
>
> Then she took the top off the Smarties tube and turned it upside down and a little red pencil came out and she laughed and I said, 'It's not Smarties, it's a pencil.'
>
> Then she said, 'If your mummy came in now and we asked her what was inside the Smarties tube, what do you think she would say?'. . .
>
> And I said, 'A pencil.'
>
> That was because when I was little I didn't understand about other people having minds. And Julie said to Mother and Father that I would always find this very difficult. (Haddon, 2003, pp. 115–116)

The theory of mind deficit is an important theoretical perspective in research on ASD because it is uniquely able to explain this pattern of impairments (Tager-Flusberg, 2000). For example, one of the components of theory of mind is the shared attention mechanism (Baron-Cohen, 1995), or joint attention, which is the ability to form a triadic representation between the self, another, and an object by monitoring the eye direction of the other agent to interpret mental states. In lay terms this means that in conversation most people monitor each other's eye gaze, and look in the direction that their conversational partners are looking in order to see what the conversational partner is attending to. While children with ASD can understand that motion serves a goal or a desire (for example, reaching for something may mean one wants it), and can detect people's eyes and infer that those people see what they are looking at, they appear to have an impairment concerning joint attention and do not understand that the activities of the other may be intended to make meaning for the child. Thus, children with ASD do not demonstrate gaze monitoring, nor do they attempt to direct the attention of another person (Baron-Cohen, 1995). The absence of joint attention causes a problem because it forms a critical scaffold to learning. For example, vocabulary is learned during episodes of joint attention (such as when a mother says 'that's a dog' and directs her eyes to the animal), and joint attention also plays a key role in pretend play (Jones and Carr, 2004).

8.1.1 **Prevalence of Autism Spectrum Disorder**

The National Autistic Society (UK) estimates the total rate of prevalence of autism spectrum disorders in the UK to be approximately 1 in 110 (NAS, 2005). The Autism Society of America estimates a rate of autism of 1 in 166, or 1.5 million Americans

(ASA, 2005). Because clinicians and researchers are seeing increasing numbers of children for assessment, diagnosis, and treatment of autism spectrum disorders, there is a strong sense that ASD has become more prevalent in recent years (Prior, 2003). In fact, up until 1990, ASD was considered a rare disorder with an occurrence of 4 per 10000 children. However, it is debatable how much these increases represent an actual rise in the disorder (Prior, 2003). Possible alternative explanations include changes in diagnostic practices, heightened awareness and acceptance among parents and educators, and improved services for children with ASD, such that parents may be willing to bring their children in for diagnosis (Charman, 2002; Prior, 2003).

8.1.2 Social Skills Deficits

Although children with ASD may manifest a number of differences from their typically developing peers, the current chapter focuses on social skills. More exactly, we focus on social communication and reciprocal social interaction – that is, the ability to make oneself understood to another person, to use communication to achieve a common goal with another person, and the ability to behave in ways that demonstrate mutuality or joint work in conversation. These particular deficits in children with ASD can impact children's personal relationships, education and employment opportunities (Webb *et al.*, 2004), and have been particularly resistant to intervention, making them an area that needs further research. In addition, the perceived value of social skills instruction is high. In a survey of maternal perceptions of the importance of needs and resources for children with Asperger syndrome and nonverbal learning disorders, 78% of mothers rated social skills training as extremely important. The study also concluded that schools are not providing sufficient social skills training (Little, 2003).

When reciprocal social interaction is successful, communication is seamless, and the participants may even experience an increased feeling of rapport with the conversational partner, which itself serves as a foundation for learning. Successful communication of this sort, however, is composed of exactly the kinds of behavior that are difficult for individuals with ASD: joint attention, positivity toward the other as demonstrated in words and nonverbal behavior, and coordination of speech behavior and social interaction (Tickle-Degnen and Rosenthal, 1990). We have examined some of this work in our implementation of an 'embodied conversational agent' that engages in small talk and social dialog (Cassell, 2002; Bickmore and Cassell, 2005). We translated the concepts verbally into shared patterns of speech, and increasing coordination in speaking, and nonverbally into behaviors such as body postures that signal accessibility, smiling, head nodding, postural mirroring, and interactional synchrony. Our results showed that users demonstrate increased trust of an interaction with a virtual human when that virtual human engages in these relational behaviors. In the current work, we hypothesize that one of the ways that we can address impairments in theory of mind in ASD is by modeling these surface-level rapport behaviors in embodied virtual peers, allowing the children to tweak the behaviors themselves and observe the outcome on communication.

8.2 Interventions for Children with Autism Spectrum Disorder

Nontechnological approaches that target the social interaction deficits of ASD have existed for quite some time with fairly good results (Faherty, 2000). For reciprocal social interaction, such as gaining a listener's attention, initiating topics, maintaining topics, and expressing ideas, approaches have included social groups, peer partnerships, formal social skills training programs, and narrative and/or pictorial approaches such as social stories or comic strip conversations.

8.2.1 Social Groups

Social groups target improvement in social skills such as perspective-taking, reciprocal interactions, listening skills, turn-taking during games and conversations, etc. (Faherty, 2000). Social groups vary in how much structure they provide on social interactions, and sometimes involve typically developing peers. Social groups are used with individuals with autism of all ages, including young children, adolescents, and adults. Some groups are organized around a common interest, such as exploring computers, or may have a dual focus of providing a social event and discussing issues encountered by the participants related to their disorder. Activities used to structure the social group may include games, sports, crafts, or music. Some general guidelines often followed by social groups include: meeting on a consistent basis, keeping the group small, beginning each meeting with a common routine, displaying a schedule of events, providing structure and visual cues, using social stories (below) to clarify problematic situations, including a snack or meal, discussing and voting on what the group will do next, and concluding with a familiar routine (Faherty, 2000).

LeGoff (2004) studied a social group that used Lego as a medium to develop social skills in children with autism. A key feature of Lego as a therapeutic tool is that the medium has a 'constructive application' – it relies on children's natural interests to motivate learning and behavior change. The goal of Lego therapy is to increase social competence along three dimensions: (1) motivation to initiate social contact with peers; (2) ability to sustain interaction with peers for a period of time; and (3) overcoming autistic symptoms of aloofness and rigidity. A key strategy involves dividing the task of building into two roles: the 'engineer' and the 'builder.' Much of the communication requires nonverbal behavior, with an emphasis on joint attention, eye contact, and 'mind-reading.' The unique aspects of the Lego therapy are: (1) blending of individual and group therapies; (2) use of play materials (Lego) which were inherently interesting and motivating to the clients, and providing a medium for promoting social interaction, collaboration, and interactive play; and (3) creation of a social group.

8.2.2 Peer Partnerships

Identifying 'buddies' or 'peer helpers' is another technique used to facilitate friendship and interaction skills in children with autism. Peer partners may fill a variety of roles such as peer tutor, project partner, extracurricular activity buddy, etc. Successful relationships are based on common interests and experiences. The peer is taught to understand autism and any structured strategies used by the child with autism (Faherty, 2000).

8.2.3 Social Skills Training Programs

Social skills training programs such as the SCORE Skills (Vernon *et al.*, 1996), Skillstreaming (McGinnis and Goldstein, 1984, 1990) and Social Effectiveness Training (Jackson *et al.*, 1991) explicitly teach social skills. The SCORE Skills Training Program focuses on a set of five skills that are needed for effective cooperative group work: 'share ideas,' 'compliment others,' 'offer help or encouragement,' 'recommend changes nicely,' and 'exercise self-control.' The skills are taught by asking participants to memorize the steps of each social skill and practice using the skills in role play situations. As skills are practiced, it should become more natural to carry out the skill steps. A recent study demonstrates the effectiveness of using the SCORE Skill Program with adolescents with high-functioning autism (Webb *et al.*, 2004).

Similarly, Skillstreaming (McGinnis and Goldstein, 1984, 1990) uses structured learning techniques of modeling, role playing, performance feedback, and transfer of training to teach children specific pro-social behaviors. The program groups skills into: beginning social skills, such as 'listening' and 'asking for help'; school-related skills, such as 'asking a question' or 'following directions'; friendship-making skills, such as 'joining in' and 'sharing'; dealing with feelings, such as 'asking to talk' or 'showing affection'; alternatives to aggression, such as 'dealing with teasing' and 'being mad'; and dealing with stress, such as 'being honest' and 'saying no.' Social Effectiveness Training (Jackson *et al.*, 1991) uses five specific teach strategies to help children develop social skills: Positive Feedback, Ignore–Attend–Praise, the Teaching Interaction, the Direct Prompt, and Sit and Watch. Groups of six to eight clients meet with two instructors for one to two hours weekly or biweekly. Each session reviews one or two specific social skills, such as 'interrupt the right way' or 'join in.'

8.2.4 Narrative and Pictorial Interventions

A common intervention employing narratives that model social competencies is the 'social story,' developed by Carol Gray in 1991. A social story defines relevant cues in a social situation and describes appropriate responses (Gray, 1994b). For example, a social story can involve a specific activity, such as homework time. The child's behavior during this activity is analyzed to determine what situations cause undesirable behaviors, such as crying and hitting. These situations are described in the story and inappropriate behaviors are contrasted with correct actions. For example, if a homework problem is hard, the child should not scream, but rather ask someone for help. The components of the strategy include: social modeling, task analysis, visual aides, practice with corrective feedback, and priming. Figure 8.1 gives an example of a social story written to support a student in following her daily schedule.

A small amount of recent research has provided empirical evidence on the effectiveness of social story interventions (Adams *et al.*, 2004; Barry and Burlew, 2004). Both these studies described case studies where social story intervention was effective for the situation target, and even transferred to other situations.

Comic Strip Conversations use simple drawings to represent a conversation between two or more people. By using stick-figure illustrations and text to represent speech and thought, the drawings illustrate an ongoing communication and help students improve their understanding and comprehension of conversation (Gray, 1994a). Comic Strip Conversations use a set of eight symbols to represent basic conversational skills, including 'listening,' 'interrupting,' 'loud' and 'quiet words,' 'talk,' and 'thoughts.' Thus the drawings can represent not only what people are saying and doing but also emphasize what people may be thinking. Comic Strip Conversations are said to leverage visualization and visual supports, techniques found useful in structuring learning in students with autism.

A similar technique, Social Skills Picture Stories, uses digital pictures of actual children demonstrating various social skills (Baker, 2001). The pictures are combined with text and cartoon bubbles to denote what the children are saying and thinking. Social Skills Picture Stories break down social skills, such as asking for help and initiating or joining conversations, into their components and make explicit what to say and do in social situations.

Figure 8.1 *Example social story written to support a student in following her daily schedule. Written by Nicole Ruschmeyer, M.A., CCC-SLP/L, Speech-language Pathologist, Clinical Assist, Ltd. The Picture Communication Symbols ©1981–2006 by Mayer-Johnson LLC. All Rights Reserved Worldwide. Used with permission. Boardmaker is a trademark of Mayer-Johnson LLC.*

8.3 Technology and Autism Spectrum Disorder

There has been a recent increase in computational systems for children with ASD. Often these projects rely on proven techniques to address the social and learning needs of children with ASD: story telling (Davis *et al.*, 2004), animated cartoon characters (Bosseler and Massaro, 2003; Cole *et al.*, 2003; Wise *et al.*, in press), socially situated learning (Dautenhahn *et al.*, 2002; Kerr *et al.*, 2002; Dautenhahn and Weery, 2004; Parsons *et al.*, 2004; Robins *et al.*, 2004), and tracking and evaluations of treatments (Hayes *et al.*, 2004).

Davis *et al.* (2004) created a system called Touch Story to explore the ability of children with ASD to build coherent stories. The system tested whether children with ASD could select the third frame in a five-frame picture story. While their research demonstrates the use of storytelling in interventions for children with ASD, it does not go further in exploring storytelling as a context for exploration of language, imagination, or social interaction.

The Aurora project (Dautenhahn and Weery, 2004) built a series of autonomous robots that can engage children in interactions which demonstrate important aspects of human–human interaction, such as eye-gaze, turn-taking, and imitation games. They have found that children with ASD will proactively approach robots (Dautenhahn *et al.*, 2002), and that robots can be used to elicit joint attention episodes between children with ASD and an adult (Robins *et al.*, 2004). In addition, by slowly increasing the repertoire and unpredictability of the robot's behavior, the robot can be used to guide a child to more complex forms of interaction (Dautenhahn and Weery, 2004). Similarly, Michaud and Theberge-Turmel (2002) describe several robots that offer different behaviors and rewards to appeal to different children. Their goal is to design robots that can evolve with the child from simple machines to robots that demonstrate more complex behaviors.

These different robot therapies demonstrate two key features of systems for children with ASD: (1) because of the diverse profiles that characterize children with autism, the system must be highly personalizable to adapt to the needs, interests, and abilities of each child that interacts with it; and (2) even more than for typically developing children, it is helpful if the system can provide a scaffold for learning that is withdrawn little by little as the child's competencies grow.

Virtual environments have proven to be another active area of research for social skill interventions. Kerr *et al.* (2002) have designed a number of single-user and collaborative virtual environments that teach social skills for adolescents and adults with Asperger syndrome. They emphasize the importance of scaffolding in the system that can guide users through the learning process. In addition, they use two scenarios, a virtual café and a virtual bus, which share a common goal (to find a seat) to explore transfer of learning from one context to another.

Similar research evaluates a desktop virtual environment for people with ASD, where users were represented by avatars (Parsons *et al.*, 2004). This environment proved to be intuitive to individuals with ASD, who were able to learn to use it quickly. In fact, the users with ASD were able to interpret the environment in a nonliteral way, for example by concluding that two figures standing by a bar in a virtual café were talking. Interestingly, participants with ASD were more frequently rated as walking between or bumping into the people at the bar and more likely to be judged as having 'low intention to avoid' a couple at the bar, compared with matched counterparts. The authors conclude that this reflects a weak understanding of appropriate behavior concerning personal space in people with ASD that even translates into the virtual environment.

Bosseler and Massaro (2003) evaluated the effectiveness of an animated cartoon agent vocabulary tutor for children with ASD. The studies found that children were able to learn new vocabulary words, retain much of the learned material over time, apply the words to new images, and apply the words outside of the computer program context. Massaro's Baldi system has recently become a commercial product where an animated adult face gives feedback and motivates the child to continue working through exercises that include demonstrating understanding of stories that deal with social problems, sequencing of frames in stories, and practicing language skills (Animated Speech Corporation, 2002, 2005). The Center for Spoken Language Research at the University of Colorado (Wise *et al.*, in press) has also tested a literacy education system for children with ASD. The system uses a cartoon face to give hints and explanations to children as they complete phonological awareness, reading, spelling, and comprehension exercises. In both of these cases, an animated tutor motivates children, and gives them immediate feedback on their performance. However, neither project provides the *peer* context that is so important to learning about social skills and about literacy, nor a full-bodied animated agent that can allow children with ASD to learn about the role of the body in social interaction. And, in both projects, content is authored by the teachers, and there is not room for children to explore imaginative play or the behaviors of reciprocal social interaction by authoring their own stories – and their own animated agents.

CareLog uses automated capture techniques to track the effectiveness of educational and therapeutic interventions for children with ASD (Hayes *et al.*, 2004). This software enables members of care teams for an individual child to automatically capture, measure, mine, and analyze behavior and learning data. The system helps coordinate caregivers, and uses data to affect treatment and future data capture.

8.4 Guidelines for Using Technology in Social Interventions

The researchers who have implemented and evaluated these previous technological and nontechnological social skill and language interventions emphasize a certain number of features that appear to be key to success in designing for the population of children with ASD. These features include:

- *Interventions are highly personalizable.* Social stories, for example, are tailored to a specific child's behavior in a particular situation (Gray, 1994b; Adams *et al.*, 2004; Barry and Burlew, 2004). The robots described by Michaud and Theberge-Turmel (2002) exhibited different behaviors and reward sequences to appeal to the preferences of children.

- *Systems scaffold the child*. In the Aurora project (Dautenhahn and Weery, 2004), the behaviors first exhibited by the robots are simple and predictable. As children interact more with the robots they become more complex. This progress from simple, predictable behaviors to more complex interactions is common in therapies designed for children with ASD, and adapts children to social interaction.
- *Artifacts have constructive applications*. The success of the Lego therapy was greatly influenced by the natural appeal of the Lego artifact (LeGoff, 2004).
- *Using roles helps children with ASD practice social interactions*. By taking on roles of 'engineer' and 'builder' during the Lego therapy, children were encouraged to interact to complete a task (LeGoff, 2004). Also, the roles provide a script the children can learn and follow to scaffold their interaction.
- *Social contexts provide an environment for practicing social skills*. Virtual environments use the context of a café or bus to practice behavior in a social situation (Kerr *et al.*, 2002; Parsons *et al.*, 2004). Social groups create a safe space for practicing peer interaction.
- *Evaluation considers the transfer of behaviors to other contexts*. That children with ASD have trouble transferring learned behaviors to different contexts must be remembered when designing systems and revisited in their evaluation.

Our goal is to design a technology intervention that incorporates these features but adds three additional features that we know to be important from research on typically developing children: (1) a peer context, rather than a virtual parent or teacher, so that children can practice peer social interaction skills; (2) a personally meaningful storytelling task for practicing imagination and language; (3) a system that is authorable by the child, to allow the child to literally build appropriate social skills from the ground up.

8.5 Virtual Peer Support for Learning

A virtual peer is a life-sized, full-body computer-generated animated character that looks like a child and is capable of interacting with children by sharing real toys and responding to children's input. Sam, the virtual peer shown in Figure 8.2, was developed as a way to promote language and literacy development in children by leveraging oral storytelling and communication skills, engaging children in peer play, and supporting imaginative play (Ryokai *et al.*, 2003; Cassell, 2004). Sam's speech and body behaviors are modeled after the storytelling roles and turn-taking behaviors that children use when interacting with each other.

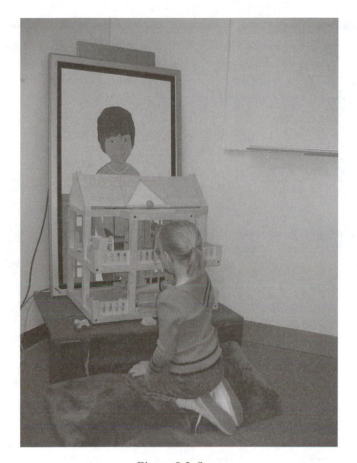

Figure 8.2 Sam.

Sam tells stories with children using a castle placed in front of the child that 'extends' into Sam's virtual world, and toys that pass between the virtual and physical world through a 'magic portal' in the castle. Sam has been implemented in Macromedia Flash. 3D animations are created using a character animation tool, and then imported into Flash, where they are edited so that the body parts can be controlled independently. Sam's voice is a set of pre-recorded audio clips, which offer more realism than text-to-speech. Some of Sam's behaviors are generated automatically, such as Sam's eyebrows, which rise for emphasis with changes in pitch in the speech, and Sam's lips, which move as a function of the sounds of the words that Sam utters. Other behaviors are scripted by hand.

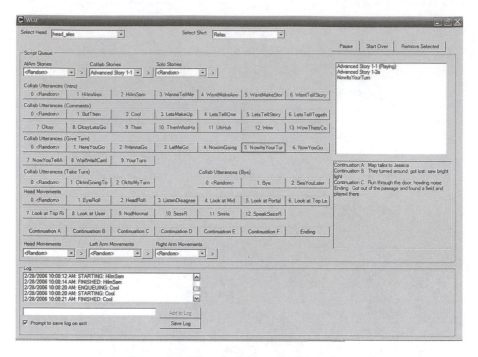

Figure 8.3 *Wizard of Oz control interface.*

Since speech recognition of children's voices is very difficult, the Sam system relies on an audio threshold to determine when the child is speaking. RFID tags on the toys and sensors in several rooms of the house are used to direct Sam's head animations so s/he is always looking where the child is playing, and as a clue to turn-taking when children put the toys back into the 'magic portal,' completing a storytelling turn.

To evaluate Sam's interactions with children, we rely on a Wizard of Oz (WOZ) control interface (Figure 8.3) that enables the experimenter to select Sam's pre-recorded responses and story segments. The experimenter is trained to select responses based on the same algorithm used by the autonomous system.

8.6 **Storytelling**

Because literacy is fundamentally about producing language in a way that others can understand, and understanding language that others have produced, the audience or listener plays an essential role in literacy learning. For this reason, typically developing children first acquire literacy skills in social contexts such as language play and storytelling, and many of these skills are acquired in the context of children's interactions with peers (Snow, 1983). Peer storytelling is a particularly relevant context for literacy development because it encourages children to produce 'decontextualized language.' Decontextualized language is language for an audience that does not share the same temporal and spatial context (Snow, 1983). For example, 'tomorrow' and 'here' are contextualized language because the listener must share the same time and place as the speaker to understand the meaning. 'One Spring day' or 'in the library at Northwestern University' are examples of decontextualized language because they convey a place or time that can be understood without knowing who the speaker is, or when s/he has spoken. Storytelling requires children to hold the audience's perspective in mind while relating the context of a story (Cameron and Wang, 1999). In addition, children are demanding listeners, co-authors, and critics of one another (Preece, 1992; Sawyer, 2002), meaning that peer storytelling is also a social interaction exercise.

Lack of awareness of audience and inability to collaborate with peers to make meaning are considered to be key signs of ASD. In fact, children with ASD produce impoverished narratives when compared with typically developing children matched for mental age, and may not provide causal explanations for the events in the stories (Tager-Flusberg, 1995). Loveland *et al.* (1990) found children with ASD are less able to consider the listener's needs when constructing stories, and produce more bizarre or inappropriate utterances.

These deficits in narrative ability have been interpreted as reflective of autism's underlying deficits in theory of mind (Tager-Flusberg, 2000). Capps *et al.* (2000) investigated the relationship between social competence and narrative in more detail. They found that theory of mind abilities are related to two fundamental aspects of narrative: (1) narrative as a social activity that involves monitoring and maintaining listener involvement; and (2) narrative as a means of elaborating a point of view concerning characters' emotions, thoughts, and actions. Thus, creating a collaborative storytelling task that enables children with ASD to develop their narrative skills addresses the underlying theory of mind deficits of ASD. At the same time, it creates a peer context for observing and practicing social skills. Although psychologists often use open storytelling as a diagnostic tool for children with ASD, and reading or retelling stories appears in many interventions for children with ASD, few interventions ask the children to collaborate to tell unconstrained and personally meaningful stories, and none to our knowledge allow children to engage in the key developmental task of collaborative storytelling with peers. And yet, the research described above leads us to believe that storytelling with a virtual peer can allow children to practice turn-taking behaviors, take on conversational roles, address the beliefs of peers, and stretch their imaginations.

8.6.1 PAT: a Virtual Peer Authoring System for Children with ASD

On the basis of the research reviewed above, and the key features extracted from interventions designed by others and our own previous work on typically developing children, we are designing, creating, and evaluating the use of a new kind of 'authorable,' life-size, full-body virtual peer for children with ASD: PAT (Play and Tell). PAT is used in three modes. Children with ASD interact with the virtual peer by telling stories. In a second mode, children also control the virtual peer by using the Wizard of Oz interface to select predefined responses, thus practicing and observing different behaviors through the agent. Finally, in the third mode, children author the virtual peer by creating new behaviors and responses. These interactions occur cyclically, as illustrated in Figure 8.4, and scaffold children from simple, predictable interactions with the system to more complex, social interaction with the system. The authorable virtual peer offers children with ASD a space to play with social communication, social interaction, and imagination – exactly the areas of impairment that characterize the deficits of ASD. We believe that collaborative storytelling with a virtual peer will help children with ASD develop narrative and social interaction skills.

Each mode of the system is controlled by a different interface. In *interact* mode, children tell stories with the virtual peer while the virtual peer is controlled by an experimenter, or a peer, using a WoZ interface. For the *control* mode, in conjunction with the children themselves, we are developing a child-friendly version of the experimenter's WoZ interface so that the children can control the behaviors of the virtual peers. Children can turn on and off the nonverbal behaviors of the agent, such as eye gaze, hand gestures, head nods, and observe the effects on interaction. A pilot study demonstrated that even the adult-oriented Wizard of Oz control panel that we

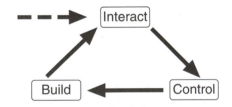

Figure 8.4 Authorable virtual peer interactions.

currently use is intuitive for some children with ASD, who were very interested in using the interface to control the behaviors of a virtual peer.

Finally, for the *author* mode we are creating child-friendly story- and behavior-authoring tools for virtual humans. Currently, stories are scripted by hand by timing gestures to audio files by the millisecond. With new authoring tools, children will be able to record or type story segments, and select sequences of gestures to accompany the utterances. Building their own virtual storytellers enables the children to practice decentering, or imagining the interaction from the point of view of the conversation partner.

The authoring tools will use a flow-chart framework that helps children with ASD understand social skills and conversational goals by making the skills explicit. Computational objects (pictures of the behavior) are used to specify nonverbal behaviors, such as gestures and head nods, and to record plot segments of the conversational narrative, including greetings or specific social acts such as 'share' or 'compliment.' A story might, for example, be scripted to start with a 'greeting' object, followed by a 'share idea' object that includes a recorded portion of a personal narrative. The next object would indicate to wait for a response from the user, followed by a choice of responses for the virtual peer that can be selected in control mode. Figure 8.5 depicts the authoring of such a story.

The actual intervention is a series of interactions with the system and an adult. First, children interact with the virtual peer to get an idea of what the system does.

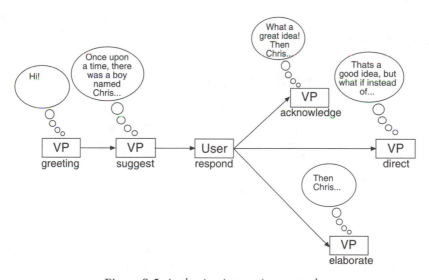

Figure 8.5 *Authoring interaction example.*

Then children control the virtual peer and choose its reactions. The control mode allows children to rehearse and observe interactions. Children then learn how to create their own stories and behaviors using the author mode by creating storytellers for their peers to interact with. Finally, children share their virtual peers, by controlling their own virtual peer, selecting its responses, while another child interacts with it. These interactions will lead children to go back and redesign their system.

This authoring technique has been used with typically developing children in the Storyteller Agent Generation Environment (SAGE) project, with good success (Umaschi-Bers and Cassell, 2000). SAGE is a storytelling system that enables children to tell stories, find personal relevance in other people's stories, and design and build their own storytellers. Interacting with SAGE empowers children to explore their own identity as well as how they wish to present themselves to others.

The authorable virtual peer casts children in the role of technologists by asking them to program the behaviors of a virtual character. When creating these interactions for the virtual peer, children are constructing their own understanding of the interaction and able to observe the effects of what they program on social interaction. In this way we are providing a scaffold to these social interactions. This process of authoring virtual peers has its roots in the *constructionist* tradition – the use of technology as 'objects to think with' (Harel and Papert, 1991), whereby children learn concepts such as geometry by programming robotic turtles to walk in circles, or learn about physics by building machines with levers and gears. However, while research in this tradition has concentrated on the learning of math and science, in our own work, we are extending the constructionist paradigm to learning about language and social interaction through building communicating virtual humans.

8.7 Virtual Peer Methodology

The methodology we use to design our virtual peers informs both our understanding of children and the design of our systems. The design of our virtual peers is informed by first carefully studying human behavior. Thus, for the PAT project, first we want to know how the collaborative storytelling behaviors of children with ASD differ from our model of typically developing children's collaborative storytelling. For example, do children with ASD use storytelling roles? What speech acts and turn-taking behaviors do they use?

In this context we are conducting a study to carefully observe and analyze the collaboration skills, nonverbal behavior, and storytelling roles used by children with ASD during an interactive narrative task. We elicit collaborative storytelling from children, videotape children as they tell stories, and then analyze the data. Our analysis is focusing on collaborative speech and turn-taking behaviors (Wang and Cassell, 2003) based on our model of typically developing children, use of decontextualized language (Ryokai *et al.*, 2003), and uses of social skills such as sharing ideas, complimenting others, and recommending changes nicely (Webb *et al.*, 2004). From this data we create a formal model of these collaborative storytelling behaviors in children with ASD. Comparing collaborative storytelling in children with ASD to an existing model of collaborative storytelling in typically developing children (Wang and Cassell, 2003) reveals what needs to be made explicit in the subsequent computer intervention.

As we build the interfaces for our system, we use an iterative design process that relies on prototyping a system and then continuing to revise the design by having children with ASD interact with the system. This allows us to design an interface that is maximally intuitive to the child, and maximally successful.

Finally, we will evaluate the system to examine how children with ASD use the system in each of the modes of control, author, and interact, as well as to measure effects of the intervention. Our evaluation of the treatment will employ a within-subjects design, so that we can account for the individual differences among children with ASD, and a between-subjects design to compare interactions with the virtual peer to: (a) the child's baseline treatment; and (b) interactions with typically developing peers. Within these comparisons, we will investigate whether interactions with the virtual peer improve communication and reciprocal social interaction skills. A pre-/post-test design will specifically target communication, reciprocal social interaction, and theory of mind skills, as well as transfer of communication skills from conversations with the virtual peer to conversations with others.

For the purposes of this project, we are working primarily with children with high-functioning autism (defined as IQ above 80, including children with Asperger syndrome and PDD-NOS) to maximize opportunities for participation from the children and to allow for optimal feedback from the participants. Future work will extend the use of authorable virtual peers to a broader range of ASD.

8.8 Pilot Studies

Our system and studies are still under development. However, we have conducted two pilot studies to evaluate feasibility and design constraints of using virtual peers to practice social interaction. The goals of the first study's pilot sessions were to observe a child with a social skills disorder interacting with a virtual peer system, and then controlling the virtual peer himself; test authoring task ideas; and gain insight into potential technical design issues of the proposed system. The second study investigated verbal and nonverbal behaviors of interaction with a virtual peer through structured observations of a child with Asperger syndrome.

8.8.1 Pilot Study 1: Task and Technical Evaluation

Our first pilot participant was Tom,[1] a 10-year-old boy with a nonverbal learning disorder. The pilot systems we used included the current Sam virtual peer system and an off-the-shelf development environment for talking heads. As described earlier, the Sam system uses prerecorded story segments to collaboratively tell stories with a child, and a complex Wizard of Oz interface to enable an adult to select Sam's responses. The off-the-shelf development environment creates dialog utterances that are then spoken by an animated character. Unfortunately, this development environment did not allow control over the gestures of the talking head, which were automatically selected.

Tom spent one session telling stories with Sam and then controlling Sam. He then spent five sessions interacting with the development environment. His first development environment task was to modify one of the demos that came with the system, and make it complete a task of his choosing. The demo was a pizza ordering system that first asked a question with three choices for an answer, followed by a question with four answer choices, followed by a yes/no question. Tom typed in new dialog prompts for each question that were spoken by the speech-generation feature of the system, and modified the possible answers from the user. Tom modified the system to have an alien/science fiction theme.

Next, Tom spent two sessions developing a dialog system from scratch. This time we used the voice recording features of the system instead of speech generation. Tom enjoyed using a variety of accents for recording dialog prompts. Tom decided to make a system for his father that told him to remember a phrase, and then asked a series of questions. After Tom created several question nodes, he got to the last node. Instead of simply asking the users to say back what they were told to remember, Tom had the system ask, 'What is the penultimate word of the sentence I asked you to remember?'

In the final two sessions, Tom wrote a creative story for his sister using the development system. His story concerned two children who go into a chicken coop that turns into a spaceship. The chickens turned out to be aliens. The children get hungry, and go into the kitchen and discover gray paste that turns itself into whatever you want. After eating, they command the gray paste to turn into guns to fight the aliens. Tom gave the user the option of deciding what the children in the story would do next, and created two different endings for the user to choose from.

These pilot sessions revealed some important design constraints for work with this population:

---

[1] Names have been changed.

- *Avoid speech recognition.* Speech recognition, with its attendant break-downs, was particularly frustrating for Tom to use.
- *Provide a more structured design environment.* The off-the-shelf development environment, meant for designers of dialog systems, is complex and offers many options that are distracting to the task. For children of this population, a structured sequence of steps for composing utterances facilitates story authoring.
- *Provide flexibility in character design.* The system we used offered several choices of characters. Tom was taken by the ability to choose his character.
- *Enable typing OR speaking dialog segments.* The development toolkit requires designers to type a response for both the speech synthesis and speech recording features. While requiring both for recorded speech is tedious, Tom did indicate that he likes having the flexibility of using either feature.

In general, this pilot indicated the importance of balancing flexibility with structure – allowing the child to design his own personally meaningful stories and characters, while not leaving the task unconstrained. And most importantly, these pilot sessions suggested that controlling and designing a character is an extremely engaging activity, with clear benefits for understanding how social interaction works. At the end of the first session, for example, Tom enthused, 'you can make him say funny things. Plus, normally, you don't get to control people. . .' During a subsequent session, we were struck by Tom's ability to remain focused on the task, his ability to iteratively improve the look and behaviors of his virtual character creation, and his desire to test his creation on his mother, father, sister. . . and anyone who came by the lab. Finally, Tom was clearly quite focused on the full-body behaviors of the virtual peer, and their meaning. At one point, Tom spent considerable time discussing with us whether Sam was a boy or a girl, and as part of his discussion, jumped to his feet and mimicked for us the nonverbal behaviors that the virtual peer demonstrated.

8.8.2 Pilot Study 2: Structured Observation of Virtual Peer Interactions

Our second pilot participant was Mary, an 8-year-old girl attending a school for children with ASD. This study focused on characterizing Mary's interactions with a virtual peer through structured observations of a single session. After the experimenter introduced Mary to Sam, Mary and Sam told two collaborative stories together where Mary and Sam took turns adding to the story, Mary initiated one story with Sam, and then Mary requested that Sam continue telling stories for two stories. We transcribed the session and coded Mary's speech for types of collaborative speech acts, and reciprocal social nonverbal behaviors including eye gaze, play gestures with the toys, and head nods. Our goal is to set up a coding scheme that allows us to compare the behavior of children with ASD to our model of collaborative storytelling for typically developing children, and to test that coding scheme on one child with ASD. Behaviors that are different from our model suggest the kinds of interactions the virtual peer intervention can target.

Our model of collaborative storytelling in typically developing children consists of three elements – the roles of collaborative storytellers, their speech acts, and their turn-taking behaviors – and is summarized in Table 8.1 From this model, we focused on the specific speech acts Mary used, assigning one code to each of Mary's turns, and her eye gaze, gestures with the physical toys, and head nods. We then looked at co-occurrences of speech acts with the different nonverbal behaviors. Our codes are summarized in Table 8.2.

Mary engaged with Sam with notable enthusiasm, exclaiming after Sam spoke for the first time, 'It interacts to us!' This is in stark contrast to interactions with her peers which are marked by avoidance of social groups. Her speech acts, summarized in Table 8.3, were mainly collaborator-elaborate and response-Sam, demonstrating her ability to, and interest in, listening and responding to Sam. In addition, when Sam asked her to tell a story, she facilitated her own story. However, notably missing from her interactions are speech acts including role-playing as a co-author, and suggesting, directing, questioning, or acknowledging as a facilitator, collaborator, author, or critic.

When Mary engaged in a similar storytelling task with another child with autism, she interacted in a manner actually quite similar to her interactions with Sam. The children seemed interested in collaborating with each other, and were able to facilitate and elaborate story segments. Their collaborations were locally contingent, building on each other's utterances. For example, their interaction began with one child introducing one of the girl dolls as herself and another as Mary. Mary responded to her by disagreeing and suggesting an alternate assignment of the characters. This interaction demonstrates that the two children are able to attend to one another's pretend behaviors. However, the two children were less able to collaborate on the construction of a narrative structure together. For example, while they talked about Build-a-Bear in their story, they were not able to fully develop a narrative about Build-a-Bear. Other speech acts, such as 'direct' to propose a storyline about Build-a-Bear, could have been used to construct a narrative goal. Using the technology to elicit different collaborative speech acts will strengthen the potential of a virtual peer intervention and the children's interactions with each other. Role-playing enables children to practice imaginative play, while suggesting, directing, questioning, and acknowledging are all reciprocal social interaction speech acts.

Table 8.1 Taxonomy of children's collaborative speech acts

Roles	Speech act	Speaker	Function	Turn-taking behaviors
Critics and authors	Suggest	Critic	To suggest an event or idea to the story	Eye gaze toward author, author may use paralanguage drawls and socio-centric sequences like 'uhh'
	Correct	Critic	To correct what's been said	Eye gaze toward author
	Question	Both	To seek clarification or missing information	Eye gaze toward other, lack of backchannel feedback like head nods, increased body motion, author stops gesturing
	Answer	Both	To clarify or supply missing information	Eye gaze toward other, rising pitch, question syntax, author stops gesturing
	Acknowledge	Author	To acknowledge a suggestion or correction	Eye gaze toward critic, backchannel feedback like 'mm-hmm', author stops gesturing
Facilitator and collaborator	Direct	Facilitator	To suggest storylines and designate roles	Eye gaze toward collaborator, socio-centric sequences like 'OK', both stop gesturing
	Acknowledge	Collaborator	To acknowledge a role designation or storyline suggestion	Eye gaze toward facilitator, backchannel feedback like head nods, both stop gesturing
	Elaborate	Both	To narrate following suggested script	Eye gaze toward other, may start gesturing
Co-authors	Role-play	Both	Play the role of characters in the story	Eye gaze toward action, prosody of in-character voice, gesture with prop
	Simultaneous turns	Both	Compete for turn	

Table 8.2 Collaboration code scheme

Speech acts

    Author-Acknowledge
    Author-Answer
    Author-Question
    Critic-Answer
    Critic-Question
    Critic-Correct
    Facilitator-Elaborate
    Facilitator-Direct
    Collaborator-Elaborate
    Collaborator-Acknowledge
    Coauthor-SimultaneousTurn
    Coauthor-RolePlay
    Nonstory-Comment
    Response-Sam

Eye gaze
    EGToSam
    EGToPhysicalToys
    EGToVirtualToys
    EGToHuman
    EGAway

Gestures
    Non-narrative
      Hold
      Move
      Examine
    Narrative
      ChildCharacterSpeak
      ChildStoryNarration
      SamCharacterSpeak
      SamStoryNarration
Head nods

Mary's eye gaze and play gestures further illustrate her engagement with Sam. Our model of collaborative storytelling describes elaboration speech acts as characterized by 'eye gaze towards the other' and 'may start gesturing.' When Mary used these speech acts, her gaze moved back and forth between Sam and the physical toys, and she incorporated gestures with the toys into her stories, as illustrated in Table 8.4. Likewise, during Sam stories, Mary's gaze moved back and forth between Sam and the

Table 8.3 Total count of speech acts performed by Mary

Speech act	Count
Non-story comment	3
Response-Sam	7
Collaborator	
Elaborate	7
Acknowledge	0
Facilitator	
Elaborate	1
Direct	0
Author	
Acknowledge	0
Answer	0
Question	0
Critic	
Answer	0
Question	0
Correct	0
Suggest	0
Co-author	
Simultaneous turn	0
Role play	0

Table 8.4 Summary of eye gaze, gestures and head nods co-occurring with Mary's speech acts

	Non-story comment	Response-Sam	Collaborator-elaborate	Facilitator-elaborate
Eye gaze				
To Physical Toys	1	1	6	5
Away	1			
To Sam	2	7	10	5
Gesture				
Non-narrative				
Hold	1	4		1
Move		2		
Examine	2		1	
Narrative				
Child Story Narration			4	1
Sam Story Narration			1	
Head nod		1		

Table 8.5 *Total count of eye gaze and gesture co-occuring with Sam's story narrations*

	Count
Gesture	
Non-narrative	
Hold	9
Move	5
Examine	8
Narrative	
Child Character Speak	
Child Story Narration	
Sam Character Speak	6
Sam Story Narration	1
Eye Gaze	
To Physical Toys	22
To Virtual Toys	1
To Human	
Away	
To Sam	21

physical toys, which she was using to act out the story that Sam was telling, as illustrated in Table 8.5.

Our results show that Mary engaged with the virtual peer and practiced collaborative behaviors that she also uses in interactions with her real peers. We hypothesize that the virtual peer authoring tools will enable children with autism to practice and construct reciprocal social interactions, and will encourage them to experiment with skills that they are not able to easily use with real peers. The personalizability of Sam is maximized by a design whereby each child is first tested in conjunction with a real peer, so that Sam can then be tuned to work with the individual deficits manifested by that child.

8.9 Current Status and Future Directions

We are currently designing and developing new *control* and *build* interfaces for our authorable virtual peer system as described above. In addition, we are continuing to collect pilot data on interactions between pairs of children with ASD as well as children with ASD interacting with our current virtual peer, Sam. These studies will build on the knowledge gathered in our early pilot studies described above and will further inform the design of our system.

In addition to developing new interfaces for children to control and author virtual peers, this project has also led us to create a new, flexible system for developing embodied conversational agents (the technology underlying virtual peers). This system will provide the framework for coordinating gestures and speech that comprise a virtual peer's stories.

If the authorable virtual peer is successful with high-functioning children with ASD, we hope to extend the work to support individuals in a broader range of the autism spectrum. In addition, we will apply cognitive neuroscience techniques, including cognitive psychology, neuroimaging, and neurophysiology, to understand the mechanisms underlying change in response to interactions with the authorable virtual peer.

8.10 Implications for Designers, Researchers, and Policymakers

Our research holds implications for designers, researchers, and policymakers. By employing new methods in artificial intelligence and computer graphics for designing and implementing autonomous virtual characters, we offer designers an improved method for using full-body virtual characters in their systems. In addition, by creating new kinds of interfaces that are suitable for young children, for children with disabilities, and perhaps in the future for other nonliterate populations, we are advancing the study of human–computer interaction.

Our studies also add to the understanding of ASD itself and to the design of interventions for children with ASD. More generally, we offer new directions for the use of technology to facilitate communication and learning for children with disabilities.

Finally, our research supports the importance of both computers and social skills instruction in the lives of children with ASD. We thus offer support to education policy reform that seeks to provide improved access to these resources for children with ASD and related disorders.

8.11 Conclusion

In this chapter we have discussed the motivation, design, and implementation of PAT (Play and Tell), an authorable virtual peer for children with ASD. Based on research on the triad of impairments that characterize autism spectrum disorder, and how these impairments may be linked to a deficit in theory of mind, we have discussed a set of key features that we believe are important to interventions for children with ASD: (1) a peer context, rather than a virtual parent or teacher, so that children can practice peer social interaction skills; (2) a personally meaningful storytelling task for practicing imagination and language; (3) a system that is authorable by the child, to allow the child to literally build appropriate social skills from the ground up.

These features are instantiated in an authorable, life-sized, full-body virtual peer that uses a peer context and collaborative storytelling task to give children with ASD a space to play with social interaction, communication, and imaginative play behaviors. Children interact with the virtual peer by telling stories with the system, control the virtual peer by selecting predefined responses, and author the virtual peer by creating their own content. Our evaluation of PAT will focus on the effects of the interactions on children's social skills both within a storytelling task and in transfer to other contexts, such as their home.

References

Adams, L., Gouvousis, A., VanLue, M. and Waldron, C. (2004) Social story intervention: improving communication skills in a child with an autism spectrum disorder. *Focus on Autism and Other Developmental Disabilities* **19**(2), 87–94.

Animated Speech Corporation (2002) *Team Up with Timo* San Francisco, CA.

Animated Speech Corporation, (2005) *Team Up with Timo* San Francisco, CA.

ASA (2005) Autism Society of America, `www.autism-society.org`.

Baker, J. (2001) *The Social Skills Picture Book*. Future Horizons, Inc. Arlington, TX.

Baron-Cohen, S. (1995) *Mindblindness: An Essay on Autism and Theory of Mind*. MIT Press, Cambridge, MA.

Barry L.M. and Burlew, S.B. (2004) Using social stories to teach choice and play skills to children with autism. *Focus on Autism and Other Developmental Disabilities* **19**(1), 45–51.

Bickmore, T. and Cassell, J. (2005) Social Dialogue with Embodied Conversational Agents. In Kuppevelt J.V. Dybkjaer L. Bernsen N. (eds.), *Natural, Intelligent and Effective Interaction with Multimodal Dialogue Systems*, Kluwer Academic, New York.

Bosseler, A. and Massaro, D.W. (2003) Development and evaluation of a computer-animated tutor for vocabulary and language learning in children with autism. *Journal of Autism and Developmental Disorders* **33**(6), 653–672.

Brill, M.T. (2001) *Keys to Parenting the Child with Autism*, Barron's Educational Series, Inc., Hauppauge, NJ, 2nd edn.

Cameron, C.A. and Wang, M. (1999) Frog, where are you? Children's narrative expression over the telephone. *Discourse Processes* **28**(3), 217–236.

Capps, L., Losh, M. and Thurber, C. (2000) The frog ate the bug and made his mouth sad: narrative competence in children with autism. *Journal of Abnormal Child Psychology* **28**(2), 193–204.

Cassell, J. (2002) We have these rules inside: the effects of exercising voice in a children's online forum in Calvert S.L., Jordan A.B., Cocking R.R. (eds.), *Children in the Digital Age: The Role of Entertainment Technologies in Children's Development*, Praeger Press, New York, 123–144.

Cassell, J. (2004) Towards a model of technology and literacy development: story listening systems. *Journal of Applied Developmental Psychology* **25**(1).

Charman, T. (2002) The prevalence of autism spectrum disorders: recent evidence and future challenges. *European Child and Adolescent Psychiatry* **11**, 249–256.

Cole, R., van Vuuren, S., & Pellom B. et al. (2003) Perceptive Animated Interfaces: First Steps Toward a New Paradigm for Human Computer Interaction. *IEEE: Special Issue – Multimodal Human Computer Interface.*

Dautenhahn, K. and Weery, I. (2004) Towards interactive robots in autism therapy. *Pragmatics Cognition* **12**(1), 1–35.

Dautenhahn, K., Werry, I., & Rae J. et al. (2002) Robotic playmates: analysing interactive competencies of children with autism playing with a mobile robot In Dautenhahn K., Bond A., Canamero L., Edmonds B., (eds.), *Socially Intelligent Agents – Creating Relationships with Computers and Robots*, Kluwer Academic Publishers.

Davis, M., Dautenhahn, K., Nehaniv, C. and Powell, S. (2004) Towards an interactive system facilitating therapeutic narrative elicitation in autism, *Paper presented at the Third International Conference on Narrative and Interactive Learning Environments (NILE 2004), August 10–13*, Edinburgh, Scotland.

Faherty, C. (2000) *Asperger's. What Does it Mean to Me?* Future Horizons, Inc., Arlington, TX.

Ghaziuddin, M. and Mountain-Kimchi, K. (2004) Defining the intellectual profile of Asperger syndrome: comparison with high-functioning autism. *Journal of Autism and Developmental Disorders* **34**(3), 279–284.

Gratch, J. (2000) Emile: marshalling passions in training and education, *Paper presented at the 4th International Conference on Autonomous Agents,* Barcelona, Spain.

Gray, C. (1994a) *Comic Strip Conversations: Colorful, illustrated interactions with students with autism and related disorders,* Furture Horizons, Inc., Arlington, TX.

Gray, C. (1994b) *The New Social Story Book,* Future Horizons, Inc., Arlington, TX.

Haddon, M. (2003) *The Curious Incident of the Dog at Night-time.* Vintage Books, New York.

Harel, I. and Papert, S. (1991) *Constructionism: Research Reports and Essays 1985–1990.* Ablex Publishing Corp., Norwood, NJ.

Hart, M. (2005) Autism/Excel Study, *Paper presented at ASSETS 2005, the Seventh* International ACM SIGACCESS Conference on Computers and Accessibility, Baltimore, MD.

Hayes, G.R., & Kientz, J.A., et al. (2004) *Designing Capture Applications to Support the Education of Children with Autism.* Paper presented at UbiComp.

Jackson, D.A., Jackson, N.F., & Bennett M.L. et al. (1991) *Learning to Get Along: Social Effectiveness Training for People with Developmental Disabilities* Research Press, Champaign, IL.

Johnson, D.J. and Carlisle J.F. (1996) A study of handwriting in written stories of normal and learning disabled children. *Reading and Writing: Interdisciplinary Journal* 8, 45–59.

Jones, E.A. and Carr, E.G. (2004) Joint Attention in Children with Autism: Theory and Intervention. *Focus on Autism and Other Developmental Disabilities* 19(1), 13–26.

Kerr, S.J., Neale, H.R. and Cobb, S.V.G. (2002) Virtual environments for social skills training: the importance of scaffolding in practice. *Paper presented at the Assets, July* 8–10. Edinburgh, Scotland.

LeGoff, D.B. (2004) Use of LEGO as a therapeutic medium for improving social competence. *Journal of Autism and Developmental Disorders* 34(5), 557–571.

Lester, J.C., Converse, S.A., & Kahler S.E. et al. (1997) The persona effect: affective impact of animated pedagogical agents, *Paper presented at the CHI 97,* Atlanta, GA.

Little, L.(1999) The misunderstood child: the child with a nonverbal learning disorder *Journal of the Society of Pediatric Nurses* 4(3), 113–121.

Little, L. (2003) Maternal perceptions of the importance of needs and resources for children with Asperger syndrome and nonverbal learning disorders. *Focus on Autism and Other Developmental Disabilities* **18**(4), 257–266.

Loveland, K.A., McEvoy, R.E. and Tunali B. (1990) Narrative story telling in autism and Down's syndrome. *British Journal of Developmental Psychology* **8**, 9–23.

McGinnis, E. and Goldstein, A.P. (1984) *Skillstreaming the Elementary School Child,* Research Press Company, Champaign, IL.

McGinnis, E. and Goldstein, A.P. (1990) *Skillstreaming in Early Childhood,* Research Press Company, Champaign, IL.

Michaud, F. and Theberge-Turmel, C. (2002) Mobile robotic toys and autism in Dautenhahn K., Bond A.H., Canamero L., Edmonds B., (eds.), *Socially Intelligent Agents: Creating Relationships with Computers and Robots,* Kluwer Publishersm, 125–132.

NAS (2005) National Autistic Society, `http://www.nas.org.uk`.

Parsons, S., Mitchell, P. and Leonard, A. (2004) The use and understanding of virtual environments by adolescents with autistic spectrum disorders. *Journal of Autism and Developmental Disorders* **34**(4), 449–466.

Paul, R., Miles, S., Cicchetti D. et al. (2004) Adaptive behavior in autism and pervasive developmental disorder-not otherwise specified: microanalysis of scores on the vineland adaptive behavior scales. *Journal of Autism and Developmental Disorders* **34**(2), 223–228.

Preece, A. (1992) Collaborators and critics: the nature and effects of peer interaction on children's conversational narratives. *Journal of Narrative Life Histories* **2**(3), 277–292.

Prior, M. (2003) Is there an increase in the prevalence of autism spectrum disorders? *Journal of Paediatric Child Health* **39**, 81–81.

Robins, B., Dickerson, P., Stribling P. and Dautenhahn, K. (2004) Robot-mediated joint attention in children with autism: a case study in robot–human interaction. *Interaction Studies* **5**(2), 161–198.

Ryokai, K., Vaucelle, C., & Cassell, J. (2003) Virtual peers as partners in storytelling and literacy learning. *Journal of Computer Assisted Learning* **19**, 195–208.

Sawyer, R.K. (2002) Improvisation and narrative. *Narrative Inquiries* **12**(2), 319–349.

Shneiderman, B. (2000) Universal usability. *Communications of the ACM* **43**(5), 85–91.

Si, M., Marsella, S. and Pynadath, D. (2005) Thespian: using multi-agent fitting to craft interactive drama, *Paper presented at the International Conference on Autonomous Agents and Multi Agent Systems.*

Snow, C.E. (1983) Literacy and language: relationships during the preschool years, *Harvard Education Review* **53**(2), 165–189.

Tager-Flusberg, H. (1995) 'Once Upon a Ribbit': stories narrated by autistic children. *British Journal of Developmental Psychology* **13**, 45–59.

Tager-Flusberg, H. (2000) Language and understanding minds: connections in autism in Baron-Cohen S., Tager-Flusberg H., Cohen D.J. (eds.), *Understanding Other Minds: Perspectives from Developmental Cognitive Neuroscience,* Oxford University Press, Oxford, 2nd edn.

Tickle-Degnen, L. and Rosenthal, R. (1990) The nature of rapport and its nonverbal correlates. *Psychological Inquiries* **1**(4), 285–293.

Umaschi-Bers, M. and Cassell, J. (2000) Children as Designers of Interactive Storytellers: "Let me tell you a story about myself . . . ." In K. Dautenhahn (Ed.), *Human Cognition and Social Agent Technology.* John Benjamins, The Hague, pp. 61–85.

Vernon, D.S., Schumaker, J.B. and Deshler, D.D. (1996) *The SCORE Skills: Social Skills for Cooperative Groups,* Edge Enterprises, Inc., Lawrence, KA, 2nd edn.

Wang, A. and Cassell, J. (2003) Co-authoring, corroborating, criticizing: collaborative storytelling between virtual and real children. *Paper presented at the Workshop of Educational Agents: More than Virtual Tutors,* Vienna, Austria.

Webb, B.J., Miller, S.P., Pierce T.B. et al. (2004) Effects of social skill instruction for high-functioning adolescents with austism spectrum disorders. *Focus on Autism and Other Developmental Disabilities* **19**(1), 53–62.

Wise, B., Cole, R., Vuuren, S.v., et al. (in press). Learning to read with a virtual tutor: foundations to literacy In *Interactive Literacy Education: Facilitating literacy learning environments through technology,* C. Kinzer and L. Verhoeven (eds). Lawrence Erlbaum Associates, Mahway, NJ.

Evidence-Based Computer-Assisted Instruction for Autism Spectrum Disorders

9

Christina Whalen[a], Lars Lidén[a], Brooke Ingersoll[b], and Sven Lidén[a]

[a] TeachTown, Inc.
[b] Department of Psychology, Lewis and Clark College, USA

Summary

Current trends in treatment and education for children focus on the importance of using evidence-based practices (e.g. Reichart, 2001). Because of the numerous treatment and education options available for children with autism, many of which are not supported by research, the use of evidence-based practices is particularly important (Perry and Condillac, 2003) and many schools are mandating these practices. With recent advances in computer technology, there has been a strong interest in the use of computer-assisted instruction (CAI) in the treatment and education of children (Parkin, 2006). Due to the unique characteristics and learning styles of children with autism, the interest and need for CAI is especially strong (e.g. Goldsmith and LeBlanc, 2004). In this chapter, evidence-based practices for autism, particularly applied behavior analysis (ABA), will be reviewed as well as the research on technology and computers for this population. The importance of developing evidence-based technology for children with autism and other special needs will be discussed along with the implications for designers and researchers.

9.1 Introduction

9.1.1 Autism Spectrum Disorders

Autism spectrum disorder (ASD) is a heterogeneous class of disorders that is manifested quite differently in each child; however, there are strong and consistent diagnostic commonalities (National Research Council, 2001). ASD includes autism, pervasive developmental disorder not-otherwise specified, Asperger's disorder or syndrome, and childhood disintegrative disorder. Rett's syndrome is also often included as an ASD, however, due to its special characteristics and unique needs, it will not be considered as an ASD in this chapter.

ASD is present early in development (possibly at birth) and has lifelong effects on the child's behavior and learning, although many researchers report that autistic behavior is most pronounced between 2 and 5 years (Wing, 2001). ASD is characterized by profound deficits in communication, social interaction, and restricted interests and repetitive behaviors (APA, 2000). Only 50% of individuals with autism develop functional speech, and those who do, exhibit deficits in pragmatic skills such as inappropriate use of speech, use of language as a means rather than an end, disregard for the audience, and poor prosody (Rogers and Pennington, 1991). In addition, autistic language is often characterized by unusual features such as echolalia (the nonfunctional repetition of previously heard speech), pronomial reversal, jargon, and idiosyncratic speech (APA, 2000). The pragmatic deficits also extend to nonverbal communicative behavior. Joint attention, the coordination or sharing of attention with a social partner regarding an object or event, is greatly impaired in autistic children (i.e. Loveland and Landry, 1986; McArthur and Adamson, 1996), as is the use of descriptive gestures (Bartak *et al.*, 1975).

Individuals with autism also exhibit significant difficulty with the development of social interaction. They may seem to be indifferent to others or may actively avoid contact. Some individuals actively seek out interactions, but do so in odd or inappropriate ways (Wing and Gould, 1979). Studies have indicated that children with autism are less likely to initiate play (Hauck *et al.*, 1995; Lord and Magill-Evans, 1995; Sigman and Ruskin, 1999) and accept peer invitations to play (Sigman and Ruskin, 1999) than children with developmental delays. In addition, they have difficulty understanding the intentions (Phillips *et al.*, 1998) and mental states of others (Baron-Cohen *et al.*, 1985).

Finally, individuals with autism often express unusual interests. Interests are typically unusual in their focus (e.g. calendar dates, bus schedules) or degree. In addition, many individuals with autism exhibit repetitive motor mannerisms involving the hands (e.g. hand flapping or posturing) or entire body (e.g. rocking, toe walking; Lewis and Bodfish, 1998). Many individuals with autism are also reported to be over- or under-responsive to sensory stimulation (Rogers *et al.*, 2003). Finally, autism is characterized by compulsions and insistence on sameness (Lewis and Bodfish, 1998). These characteristics may lead to behavior problems (i.e. tantrums) and typically interfere with the development of more appropriate behaviors.

What was once considered a rare disorder, 4.5 out of 10 000 births (Lotter, 1966), is now considered a national epidemic by many experts, now that ASD is affecting between 34 (Centers for Disease Control and Prevention, 2002) to 60 (Fombonne, 2003) out of 10 000 births. This means that approximately 425 000 children under the age of 18 have a diagnosis of ASD with about 114 000 under the age of 5 years in the USA (Fombonne, 2003). The numbers have increased over the past 40 years by three to four times and the reasons for this alarming increase have scientists baffled. Although there is no consensus, several possible reasons have been posited in the literature about this increase in ASD diagnoses, including: (a) widening of the definition of ASD, (b) earlier and better diagnosis, and (c) a real increase in the disorder (Wing, 2001). If there has, in fact, been a substantial increase in the number of cases of ASD, it is unclear why this might be happening.

Although it was originally believed that parent behavior was the primary cause of autism (Bettleheim, 1967), researchers now agree that the disorder relates more to biological, genetic, and possibly environmental factors. As early as 1971, scientists began to discuss autism as an organic brain disorder (Rutter and Bartak, 1971). Since then, many neuropsychiatric (e.g. Zwaigenbaum *et al.*, 2002) and genetic (e.g. Folstein and Rutter, 1977; Yonan *et al.*, 2003) studies have supported that ASD is caused by biological factors. Less consensus is available on potential environmental triggers. Regardless of the reasons for the increase in this disorder, few would argue that intervention (particularly early intervention) is essential for the future success of these children.

9.1.2 Evidence-Based Treatments

Evidence-based or scientifically supported practices are important for all children but they are especially important for ASD due to the large number of options available and the controversies over these treatment options (Perry and Condillac, 2003). 'Evidence-based practices' can be described as 'the integration of best research evidence with clinical expertise and [client] values' (Sackett *et al.*, 2000). It is difficult for parents and even teachers and clinicians to sort through these treatment options and to critically evaluate which practices are appropriate. In fact, although many new interventions are promising, they often lack the scientific integrity that is necessary and sometimes may cause more harm than good (Perry and Condillac, 2003). Behavioral interventions are the best studied and empirically validated interventions for children with autism to date (Sulzer-Azaroff and Mayer, 1991). These interventions do not cure the disorder, however they can significantly improve children's functioning and long-term outcomes and are currently considered the most effective treatment for children with autism (National Research Council, 2001). Using programs based on the principles of applied behavior analysis (ABA), researchers have shown that they can often improve the quality of life for many children with autism and help them integrate more successfully into society.

The use of behavioral interventions in the treatment of autism began in the early 1960s (e.g. Ferster and Demyer, 1961, 1962). Since that time, a wide variety of behavioral interventions have been developed for use with children with autism and other developmental disorders. These interventions range from very structured, adult-directed approaches to less structured, child-directed approaches. All behavioral interventions are based on learning theory and thus, share the assumption that new appropriate skills can be taught through the systematic use of reinforcement and specific teaching procedures such as prompting, fading, shaping, and chaining.

Discrete trial training (DTT) is most closely aligned with the original learning literature and is most often associated with Ivar Lovaas, who was the first to develop a systematic, comprehensive curriculum for children with autism using this teaching approach. Although there are multiple discrete trial programs in use around the country, all structured techniques share the following elements. The learning environment is highly structured and controlled by the therapist, usually with the child and therapist facing each other in child-sized chairs. The use of structure and reduction of distraction is thought to facilitate learning because children with autism have difficulty learning in the natural environment. New skills are taught in a logical sequence building on previously learned skills. The concepts to be taught are broken down into discrete sub-skills which are then targeted for instruction. Each instructional session consists of a series of discrete trials. A discrete trial involves a four-step sequence: (1) instructional cue, (2) child response, (3) consequence (a positive reinforcer), and (4) pause. Shaping is used such that the child must produce a response that is equal to or better than the child's previous response in order to get the reinforcement. In addition, a variety of prompts are used to help the child produce the target response. Data is collected to monitor the child's progress and to help determine when a preset criterion has been reached.

Structured approaches have been shown to produce a wide variety of gains in children with autism (e.g. Lovaas, 1987) and accelerated skill acquisition (Miranda-Linne and Melin, 1992). In 1987, Ivar Lovaas reported that 47% of preschool-aged children with autism who had received intensive (40 hours per week) DTT instruction for at least 2 years achieved normal intellectual and educational functioning. In contrast, only 2% of the children who received less intensive intervention (10 hours per week) made similar gains (Lovaas, 1987). Although this study has been criticized for several methodological flaws (e.g. lack of random assignment, use of only verbal subjects; Mesibov, 1993), it highlights the potential benefit of structured behavioral techniques in the instruction of children with autism. A more recent, well-controlled study examining the effectiveness of discrete trial training found similar, yet much less dramatic results (Smith *et al.*, 2000). Another recent controlled study showed that when DTT was compared with eclectic treatment approaches (e.g. traditional school-based instruction), DTT was more effective (Eikeseth *et al.*, 2002). Despite the success of DTT, the research is not conclusive and has not been sufficiently replicated. In fact, eight out of ten single-subject studies which compared structured teaching such as DTT with more naturalistic interventions showed that naturalistic teaching for language is not only more effective but also results in more positive affect from the parents than during DTT (Delprato, 2001). Basically, the jury is still out as to which type of intervention is more effective. Many researchers and clinicians today are advocating for blended approaches or individualizing treatment to meet the unique needs of each child.

Naturalistic behavioral interventions, such as pivotal response training (PRT; Koegel *et al.*, 1987, 1989) and incidental teaching (e.g. McGee *et al.*, 1999) have been used to teach skills in a less structured environment with the goal of increasing the generalization of new skills and the children's motivation to perform the behaviors being taught. For example, PRT works to increase motivation by including components such as child choice, turn-taking, reinforcing attempts, and interspersing maintenance tasks. PRT and other naturalistic ABA approaches have been shown to be effective for increasing language (Koegel *et al.*, 2001), play (Stahmer, 1995), imitation (Ingersoll and Schreibman, 2006), social skills (Pierce and Schreibman, 1995), and joint attention (Whalen and Schreibman, 2003) in children with autism and other developmental disorders. Generalization is almost always shown in these studies, and in addition, some of these studies have even shown collateral effects of treatment to untargeted behaviors (e.g. Pierce and Schreibman, 1995; Whalen *et al.*, 2006b). However, no large-scale clinical trials have been done on the efficacy of more naturalistic ABA approaches and it is still not clear what the best type of treatment is for children with autism. Many researchers now advocate for individualization of treatment (i.e. identifying child characteristics which may predict success in a particular type of treatment).

Although there is some debate on the best ABA teaching method for young children with autism, there is a strong consensus across researchers and practitioners alike that intensity and timing (i.e. early intervention) of services is crucial. The National Research Council (2001) recommends a minimum of 25 hours per week of intensive intervention year round for children with autism, beginning as soon as diagnosis is made. This level of intensity often makes the acquisition of appropriate services prohibitive to many families due to lack of financial resources and available professionals, highlighting the need for novel service delivery models.

There has been an evolving interest in incorporating visual supports in the provision of behaviorally based treatments. Visual supports have some intrinsic appeal as an instructional tool for this population. Although not well documented in the literature, researchers and clinicians have often suggested that children with autism are visual learners and excel in treatment modalities that rely on visual stimuli (e.g. Charlop and Milstein, 1989; Campbell *et al.*, 1995; Schreibman *et al.*, 2000). For example, picture schedules which depict up-coming events or present the individual steps in a complex chain of behaviors have been shown to help individuals with autism and other severe disabilities transition to new activities and build self-help skills (e.g. Wacker and Berg, 1983; Pierce and Schreibman, 1994). Picture or iconic systems have also been used to teach functional communication to children with autism who fail to acquire verbal language. The Picture Exchange Communication System (PECS), the most widely used iconic system for nonverbal children (Bondy and Frost, 1994), has been shown to be easier to acquire than sign language (Anderson, 2002) and leads to increases in vocal speech (Charlop-Christy *et al.*, 2002). The use of video has also been found to be very effective for teaching children with autism. Video modeling, the most well researched form of video instruction, presents target behaviors in video format and has been shown to improve various skills in individuals with autism (e.g. Charlop-Christy *et al.*, 2000). Research has suggested that video modeling promotes faster acquisition and better generalization of new behaviors than live modeling (Charlop-Christy *et al.*, 2000).

9.1.3 **Using Computers for Intervention**

Research that has examined the effectiveness of CAI for teaching children with autism and other developmental disorders has been promising (e.g. Moore and Calvert, 2000; Bernard-Opitz *et al.*, 2001; Williams *et al.*, 2002; Coleman-Martin *et al.*, 2005). For example, recent findings demonstrated efficacy in teaching receptive language, social understanding, and cognitive skills to children with autism and other developmental disabilities using a prototype of the TeachTown software program (see below) (Whalen *et al.*, 2006a). Computerized techniques have also been shown to be effective for teaching social understanding to children with autism via computerized social stories (Bernard-Opitz *et al.*, 2001). In both of these studies, concepts taught on the computer generalized to novel computer-presented stimuli.

There has also been some evidence that information learned during CAI generalizes to the natural environment. For example, Bosseler and Massaro (2003) developed and assessed a computer-animated tutor to teach vocabulary and grammar to eight children with autism. Their program included receptive and expressive language activities. This program was successful in teaching language to all participants and the children generalized their use of skills to receptive and expressive labeling tasks presented by a teacher not present during computer instruction. In another study, inappropriate verbalizations were decreased and functional communication was increased using a computerized intervention and these skills generalized to a classroom environment (Hetzroni and Tannous, 2004). Similarly, Hetzroni and Shalem (2005) found that a computer-presented fading procedure was effective for teaching children with autism to recognize sight words. For most children, this skill generalized to the natural environment. However, one study examined the effect of teaching two children with autism to identify object labels using a DTT computer program. One child was able to generalize these skills to labeling 3D objects outside of the computer setting, but the other child was not (Schilling *et al.*, 2005).

Research is beginning to emerge which demonstrates that CAI may be more effective for teaching certain skills than direct instruction provided by a trained teacher. For example, Williams *et al.* (2002) compared CAI and teacher implemented instruction for teaching sight word reading to eight children with autism in a cross-over design. The children learned significantly more sight words in the computer condition than the direct instruction condition. In addition, it was found that the children attended significantly more during the CAI condition than direct instruction, suggesting that CAI was more motivating to the children with autism. In a similar study, Moore and Calvert (2000) compared CAI and teacher instruction for teaching basic vocabulary skills. The children in the CAI condition learned significantly more vocabulary words than the children in the direct instruction condition. In addition, the children in the CAI condition attended more and were more motivated than the children in the direction instruction condition. Across children, the amount of time on task was positively correlated to the number of words learned. Increased interest was also observed in a recent study using the *TeachTown: Basics* program (Whalen *et al.*, 2006a).

Taken together, these studies suggest that children with autism are able to learn new skills effectively on the computer. In addition, CAI may be more effective than direct teaching for many children with autism. This finding is consistent with research on video modeling, which has demonstrated that skills taught via video modeling promotes faster acquisition and better generalization of new behaviors than live modeling (Charlop-Christy *et al.*, 2000). Finally, there is some preliminary evidence that many of skills learned via CAI generalize to the natural environment. However, more research on the generalizability of skills taught via computer is necessary.

The majority of research on the use of CAI with children with autism has been conducted using lab-based computer programs that are not, as of yet, commercially available. However, there are a variety of commercially available products on the market that purport to teach new skills, primarily language, reading, and mathematics. Most of these products fall under the umbrella of 'edutainment' meaning that they are developed primarily for entertainment purposes and include learning elements. There are a handful of evidence-based programs that have successfully produced commercial products and continue to do the research that is necessary to support these products. For instance, in one study, *FastForWord* and *Laureate* language products were compared. Both demonstrated efficacy including increased standardized language scores and changes in MLU (mean length of utterance); however there was no difference in outcome between the two products (Gillam *et al.*, 2001). Other companies have successfully helped bridge the gap between research and consumers by creating evidence-based computer programs for reading. One of the most successful and innovative of these products is *Headsprout* which, similar to *FastForWord* and products by *Laureate*, was developed by professional speech, language, and behavioral therapists and researchers. Some of these products have been used clinically for children with autism although most of these products are not grounded in the science of ABA and have not been tested specifically with this population.

Despite the trend for evidence-based products being made for language, reading, and mathematics which are commercially available, there is still a large gap in the number of commercially available products for ASD which are based on rigorous evidence-based practices (e.g. ABA). Two such products, the *Discrete Trial Trainer* and the *PALS* program, use ABA (specifically discrete trial) to teach language and cognitive skills to children with ASD. Although some of these products have received positive reviews and are based on ABA practices (e.g. Butter and Mulick, 2001), limited data are available on their efficacy. There are a small number of programs that address the social deficits in autism including *Social Skills Builder* but more research is also needed on the use of these programs for children with ASD.

9.2 TeachTown and *TeachTown: Basics*
9.2.1 Product Design and Development

TeachTown was conceptualized by the first author, who is a researcher and clinician for children with ASD. Dr Whalen approached two professional software developers and designers from the video game industry, including the second author, an expert in cognitive and neural systems. Five years of research and development went into the design of the company's first product, *TeachTown: Basics*. TeachTown's intervention is based on the principles of applied behavior analysis and incorporates teaching procedures from both discrete trial and pivotal response training. Substantial development time was spent on the interface design and the learning protocol to ensure that the program was based on scientifically validated behavior programs. In addition to experts in behavioral treatment techniques, parents, teachers, and therapists were consulted to ensure that the interface was easy to understand and usable by nonexperts. Both mouse and touchscreen technologies were tested to ensure usability for young children and children with motor difficulties.

The curriculum for the first product, *TeachTown: Basics*, was with review and advice from an advisory board of experts in applied behavior analysis, special education, developmental and clinical psychology, and speech pathology. Learning domains were selected based on previous research and curricula designed for use in direct instruction behavioral programs and from education curricula (e.g. Maurice *et al.*, 1996; Partington and Sundberg, 1998; Leaf and McEachin, 1999; Quill, 2000; Johnson-Martin *et al.*, 2004). The *TeachTown: Basics* program includes a comprehensive curriculum intended to teach a variety of skills across several domains, including vocabulary, matching, sequencing, phonics and early reading, mathematics, time, money, emotion identification, matching feelings to events, face matching, following eye gaze, friendship, safety awareness, personal needs, etc. TeachTown uses a client server architecture which allows new lessons to be added to the curriculum on a continuous basis and allows for regular refinement of existing lessons (similar to a high quality ABA program).

Although computer-based learning has shown promise as a learning tool, an equally important component of the TeachTown program is the inclusion of 'off-computer' learning activities with adults and other children. The *TeachTown: Basics* program includes developmentally appropriate *Generalization Activities* which can be printed out and used with a child. The program recommends that as much time as the child spends on the computer, an equal amount of time should be spent interacting with the child using 'naturalistic' learning activities (either the *Generalization Activities* included in this program or other developmentally appropriate activities). The combination of structured learning and naturalistic teaching is intended to optimize the child's treatment program.

For any ABA intervention to be effective, it is critical that the therapy is matched with the student's developmental level. *TeachTown: Basics* was designed to teach skills to developmental ages 2–7 years. This means that older children can use the program if they are functioning within that developmental range. However, determining what is developmentally appropriate is very difficult for a nonexpert. One of the most important features of the TeachTown program is its ability to individualize the program to suit the needs of each child without requiring external expertise. When creating a new account for a child, the adult facilitator answers a series of

Figure 9.1 Recommended lessons.

questions about the child's abilities. This 'ranking' questionnaire is used to place the child at a developmentally appropriate level within the TeachTown curriculum. The software will then automatically adjust the child's starting point in the curriculum based on the child's performance in initial pre-tests. The curriculum is then continually adjusted based on the child's ongoing performance without requiring further facilitator input (Figure 9.1).

When a new lesson is introduced, a pre-test assessment is administered, consisting of 25 trials with noncontingent reinforcement. If the child demonstrates 80% accuracy or better, they 'pass' the lesson and move on to the next lesson in the curriculum. If they receive less than 80%, they begin training exercises (described below) for the lesson. Following training exercises, the child will take a post-test to determine mastery of those concepts. The TeachTown software tracks and records the child's responses, and produces detailed progress graphs for facilitators (Figure 9.2(a) and (b)).

One of the challenges with this population is that some children can be very talented at memorizing individual exemplars but have difficulty with generalization. For example, a child might learn that an image of a baseball is a 'ball' and an image of a tennis ball is a 'ball', but not be able to generalize to an image of a racquet ball. Getting a sufficient number of exemplars to ensure generalization is particularly challenging in conventional one-on-one therapy, where the therapist needs physical examples or cards with pictures to show the child. Software-driven interventions, such as TeachTown, are able to employ thousands of unique stimuli (i.e. images and animations) to improve generalization. TeachTown facilitates generalization by drawing from a large database of images, and by using distinct sets of images in for testing and training exercises, helping to decrease the probability of rote memorization.

Individualization of treatment is also achieved by grouping lessons into four 'Learning Domains' (receptive language, social understanding, cognitive/academic, and life skills). The receptive language domain teaches an immense amount of vocabulary including nouns, adjectives, pronouns, yes/no, attributes, and verbs. The social understanding domain teaches emotion identification, joint attention, face processing, friendship, and social rules. (This is the most important domain for doing the off-computer

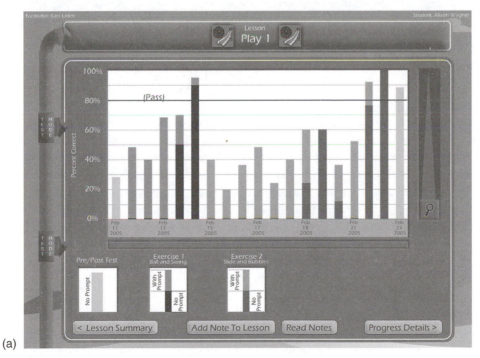

(a)

Figure 9.2 *(a) Lesson progress graph. (b) Domain progress graph.*

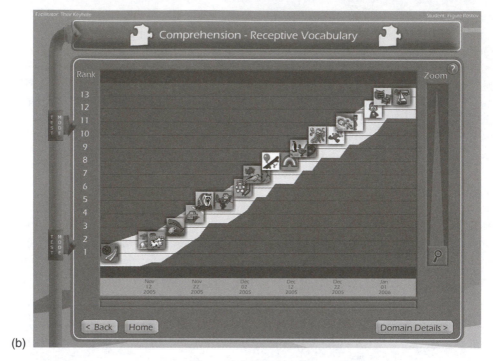

Figure 9.2 (continued)

activities.) The cognitive/academic domain teaches matching, categorization, letters, numbers, phonics, shapes, sight words, opposites, and quantity. The life skills domain teaches body parts, identification of personal needs, time, money, safety, etc. Off-computer activities are also extremely critical for success in this domain. If a child excels in one domain and shows limitations in another domain, the program will focus on the domain where the child needs the most help. This way the program does not cater to the child's deficit but instead, strives for a balance of skills across all four domains.

During a computer teaching session, which can be as short as 8–10 minutes or as long as an hour, the student's home page consists of a small town scene (Figure 9.3). The student can choose which lesson they would like to study by selecting from one of five buildings that highlight when rolled over with the mouse or touched using a touchscreen monitor. Research has demonstrated that this child-choice technique keeps motivation high (Koegel *et al.*, 1987; Dunlap *et al.*, 1994). When the child selects a building, a lesson begins and the child earns reinforcers (i.e. short video games or animations) approximately every three correct responses. A large variety

Figure 9.3 *Student interface.*

of reinforcers consisting of short, professionally designed games are available for the child to select (Figure 9.4). Anecdotal data from early product testing demonstrated high motivation for children to get access to these reinforcers. Although the student can select which building they would like to enter, the software determines the list of lessons that are available in the building based on the student's current developmental needs. Because of the child choice for lessons, the varying ability levels of children, the time chosen by the adult, and the reinforcers chosen by the child, every child's experience with the program is unique and individualized.

Each lesson consists of 15 trials. Lessons include 'maintenance trials,' during which the student is presented with material from previously mastered lessons. Maintenance trials are used to help the student preserve previously learned skills as well as to increase student motivation (Dunlap, 1984; O'Connor *et al.*, 2000). After the trials are completed the student returns to the town where he/she chooses another building, containing a new lesson. The process repeats until the session timer runs out.

Correct answers are systematically reinforced on an intermittent schedule. This has been shown to be the most effective schedule for keeping responses high during

Figure 9.4 Sample reinforcement game.

a task (Neef and Lutz, 2001). For incorrect responses, the correct answer is presented but no negative consequence is given, decreasing the likelihood of a child perseverating on incorrect responses. Data on the child's progress is systematically tracked by the program, and the software adjusts the curriculum and the difficulty of individual exercises dynamically to match the needs of the student.

Difficulty level within a trial is controlled by several layers of prompting (through the fading of distracters on the screen) (Figure 9.5(a) and (b)). When a child is having a particularly difficult time, TeachTown utilizes errorless discrimination training, a discrimination procedure in which the stimuli are introduced in a weak (e.g. faded images) form and gradually strengthened (e.g. saturated images) (Figure 9.5(c)). This has the advantage of gradually introducing distracters at the child's pace to help maximize learning and minimize errors so that the child can learn to discriminate one stimulus from another (e.g. knowing which picture is a cat) (e.g. Pérez-González and Williams, 2002). Effective prompting is achieved by dynamically adjusting the difficulty level of each trial based on the child's performance using empirically supported prompting strategies. With the addition of incorrect choices (or distracters) the student is given trials where errors are possible. Prompting decreases as the student

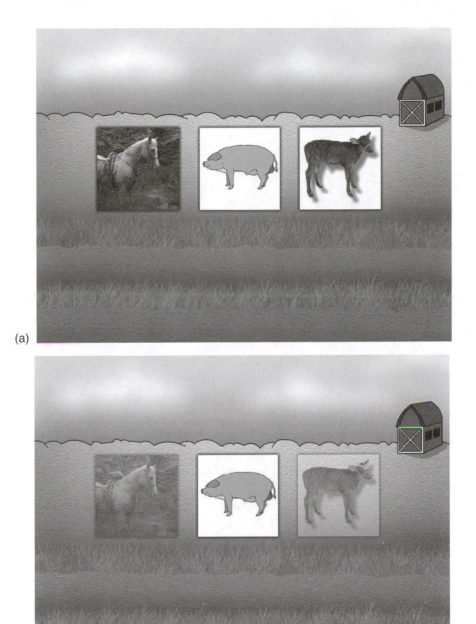

Figure 9.5 *(a) Trial without prompting (b) Trial with prompting (c) Trial with errorless learning.*

(c)

Figure 9.5(continued)

improves or increases if the student is having difficulty. Due to the immense variability in this population, failure criteria is not based simply on the number of attempts, but by a least-squares regression model, which gives a more accurate indication of trouble spots. If particular lessons are causing problems for the student, the software will recommend complementary off-computer *Generalization Activities* to the child's facilitator.

Many children with ASD have a team of individuals that contribute to their therapy program including teachers and aids at school, one or more clinicians trained in ABA, a speech therapist, the parents at home and one or more home therapy assistants. The TeachTown program is 'portable,' intentionally designed to be used in multiple settings, including home, school, speech therapy, behavioral therapy, occupational therapy, or virtually any setting where services might be appropriate for that child. The number of hours per week that this program is used will depend on the individual child's needs and this decision should be made with the entire team. Some children may only use the program for a few minutes a day to supplement other programs while other children may use it several hours a day to meet the needs of their program. Again, it is important to emphasize that the 'program' includes on and off-computer

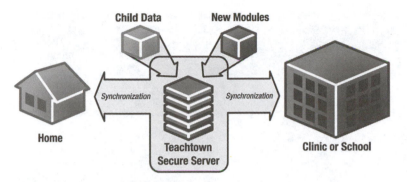

Figure 9.6 *Internet synchronization.*

activities, it is not suggested that the child use the computer several hours per day every day with no other kind of 1:1 or group instruction.

Effective communication is often a major challenge for members of a child's team. Conventionally, communication is handled via email and by physically passing the child's data sheets back and forth between members of the team (often in a physical folder that travels with the child). This method is problematic: data can easily be lost or binders misplaced; and not every member of the team has timely access to the latest data. Email is also not always effective as a child's facilitator may forget to include other members of the child's team in the communication and because there tends to be quite a bit of turnover among team members and/or transitions for the child to new service providers.

TeachTown solves the communication problem by 'attaching' all communication to the child's account, storing it electronically on a secure central server (Figure 9.6). After signing an electronic confidentiality agreement, any invited member of the child's team can access the child's most recent data via the Internet. Practically this means that after a child performs some lessons at school and the teacher leaves a note about the session, a parent (or clinician) could start TeachTown at another location, see exactly what the child did at school, read any notes left by the teacher, and even take over the therapy where the teacher left off.

'Notes' are a variant of the email paradigm, designed to facilitate communication among a child's team. Team members can leave notes on computer lessons, off-computer activities or general session notes (Figure 9.7). Each facilitator must be invited to join the team by the parent or legal-guardian (or someone with permission from the parent or legal guardian). Facilitators may include parents, teachers, behavioral therapists and consultants, speech and language therapists, occupational

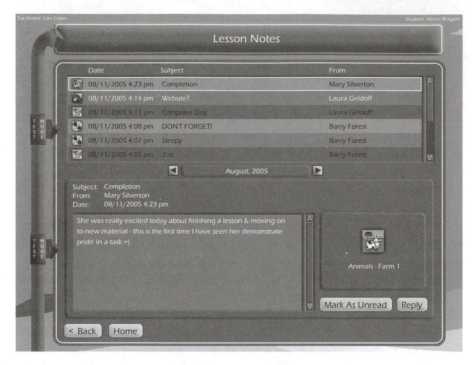

Figure 9.7 Note interface.

therapists, researchers, or agency representatives (e.g. state regional centers). Notes and progress data become instantly available to anyone who joins the child's team. This means that any new facilitator joining the team has access to all prior information about the child. Furthermore if an individual leaves the child's team they will no longer have access to any of the child's data or notes.

The *Generalization Activities* referenced earlier are an important aspect of the TeachTown program, intended to enhance target skills between the parent (or professional) and the child in a naturalistic setting. The term 'generalization' in this context refers to the transfer of a response learned from one stimulus to a new stimulus. For example, if a child learns to label several images of a tree and is then able to identify a new tree that he has never seen before. *Generalization Activities* were developed by the first author and other professional behavioral clinicians to be used in conjunction with the software-component of the program. Each activity consists of a set of very simple 'recipe-like' instructions for performing a hands-on learning activity with the child. (Figure 9.8).

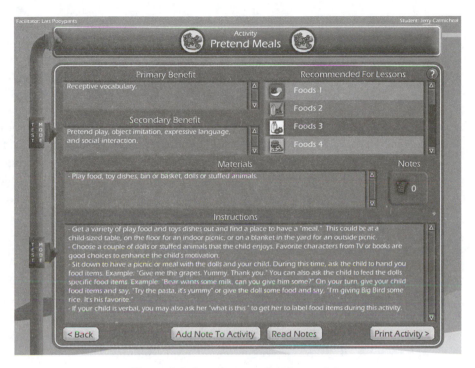

Figure 9.8 *Sample generalization activity.*

Activities enhance generalization of targeted skills while providing additional learning opportunities not possible on the computer. Activities are designed to be age-appropriate for the child and natural to the parent–child relationship. Instructions are written in an easy-to-follow language for nonexperts (e.g. an older sibling). Although software alone is an excellent way to quickly build skills, structured and unstructured activities are equally important. Quality face-to-face interaction (especially with parents) is critical to the success of the TeachTown program and to the child's long-term treatment outcome. For optimum treatment it is important that users implement a 1:1 ratio between the software and the *Generalization Activities* (which can be substituted with other appropriate, naturalistic activities).

9.2.2 **Evaluation of Usability and Appropriateness**

A prototype of the *TeachTown: Basics* program was tested for efficacy and ease of use in a 6-month research project supported by a research grant from the Department of Education. One of the goals of this research was to collect information and feedback from the facilitators as well as researchers in the field of autism, psychology, and education to make the intervention as effective as possible. Prior to seeing the demo of the software, 15 participants (five parents, five educators, and five autism specialists/researchers) were asked to complete a questionnaire to assess their child's current treatments and to determine their interest in a computerized intervention. After completing the initial questionnaire, the adults were shown the prototype of the TeachTown software and were asked to complete another short Likert-scale questionnaire (ratings between one and five with one being unfavorable and five being the most favorable). Adult participants received a sample of the off-computer *Generalization Activities*. They were asked to review the activities and try them out with their child. After 1 week, the adults were interviewed and asked to rate these activities. Parents, teachers, and clinicians rated the look and feel of the program very high (avg. 4.7 out of 5). They also felt that the program generated appropriate goals (avg. 4.6 out of 5) and that the program of on- and off-computer activities was a good model for treating symptoms of autism (avg. 4.7 out of 5).

The second goal of the study was to obtain pilot data on the usability and efficacy of the product. Eight children (four with autism, three with Down Syndrome, and one with Soto's Disorder) participated for 2–4 months. Children with autism were chosen as the program was specifically designed for this population. The other four children were chosen to see if children with other special needs might also benefit from the program. Also, we wanted to see if behavioral patterns were different with children with other disabilities. Down Syndrome was chosen specifically because these children often demonstrate opposite social behavioral patterns from children with autism. The children ranged in age from 3 years, 11 months to 5 years, 10 months (six boys and two girls both with Down Syndrome). All participants demonstrated language delays (developmental range: 1 year, 2 months to 2 years, 4 months) according to parent reports. Participating children were observed and videotaped in a baseline interaction with their parent prior to beginning the *TeachTown: Basics* program. Communication, social skills, and behavior were coded. Following pre-treatment measures, each family was given a pilot version of the *TeachTown: Basics* software and asked to have their child play it for 15 minutes at a time, three times per week, and to work on off-computer *Generalization Activities* with their child for an additional 15 minutes at a time, three times per week (a total of 1.5 hours/week of intervention).

Significant changes from pre- to post-tests were observed for the eight participants using the *TeachTown: Basics* software (Figure 9.9). In addition, positive collateral changes were observed including increases in spontaneous commenting, length of sentences, positive affect, and looking at the adult. Decreases in inappropriate language

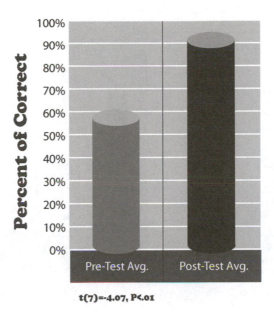

Figure 9.9 *Average pre-test and post-test scores.*

and behaviors were also observed (Figure 9.10) (Whalen *et al.*, 2006a). Spontaneous commenting was scored when the child expressively commented on something (e.g. 'look, a rocket ship') without hearing it first from the computer or an adult. Requests such as 'I want more computer' were not scored as comments. Length of sentences was measured by counting the number of words the child used in each sentence and taking an average for each 15-minute observation. If a word was repeated (e.g. 'no, no, no') this was only scored as 1 word. Positive affect was coded when the child smiled while either looking at or talking to the adult or in response to something that the adult did. It was not counted when the child smiled or laughed in response to an object as this was often inappropriate and not social in nature. Looking at the adult was scored whenever the child turned their face in the direction of the adult. Eye contact was not scored as the video equipment was not sophisticated enough to capture subtle eye movements. Inappropriate language was defined as any nonsensical or out-of-context remarks (e.g. talking about a motorcycle when others were talking about animals). Inappropriate behaviors included crying, running away from the adult, throwing objects, screaming, hitting self or others, etc.

Standardized measures of behavior were not used as treatment outcome measures due to the brief period of time children participated in treatment (2 months at only

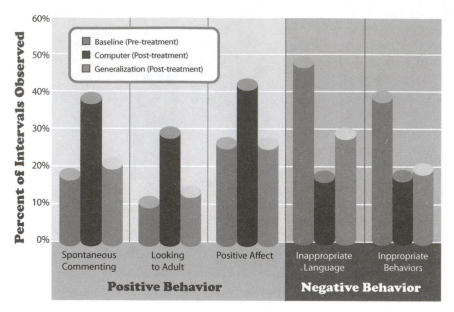

Figure 9.10 Behavioral results.

1.5 hours/week). However, data were recorded via videotape using 10-second inter-vals as is standard in applied behavior analysis studies (e.g. Whalen and Schreibman, 2003). Also, interobserver reliability was recorded for more than 33% of sessions with kappa statistics (which account for chance reliability) between 79% and 91%.

Most participants easily adapted to the use of the computer although some required some initial training from their parents (e.g. how to point or use the mouse). No difficulties were encountered while videotaping sessions in the home, but cancel-lations were often a problem with some families due to high stress levels and busy schedules.

Larger-scale usability issues and social validity were tested through a series of beta-test programs with a group of approximately 150 children. Feedback was col-lected from parents, teachers, speech pathologists, behavioral therapists, and researchers to help tailor the program to the specific needs of the ASD consumer. Beta-trials involved many phone conversations and on-site visits to help set up the programs, problem-solve issues (primarily technical difficulties with older computers in the schools), and listen to suggestions from beta users for final changes prior to product release. Focus testing with adult users (i.e. parents, teachers, clinicians) was another key factor in development. Approximately 20 novice users were brought in throughout the development of the software to test interface usability and to determine what features were important to users. One of the key findings was that users prefer fewer configuration options. Often teachers or parents have limited time to work with their children, so software that starts rapidly and requires little setup is valuable. Although the software implements a sophisticated therapeutic protocol, users are shielded from needing to understand the details. The suggestions from our beta with children and focus testing with adults included: (1) including a way to enter in session notes; (2) allowing a way to print off-computer activities and data; (3) allowing for a way to see the entire curriculum so that programs could be better planned and IEP goals could be developed from the curriculum list; (4) adding a glossary to help explain some of the terminology; (5) several reinforcer ideas such as a solar system, dinosaurs, cars, etc.; and (6) having the cursor automatically move off the screen after each trial so that it was not on one of the images (accidentally prompted children and confused them). These changes and many more were incorporated into our original release and into Version 1.1. Recent suggestions from teachers and clinicians finishing up their beta trials include: (1) allowing to customize and build lesson plans for the child (but also have automatic curriculum planning) and (2) including a 'learning to learn' module that helps children learn to use the program before teaching trials begin. These changes are currently being tested and will be available in the next update.

9.3 Implications for Designers

Significant design work went into building an architecture that allows TeachTown to rapidly prototype and develop new learning modules. The software consists of a central engine that runs the treatment and tracks an individual student's progress, a set of plug-in modules for each learning domain and a set of plug-in reinforcer modules. The entire system is data-driven, meaning that the engine, as well as the plug-in lesson and reinforcer modules, are agnostic with regards to data. They are capable of generalizing to new learning modules with only modest software development overhead.

In addition to producing the software, TeachTown created a sophisticated set of development tools. In most cases the development tools can be used to generate new lessons and reinforcer content without the need for any additional software development (Figure 9.11). This makes it easy to rapidly create new lessons and learning modules without additional software development time. Generalization is enhanced by the utilization of tens of thousands of images and animations. To make maintenance of such a large database of content manageable a content database was created with keywords, copyrights, and lesson tags (Figure 9.12).

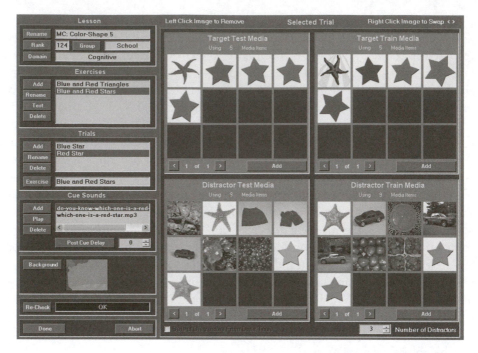

Figure 9.11 *Lesson editing.*

Conventional educational software frequently misses subtle interface features which can render the software virtually useless for a child with ASD. For example, in many software programs a selectable interface item highlights when the mouse rolls over it. However some children with ASD may perseverate (i.e. engage in repetitive actions) on this highlight. In particular, a child might roll the mouse back and forth over a selectable item just to see the highlight turn on an off. In TeachTown, the amount of highlighting that occurs when the mouse is rolled over a selectable interface decreases each time the interface element if rolled over. This prevents the child from perseverating on the highlight.

Another important factor to consider in software design for this audience is that a significant portion of users will be using outdated computer hardware. Many schools are still running Windows 98 (and even Windows 95) on machines with limited memory and processor speeds. A careful balance must be maintained to give the children the best software that current technology can offer, but to also support older machines as much as possible. It is acceptable for the facilitator interface to run slowly on older machines, but the child interface must respond rapidly to child input.

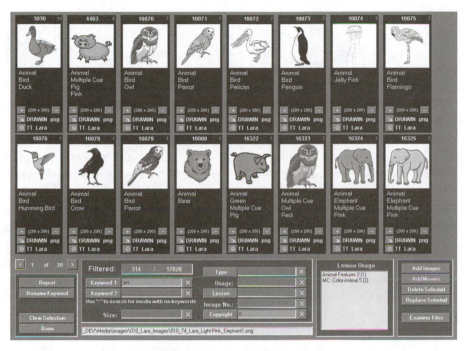

Figure 9.12 *Media selection tool.*

Because TeachTown is dealing with data that may be considered sensitive, in particular the performance data for the child and notes shared between members of the child's team, it is important that such information is stored and transferred in a secure matter. Careful steps were taken to store performance data in a manner that isn't easily interpretable and all data transferred over the Internet is encrypted using the same technology used by bank and credit card companies for dealing with personal information.

9.4 Implications for Researchers

Computer-based interventions are becoming increasingly popular but many research studies are still needed to determine the efficacy of various methods of computer-based treatments. Perhaps the most important question that needs to be answered is to what degree to skills learned via CAI generalize to the natural environment. Most existing studies have assessed generalization using adult-presented tasks which are very similar to tasks presented on the computer. While these studies have typically found generalization, it is unknown whether children are able to apply the concepts to completely novel situations. Additionally, while research suggests that certain cognitive and receptive language skills, particularly receptive object labels, generalize well to the natural environment, there is much less research that has examined how well expressive language and social skills generalize to natural interactions.

Research is also needed to determine which skills are most appropriately targeted via CAI and which skills are better taught via more traditional teaching methods. Research which can determine the most effective methods of instruction are also needed. Programs vary significantly on their interface, method of presentation, reinforcement schedule, and mastery criteria. Computer-based treatments provide entirely new tools unavailable in traditional intervention methods, such as animated cues and targets, new ways of prompting and a much wider array of target images. To fully capitalize on the power of such interventions research is required to see how the new tools can be used most effectively.

Research is also necessary to optimize CAI procedures such as types of prompting, reinforcement schedules, interface designs, etc. Using data to determine how to best design CAI will ensure that higher quality programs are developed and that these programs are evidence-based and usable by the consumers.

Next, additional research is needed to determine which children with autism are most likely to benefit from CAI. Although many children with autism enjoy the computer, there is likely a segment of the population for whom it is less effective. Research which can determine *a priori* which children are most likely to benefit will likely improve treatment outcomes.

Another very important aspect of the *TeachTown: Basics* program is the built-in naturalistic generalization activities that are off-computer. Although these activities are based on existing research and clinical practice, research is needed which assesses the efficacy of these activities as well as treatment adherence (i.e. are parents, teachers, and clinicians doing the activities or only using the computers?). Also, researchers can help to identify strategies for helping users to adhere to the complete program and optimizing the activities to the child's various learning environments.

9.5 Implications for Users

It is very important for users of CAI to provide a way for all users of the program to communicate with one another, whether this is through the technology itself (such as in *TeachTown: Basics*) or through other means (e.g. written notes, email, etc.). Having frequent communication among team members will help keep the child's program consistent and moving forward in all of the child's environments.

Users of the *TeachTown: Basics* program should keep in mind the intended purpose of the program and try to use all elements of the program to best benefit the child: (1) the generalization activities should be done just as much or more than the computer part of the treatment; (2) notes should be put in regularly to best track the child's overall progress; (3) any adult that is working with the child on learning activities of any kind should be added as facilitators whether or not they use the program in their teaching – this will keep everyone in the loop and help to keep the child's program consistent; and (4) data should be monitored regularly to make sure the child is benefiting from the program.

Anyone using *TeachTown: Basics* should understand that although it is good to see progress on the computer, assessing the child's skills and behavior in the natural environment is the best indicator of treatment success. Just because a child has mastered many skills on the software does not mean that the child can use all of these skills in the real world. Using the generalization activities and monitoring the child's progress in natural situations is the best way to ensure that the child is truly making progress.

One nice aspect of TeachTown is our passion for staying in frequent communication with our customers and helping them to get the most out of the program. Our web site is updated frequently and users can also subscribe to our online journal (i.e. blog) (http://drchris.teachtown.com) which provides constant information about TeachTown, autism, and child development. In this journal, we post tips for using the *TeachTown: Basics* program based on questions or concerns from our customer support department. The posting are written by Dr Whalen or by Manya Vaupel, a board certified behavior analyst and the Education Director for TeachTown. Few researchers or clinicians in the field of autism provide this kind of service to the community and more professionals and researchers should consider doing this to further educate those affected by or working with people with autism.

9.6 Implications for Policymakers

Educating consumers about new research and effectiveness of existing treatment programs is one of the most important things for policymakers to focus on today for children with autism. Much of the focus of policymakers is to develop research programs for finding a cause and a cure for autism. While this is important, there is little emphasis on funding or programs for the children who are diagnosed today. Most treatment is through private agencies and it is difficult for families to determine the most appropriate intervention.

Funding intervention for the children who are diagnosed today is also a concern. The majority of funding for research is for finding the cause and the cure for autism.

This is very important research, but developing effective interventions for the children who have autism today should also be a high priority. In addition, most insurance companies do not cover treatment services for autism and when they do, they typically only cover medical interventions, speech therapy, and occupational therapy. ABA is rarely covered by insurance, despite the fact that it has more research demonstrating efficacy than any of the other types of treatment. CAI is not typically covered by any insurance companies, although it is something for policymakers to consider due to the accessibility and affordability of it, especially for rural families. Policymakers should consider offering scholarship programs to help rural and low-income families with treatment, including CAI, as it may offer more accessibility and affordability to these families.

There is also a critical need to determine how to best disseminate CAI to relevant consumers. For example, computer hardware has improved rapidly over the last 10 years, allowing for the creation of sophisticated graphical displays and the rapid processing of data. However, schools frequently only have access to outdated computer hardware (often as old as 6–8 years) severely limiting what they can provide for their students and many parents either do not have computers in their homes or have outdated computers that are not optimal for using the latest technology for CAI. Better funding for modern computer equipment would increase the accessibility to the latest in treatment technologies.

9.7 Conclusion

Despite the fact that computer-assisted interventions for children with autism are relatively new and research is still in its infancy, CAI offers a promising intervention tool. CAI can increase the accuracy of intervention implementation, can increase children's interest and motivation, and can provide intervention at a significantly reduced cost. In addition, it may be an excellent option for rural, low and middle-income families who do not have access to trained professionals or who cannot afford the services. As more research is conducted, CAI interventions will undoubtedly improve.

Acknowledgments

We would like to thank Kevin MacDonald, Eric Dallaire, Manya Vaupel, Eric Dashen, Lara Schneider, Thomas Rockstrom, Sascha Broomberg, Chris Marshall, Sally Vilardi, Kate Kennedy, Richard Dormer, Derek Becker, Joel Walden, Scott Kennedy, Destiny Bassett, and Brad McGuire for their valuable feedback and assistance in the development of *TeachTown: Basics* and their dedication to making TeachTown a success. We are also grateful to our scientific and business advisory board members for their ongoing support and advice.

References

American Psychiatric Association (APA) (2000) *Diagnostic and Statistical Manual of Mental Disorders*, 4th edition, text revision. American Psychiatric Association, Washington, DC.

Anderson, A.E. (2002) Augmentative communication and autism: a comparison of sign language and the picture exchange communication system. Doctoral dissertation, University of California, San Diego, 2001. *Dissertation Abstracts International* **62**, 4269-B.

Baron-Cohen, S., Leslie, A.M. and Frith, U. (1985) Does the autistic child have a 'theory of mind'? *Cognition* **21**, 37–46.

Bartak, L., Rutter, M. and Cox, A. (1975) A comparative study of infantile autism and specific developmental receptive language disorder. *British Journal of Psychiatry* **126**, 127–145.

Bernard-Opitz, V., Sriram, N. and Nakhoda-Sapuan, S. (2001) Enhancing social problem solving in children with autism and normal children through computer-assisted instruction. *Journal of Autism and Developmental Disorders* **31**(4), 377–384.

Bettleheim, B. (1967) *The Empty Fortress: Infantile autism and the birth of the self*, Free Press, New York.

Bondy, A.S. and Frost, L.A. (1994) The Picture Exchange Communication System. *Focus on Autistic Behavior* **9**, 1–19.

Bosseler, A. and Massaro, D. (2003) Development and evaluation of a computer-animated tutor for vocabulary and language learning in children with autism. *Journal of Autism and Developmental Disorders* **33**(6), 653–672.

Butter, E.M. and Mulick, J.A. (2001) ABA and the computer: a review of the Discrete Trial Trainer. *Behavioral Interviews* **16**, 287–291.

Campbell, J.O., Lison, C.A., and Borsook, T.K. et al. (1995) Using computer and video technologies to develop interpersonal skills. *Computers and Human Behavior* **11**, 223–239.

Centers for Disease Control and Prevention (2002) National Center on Birth Defects and Developmental Disabilities, Autism and Developmental Disabilities Monitoring Network. Available at `http://www.cdc.gov/ncbddd/dd/aic/states/default/htm#addm` [accessed 10 December 2002].

Charlop-Christy, M., Carpenter, M., and Le, L. et al. (2002) Using the Picture Exchange Communication System (PECS) with children with autism: assessment of

PECS acquisition, speech, social-communicative behavior, and problem behavior. *Journal of Applied Behavior Analysis* 35, 213–231.

Charlop-Christy, M.H., Le, L. and Freeman, K.A. (2000) A comparison of video modeling with in vivo modeling for teaching children with autism. *Journal of Autism and Developmental Disorders* 30, 537–552.

Charlop, M.H. and Milstein, J.P. (1989) Teaching autistic children conversational speech using video modeling. *Journal of Applied Behavioral Analysis* 22, 275–285.

Coleman-Martin, M., Heller, K., Cjhak, D. and Irvine, K. (2005) Using computer-assisted instruction and the nonverbal reading approach to teach word identification. *Focus on Autism and Other Developmental Disorders* 20(2), 80–90.

Delprato, D.J. (2001) Comparisons of discrete-trial and normalized behavioral language intervention for young children with autism. *Journal of Autism and Developmental Disorders* 31(3), 315–325.

Dunlap, G. (1984) The influence of task variation and maintenance tasks on the learning and affect of autistic children. *Journal of Experimental Child Psychology* 37, 41–46.

Dunlap, G., dePerczel, M., Clarke S. et al. (1994) Choice making to promote behavior support for students with emotional and behavioral challenges. *Journal of Applied Behavioral Analysis* 27, 505–518.

Eikeseth, S., Smith, T., Jahr, E. and Eldevik, S. (2002) Intensive behavioral treatment at school for 4–7 year-old children with autism: a 1-year comparison controlled study. *Behavioral Modifiers* 26(1), 49–68.

Ferster, C.B. and Demyer, M.K. (1961) The development of performances in autistic children in an automatically controlled environment. *Journal of Chronic Diseases* 13, 312–345.

Ferster, C.B. and Demyer, M.K. (1962) A method for the experimental analysis of the behavior of autistic children. *American Journal of Orthopsychiatry* 32, 89–98.

Folstein, S. and Rutter, M. (1977) Infantile autism: a genetic study of 21 twin pairs

Journal of Child Psychology and Psychiatry, 18(4), 297–321.

Fombonne, E. (2003) The prevalence of autism. *Journal of the American Medical Association* 289(1), 87–89.

Gillam, R.B., Crofford, J.A., Gale, M.A. and Hoffman, L.M. (2001) Language change following computer-assisted language instruction with Fast ForWord or

Laureate Learning Systems Software. *American Journal of Speech-Language Pathology* **10**, 231–247.

Goldsmith, T. and LeBlanc, L. (2004) Use of technology in interventions with children with autism. *Journal of Early Intensive Behavioral Interventions,* **1**(2), 166–178.

Hauck, M., Fein, D., Waterhouse, L. and Feinstein, C. (1995) Social initiations by autistic children to adults and other children. *Journal of Autism and Developmental Disorders* **25**, 579–595.

Hetzroni, O.E. and Shalem, U. (2005) From logos to orthographic symbols: a multi-level fading computer program for teaching nonverbal children with autism. *Focus on Autism and Other Developmental Disabilities* **20**(4), 201–212.

Hetzroni, O.E. and Tannous, J. (2004) Effects of a computer-based intervention program on the communicative functions of children with autism. *Journal of Autism and Developmental Disorders* **34**, 95–113.

Ingersoll, B. and Schreibman, L. (2006) Teaching reciprocal imitation skills to young children with autism using a naturalistic behavioral approach: effects on language, pretend play, and joint attention. *Journal of Autism and Developmental Disorders.*

Johnson-Martin, N.M., Hacker, B.J. and Attermeir, S.M. (2004) *The Carolina Curriculum for Preschoolers with Special Needs,* 2nd edn. Paul H. Brookes Publishing Co., Baltimore, MD.

Koegel, R.L., Koegel, L.K. and McNerney, E.K. (2001) Pivotal areas in intervention for autism. *Journal of Clinical Child Psychology* **30**(1), 19–32.

Koegel, R.L., O'Dell, M.C. and Koegel, L.K. (1987) A natural language teaching paradigm for nonverbal autistic children. *Journal of Autism and Developmental Disorders* **17**, 187–200.

Koegel, R.L., Schreibman, L. and Good, A., et al. (1989) How to teach pivotal behaviors to children with autism: a training manual.

Leaf, R. and McEachin, J. (eds.), (1999) *A Work in Progress: Behavior Management Strategies and a Curriculum for Intensive Behavioral Treatment of Autism,* DRL Books, Inc., New York.

Lewis, M.H. and Bodfish, J.W. (1998) Repetitive behavior disorders in autism. *Mental Retardation and Developmental Disability Research Review* **4**, 80–89.

Lord, C. and Magill-Evans, J. (1995) Peer interactions of autistic children and adolescents. *Developments in Psychopathology* **7**, 611–626.

Lotter, V. (1966) Epidemiology of autistic conditions in young children. *Society of Psychiatry and Psychiatric Epidemiology,* **1**(3), 124–135.

Lovaas, O.I. (1987) Behavioral treatment and normal educational and intellectual functioning in young autistic children. *Journal of Consulting Clinical Psychology* **55**, 3–9.

Loveland, K. and Landry, S. (1986) Joint attention and language in autism and developmental language delay. *Journal of Autism and Developmental Disorders* **16**, 335–349.

Maurice, C., Green, G. and Luce, S.C. (eds) (1996) *Behavioral Intervention for Young Children with Autism: A Manual for Parents and Professionals.* Pro-Ed, Inc., Austin, TX.

McArthur, D. and Adamson, L. (1996) Joint attention in preverbal children: autism and developmental language disorder. *Journal of Autism and Developmental Disorders* **26**, 481–496.

McGee, G.G., Morrier, M.J. and Daly, T. (1999) An incidental teaching approach to early intervention for toddlers with autism. *Journal of the Association for Persons with Severe Handicaps* **24**(3), 133–146

Mesibov, G. (1993) Treatment outcome is encouraging. *American Journal of Mental Retardation* **97**(4), 379–380.

Miranda-Linne, F. and Melin, L. (1992) Acquisition, generalization, and spontaneous use of color adjectives: a comparison of incidental teaching and traditional discrete-trial procedures for children with autism. *Research into Developmental Disorders* **13**, 191–210.

Moore, M. and Calvert, S. (2000) Brief report: vocabulary acquisition for children with autism: teacher or computer instruction. *Journal of Autism and Developmental Disorders* **30**(4), 359–362.

National Institute of Mental Health (2004) Autism spectrum disorders research at the National Institute of Mental Health: Fact sheet. Department of Health and Human Services.

National Research Council (NRC) – Division of Behavioral and Social Sciences and Education (DBASSE) (2001) Educating Children with Autism – Commission on Behavioral and Social Sciences and Education (CBASSE), 'Characteristics Of Effective Interventions', p. 6.

Neef, N.A. and Lutz, M.N. (2001) A brief computer-based assessment of reinforcer dimensions affecting choice. *Journal of Applied Behavioral Analysis* **34**(1), 57–60.

O'Connor, J., French, R. and Henderson, H. (2000) Using physical activity to improve behavior of children with autism. *Palaestra* 16(3).

Parkin, A. (2006) Computers in clinical practice: applying experience from child psychiatry. *British Medical Journal* **321**, 615–618.

Partington, J. and Sundberg, M. (1998) The Assessment of Basic Language and Learning Skills (ABLLS), Behavior Analysts, Pleasant Hill, CA.

Pérez-González, L.A. and Williams, G (2002) Multicomponent procedure to teach conditional discriminations to children with autism. *American Journal of Mental Retardation* **107**(4), 293–301.

Perry, A. and Condillac, R. (2003) Evidence-based practices for children and adolescents with autism spectrum disorders: review of the literature and practice guide, Children's Mental Health Ontario, Toronto, Ontario.

Phillips, W., Baron-Cohen, S. and Rutter, M. (1998) Understanding intention in normal development and in autism. *British Journal of Developmental Psychology* **16**, 337–348.

Pierce, K.L. and Schreibman, L. (1994) Teaching daily living skills to children with autism in unsupervised settings through pictorial self-management. *Journal of Applied Behavioral Analysis* **27**, 471–481.

Pierce, K. and Schreibman, L. (1995) Increasing complex social behaviors in children with autism: effects of peer-implemented pivotal response training. *Journal of Applied Behavioral Analysis* **28**(3), 285–295.

Quill, K.A. (ed.), (2000) *Do-Watch-Listen-Say: Social Communication Intervention for Children with Autism*, Paul H. Brookes Publishing Co., Baltimore, MD.

Reichart, R. (2001) Toward a comprehensive approach to teacher quality. Mid-Continent Research for Education and Learning, November 2001, pp. 1–11.

Rogers, S.J., Hepburn, S. and Wehner, E. (2003) Parent reports of sensory symptoms in toddlers with autism and those with other developmental disorders. *Journal of Autism and Developmental Disorders* **33**, 631–642.

Rogers, S. and Pennington, B. (1991) A theoretical approach to the deficits in infantile autism. *Developmental Psychology* **3**, 137–162.

Rutter, M. and Bartak, L. (1971) Causes of infantile autism: some considerations from recent research. *Journal of Autism and Developmental Disorders* **1**(1), 20–32.

Sackett D., Straus S., Richardson W. et al. (2000) Introduction, *Evidence-Based Medicine: How to Teach and Practice EBM*, 1.

Schilling, J., Hoch, H., Lengel, K. and Taylor, B. (2005) Assessing generalization from the computer to 3-D objects using Discrete Trial Trainer computer program, Poster Session: Association for Behavior Analysis Convention.

Schreibman, L., Whalen, C. and Stahmer, A. (2000) The use of video priming to reduce disruptive transition behaviors in children with autism. *Journal of Positive Behavioral Interventions* 2(1), 3–11.

Sigman, M. and Ruskin, E. (1999) Continuity and change in the social competence of children with autism, Down Syndrome, and developmental delays. *Monographs of the Society for Research in Child Development* 64, 1–114.

Smith, T., Groen, A.D. and Wynn, J.W. (2000) Randomized trial of intensive early intervention for children with pervasive developmental disorder. *American Journal of Mental Retardation* 105(4), 269–285.

Stahmer, A. (1995) Teaching symbolic play skills to children with autism using pivotal response training. *Journal of Autism and Developmental Disorders* 25(2), 123–141.

Sulzer-Azaroff, B. and Mayer, R. (1991) *Behavior Analysis for Lasting Change*, Holt, Reinhart & Winston, Inc., Fort Worth, TX.

Wacker, D.P. and Berg, W.K. (1983) Effects of picture prompts on the acquisition of complex vocational tasks by mentally retarded adolescents. *Journal of Applied Behavioral Analysis* 16, 417–433.

Whalen, C. and Schreibman, L. (2003) Joint attention training for children with autism using behavior modification procedures. *Journal of Child Psychology, Psychiatry and Allied Disciplines* 44(3), 456–468.

Whalen, C., Liden, L., Ingersoll B. et al. (2006a) Behavioral improvements associated with computer-assisted instruction for children with developmental disabilities. *Journal of Speech Language Pathology and Applied Behavioral Analysis*.

Whalen, C., Schreibman, L. and Ingersoll, B. (2006b). The collateral effects of joint attention training on social initiations, positive affect, imitation, and spontaneous speech for young children with autism. *Journal of Autism and Developmental Disorders*.

Williams, C., Wright, B., Callaghan, G. and Coughlan, B. (2002) Do children with autism learn to read more readily by computer assisted instruction or traditional book methods? A pilot study. *Autism* 6(1), 71–91.

Wing, L. (2001) *The Autistic Spectrum: A Parent's Guide to Understanding and Helping Your Child*, Ulysses Press, Berkely, CA.

Wing, L. and Gould, J. (1979) Severe impairments of social interaction and associated abnormalities in children: epidemiology and classification. *Journal of Autism and Developmental Disorders* **9**, 11–29.

Yonan A.L., Alarcón M., Cheng R. et al. (2003) A genomewide screen of 345 families for autism-susceptibility loci. *American Journal of Human Genetics* **73**, 886–897.

Zwaigenbaum L., Szatmari P., Jones M.B. et al. (2002) Pregnancy and birth complications in autism and liability to the broader autism phenotype. *Journal of the American Academy of Child and Adolescent Psychiatry* **41**(5), 572–579.

Making Software Accessible for Users with Dementia

10

Norman Alm[a], Richard Dye[a], Arlene Astell[b], Maggie Ellis[b], Gary Gowans[c], and Jim Campbell[c]

[a] School of Computing, University of Dundee, Dundee, Scotland
[b] School of Psychology, University of St Andrews, St Andrews, Scotland
[c] Department of Computer-Aided Design, School of Design, University of Dundee, Dundee, Scotland

Summary

Good practice in interface design takes into account the limitations on a user's working (short-term) memory capacity. This applies to how much is presented on the screen as well as how many navigation levels are required to be held in memory. With conditions such as dementia, the working memory can be so impaired as to be virtually nonoperative. This presents a significant challenge in designing interactive systems for people with this condition. If the difficulties in such an extreme case as this can be overcome, such systems could offer the possibility of improving the communication abilities of people with dementia, and eventually providing them with satisfying activities that can be carried out unaided. We report on a project that has developed a hypermedia reminiscence-based communication support system for older people with dementia, which has been designed to compensate to some degree for their working memory deficits. The system has proved remarkably effective in restoring a degree of equality in the communication between a person with dementia and a carer or relative. The results from this work may have implications for designing interfaces for other people with cognitive difficulties, and for the wider population of users who may experience a temporary loss of cognitive focus.

10.1 Interface Design and Working (Short-Term) Memory

An important principle of good interface design is to take into account limitations in the user's working (short-term) memory. A number of heuristics have been developed to help ensure that the demands on the user do not push working memory capacity uncomfortably past its limits. Care must be taken in the number of items presented at any one time for the user's attention, and also in the number of navigation levels the user must traverse (Miller, 1956; Shneiderman, 1998). Of course trade-offs are inevitable in the design process. Overlarge menus and systems that require multiple uses of the back button will still in some cases be the only solution. Elegant and efficient interface design, however, requires that attention be paid to the limits on the user's ability to hold a number of items in memory while they travel within the structure provided. People who have cognitive problems leading to impairment or loss of working memory thus present a particularly challenging group for an interface designer.

As with all efforts to meet the needs of 'extraordinary' people, experience suggests that we will no doubt find that in addressing this user population, we discover techniques and approaches which prove useful for the wider population as well (Newell, 1995). In the case of working memory impairment, all of us may suffer temporary problems, through haste, preoccupation, or stress. For a temporary period we may find ourselves in the same position as someone with a permanent impairment of this sort. Someone who is temporarily without the use of one arm might make use of the 'sticky keys' feature on their keyboard which is now incorporated into commercially available operating systems. This replaces the use of simultaneous key presses (such as Control key actions) with a sequence of single key presses. Similarly, interfaces which take account of cognitive deficits could prove helpful for all of us when suffering from a temporary loss of cognitive focus.

We have addressed the problem of designing an interface to be used by older people with dementia. With the increasing proportion of the human population in the older age range, dementia is a growing problem. The aim of our research group is to create a range of computer applications helpful for people with this problem. We began by developing a system to assist people with dementia to continue to hold conversations with carers and relatives. We decided to start with this application because it allowed us to begin by addressing the slightly more tractable problem of designing a system which could be used with the help of a carer. This would give us valuable data and insights useful in moving on to develop systems which could be used by the person with dementia on their own, without assistance.

The other reason we decided to start with supporting communication in dementia was its importance as a serious issue for families and carers. The origin for this project was an interview with the head of a residential home for people with dementia who described how dispiriting it was for families to visit a relative with dementia, and, in an entire afternoon, not to have any sort of satisfying communication with them. She said, 'If you people at the university could come up with something that provided even a spark of positivity for my families that would be a big help.'

10.2 **Dementia and Working Memory**

Dementia in older people consists of a group of symptoms involving impairment of cognitive abilities. The two major causes of dementia are Alzheimer's disease, which is a progressive loss of nerve cells, and vascular dementia, which is loss of brain function caused by small strokes. The impairment of working (short-term) memory is often the first symptom of dementia to be noticed.

The loss of working memory as a result of dementia is a very serious problem for the person and for their family and carers. Many social activities and interactions become increasingly difficult as the condition progresses, since they depend on working memory for effective participation. As a result people with dementia can become socially isolated and deprived of the range and variety of social interactions that characterize everyday life for unimpaired people. This can have a profound effect on their sense of well-being, and put a severe strain on family and carers.

There are currently 24.3 million people worldwide with dementia, with 4.6 million new cases every year (a new case every 7 seconds). The number of people affected is predicted to double every 20 years to 81 million by 2040. Numbers in developed countries are forecast to increase by 100% between 2001 and 2040, and by more than 300% in India, China, and their south Asian and western Pacific neighbors (Ferri *et al.*, 2005).

10.3 **The Difficulty of Communication with Dementia**

One of the disabling results of working memory impairment is its effect on communication of even the most casual kind. Without working memory it is not possible to carry out any kind of conversation. Typically the person with dementia repeats themselves continually, trapped in a time frame that may only be a few seconds long. It is difficult enough when everyday tasks become impossible through dementia, but the loss of the ability to chat to family, friends, and carers is quite devastating. Everyday conversation is fundamental to human social interaction.

Ways of structuring conversations for people with dementia have been investigated, for instance with the use of specially prepared memory books that contain autobiographical material, daily schedule information, and problem resolution information. When such material is individually prepared, and when staff are trained in using it, communication improves between the carers and people with dementia (Bourgeois *et al.*, 2001).

Reminiscence sessions are also a useful way to structure interaction so as to maximize the positive contribution that can be made by a person with dementia. Although working memory is impaired, the long-term memory of a person with dementia is often still functioning even at the latter stages of the disease. In fact, it is becoming clear that different parts of the brain and possibly even different physiological mechanisms are involved in the process of laying down short- and long-term memories (Calvin and Ojemann, 1980; Kandel, 2006). By guiding and supporting the person to take advantage of long-term memory they can be helped to take a more active part in conversations (Baines *et al.*, 1987; Feil, 1993; Woods, 1994; Finnema *et al.*, 1999). Reminiscence sessions can be pleasurable and empowering for the person with dementia, but the experience for the carer is far from a relaxed natural interaction, since they are having to continually support the conversation by prompting and encouraging the person with dementia to make use of their long-term memories.

10.4 A Support for Communication Based on Hypermedia and Reminiscence Material

In order to develop this system we assembled a multidisciplinary team from the fields of psychology, software engineering, and design. The psychologists on the team were experienced in the problems of dementia, and in particular were keen to find ways to maximize the potential of people with dementia. The software engineers were experienced in rehabilitation engineering, user-centered design, and human–computer interaction. The designers came into the project with a considerable background in interactive systems design, as well as in print and 2D and 3D graphic design. Interestingly, the nonpsychologists on the team all had some family experience with dementia (as do more and more of us as the prevalence increases with the aging population profile in most countries).

The system we have created consists of a hypermedia structure with reminiscence material as content. The system attempts to relieve the carer or relative of the job of continually supporting the person with dementia in a conversation. An obvious advantage of a computer-based system over using traditional materials is the bringing together of the various media into one easily accessible system. But we also have explored ways in which hypermedia could in some way mimic the way memory is used in conversations, thus presenting the material in a way that seems natural in the context of a conversation.

When two people sit down to have a casual conversation, if they start on one particular topic, at the end of the conversation they will typically be on a completely different one. The way we move from topic to topic in a conversation has been called 'step-wise progression' (Jefferson, 1984). A speaker does not abruptly end one topic and start another. It is expected that the speaker will establish some sort of link between one topic and the next. After several such links we may be far from the original subject, but a trail of plausible links has led us to this point. One of the authors has experimented with a number of different ways to model such stepwise conversation links, in the context of supporting the communication of people with severe physical disabilities who are unable to speak, and use a computer voice output system for communication. Prototypes were developed involving text-databases, fuzzy information retrieval, intersecting conversational perspectives, and hypertext (Alm and Arnott, 1998). The work on a hypertext-based conversation aid in particular seemed to model most closely the flexibility within a set of topic constraints of free-flowing conversation. The system we have developed has built on this work, and extended the support offered beyond text into multimedia. The addition of graphics, photos, music, and video introduces the possibility of more richly modeling, to some degree, associative links in memory (Brown and Schopflocher, 1998; Conway and Pleydell-Pearce, 2000).

It is unrealistic to expect people with dementia to acquire new skills, as their working memory problems normally preclude this. For the current generation of older people with dementia, therefore, using a mouse to interact with a system (or a keyboard, if the person has not been a typist) would not be suitable. A touchscreen, however, provides a more intuitive way to interact with material on the screen. It is does not require fine muscle control to operate. Importantly, the user is not required to split their attention between the screen and the input device. This would be problematic for people with dementia. Previous work, by ourselves and others, has established that people with dementia can usually manage to make use of touchscreens. Also their attention can be more readily engaged when another person is operating a touchscreen, compared with the more indirect control of events on the screen produced by using a mouse or keyboard. The direct sense of manipulation of a touchscreen seems to offer enough affordance that, with encouragement, they work very well even with people who have fairly severe dementia (Alm *et al.*, 2001, 2004).

Because vision problems are common with elderly people, and since the display was to be shared during a reminiscence session, it was decided to use the largest available (21″) flat panel touchscreen. This size of screen was also chosen to create a more engaging experience than that offered by standard TV screens, but still staying on the table top, with a screen that suggested active use, and not just passive viewing of a large public screen on the wall. Our intention was to have the screen look big enough to be unusual, and thus attract interest, without being so big that it suggested a passive viewing experience, such as when watching a film. The screen in use is shown in Figure 10.1. Sound output was provided using a standard computer sound card together with speakers.

Figure 10.1 *The large panel touchscreen used for presenting the system. Photo in montage on screen © National Museums of Scotland Licensor,www.scran.co.uk.*

10.4.1 **Prototype Development**

An iterative design approach was used to develop the first prototype. Forty people with dementia were identified who expressed an interest in helping us to design and evaluate the system. Thirty relatives and carers also agreed to take part as advisors and evaluators for the project. As a first step, we asked the group to comment on suitable content for the system. Ideas for themes which the system might include (such as national events, local industries, street life, celebrations) were elicited using high-quality photographs.

The system was developed using Macromedia Director. Director was chosen because it is a cross-platform development package that allows rapid development of complex multimedia systems. It also has its own programming language which allows it to be interactive and to be connected to a database. The completed system was given the name CIRCA, standing for Computer Interactive Reminiscence and Conversation Aid.

10.4.2 **Description of the Interface**

Consultation with experts on dementia had established that the interface would need to be as simple as possible while still being attractive and encouraging interaction. One problem that people with dementia have is an inability to cope with too many items that compel attention. In this state the user often will focus on one item and stay with it, not being able to scan easily over the other possibilities. To cope with this, we designed the interface so that the background and navigation features are in muted colors. In most cases only one item of interest is shown at a time. In this way, even a black and white photograph stands out clearly as the point at which the user's attention should be directed. In order to keep the navigation process as simple as possible it was decided to have just three themes to choose from, and for each theme to have three media types that could be chosen. Each theme was associated with a different color scheme. When a theme was selected the background color and color of all the buttons were changed to reflect the selected theme. When the carer or the person with dementia selected one of the three themes, they were then offered a choice of photographs, video, or music.

10.4.3 Media Content of the System

Based on feedback from our user population, the three themes chosen for the prototype were; Recreation, Entertainment, and Dundee Life. The Recreation theme focused on UK material with an emphasis on Dundee and Scotland. The Entertainment theme contained both US (movies and music) and UK material (TV and music). The Dundee Life theme focused on local material. In total the system contained 80 photographs, 10 videos, and 23 music items.

Photographs are often used in reminiscence sessions as they are easy to source. There are many photograph archives and libraries available, covering many themes and time periods. It was therefore relatively easy to add a large number of photographs to the prototype. As it is usual to view photographs in short sequences, the photographs within each theme were grouped into categories. Two navigating buttons, 'Next picture' and 'Previous picture' were provided for stepping through the photograph sequences (see Figure 10.2).

The system allowed the users to select and play video clips related to the theme selected. People with dementia may not be able to follow a long video clip because of their working memory problems. The video clips had a short duration for this reason and also because they were intended to act as conversation prompts and not be too immersive.

The system allowed the users to select and play music related to the theme selected. Music has proved to be a powerful stimulant to long-term memory. Often people with dementia who have stopped speaking can be engaged by music and can proceed to sing entire songs word perfect with evident enjoyment. The difficulty in presenting musical prompts is the physical process of accessing a particular song and playing it

Figure 10.2 Sample screen shot from the Photographs section in the Dundee Life theme.
The menu bars of the touchscreen were at the bottom for easier reaching for older users.
Visible are the three themes, the three media choices, and simple navigation buttons.
Photograph © Archive Services, University of Dundee.

without having to set up equipment and materials beforehand. Having touchscreen
access to songs and music provided an instant way to produce a wide variety of musical prompts. Work by another research group on a touchscreen 'Picture Gramophone'
with images as buttons to access music has established the usefulness of making
familiar music instantly accessible for people with dementia (Topo *et al.*, 2004). In
our system, rather than simply having a static screen while the music played, the type
of device that particular music would normally be coming from was displayed, with
animated movement where appropriate. A record player, radio, or tape recorder was
depicted depending on the theme selected, as shown in Figure 10.3. We found this
representation of the music producing device can also act as a conversation prompt
in itself.

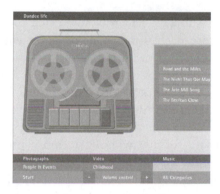

Figure 10.3 *Music was accessed through representations of the type of player that might have produced it in times past. The record player and the reel-to-reel tape recorder were animated to give the impression of working while the song was played.*

10.5 Evaluating the Prototype

A series of evaluations were performed during the development of the prototype, and of the final prototype version. The prototype was tried out with people across the range of dementia severity. The severity of dementia is described in three stages: mild, moderate, and severe. At the mild stage, a person might have difficulty dealing with complexity, and remembering daily tasks. At the moderate stage, they may have increasing difficulty recognizing family, friends, or familiar places, and will need more help with everyday activities. In the severe stage communication can become very difficult and a great deal of help is required for daily tasks. It is estimated that 30% of people with dementia have mild dementia, 42% are at a moderate stage, and 28% have severe dementia (Roth *et al.*, 1998).

People with mild to moderate dementia were able to make full use of the system. More severely affected people could not actually engage with changing the system display, but did show a marked reaction to any musical items which came up. The fact that music can reach even those with severe dementia is well known, but the difficulty of accessing music without setting up an organized session for it means that less music is used than carers would ideally like. The system was used both in one-to-one sessions and as the center of a group activity. It was used under conditions of close observation and also left at a residential facility for an extended period, with staff instructed to make whatever use of it they liked. Comparisons were made between sessions involving other enjoyable activities and sessions using the prototype.

One particular question we had was how using the prototype would compare with traditional reminiscence sessions. One of our intentions was to make the running of such sessions easier by means of multimedia accessed through a touchscreen, and also to establish whether an interactive system had advantages over traditional reminiscence sessions. In a series of videotaped, transcribed, and coded evaluation runs, the system was compared directly with traditional reminiscence sessions. In a traditional session, the carer takes the responsibility for guiding the session, and at all points must compensate for the working memory problems of the person with dementia. We designed the system so that it hopefully would be able to take over the role of supporting the cognitive abilities of the person with dementia, freeing the carer to take part in the session more naturally. Each person with dementia and their carer undertook a 20-minute reminiscence session: half using the prototype, and half using traditional reminiscence methods. As expected, the carers did most of the direct operation of the touchscreen. However, both had their attention held by the displays on the screen and the carer was often prompted and directed by the person with dementia. With encouragement a number of people with dementia also made direct use of the touchscreen to make selections.

The carers were asked to complete a questionnaire at the end of each session. All the sessions were video recorded, transcribed, and coded. All the items accessed using the prototype were logged. As part of the coding process, a protocol was developed for observing and recording behavior during the sessions in order to identify the degree of participation, engagement, and enjoyment of the experience.

Eighteen people with dementia took part in this evaluation, 13 women and 5 men. Nine participated in CIRCA sessions and 9 participated in traditional reminiscence sessions. The age range was 65–95 years. The Mini Mental State Examination (MMSE) is a rough measure of degree of severity of dementia ranging down from 30 (no measured cognitive impairment) to 0. The MMSE range of the participants was from 2 to 23.

Profile of participants:

CIRCA sessions		Traditional sessions	
Age		*Age*	
Mean	82.00	Mean	81.88
Standard deviation	7.93	Standard deviation	6.17
Range	65–95	Range	71–89
MMSE		*MMSE*	
Mean	14.88	Mean	16.00
Standard deviation	6.71	Standard deviation	6.14
Range	2–22	Range	5–23
Carers ($N = 12$)			

A between-subjects protocol was used (Mann–Whitney test).

All the people with dementia were able to make sense of the material the system was presenting, and showed an understanding of how it worked. Some spontaneously commented several times that they were enjoying using CIRCA. One person said, 'It takes you back and refreshes your memory.' Other spontaneous comments were: 'This covers everything,' 'Good thing, this,' 'It's good to remember things,' and 'That's entertainment!' One person said she certainly would like to use the system again. She said she thoroughly enjoyed it and found it very interesting and 'something new.' Another person commented that she enjoyed using the system herself.

In comparing CIRCA with using traditional reminiscence aids, we found that the person with dementia was offered a choice of reminiscence subject/materials more often when using CIRCA ($U = 1.50$, $p < 0.001$). We also found that the person with dementia chose reminiscence subjects/materials more often when prompted when using CIRCA ($U = 3.60$, $p < 0.001$). The traditional sessions were characteristically a series of one question from the carer followed by one response from the person with dementia. The CIRCA sessions were more of a conversation, with each person contributing an equal amount, and control of the direction of the conversation being shared. The carers asked more direct questions when using traditional reminiscence methods ($U = 5.00$, $p = 0.01$).

We had expected that providing reminiscence materials in a multimedia format on a large but not intimidating touch panel would have some advantages over traditional methods of delivering a reminiscence session. From our contacts with carers and relatives, and people with dementia, we knew that reminiscence sessions had proved very valuable, but were not carried out as frequently as would be desirable, because of the preparation time necessary. Also they were normally performed as a group activity, because of considerations of the economies of staff time and availability. One-to-one reminiscence sessions could be very successful, but were not often possible in care settings. In demonstrating and evaluating the system we encountered entirely positive reactions from care staff and relatives. We had wondered if there would have been a degree of reluctance to adopt this sort of unfamiliar technology. The enthusiasm of care staff was quite striking, and made us realize the extent to which they would like to do more of this type of activity, and saw CIRCA as a way of making that a practical possibility.

Another finding that took us by surprise was the ability of the system to assist the person with dementia to take more control of the conversation, and to make the interaction more one of equal partners than is possible without the technology. In this way, the sessions with the system were definitely superior to the traditional sessions. Even with the most skilful handling, the working memory problems of participants meant that these sessions tended to be channeled into a single question/single answer sequence. We also observed that one advantage the system had over traditional methods was the richness of items it could present easily and attractively, thus increasing the chances of a 'hit' on a long-term memory.

In order to determine the effects of familiarity by staff with the system, we arranged for it to be installed in an easily accessible place at a residential facility. Staff were given a demonstration of how the system worked and then left to make whatever use of it they liked over the next few weeks. We found that a number of the staff took a particular interest in the system and used it frequently with residents. These staff, after they became familiar with the contents of the system, then tended to direct residents toward particular sections. This, while entirely understandable, and even laudable, had the effect of weakening the equality of participation which we had observed when the contents were equally new to both parties.

The system logged and timed every event that took place during the sessions. From these logs we were able to measure the use made of different sections, and thus, we hoped, judge the popularity of the various offerings. Consistently we found that one of the themes was the most accessed. At first it seemed obvious to suppose that this was the most popular theme. In discussing it we realized that in the display of on-screen buttons, this theme was displayed furthest on the right. Carers would commonly read out the choices to the person with dementia, one after another from left to right. When this sort of procedure is followed with people who have dementia, it is commonly observed that the person tends to choose the last item, that being the one they can most easily remember.

In order to counteract this, and also to ensure that we retained the important effect we had produced of the person with dementia able to maintain an equal control over the conversational direction, we introduced a randomizing feature to the system. We increased the number of themes from three to seven, and had the system make a random choice of the three themes it would offer each time it was started up. We then introduced extra material to each theme and had the system make a random selection from amongst the possible items to display. In this way, the experience became unpredictable for both the carer and the person with dementia. We have found that this randomization plus a wider store of items does have the desired effect of ensuring the equality of control by both users.

10.6 Conclusion

We have designed an interactive system which has proved to be usable by people with dementia. They were engaged by it, understood how it operated, directed the carers to touch the screen to make changes, and in many cases were able to make use of the touchscreen themselves. Their problems with working memory did not stop them from understanding the material presented to them, and figuring out how to navigate to other material, either by directing the carer or using the touchscreen themselves. The system facilitated a more equal participation in communication for the person with dementia, as compared with traditional reminiscence. Because of the richness of choice in any easy to navigate structure, the carer could hand over more of the control of the session to the person with dementia. By choosing reminiscence items themselves, the person with dementia guided the session. In this way, people with dementia could set the agenda and pace of the interaction.

10.6.1 Implications for Users

For potential users, people with dementia, and their carers, this research has demonstrated that residual communicative abilities of a person with dementia can be tapped by an appropriately designed interactive system. The CIRCA system did not provide a total solution to the problem of communication with impaired working memory, but it did demonstrate that an approach which capitalizes on positive abilities which remain can provide a real help.

10.6.2 Implications for Researchers

For researchers seeking to find ways to support people with dementia in living as fully as possible despite declining cognitive abilities, this project suggests that a multidisciplinary approach is certainly a successful plan, and it may be an essential plan, to achieve such a complex goal. The CIRCA team needed to draw on expertise in software engineering, design, and psychology to produce a usable system. The method in which the team worked together is one we would recommend. Deliberate efforts were made from the outset to meld a team from varying disciplines, which worked together daily as a team. This is not an easy task, but it is worth persevering to overcome initial issues of boundaries, ownership, and terminology, in order to achieve an easy working relationship.

10.6.3 **Implications for Designers**

For consideration by designers of systems for people who may have cognitive difficulties, we have found that the following features of interface design make a system which can be used by people with dementia.

(1) *Touchscreen*. We confirmed the finding of other research groups that touchscreens, although usually an unfamiliar technology to older people with dementia, are nevertheless so obvious in the connection between cause and effect that they are readily understood when the carer operates them, and are usable with support by the people with dementia themselves. It is clear that the same material, controlled by a carer using a mouse, would provide a completely different experience for the person with dementia. What they would see would be a succession of media items changing without any apparent cause. The connection between the user and the multimedia display would be broken.

(2) *On-screen controls at the bottom of the display*. We found that if the controls were at the top of the screen, users got fatigued holding their arms up for extended periods. Moving the buttons to the bottom of the screen made an immediate difference.

(3) *Large format screen with large font sizes*. The large screen compelled attention but also invited participation through touching the on-screen buttons. Font sizes need to be large enough to be readable by people who are likely to have some vision problems.

(4) *Minimal amount of text*. Even with working memory loss, reading ability is still present. The problem is remembering what was at the beginning of a long passage when you reach the end. Short text items are feasible and useful for labeling graphics and providing explanations and prompts.

(5) *A hypermedia structure with a limited range of choices*. Hypermedia structures have become familiar through the popularity of the World Wide Web.

The highly flexible and multidimensional nature of hypermedia, which has been cited as a potential navigation problem for users, may in fact be of benefit in a system such as this, in that it does not put any penalty on 'losing the place' (Conklin, 1987; Alm *et al.*, 1990; McKerlie and Preece, 1992). Whatever place the user is in is the right place to be. Exploring and 'getting lost' can be actively encouraged as strategies to enjoy experiencing the material. In contrast with navigating through a structure with the purpose of finding some specific information, the process which casual conversation more closely resembles is the browsing experience, where serendipity and chance encounters are welcome features. Usefully, this maps onto the concern in dementia care to make sure that activities for people with dementia are as far as possible 'failure free' (Sheridan, 1987; Feil, 1993). Ensuring this can take a great deal of sensitivity and skill on the part of cares and relatives, and can be an exhausting effort. Because of the way hypermedia can simulate memory links and topic-based conversation, the software we have developed provides a failure-free experience which the person with dementia can enjoy, which empowers them, and which allows the carers to relax and become an equal participant in the interaction.

(6) *An attractive design to please, surprise, and engage the user*. One manifestation of the multidisciplinary aspect of this project is the attractive and interesting look that the system has, which was produced by an experienced team of designers. The look and feel of the system is inviting, polished, and professional. We are convinced that the appearance of the system encourages engagement in a way that a less aesthetically pleasing interface might not. This relates to what has been called the 'aesthetic–usability effect.' Aesthetic designs tend to be perceived as easier to use than less-aesthetic designs (Kurosu and Kashimura, 1995; Norman, 2002; Lidwell *et al.*, 2003). Since the aim of this system is to engage the continued attention and involvement of people for whom this has proved difficult, this is not just a matter of a desirable extra feature.

10.6.4 Implications for Policymakers

The implications for policymakers of the research are that people with dementia are not beyond reach, even with significant cognitive problems. This of course has always been argued by those campaigning on their behalf, but a system such as this provides a means for all carers, and not just the most skilful or knowledgeable ones, to have an interaction with a person with dementia which is satisfying to both parties.

10.6.5 **Next Steps**

The next stage for this research is to study in more detail the videotapes we have made of people using CIRCA, with the aim of identifying ways to improve future versions of the system. Also a commercial partner is being sought to make the system widely available. Having developed a way to support communication in dementia, the next task of the team will be to address the problem of occupying a person with dementia with an interesting and entertaining experience which they could control on their own, without assistance from a carer. The content for such a system, and a way of prompting the user continually, will be the focus of this project.

Acknowledgments

We would like to acknowledge the essential participation in this work by people with dementia, their relatives, and carers. Alzheimer Scotland and Dundee City Council Social Work Department were active and supportive partners in the project. The project was funded by the UK Engineering and Physical Sciences Research Council.

References

Alm, N. and Arnott, J.L. (1998) Computer-assisted conversation for non-vocal people using pre-stored texts. *IEEE Transactions on Systems, Man and Cybernetics,* **28,** 318–328, Part C No. 3.

Alm, N., Arnott, J.L. and Newell, A.F. (1990) Hypertext as a host for an augmentative communication system. *In Proceedings of the European Conference on the Advancement of Rehabilitation Technology,* ECART, Maastricht, The Netherlands, 14.4a-14.4b.

Alm, N., Dobinson, L., Massie, P. and Hewines, I. (2001) Computers as cognitive assistants for elderly people. In Hirose F.M. *Proceedings of Human-Computer Interaction – INTERACT'01,* Tokyo, July, IOS Press, Amsterdam, pp. 692–693.

Alm, N., Ellis, M. and Astell, A. *et al.* (2004) A cognitive prosthesis and communication support for people with dementia. *Neuropsychological Rehabilitation,* **14**(1/2), 17–134.

Baines, S., Saxby, P. and Ehlert, K. (1987) Reality orientation and reminiscence therapy: a controlled cross over study of elderly confused people. *British Journal of Psychiatry,* **151,** 222–231.

Bourgeois, M., Dijkstra, K., Burgio, L. and Allen-Burge, R. Memory aids as an augmentative and alternative communication strategy for nursing home residents with dementia. *Augmentative Alternative Communications,* **17**, 196–210.

Brown, N.R. and Schopflocher D. (1998) Event cueing, event clusters and the temporal distribution of autobiographical memories. *Applied Cognitive Psychology,* **12**(4), 305–319.

Calvin, W.H. and Ojemann, G. (1980) *Inside the Brain: Mapping the Cortex, Exploring the Neuron,* New American Library, New York.

Conklin, J. (1987) Hypertext: an introduction and a survey. *IEEE Computer,* 17–41.

Conway, M.A. and Pleydell-Pearce, C.W. (2000) The construction of autobiographical memories in the self-memory system. *Psychological Review,* **107**(2), 261–288.

Feil, N. (1993) *The Validation Breakthrough,* Maryland, Health Professions Press.

Ferri, C., Prince, M. and Brayne, C. (2005) Global prevalence of dementia: a Delphi consensus study. *Lancet,* **366**, 2112–2117.

Finnema, E., Drö, R.-M., Ribbe, M. and Van Tilburg, W. (1999) The effects of emotion-oriented approaches in the care for persons suffering from dementia: a review of the literature. *International Journal of Geriatric Psychiatry,* **15**, 141–161.

Jefferson, G. (1984) On stepwise transition from talk about trouble to inappropriately next-positioned matters. In Atkins, J. & Heritage, J. (Eds.). *Structures of Social Action – Studies in Conversation Analysis,* Cambridge University Press, London, 191–222.

Kandel, E. (2006) *In Search of Memory: The Emergence of a New Science of Mind.* Norton, New York.

Kurosu, M. and Kashimura, K. (1995) Apparent usability vs. inherent usability: experimental analysis on the determinants of the apparent usability. *Proceedings of CHI'95,* 292–293.

Lidwell, W., Holden, K. and Butler, J. (2003) *Universal Principles of Design.* Rockport Publications, Gloucester, MA.

McKerlie, D. and Preece, J. (1992) The hypermedia effect: more than just the sum of its parts. *Proceedings of the St. Petersburg HCI Conference,* St. Petersburg, pp. 115–127.

Miller, G.A. (1956) The magical number seven plus or minus two: some limits on our capacity for processing information. *Psychological Review,* **63,** 81–97.

Newell, A.F. (1995) Extra-ordinary computer operation. In Edwards, A. (Ed.). *Extra-ordinary Human Computer Interaction,* Cambridge University Press.

Norman, D.A. (2002) Emotion and design: attractive things work better. *Interactions Magazine,* ix(4), 36–42.

Roth, M., Huppert, F., Tym, E., and Mountjoy, C. (1998) *CAMDEX, the Cambridge Examination for Mental Disorders of the Elderly*, Cambridge University Press.

Sheridan, C. (1987) *Failure-Free Activities for the Alzheimer Patient: A Guidebook for Caregivers*. Cottage Books, Oakland, CA.

Shneiderman, B. (1998) *Designing the User Interface*, Addison Wesley, New York.

Topo, P., Mäki, O., and Saarikalle, K. (2004) Assessment of a music-based multimedia program for people with dementia. *Dementia,* **3,** 331–350.

Woods, R.T. (1994) Management of memory impairment in older people with dementia. *International Reviews in Psychiatry,* **6,** 153–161.

Designing a Cognitive Aid for and with People Who Have Anterograde Amnesia

11

Mike Wu[a], Ron Baecker[a,b], and Brian Richards[b]

[a] Department of Computer Science, University of Toronto, Canada
[b] Department of Psychology, Baycrest, Toronto, Canada

11.1 Introduction

Anterograde amnesia (Curran and Schacter, 2000) is a selective memory deficit that impairs an individual's ability to register, and consciously retrieve, new facts or events following a brain injury. For example, being unable to recollect attendance at your parent's 50th wedding anniversary on the previous week would constitute a failure of anterograde memory. There are a number of conditions capable of damaging the brain's memory structures, including oxygen deprivation (for example, following a heart attack), stroke, encephalitis, tumor, alcohol abuse, or a blow to the head. Anterograde memory failure undermines the ability to perform everyday tasks and engage in social interactions due to difficulty remembering relevant information. In addition to the frustration faced by the memory-impaired individual, it is extremely taxing for caregivers, who must devote considerable energy to remembering appointments, providing reminders when necessary, or acting as an external memory aid for their loved one. These stresses can have a long-term negative impact on the relationships.

Depending on the site of the brain injury, anterograde amnesia may co-occur with retrograde amnesia. Retrograde amnesia relates to difficulty retrieving memories of events that occurred prior to the injury. Retrograde amnesia is typically characterized by a temporal gradient in which remote memories are better recalled than information acquired closer to the time of the injury. Well-established knowledge and skill sets are largely preserved. Finally, the amnesic syndrome is characterized by preserved intellectual ability and problem solving and this differentiates amnesia from dementia.

To our knowledge there are no published statistics on the incidence and prevalence of amnesia. This reflects that, until recently, amnesia was considered an untreatable condition and very little professional attention was paid to it. A pilot study conducted in the province of Ontario in Canada polled 35 neurologists and neurosurgeons who indicated that in a 12-month period between 2002 and 2003 they reported having seen 2050 individuals with diagnoses that typically result in amnesia and of those, 425 were rated as having severe memory impairments. There is no medical intervention capable of restoring the function of damaged brain regions that support memory. Consequently the focus has been on compensatory cognitive rehabilitation (Sohlberg and Mateer, 2001; Wilson, 2002).

Our project (Wu *et al.*, 2004, 2005) involves the design of a cognitive aid with and for people who have anterograde amnesia. We felt that individuals with amnesia needed to be active participants in the design team in order to ensure that what we designed was directly aligned with their expressed needs. To this end, we adopted a participatory design method and involved six individuals with amnesia in our design team. We present our motivations, experiences, and outcomes from this project.

We first describe insights gathered from a series of interviews with persons having amnesia and their family members to better understand how memory deficits affect their lives. We report on key problems that our field study uncovered and some of the coping strategies that were devised in response. Using our findings, we adapted participatory techniques and methods to suit the needs of our design participants who had amnesia. We needed to develop mechanisms to support the reliable transference of information from one design session to the next in order to move the design process along. These mechanisms included four techniques that we used to directly support memory *during* and *in between* design sessions: incorporating structure in review and activity, creating environmental support, emphasizing physical artifacts, and documenting design history.

Our participatory design team envisioned a novel application, called the OrientingTool (see Figure 11.1), that presents situational information (for example, time of day, location, user intentions, and goals) to assist people with amnesia when disoriented and help them get back on mental track. Even when traveling with caregivers, individuals with amnesia are susceptible to feeling lost and disoriented in various settings because of their difficulty in recalling recent events. Such episodes are typically accompanied by anxiety and panic, often compounded by the rush of noise and commotion in unfamiliar public settings. People with amnesia have few established strategies for dealing with such scenarios. If caregivers are present, they often will cue the person with amnesia and help them re-establish equilibrium by informing them of the details of the current situation, but when they are alone – even

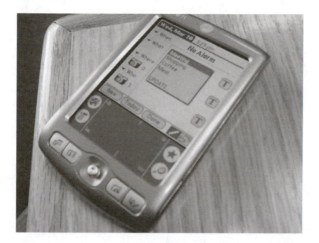

Figure 11.1 The OrientingTool running on a Palm Zire 71.

temporarily – this supportive intervention is not available. Because they have difficulty thinking back through the day's events to try to reason what is going on, people with amnesia may call for police assistance or even wander around the city looking for a familiar landmark that might give a clue to where they are and what it is they are supposed to be doing. In either case, their loved ones often helplessly wait and worry.

We conducted two user studies to evaluate the effectiveness of the tool in ecologically valid contexts: a short-term focused study on usability and a medium-term freeform study on usefulness. The short-term study was conducted in a local shopping mall and the freeform study was performed by the individual with amnesia in settings of their choice where researchers were not present. Our findings suggest that our tool increases self-efficacy and independence in managing new locations or unanticipated situations.

Finally, we reflect on our participatory design experiences and discuss the implications of amnesia on the design cycle as well as its influence on the tool we built. In particular, we consider the implications of training on the design cycle as well as issues in the use of mainstream hardware for memory rehabilitation.

11.2 Field Study

To better understand the domain, we conducted a set of semi-structured interviews. A total of 18 people participated in these interviews: eight people with amnesia, eight caregivers, one health care worker, and one occupational therapist. It was important *not* to solely rely on the responses from those with amnesia because their memory deficits could distort aspects of data collection. Yet they are our primary informants, and with the exception of memory impairment their cognitive and intellectual abilities are preserved, so we needed to hear their voices.

We recruited our interviewees from a group of individuals with amnesia and their families who were participants in the Memory-Link program (Baycrest Directory, 2005) at Baycrest Center. The Memory-Link program is an outpatient service that trains and supports people with amnesia and their families. The program includes participation in a psycho-educational support group, skills training for memory aid use, and links to other relevant services in the community. The people with amnesia who we interviewed had been utilizing memory aids that were developed at Baycrest. In particular, paper-based memory books (Richards *et al.*, 1990) and more recently PDAs were utilized.

Oftentimes, good memory strategies that are well integrated into one's life may work so seamlessly that they can be overlooked during self-reports. In an attempt to learn about these strategies and why they are effective, we arranged the interviews as site visits, in which a researcher would visit the homes of the persons with amnesia and their families to learn more about memory issues and how they impact their lives. This also allowed us to collect detailed information that may be forgotten or omitted by those with amnesia when reporting out of context. Many of the key insights gathered from these interviews were used in the development of the design process and the design of the software tool.

Table 11.1 summarizes some of the results gathered from the interviews. The following subsections describe each of these results and explain themes that unify what we have learned from our field study.

11.2.1 General Memory Issues Since Onset of Impairment

The most prominent problems since the onset of the memory loss can be broken down into two categories: those that occur inside the home and those that occur outside. The issues occurring outside of the home can more easily lead to dangerous situations because the individual with amnesia is often alone in those cases.

In the home, a lack of memory can lead to:

- The misplacement of objects like glasses, papers, keys, telephone messages.
- The inability to complete day-to-day chores (being distracted and forgetting to return to a task that has been interrupted).
- Going into a room but then forgetting why upon arrival.

Table 11.1 *Summary of interview results*

Item	Person with amnesia and family							
	A	B	C	D	E	F	G	H
Degree of Independence								
Living alone						✠		
Living with family	✠	✠	✠	✠	✠		✠	✠
Travels alone	✠	✠	✠	✠	✠	✠	✠	
Travels with family	✠	✠	✠	✠	✠		✠	✠
Schedules own appointments	✠	✠	✠	✠	✠	✠	✠	✠
Has assistance scheduling own appointments				✠			✠	✠
Reviews scheduled appointments with family	✠	✠		✠			✠	✠
Family also reminds individual with amnesia about family events or appointments	✠	✠	✠	✠	✠		✠	✠
Artifacts								
Uses family scheduling calendar				✠	✠		✠	✠
Uses message log book by telephone	✠	✠	✠	✠	✠		✠	✠
Uses lists for keeping track of things		✠	✠	✠		✠		✠
Uses PDA	✠	✠	✠		✠	✠		✠
Uses paper memory book				✠			✠	
Uses a purse, special belt, or custom designed bag for preventing loss of items	✠	✠		✠		✠	✠	
Carries cell phone	✠	✠		✠	✠			
Being Lost								
Experienced at least one situation where completely lost	✠	✠		✠	✠	✠	✠	
Experienced at least one situation where temporarily lost (confused, 30 minutes)	✠	✠	✠	✠	✠	✠	✠	✠
Situation required police assistance				✠			✠	

- Not knowing what is coming up next.
- Not varying the choices of food eaten each day (which can be the same for many meals).
- The inability to recall the plot from a novel while reading it.

Memory impairment can severely affect the following tasks that are often done outside of the home:

- The recall of simple facts that result in repetitive tasks such as walking the dog several times a day.
- Forgetting where one is going, who they are with, or why they are there.
- Misplacement of objects like identification or keys.
- The inability to go somewhere independently.
- The inability to relate back to what was talked about before at social outings.
- Forgetting major events and details (such as family weddings or parties).
- The inability to maintain a job in the competitive workforce, though we note that some of the individuals who have amnesia volunteer at schools or community centers.

11.2.2 Themes

There were many similarities between the lives of our interviewees. The themes that emerged included: a strong dependence on family members, effective family communication and planning, useful structure and routines, a strong dependence on external objects, and good organization to prevent object misplacement. In particular, our interviewees were found to be extremely vulnerable to disorientation, which was a major concern.

A Strong Dependence on Family

Seven of the eight persons with amnesia that we interviewed lived with one or more family members. They relied on family members to provide prompts for such things as medication and appointments. In the lone case where the person with amnesia was living on her own, she still utilized people who were aware of her needs. Though she was initially embarrassed about this, she got over this embarrassment when she realized that she could not function without assistance. Thus, she asked her friends to remind her of dinner or sporting events as needed.

In five of the eight interviews, the person with amnesia reviewed their appointments with a family member. In one case, the family member would casually check the desktop computer once the PDA had synchronized its data to the machine. In another case, the family member sat down with the individual who had amnesia at the start of each month to go over all the scheduled appointments for that month, meeting once a week thereafter to update this overall schedule. Furthermore, for more spontaneous activities (i.e. the person with amnesia deciding to do something not listed in their schedule), updates were made by conversation over cell phones.

This scheduling was very important to the caregivers because it allowed them to know at all times where their loved ones could be found.

Effective Family Communication and Planning

Our interviewees made extensive use of family communication and planning protocols, in the form of designated communication areas, telephone message log books, and family monthly calendars. Several families used a designated communication center (for example, the exterior of a fridge door, or a specific corner of the kitchen table) to transfer notes (such as a shopping list) between members of the family. A telephone message book was commonly used by all families to record and relay phone messages to others. Four of our eight families also made use of some form of family calendar which was kept in a high traffic room, most often the kitchen. This family calendar took the form of a large wall calendar where each page displayed a month. All family members wrote their own schedules and appointments onto the calendar. In this way, an individual could see how planning an activity affected other members of the family. Tick marks were used to indicate when something was completed. This supported planning ahead as well as enabling someone to see if things still need to be carried out for any given day. At the end of each day, it was the person with amnesia who crossed off the day from the calendar so that when they approached the calendar the next morning, they could easily determine the current day. An important aspect of the calendar and phone message book was that once the month was over or the log book page full, the page was torn off and stored away instead of being thrown out. This was a way to record histories of past events as well as details.

Useful Structure and Routines

Our interviews suggested that persons with amnesia made use of structure to increase their ability to function. All of our interviewees currently make use of a paper planner/scheduler or digital scheduling application for managing important appointments. This is because each of them has been involved with Memory-Link. This structured way of handling prospective memory tasks has allowed them to overcome many of the disadvantages of the paper note system to which they were originally accustomed.

Also, daily routines were useful for some people with amnesia – some of whom managed to take their own medication using pillboxes with built-in alarms.

A Strong Dependence on External Aids and Artifacts

All our interviewees who have amnesia relied on external aids and artifacts to compensate for their memory loss. Before joining the Memory-Link group, many of them made use of small pieces of paper to record notes for themselves. For example, these notes included phone numbers, messages, or appointments. These pieces of paper were kept all over the place – in books, pockets, and even left on top of study desks. Oftentimes, the individuals with amnesia would forget that they wrote the information down and thus neglected to check the notes. Essentially, there was much trouble remembering *what* information was written on *which* piece of paper. This resulted in them missing appointments or messages, resulting in their greater dependence on others. However, many of our interviewees use PDAs because of their involvement in Memory-Link. Six of our eight interviewees have been trained to use PDAs to schedule appointments, while the other two make use of a paper memory book. The PDA is mostly used outside of the home.

Lists or journals are also used to keep track of things that may be forgotten. One person with amnesia maintains a menu list so that he can check off what he eats each day to ensure that the same food item is not consumed several days in a row. Another person with amnesia keeps and updates a list of books that he has read so that he does not read the same novel twice. Yet another individual will take notes in a journal to help remember key plot points in a novel so that he can read over his notes to refresh his memory when necessary.

Organization to Prevent Object Misplacement

Almost all interviewees who have amnesia faced issues of misplacing or losing objects. Organization helped to minimize this problem.

Commonly misplaced items were often left in specific locations as decided by the family member and person with amnesia. When these items were found outside of their designated locations, caregivers moved them as appropriate.

In terms of preventing misplacement of commonly used items, five of the eight interviewees made use of a purse, special belt, or custom-designed carrying bag with shoulder strap. The bag was used to carry key equipment such as a cell phone, a PDA, keys, bus tickets/schedules, medication, a first aid package, and/or snacks. One of the individuals with amnesia used string to attach their cell phone, PDA, and keys to the purse in order to significantly decrease their chances of being misplaced. Original documentation such as a health card or a driver's license is never taken outside the home (photocopies are used instead). One interviewee made use of a belt on which his PDA was holstered. The PDA was put back onto the belt immediately after being used.

Disorientation

We have found strong evidence of wandering due to disorientation in all our subjects who have amnesia. The majority of family members considered that losing their loved ones in a crowd was one of their primary fears. Six of eight people with amnesia have experienced situations in which they have become completely disoriented while out on their own. The remaining two have had less intense disorientating experiences lasting minutes, primarily because their family members keep a very tight watch over them and were around to cue them when they become disoriented. While all the interviewees who have amnesia indicated that they had experienced these smaller disorienting incidents, they occurred at varying frequencies. These episodes were often observed by the caregivers when the person with amnesia asked, 'Why are we here again?' or 'What are we supposed to be doing?' All of our subjects with amnesia encountered this disorientation when out of the home, and sometimes in their house as well.

Novel settings or environments can often lead to disorientation in memory impaired individuals. Some examples of novel locations where our interviewees have got lost include: new campsites, different cities while on vacation, and in one case on the way to a community swimming pool that the person with amnesia had only visited once before.

In one example, during a vacation one caregiver reported to the local police that his family member was gone for most of the day and had not returned home as expected. The caregiver waited at his hotel for hours and in the late hours of the night, the person with amnesia was found – on the other side of the island. The person with amnesia had somehow walked 10 miles to another hotel of the same name. Fortunately, the hotel staff helped send this person back by sending a taxi.

Most persons with amnesia stick to familiar activities and routes for fear of becoming disoriented and then lost. Thus, they often will learn the minimal amount of routes and add to them progressively. Once this set of routes become manageable, more routes are added, but with care to avoid overloading. However, an individual having amnesia is still susceptible to being lost in familiar places, such as public settings which can be crowded. Some examples include a grocery store, a hockey arena, a theme park, and a movie theater. Two examples are elaborated upon.

One person with amnesia was leaving a building using the same route that she always uses. However, on this occasion she ran into a friendly staff member who worked in the building. After some conversation in the elevator, he asked her where she was heading and offered to show her the building exit. The person with amnesia followed this staff member but she did not realize that the exit would be different from the one with which she was familiar. When the staff member left her at the exit, she did not recognize her surroundings and did not know where she was.

An individual with amnesia was at mall with his spouse. They decided to momentarily split up and do some independent shopping. The person with amnesia made his way to the nearby grocery store. Upon arriving at the store, he saw that the line-ups were long and so he decided against shopping there. At that point, he forgot why he was there or who he was with. His response was to immediately find a phone to call his spouse. After this incident, this person now becomes anxious just thinking about going to the mall. He explains, 'I can't focus because so much is going on around me and when I can't focus, I panic.'

Strategies to Handle Disorientation

Our interviewees with amnesia each had different techniques for handling the situation when lost. The responses following an episode of disorientation are unpredictable, and different families deal with the situation in different ways. One interviewee acknowledged that he tried to wander around to see if he could recognize any landmarks. In contrast, two other interviewees keep a basic rule of staying within the same building when lost. One person with amnesia once called a taxi when she was lost in order to return to familiar territory. Four of the eight individuals with amnesia carry cell phones, and call home when disoriented, asking family members to cue them in to their present activities and whereabouts. Unfortunately, these severely memory-impaired individuals often forget to bring their cell phones with them, or neglect to turn them on (and thus cannot be reached by the caregivers). While cell phones were seen as useful in such situations, their utility was offset by the proneness of people with amnesia to lose items (i.e. replacement costs would have been prohibitive to practical use). In three incidents (two occurring with one particular individual), we noted that police assistance was required after the person with amnesia felt lost.

11.3 **Related Work**
11.3.1 **Background**

Our current project has been preceded by over a decade of work by clinicians from Baycrest who have developed techniques to minimize the deleterious impact of amnesia on individuals and families. Their clinical and research agenda focused on developing nontechnological compensatory strategies for people who have memory impairments. Richards *et al.* (1990) developed a paper memory book to assist memory-impaired individuals in carrying out prospective memory tasks. These tasks include scheduling appointments, storing contact information, and recording messages for others. The memory book consists of a specialized alarm mechanism and a binder with paper-based day planner enclosed (see Figure 11.2). The day planner is used to record task-oriented events for a particular day, while the alarm can be set to ring at specified intervals. Researchers (Sohlberg and Mateer, 1989; Kime *et al.*, 1996; Richards, 1990) have shown that it is possible to teach memory-impaired individuals to associate the ringing of an alarm with the opening of the attached day planner so that tasks can

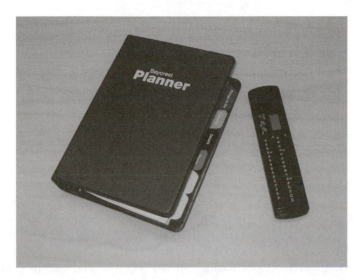

Figure 11.2 *The Baycrest paper-based memory book. The alarm is detached from the book in the diagram, but in actual usage the alarm can be found attached to the back of the front cover.*

be managed. More recently, Richards *et al.* and colleagues (1990) have extended this work by successfully training individuals with amnesia to move from their paper-based memory book to an electronic PDA. They used mainstream scheduling software, and adapted training techniques for electronic media based on the techniques they developed for the paper artifacts. This is the context of our current research.

Our field study revealed the need for supporting persons with amnesia when they are disoriented. The goal of our current research was therefore to develop a system (which we later named the OrientingTool) that could be used to help someone get back on track after becoming disorientated. Unfortunately, current electronic orientation and memory aids are not adequate. We explain why below, and then follow by introducing a design approach called participatory design, how it has been used under varying contexts, and how it can assist in addressing the needs of those with anterograde amnesia.

11.3.2 **Electronic Orientation and Memory Aids**

Research into orientation devices has typically been limited to wayfinding and obstacle avoidance (Blasch *et al.*, 1997; Busboom and May, 1999; Kray *et al.*, 2003). Such systems provide location and position awareness. In developing several wearable orientation and wayfinding interfaces, Ross and Blasch (2002) noted that orientation information should include: current location and heading, distance and direction, overall layout of the surroundings, and things of interest to the user in the environment. The first three items aid spatial orientation and mobility; the last item suggests that additional information relevant to the current situation is needed. We believe that situational information such as intent of a user's actions and context should also be included in orientation. Some of this information can be provided by memory aids.

Researchers have argued for the use of electronic devices as external memory aids in the rehabilitation of memory-impaired individuals (Kapur *et al.*, 2004; LoPresti *et al.*, 2004). Many such devices use built-in alarms to remind patients to carry out tasks at particular times while messages are displayed to provide details of the task. For example, NeuroPage (Hersh and Treadgold, 1994; Wilson and Evans, 1996) is a pager system for assisting memory-impaired individuals in remembering tasks. A caregiver uses a desktop computer to input prompting times and messages. At the appropriate times, the pager transmits those messages to the wearer through a small display on the pager. MAPS-LifeLine (Carmien and Gorman, 2003) is a guided prompting system that supports diminished executive and memory functions by allowing caregivers to track and support clients in remote locations. A caregiver uses a web browser on a desktop computer to create support scripts that can then be used on a client PDA while clients perform day-to-day activities such as shopping. Both NeuroPage and MAPS-LifeLine are distributed support systems in which caregivers must be able to create plans in addition to ensuring successful task completion. In contrast, the goal of our work is to focus on improving self-sufficiency and thus independence in memory-impaired individuals. We hope to support them as they manage their own plans, thereby interactively participating in their own rehabilitation.

Perhaps the most promising orientation aids are mainstream PDA applications. Reminding software such as Note Pad (in the PalmOS), BugMe! (http://www.bugme.net/bugme/), and DiddleBug (http://diddlebug.sourceforge.net/) allow someone to store short notes on their PDA, which can later be displayed through an alarm. These notes can take the form of prospective tasks such as a mental note to remind oneself that a task needs to be completed at a later time. As a result, these applications can be used for storing notes that convey orientation information. However, none of these general-purpose applications have been designed for memory rehabilitation nor do they allow management of a situation in a structured way.

11.3.3 Participatory Design with Populations Having Specific Needs

Participatory design is a specific user-centered design approach where end users join the design team and make design decisions by consensus (Greenbaum and Kyng,

1991). We briefly review how participatory design has been used with populations having specific needs.

Children have preferences and needs that are not necessarily the same as those of adults (Farber *et al.*, 2002). Although there has been significant work in developing a form of contextual inquiry for designing with children (Druin, 1999, 2002; Druin *et al.*, 1998), there is little research focusing on participatory design with people who have cognitive deficits.

Many researchers have developed assistive technologies (LoPresti *et al.*, 2004), but most systems have not been shaped using a participatory design approach. A few notable projects have deemed themselves to be participatory.

Cole and coworkers (Cole *et al.*, 1994; Cole and Dehdashti, 1998) have explored interface design with traumatic brain injured patients by using a single subject case study approach commonly applied in cognitive rehabilitation (Sohlberg and Mateer, 2001). Patients guided the designers in decisions about interface parameters such as text and instructions. Clinicians were involved in design sessions focused upon correcting interface characteristics. A clear majority of the accepted interface changes and functionality in the final product were requested by the patients and clinicians during the development of the system.

Fischer and Sullivan (2002) reported on a participatory approach to design transportation systems for persons having cognitive disabilities. Their research methodology involved conducting field studies that examine socio-technical solutions in light of real-world constraints and cognitive issues. Though their design team was composed of individuals from a very diverse set of stakeholder communities (including assistive care specialists, family support organizations, urban transportation experts, technology designers, and university researchers), the group did not include any persons who had cognitive impairments.

More recently, McGrenere *et al.* (2003), Moffatt *et al.* (2004) have begun the design of assistive technologies while working with persons who have aphasia, a cognitive disorder that impairs speech and language. They made two observations relating aphasics to the design process. First, the fidelity of their prototypes had a very large impact on aphasic individuals. Second, by using nonaphasic participants to help solve general usability problems, the time with aphasics could be spent focusing on language-specific issues.

There are two dimensions along which these projects are situated. They are illustrated through the following questions: (1) to what degree does the cognitively impaired user influence design, and (2) how many impaired users are included in the design team?

All the above investigations have concluded that no single perspective or technique can yield a complete solution. These projects have been deemed 'participatory' by having the disabled user or related stakeholders play a role in the initial design and on-going redesign of the system. Yet in many cases, design teams involving users with disabilities were kept to single-subject sessions (of researcher and user) because the variability of the disorders were extraordinarily wide-ranging, thereby making collaboration between impaired users extremely difficult to manage and operate.

Our research builds upon these important explorations, but may be distinguished from them methodologically. We attempt to more intimately involve cognitively impaired individuals by giving them the ability to *make key decisions by consensus* throughout the design lifecycle rather than just *influencing external designers* through suggestions/feedback at various stages of design. We achieve this by creating a design team that includes six cognitively impaired participants who actively engage in collaborative design discussions. This is very different from prior research (which typically involves only a researcher and a single subject in design sessions). By bringing together *a number* of memory-impaired individuals, we follow more strongly the philosophy of participatory design than have past researchers.

Furthermore, because such severe memory disorders present unique challenges to group work, it is not clear what techniques can be used with people who have amnesia. We overcame these challenges by using a combination of design techniques that were carefully adapted to accommodate these special cognitive needs.

11.4 Participatory Design Approach

In the design of our cognitive aid, we decided to take a participatory design approach for several reasons. People with cognitive deficits have often been marginalized and thereby disadvantaged, but the principles of participatory design advocate respect for all collaborators and thus encourage all participants to contribute. Also, personal expertise is extremely important when cognitive functioning is considered. It can be extremely difficult for designers to imagine the experience of coping with a cognitive impairment, resulting in a gulf in understanding between the impaired and nonimpaired individuals' experiences of the world. This gulf can be bridged through mutual learning (Bødker *et al.*, 1987), a key tenet of participatory design.

We assembled a multidisciplinary design team that consisted of six people with amnesia, one neuropsychologist (third author), and one computer scientist (primary author). Our design team was diverse in age (ranging from 25–55) and past occupations (including a judge and power tools designer). Our participants were selected from a larger group of people having amnesia who were involved with Memory-Link. We decided upon this team composition rather than a single-subject or a larger group in order to establish a critical mass conducive to brainstorming, and a context where

Table 11.2 The design stages in our case study

Design stage	Week
Project overview and goals	1
Needs analysis	2
Requirements analysis	3–4
Concept development	5
High-level design	6–8
Low-level design	9–12

participants could play off other members' ideas. Having multiple team members also meant that design decisions could be made by consensus. This led us to select participants whose level of memory function enabled them to retain some memory for workable periods of time, rather than involving those most severely impaired and unable to retain information for more than a few minutes. Our participants have been living with amnesia for some time and are aware of their own cognitive strengths and weaknesses. They provided many first-hand experiences and insights into their memory difficulties.

The design team participated in early design stages involving: definition of problem statement and goals, requirements analysis, concept development, and high-level and low-level design. Every week, we held a participatory design session lasting one to two hours. We ran these sessions over a period of 3 months. A breakdown of the design stages over time can be seen in Table 11.2.

Doing participatory design in the face of memory impairments was challenging, so we architected the design process to accommodate working with people who have amnesia. In the next few subsections, we present four techniques that we used to directly support memory during and in between design sessions: incorporating structure in review and activity, creating environmental support, emphasizing physical artifacts, and documenting design history.

Incorporating Structure in Review and Activity

For a person with amnesia, the general sense of a presented fact is often available during the entirety of the design session but the details quickly fade or degrade over time. For example, in the middle of a meeting, one of our design participants might know that we spoke about interface components at the beginning of the session but may not be able to recall what was said about those components. It is important to address this as many design decisions are based on a collection of arguments that may be presented over a lengthy period of time.

The most obvious solution to this problem of forgetfulness is to review items throughout a meeting, using redundancy to advantage. Going over the material and design decisions increases the chances that the content becomes *familiar* to the design participants. Also, we have found through our interviews that presenting details at a later stage can help trigger recall of the larger memory encompassing those details. We made use of three reviewing techniques:

1. **Review to prepare** (for supporting memory during session). At the beginning of each session, we verbally reviewed the key components from the previous session to put the current meeting into context.
2. **Review to sustain** (for supporting memory during sessions). At key points during a meeting, such as before a consensus decision was to be made, we would review key details, including arguments from different perspectives.
3. **Review to summarize** (for supporting memory between sessions). At the end of each session, we spent some time discussing and highlighting all the choices that were made during the meeting. We observed that this was an opportunity for new insights to be added in the context of the larger picture. This summary also served as a good way to begin the next meeting.

Though reviewing had the potential to increase familiarity with material, an individual who has amnesia will have difficulty in *remembering specific details*. This was a fundamental challenge. From our interviews, we learned that people with amnesia often deal with problems in a structured manner to increase the chances of successfully completing a task. We thus tried to use activity structuring as much as possible. For example, in one of our meetings, content was divided into sections, and each section had one or more goals that were to be addressed. Since each section was independent of the others, there was no need to recall earlier details of the meeting at later points of the session.

Creating Environmental Support

Some research has specifically used a person's environment to reduce the demands on memory (Craik *et al.*, 1995; Kapur, 1995; Sohlberg and Mateer, 2001). A simple illustration is the use of name tags that allow people to refer to one another by name. The tags remain with their wearers and constitute a part of the environment. We have utilized this theme of environmental support to architect a space for design sessions intended to support memory by reducing the demands on it during meetings.

One example of how we made use of environmental support is in the location we decided upon for our design meetings. We arranged to use a board room at

Figure 11.3 The Baycrest meeting room used for psycho-educational support group meetings.

Baycrest. All of our design partners agreed that the room conveyed a feeling of importance.

The participants in our design group continue to attend weekly psycho-educational support group meetings in a meeting room (Figure 11.3) at Baycrest. They are familiar with the route to the building and room. We wanted to leverage this as much as possible by holding our participatory design meetings in this room instead of a completely new location. However, one problem we faced was that by holding both the psycho-educational group support sessions and design sessions in the same building, we ran the risk of making it harder for our participants to distinguish the *temporal sequence* of memories that may have been retained from the previous week. In essence, even if memories were recalled, they may be of little use if the ordering of them were mixed. When we referred to details from previous weeks, it seemed more difficult to determine from which session the idea originated. To respond to this issue, we instead arranged to use a board room at Baycrest (Figure 11.4) for holding our participatory design meetings. The board room is a very distinctive space that conveys a feeling of importance as many people associate board rooms with prominent executive meetings. While Baycrest is a familiar location, none of the design group members have worked in the board room before.

We argue that our choice in location for the design meetings supports memory by providing distinctive contextual cues that serve to promote discriminitability. Using a

Figure 11.4 The Baycrest Exton board room used for design group discussions.

different space does introduce new issues – one point being that the unfamiliar space can lead to disorientation. To deal with this, we all met at the original familiar meeting spot and went to the board room as a group, thus removing the time-consuming need to teach each individual the route to the new room. One participant noted early on that though the board room was unfamiliar, she recognized the design partners from the normal weekly psycho-educational support group, and so felt grounded and comfortable, even at times when she felt a little disoriented at the meeting. For the majority of the participants in our design meetings, details of the meeting decayed and were not retained between weeks. After several sessions, however, many recognized the location and understood that a meeting, of which they were members, took place in that space. They knew that they were selected for this work and many could, though inconsistently, recall fragments of discussion when cued with other fragments that helped to trigger the recall.

Another way that we made use of environmental support was through utilizing whiteboard space along with poster stands and physical artifacts to provide distinctive contextual cues to aid memory. We wrote what happened in the meetings onto large pages from a flipchart (see Figure 11.4) and then taped up the pages to stands around the table, arranged in chronological order. We avoided erasing notes from the whiteboards until the design meetings were over. In this way, it was possible to make use of the information written in the room to try to figure out generally what had happened in the meeting should someone forget halfway through the meeting.

Emphasizing Physical Artifacts

As with past neuropsychological case studies (Wilson, 1999), our field studies have shown that people with amnesia rely heavily on external memory aids, such as a calendar or an action item list. This is somewhat equivalent to memory triggers, for example strings on fingers, which people use to remind themselves to do something. With a person having amnesia, however, using a strategy such as a string on their finger will likely fail because remembering the original message attached to the trigger is difficult. Thus, though physical artifacts can aid memory, they must be used in a specific way. We used two different kinds of artifacts in our participatory design sessions:

1. **Paper documents**. Paper documents were used extensively for guiding discussions. Some examples include: meeting agendas, summaries from past weeks, use case scenarios, and options listings. For example, whenever we had a set of choices that needed to be considered by our team, printed materials that detailed the relevant options were brought to the meeting. Oftentimes, going through each option involves a significant amount of discussion. After discussing each item in turn, an individual with amnesia may forget some of the details presented in earlier options. Thus, having this detail readily available on paper assists the decision-making process. Though we often summarize the details by reviewing the options before making a decision, summaries tend to omit specific detail.

2. **Design artifacts**. We created various physical artifacts such as storyboards (see Figure 11.5) where appropriate throughout our design. We often included these

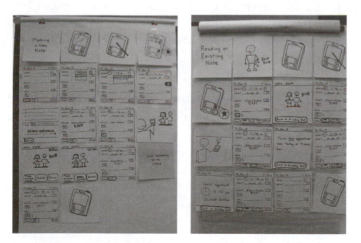

Figure 11.5 Two example storyboards illustrating device usage.

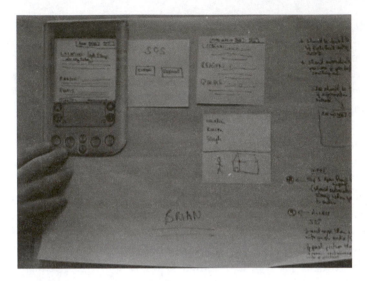

Figure 11.6 *An example of a paper prototype design artifact.*

artifacts while summarizing our meeting by referring to salient elements of the object relevant to our discussion. We also used paper prototyping (Snyder, 2003), which resulted in paper design artifacts (see Figure 11.6 for an example). These physical artifacts were brought to subsequent meetings to supplement reviews, offering a richer context to help trigger recall. From time to time, we arranged objects from past meetings in a linear fashion on the table to illustrate our progression in the design process. The long table of our board room (see Figure 11.4) afforded this ability.

Documenting Design History

Supporting memory between design sessions is one goal in the field of design rationale, which seeks to capture and maintain documentation detailing how designers reason and arrive at their decisions (Moran and Carroll, 1996). Though creating documentation can be tedious and time-consuming, it becomes vital when working with people who have amnesia.

One way of supporting memory between weeks is to allow each participant to take the contents of the meeting with them when they leave, so as to allow review in between sessions. We initially wanted to pass around physical journal books, in which participants could record meeting information. However, as we have noted from our site visits as well as our own attempts at giving out homework packages, objects could be misplaced if the individuals with amnesia were not trained to use them regularly. We have

Figure 11.7 *A few of the PDAs used by the participants on the design team.*

found that such training could take as long as 2 to 3 months, depending on the individual. The thought of putting the information online was considered in response to this, but this was not possible as many of the group members were not comfortable using a desktop computer, nor had convenient access to the Internet.

Before the formation of our design group, a researcher (the third author) had trained the participants in our team to use a Palm Pilot PDA for scheduling appointments and managing lists of action items as part of a rehabilitation program independent of our design project. This training made use of procedural memory systems (Squire, 1982). As such, each member of our design group used a Palm device on a daily basis (see Figure 11.7). We wanted to utilize this training by synchronizing meeting notes into the Palm. In this way, members could take home the minutes and would have access to them throughout the week. Since the memo application was frequently used, the likelihood of reviewing the material from our meetings was reasonably good.

The main problem with this idea was that typing up meeting details was something to be done at a computer after everyone left the meeting. As we held meetings every week, this meant that one week's meeting notes would not be available until the following week. We overcame this by creating two different sets of notes that were staggered in how they were distributed:

1. **Summary notes.** One set of notes described the meeting summary (approximately 100–200 words) along with key homework questions, which were typed up on a

laptop at the end of each meeting while the key points were being reviewed and summarized. After this was completed, the summaries were transferred from laptop to one of the Palms by HotSync. We then used the infrared beaming function of the Palms to pass the notes around to the rest of the group, thereby allowing everyone to leave the meeting with the meeting summary. Making the information immediately available was beneficial in other respects as well; one design partner made this comment of our process: 'This is great. I can show this to my wife. She always asks me what I did that day and I can't remember.' The summary notes were kept short on purpose to avoid the necessity of reading through large amounts of text on a small screen device to get the overall understanding of what occurred.

2. **Detailed meeting minutes**. The second set of notes was a more detailed version of the meeting minutes (typically 300–700 words) that included rationale and justifications for design decisions that were made. These minutes were typed up after the meeting and transferred to the Palm devices the following week. We video recorded each design meeting and occasionally added detail collected from the tapes to the minutes as necessary.

11.5 Orienting Tool Application

The motivation for our work arose from discussions with our participants during the interviews. One individual having amnesia described a situation during which he experienced disorientation and high levels of anxiety as a result. He was on vacation in an unfamiliar city. On this particular day, he was in a casino. As he exited the restroom facilities of the casino, he suddenly realized he had no idea where he was, what he was previously doing, or even who he was with. Looking about, he knew that he was in a casino, but did not recognize any landmarks. He tried to think back and trace through what happened that day, but could not recall anything. Becoming very anxious and feeling lost, he literally shut down and decided to stay where he was, figuring someone would eventually come and find him. Fortunately, his wife, who was concerned about his long absence, went to look for him and did indeed find him.

This issue of sudden disorientation was more prevalent than we at first believed. We found compelling evidence of wandering due to disorientation in all our interviewees. The family members considered that losing their loved one in a crowd was one of their primary fears. As stated earlier, six of the eight interviewees with amnesia have experienced situations in which they have become totally disoriented while out on their own. The remaining two have had milder disorienting experiences lasting minutes, mainly because their family members tend to keep a tight watch over them and are usually around to cue and reorient them.

We wanted to develop a system to support people with amnesia when lost. The basic premise behind our project was that users with amnesia would carry around PDA software that would provide contextual information to cue them to their current situation when disoriented. Our approach was to have the user enter contextual information into their portable system before they begin an activity that has the potential to lead to disorientation and then have the system return that information later when needed. This required that an individual with amnesia must make a conscious effort to input the data beforehand, but how can someone know in advance that they will get lost? Through our interviews we learned that people with amnesia are often aware of their own limitations and are good at recognizing situations in which they may be vulnerable. Persons with amnesia have comfort zones, or routines and places with which they are familiar. Oftentimes, it is the deviation from these zones that leaves them susceptible to being lost or confused. The ultimate vision of our system was that it would allow someone to push beyond their comfort zone and independently explore new spaces and new situations. Reliability of the device would instill more confidence in one's ability to expand their experiences and situations, rather than solely sticking to what is currently comfortable or known.

Our design participants each owned and operated Palm devices, so our design team chose to design for the Palm platform. We used the Palm Zire 71 (http://www.palmone.com/) as the PDA hardware for prototyping (see Figure 11.1). The software application was developed using C++ and runs on the PalmOS 5 platform. Our application was also programmed to be backwards compatible with PalmOS 3.5 and will thereby run on the majority of existing Palm devices on the market.

11.5.1 Basic functionality

Once the OrientingTool is launched, its main form is displayed (see Figure 11.8). This form is used to record the current situation. It is also the same screen that is shown for cueing the user. The main form always shows the current day and time at the top of the screen. The body of the form is organized into four sections, labeled: When, What, Where, and Who. The What, Where and Who sections each contain a labeled pop-up trigger, a text field, and a button. The text fields are filled in with appropriate information pertaining to the situation. A set of buttons are listed at the bottom of the screen. The New button clears the form completely. The Today button retrieves and displays all appointments on the current day from Palm's Calendar application (Calendar is an application provided by the Palm). The Done button signals that a complete note has been entered into the application.

Figure 11.8 (left) The OrientingTool main form. (right) A shortcut menu is displayed when the What trigger is tapped.

Having all the details on one screen allows the user to see the pertinent information all at once, decreasing the chance that the user misses some information because of inaction or lack of adequate exploration.

Tapping on one of the four triggers will activate a menu of options. For example, the What shortcuts are displayed on the right in Figure 11.8. For the What, Where, and Who triggers, the menu lists a set of shortcut options. Tapping on a shortcut will insert text into the text field. Similarly, the Who trigger pops up a list of names and a subsequent tap on a listed name dismisses the menu and appends the selected name to the text field. We incorporated these shortcuts for commonly used phrases to help reduce the total interaction time because entering words through a digital keyboard can be slow.

Tapping on one of the buttons (labeled T) beside a text field will bring up the system keyboard so that customized text can be appended into the associated text field.

The When pop-up trigger is used to set an optional alarm for external prompting to request user attention. This feature is intended for spontaneous meeting arrangements, rather than scheduled appointments (like meetings with a doctor) that are kept in the Calendar. When the trigger is tapped, a list of durations is presented (1 minute, 5 minutes, 10 minutes, etc.). As opposed to how an alarm is set with the Calendar, where a time (precise to the minute) is explicitly set using at least seven taps, the alarm in the OrientingTool is set using only two taps (one to trigger the menu, one to select the interval). After the user selects one of the options, the system calculates the time that the alarm will ring and displays this time to the right of the trigger. When the alarm is triggered, a series of reminder screens that is consistent with how Calendar behaves is presented to get the attention of the user.

11.6 **Evaluation**

One of the fundamental difficulties (Madsen, 1996) in evaluating the effectiveness of cognitive aids is demonstrating ecological validity. This is largely because many experiments require that variables be controlled, a feat easier to achieve in the laboratory. While demonstrating use of a system in a laboratory environment is useful, this may shed little light on effective deployment and use of a device in real situations. We wanted instead to observe OrientingTool usage in ecologically valid contexts.

We conducted a pair of user studies: one short-term focused evaluation, and the other a medium-term freeform study. We were interested in how the application would be used in real settings, but we faced an unusual dilemma. The goal of the OrientingTool is to help people with amnesia when they are feeling lost or disoriented, but we wanted to avoid placing them under any source of anxiety during our evaluations. Therefore, in our first study we orchestrated some reasonable situations and made direct observations. In our second study, we installed the OrientingTool on our study participants' Palm devices so that it could be used with their families in real situations. However, it was made clear to each participant that the tool was only to be used in situations with which all parties felt comfortable.

11.6.1 **Training**

There is now robust evidence that procedural memory is preserved in amnesia (Squire, 1982; Squire and Frambach, 1990; Muller *et al.*, 1997). Procedural memory refers to the ability to learn new skills and associations based on prior experiences without the conscious recollection of those experiences. Another term for this is learning without awareness. Procedural memory forms the basis of our ability to acquire skills and habits that require repeated practice (i.e. swimming, touch typing). Capitalizing on this preserved memory system and enhancing learning through a combination of errorless learning (Wilson, 2002) and vanishing cues (Gliskey *et al.*, 1986) formed the basis of our training technique.

Participants first underwent training in the skill set needed to utilize the OrientingTool. Once the fundamentals were acquired we employed role playing techniques to mirror potential situations where OrientingTool use would be appropriate.

In total, seven people with amnesia participated in hour-long training sessions. Each session consisted of two blocks of ten trials. Training was individualized and participants varied in the number of sessions required to reach a criterion of 95% correct responses on two successive sessions.

The dips in Figure 11.9 correspond to places where either there were many different responses possible or the next step was not immediately obvious from the

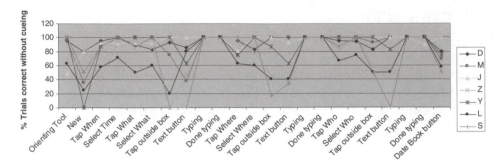

Figure 11.9 *Average training data for all seven participants in their initial 20 trials of training. This was when the participants were first learning tool use. Each trial is broken into 24 interaction steps.*

interface. These stumbling blocks indicate elements of the interface that were unintuitive and did not provide enough support for someone to logically reason out what the next step might be. As training continued, these dips became less pronounced and eventually disappeared. One source of confusion that our training identified was the difficulty in canceling a shortcut menu by tapping outside of the menu. This might be necessary if no shortcut item was appropriate for the given scenario. Our trainees stumbled at this point, which we believe is the result of the system not providing enough environmental support for the action. This difficulty resolved as the participants approached the criterion in their training (see Figure 11.10), but one interface improvement may be to embed a text entry option in the shortcut menu.

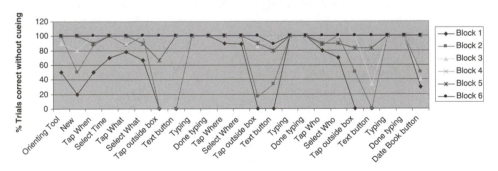

Figure 11.10 *Progression of improvement. The first six blocks (60 trials) of one of our study participants, demonstrating the amount of cueing needed at different interaction steps. Fewer cues were needed as the participants performed more trials.*

From our training, we realized that we needed a way for the users to signify completion of note input. Though this was not technically required for the tool to function, all our trainees were unsure what to do once they finished inputting their notes into the OrientingTool (this is before we added the Done button). Most of our trainees expected to turn off the device at this point. However, when the Palms are reactivated, the last run application (our tool in this case) is displayed. This is a problem because the majority of our participants expect the Calendar to be opened to the current calendar day when they turn on their device, as it is their usual center of operations. We organized a design session to discuss this and decided to make a slight system change before further training. We added a button to the main form (labeled Done) that switches the current application to the Calendar. Adding a button to close the OrientingTool is not consistent with Palm's User Interface guidelines (Palm OS, 2005), in which applications are not closed. However, we felt that this was an important exception to the rule of thumb.

11.6.2 Evaluation Phase 1: Short-term Focused Study

We planned a 2-hour evaluation of the OrientingTool in a local shopping mall to test tool use in a highly distracting real-life environment. A total of 15 people were involved in this evaluation: six people with amnesia, seven confederates, and two observers. We were curious to know if there might be a difference in reactions to the OrientingTool between designers in our group and people with amnesia who were not involved with design. As such, of the six study participants, three were from our design team and three were not. One of the participants (F) acted as a control in our evaluation. He had not been previously trained to use PDAs, but made use of a paper memory book (Richards *et al.*, 1990; Kime *et al.*, 1996).

Each participant had the OrientingTool loaded onto their Palm, and was paired with a confederate partner. The paired teams were to meet at designated times and locations throughout the mall, but before these meetings, the teams were to engage in shopping activities that included: product price matching, finding a gift or item, and collecting specific product details. We chose these activities as they are common shopping tasks. The activities were presented to the teams as a scavenger hunt, to be completed as the partners worked together. Each team received a different selection of activities. We ran three trials in total, with each trial lasting for 30–40 minutes. All the pairs had to meet together at the same time. We chose this format instead of meetings between two pairs because we did not want any groups waiting around should one of the groups miss their meeting. No participant worked with the same confederate more than once. This allowed us to examine each person's tool usage from at least three perspectives.

The confederates were to stay with their partners to ensure that they did not get lost, and they also helped as direct observers, distracters, and prompters. At the end of each trial, the confederates recorded notes about usage of the OrientingTool. During trials, in order to prevent the participants from consciously concentrating on remembering that a meeting was scheduled, the confederate partner acted as a distracter by engaging the participants in shopping activities. If after 10–15 minutes the person with amnesia did not inquire about what should be done next, the confederate casually asked if they remembered what should be done next. By doing so, we observed if the prompting led to access of the OrientingTool. We also wanted to know whether or not the notes could trigger a correct recall of the situation, how much prompting and intervention was needed to use the device, and if there were any spontaneous unguided accesses to the OrientingTool.

During the trial, some confederates asked their partners if they knew what was to happen next, and watched to see if the OrientingTool would be used. Confederates also watched for any checking of the tool without external prompting. We paid attention to the alarms, errors in tool use, and whether or not additional reinforcement from the confederate was needed when the user made an orienting note.

11.6.3 **Evaluation Phase 1 Results**

Ambient Noise Obscuring the Alarm Cue

We did not anticipate that the ambient noise in the shopping mall would interfere with the Palm alarm, but the alarm was heard in only seven of the 15 trials despite being set to maximum volume. In one of these trials, only the study participant heard the alarm while the confederate did not. In the six other cases when the alarm was noticed, the pairs were either away from the traffic of people or walking inside less busy stores. In the cases when the alarm was not heard, the confederate prompted their partner 5 minutes after the meeting time asking them if they knew what was to happen next. In every case that this was asked, the participant took out their Palm and checked. Upon activating their Palm, a reminder screen was already displayed (as in the default behavior of the Calendar) that was used to see the last input OrientingTool note. In 12 of the 15 trials, the participant then mentioned relevant information to the confederate.

Spontaneous Use of the Tool

We observed two instances in which a participant spontaneously checked their device without an alarm or confederate providing the cue. In the first case, subject Y wanted to check the meeting time before proceeding onto the next shopping activity. He checked his Palm and realized that the alarm had already gone off. In the second case, the confederate partner of subject M wanted to sit down briefly to jot down a few quick notes. As the confederate sat down, subject M asked aloud what time the next meeting was scheduled for while pulling out his Palm. He saw that the meeting was to happen soon and voiced the location to the confederate. Shortly thereafter, another pair (Y and confederate) walked by and subject M pointed out to them that they were heading in the wrong direction for the next meeting. Subject Y then pulled out his Palm and confirmed this. This sharing of information by the participants occurred in three of 15 trials (two of these were as a result of spontaneous access to the tool).

Dependence

In the first trial, only half of the pairs made it back to the meeting location in under 30 minutes. The confederates did not know the meeting times or locations until they were announced to all the pairs. In one instance, the confederate was actually relying on the Palm to ring at the proper meeting time (she forgot the group meeting time).

There was a notable difference between the pairs using the OrientingTool and the subject that did not. Subject F relied almost entirely on the confederate to remind him of the meeting. The confederate used his watch for timing. In all trials, subject F did not want to use his paper memory book, saying that it was used for other things (scheduling, phone numbers, etc.). He did write the meeting details on the mall map that he carried. However, this was not reliable because he forgot to check the map. Not surprisingly, the reliance on the confederate added greater responsibility and a larger mental load on that individual.

Errors

In six of the 15 trials, the participant initially started to use the Calendar to schedule the meeting. In five of those cases, the confederate pointed out that there was something else that could be used, and upon hearing this, each of the participants made use of the OrientingTool. In the lone case where the confederate did not realize this, subject J used the Calendar to schedule the meeting. However, the alarm in the Calendar was not set, and so when it came time to meet there was no cue. Upon closer examination of how the Calendar was used, no contextual information was added other than the meeting location. He neglected to specify that there would be a meeting, nor did he mention who would be present.

11.6.4 **Evaluation Phase 2: Medium-term Freeform Study**

A second evaluation (running 3 weeks) was planned to explore real situations in which the OrientingTool might be spontaneously used. We wanted to better understand how the tool is utilized, in what situations, and how often the caregivers provided cues or prompts. We realized that any solution that would be integrated into the lives of people with amnesia should involve the caregivers or family, who must be constantly present for prompting until the behavior is learned. We handed out observation sheets to each of the family members for recording every instance of tool use.

We installed the OrientingTool onto the Palms of five people with amnesia and asked them to make use of the device in situations with which they felt comfortable. Four individuals who participated in this study were from our design team (D, M, J, L). Person Y was not a designer, and lived independently; as we noticed that he had used the tool spontaneously in the first evaluation phase, we included him in Phase 2.

We held two general group meetings, one after the first week and the other at the end of the 3 weeks. All the family members and the study participants were invited to discuss their experiences with the OrientingTool and suggestions for interface or functionality improvements. For those members who missed any one of the meetings, phone interviews were arranged. In addition to these direct discussions, some computer logging was also done and this data showed that there was consistency between what the people having amnesia and their caregivers reported.

11.6.5 Evaluation Phase 2 Results

In our first user study, we knew that some of the participants might be cued to use their tool by other users who immediately used it within their proximity when the meeting times and locations were announced. In contrast, this second study paid closer attention to whether or not the tool would be spontaneously accessed for input as well as checking without external cues.

There were at least 11 uses of the OrientingTool during the 3-week period. The situations included setting up a lunch meeting, getting back to finish the laundry, returning from a biking trip, shopping, walking the dog, and waiting for an appointment. M's caregiver observed that once they become more accustomed to using the tool, they would be able to use it much more often. L mentioned, 'I use it . . . oh . . . about two times a day,' becoming '. . . very comfortable using it.' He had used the OrientingTool very much independently from his family member, who did not supervise use of the tool at all, but noticed through casual observance and discussion that it was being utilized daily.

Sample Personal Accounts

On the first day after the tool was installed, L was waiting by himself at Baycrest for a doctor's appointment at 3:00 p.m. He arrived early at 2:20 p.m. and decided to stay in the main lobby as there was a piano performance in the public space. Once that ended, L read a book on one of the benches. At 2:50 p.m., he began to wonder why he was there. He knew where he was, but did not know for what purpose. Reasoning that he was not there for a board meeting as he was wearing shorts, he figured that he was probably there for a doctor's appointment but still did not know with whom or when. Without external cueing, he took out his Palm device and started the OrientingTool – this reoriented him in to what was going on.

Participant L took his father to a dentist appointment, which lasted 40 minutes. While waiting for his father, he decided to get a cup of coffee from the coffee shop across the street from the dentist. Before leaving the dentist's office, he utilized the OrientingTool and simply used the What field to say that he was waiting for his father who was in a dentist appointment. He did not use an alarm. While sipping his coffee, he placed his Palm on the table where he could see it. After finishing his coffee, he checked his device and saw that he was to pick up his father from the dentist. This allowed him to return to the dentist's office.

Participant J and his family member used the OrientingTool in a few shopping scenarios. In one case, they used it for a grocery shopping task. The family member prompted J to input the note into his Palm before leaving the house. When they arrived at the grocery store, the family member asked if J knew what they were doing there. He replied that he knew they were to go to the grocery store, but he forgot why. He automatically took out his Palm without further cueing and launched the OrientingTool, where he saw what he needed to do. He then proceeded to enter the store and pick up a food item while the family member observed him through the large store windows from the outside.

Participant D went bicycling with his daughter a couple of times. In both cases, D's wife wanted him and their daughter to return in half an hour, and suggested that he use the OrientingTool. In the past, D's wife had to go out to find them because they would not return from their excursion. 'He argued it for a second,' said D's wife, 'but then I know he'll be back.' On both these occasions that the tool was used, D returned with his daughter on time.

We were surprised to see that participant Y made use of the OrientingTool, particularly because he did not have a family member to prompt his usage of the tool. He used the OrientingTool while doing his laundry. After putting his clothes into the washing machine, he marked a 15-minute alarm into his device and wrote in 'laundry.' When asked about his first impressions of the tool, he claimed, 'In many ways, I thought it was useless – but you know what? It actually helps. It does make a difference – *for me*.'

Initial reservations

There were some initial reservations from three participants (D, Y, L) because they felt that the OrientingTool was a duplication of the Calendar functionality, but when they started to use the OrientingTool, they began to understand the differences and found the tool useful. A caregiver observed, 'When he finds it helps, then he'll use it. First he thought it was the stupidest thing . . . He thought it was duplication, and now he sees the use for it.' At the same time, one individual having amnesia was reluctant to use his OrientingTool when he was prompted because he felt he would remember the detail. His family member commented, 'He'll get mad at me because he thinks he can remember that one little thing. Like if he wants to do the laundry or something around the house, he thinks he'll remember and I can't sort of remind him because he'll get mad at me . . . Even with this new tool, he got mad at me the first couple of times we tried it . . . But he goes "You know what? This works." And then he did it on his own because he went to take the laundry out and there wasn't anyone to go with him, and he used it – on his own.'

Spontaneous Use of the Tool

Spontaneous use of the OrientingTool is a vital step for autonomous functioning. At least five cases were spontaneous in that the person with amnesia chose to use the device without prompting from another person. Of these uses, two were for completing a laundry task, two were for waiting for an appointment, and one was for setting up a lunch meeting. L mentioned that he used the tool by himself at least twice a day. This was confirmed by the family member who did not prompt him at any point during the 3-week period.

Support for Short-duration Tasks

We found that some of our participants were making use of the OrientingTool in a way that was slightly different from how we expected they would use it. We started our designs by focusing on helping people with amnesia with orientation when they were lost. However, it seems that through actually using it, the use of the device has shifted away from assistance with disorientation to assistance with keeping on track for shorter-duration tasks (lasting around 10–30 minutes), such as doing the laundry or mailing a letter while walking the dog. These particular tasks were not mentioned during training sessions or design meetings. This is a more functionally driven use of the OrientingTool rather than a preventative focus. On this realization, one caregiver mentioned, 'Yeah, we can use this everyday – like a couple of times everyday . . . Practically, it's got more uses than you [originally] thought.' This may be an important step toward eventual integration of the tool in real life. As this usage pattern is frequent and habitual, it improves the tool's readiness and availability when needed for situations that could potentially lead to disorientation.

Confidence and Assurance

One of the goals of our work is to improve the confidence and autonomy of our participants. On this matter and on the OrientingTool, M commented, 'Pretty unique. Certainly gives you a feeling of confidence . . . that helps develop independence again . . . independence is really my ultimate goal.'

At the same time, the OrientingTool provided much comfort and assurance for the family members of those having amnesia. One caregiver recalls, ' . . . we've gone to a trade show or one of those big places where you could get lost. You'd [normally] say "I'll meet you at [location]," but I could never do that with him. We relied on the cell phone – we always had a cell phone. But now I know for sure [that] if the cell phone doesn't work in the building or something, I don't have to worry – he'll know where to meet me.' This reassurance was echoed by all the other caregivers in our group. 'I can't think how many times we were at [a store] that [he] wanted to go wandering and he'll say I'll meet you in 15 minutes, and I'm walking – *looking at him* because I have to keep an eye on him . . . And now I have confidence that he'll know where to meet me . . . At the book aisle or the cash . . . It's huge for that.'

11.7 Issues and Discussion

We faced some issues and barriers which we discuss in this section. The acceptance of technology may be influenced by how the technology is perceived by others, general-purpose tools are not necessarily suited to support memory-impaired individuals despite training being a solution, and the need to train usage can lead to a decreased ability to explore radical design ideas. We also reflect on our participatory design experience and discuss various implications for users, developers, researchers, and policymakers.

11.7.1 Acceptance

Though assistive devices can be invaluable, people with cognitive deficits may be reluctant to use them in public if this may label them as impaired or disabled (Fluharty, 1993; Kime *et al.*, 1996). As a result, there is often a stigma associated with assistive technologies (Keates *et al.*, 2000), leading to lower acceptance rates of such devices. We did not observe this response from our design partners who were in fact very excited about the prospects of the OrientingTool. This might have been due in part to the nature of their involvement in this project, as some researchers have suggested that consumer involvement improves acceptance of the device (Wilson *et al.*, 2001). We also posit that the decision to use Palm hardware positively contributed to their perceptions of the orientation application. PDAs are used by a broad range of people for a variety of different reasons such as games or appointment scheduling, and so being associated with something like a Palm Pilot in no way labels the user as impaired. Thus, the use of a mainstream hardware platform for our software seems to have reduced the barrier to its acceptance as a memory aid.

11.7.2 Special-Purpose vs. General-Purpose Tools

Given that our users must train before they are able to effectively use an application, we could have conceivably trained them to use a general-purpose application instead of the OrientingTool. The problem with this is that general-purpose applications were not built with the needs of someone with severe memory impairments in mind, and so conventional systems often follow other guidelines that are based on a different value system. For example, if we had trained users to use Palm's Memo Pad application in a manner similar to the OrientingTool, they might write paragraphs of text to describe their situations, but because the application is freeform with no logical structure, we conjecture that there is an increased potential for error through leaving out important details.

11.7.3 Implications of Training on the Design Cycle

Training our participants was a necessary step toward effective use of our tool. One result of this was that all our users became experts with the interface before the tool was deployed for evaluation. This has serious implications on the duration of design cycles. Design is inherently iterative, involving cycles of system design, development, and testing. In our project, training can take a large amount of time and thus there exists a lag between prototype development and testing. It is important to identify if there may be ways to shorten this lag and thus the duration of the design cycle. One thought is to break the prototype into chunks that can be trained in a staggered manner so that the entire system need not be built before portions of it are evaluated.

As design is iterative, recommendations to change the interface between cycles necessitates that new skills must be acquired and old skills corrected. While training is essential, researchers have also argued for minimal training of memory-impaired people, since past skill sets may interfere with new ones (Wilson and Evans, 1996). Since we spent a nontrivial amount of time on training, we cannot test a prototype, make an interface change, and test it again in a reasonable time frame. We have tried to address this problem by considering possible interface conflicts in the early stages of design. However, iterations must build upon each other carefully, and this issue reduces a team's ability to explore vastly different design ideas once a prototype is developed.

11.7.4 **Reflection on Participatory Design Experience**

We have had major contributions from all members of our team. Active participation in the design sessions led to at least one participant from our group feeling more confident in his ability to handle disorientation incidents. In one instance when participant L made use of the OrientingTool, he remembered having discussed the OrientingTool extensively during design meetings and felt confident in the tool's ability to keep him on track. His confidence appeared to encourage him to use the tool more often.

One way of examining whether our participatory design approach was appropriate in our project is to examine the end results and product. The fact that the design team worked together as a cohesive unit, despite differences in opinion at times, was encouraging. As well, the success of the OrientingTool as a product of our design suggests that we succeeded in achieving our design goals. In terms of mutual learning, the two design members without amnesia (i.e. the author and neuropsychologist) learned a great deal about amnesia from those living with memory impairments. Likewise, though the individuals with amnesia had difficulty remembering the specific details of their design group experience, they developed an appreciation for the design work in which they were direct contributors. In another incident, participant S was shocked to see the initial electronic prototype of the OrientingTool being demonstrated on a Palm. When asked why she was surprised since the team had been designing the tool for a couple of months, she commented that she had previously been in many meetings that resulted in a lot of talk, but with little action or results.

The majority of our design team had amnesia (six of eight individuals), but in actuality everyone in the team experienced memory lapses during our design sessions. The participants with amnesia were relieved to see that those without the impairment (i.e. the author and neuropsychologist) could make mistakes based on poor memory, and derived enjoyment from lighthearted joking about the situation. We sometimes used these episodes of memory failure as common ground with our participants, and as a way to remind them that our design work may have implications for those with normal memories as well.

11.7.5 **Implications for Users, Developers, Researchers, and Policymakers**

Individuals with amnesia usually show good physical and intellectual recovery but their memory deficits prevent them from functioning independently. This, in turn, places significant burden on their families, the health care system, and society.

Consequently, there is a need for policymakers to develop more effective ways of dealing with amnesia. Emerging electronic technology provides an unparalleled opportunity to develop practical solutions through the design and development of memory aids. With regards to the design process, our research has demonstrated that users with cognitive impairments can play vital roles in designing their *own* technological aids. This is particularly encouraging as it suggests that people with cognitive impairments can be active participants in driving their own rehabilitation. Our work draws researchers' attention to the notion of utilizing of the users' unique strengths to offset their deficits. For example, researchers should be aware that cognitively impaired users may have intact procedural learning systems that can enable them to use complex technology. Finally, both researchers and developers can make use of participatory design as a method for understanding the population for whom they intend to design, and may find it satisfying to learn from and work closely with their user population.

11.8 Conclusion

We have demonstrated that participatory design is a viable option for populations having memory impairments. For the most part, participatory design teams with cognitively impaired populations have in the past involved single-subject cases in which the design partners offered suggestions to an external designer, but did not act the role of the designer. Our team consisted of six people with amnesia and two others who collectively made design decisions by consensus and solved problems together. We developed four techniques that supported memory during and in between our sessions.

Through our participatory design sessions, we have designed and developed the OrientingTool for Palm devices, specifically created to accommodate the needs of people having amnesia. This tool assists people with amnesia when they feel lost or disoriented by providing information as to their whereabouts and their intent for being where they are. We have successfully trained a group of people with amnesia for interaction with the tool and have evaluated it under both a designed situation and more realistic settings. Our results suggest that it allows people with amnesia to effectively manage situations in which disorientation would otherwise provoke high levels of anxiety.

11.8.1 Current status and future directions

The OrientingTool is now being regularly used by the participants of our study in their daily lives. We will be training new clients how to use it and anticipate conducting long term follow up studies of the tool's everyday application.

Our case study of amnesia may also inform the design of systems for those who have normal-functioning memory. It is not difficult to imagine situations in which past meeting content is forgotten due to incomplete documentation, information overload, or simply a long break since the last meeting. Such circumstances can easily arise when participants are placed under stressful deadlines or settings. While this loss of information is not attributed to amnesia, the resulting effect is similar. We will continue developing this branch of research with the goal of demonstrating how our design techniques and outcomes have greater applicability beyond amnesia.

References

Baycrest Directory of Programs and Services (2005). *Memory-Link*. Retrieved October 24th, 2005 from `http://www.baycrest.org/directory/directory_memory_link_se12.asp`.

Blasch, B., Wiener, W. and Welsh, R. (1997) *Foundations of Orientation and Mobility*. 2nd edn, American Foundation of the Blind.

Bødker, S., Ehn, P., Kammersgaard, J. et al. (1987) A UTOPIAN experience: on design of powerful computer-based tools for skilled graphic workers. In Bjerknes, G., Ehn, P., & Kyng, M. (Eds.). *Computers and Democracy – A Scandinavian Challenge*, 251–278

Busboom, M. and May, M. (1999) Mobile navigation for the blind. *Proceedings of ICWC 1999*.

Carmien, S. and Gorman, A. (2003) Creating distributed support systems to enhance the quality of life for people with cognitive disabilities. *Proceedings of UbiHealth* 2003.

Cole, E. and Dehdashti, P. (1998) Computer-based cognitive prosthetics: assistive technology for the treatment of cognitive disabilities. *Proceedings of the International ACM Conference on Assistive Technologies*, pp. 11–18.

Cole, E., Dehdashti, P., Petti, L. and Angert, M. (1994) Participatory design for sensitive interface parameters: contributions of traumatic brain injury patients to their prosthetic software. *Proceedings of the SIGCHI Conference on Human Factors in Computing Systems*, pp. 115–116.

Craik, F., Anderson, N., Kerr, S. and Li, K. (1995) Memory changes in normal ageing. In Baddeley, A., Wilson, B., & Watts, F. (Eds.). *Handbook of Memory Disorders*, John Wiley & Sons, 211–241.

Curran, T. and Schacter, D. (2000) *Cognitive Neuropsychological Issues, Patient-Based Approaches to Cognitive Neuroscience*, M. Farah & T. Feinberg (Eds.). The MIT Press, 291–299.

Druin, A. (1999) Cooperative inquiry: developing new technologies for children with children. *Proceedings of the SIGCHI Conference on Human factors in Computing Systems,* ACM Press, pp. 223–230.

Druin, A. (2002) The role of children in the design of new technology. *Behavioral Inference Technology,* **21**(1), 1–25.

Druin, A., Bederson, B. and Boltman, A. (1998) Children as our technology design partners. In *The Design of Children's Technology: How We Design and Why?* A. Druin (ed.). Morgan Kaufmann, 51–72.

Farber, A., Druin, A., Chipman, G. et. al. (2002) How young can our design partners be? *Proceedings of the Participatory Design Conference,* pp. 272–277.

Fischer, G. and Sullivan, J.Jr. (2002) Human-centered public transportation systems for persons with cognitive disabilities. *Proceedings of the Participatory Design Conference,* pp. 194–198.

Fluharty, G.P.D. (1993) Methods of increasing client acceptance of a memory book. *Brain Injury,* **7**(1), 85–88.

Gliskey, E.L., Schacter, D.L. and Tulving, E. (1986) Learning and retention of computer-related vocabulary in memory-impaired patients: method of vanishing cues. *Journal of Clinical and Experimental Psychology,* **8**(3), 292–312.

Greenbaum, J. and Kyng, M. (1991) *Design at Work: Cooperative Design of Computer Systems,* Lawrence Erlbaum Associates, Mahwah, NJ.

Hersh, N. and Treadgold, L. (1995) NeuroPage: the rehabilitation of memory dysfunction by prosthetic memory and cueing. *Neurorehabilitation,* **4**, 187–197.

Kapur, N. (1995) Memory aids in the rehabilitation of memory disordered patients. In Baddeley, A., Wilson, B., & Watts, F. (Eds.). *Handbook of Memory Disorders,* John Wiley & Sons, 533–556.

Kapur, N., Glisky, E. and Wilson, B. (2004) Technological memory aids for people with memory deficits. *Neuropsychological Rehabilitation,* **14**(1/2), 41–60.

Keates, S., Clarkson, P.J., Harrison, L. and Robinson, P. (2000) Towards a practical inclusive design approach. *Proceedings of CUU 2000,* pp. 45–52.

Kime, S.K., Lamb, D.G. and Wilson, B.A. (1996) Use of a comprehensive programme of external cueing to enhance procedural memory in a patient with dense amnesia. *Brain Injury,* **10**(1), 17–25.

Kray, C., Elting, C., Laakso, K. and Coors, V. (2003) Presenting route instructions on mobile devices. *Proceedings of IUI 2003,* 117–124.

LoPresti, E.F., Mihailidis, A. and Kirsch, N. (2004) Assistive technology for cognitive rehabilitation: State of the art. *Neuropsychological Rehabilitation,* **14**(1/2), 5–39.

Madsen, K. (1996) Initiative in participatory design. *Proceedings of the Participatory Design Conference,* pp. 223–230.

McGrenere, J., Davies, R., Findlater, L. et al. (2003) Insights from the aphasia project: designing technology for and with people who have aphasia. *Proceedings of the ACM Conference on Universal Usability,* pp. 112–118.

Moffatt, K., McGrenere, J., Purves, B. and Klawe, M. (2004) The participatory design of a sound and image enhanced daily planner for people with aphasia. *Proceedings of the SIGCHI Conference on Human Factors in Computing System,* pp. 407–414.

Moran, T.P. and Carroll, J. (1996) *Design Rationale: Concepts, Techniques and Use.* Lawrence Erlbaum Associates.

Muller, M., Halkswanter, J. and Dayton, T. (1997) Participatory practices in the software lifecycle. In Helander, M., Landauer, T., & Prabhu, P. (Eds.). *Handbook of Human–Computer Interaction,* 2nd edn, Elsevier, 255–313.

Palm, O.S. (2005) User Interface Guidelines. Retrieved October 24th, 2005 from `http://www.palmos.com/dev/support/docs/ui/UIGuide_Front.html`.

Richards, B. (2007) Use of external memory aids in the rehabilitation of severe memory impairment. *Proceedings of the 17th Annual Rotman Research Institute Conference, Brain and Cognition.*

Richards, B., Leach, L. and Proulx, G. (1990) Memory rehabilitation in a patient with bilateral dorsomedial thalamic infarcts. *Journal of Clinical and Experimental Neuropsychology,* **12**, 395.

Ross, D.A. and Blasch, B.B. (2002) Development of a wearable computer orientation system. *Personal Ubiquitous Computing,* **6**(1), 49–63.

Snyder, C. (2003) *Paper Prototyping: The Fast and Easy Way to Design and Refine User Interfaces,* Morgan Kaufmann Publishers.

Sohlberg, M.M. and Mateer, C.A. (1989) Training use of compensatory memory books: a three stage behavioral approach. *Journal of Clinical and Experimental Neuropsychology,* **11**, 871–891.

Sohlberg, M.M. and Mateer, C.A. (2001) *Cognitive Rehabilitation: An integrative neuropsychological approach.* The Guilford Press, 2001.

Squire, L.R. (1982) The neuropsychology of human memory. *Annual Review of Neuroscience,* **5**, 241–273.

Squire, L.R. and Frambach, M. (1990) Cognitive skill learning in amnesia. *Psychobiology,* **18**, 109–117.

Wilson, B.A. (1999) *Case Studies in Neuropsychological Rehabilitation.* Oxford University Press.

Wilson, B.A. (2002) Memory rehabilitation. In Squire, L. & Schacter, D. *Neuropsychology of Memory,* 3rd edn, The Guilford Press, 263–272.

Wilson, B.A. and Evans, J.J. (1996) Error-free learning in the rehabilitation of people with memory impairments. *Journal of Head Trauma Rehabilitation,* **11**, 54–64.

Wilson, B.A., Emslie, H.C., Quirk, K. and Evans, J.J. (2001) Reducing everyday memory and planning problems by means of a paging system. *Journal of Neurology and Neurosurgical Psychiatry,* **70**(4), 477–482.

Wu, M., Richards, B. and Baecker, R. (2004) Participatory design with individuals who have amnesia. *Proceedings of PDC 2004 Participatory Design Conference,* pp. 214–223.

Wu, M., Baecker, R. and Richards, B. (2005) Participatory design of an orientation aid for amnesics. *Proceedings of the SIGCHI conference on Human Factors in Computing System,* pp. 511–520.

Memories of a Life: A Design Case Study for Alzheimer's Disease

12

Tira Cohene[a], Ron Baecker[a], Elsa Marziali[a], and Simona Mindy[b]

[a] Department of Computer Science, University of Toronto, Canada, and Baycrest, Toronto, Canada
[b] Department of Computer Science, University of Toronto, Canada

12.1 Introduction

Technology can be a powerful support tool, leveraging media in order to enhance the lives of individuals affected by disabilities. Unfortunately, the design of this technology can be a complex and challenging process. In this chapter we present research in which we are designing interactive multimedia life stories for families affected by Alzheimer's disease (AD). AD is a degenerative brain disease that causes the deterioration of cognitive abilities such as memory, language, communication, reasoning, and judgment (Alzheimer's Association, 2005). As time progresses the severity of the symptoms increases and the disease advances through the early, mid, and late stages. The expression of the symptoms can range for each individual and at each stage. Currently, there is no cure for the disease, however, there are ways in which the symptoms can be treated.

Our memories are important because they help shape our experiences, our relationships, and our sense of self. The loss of them can be devastating and can cause changes in personality and behavior (Kasl-Godley and Gatz, 2000; Woods, 2001; Alzheimer's Association, 2005). In addition, individuals with AD become increasingly dependent on a caregiver for activities of daily living. Thus the caregiver, who is often a family member, is also very much affected by the disease (Kasl-Godley and Gatz, 2000; Czaja and Rubert, 2002; Alzheimer's Association, 2005). Nearly half of individuals over the age of 85 show symptoms of AD (Alzheimer's Association, 2005). As a result, it is becoming increasingly important to provide social support for the many people who are affected by this pervasive and complex disease.

In order to help cope with these issues, health care communities offer intervention methods. They may focus on memory training, memory support, assisting life aspects strained by memory loss, or facilitating the responsibilities of the caregivers.

Intervention can enhance the well-being of individuals' lives (Kasl-Godley and Gatz, 2000; Spector *et al.*, 2003) and can in some cases slow down the progress of the disease (Wilson *et al.*, 2002). Reminiscence therapy is an example of an intervention activity that can reveal and support a person's identity. Even the family can participate and play a major role to support their relative (Woods, 2001; Marziali, 2003).

Intervention technology refers to technology that provides support or other non-medicinal treatment. Most intervention technology is designed to help individuals perform everyday activities, such as memory aids or planning tools (LoPresti *et al.*, 2004). To date, little attention has been given to the design of technological tools for social support. Elders with cognitive decline can benefit from social support tools, and recent ethnographic research provides insight into the design of such systems (Morris *et al.*, 2004). Several intervention technologies focus on supporting the caregiver, such as specialized telephone and video conferencing applications (Czaja and Rubert, 2002; Marziali, 2003). Few intervention technologies focus on psychosocial support for the patient.

In September 2004 we began a project to create digital personal life stories for families affected by AD. The project is based on a previous pilot study involving nondigital life stories. Researchers created and presented a VHS video life story to an AD individual (Marziali, 2004). The work from the VHS pilot study has inspired the project to create digital life stories, which began with the case study described in this chapter. The digital multimedia content includes digital video, images, photographs, and audio. Interactive components allow the individual to actively participate with the multimedia. We are conducting this research at Baycrest in Toronto, Canada with a multidisciplinary team of social workers, interaction designers, health care providers, and participating families.

Our goal is to understand how interactive reminiscent media can play a role in intervention for families affected by AD. Our hypothesis is that the intervention technology will provide stimulation while reinforcing the individual's positive self-identity. In the first year of our research we (i) investigated and documented the process of creating interactive multimedia life stories, (ii) investigated potential effects that the intervention may have, and (iii) explored how to encourage and support system interaction via system instructions, navigation, and input methods.

In this project we have experienced many challenges for the user-centered design of our system. A significant challenge is our unique user group, and the ability to communicate and interact with them. Short-term memory loss is one of the most significant symptoms of AD. However, other symptoms can also hinder communication and interaction with the individual. For example, a mid-stage individual may have difficulty following instructions, making decisions, or recalling words.

A second challenge is accessibility to participants. The researchers were very concerned about disrupting the individual's daily activities, disrupting health care staff, as well as other ethical concerns. Issues such as cognitive decline in the user population and limited access to participants have great impacts on the entire design processes for our system.

A third challenge is to meet the needs of our broad range of stakeholders. The term 'stakeholder' refers to anyone who is affected by the system. In our case this includes relatives, friends, and health care providers. We need to meet each group's differing needs, abilities, and roles in this project. Not only is it a challenge to meet the needs of all of our stakeholders, it is also a challenge keeping stakeholders involved in the process.

Given these challenges, how can we elicit the necessary information and requirements to tell the story of someone's life in a stimulating and interactive way? In this chapter we begin to answer these questions based on our experiences from an exploratory case study. We begin with a brief discussion on related background research. While assistive technology for cognition is promising, much more development is required, particularly for assistive technology for psychosocial support.

We discuss our needs and requirements analysis process and how we had to modify several common design methodologies to address the challenges. We iteratively designed, prototyped, and tested the multimedia life story system with one participant with AD as well as secondary stakeholders. We describe our preliminary findings, and suggest that interactive participation has the potential to be stimulating, empowering, and trigger reminiscence in a different manner than noninteractive participation in intervention reminiscence activities. We also discuss our lessons learned from the project. Since this exploratory case study does not consider the long-term effects on a large sample size, we do not intend to broadly generalize our results. However, we do intend to inspire further research in related areas. For a more detailed description of the work described in this chapter, see Cohene (2005).

12.2 Background

Memory loss is often associated with aging or age-related conditions such as dementia or AD. The Alzheimer's Association defines AD as an irreversible progressive disorder that causes the gradual loss of brain cells (2005). AD is the most common form of dementia, a term used to describe various diseases or conditions involving the progressive deterioration of brain tissue and the related cognitive faculties (Zec, 1993). Dementia can occur in conditions aside from AD including senility, cerebrovascular disease, Huntington's disease, Parkinson's disease, and Pick's disease (Burns and Zaudig, 2002).

Alzheimer's is known for its high frequency in the aging population. According to reports conducted by the Alzheimer's Association (2005), one in ten people over the age of 65, and nearly half of those over the age of 85 show symptoms of AD in North America. Due to the aging population, the diagnosis rate is expected to triple by 2050 (Alzheimer's Association, 2005). The worldwide incidence is projected to grow from a current level of 18 million to 34 million by 2025. The worldwide incidence of dementia may grow to 42 million by 2020 (Ferri *et al.*, 2005).

Although AD often has strong associations with memory loss, it is important to recognize all of the symptoms of cognitive degeneration. Common symptoms indicated by Alzheimer's Association (2005) include a gradual loss of memory, problems with reasoning or judgment, disorientation, difficulty in learning, loss of language skills, and a decline in the ability to perform routine tasks. The memory loss is more severe for short-term memory and prospective memory. The AD symptoms express themselves more severely as the disease progresses through early, mid, and late stages. Table 12.1 gives examples of how these symptoms might be expressed. More

Table 12.1 *Symptoms of Alzheimer's disease (adapted from the Alzheimer's Association, 2005)*

Symptom	For example, a person may:
Memory loss	Repeat stories or questions
	Have trouble recalling familiar people, things, or recent activities
	Frequently misplace objects
Problems with reasoning or judgment	Have difficulty performing or prioritizing common tasks
	Be unable to follow directions
	Rely on others to make decisions or answer questions
Disorientation	Get disoriented about time, people, and places
	Become lost in familiar places, wandering frequently
Difficulty in learning	Be unable to think clearly
Loss of language skills	Have difficulty in speaking, reading, or writing
Decline in ability to perform routine tasks	Forget how to cook, perform routine chores, or play cards
	Have difficulty brushing teeth, combing hair, or making a bed
Changes in behavior	Experience high levels of grief, fear, confusion, or mood swings

information on AD and each of the stages of the disease is available from the Alzheimer's Association (2005).

When an individual begins to experience cognitive loss there may be various behavioral consequences. They may experience changes in personality, a lesser sense of self, or a loss of independence (Kasl-Godley and Gatz, 2000). This can lead to symptoms such as high levels of depression, grief, fear, and frustration, all of which have a significant impact on the well-being of the individual.

In order to deal with both the cognitive and behavioral symptoms, health care professionals may provide various medicinal treatments. Nondrug intervention approaches such as support and training can also help decrease the symptoms of AD and dementia. Health care providers offer various coping strategies and tips (The Alzheimer Journey, 1998; Alzheimer's Association, 2005). For example, experts suggest maintaining meaningful activities that focus on the individual's remaining abilities and help the person feel active and empowered.

The term 'intervention' refers to the specific application of techniques intended to change knowledge, attitudes, beliefs, or behaviors (Eprevco, 2005). Psychosocial interventions refer to therapy and techniques designed to enhance an individual's well-being. Each intervention method may have specific goals, such as to activate memories, strengthen intact abilities, alleviate distress, facilitate coping, or enhance behaviors. Examples of intervention methods include memory training, support groups, reminiscence and life review, psychodynamic approaches, reality orientation, and cognitive and behavioral therapy.

Reminiscence and life review therapy aims to improve an individual's well-being by bringing past experiences and unresolved conflicts into awareness (Woods *et al.*, 1992). Examples include telling stories, using photographs and memorabilia as prompts, creating autobiographies, creating scrapbooks, or going on pilgrimages and reunions. Despite the many potential benefits of conducting life story work, formal studies to date have not shown empirically significant results in terms of specific benefits (Spector *et al.*, 1999). Despite this, they do show slight interpersonal and intrapersonal benefits (Baines *et al.*, 1987; Kasl-Godley and Gatz, 2000). The reported interpersonal benefits include enhanced caregiver–patient relationship, socializing with others, and leaving a legacy (Baines *et al.*, 1987; Woods, 1994). These benefits are especially useful for individuals with moderate stage AD. Reported intrapersonal enhancements include self-awareness, personal stability, and life meaning. These benefits are more common among individuals with mild impairment (Kasl-Godley and Gatz, 2000).

It is particularly important for AD individuals to be able to support and maintain their personal identity. Reminiscent activities provide a means for defining and supporting one's personhood, which may help deter negative behavioral symptoms (Tobin, 1999). Life stories have many interesting factors that contribute to the individual's identity. Although the participant may not recall all of the life stories, some may evoke recognition or reminiscence. The experience may elicit different responses such as joy or discomfort. They may offer new perspectives, or help make lives seem more coherent or continuous. Some of the content may prompt rare thoughts or additional support in comparison to everyday activities. The stories can also affect others by providing a legacy, a vehicle for communication, or a shared experience. They may also involve difficulties, such as unpleasant memories or feelings.

In 2003, Dr Elsa Marziali, Schipper Chair in Gerontological Social Work at Baycrest, began research on the effects of personalized video life histories on individuals with AD and their caregivers and families (Marziali, 2004). The hypothesis is that the video intervention may provide stimulation, provide distraction from negative stimuli, reinforce the individual's positive self-identity, and diminish problematic behaviors. In addition, potential outcomes for the caregiver include relief from stress, frustration, and reduction in caregiver burden.

The researchers conducted a pilot study, creating the life story video intervention for one mid-stage AD participant. We call this the VHS pilot study. Caregivers and family members collaborated on the filming, editing, and viewing of their relative's life story. The VHS video included interviews, photographs, as well as other prompts and cues such as visual and auditory stimuli to represent retrospective memories. The story progressed through the participant's life, including milestones, relationships, and personal interests. Unfortunately, the researchers were unable to measure any significant positive results from the VHS pilot study. Yet they saw the need for more research to learn how to maximize the positive outcomes for both the patient and family.

Assistive Technology for Cognition, or ATC (LoPresti *et al.*, 2004), refers to technological interventions that assist people with cognitive and neuropsychological disabilities. In most ATC projects, the assistance is geared toward the rehabilitation of performing everyday activities. One of the major benefits claimed for ATC is that of increasing the individual's independence, since they are less likely to rely on others to recall things or perform tasks. ATC are also known as 'cognitive prosthetics' or 'cognitive orthoses' (LoPresti *et al.*, 2004). For a review on ATC designed for individuals with various cognitive impairments, such as memory aids or planning devices, see LoPresti *et al.* (2004).

ATC can be designed for individuals who are affected by dementia, but not afflicted with it. AD impacts both the people with the disease and the people who interact with them. Almost 90% of people with AD receive home care by a family member

(Alzheimer's Association, 2005). Studies show that caregivers often neglect their own health and well-being as a result of the stress of caregiving (Czaja and Rubert, 2002). Many older individuals are socially isolated due to a shrinking network of family and friends (Morris *et al.*, 2003). Many caregivers also cannot leave their ill spouses unattended (Marziali, 2003). Studies confirm that caregivers feel isolated and experience high levels of depression and anxiety (Haley *et al.*, 1995). Support networks are invaluable for providing communication, compassion, advice, and consolation.

Examples of ATC support networks include the Telephone-Linked Care system and the Caring for Others project. The Telephone-Linked Care (TLC) system links a telephone to an Alzheimer's communication and information network. The TLC system facilitates access for caregivers to resources and information (REACH, 2003) through dedicated voicemail services, teleconferencing family therapy sessions, and teleconferencing discussion groups. Caring for Others (CFO) is a web-based support tool for seniors who care for their spouses with dementia (Marziali *et al.*, 2005, in press; Marziali and Donahue, in press). The CFO site is a portal for access to information, training, and videoconference support groups. Both the TLC and CFO systems offer a wide range of benefits (Czaja and Rubert, 2002; Marziali *et al.*, 2005) including enhancing communication, managing the stress and burden of caregiving, and reducing the amount of resources in comparison to face-to-face intervention.

At this time, there does not exist substantial development in psychosocial ATC designed for the AD individual as the end user. One exception is CIRCA (Computer Interactive Reminiscence and Conversation Aid), which explores the effects of interactive multimedia on AD individuals (Gowans *et al.*, 2004). A goal of CIRCA is to stimulate conversation in reminiscent therapy sessions. The project uses a database of audio, video, animation, and QuickTime VR media content with a touchscreen interface. The media is not personalized for each participant and can therefore be presented to all participants. For an image of the CIRCA system see Figure 10.2 (p. 306). The media are displayed on a touchscreen with menu items including alternative themes, media choices, and navigation. Their studies show that the system provides a mechanism for eliciting more natural, less repetitive, and sometimes entirely new responses from the participants in reminiscent therapy sessions (Gowans *et al.*, 2004). A particularly significant finding from this work is that many participants were able to interact and operate the system themselves, even though it was initially designed to be used with the aid of a therapist.

The researchers decided not to use personalized content from individual participants because it involves several risks (Gowans *et al.*, 2004). In the health care environment, researchers must maintain participant privacy and restrict public access to personal data. There is also a risk of upsetting participants by emphasizing their forgotten memories and their cognitive deficit. In CIRCA, the researchers are able to support communication without the use of personal data. Although it is risky and requires more customization for each participant, using personalized information (such as in the case of Marziali's VHS life story work) may have powerful benefits including being more stimulating and meaningful for both the participant and the relatives.

12.3　How this Project Helps the Targeted User Population

In this project we wish to support an individual's personhood through a technological intervention. We are creating personalized multimedia systems. We believe that an intervention method that reinforces a self-identity can have positive effects for both the individual and the family caregiver. For example, the activity may bring a sense of well-being or even joy to the entire family. It may have calming effects, or may reduce disruptive behavior for the individual suffering from AD.

Inspired by the VHS pilot study, we were interested in learning how we could maximize the positive outcomes for both the patient and family. We saw the potential for using technology and interactive multimedia in this research and decided to create digital life stories. In order to obtain the information necessary for the successful conduct of a large-scale research project, we began the digital multimedia research with an exploratory case study. This case study is the focus of this chapter.

Similar to the VHS pilot study, one of our research objectives is to investigate if and how recollecting and reinforcing memories of the individual and family history could have beneficial effects for both the participant and her family. In comparison to the VHS pilot study, we were also interested in exploring how to encourage and support system interaction via system instructions, navigation, and input methods.

With technology and multimedia, the life story activity can become interactive. It can be an active event involving participation and varied presentation formats. In comparison, VHS videos are restricted to a linear nondynamic presentation format. Digital video can be presented nonlinearly, opening up new possibilities for storytelling and sharing experiences. For example, the person viewing the biography can be given the option to select the particular stories that he or she would like view at that time. This interaction may help promote a positive and stimulating experience, potentially more stimulating than viewing noninteractive linear life stories. Contributing to the reminiscent activity may even promote empowerment through feelings of control and value. The media can stimulate many senses including sight, sound and even touch with opportunities to physically participate. This multi-modal sensory stimulation may also add to the effects of viewing the life stories. In addition, the participant's responses to the opportunities to interact will offer an additional variable to observe and measure.

The first participating family consists of a 91-year-old female participant, Laura, with mid-stage AD, living in a long-term care facility. To maintain the participants' anonymity all names have been changed. Laura moved from South Africa to Canada at the age of 86 to be with her two daughters and was diagnosed with AD one year later. The two daughters are both very much active in this project. Cathy and Margaret are in their mid-sixties, work full time, and have families and grandchildren of their own.

12.4 How this Project was Developed

To pursue the exploratory case study, we began with a user needs and requirements analysis process. We obtained initial insights by conducting extensive research on the disease, memory and cognitive loss, intervention methods, digital storytelling, and previous ATC research. We then employed common user-centered design methodologies including ethnography, interviews, contextual exploration, participatory design, and iterative prototyping. However, because of limitations in our ability to communicate with an AD individual we had to make adaptations to these methods. We introduce our atypical use of research methods in Cohene et al. (2005), and provide additional information in this chapter.

When the end user's environment is accessible, ethnography can be an excellent means of learning about the stakeholders and their needs. Ethnography involves immersion in the users environment and participation in relevant activities (Suchman, 1987; Hughes et al., 1993; Beyer and Holtzblatt, 1998). We had a limited amount of accessibility to AD individuals at Baycrest due to participant health conditions, ethics, privacy, and administrative issues. Given that we had a moderate amount of access, we conducted research that was inspired by ethnography but limited by these conditions. We call this moderated ethnographic research. We interacted with groups of individuals in moderated recreational therapy activities. The groups ranged from 5 to 35 mid- and late-stage AD individuals, and were moderated by health care staff and several volunteers. Over a 3-month period we played games, made crafts, joined sing-alongs, and observed meal times. In comparison to traditional ethnographic research, we did not observe individuals privately or visit participants in their personal spaces.

These noninvasive activities gave us insight into the communication needs and abilities of the AD population. Instead of merely focusing on the disabilities due to cognitive decline, we also made many observations related to the intact abilities.

Many individuals are able to react to instructions and respond to activities, such as a game of bingo. However, the abilities range among individuals and even among day-to-day interactions. There is also a wide range and complexity within the individual's own abilities. For example, even though the person may mark squares on the bingo card, they may not become aware they have won a game.

Observations such as these have stressed the importance of simplicity, consistency, and minimizing over-stimulation. These principles can be applied to the multimedia life story content as well as the interactive design. With these understandings we can leverage the individual's abilities in the system design.

Unfortunately, the severity of the disease prevented us from conducting meaning-ful interviews with the participant. In order to elicit as much information as possible we interviewed and consulted with many secondary stakeholders. We consulted experts from the Baycrest health care staff including social workers and recreational therapists. We also conducted interviews with members of a spousal caregiver sup-port group. We then spoke with experts outside of the Baycrest community including representatives of the Toronto Alzheimer's Society, colleagues researching other ATC projects, ethnographers, and life story authors. These interviews contributed a gener-al understanding of the AD individual's capabilities and potential limitations in their ability to interact with the communication provided by the life story presentation. It also helped determine general life story content, themes, and media that could be included to create a stimulating experience, listed in Table 12.2.

Personal content and specific needs were determined in the following stage, in col-laboration with the participating family. We conducted interviews with Laura's rela-tives, particularly with her daughters, Cathy and Margaret, in order to collect the necessary information to tell the life stories. We presented a workbook to introduce

Table 12.2 Life categories and life themes

Time periods and experiences	Personhood	Interests and accomplishments	Social factors
Childhood	Personality	Achievements, Strengths	Family
Youth	Values, Religion, Spirituality	Culture, Languages	Friends
Education	Rituals	Hobbies	Social history
Profession	Health history	Leisure activities	Celebrations
Middle age	Losses, Tragedy		Community
Life today			

the family to the research project called the Family Workbook. The Family Workbook aimed to foster a discussion on the project goals and the potential benefits of reminiscing through life stories.

We used this opportunity to elicit the most important goals from the family, including personal project outcomes that were the most meaningful to them. One of the goals in collecting the information necessary to tell a life story is to collect information other than lifetime events or milestones. In addition to important events such as graduations and births, we wanted to convey characteristics, habits, and values in the life story content. We call all of this information a life theme. In order to help the family elicit appropriate life themes, we asked questions to prompt the elicitation of stories regarding each life category and theme in Table 12.2. For example, the 'Time Periods' section in the Family Workbook began with several questions aimed at prompting life stories for the participant's childhood.

The Family Workbook essentially acted as an open-ended questionnaire with 21 life theme prompts, as well as details on user goals, media content preferences, and other requirements. As a result of this questionnaire, the relatives filled out 15 life theme sections and we gathered an immense amount of data about lifetime milestones, day-to-day life, and the participant's personality. For example, Cathy and Margaret told stories about entertaining guests in their home, recalling the scent of their mother's perfume, and being tucked into bed at night. These stories may help trigger emotions related to memories of frequently experienced moments.

The Family Workbook played a major role in the elicitation process for the life story system design. Based on the interviews and consultations with the secondary stakeholders, none of the relatives or health care providers expressed confidence that a mid-stage AD individual would be able to physically interact with the life story system. This is despite their universal support for the project. In the next stage we met with the participant at the long-term care facility in order to learn how we could support and promote system interaction.

In order to elicit the necessary information for a personalized life story system we needed to carry out design methods that would give us an intimate understanding of our participant. We employed principles from contextual inquiry (Beyer and Holtzblatt, 1998) and observed relevant tasks in the participant's natural settings. Conducting tasks can be a challenge because they often rely on cognitive abilities. As well, if we highlight declining memories it might frustrate or upset the participant. To cope with this, we focused on failure-free exploratory tasks and we were sensitive to the participant's abilities and feelings. We call this contextual exploration.

We visited Laura in her room at the care facility and conducted a reminiscing session with her relatives in order to learn how personal photographs might stimulate her.

First, Laura independently explored a stack of photographs. There were a variety of outcomes to viewing each photograph including positive and negative responses, or no response at all. For example, Laura enjoyed looking at photographs of some people but not others, regardless of their relation to her. Some photographs elicited more meaningful conversation than the relatives expected. They were quite surprised that she recalled names of several old friends and enjoyed reminiscing about her home town. When we presented two photographs to Laura, and asked her which she preferred, she responded with a smile, and did not answer the question. As mentioned, it is common for mid-stage AD individuals to have difficulty making decisions.

We also considered some other activities aside from browsing photographs. The relatives were surprised to find that Laura could still physically demonstrate how to stand in a position from her sporting career. She could also play certain card games, a favorite and common activity throughout her life. We demonstrated to Laura how to turn off the television, however, after some time she could not recall how to turn it off on her own. Throughout these activities we also noticed some communication difficulties. For example, Laura sometimes used incorrect words to describe items. Throughout the contextual exploration the social workers were conscientious to the length of the activity, and we ended sessions if the participant showed any signs of possible distress such as discomfort, confusion, or irritation.

As a result of this contextual exploration we uncovered many requirements specific to our participant. Although she was unable to follow instructions from a short time prior, she maintained a significant amount of procedural memory for activities that occurred often throughout her life. We also learned that the participant could be meaningfully stimulated by activities involving personal life stories. Since we observed a range of responses from the participant, we learned how we could design the system to maximize the amount of positively stimulating content, while minimizing the amount of negatively stimulating content. At the same time, we suspected that the participant might respond differently from one day to another. This motivated us to design a system in which the participant would be able to control the content that is presented in the life story multimedia.

In participatory design there is active involvement with the end users in the design process, and the end user participation is often considered a prerequisite for good design (Kensing and Blomberg, 1998). However, stakeholders other than end users can also provide very valuable input. When designing for a user group that includes persons with disabilities, another group can act as a proxy in the participatory design process (Fischer and Sullivan, 2002). To foster creativity among the relatives, we created a participatory activity based on 'probes' (Gaver *et al.*, 1999). Probes are packages of tools that help elicit imaginative and inspirational responses. Our probes

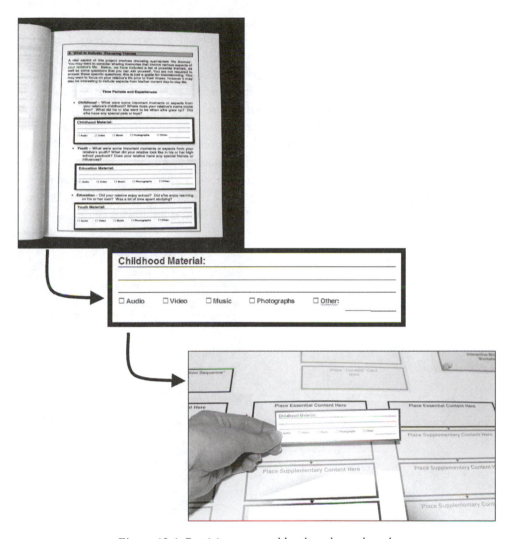

Figure 12.1 Participatory workbook and storyboard.

included a workbook (previously discussed), life theme cards, a storyboard, script forms, sticky notes, and clear plastic bags.

As mentioned, the Family Workbook introduced the family to the research project. The sections that could be filled out were actually removable cards. A sample card is shown in Figure 12.1. The cards were lined with adhesive reusable glue, similar to the glue on 'Post-It' notes.

Once the relatives completed the card forms in the workbook, they were able to place all of the cards on a storyboard. The storyboard included rectangular blocks stating 'Place [content] here,' where 'content' referred to specific card forms from the workbook, including project goals, multimedia content preferences (such as music, photographs, or videos), and life story content. The cards were arranged in a flow chart to represent the relationships between different life stories. Since the multimedia life story system is interactive, the content does not need to be presented to the viewer in a linear manner. Depending on the response from the viewer, the life story sequence can change. Therefore, it was essential that we understand the relationships between each story and establish navigation sequences for the life story content.

The red line in Figure 12.2 traces a path along the introduction content, essential life story content, and the conclusion content. We asked the relatives to determine the

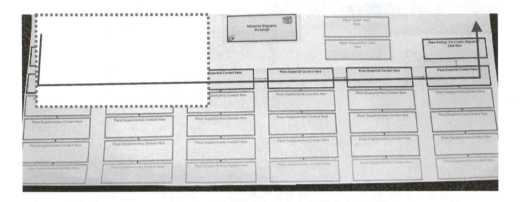

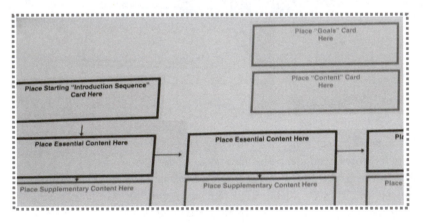

Figure 12.2 *The storyboard navigation and enlarged view.*

most important life stories theme cards and place them in the essential spots, in an order that was meaningful to them. We limited the number of spaces to six cards, forcing the relatives to prioritize the stories. We also asked them to place less essential stories (that we called supplementary content) below one of the six essential life stories.

Together with the relatives, we arranged and rearranged the cards, and marked up the storyboard with notes. We continued organizing and interconnecting the cards until they represented cohesive stories. A section of the completed storyboard is shown in Figure 12.3.

Corresponding to each life theme card, the family filled out a form to write down an interview script. The script form included space for describing the story, listing the related media (e.g. specific photographs), and describing information on the media (e.g. names of people in photographs). We then placed the scripts with their related photographs and memorabilia in clear plastic bags. We used these bags as kits for

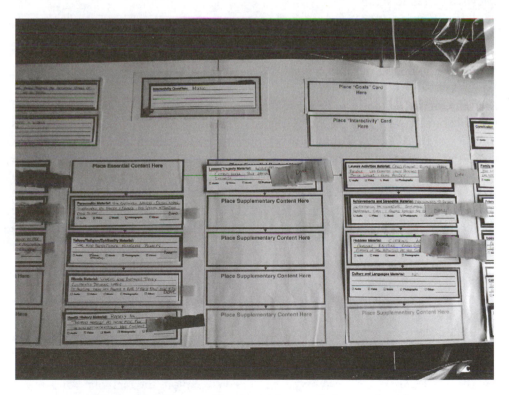

Figure 12.3 The completed participatory design storyboard.

creating each scene of the life stories. We interviewed the relatives on camera, photographed memorabilia, scanned family photos, digitized home videos, and collected music.

We developed a conceptual model based on the results of the requirements and needs analysis. To test the conceptual model we developed some prototypes using rapid prototyping methods such as paper prototypes and HTML. We then iteratively modified our design concept with further prototypes that we presented to secondary stakeholders. At this stage we addressed challenges in our design process such as maintaining the anonymity of our participant while trying to elicit feedback from colleagues, health care providers, and other stakeholders. In order to ensure this, several demos included the life story of one of our researchers, instead of the participant. By shifting the context of the project we risked eliciting less useful feedback. However, we found that the reactions valuably informed the next iteration of our design, with new design metaphors and input methods (such as photo albums and television channels).

In the next iteration, we developed prototypes on the platform of the deliverable system. We decided to make the multimedia in a DVD format because DVD players are less expensive than PCs, DVDs can be easily shared and distributed, and our designers could easily customize the DVD navigation sequences to fit the life stories. We created our own specialized input devices from standard remote controls. We used the digitized content to create multimedia scenes and implemented a number of possible navigation paths for the multimedia scenes. We created multiple prototypes in order to test different stories, different media content (music, video, photographs, etc.), and different input devices. For example, in one prototype we interspersed life story scenes with video-based instructions describing the next options. Between each scene there was a short video in which a daughter would say, 'Hi mom, it's me [*name*], did you enjoy watching [*scene name*]? If you did press the button, otherwise we'll move on to other stories.' Figure 12.4 outlines a portion of the navigation path for this particular prototype.

We rewired the DVD remote control and replaced the small buttons with one large soft button (Figure 12.5a). If the participant pressed the button, the DVD automatically navigated to a story with similar content. If the participant did not press the button, the DVD automatically navigated to a story with different content.

In another prototype, we presented an interactive photo album. Each page contained one photograph corresponding to a life story scene. As the participant turned the pages of the album the corresponding life story appeared on the television monitor (Figure 12.5b). In this prototype we hoped to explore the metaphor of a photo album and the implicit control of the multimedia.

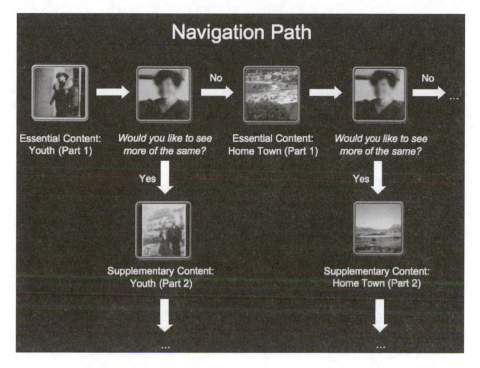

Figure 12.4 Navigation path for one of the prototypes.

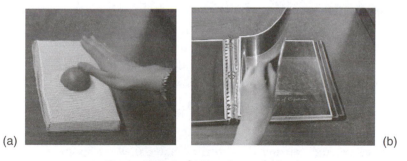

(a)   (b)

Figure 12.5 (a, b) Two input devices.

12.5 **How this Project was Evaluated for Usability and Appropriateness**

As discussed, this exploratory case study was conducted with one participant in order to uncover and inspire further research in this area. We evaluated the usability and desirability of the interactive life story multimedia specifically for our participant and her family. Although we cannot generalize our results to the entire Alzheimer's community, we believe that the results provide groundwork for future research.

We hoped to learn how Laura was stimulated by the multimedia and how to optimize the stimulation for her. We had many questions for this case study. Would Laura interact with the life stories (for example, by pressing the button or turning the pages)? Would she make verbal comments about the stories? Would the comments be relevant and meaningful? And how would the family respond?

We presented the life story multimedia to the participant and her relatives and conducted post-study interviews with relatives. We tested and iterated the prototypes with our participant in eight trials over the course of 4 weeks and filmed her reactions. Laura watched the presentations under various conditions such as on different days and with different guests in her room. We found that she responded more positively and enthusiastically to particular life stories, media content, and input methods. For example, we found that the interactive photo album was too cognitively demanding because it involved diverting attention from the photo album to the television monitor. Laura was only able to concentrate on one form of media at a time, losing the benefit of the other. As a result, Laura was less responsive to this prototype so we did not continue testing and iterating on it. Based on Laura's reactions throughout the trials we made several other minor (but significant) enhancements to the multimedia and the remote control.

Overall, Laura was delighted and engaged by the multimedia. In response to some scenes Laura made comments such as 'Lovely!' 'Look at this!' and 'Not bad, eh?' However, in response to other scenes she consistently made few or no comments. We determined that the reason for this difference was not just the content but also the format and quality of the content. Our intention was to provide meaningful, clear, and comprehensible information. However, after observing Laura's responses to the life stories we were able to isolate several problematic areas. Some footage was too vague while other scenes were too busy. We realized that certain scenes might have been too linguistically complex or over-stimulating. In response to this we edited the content by slowing down the speed of the footage, adding short pauses between sentences and scenes, and deleting nonessential material. We also created more scenes focusing on music and visuals as opposed to conversations. We interspersed the videos with meaningful, clear, and colorful photos to add to the visual stimulation. We also focused on salient aspects of photographs using various editing techniques. After making these changes we presented the stories and found that Laura made more meaningful verbal responses to the content. In addition to comments such as 'Lovely' and 'Look at this!' Laura made more comments regarding specific people, items, or memories. She said things like 'That's in [home town],' 'That was a good day,' and 'You ever hear from them?'

Despite being engaged by the life stories, Laura did not initially respond to the video instruction sequences by pressing the single button remote control. After viewing several instruction sequences, and receiving additional prompting from her family, Laura pressed the button. At one point she stated, 'Don't forget, got to press the button.' We noted the points in time when the family would provide additional support and edited the videos to include additional prompts and cues for pressing the button. For example, after showing the scene of the relative giving instructions, we presented an image of the remote control and caused a 'beep' to emit from the remote in Laura's hand. We also redesigned the remote control to be more ergonomic (Figure 12.6). We made it smaller so that it could fit better in her hands and covered it in softer fabric. In the next iterations of testing we found that Laura held onto the remote with more enthusiasm and pressed the button with less prompting from others.

Figure 12.6 Redesigned remote control.

She pressed the button at nearly every opportunity, and in once case she did not press the button and mentioned that she would prefer to lie down.

As we iterated through the multimedia designs we found that Laura responded more often and more meaningfully to the life stories. Although there are many variables to consider, we were inspired by Laura's increasingly positive reactions and hope that these are indicative of improvements in the design. As a baseline, we presented the same life stories in a linear noninteractive version of the life stories (such as viewing linear VHS films) in order to gauge and compare her responses to a passive, noninteractive activity. Interestingly, Laura's responses to these presentations did not result in as many verbal responses nor as many meaningful responses.

We also saw how the entire process impacted the relatives. The relatives seemed initially frustrated by watching their relative reminisce. At times, they seemed disappointed when Laura could not recall specific memories. However, in retrospect they reacted positively to this collaborative activity. They were interested in seeing Laura reminisce, communicate, and react to the activities. After the first reminiscing activity, a daughter wrote in a letter:

. . . I hadn't realized how much pleasure seeing these photos would give her . . . [Yet] she didn't know my name and that we were her daughters . . . I saw that different things can trigger her memory, and obviously [her] career lit a spark. So hopefully seeing some video of earlier times will light something up for her, and she'll enjoy those memories. What a thrill that would be.

In the 3-month follow-up interviews with Cathy and Margaret, we asked the daughters whether they observed any changes in Laura's behavior outside of the viewing sessions. One daughter mentioned that Laura was more likely to use people's names and less likely to ask to return to her room, on the days that she viewed the life story.

We also learned how the family and friends are affected by participating in this project. In our project, we hypothesized some potential benefits for the relatives including leaving a legacy, gaining perspective, enhancing generational bonds, sharing experiences, and communicating. In the follow-up interview, the daughters voluntarily discussed every one of these aspects. Both daughters asked for additional copies of the life stories, to distribute to each of their own children.

In a 6-month follow-up interview the daughters mentioned that their mother continues to watch the life stories between 2 to 5 times per week. Laura watches the noninteractive version because it's significantly longer and does not require as much supervision. They find that their mother is able to stay focused on the life stories, whereas in other activities she often appears distracted. Based on her reactions, they feel that she enjoys the stories and finds them fulfilling:

But maybe this is something that just – when she saw it – unlocked it for her, or if it was just luck that day that the words came back to her I don't know. But I think bringing the family all the time up to her in front of her the whole time – it keeps her happy. And that to me is the greatest benefit of it all. Is that she's happy.

The stories also provide a legacy of memories:

And even now to see the pleasure that she gets from the video and to see her enjoyment. I mean for us this is going to be something that we're going to treasure . . . and we've given copies to all the grandchildren and hopefully that they're going to treasure.

And they have helped shed new perspectives on coping:

Before [the project] I think I just got all upset when she said garbled things and I couldn't work out what she's saying. And maybe now I've become more tuned in.

I've also learned now how to cope with it . . . I'm learning to cope in different ways . . . So I think this whole project and everything has been a wonderful experience for us to – but also to help the family really.

The relatives gained perspective and expressed personal growth regarding managing their own feelings and responding to their mothers disease. One daughter even expressed how the stories helped her see positive qualities that she acquired from her mother. In addition, both greatly appreciated the opportunity to share experiences and communicate. In the large-scale study we will further explore the persistent effects of this project, such as more attentive and calm behavior throughout the day.

12.6 Lessons Learned and Guidelines

We analyzed the results of the study in order to suggest design guidelines and enhancements for the main study.

12.6.1 An AD Population Requires New Design Methodologies

Impaired cognition affects a range of thinking abilities that are often taken for granted. These lead to communication and interaction obstacles that make many design methods impractical. In addition, ethics and administrative issues can prevent practitioners from conducting design methods as they are intended. We adapted traditional methods in order to conduct our research so we could gain insight about our stakeholders. We made use of many secondary stakeholders during the interviewing and participatory design activities. During the ethnographic and contextual inquiry activities, we were sensitive to the cognitive and psychosocial needs of our participants. Despite challenges in being able to communicate and interact with our AD participant, we were able to elicit needs and requirements by making adaptations to our design methods.

12.6.2 An AD Population Requires New Design Principles

One of our goals has been to learn more about the needs of the user population when designing psychosocial ATC. Based on our case study results, we have begun to uncover some additional design principles for Laura that may also be useful for other cognitively impaired users. Examples include:

- Appealing to a range of cognitive processes and modalities.
- Supporting tasks at lower levels.

In our testing we saw how different multimedia content can evoke different reactions from our participant. Many guidelines from AD research suggest the importance of communicating clearly. However, it can be very difficult to anticipate the communication needs of each individual. Through iterative testing and design with Laura we were able to isolate specific factors in the multimedia design that would support clear communication. In particular, by appealing to different cognitive processes and modalities we were able to support a more stimulating experience.

We learned that the multimedia should include as much meaningful content as possible and appeal to a range of cognitive processes such as communication, recognition, imagery, and music. Drawing upon a larger range of cognitive process will ideally enhance the ability to stimulate the participant. The content should appeal to a range of senses, including physical touch, such as something soft to hold on to. The factors that require cognitive functioning should be seamless and minimize distractions.

Prompts are very important and can be used to support tasks. A task, such as pressing a button, may seem straightforward for a noncognitively impaired person. However, this task may be much more complex for and individual with a cognitive disability. In the example of pressing the button, the participant needs to:

1. Focus on the video instruction.
2. Comprehend the instruction.
3. Make a decision based on the instruction.
4. Locate the button.
5. Recall the instruction.
6. Associate the instruction with the button.

7. Physically push the button.
8. Focus on the video.

When we break down the tasks to these lower levels, we can better see how to support the interaction through the system design. For example, going from steps 3 to 4 involves redirecting attention from the monitor to the input device. One way in which we facilitated this was by providing an audio cue in the input device, to attract the participant's attention. This form of task analysis has helped us support complex tasks.

12.6.3 AD Participants can Interact with Multimedia

One of our objectives in this feasibility study has been to support and encourage system interaction through system instructions, navigation and input devices. In relation to this, a major research question has been will the participant press the button? When we began this project, the AD experts from our interviews and consultations, as well as the relatives, did not believe that the participant would physically interact with the system (i.e. by pressing the button). We were aware that the participant could press a button on a remote control only after precise, persistent guidance and prompting from another person.

Our goal was to implement a system that would provide precise and persistent guidance, and provide the opportunity to express her preferences in viewing the life stories. Social workers and relatives believed that the cognitive skills used in these activities could not be transferred to an interactive technical medium. In our feasibility study, we began with the assumption that interaction could be possible. We found that Laura was positively stimulated by the content on the new medium of an interactive multimedia platform. Remarkably, Laura did in fact press the button! Although we could not discern whether she interacted based on a cognitive decision involving reasoning and judgment, or whether she interacted based on the instructions and prompting alone, we now know that she was capable of interacting by responding to prompts and cues.

12.6.4 Active Participation is more Stimulating than Passive Participation

In our testing we saw how different types of activities can evoke different reactions from our participant. As we iterated through the designs and enhanced the life story multimedia we saw a growth in positive responses from our participant. We believe that the design of the interactive device can either impede or facilitate the effects of the intervention activity. It is possible that our earlier designs relied more on the diminishing cognitive abilities, resulting in an activity that was too complex or distracting. However, in later iterations we redesigned the multimedia to better meet the special needs of our participant and we saw positive results.

In addition, taking part in the passive noninteractive presentation had a different effect on Laura than participating with the interactive life story system. We found that Laura expressed more meaningful responses when viewing the interactive life story systems, in comparison to the linear noninteractive presentations. She showed more interest (through her body language and facial expressions) when she had the remote control in her hands. One possible explanation for this is that the interactive activity is empowering. We believe that further research should explore whether interactive stimulation affects the participant's ability to communicate meaningfully.

In our hypothesis, we proposed that active participation might be empowering because it promotes feelings of control and value. Prior to conducting this study, we believed that being able to make a decision to control the presentation would be empowering. However, this assumed that the individual could make the cognitive decision, a process that requires reasoning and judgment. In this study, we were at times unsure whether Laura pressed the button as a result of the decision (to see more scenes, or to skip scenes) or from the prompting. It is possible that when the participant interacted successfully, she was merely responding to the instructions without using any reasoning or judgment. Despite the uncertainty of whether the participant was making the decision, we believe that the act of participating itself was empowering for several reasons. First, the interaction added a sense of control to the activity. Even if she was at times unable to make a cognitive decision, the participant was aware of her responsibility and control over the activity. This is particularly evident from her comment, 'Don't forget, got to press the button.' In addition, the activity added physical stimulation through touch and motion. Another factor is that this activity evoked support and positive responses from her family. We believe that these observations inspire further research on interactive psychosocial support tools as an empowering and stimulating activity.

12.6.5 **Different Stakeholders Experience Different Effects**

As the family became more involved in the project, it became apparent that their needs (though different from their relative's needs) should be addressed throughout the project. It could be clinically contraindicated to focus purely on one stakeholder or one end user, since this project touches the lives of many people. Having a clinician who is trained to work with AD patients and their families throughout the development and evaluation of the project was essential for monitoring possible clinical issues that could arise and that would need to be dealt with from a clinical perspective. We also addressed the needs of the relatives through the participatory design process and encouraged the family to share memories and gain perspectives. We also distributed copies of the life story, providing legacies that they themselves can view with their mother or their own families. In this project, user-centered design involves exploring how to provide support and opportunities, throughout the entire design process, for all individuals affected by AD.

12.7 Current Status and Future Directions

We are now in the process of conducting the large-scale research project. Our goals are to (i) study life story multimedia with 12 participants over a period of 24 months, and (ii) research methods for scaling the design process. With more participants we will be able to further test our hypotheses. As we create more life stories we hope to learn how to better scale the project to require less time and resources so that more people can benefit from similar projects. The development and evaluation of effects of the large-scale research project is based on this initial project. The follow up strategies are more structured and have longer durations. In addition, we are asking the families to show the videos at specific intervals and to record their observation of the AD patient's response over a period of a year.

We have now produced two additional digital life histories, and have three more underway. A second family was recruited after the conclusion of our active work with Laura and her daughters. The new participant, Michael, was an 87-year-old man diagnosed with mid-stage AD (names have been changed to maintain the participants' anonymity). Unfortunately, Michael passed away before our project completed, and we were only able to complete an abbreviated 10-minute version. Despite this unfortunate event, we gained important experience and knowledge from working with Michael and his family. We refined our research methods that were developed during our work with Laura and we investigated the impact of including Michael in the design process.

Although we could not conduct structured interviews with Michael, we found that Michael could provide valuable input by being present for the interviews with his relatives. He showed enthusiasm, preferences, and at times he made contributions to conversations. Although the nature of this interaction will be limited as AD progresses, this input can valuably guide the production process, possibly resulting in a more stimulating biography.

We were also able to streamline the design process from the initial project by developing templates and creating semi-customized life stories. When possible, we are also encouraging the relatives to take on larger roles by working with the digital media and focusing more on photographs and music (since video requires more resources). When relatives review and organize the media themselves the development process becomes more efficient and reduces the multimedia editing time. These are just a few of the improvements that we are investigating for this research.

We also created an interactive biography for an individual with vascular dementia. Preliminary findings suggest the result was well received; the participant made numerous positive comments while watching the DVD, and made attempts to interact with the system. Unfortunately, follow-up proved difficult because family circumstances made it impossible to guarantee regular showing of the biography.

We believe that this program has the potential to benefit individuals afflicted with a wide variety of cognitive impairments. Hence future research may include individuals afflicted with other types of dementia, as well as earlier stages of AD and mild cognitive impairment (MCI), and may explore a system that is controlled by different stakeholders. More complex interaction methods may be possible in these cases. Such methods would allow researchers to explore the impact of new variables such as early prevention. Further, researchers can study correlations between the effects of media and different behavioral effects, and use this information to enhance the intervention activity. For example, if a participant is feeling agitated, we can present specific content that is known to manage agitated behaviors.

12.8 Implications for Designers, Researchers, Policymakers, and Participants

12.8.1 The Research is Extremely Resource-Intensive

Conducting the case study requires resources such as intricate recruiting, various research and development, and ongoing production costs. For example, the case study required 6 weeks of ethical review, as well as a variety of technical equipment and software. In addition to these one-time resources, the case study included approximately 200 hours of research and development, and 10 gigabytes of storage space.

12.8.2 This Research is Very Emotionally Intensive

This project has been emotionally intensive for both the stakeholders and researchers. Recruiting families took at least 3, and up to 8 weeks because many families who are coping with the loss of a relative do not feel that they have the time or emotional stamina needed to participate in this project. Even after completing the life stories, the participating relatives continue to experience the many effects of taking part in the project. In addition, this research exemplifies the value of working in multidisciplinary teams, since each researcher is contributing valuable work. In particular, it is essential that social workers are present to provide expertise and professional guidance. They can help the team understand the emotional implications while monitoring possible issues that could need clinical attention.

12.8.3 The Project should be Accessible but Practical

As the number of participants increases it becomes import to be able to manage and streamline the project. It is unlikely that a health care system would have the resources to replicate this approach with AD families and patients. Similarly, not many families can afford to have this project conducted for their relative. Creating a technological product is a great option. However, this is likely to require more commitment, time, multimedia equipment, and computer skills from the family. In addition, the streamlined method should include a social worker to ensure support and value for the relatives. We intend to develop several practical resources to help conduct life story development, such as producing a guidebook for developing the life stories in a simplified form. The book could be geared toward families with children or grandchildren who have computer skills and could deal with digital information readily.

12.8.4 Standards for Evaluations of Interventions are Needed

We also believe that the research community may need to modify and develop standards for evaluations of intervention methods. Normally, large-scale clinical studies are required for showing validity and value. Unfortunately, large-scale studies are not currently possible for these types of research projects. Despite this we aim to conduct research on intervention technologies that can impact the health care community.

12.9 Conclusion

We have designed interactive life story multimedia for families affected by AD. By employing user-centered design principles we have explored how to encourage and support system interaction, particularly through our application of modified design methodologies and new design principles. We have shown that a mid-stage AD individual can interact with multimedia. However, participant interaction is dependent on a number of factors, including the state of the disease and the design of the system.

We discussed several factors that affected the design in our case study, such as simplicity, stimulation, and active participation. We believe that many individuals will benefit from the empowerment offered by participating in this project and interacting with the media. We also believe that creating more effective designs of psychosocial ATC may lead to enhanced intervention programs. This case study also offers an exciting foundation for future research on the interactive life story multimedia project, as well as other related future work. For example, researchers can study the power of interacting and actively participating during reminiscent intervention activities with families affected by AD.

Acknowledgments

Many thanks to the funding provided by the Alzheimer's Association through the ETAC-04-1003 grant, Alison Sellors, and other researchers and colleagues at Baycrest and the University of Toronto.

References

Alzheimer's Association (2005) 'What is Alzheimer's Disease?' `www.alz.org/AboutAD/WhatIsAD.htm` (accessed February 2005).

Alzheimer Journey (1998) *The Alzheimer Journey: Videos 1 through 3*. Alzheimer Society of Canada, Toronto.

Baines, S., Saxby, P. and Ehlert, K. (1987) Reality orientation and reminiscence therapy: a controlled cross-over study of elderly confused people. *British Journal of Psychiatry,* **151**, 222–231.

Beyer, H. and Holtzblatt, K. (1998) *Contextual Design: Defining Customer-Centered Systems*. Morgan Kaufmann, San Francisco, CA.

Burns, A. and Zaudig, M. (2002) Mild cognitive impairment in older people. *Lancet,* **360**, 1963–1965.

Cohene, T., Baecker, R. and Marziali, E. (2005) Designing interactive life story multimedia for a family affected by Alzheimer's disease: a case study. *Proceedings in CHI 2005*, ACM Press, pp. 1300–1303.

Cohene, T. (2005) The design of interactive life story multimedia for an individual and family affected by Alzheimer's disease: a case study. *Unpublished Master's Thesis,* University of Toronto, Toronto, Canada.

Czaja, S.J. and Rubert, M. (2002) *Telecommunications technology as an aid to family caregivers of persons with dementia.* Psychosometric Medicine, **64**, 469–476.

Eprevco (2005) Electronic community prevention organizer. `www.eprevco.com/supporttutorial/document1/glossary.asp` (accessed January 2005).

Ferri, C., Prince, M. et al. (2005) Global prevalence of dementia. *Lancet,* **366**, 2112–2117.

Fischer, G. and Sullivan, J.F. (2002) Human-centered public transportation systems for persons with cognitive disabilities – challenges and insights for participatory design. *Participatory Design Conference,* 194–198.

Gaver, W., Dunne, T. and Pacenti, E. (1999) *Cultural Probes: Interactions.* ACM Press, 21–29.

Gowans, G., Campbell, J., Alm, N. et al. (2004). Designing a multimedia conversation aid for reminiscence therapy in dementia care environments. *Proceedings of CHI 2004,* ACM Press, pp. 825–836.

Haley, W.E., West, C.A.C. and Wadley, V.G. (1995) Psychological, social, and health impact of caregiving: a comparison of black and white dementia family caregivers and noncaregivers. *Psychology of Aging,* **10**, 540–552.

Hughes, J.A., Sommerville, I. and Randall, D. (1993) Designing with ethnography: making work visible. *Interactive Computing,* **5**(2), 239–253.

Kasl-Godley, J. and Gatz, M. (2000) Psychosocial interventions for individuals with dementia: an integration of theory, therapy, and a clinical understanding of dementia. *Clinical Psychology Review,* **20**(6), 755–782.

Kensing, F. and Blomberg, J. (1998) Participatory design: issues and concerns. *Computer Supported Cooperative Work,* 167–185.

LoPresti, E.F., Mihailidis, A. and Kirsch, N. (2004) Assistive technology for cognitive rehabilitation: state of the art. *Neuropsychological Rehabilitation,* **14**, 5–39.

Marziali, E. (2004) *Effects of Personalized Video-Taped Retrospective Life Histories on Persons with Alzheimer's Mood and Agitated Behaviours.* Unpublished report.

Marziali, E. (2003) Seniors Use Internet to Reduce Stress of Caring for a Spouse with Dementia. *The Baycrest Bulletin* 2(1), August. `www.baycrest.org/reports/bulletin_aug2003.pdf`.

Marziali, E., Donahue, P. and Crossin, G. (2005) Computer-Internet health care support interventions for family caregivers of persons with dementia (Alzheimer or other), stroke, or Parkinson disease. *Families Society,* **86.**

Marziali, E. and Donahue, P. (2006) Caring for others: Internet, video-conferencing group intervention for family caregivers of older adults with neurodegenerative disease. *The Gerontologist,* **46,** 398–403.

Marziali, E., Damianakis, T. and Donahue, P. (in press) Virtual support for family caregivers: theoretical framework, intervention model and outcome. *Journal of Technology and Human Service* (in press).

Morris, M., Lundell, J. and Dishman, E. (2004) Catalyzing social interaction with ubiquitous computing: a needs assessment of elders coping with cognitive decline. *Conference on Human Factors in Computing Systems,* ACM Press, 1151–1154.

REACH (Resources for Enhancing Alzheimer's Caregiver Health) (2003) Description of resource projects. `www.edc.gsph.pitt.edu/reach` (accessed September 2003).

Spector, A., Orrell, M., Davies, S. and Woods, R.T. (1999) Reminiscence for dementia (Cochrane review). In *The Cochrane Library.* Update Software: Oxford.

Spector, A., Thorgrimsen, L., Woods, B. et al. (2003) Efficacy of an evidence-based cognitive stimulation therapy programme for people with dementia: randomised controlled trial. *British Journal of Psychiatry,* **183,** 248–254.

Suchman, L.A. (1987) *Plans and Situated Actions: The Problem of Human-Machine Communication.* Cambridge University Press, Cambridge.

Tobin, S.S. (1999) *Preservation of the self in the oldest years: with implications for practice.* Springer, New York.

Wilson, R.S., Mendes De Leon, C.F., Barnes, L.L. et al. (2002) Participation in cognitively stimulating activities and risk of incident Alzheimer disease. *JAMA,* **287,** 742–748.

Woods, B., Portnoy, S., Head, D. and Jones, G. (1992) Reminiscence and life review with persons with dementia: which way forward?. In Jones, G.M.M. & Miesen, B.M.L. (Eds.). *Care-giving in Dementia: Research and Applications,* Tavistock/Routledge, New York, 137–161.

Woods, B. (1994) Management of memory impairment in older people with dementia. *International Review of Psychiatry,* **6,** 153–161.

Woods, R.T. (2001) Discovering the person with Alzheimer's disease: cognitive, emotional and behavioural aspects. *Aging and Mental Health,* S7–S16.

Zec, R.F. (1993) Neuropsychological functioning in Alzheimer's disease. In Parks, R.W., Zec, R.F., & Wilson, R.S. (1993). *Neuropsychology of Alzheimer's Disease and Other Dementias,* Oxford University Press, New York, 3–80.

Interaction Techniques for Users with Spinal Cord Injuries: A Speech-Based Solution

13

Jinjuan Feng[a] and Andrew Sears[b]

[a] *Department of Computer and Information Sciences, Towson University, USA*
[b] *Interactive Systems Research Centre, Information Systems Department, UMBC, USA*

Summary

This chapter discusses hands-free speech-based technologies that support users with spinal cord injuries and other similar impairments that may hinder interactions using a keyboard and mouse. Although speech recognition is expected to be a fast, easy-to-learn, and natural way of interacting with computers, the majority of users abandon speech-based systems in the early stages of interaction. One major obstacle that deters wide adoption of these systems is the high rate of speech recognition errors coupled with cumbersome navigation and error correction techniques. Through a series of studies involving users with spinal cord injuries, we investigated the challenges posed by traditional speech-based navigation and error correction techniques. Two sets of improvements were proposed and evaluated. First, traditional target- and direction-based techniques were refined, significantly lowering command failure rates, reducing the amount of time spent on navigation, and improving productivity by approximately 40%. Second, we proposed a new anchor-based navigation technique that has been shown to be efficient, especially for novice users. Based on the results of these studies, we propose a solution to support seamless interaction with standard desktop applications.

13.1 Introduction

As computing devices become indispensable components of workplaces and education facilities, as well as homes, the accessibility to use those devices is crucial for building careers, pursuing higher education, and social interactions. However, physical impairments (PI) may prove detrimental to an individual's ability to use computing devices. According to the *International Classification of Impairments, Disabilities, and Handicaps* published by the World Health Organization (WHO, 2006), PI refers to a loss of muscle power, reduced mobility of a joint, uncontrolled muscle activity, or absence of a limb. In this chapter, we focus on PI that hinders an individual's ability to use computing devices, specifically those that affect the motor functions in an individual's hands and arms. Examples of PI addressed in this chapter include spinal cord injuries (SCI), repetitive strain injuries (RSI), loss of limbs, and locked-in syndrome, but the primary focus of this chapter is SCI and impairments that result in comparable challenges.

Individuals with PI that affect the hands and arms often find it difficult to use the standard keyboard and mouse. A significant body of research focuses on improving existing keyboard and mouse techniques, such as the use of haptic feedback, and some of the proposed solutions do reduce error rates and improve productivity. However, since these solutions still depend on motor capabilities, the fundamental problems introduced by the PI remain unaddressed. Other solutions examine the use of human capabilities other than the motor functions of the hands and arms. Examples include head-, eye-, and electrophysiologically controlled solutions, each with specific advantages and disadvantages. For instance, both head- and eye-controlled techniques are quite effective for target selection tasks, but extremely slow for generating text. The cost of both techniques is relatively high, making them less accessible for the average user. Similarly, the cost of existing electrophysiological solutions is prohibitive and error rates remain high, limiting the efficacy of these solutions for many tasks.

In contrast, speech-based techniques have various advantages. Unlike the traditional keyboard which requires some degree of learning, speech is a skill that most people learn naturally as children. Therefore, it is expected that most users would find speech-based techniques easy to learn and natural to use. Even better, people speak (normally 120 to 150 words per minute) much faster than they can type (normally 15 to 30 words per minute). The large gap between the speed of speaking and typing makes speech an attractive alternative. In addition, effective speech-based solutions can completely replace keyboard and mouse so the users' hands and arms are not tied to the interaction devices. For able-bodied users, this means that their hands and arms can be free to complete other tasks, such as driving or completing medical procedures. For users with PI who have difficulty using a keyboard and mouse, speech has the potential to provide an effective solution for interacting with computing devices.

Even with all these potential advantages, multiple studies have found that the majority of users continue to abandon speech-based systems shortly after they begin to use them (e.g. Koester, 2003). The high abandonment rate of speech systems reveals intrinsic limitations of speech-based interactions, such as disturbing co-workers, privacy issues, increased cognitive workload, and recognition errors. Among these limitations, recognition errors are a significant barrier to the wide adoption of speech-based technologies. Speech recognizer output is based on complicated statistical models that consider phonetic signals, grammar, and contextual information while the input to a speech recognizer is often mixed with significant noise. Many factors contribute to high error rates, including the fact that human speech is ambiguous, inconsistent, highly context-dependent, with numerous words sharing a common pronunciation (e.g. 'too,' 'two,' and 'to'). As a result, recognition errors are inevitable, especially when the available vocabulary is large. In addition to user and system issues, many contextual sources can also introduce recognition errors, such as environment noise.

Unfortunately, existing speech-based error correction techniques are extremely troublesome. Karat *et al.* (1999) observed that users with extended experience of speech systems still spent an average of 75% of their time selecting and correcting errors. More recently, Sears *et al.* (2001) found users spent one-third of their time just selecting words to be corrected and another one-third correcting the words. The significant time spent on error recovery dramatically reduces productivity, offsetting the theoretical time savings associated with speaking faster than typing. To address this problem, Sears *et al.* conducted a series of studies investigating speech-based navigation and error correction techniques. Several major difficulties with existing speech-based navigation techniques were identified. Refining the existing solutions significantly reduced error rates for the navigation commands, increasing productivity by nearly 40%. In addition, a new anchor-based navigation technique was developed and evaluated. Initial results suggest that this technique can be both efficient and reliable, a combination of attributes that is missing from more traditional speech-based navigation solutions. Based on these results, we proposed a hands-free solution using multiple speech-based navigation techniques to support seamless interaction with standard desktop applications.

In the following section, we summarize previous research involving users with SCI, providing readers with key background information regarding the challenges that must be addressed and existing interaction solutions used by individuals with SCI. In the subsequent section, we discuss our studies of existing speech-based navigation solutions and introduce the proposed interaction model. In the final sections, we discuss the implications of our research and lessons learned regarding research involving individuals with SCI.

13.2 Related Research

Spinal cord injuries occur when the spinal cord (a collection of nerves extending from the base of the brain through the spinal column) is compressed, cut, damaged, or affected by disease (Stiens *et al.*, 1997). The spinal cord contains motor nerves that control movement and sensory nerves that provide information such as temperature, pain, position, and touch. The consequences of an SCI depend upon the level (the nerves that are affected) and the completeness of the injury. The spinal column is divided into four areas: cervical (neck), thoracic (chest), lumbar (lower back), and sacral (tail bone). For the purpose of this chapter, we are concerned with injuries to the cervical vertebrae (C1–C7) and thoracic vertebrae (T1–T12) as injuries in the lumbar or sacral regions will not affect the arms or hands. The level of an SCI refers to the location of the damaged nerves. In general, injuries higher on the spinal cord will result in greater impairments (Sears and Young, 2004).

In the United States, there were nearly 250 000 people living with SCI in July 2005, with approximately 11 000 new cases occurring each year (SCI Information Network, 2006). SCI primarily affects younger adults, with the average age of people with SCI being approximately 38 years in 2000 (SCI Information Network, 2006), suggesting that many of these individuals have employment potential after the injury. Statistics suggest that following an SCI, approximately 33% of people with lower-level injuries are employed, while just 25% of those with high-level injuries are employed (SCI Information Network, 2006). Allowing for more effective interactions with computers and computer-related devices may help those who are unemployed start a career and those who are already employed be more productive.

Many studies have examined how individuals with SCI or other upper body PI interact with information technology. In this section, we focus on studies involving users with SCI as well as impairments in hands and arms that may result in similar consequences and challenges. This includes research that focuses on improving the effectiveness of the standard keyboard and mouse as well as studies of alternative solutions such as head-, eye-, brain-, and speech-based interactions.

13.2.1 **Standard Keyboard and Mouse**

The keyboard and mouse are by far the most popular solutions for interacting with computing devices. A large number of individuals with PI use a keyboard and mouse as their primary interaction solutions, but this often results in significant difficulties. Numerous studies have focused on identifying specific challenges experienced by users with PI as well as possible improvements.

Casali (1992) investigated the efficacy of five cursor control devices when used by individuals with SCI. Thirty participants were divided into three groups of ten: PI users with low motor skills, PI users with high motor skills, and participants with no PI. Each participant used a trackball, mouse, tablet, joystick, and the cursor keys to complete a series of tasks involving selecting or dragging a target.

Participants in the low motor skill group took longer to complete the tasks than those with no PI, but there was no difference between participants in the high motor skill group and the no PI group. The rank ordering of the devices, with respect to target acquisition time, was the same for all three groups. The order of the task completion time was also the same for all groups, with the mouse, trackball, and tablet resulting in the shortest task completion times. The cursor keys were slower, and the joystick was the slowest device. Target size was more important as motor skills decrease.

Encouragingly, all participants were able to complete the tasks with all five devices with minimal system customization. However, participants in the low and high motor skill groups did experience substantial difficulty using the mouse. The majority of these individuals found holding the mouse button down while moving the mouse difficult and ended up relying on a toggle switch customization to complete the task.

Koester and Levine (1994) investigated the ability of keystroke-level models to predict performance of individuals with SCI using word prediction software to enter text. Twelve individuals participated in the study, including individuals with and without high-level SCI. Participants with SCI used their normal method of interacting with a keyboard (two used a mouthstick, four used hand splints). Participants without PI all used a mouthstick to interact with the keyboard even though they did not have previous experience using a mouthstick. Two prediction models were evaluated. One used generic, user-independent, parameters. The second was customized based on data gathered for each individual.

The user-driven model was more accurate than the generic model, resulting in an average error rate of approximately 6% for all participants while the generic model resulted in error rates of 53% and 11% for participants with and without PI. Overall the models predicted modest improvements in performance (ranging from slight decreases to improvements of over 40%), but participants with PI showed a consistent, large decrease in data entry rates when using word prediction (ranging from approximately 20–50%).

Keates *et al.* (2000) studied the possibility of using force feedback to cope with the needs of individuals with PI. Six individuals with various upper body PI (e.g. cerebral palsy, spasm, tremor) participated. Pointer trails (e.g. showing the path the cursor followed), changing the color of the target and vibrating the mouse when the cursor was over the target, and gravity wells were all tested. Gravity wells are unseen circles around the target that define a gravity field. Entering the gravity well causes the cursor to be pulled toward the target.

Gravity wells reduced the time needed to select the targets by approximately 10–20%. The largest improvements were observed for more severely impaired users. In contrast, vibrating the mouse caused selection times to nearly double. While this study confirmed the potential of gravity wells, there were few targets on screen at any given time. As a result, it is unclear if gravity wells would be useful in a typical user interface where many targets can be present on screen at the same time.

Hwang *et al.* (2003) expanded on these results, investigating the performance of gravity wells when an undesired distracter target was present. Individuals with and without PI participated. Gravity wells resulted in improved selection times and error rates, especially for the most impaired users. However, the presence of multiple targets (and their corresponding gravity wells) did cause users to experience undesirable forces, hindering progress and leading to poorer performance.

These studies confirmed that individuals with SCI had great difficulty manipulating the standard keyboard and mouse. Gravity wells helped, but users still experienced difficulties because the revised solutions continued to rely on the motor functions of the hands and arms. To address this issue, alternative technologies that depend on other body functions have been examined.

13.2.2 Head-Controlled Interaction

Some SCI users have no or very limited control over their hands but retain effective control of their necks. For these individuals, head-controlled interaction techniques can be an effective alternative.

LoPresti and Brienza (2004) investigated the use of head-controlled devices by people with SCI. To address challenges associated with limited neck control, the authors developed software that automatically adjusted the interface sensitivity to the needs of individual users. The software was evaluated in two stages. The first stage involved 16 novice users with SCI or multiple sclerosis, confirming that icon selection speeds increased significantly. The second stage involved five users with PI who were experienced users of head-controlled devices. Only one participant experienced an improvement in performance. The limited success of these more experienced users was attributed to the fact that calibrating the system required five steps.

Other studies which have investigated the use of head-controlled devices by individuals without PI will not be discussed here. In general, head-controlled techniques can be useful for individuals with SCI, but several significant challenges must be addressed. First, text generation using head-controlled interactions is slow. Second, existing head-controlled devices are only effective if they are calibrated, but this process can be complicated for individuals with limited computing experience. Third, extended use of head-controlled devices may cause fatigue in neck and related muscles.

13.2.3 **Eye-Controlled Interaction**

Numerous studies explored the use of eye trackers as a navigation technology. For instance, Sibert and Jacob (2000) developed eye tracking algorithms that took advantage of knowledge about how human eyes behave, allowing users to select targets more quickly than with a mouse. Their results suggest that eye tracking may be an effective solution for users who have limited use of their hands as well as individuals who are completing hands-busy tasks. However, the system was evaluated by individuals without PI and no data regarding errors were presented.

Lankford (2000) integrated eye tracking technology in a Windows environment to support a full range of mouse actions. System accuracy was limited to between one-half of a centimeter and one centimeter when the users were roughly 60 centimeters from the monitor, but the precision needed to reliably control Windows was approximately one millimeter. This suggests that effective control of Windows is unlikely without specialized interaction solutions. Therefore, the researchers developed a zooming technique to make targets larger with the goal of reducing errors. Testing with participants with disabilities confirmed the effectiveness of the system.

Despite these efforts, eye tracking still suffers from fundamental challenges. One significant challenge is the limited accuracy that can be achieved. Current eye tracking techniques provide a resolution much more coarse than the mouse, making it difficult to effectively support many common interaction tasks. Further, the range over which the eye can be effectively tracked is fairly limited.

In addition to eye tracking, some researchers investigated the use of eye lid movements to interact with computers. For example, Shaw *et al.* (1995) developed a system that monitored eye lids as input to control various devices including computers. An empirical evaluation using wheelchair controls demonstrated significant potential in the context of simple interactions. However, their result also suggested that it was unlikely that the eye-lid control could be used to efficiently complete more complicated activities such as navigation within a text document.

13.2.4 **Electrophysiological Solutions**

In recent years, dramatic progress has been made in using various electrophysiological signals to communicate with computing devices. These solutions have the potential to benefit users with various motor impairments, but in their current form these solutions are most useful for individuals with severe PIs, such as locked-in syndrome. Locked-in syndrome is a state in which the individual is conscious and able to think but is so severely paralyzed that communication is often possible only by opening and closing the eyes in response to questions (Berkow, 1997).

Lisogurski and Birch (1998) and Bozorgzadeh *et al.* (2000) described a brain-controlled switch that could be activated by imagining finger movement. Their system was evaluated by individuals with no PI with results suggesting that the system could effectively identify both real and imagined finger movements. These results indicate that such a system has the potential to benefit individuals who have lost motor function in the hands or arms.

Building on their earlier results, Birch and colleagues discussed a study involving two individuals with high-level SCI (Birch *et al.*, 2002; Mason *et al.*, 2002). Neither participant had any residual motor or sensory function in their hands. Their results indicated false-positive rates of less than 1% (i.e. the system detected activity when none was intended) and hit rates of 35–48% (i.e. the system detected activity when it was intended). Although higher hit rates are desirable, these results are promising in that they confirm that individuals with no residual motor or sensory function in their hands could activate the system by imagining finger movements. Furthermore, these results were obtained with relatively little training and no calibration for the individual participants. Significant improvements in performance could be achieved with sufficient training and calibration.

More recently, Moore and Dua (2004) developed a biometric input device using galvanic skin response (GSR), a change in the conductivity of the skin caused by increased activity of the sweat glands. GSR can be affected by various emotional responses such as fear, excitement, and anxiety. A user with locked-in syndrome who had lost the ability to use a brain computer interface tested the system for 1 year in an online study. The user achieved 62% accuracy within several days of using the technology, demonstrating that GSR has the potential to be used by people with severe motor impairments.

Despite significant improvements in electrophysiological techniques, crucial limitations remain. First, complicated and expensive equipment, and in some cases medical procedures, are required to collect and analyze electrophysiological data. Second, since these are recognition-based technologies and electrophysiological signals are inherently noisy, system-induced errors will be a significant problem. Third, use of electrophysiological data often causes concerns about privacy due to the fear of electrodes that can read an individual's mind. These real and perceived concerns must be addressed if electrophysiological solutions are to be widely adopted.

13.2.5 **Speech-Based Interactions**

Speech-based solutions are promising for individuals who have limited control over their hands and arms but intact speech capabilities. Numerous studies have investigated the use of speech for both text generation and target selection tasks including several studies involving users with SCI or similar impairments. Manaris *et al.* (2002) developed a speech interface that provided access to all of the capabilities of a traditional keyboard and mouse. For example, to click the left mouse button, the user said 'click left mouse button.' A usability study was conducted evaluating the efficacy of the interface for keyboard access and mouse control. Three disabled users with upper body PI that interfered with the use of standard keyboard and mouse participated in the pilot study. In the first trial, participants used their preferred input method (e.g. typing with one hand, dictating to an assistant, or using a mouthstick) to type a 38-word paragraph. After the training session, participants generated a 41-word paragraph using the speech interface. The results indicated that all participants were comfortable with the speech-based interactions. Data entry rates were comparable for the speech interface and the participants' preferred input methods. Considering the significant training participants had with their preferred input mode, and the limited training provided for the speech interface, these results are considered encouraging.

Their second study compared the speech interface to a handstick. A handstick allows individuals with PI who are not able to use a keyboard and mouse, but have some residual motor capabilities in their hands and arms, to interact with computing devices by pushing one button at a time. Forty-three able-bodied users participated in this study, transcribing one paragraph using a handstick and a second using the speech interface. Their results showed that the speech interface allowed for a 37% decrease in task completion time, 74% increase in typing rate, and 63% decrease in error rate.

Karat *et al.* (1999) conducted a study in which participants without PI composed text documents using commercial speech recognition software. The results revealed significant problems with existing speech-based navigation and error correction techniques. On average, participants only spent 25% of their time dictating text. While dictating text should have been the primary focus of the participants, they spent 75% of their time selecting and correcting errors. Since all participants had extended experience using speech-based dictation software, these results suggest that novice users would likely encounter even more problems with navigation and error correction. These results, which confirm that users spend the vast majority of their time dealing with recognition errors, may provide insights as to why others have reported that the majority of users abandon speech recognition products shortly after they begin using them (Newman, 1999).

Koester (2003) provides additional data regarding the abandonment of speech recognition systems. Eight participants without previous experience using speech recognition used Dragon NaturallySpeaking or Dragon Dictate at home or in their offices. Seven had PI that affected their use of the standard keyboard and mouse. One had difficulty writing and reading using traditional orthography. After 6 months, 87.5% of the participants had stopped using the speech recognition software. Once again, high recognition error rates played a significant role. All participants were observed during two sessions, once during week 4 and again during week 6. The average recognition error rates during these sessions were 14% and 17%. Interestingly, the only participant who was still using the system at the end of the study is also the only individual who experienced a recognition error rate of less than 10% during these two sessions. In addition to recognition errors, other major causes for abandonment included preference for nonspeech input methods and difficulties with technical implementation of the speech system. For comparison purposes, average text entry rates for the two sessions were approximately 17 and 20 words per minute.

These studies confirmed the potential of speech-based solutions for individuals with impairments that resulted in limited motor functions in hands and arms. Compared with highly error-prone, expensive, brain-controlled techniques, speech-based solutions are both more accurate and less expensive. Compared with head- or eye-controlled techniques, speech-based interactions are more efficient for generating text and in most instances cost less.

On the other hand, these studies also highlighted significant challenges, especially when correcting recognition errors. In the next section, we focus on the challenges associated with speech-based navigation and identify several possible improvements to existing techniques. We also present a solution that provides effective support for hands-free speech-based navigation that builds on the results of several user studies involving individuals with and without SCI.

13.3 A Seamless Speech-Based Navigation Solution for Users with SCI

A series of studies were conducted with the goal of providing a seamless, hands-free, speech-based navigation solution. In the first study, we examined how SCI users composed text documents using speech, with a particular focus on traditional navigation and error correction techniques (Sears *et al.*, 2001). Based on the results of this study, traditional speech-based navigation solutions were revised and evaluated through a longitudinal study (Sears *et al.*, 2003). This study confirmed the efficacy of the changes, but also revealed interesting patterns as participants learned to compose documents using speech (Feng *et al.*, 2005). In a third study, a new speech-based navigation technique that uses carefully selected navigation anchors to expedite navigation was evaluated (Feng and Sears, 2004). We also investigated the effectiveness of speech-controlled continuous cursor movements (Karimullah and Sears, 2002) as well as a grid-based solution (Dai *et al.*, 2004). Integrating the results of these studies, we propose a comprehensive speech-based navigation solution that could be used by individuals with impairments that affect the use of the hands and arms. As appropriate, we also address issues related to error correction and dictation.

13.3.1 Target- and Direction-Based Navigation

In our first study, we used a commercial speech recognition engine and a custom application that provided all of the standard interaction solutions available in state-of-the-art commercial dictation products (Sears *et al.*, 2001, 2003). One significant focus was the efficacy of speech-based navigation as used for text editing tasks including both:

1. Target-based navigation which allows users to specify the word they would like to select, such as 'select Friday' or 'correct boy.'
2. Direction-based navigation which, as implemented, lets users specify the direction and distance the cursor should move, such as 'move up four lines' or 'move right three words.'

Target-based navigation, if successful, can allow users to select any words that appear on the screen with just one command. If the target appears on the screen more than once, additional commands may be required to clarify which instance of the word is desired. In contrast, direction-based navigation can only move the cursor horizontally or vertically so most tasks will require two successful commands. The target-based approach is very powerful, but the larger vocabulary associated with this solution would suggest that recognition errors will be more common. The direction-based approach uses a smaller vocabulary, but each command involves three variables: a number, a direction, and the unit of movement. As a result, direction-based navigation may also result in higher error rates than one might desire. In this study, individuals with and without SCI composed text documents using speech-based dictation, navigation, and correction techniques.

Method

Fourteen native English speakers with prior experience using commercial speech-based dictation software were recruited to participate in this study. Seven participants had no documented physical impairments that would hinder their ability to use the keyboard or mouse. The other seven participants had spinal cord injuries at or above

C6 with American Spinal Cord Injury Association (ASIA) scores of A or B, indicating that there was no or very limited residual motor function in their hands and arms. Thirteen participants were male, the participants' average age was 34.4 (st. dev. 11.7), and participants averaged 15.6 years of computing experience (st. dev. 6.8).

Participants utilized a Gateway Solo Pro 9300 laptop computer with a 600 MHz Pentium III processor, 128 M of memory, and a VXI Parrot 10-3 microphone. Participants interacted with a custom speech recognition application, TkTalk Version 1.0 that used IBM's ViaVoice Millennium Edition speech recognition engine. TkTalk allows users to dictate and edit text using a full range of speech-activated editing capabilities, including target and direction-based navigation commands. During training, participants were introduced to all of the commands available in TkTalk.

Participants were guided through the standard enrollment process, completing one training passage, to ensure that the recognition engine had an equivalent amount of information about each participant's speech patterns. Participants were guided through 30 minutes of training during which they completed two sample tasks (one transcription and one composition). The experimenter guided the training and practice to ensure that all participants were exposed to all of the capabilities of TkTalk. Once the training session was complete, the participant was left alone to complete the experimental tasks independently.

Each participant completed four experimental tasks: two transcription tasks of approximately 70 words each and two composition tasks which required them to respond to several questions posed in a hypothetical email (three and four questions, respectively). Responses for composition tasks could be as brief or lengthy as the participant desired. Participants completed either the two composition tasks first or the two transcription tasks first, with the order of each pair of tasks being randomized. Participants were given one task at a time to ensure that the tasks were completed in a predefined order. After each task, participants responded to questions about the ease of use of the software and their satisfaction with the amount of time required to complete the task. After completing all four tasks, participants completed a final questionnaire regarding their overall satisfaction with the software.

Results
Productivity and Time Allocation

There were no significant differences between the two groups with regard to task completion times, recognition error rates, and overall productivity. Text was composed at a rate of approximately 13 words per minute with an average recognition error rate of approximately 17%. These findings were quite consistent with the results reported more recently by Koester (2003).

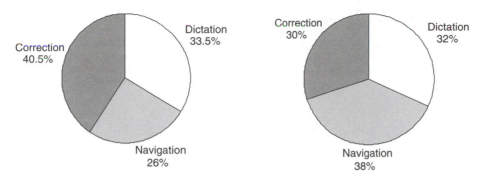

**Proportion of time spent on different tasks
– SCI users**   **Proportion of time spent on different
tasks – Users without PI**

Figure 13.1 Proportion of time spent on different tasks – participants with and without PI.

Participants spent approximately one-third of their time dictating, one-third issuing navigation commands, and one-third issuing error correction commands. The fact that participants spent such a large portion of their time dealing with recognition errors confirmed that there were serious problems with the existing speech-based navigation and correction techniques. Interestingly, participants without PI spent more of their time navigating as compared with SCI users. As indicated in Figure 13.1, participants without PI spent 38% of their time navigating within the documents they were creating while SCI participants spent just 26% of their time on comparable activities.

More detailed analysis confirmed that this difference could be attributed to the different interaction strategies employed by the two groups of users. Participants without PI tended to delay error correction, using navigation commands to move back to earlier errors that needed to be corrected. In contrast, SCI participants tended to correct errors as soon as they occurred, causing navigation commands to be used less frequently. This finding revealed important differences between the two groups of users and suggested that improvements in navigation and correction techniques would likely impact the two groups of users in different ways.

Navigation command failures

A significant portion of both target- and direction-based navigation commands failed, causing a variety of unexpected outcomes. The failure rates for target- and direction-based techniques were 15% and 19%, respectively, suggesting that neither technique was particularly reliable.

Table 13.1 *Distribution of unexpected outcomes of failed target and direction-based commands*

	Change content	Move cursor	No change	Other change
Target-based technique	7.8	6.8	1.1	0.0
Direction-based technique	8.8	2.4	7.3	0.7

A more detailed analysis revealed that both system errors (i.e. recognition errors) and user errors contributed to the difficulties users experienced with speech-based navigation. System, or recognition, errors are best illustrated by a simple example where 'select toy' is incorrectly recognized as 'select boy.' User errors could be associated with one of two basic problems. Sometimes, users paused too long while issuing a command: 'move up. . . . . . four lines.' This typically resulted in the first part of the command being treated as an incomplete command which is simply rejected by the system while the second part is treated as text which is inserted into the document.

Our results confirmed that failed commands resulted in a variety of consequences and that the specific consequences users encountered could have a major influence on task performance. We found that failed navigation commands normally caused one of three major consequences (see Table 13.1), including inappropriately modifying the text in the document, moving the cursor to the wrong location, or simply ignoring the command. Modifying text is viewed as the most severe consequence given the time and effort required to correct the text before resuming the navigation activity. Moving the cursor to an incorrect location is a less severe consequence, but is more severe than simply ignoring the command because the cursor has been moved and the users must reorient themselves within the document. Approximately one-half of all failed target- and direction-based navigation commands caused the most severe outcome, suggesting that user experience could be improved either by reducing the number of failed commands or by reducing the severity of the consequences associated with failed commands.

Command usage strategy

We also investigated the context in which both direction- and target-based navigation commands were used. We began by defining the concept of a navigation sequence as a series of navigation commands that moved the cursor from the starting location to the desired target. Since the first command in each sequence reflects the user's initial

> I would be in charge of all those department heads in
> my health care company and think of health care packages that
> are affordable and cover most health problems. I would also
> be working hand-in-hand with the accountants, lawyers, and
> probably a *mentor* in the *insurance* business, so that I would be
> able to run my company to the best of my knowledge.
> Hopefully, I would have the **several** branches so that I would
> be able to make lots of money. I would have branches in
> populated areas on the eastern coast of the United States. The
> best part would be, that I would be able to run the company in
> my own home. From time to time, I would the visit to my own
> companies to see if my business was running smoothly.

Figure 13.2 Demonstration of navigation distance.

decision as to how to relocate the cursor after observing the context, navigation sequences were categorized as target- or direction-based sequences based on the first command issued. We define navigation distance as the number of steps required to reach the target location if the cursor were moved one word or one line at a time. As shown in Figure 13.2, moving the cursor from 'insurance' to 'several' requires two steps (move down, move down), resulting in a distance of two. Similarly, the navigation distance between the word 'mentor' and 'several' is five.

The average distance traversed using target- and direction-based navigation sequences was 3.7 and 3.0, respectively. A Wilcoxon Signed Ranks test confirmed that there was no significant difference when comparing the distance traveled using target- and direction-based sequences ($Z(10) = 0.533$, n.s.), suggesting that users did not develop a clear distance-based strategy as to when to use one type of navigation command versus the other.

Revising Target- and Direction-Based Navigation

Based on a detailed analysis of the successful and failed navigation commands, three revisions were made to the traditional navigation commands. First, we allowed a longer pause while issuing commands. By recognizing that users naturally paused after successful commands, we could allow users to pause much longer (i.e. 750 ms as compared with the original threshold of 250 ms) without causing commands to fail. Based on our existing data, it was expected that this change would allow approximately 78% of the commands that had failed due to unacceptably long pauses to succeed. The consequence of this change is that users would be required to pause longer after each command.

The second revision focused on reducing the severity of the consequences associated with failed target-based commands. Specifically, each time a target-based navigation command was recognized, we compared the confidence scores of the target words to a predefined threshold. If the confidence scores were too low, the command was ignored. Otherwise it was processed normally. In theory, this revision would allow the system to ignore approximately 22% of the target-based commands that would otherwise move the cursor to the wrong location. The consequence of this change was that approximately 1% of the target-based commands that would have been successful would also be ignored.

The third change focused on improving the reliability of the direction-based navigation solution while simultaneously assisting users in developing more effective strategies as to which navigation solution to use in any given situation. Originally, both target- and direction-based solutions could move the cursor large distances quickly, but both techniques are also quite error-prone. The distance the cursor had to move did not provide a clear indication of which commands would be most effective and users spent significant time just deciding which approach to use. To address these problems, we dramatically simplified the direction-based solution, providing four short commands that should be substantially more reliable than the existing solution: 'Move up,' 'Move down,' 'Move right,' and 'Move left.' In addition to being more reliable, these simplified direction-based commands are no longer logical solutions when a large distance needs to be traversed. Therefore, it was anticipated that users would develop more effective navigation strategies, using target-based commands when moving larger distances and direction-based commands to move shorter distances.

Evaluating the Revisions

A longitudinal empirical study was used to evaluate the efficacy of the three revisions. Fifteen native English speakers with no PI and no previous experience using speech-based dictation software completed nine trials in a period of 10 to 20 days. In each trial, participants used a newer version of TkTalk to compose a text document of approximately 400 words. The newer version of TkTalk integrated the three revisions to target- and direction-based navigation commands described above. The first trial was used as a training session. Results for the final trial from the current study, representing experienced usage, were compared with results for participants without PI from the first study.

The revised target- and direction-based commands resulted in significantly lower failure rates and less severe consequences when commands did fail. More importantly, simplifying the direction-based commands did help users develop an effective strategy, using target-based commands to move larger distances and direction-based commands to move shorter distances (see Figure 13.3).

In addition, participants spent significantly less of their time navigating and more of their time dictating text. As shown in Figure 13.4, the percentage of time spent on

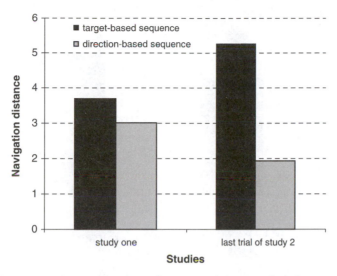

Figure 13.3 *Average navigation distance of target- and direction-based sequences by partici-pants for study 1 and last trial of study 2.*

navigation dropped from 38% in study one to just 12% in the current study. At the same time, the percentage of time spent dictating increased from 32% to 62%. These changes suggest that the three revisions were successful, allowing users to spend much more of their time on the primary task of composing text.

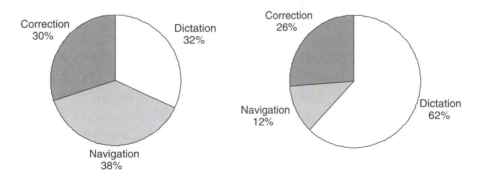

Proportion of time spent on different tasks using traditional navigation techniques

Proportion of time spent on different tasks using revised navigation techniques

Figure 13.4 *Proportion of time spent on different tasks – study 1 and last trial of study 2.*

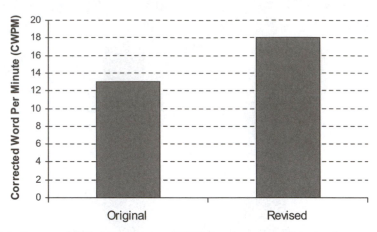

Figure 13.5 *Corrected Word Per Minute (CWPM) using original navigation commands and revised navigation commands.*

Overall, the revised navigation commands allowed for a significant increase in productivity. As shown in Figure 13.5, data entry rates increased from 13 words per minute to 18 words per minutes, which was an increase of nearly 40%. The first study confirmed that traditional speech-based navigation techniques were ineffective, provided insights into the underlying problems users were experiencing, and suggested two methods of improving the user's experience: reducing failure rates and reducing the severity of the consequences experienced when commands do fail. The second study confirmed the efficacy of several revisions to traditional navigation techniques, resulting in a 40% increase in productivity.

13.3.2 Anchor-Based Navigation Technique

Although revising the traditional target- and direction-based commands allowed for significant improvements, both solutions continue to have limitations. Target-based commands are efficient but error prone while direction-based commands are reliable but inefficient when the cursor must be moved more than a couple of words. Ideally, users would have access to a single solution that is both reliable and efficient. To address this goal, we developed a new anchor-based navigation technique (Feng and Sears, 2004). Navigation anchors are strategically selected words within a text document that can be reached using a set of highly reliable commands. Various methods could be used to define navigation anchors, but our initial implementation was based on the confidence scores of the words produced by the recognition engine, including

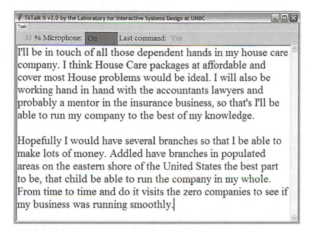

Figure 13.6 *Demonstration of anchor-based navigation technique – dictation mode.*

both those words that are displayed to the user and the alternatives produced by the recognition engine that are not displayed.

TkTalk 2.0 supports anchor-based navigation, providing two basic modes of operation. In the dictation mode (see Figure 13.6), users can dictate new text but cannot edit the text they produce. At any time, but preferably after dictating a paragraph or more of new text, users can issue the 'proof document' command to enter the proof document mode (see Figure 13.7). In this mode, navigation anchors are displayed using gray text and users have access to six simple navigation commands.

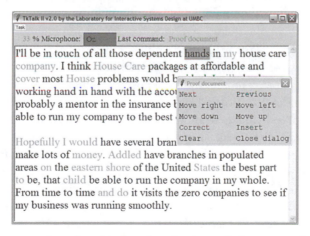

Figure 13.7 *Demonstration of anchor-based navigation technique – proof document mode.*

'Next' and 'Previous' cause the cursor to jump forwards or backwards to the next anchor. 'Move right,' 'Move left,' 'Move up,' and 'Move down' move the cursor one word or line in the corresponding direction. In a full implementation, users would be able to modify or delete the highlighted word or insert a new word nearby. In the current prototype, users simply indicated which corrective action they would take before proceeding to the next error.

An Empirical Evaluation

Our initial evaluation of the new anchor-based navigation technique included 12 participants without any disabilities. All participants were native English speakers with no previous experience using speech-based dictation software. Participants used TkTalk 2.0 to compose a text document of approximately 400 words. Since our focus was on the efficacy of the new navigation technique, participants simply selected the incorrect words and indicated the type of change that was desired (i.e. 'correct,' 'insert,' or 'clear').

The results confirmed that users could navigate to erroneous words efficiently, reaching each target using an average of just 2.25 navigation commands. As expected, failure rates were quite low. For example, the 'Next' commands accounted for 53% of all navigation commands and only failed 0.8% of the time. In addition, the consequences experienced when commands did fail were minimal, with over 90% of the failed commands being ignored by the system. Responses to questions regarding satisfaction indicate that users felt that the technique was both easy to use and efficient. A preliminary comparison showed that the new technique performed better than the revised target- and direction-based techniques in terms of command failure rates, failure consequences, navigation efficiency, and user satisfaction (Feng and Sears, 2004).

Due to the novelty of the navigation technique being evaluated and the goals established for this study, several limitations were introduced that should be acknowledged. While our primary goal is to develop more effective hands-free solutions for individuals with PI that hinder their use of a keyboard and mouse, our earlier studies confirmed that the number of individuals who fit this description that could be recruited to participate in our studies is limited. Therefore, participants for this study were not drawn from the limited population of target users (e.g. individuals with limited motor functions in hands or arms), allowing us to reserve the target population for more comprehensive studies. At the same time, our earlier studies highlighted differences between individuals with and without PI that must be considered in these situations. Second, the participants dictated text and indicated which words needed to be corrected but were not required to correct the errors that they identified. Since the efficacy of this new navigation technique has been established, future studies should seek to have representative users complete the entire dictation, navigation, and error correction process.

13.3.3 Grid-Based Navigation

Dai *et al.* (2004, 2005) investigated grid-based solutions for speech-based navigation. This approach uses recursive *n* by *n* grids to allow users to 'drill down' to select targets. Figure 13.8 illustrates the grid-based navigation technique. To reach the gray square, the user can say 'one' first to reach the top left grid, then another 'one' to further drill down to the square. This process is repeated until the desired target can be selected. Dai *et al.* (2005) compared two variations of the grid-based solution. The first provides users with nine cursors on screen with one in the center of each cell of the grid. The second, more traditional, solution provides a single cursor in the middle of cell number five. The result shows that the nine-cursor solution allowed users to select targets more quickly while the single-cursor solution resulted in lower error rates.

Unlike target- and direction-based techniques, grid-based navigation ignores information about the context in which the navigation is occurring (e.g. the application, the fact that words appear on the screen), focusing entirely on the spatial location of the desired object. The major advantage of grid-based navigation is that it is context-free, allowing users to position the cursor anywhere on the screen. On the other hand, being context-free is also a disadvantage since knowledge that you are trying to select a word could make navigation more efficient. For example, users can typically reach a word in a text document using just one or two successful target- or direction-based commands but five or more grid-based commands may be required. Therefore, grid-based navigation appears to be most effective when the user may need to place the cursor anywhere on the screen and targets are not predefined (e.g. editing graphics).

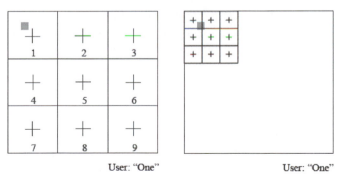

User: "One"   User: "One"

Figure 13.8 *Illustration of grid-based navigation technique.*
Source: From Dai et al. (2004). Copyright 2004 by ACM Press.

13.3.4 **Continuous Navigation Techniques**

The speech-based techniques discussed previously accomplish navigation via discrete movements. Another approach is through continuous cursor movements, which typically includes commands that cause the cursor to begin moving in a predefined location such as 'Up' or 'Move left' as well as commands to stop the cursor like 'Stop' or 'Click.' Karimullah and Sears (2002) conducted a study examining continuous speech-based navigation which indicated that error rates were quite high when targets were small or when the cursor moved too quickly. These difficulties were attributed, in large part, to the brief processing delay that is unavoidable when using speech recognition systems. Several revisions were made, such as allowing users to adjust the speed of the cursor and presenting a second cursor that indicated where the actual cursor should stop if the user issued selection commands such as 'Stop.' The second, predictive, cursor did not prove useful but allowing users to control the speed at which the cursor moved did improve performance (Sears *et al.*, 2002). However, even with these improvements, speech-based navigation that supports continuous cursor movements does not appear to be a promising alternative.

13.3.5 **A Seamless Speech-Based Navigation Model**

Based on the results summarized above, we proposed an interaction solution that will allow users to navigate efficiently regardless of the application being utilized (Goldman *et al.*, 2005). As indicated in Figure 13.9, grid-based navigation would be available, especially for navigation within GUI interfaces, such as Microsoft Windows. Grid-based solutions enable users to select icons or graphic links in any location, even when there is no text accompanying the target. Target-based navigation could also be available, when targets are predefined and named.

Several solutions can be provided to support navigation within applications. Which solutions are appropriate depend on the nature of the application. The first includes the revised target- and direction-based techniques discussed above. This approach provides effective navigation while providing users with a great deal of flexibility. This approach is likely to be preferred by more experienced users who have predefined strategies for working with different applications. This combination of navigation solutions can allow users to interact with a wide variety of applications including word processors, spreadsheets, and email. An alternative for editing text documents would be to support anchor-based navigation, which has been shown to be both simple and easy to learn. Anchor-based navigation is more likely to be useful for novices, who have limited experience using speech-based solutions. Grid-based navigation is a safe solution that can be supported when other approaches are not

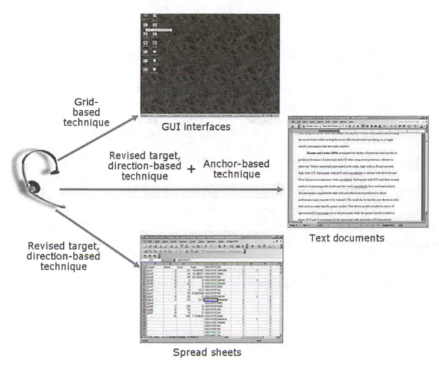

Figure 13.9 *A theoretical interaction solution for hands-free speech-based navigation tasks.*

viable. For example, in a graphics application, targets may not be defined in advance and the cursor can be placed anywhere on the screen, making anchor- and target-based navigation inappropriate. Direction-based navigation may be viable, but the high resolution requirements of graphics applications make this unlikely. A comprehensive solution that combines target-, direction-, anchor-, and grid-based navigation would provide a powerful, reliable, and flexible solution that could address the varying needs and preferences of individual users.

13.4 **Implications for Developers**

Speech-based solutions have unique advantages as well as inherent limitations. Our studies confirmed that speech-based dictation systems were error prone and that it was extremely time consuming for users to correct those errors. Although our revisions significantly reduced the amount of time spent on navigation, dictation still accounted for less than two-thirds of the user's time. The resulting data entry rate (18 words per minute) is still quite slow compared with the normal speech (120 to 150 words per minute), but is reasonably competitive with the rate at which people compose text when using a keyboard and mouse (Karat *et al.*, 1999). The large gap between the current data entry rate and how fast people normally talk suggests that there is great potential for further improvements in speech-based dictation systems. We envision the process of actually correcting recognition errors, which still accounts for one-quarter of the user's time, is an area where considerable improvements are possible.

13.5 Implications for Researchers

Conducting user studies that include participants with SCI or similar impairments can introduce a number of new requirements and challenges for researchers. Based on our experiences, we suggest that researchers consider each of the following issues carefully as they prepare to conduct such studies.

13.5.1 Specifying the Appropriate Participants

Many studies that focus on improving technologies for individuals with disabilities use participants without disabilities, assuming the results will generalize to the target population. In our experience, this assumption can lead to questionable conclusions. Even if the specific functionality provided by the interaction technique is not affected by the users' disabilities, the disabilities affect the way the users interact with the technology, user expectations, and user satisfaction with the experience. For instance, in our first study, users with and without PI were able to achieve comparable data entry rates. However, users with PI adopted different strategies, used different commands, and expressed greater satisfaction with the system. There are times when it makes sense to use participants that are not from the target population, but this must be done carefully. Ideally, there will be pre-existing knowledge of the similarities and differences that should be expected between the population studied and the target users.

13.5.2 Recruiting Participants

Recruiting participants with disabilities can be a difficult task. Researchers typically begin without convenient contacts with the target population. Even if a list of possible participants is available, it can be hard to establish trust with the participants and for the participants to communicate freely with the researcher within the short period of time that most studies involve. Cooperating with health care organizations and other groups that have already established a relationship with the target users can be helpful. These groups can assist in recruiting and communicating with potential study participants, as well as introducing the researchers to participants. Health care providers and support groups are often aware of the potential benefits that technologies can provide, so they are often supportive of collaborative projects of this nature. Most of our projects involve a local rehabilitation center, which provides valuable insights regarding our target users, facilitates the recruitment process, and helps establish trust between study participants and researchers.

13.5.3 Challenges of Off-Site Studies

Most of our studies involving participants without PI are run at our site in one of several permanent usability labs. This is convenient since the necessary equipment can be configured and tested in advance. In addition, the lab provided good control over the physical environment including noise, lighting, and temperature. However, participants with SCI often find transportation to our site challenging, making off-site studies at participants' homes, places of work, or local rehabilitation facilities a necessity. When scheduling sessions for off-site studies, especially for locations controlled by third parties, it is important to confirm that the locations are appropriately accessible. The Americans with Disabilities Act Accessibility Guidelines provide useful guidance (Access Board, 2006). The researcher should ensure that the path to the room being used is accessible as well as the restrooms and any other spaces that participants may need to use. Door openings should be wide enough to allow wheelchair passage and other needs may need to be accommodated, such as service animals.

The inability to control the physical environment is particularly important and can cause significant challenges. When conducting studies in various locations such as participants' homes, rehabilitation centers, and places of work, the physical environment can differ at each location. When setting up the experiment, it is important to carefully define the requirements for the study so all locations can be made as similar as possible. For example, we typically emphasized the need for a quiet enclosed space in which we would not be interrupted.

13.5.4 Data Analysis

In addition to traditional usability measures such as time, error rate, and subjective satisfaction, we find that significant attention should be given to the interaction strategies employed. Our studies provide an excellent example. Although high-level measures such as task completion times and error rates do not differ between the participants with and without PI, process-level analyses confirmed that the two groups adopted very different strategies when completing the tasks (Oseitutu *et al.*, 2001). Unlike traditional measures, which can be relatively simple to capture and analyze, process measures require more detailed observation and a thorough understanding of the interaction technique, the interactions themselves, and the users. Based on our previous experience, we suggest that researchers consider employing additional metrics that provide insights into:

- The time allocated to subtasks.
- How interaction strategies evolve with experience.
- How quickly, how often, and why users change interaction strategies.
- Factors that are used when making decisions regarding which command or technique to employ in a given situation.

Understanding these issues can provide valuable insights into the strategies users employ as novices and how these strategies evolve with experience. Unfortunately, addressing these issues requires a more detailed examination of the users' interactions than is normal. As a result, additional time and resources should be allocated for data analysis.

13.6 **Implications for Users**

At present, it is important for all users to have realistic expectations when using speech-based systems. For example, Goette (2000) reported that the majority of users who successfully adopted speech recognition systems had realistic expectations, while most who abandoned them reported unrealistic expectations as one of the key reasons for abandonment. While speaking is quite natural, significant time and effort is often required to learn effective interaction strategies for speech-based systems.

For novice users who have not used speech recognition technology before, it is important to go through the enrollment process, which normally takes 15–30 minutes and can significantly improve recognition accuracy as well as likelihood of adoption. During the enrollment process, the user dictates specific amounts of predefined text in their normal way of speech. The recognition engine then analyzes the collected speech and creates a profile for the specific user. If multiple users are sharing one computer, the user should make sure that his or her profile is the current one being used by the speech engine. Otherwise the recognition accuracy would dramatically deteriorate.

It has been observed that users of speech technology tend to speak more loudly or slower, especially when encountering recognition errors (Oviatt *et al.*, 1999). Those adaptations, with the intention to avoid recognition errors, actually result in higher error rates since the user's speech no longer matches the profile produced during the enrollment process. Therefore, it is important that users maintain a normal speaking voice and speed when dictating.

13.7 **Implications for Policymakers**

Although dramatic improvements have been achieved, many fundamental limitations of speech-based interaction have not been effectively addressed. Those limitations significantly hinder the wide adoption of speech technology, especially in the workplace. For instance, two major problems with speech-based interactions are interference with others and privacy protection issues. Both problems raise significant concerns in a group working environment and may limit employment opportunities for individuals with high-level SCI since speech may be the most effective and economically accessible solution for those users. Therefore, we would suggest policymakers pay special attention to those problems. Possible actions that will facilitate the resolution of those problems include allocation of more research funding in this field, financial or other forms of compensations to companies and organizations to promote more speech-technology- friendly working environments, and amendment of existing laws and regulations that promote the adoption of speech technology in the workplace.

13.8 **Conclusion**

While many studies have focused on improving the effectiveness of the traditional keyboard and mouse, and the results are often promising, the resulting solutions continue to rely on the use of one's hands and arms. As a result, even these improved solutions will remain inaccessible, inappropriate, or ineffective for some users. To address these concerns, researchers explored various alternative technologies including head- and speech-based solutions as well as techniques that use electrophysiological data. We suggest, based on existing research results and the associated costs, that speech-based solutions are a promising alternative for users with PI that affect their hands and arms.

There are two major tasks when users interact with computers: text generation and navigation. Speech technology can be quite effective for generating text, but existing solutions tend to be cumbersome for spatial navigation tasks. To address the shortcomings of existing speech-based solutions for navigation, a series of empirical studies have examined traditional target- and direction-based techniques, grid-based techniques, and continuous cursor movement techniques. Several recommendations for changing existing target- and direction-based techniques were developed and evaluated, confirming dramatic reductions in command failure rates and the percentage of time spent on navigation activities. More importantly, productivity increased by 40%. These studies also led to the development of a new anchor-based navigation technique, which was shown to be both easy to learn and effective.

Working with users with SCI can be a very rewarding experience. We learned valuable lessons not only about our research and how our participants interacted with computing technologies, but about their lives as well. With regard to our studies, we experienced new challenges with participant selection and recruitment, we learned how to collaborate with health care and support communities, we discovered new issues that are introduced when running off-site studies, and the importance of process-level measures was highlighted. While these lessons may apply to all user studies, we believe they are particularly important for studies that involve users with impairments.

Acknowledgments

This material is based upon work supported by the National Science Foundation (NSF) under Grants No. EIA-0244131, IIS-9910607, IIS-0121570, and IIS-0328391 and the US Department of Education under Grant No. H133G050354. Any opinions, findings, and conclusions or recommendations expressed in this material are those of the authors and do not necessarily reflect the views of NSF or the US Department of Education.

This chapter draws heavily on material from Sears and Young (2004) as well as various journal articles published by the authors and their colleagues as referenced.

References

Access Board (2006) New ADA and ABA Accessibility Guidelines. `http://www.access-board.gov/ada-aba.htm` (retrieved 3 June 2006).

Berkow, R. (1997) *The Merck Manual of Medical Information, Home Edition.* Merck Research Laboratories, Whitehouse Station, NJ.

Birch, G., Bozorgzadeh, Z. and Mason, S. (2002) Initial on-line evaluations of the LF-ASD brain-computer interface with able-bodied and spinal-cord subjects using imagined voluntary motor potentials. *IEEE Transactions on Neural Systems and Rehabilitation Engineering,* **10**(4), 219–224.

Bozorgzadeh, Z., Birch, G.E. and Mason, S.G. (2000) The LF-ASD BCI: on-line identification of imagined finger movements in spontaneous EEG with able-bodied subjects. *Proceedings of ICASSP* 2000.

Casali, S.P. (1992) Cursor control device used by persons with physical disabilities: implications for hardware and software design. *Proceedings of the Human Factors and Ergonomics Society,* 36th Annual Meeting, pp. 315–341.

Dai, L., Goldman, R., Sears, A. and Lozier, J. (2004) Speech-based cursor control: a study of grid-based solutions. *Proceedings of ASSETS 2004,* Atlanta, GA, pp. 94–101.

Dai, L., Goldman, R., Sears, A. and Lozier, J. (2005) Speech-based cursor control using grids: modeling performance and comparisons with other solutions. *Behavior and Information Technology,* **24**(3), 219–230.

Feng, J. and Sears, A. (2004) Using confidence scores to improve hands-free speech-based navigation in continuous dictation systems. *ACM Transactions on Computer-Human Interaction,* **11**(4), 329–356.

Feng, J., Sears, A. and Law, C. (2005) Conducting empirical experiments involving users with spinal cord injuries. *Proceedings of the 3rd Interaction Conference on Universal Access in Human Computer Interaction (HCII) 2005.*

Goette, T. (2000) Keys to the adoption and use of voice recognition technology in organizations. *Information Technology for People,* 67–80.

Goldman, R., Price, K.J., Lin, M. et al. (2005) Speech interaction for mobile devices: a natural solution to a contextual conundrum. *Proceedings of the 11th Interaction Conference on Human Computer Interaction (HCII) 2005.*

Hwang, F., Keates, S., Langdon, P. and Clarkson, J. (2003) Multiple haptic targets for motion-impaired computer users. *Proceedings of CHI 2003,* Fort Lauderdale, FL, 41–48.

Karat C.-M., Halverson, C., Karat, J. and Horn, D. (1999) Patterns of entry and correction in large vocabulary continuous speech recognition systems. *Proceedings of CHI 1999,* New York, pp. 568–575.

Karimullah, A. and Sears, A. (2002) Speech-based cursor control. *Proceedings of ASSETS 2002,* pp. 178–185.

Keates, S., Langdon, P., Clarkson, J. and Robinson, P. (2000) Investigating the use of force feedback for motor-impaired users. *Proceedings of the 6th ERCIM Workshop: User Interfaces for All.*

Koester, H.H. (2003) Abandonment of speech recognition by new users. *Proceedings of Rehabilitation Engineering and Assistive Technology Society of North America (RESNA) 2003.*

Koester, H.H. and Levine, S.P. (1994) Validation of a keystroke-level model for a text entry system used by people with disabilities. *Proceedings of ASSETS 1994,* New York, pp. 115–122.

Lankford, C. (2000) Effective eye-gaze input into Windows. *Proceedings of Eye Tracking Research and Application Symposium,* 2000, pp. 23–27.

Lisogurski, D. and Birch, G.E. (1998) Identification of finger flexions from continuous EEG as a brain computer interface. *Proceedings of IEEE Engineering in Medicine and Biology Society 20th Annual International Conference.*

LoPresti, E. and Brienza, D. (2004) Adaptive software for head-operated computer controls. *IEEE Transactions on Neural Systems and Rehabilitation Engineering,* **12**(1), 102–111.

Manaris, B., Macgyvers, V. and Lagoudakis, M. (2002) A listening keyboard for users with motor impairments: a usability study. *International Journal of Speech Technology,* **5**, 371–388.

Mason, S.G., Bozorgzadeh, Z., and Birch, G.E. (2000) The LG-ASD brain computer interface: on-line identification of imagined finger flexions in subjects with spinal cord injuries. *Proceedings of ASSETS 2000,* New York, pp. 109–113.

Moore, M. and Dua, U. (2004) A galvanic skin response interface for people with severe motor disabilities. *Proceedings of ASSETS 2004,* Atlanta, GA, pp. 48–54.

Newman, D. (1999) Talk to Your Computer: Speech Recognition Made Easy. Waveside Publishing.

Oseitutu, K., Feng, J., Sears, A. and Karat C.-M. (2001) Speech recognition for data entry by individuals with spinal cord injuries. *Proceedings of the 1st International Conference on Universal Access in Human-Computer Interaction,* New Orleans, LA, pp. 402–406.

Oviatt, S.L., Bernard, J. and Levow, G. (1999) Linguistic adaptation during error resolution with spoken and multimodal systems. *Language and Speech,* **41**(3–4), 415–438.

SCI Information Network (2006) Spinal Cord Injury: Facts and Figures at a Glance. `http://www.spinalcord.uab.edu/show.asp?durki=21446` (retrieved 3 June 2006).

Sears, A., Feng, J., Oseitutu, K. and Karat, C.M. (2003) Speech-based navigation during dictation: difficulties, consequences, and solutions. *Human Computer Interaction,* **18**(3), 229–257.

Sears, A. and Young, M. (2004) Physical disabilities and computing technologies, an analysis of impairments, In Jacko, J. & Sears, A. (Eds.). *The Human Computer Interaction Handbook,* Lawrence Erlbaum Associates, 482–503.

Sears, A., Karat C.-M., Oseitutu, K. et al. (2001) Productivity, satisfaction, and interaction strategies of individuals with spinal cord injuries and traditional users interacting with speech recognition software. *Universal Access in the Information Society,* **1**, 1–12.

Sears, A., Lin, M. and Karimullah, A.S. (2002) Speech-based cursor control: understanding the effects of target size, cursor speed, and command selection. *Universal Access in the Information Society,* **2**(1), 30–43.

Shaw, R., Loomis, A. and Crisman, E. (1995) Input and integration: enabling technologies for disabled users. In Edwards, A.D.N. *Extra-Ordinary Human-Computer Interaction,* Cambridge, UK, 263–277.

Sibert, L. and Jacob, R. (2000) Evaluation of eye gaze interaction. Proceedings of CHI 2000. The Hague, Amsterdam, 281–288.

Stiens, S., Goldstein, B., Hammond, M. and Little, J. (1997) Spinal cord injuries. In O'Young, B., Young, M., & Stiens, S. (Eds.). *PM&R Secrets,* Hanley & Belfus, Philadelphia, 253–261.

WHO (2006) World Health Organization. International Classification of Functioning, Disability, and Health. `http://www3.who.int/icf/` (retrieved 3 June 2006).

Adding Gestural Text Entry to Input Devices for People with Motor Impairments

14

Jacob O. Wobbrock[a, b] and Brad A. Myers[b]

[a] The Information School, Box 352840, University of Washington, Seattle, WA 98195, USA
[b] Human-Computer Interaction Institute, School of Computer Science, Carnegie Mellon University, Pittsburgh, PA 15213, USA

Parts of this chapter appeared in Wobbrock, J.O., Aung, H.H., Myers, B.A., and LoPresti, E.F. (2005) Integrated text entry from power wheelchairs. Journal of Behavior and Information Technology 24(3): 187–203, published by Taylor & Francis. Other parts are extensions to the work in Wobbrock, J.O. and Myers, B.A. (2006) Trackball text entry for people with motor impairments. Proceedings of ACM CHI 2006, pp. 479–488, published by ACM Press.

14.1 Introduction

People with motor impairments, such as those caused by muscular dystrophy, cerebral palsy, Parkinson's disease, or spinal cord injuries, often cannot use a conventional mouse and keyboard. They may lack sufficient mobility to reach for these devices, sufficient dexterity to operate them or switch between them, or sufficient endurance to use them for more than a few minutes. However, many of these users have other input devices already at hand. Examples are joysticks and touchpads, which are found on many power wheelchairs, and trackballs, which are often preferred to desktop mice by people with low dexterity or limited motion (Fuhrer and Fridie, 2001). This chapter presents our work on adding text entry capabilities to joysticks, touchpads, and trackballs so that they may be used as integrated devices for both mouse control and text entry. In so doing, we aim to reduce the need for multiple devices, free a person's environment from device clutter, and remove the need to switch among different devices when controlling a computer. We specifically focus on providing gestural text entry in an effort to move away from the tedious and visually taxing experience of using an on-screen keyboard.

Motor impairments caused by neuromuscular disorders, injuries, or diseases manifest themselves in different ways. Accordingly, they affect people's ability to use computers differently. For example, users with muscular dystrophy (MD), who number about 250 000 in the United States, suffer from degenerative voluntary muscle control (Myers *et al.*, 2002). Accordingly, MD results in reduced strength, limited endurance, reduced flexibility, and slowed movements (Sears and Young, 2003). However, it does not often result in tremors or spasms. Thus, many users with MD remain relatively accurate in their fine motor skills, although they are slow and prone to rapid fatigue.

In contrast, people with cerebral palsy (CP) may suffer from spasms or 'intention tremors' that often magnify as they reach for objects or attempt to acquire targets (e.g. with a mouse or stylus). They may have a more difficult time using their fine motor skills than people with MD, and may also suffer from a compromised ability to speak, which reduces the utility of voice recognition systems for these users.

Other sufferers of tremors are people with Parkinson's disease (PD), which affects over 1% of the population aged 65 and over (Sears and Young, 2003). Resting tremors are common, as are stiff muscles and limited flexibility. Difficulty controlling voluntary movements often sets in as the disease progresses. Like with CP, speech impairments are also common, limiting the extent to which voice recognition software may be used.

People with spinal cord injuries (SCI) are also targets for this work. Spinal cord injuries differ depending on the position and severity of the injury. Paraplegics with SCI, for example, may be able to use computer input devices (e.g. trackballs) with their hands, but often with reduced dexterity, strength, and endurance. These users often cannot use a desktop mouse, since shuttling the mouse across the surface of a desk requires the elevation and suspension of the forearm and wrist. They also may not be able to use a physical QWERTY keyboard, since the ability to control the fingers is compromised. Usually SCIs of this sort are the result of trauma at the C6 level or lower (i.e. C6–C8, or T1) (Sears and Young, 2003).

Other motor impairments relevant to this work include repetitive stress injury (RSI) and arthritis. These ailments may benefit from alternative forms of text entry with devices that do not exacerbate pain, discomfort, or fatigue. For example, trackballs are popular among sufferers of RSI because they do not aggravate the forearm and wrist muscles in the same way that desktop mice do.

As this chapter will show, our approach to adding text entry to joysticks, touchpads, and trackballs takes into account the limitations of these user groups by providing a more accurate, physically stable means of entering text. The core idea is to use edges and corners to provide stability and higher accuracy during movement. The result is feasible gestural text input on commonly available input devices.

14.2 Motivation

14.2.1 Joystick and touchpad text entry

An estimated 1.4 million people in the United States depend on wheelchairs for mobility (Kraus *et al.*, 1996). Of these, about 10% are in power wheelchairs, about half of whom require more than one assistive technology to participate in daily activities (Cook and Hussey, 1995). A computer access solution that works with an existing power wheelchair input device, rather than one which adds to the mix of encumbering devices, would be valuable (Guerette and Sumi, 1994). Such solutions have previously been termed 'integrated control systems' (Spaeth *et al.*, 1998).

Commercial technology already exists for enabling mouse cursor control from a power wheelchair joystick (e.g. Switch-It Inc., 2005a). But mouse control is only part of a computer access solution. The ability to enter text is also a cornerstone of successful human–computer interaction. However, an integrated text entry method to accompany joystick mouse control is not readily available. Instead, text entry with a power wheelchair joystick is mouse-driven, taking the form of point-and-click or point-and-dwell on an on-screen keyboard.

On-screen keyboards can be dissatisfying for many reasons. They require precise pointing over small targets. They also consume precious screen real-estate. When editing a document, they exacerbate the need for mouse travel between the document and the on-screen keyboard. They also impose a secondary focus-of-attention, the first being where the text is being entered, the second being the on-screen keyboard itself. This requires users to repeatedly look back and forth between their document and the on-screen keyboard, which can be visually fatiguing. In short, using a joystick-driven mouse cursor to enter text from a power wheelchair with an on-screen keyboard leaves much to be desired. By comparison, a gestural text entry method for joysticks, one which allows users to 'write' by moving the joystick in meaningful letter patterns, does not suffer from the aforementioned drawbacks. This is because gestures can be done by feel. However, the main drawback with gestures is, of course, that they must be learned.

Though less common than joysticks, touchpads can also be used to control power wheelchairs (e.g. Switch-It Inc., 2005b). Touchpads usually require less strength to operate than joysticks and little or no calibration. Like joysticks, they can be used proportionally: the further a finger is from the center of the touchpad, the faster the wheelchair turns or moves. Although touchpads have been used extensively for mousing (e.g. Hinckley *et al.*, 1998; Rekimoto, 2003), they have not generally been considered text entry devices. People in power wheelchairs might benefit from an integrated device that controls their chair, mouse, and text entry. This requires a versatile text entry technique for touchpads.

As more public information terminals (i.e. kiosks) appear in building lobbies and public libraries, on streets, in subway stations, and in community centers, the ability to access these terminals becomes more important. Just as the Americans with Disabilities Act requires that many buildings have access ramps, future terminals may be required to be accessible electronically via Bluetooth or other wireless technologies. It would be advantageous to have an integrated control system where power wheelchair joysticks or touchpads could be used as input devices for mousing and text entry on these terminals. Wheelchair users could then approach public terminals with confidence, knowing that their own wheelchair will be their gateway for access.

14.2.2 Trackball Text Entry

Although they are not used to control power wheelchairs, trackballs are often preferred by individuals with motor impairments for desktop mousing. Trackballs have many desirable properties that make them more suitable than conventional mice for people with limited dexterity, strength, or endurance in their hands or arms. The amount of effort required to roll a ball is generally less than that required to shuttle a mouse across the surface of a desk. Trackballs do not require reaching or the suspension of the forearm, as do conventional mice. Further, trackballs do not suffer from the 'edge of the pad' problem, unlike mice, which sometimes must be lifted and recentered when pushed beyond a certain range. (This action is called 'clutching.') Finally, trackballs have a very small 'desktop footprint' (Card *et al.*, 1990), making them suitable for space-constrained surfaces like the kinds of trays attached to many power wheelchairs.

Not surprisingly, many of the people who prefer trackballs due to motor impairments cannot use a conventional physical keyboard. For these people, an alternative to touch-typing is required. One option is to use a trackball with an on-screen keyboard. But on-screen keyboards have the drawbacks mentioned in the previous section. Therefore, a gestural means of 'writing' with a trackball may be a desirable alternative, allowing users to accomplish mousing and text entry with the same device.

14.3 Overview of Our Approach

Clearly, joysticks, touchpads, and trackballs are very different from one another. Adding gestural text entry capabilities to them requires leveraging their individual strengths while remaining consistent across devices. Simply providing users with a handwriting recognizer and asking them to 'write' with these devices by moving a mouse cursor around would not work very well, as these devices are not well suited to making the kind of smooth, curved letters that one makes with a pencil or stylus (Sperling and Tullis, 1988; Accot and Zhai, 1999). Instead, these devices are best used for short, ballistic straight-line movements. Thus, our approach to adding gestural text entry to them must take this into account.

As a part of the Pittsburgh Pebbles PDA Project (http://www.pebbles.cs.cmu.edu), we are investigating how handheld devices, including personal digital assistants (PDAs), mobile phones, joysticks, touchpads, trackballs, and other devices, can be used to interact in novel ways with desktop computers (Myers, 2001). In our previous work (Myers *et al.*, 2002), we showed that a Palm PDA connected to a desktop PC could be effective for computer access for some people with motor impairments. This is because while many people with motor impairments, particularly MD, lack gross motor control, strength, and endurance, they retain enough finger dexterity to negotiate the small expanse of a PDA screen.

In addition, we invented a new text entry technique called EdgeWrite (Wobbrock *et al.*, 2003b). Originally developed for use with a stylus and Palm PDA, EdgeWrite uses a custom unistroke alphabet whose letters are composed entirely of straight-line segments within a square region, making EdgeWrite suitable for a variety of devices, including joysticks, touchpads, and trackballs. Specifically, we adapted EdgeWrite to work on an Everest & Jennings power wheelchair joystick, a Synaptics touchpad, and any trackball. We conducted three studies of these prototypes, comparing their gestural text entry performance to that of on-screen keyboards for real power wheelchair and trackball users.

In the first study, seven power wheelchair users, six with CP and one with multiple sclerosis (MS), used a power wheelchair joystick to enter EdgeWrite letters and letters with the on-screen keyboard WiViK from Prentke Romich, Inc. (Shein *et al.*, 1991). They also used a touchpad to enter EdgeWrite letters. The study was only a single session, and subjects had no prior experience with EdgeWrite letters, unlike with the WiViK keyboard, which may of them used daily. Nonetheless, with only 30 minutes of practice, touchpad EdgeWrite was the fastest and most preferred, joystick WiViK was second, and joystick EdgeWrite was a close third.

The second study was a follow-up to the first. Two subjects from the first study, both with CP, used the joystick and touchpad with EdgeWrite and WiViK over 10 sessions. The goal was to discover a 'crossover point' (MacKenzie and Zhang, 1999) where EdgeWrite overtakes WiViK for each device. Our results showed that the touchpad methods were faster than the joystick methods, and that EdgeWrite overtook WiViK on both devices after an initial learning period. This supports the notion that gestural text entry may be more satisfying for extended use than selection-based methods like on-screen keyboards.

In the third study, we developed trackball EdgeWrite over a series of nine participatory design sessions with a 15-year trackball veteran with spinal cord injury. The sessions were spread by at least a week and consisted of short 'checkpoint studies' in which we compared trackball EdgeWrite to our subject's preferred on-screen keyboard, the Microsoft Accessibility Keyboard, which he used with his favorite trackball. By the second session his speed with EdgeWrite was better than with the on-screen keyboard, and over the nine sessions he was significantly faster with EdgeWrite without leaving more errors. After 15 years, our subject no longer uses an on-screen keyboard, preferring instead to use trackball EdgeWrite.

In the remainder of this chapter, we tour the related work, describe the three EdgeWrite prototypes (i.e. the joystick, touchpad, and trackball), and discuss our studies and their results. We end with implications for stakeholders and some conclusions.

14.4 **Related Work**

Many devices exist for computer access, some of which can be used from a power wheelchair. Alternative physical and on-screen keyboards, head or hand switches, sip-and-puff devices, voice recognition systems, and augmentative or alternative communication (AAC) devices are just a few of the options available for computer access (Anson, 1997). But there are often obstacles to effective deployment. Many devices are prohibitively expensive. Others require extensive configuration or maintenance (Dawe, 2006). Some might be unwieldy, even on a power wheelchair. These and other reasons may be why prior research has found that less than 60% of people who indicate they need adaptations actually use them (Fichten *et al.*, 2000). Our aim in this work, by providing text entry techniques for existing power wheelchair and trackball devices, is to lower barriers to computer access by using devices already present.

EdgeWrite is related to other gestural text entry methods, most notably Unistrokes (Goldberg and Richardson, 1993) and Graffiti (Palm Inc., 1996). Numerous efforts have been made both in research and industry at improving text entry for mobile devices, many of which are relevant to EdgeWrite. For an in-depth treatment, see the article by MacKenzie and Soukoreff (2002).

A few methods besides EdgeWrite have been devised for 'writing' with a joystick (Wobbrock *et al.*, 2004). One is myText by Co-operwrite Ltd. (1997), which is meant for miniature mobile phone joysticks. Another is Weegie (Coleman, 2001), a dual-stick method for use on the X Window System, the graphical user interface shell that runs on UNIX.

As will be seen, joystick and touchpad EdgeWrite use physical edges and corners to provide stability of motion. Previous work has explored using edges in interaction techniques, such as placing buttons along screen edges for easier target acquisition (e.g. Farris *et al.*, 2001; Wobbrock *et al.*, 2003a). The classic Lisa and Macintosh user interfaces placed their menus along the top of the screen for easy target acquisition using the screen's edge (Ludolph and Perkins, 1998).

Mouse cursor control using a power wheelchair joystick has been studied previously (Romich *et al.*, 2002; LoPresti *et al.*, 2004), but not with an integrated text entry technique. Like the current work, the study by LoPresti *et al.* (2004) also used the on-screen keyboard WiViK for mouse-based text entry.

Touchpad interaction techniques have existed for some time, but few text entry techniques have been developed for touchpads. Two limited exceptions are a touchpad used for a television remote control (Enns and MacKenzie, 1998) and for numeric entry using a clock-face metaphor (Isokoski and Kaki, 2002). Neither of these, however, is a generic touchpad text entry technique like EdgeWrite. Most touchpad techniques focus on control and selection tasks (e.g. Hinckley *et al.*, 1998; MacKenzie and Oniszczak, 1998; Rekimoto, 2003). Similar to touchpad EdgeWrite, templates have been used before on touch surfaces to help guide finger motion (Buxton *et al.*, 1985).

Trackballs have also been evaluated as mousing devices, but not for text entry. Studies have generally found them to be slower and less accurate than conventional mice for able-bodied users in pointing, dragging, and steering tasks, but comparable to touchpads for steering (MacKenzie *et al.*, 1991; Accot and Zhai, 1999). One study noted that a particular problem with trackballs is that users often accidentally move the ball when trying to click (MacKenzie *et al.*, 2001). These findings suggest that using trackballs with on-screen keyboards is not optimal, as one must perform repeated target acquisitions. Studies have shown, however, that trackballs are well suited to short straight-line movements (Accot and Zhai, 1999). As will be seen, trackball EdgeWrite uses this type of motion.

14.5 EdgeWrite for Joysticks, Touchpads, and Trackballs

14.5.1 Stylus EdgeWrite for PDAs

EdgeWrite was originally designed to address the problem of text input on PDAs. The built-in methods of text entry on PDAs usually consist of either a small 'soft' stylus keyboard displayed on-screen with tiny 'keys,' or a stroke alphabet like Graffiti, Graffiti 2, or Jot. As one might imagine, these built-in methods can be very difficult for people with motor impairments (Wobbrock *et al.*, 2003b). Tremor and poor strength, in particular, affect a person's ability to acquire small stylus targets or smoothly stroke letter gestures.

Figure 14.1 *Stylus EdgeWrite on a Palm PDA.*

In contrast, EdgeWrite enables people with tremor and reduced strength to write on a PDA with over 90% accuracy, even if they are unable to write Graffiti. The core concept behind stylus EdgeWrite is that of physical edges, which are placed around the input area of a PDA in the form of a square hole (Figure 14.1). These edges provide physical stability and high accuracy (Wobbrock, 2003) as a user moves his or her stylus along the edges and into the corners according to letter patterns that mimic the feel of Roman hand-printed letters. For a thorough discussion of stylus EdgeWrite for PDAs, see Wobbrock *et al.* (2003b).

The EdgeWrite letter patterns (Figure 14.2) were devised through a formal guessability study in which subjects lacking prior knowledge of EdgeWrite were asked to guess letter patterns by connecting the four corners of a square (Wobbrock *et al.*, 2005a). Although the figure shows only one form for each letter, multiple alternate forms exist

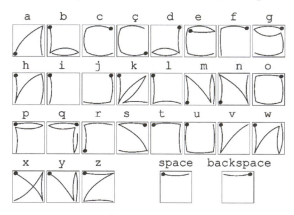

Figure 14.2 *The EdgeWrite alphabet. Bowed segments are for illustrative purposes only; all motion is ideally in straight lines along edges or diagonals and into corners.*

for most letters, which increases guessability. Subsequent comparisons to Graffiti show that the EdgeWrite alphabet is as guessable and immediately usable as Graffiti (MacKenzie and Zhang, 1997; Wobbrock *et al.*, 2005a).[1]

A key feature of EdgeWrite is that stroke recognition is not based on the overall path of motion, but on the order that the corners of the square are hit. This provides tolerance to wiggle and tremor since conventional path-based recognizers can be thwarted by jagged or tremulous strokes. Corner-based recognition also enables fast recognition, even on weak processors, as 'template' gestures can be encoded as simple integers representing corner sequences instead of more elaborate geometric shapes. It is this corner-based stroking and recognition scheme that allows EdgeWrite to easily adapt to other devices like joysticks, touchpads, or trackballs.

Prior results for stylus EdgeWrite show that it is significantly more accurate, over 18%, than Graffiti for able-bodied novices after 15 minutes of practice, and upwards of 3 times more accurate than Graffiti for some motor-impaired individuals with CP, MD, PD, or SCI (Wobbrock *et al.*, 2003b). Moreover, it is not significantly slower than Graffiti in speed. Able-bodied novices can write at about 7 words per minute (wpm), while experts can reach 24 wpm with only 2.8% errors (Wobbrock and Myers, 2005).

14.5.2 Joystick EdgeWrite

We implemented a version of EdgeWrite in C++ for an Everest & Jennings 1706–5020 power wheelchair joystick, which we removed from its chair (Figure 14.3). We attached wires to the joystick outputs in order to access the voltage signals corresponding to the absolute (x, y) position of the stick and the state of a switch. We used a National Instruments 6024E DAQCard to read the voltage signals and make them available to our software.

The joystick is polled for its position every 5 ms by the software. When the (x, y) position of the stick enters one of the four EdgeWrite corners, a character trace begins. When the joystick is briefly released and snaps back to the center, the trace is deemed complete and recognition of the stroke trace occurs. Using this snap-to-center approach for segmenting between letters worked very well. It was based on one of our previous studies (Wobbrock *et al.*, 2004), where able-bodied users of a video game joystick version of EdgeWrite committed no segmentation errors for thousands of letters.

The (x, y) position of the joystick was initially very noisy, in essence containing a great deal of electronic 'tremor' (Figure 14.4, left). To filter out this noise, we took

---

[1] A full chart with numbers, punctuation, accents, and extended characters is available at http://www.edgewrite.com.

Figure 14.3 *Joystick EdgeWrite on a power wheelchair joystick. The plastic template provides a square boundary within which EdgeWrite letters can be made.*

the last *n* points and computed a running average, treating the result as a single point (Figure 14.4, right). Trial and error yielded $n = 12$ as a value that removed sufficient noise while decreasing the inevitable stroke lag introduced by a running average.

It is important to note that the joystick is not used to drive a mouse cursor. That is, the joystick is not being used as a relative position device. Instead, the absolute position of the stick within the physical plastic square is read, so that when a user feels an edge or corner, their digital position is in agreement. For baseline comparisons, it is worth noting that able-bodied experts can write at about 12.9 wpm with this version with about 8.4% errors (Wobbrock and Myers, 2005).

Joystick EdgeWrite is a prototype system that at this time requires us to use our specific joystick. In the future, we would like to cooperate with wheelchair manufacturers

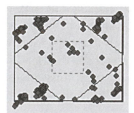 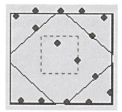

Figure 14.4 *(left) A trace of the letter 's' using joystick EdgeWrite. The absolute (x, y) position of the stick was initially quite noisy. (right) A simple running average produced a clean trace.*

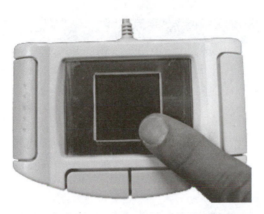

Figure 14.5 Touchpad EdgeWrite on a Synaptics touchpad with a plastic template.

to interface with their joysticks and allow our software to receive joystick inputs. EdgeWrite simply needs to know the (x, y) position of the stick in order to work, but this information is not available from most wheelchair joysticks. The EdgeWrite software receives these inputs 'in the background,' allowing the input focus to remain on any other application. EdgeWrite strokes generate key events as if they were typed on the computer keyboard, allowing joystick EdgeWrite to send text to any Windows application.

14.5.3 Touchpad EdgeWrite

We built a version of EdgeWrite in C# for use with a Synaptics touchpad (Figure 14.5). Like the stylus and joystick versions, the touchpad version used a plastic template to provide a square boundary for stability and passive haptic feedback. The edges of the touchpad's plastic template aid tremulous finger movement in the same way that physical edges aid stylus motion on a PDA. Users can feel the smooth plastic edges as they move, exerting pressure against them for stability. The touchpad surface is a capacitive sensor that detects human skin, so putting pressure on the plastic template itself does not interfere with the touchpad.

Touchpad EdgeWrite is similar to stylus EdgeWrite in that segmentation between letters is accomplished when the finger (or in the case of a PDA, the stylus) is lifted. Before a finger goes down on the touchpad, the corners are rectangular. Once a finger enters a corner, however, the corners 'deflate,' changing from rectangles into triangles. This deflation is to prevent diagonal strokes from accidentally hitting unintended corners (Figure 14.6).

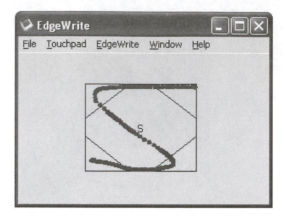

Figure 14.6 An 's' trace within the touchpad EdgeWrite square. Note the 'deflation' of the corners as triangles, which helps the diagonal part of the 's' avoid unintended corners.

Like the stylus and joystick versions, the touchpad version of EdgeWrite does not drive a mouse cursor but receives input as the absolute position of a finger within the EdgeWrite square. Synaptics drivers allow the software to read the absolute position of the finger on the touchpad's surface. With this version, able-bodied experts are able to write at about 19.1 wpm with about 4.7% errors (Wobbrock and Myers, 2005).

Touchpad EdgeWrite can send text to any application running on Microsoft Windows. With help from the Synaptics drivers, it receives touchpad events 'in the background,' so the input focus can remain on any other application window and yet EdgeWrite can receive touchpad input. EdgeWrite strokes generate key events as if they were typed on the computer keyboard, allowing touchpad EdgeWrite to send text to any Windows application.

14.5.4 **Trackball EdgeWrite**

Many people with motor impairments prefer trackballs to conventional mice because of the relatively low strength and dexterity required to roll a ball (Fuhrer and Fridie, 2001). Accordingly, many of these same users cannot touch-type on a conventional physical keyboard. We therefore built a version of EdgeWrite for trackballs. Unlike the stylus, joystick, and touchpad versions described above, trackball EdgeWrite does not work by reading the absolute position of a stylus, stick, or finger within a square. That's because trackballs do not report absolute position or even absolute rotation, but only changes in rotation (Card *et al.*, 1990). Trackball EdgeWrite therefore works

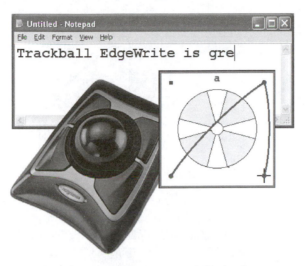

Figure 14.7 *Trackball EdgeWrite works within a virtual EdgeWrite square. The cursor itself is hidden during writing, and the input focus remains on the active window (e.g. Notepad).*

by observing the motion of a mouse cursor within a virtual EdgeWrite square that appears on-screen (Figure 14.7).

Although trackball EdgeWrite is based on the underlying mouse cursor, the cursor is not moved about the square as one would move a stylus, joystick, or finger in the other versions.[2] Instead, the cursor is hidden during writing, and users make short 'pulses' with the trackball toward the corners they desire. The angle (or vector) made by the cursor determines the intended corner, and an idealized stroke trace is drawn to that corner. Theoretically, this can be modeled as a 'crossing task,' which has been shown to be more accurate than traditional pointing (Accot and Zhai, 2002). Thus, subjects are not using the trackball as they would on an on-screen keyboard to point to targets. Instead, they are using the trackball to 'pulse' toward intended corners. Thus, a tight coupling exists between the corner users *feel* they are in, and the corner their stroke trace is *actually* in. Segmentation occurs after the trackball is left stationary for a brief amount of time, usually about 250 ms. Figure 14.8 depicts the process of writing an 's' and the underlying crossing tasks performed.

In Figure 14.8, the user's mouse, which is invisible, moves a short distance r from the top-right corner of the EdgeWrite square. The angle θ indicates the top-left corner,

---

[2]Our early prototypes were designed this way and were slow and dissatisfying. They did not 'feel like' writing because there was no correspondence between the corner the user felt he was in, and the corner the mouse cursor was actually in.

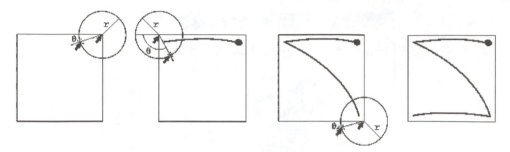

Figure 14.8 *The conceptual stages of writing an 's' with trackball EdgeWrite.*

and an idealized stroke is drawn to the top-left, where the mouse now appears. Next, the angle departing the top-left indicates the bottom-right corner, to where a stroke is subsequently drawn. Then the final angle departing the bottom-right indicates the bottom-left should be entered. This process is not unlike object pointing with only four objects (Guiard *et al.*, 2004).

Note that the stroke trace that is drawn is not a literal trace of mouse movement, but a smooth idealized trace directly connecting corners. The subjective experience for users is that they are 'pulsing' the trackball with subtle but distinct movements toward the corners they desire. Able-bodied users can write at about 12.7 wpm and 6.6% errors (Wobbrock and Myers, 2005).

Trackball EdgeWrite has been robustly engineered in C# to run on Microsoft Windows operating systems. Although we call it trackball EdgeWrite, it actually will work with any cursor-control device. DirectInput is used to poll the mouse position 'in the background' so that the input focus can remain on the active application (e.g. Notepad, Microsoft Word, Microsoft Outlook) and yet trackball EdgeWrite can still receive mouse movements.[3] EdgeWrite strokes generate key events as if they were typed on the computer keyboard, allowing trackball EdgeWrite to send text to any Windows application.

14.6 **Study 1: Novice Use of Joystick and Touchpad EdgeWrite**

This section describes our first study with seven subjects. Throughout this study we worked closely with real power wheelchair users to improve joystick and touchpad EdgeWrite.

---

[3]Normally, only the active application, that is the window with the current focus, receives mouse and keyboard events.

14.6.1 Mouse Control and The WiViK Keyboard

In order to compare EdgeWrite to a currently available means of text entry with a power wheelchair joystick, we compared joystick and touchpad EdgeWrite to the on-screen keyboard WiViK (Shein *et al.*, 1991) in conjunction with a power wheelchair joystick, the Everest & Jennings 1706–5020 (Figure 14.3). In order to allow subjects to use the WiViK on-screen keyboard, we implemented proportional mouse control for the wheelchair joystick (LoPresti *et al.*, 2004). We also enabled a switch on the joystick to simulate a mouse click. When the switch was pressed, it acted as a mouse-down. When the switch was released, it acted as a mouse-up.

We used the WiViK keyboard with the default settings, which included no 'dead space' between the virtual keys, no word prediction, and click-triggering of keys rather than hover/dwell-triggering. The keyboard consumed the entire width and about a third of the height of a 1024×768 screen. We chose the WiViK keyboard because of its familiarity to subjects as a mouse-driven on-screen keyboard.

14.6.2 Subjects

We improved the three techniques that we evaluated – joystick and touchpad EdgeWrite, and joystick WiViK – with the help of seven power wheelchair users. (We initially had eight subjects, but one was too impaired to perform any of the techniques.) Six of the seven were from the United Cerebral Palsy Center of Pittsburgh and had CP. One subject had MS. The average age of the subjects was 25.9 years, with a low of 21 and a high of 67. Subjects had been in wheelchairs for an average of 14 years, with a low of 3 and a high of 30. Two of the seven subjects were male. Four were right-handed. None of the subjects had ever used EdgeWrite, but six of seven had used WiViK. Thus, subjects were very familiar with the technique to which we would compare EdgeWrite.

14.6.3 Procedure

In order to involve subjects in the design of the techniques, we had them practice each technique before entering a single test phrase ($\sim$30 letters). Practice consisted of entering each letter four times in a row with a given technique (e.g. 'aaaa bbbb . . . yyyy zzzz'). This took about 30 minutes with the EdgeWrite techniques, and about 15 minutes with WiViK, since there was no gestural alphabet to learn. The whole test duration did not exceed 2 hours. All seven subjects used joystick WiViK and joystick EdgeWrite, but only four subjects used touchpad EdgeWrite due to time constraints. This first study did not involve using WiViK with the touchpad.

An EdgeWrite character chart was visible during the test. With the slow pace of practice and the limited endurance of subjects, we did not want to unduly burden subjects with memorizing the EdgeWrite letters. Instead, we taught them how to read the chart and observed their need to do so. Reading the chart greatly slowed them compared with their use of WiViK, which required no chart. The inter-character time – the time from the end of one character to the start of the next – gives us some idea of the delay caused by reading the EdgeWrite character chart. The average inter-character time was 6.23 seconds for the EdgeWrite methods. With more practice, this value drops dramatically, since subjects become familiar with the letters. Our second study (described below) confirms that after 10 sessions, the inter-character time drops to 3.74 seconds.

All text input was logged on the PC by a text entry test program that we wrote (Wobbrock and Myers, 2006). It was later analyzed with recently developed measures (Soukoreff and MacKenzie, 2003), which allow subjects to enter text in an unconstrained, real-world fashion, where they can choose to fix errors or not. According to this testing paradigm, subjects are merely instructed to 'proceed quickly and accurately' (Soukoreff and MacKenzie, 2003).

We solicited responses from subjects in between text entry phrases and more formally using questionnaires. In addition, many subjects offered ideas while practicing with the techniques.

14.6.4 **Results**

In this first study, slow performance and rapid fatigue during the practice phase meant that only one test sentence could be entered by each subject for each method. Thus, we do not have sufficient data for statistical significance. Speeds are reported in wpm and error rates in per cent. Standard deviations are reported in parentheses.

For text entry speed, touchpad EdgeWrite proved fastest at 1.00 wpm (0.72), joystick WiViK second at 0.84 wpm (0.36), and joystick EdgeWrite a close third at 0.77 wpm (0.57). See Figure 14.9.

Uncorrected errors are those left remaining in the transcribed string (Soukoreff and MacKenzie, 2003).[4] It is common for gestural methods to make more errors than selection-based methods like on-screen keyboards, particularly for novices

---

[4]In contrast to uncorrected errors, *corrected errors* are any letters backspaced during entry. Although corrected errors should be minimized, it is uncorrected errors that warrant real concern, since these are at odds with speed – that is, the more errors one leaves in the transcribed text, the faster one can proceed. Corrected errors, on the other hand, are subsumed in speed, since it takes time to make corrections. Thus we focus on uncorrected errors in these analyses.

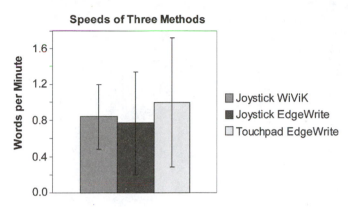

Figure 14.9 *Mean speeds of three methods after minimal practice. Error bars represent ±1 st. dev.*

(e.g. Költringer and Grechenig, 2004). This was indeed the case with EdgeWrite and WiViK. For uncorrected errors, joystick WiViK had the lowest rate at 0.46% ($\sigma = 1.21$), followed by joystick EdgeWrite at 6.05% (7.28), and touchpad EdgeWrite at 6.70% (8.24). These results are shown in Figure 14.10.

Clearly, subjects left more errors with joystick and touchpad EdgeWrite than with joystick WiViK. This is to be expected, since subjects often perform gestures incorrectly when learning them. On the other hand, to make an error with WiViK, a subject had to place the mouse cursor over the wrong key and still choose to press the switch, a lengthy perceptual-motor task that is easily avoided.

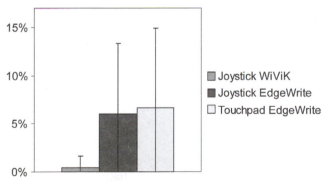

Figure 14.10 *Mean uncorrected error rates of three methods after minimal practice. Error bars represent ±1 st. dev.*

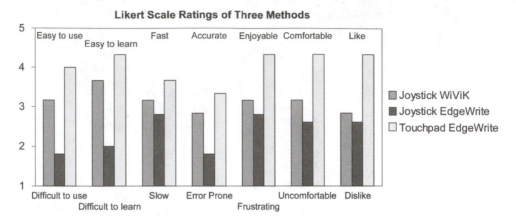

Figure 14.11 *Mean Likert scale ratings for subjective measures (1–5, worst–best).*

The questionnaire results showed that, of the three methods, subjects felt that touchpad EdgeWrite was the easiest to use, easiest to learn, fastest, most accurate, most enjoyable, most comfortable, and most liked. They rated joystick WiViK second in these categories, and joystick EdgeWrite third (Figure 14.11).

14.6.5   **Lessons Learned from Subjects**

Subject #1 was a 67-year-old retired school teacher with MS. He was notable for two reasons: he was the only person without CP, and he was only one of two subjects who was faster with joystick EdgeWrite than with joystick WiViK (1.91 vs. 1.22 wpm). The other was subject #8, who was a 22-year-old female with good fine motor control. She was only slightly better with joystick EdgeWrite than WiViK (0.52 vs. 0.50 wpm). Subject #1 showed us that the plastic template should be thicker to prevent the exposed spring on the joystick post from catching the template's edge. After using WiViK for a few minutes he said, 'It takes the patience of Job to do this.' Upon switching from WiViK to EdgeWrite he said, 'I'm much faster with this; don't you think I'm much faster?' indicating his first impression of joystick EdgeWrite.

Subject #2 was a 21-year-old student. She initially had trouble with the diagonal strokes required by joystick EdgeWrite because she would move too slowly through the center, and EdgeWrite would try to recognize her stroke to that point. She motivated us to change the center dwell time required for segmentation. If a polled joystick point falls outside the center area before the dwell time has elapsed, the dwell time counter resets. The time that worked well for subject #2 was 500 ms. However, a long dwell time was not sufficient for subject #4, a 40-year-old volunteer. She moved inconsistently with joystick EdgeWrite, sometimes making letters very quickly, other times pausing for many seconds to think. For her we added the ability to trigger segmentation explicitly with the switch, removing the need for implicit snap-to-center segmentation. She enjoyed touchpad EdgeWrite because she said it was the easiest method with which to fix mistakes. She said, 'Once you understand what you are doing, it goes completely well.' Subject #7 echoed this when she said, 'If you got used to it, you'd be really fast I suppose.'

While the females tended to interact too gingerly with the joystick, the males, subjects #1 and #3, were too forceful at first. For them, discovering the right speed and pressure to exert against the joystick template was a large part of learning joystick EdgeWrite.

A common problem was that subjects did not always start in the corner of the plastic template before making their gestures with the joystick. This was less of a problem with the touchpad. The reason may be that the joystick must be pushed from the center to reach the starting corner, whereas a finger can begin in the corner of the touchpad.

Subject #4 gave us an important insight into the design of the touchpad's plastic template. We originally beveled the edge of the touchpad template so that it was slightly rounded. But this caused subject #4's finger to slip up onto the template's surface, actuating a 'finger lift' and prematurely triggering letter segmentation. This insight led to the fabrication of a thicker touchpad template, the edges of which we left vertical and unbeveled. We also added a settable lift-tolerance for the second study (described below).

Subject #6 highlighted the importance of end-user customizability. While using touchpad EdgeWrite, this subject's finger did not always press against an edge of the physical square. Having defined the software square for ourselves by tracing along the plastic edges, we later saw that her fingers moved inside this square, and that the actual square in which she moved was smaller than the one we had defined. When we had *her* redefine the software square by tracing around the physical square herself, her accuracy improved remarkably.

Finally, the diagonal strokes were difficult for many users of joystick EdgeWrite. This is not surprising, because it is along the diagonals that the user does not have an edge to press against. The letter 'k' was particularly problematic because of its two diagonals in a row. For our second study, we designed a new form of 'k' that is still reminiscent of a Roman 'k' but without the diagonal. This new 'k' proved much easier to perform and has become a permanent part of the alphabet in all versions of EdgeWrite. In fact, all letters except 's,' 'v,' 'x,' and 'z' now have alternate forms that contain no diagonals.

14.7 Study 2: Extended Use of Joystick and Touchpad EdgeWrite

The first study largely represents 'immediate usability' (MacKenzie and Zhang, 1997; Wobbrock *et al.*, 2005a). Its findings showed that subjects needed more practice, warranting a second investigation over multiple sessions. Such a study can identify a 'crossover point' where EdgeWrite overtakes WiViK in speed or accuracy. Subjects #2 and #4 from the first investigation agreed to partake in a 10-session study over consecutive days (except weekends). About 3 months passed between the end of the first study and the beginning of the second.

14.7.1 Subjects

Subject #2 is female and 22 years old. She uses a computer more than a few hours a day, largely for email, surfing the web, and word processing. She reports being able to slowly use a standard physical QWERTY keyboard for up to 1 hour, after which she switches to an alternative method, usually a WiViK on-screen keyboard accessed with a standard mouse. She is able to write her name with a pen, though it takes her many seconds, and it is legible to others only about 80% of the time. The joystick on her power wheelchair has a short stick with a plastic ball at the top. She is right-handed.

Subject #4 is female and 41 years old. She uses a computer only about once a week for email, surfing the web, or word processing. She, too, reports being able to use a standard physical QWERTY keyboard for up to 1 hour, after which she either stops using the computer or uses the WiViK on-screen keyboard with a standard mouse. She can write her name legibly with a pen but it takes her many seconds (if not minutes), and it is legible to others about 80% of the time. The joystick on her power wheelchair is about twice as long as the one we used in the study. It also has a softer spring. Subject #4 was much weaker than #2, which affected her ability to move the joystick snugly into the corners while using joystick EdgeWrite. Presumably this would be remedied by using a joystick more like her own. This subject was also right-handed.

14.7.2 Design Improvements

Before conducting the second investigation, we made some changes to the joystick and touchpad techniques based on observations from our first study. For example, we added more 'accidental lift tolerance' to touchpad EdgeWrite. Previously, when a finger was lifted the stroke was immediately segmented. The new tolerance, which took the form of a customizable lift-delay, allowed subjects to briefly lift from the surface while stroking, thereby avoiding premature stroke segmentation. Both subjects preferred a tolerance of 275 ms.

The triangular corner regions in touchpad EdgeWrite were also reduced slightly from 47.5% of the square's width and height to 42.5%. This was because subjects would sometimes hit unwanted corners when making diagonals, particularly when moving from the bottom-left to the upper-right corners.

The area considered the 'center' for joystick EdgeWrite letter segmentation was reduced by about 11% to make accidental segmentations less common, since subjects would often move too slowly through the center region while making a diagonal. In the first study, this caused the software to think the joystick had snapped to center for segmentation between letters. We also found that subject #2 required a 500-ms center dwell segmentation time, while subject #4 required 1000 ms.

The joystick used with WiViK was rate-controlled, so the farther it was moved from its center, the faster the mouse cursor moved. The acceleration transfer function was linear from the center of the joystick to its extremes. For joystick WiViK, we reduced this acceleration from a maximum of 1.2 pixels/ms to 0.8 pixels/ms. We made this change because of some occasional target overshooting while subjects tried to acquire keys on the WiViK keyboard during the first study. With the reduced acceleration, target overshoots in the second study were rare.

Finally, for this second study we included a condition for touchpad WiViK. Thus, the study contained four input techniques, two devices crossed with two text entry methods.

14.7.3 **Procedure**

The experiment was a $2 \times 2 \times 10$ within-subjects factorial design with factors for method (EdgeWrite or WiViK), device (joystick or touchpad), and session (10 sessions). With only two subjects, the experiment was aimed less at achieving statistical significance and more at observing how long it takes subjects to become proficient at EdgeWrite.

Each subject performed all four techniques (method $\times$ device) during each session. Technique order was assigned randomly by the software for each session. Subjects warmed up with each technique before testing by entering about 10 letters. During the test, subjects transcribed two phrases of about 30 letters each for a total of about 60 letters. Subjects were quite slow, so this process took about 20 minutes per technique. Test phrases were drawn randomly from the published test corpus of 500 phrases by MacKenzie and Soukoreff (2003).

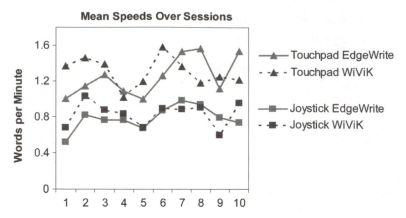

Figure 14.12 *Mean speeds over 10 sessions for two subjects.*

Unfortunately, subject #2 was unable to finish all 10 sessions due to intervening commitments. She finished six sessions with joystick WiViK due to technical problems during the seventh and eighth sessions. She finished eight sessions with the other three techniques. These limitations are taken into account in our analyses.

14.7.4 **Results**

There was a significant speedup for the two EdgeWrite methods over sessions, but no significant speedup for WiViK. This was expected, since there is more to learn with a gestural method than an on-screen keyboard already familiar to the subjects. Figure 14.12 depicts the mean session speeds for each of the four method × device combinations.

The touchpad was generally faster than the joystick for both methods at 1.27 vs. 0.81 wpm, respectively. There was no significant difference between EdgeWrite and WiViK overall (1.02 vs. 1.06 wpm), since EdgeWrite was slower in the early sessions but faster toward the end for both devices.

Overall uncorrected errors were less than 1% for all methods excluding joystick EdgeWrite in session 1 (14.6%) due to subjects refamiliarizing themselves with the technique. Average uncorrected errors for sessions 2 through 10 were 0.68% (1.41) for joystick WiViK, 0.31% (0.37) for joystick EdgeWrite, 0.28% (0.41) for touchpad WiViK, and 0.26% (0.39) for touchpad EdgeWrite. Clearly, subjects were very conscientious in correcting any errors made during entry, so speeds can be compared fairly.

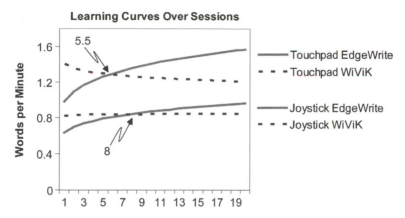

Figure 14.13 *Learning curves extended to 20 sessions for our two subjects.*

14.7.5 **Learning Rates**

It is customary in input studies to fit regression curves to speed data based on the power law of learning (Card *et al.*, 1978; MacKenzie and Zhang, 1999). Such curves are of the form $y = bx^c$, where y is speed and x is session, and b and c are regression coefficients. These performance models allow us to predict how a subject might perform in future sessions. Fitting these curves is speculative for the current data, however, since we only have two subjects. Nonetheless, the curves give a sense of how their performance may proceed beyond session 10.

The regression curves for the four method × device combinations are shown in Figure 14.13. The data is highly varied, so obtaining high correlations is not possible. But the learning curves show clear upward trends for the two EdgeWrite methods. The flat or downward slopes for WiViK are due to subjects' prior familiarity with WiViK from extended use. In addition, on-screen keyboards require little learning and offer little room for improvement. Thus, the WiViK curves are governed more by fatigue than by learning.

The power law equations and R^2 values are as follows:

$y = 0.978x^{0.1574}$	$R^2 = 0.3755$	Touchpad EdgeWrite
$y = 1.397x^{-0.0492}$	$R^2 = 0.0873$	Touchpad WiViK
$y = 0.632x^{0.1406}$	$R^2 = 0.3609$	Joystick EdgeWrite
$y = 0.819x^{0.0110}$	$R^2 = 0.0025$	Joystick WiViK

Crossover points for the touchpad and joystick techniques occur at about sessions 5.5 and 8.0, respectively, with EdgeWrite overtaking WiViK in both cases. While these curves are speculative, they do give a sense of the overall trends. The higher R^2 values for EdgeWrite suggest that more learning took place for these methods than for the WiViK methods, and would likely continue to do so with further practice.

Overall, the results for speed and accuracy confirm both the challenge of learning a gestural text input method and the potential benefits. The initially poor accuracy of EdgeWrite, particularly the joystick version, is not surprising, and could be mitigated with further design. For example, both subjects' personal power wheelchair joysticks were longer and had much weaker springs than the one used in the study. Optimizing design parameters such as these might be one way to improve users' experiences. The general advantage of the touchpad over the joystick points to this device for future inclusion in computer access solutions.

A post-test questionnaire showed similar results for the two subjects as from the first study (see Figure 14.11). Both subjects preferred touchpad EdgeWrite overall, followed by touchpad WiViK, joystick EdgeWrite, and joystick WiViK. For both devices, the WiViK methods were considered easier to learn but the EdgeWrite methods were preferred for their perceived speeds.

14.8 Study 3: Participatory Design of Trackball EdgeWrite

Our third study compared trackball EdgeWrite and on-screen keyboards. Since the requirements for the design of a trackball version were not well understood, we iterated over nine participatory design sessions with a single trackball user, obtaining feedback and incorporating it into the next version of the software. At this early stage of design, it would have been premature to run multiple subjects in a single session; so instead, we opted to run one subject over multiple sessions.

14.8.1 'Jim'

Our participatory design subject, who we will call 'Jim,' has a spinal cord injury and is in a power wheelchair. He lacks fine motor control in his hands and arms. He is 46 years old, has used trackballs for over 15 years, and prefers the Stingray trackball from CoStar Corporation (Figure 14.14).

Jim has two methods for entering text. For long sections of prose, like lengthy emails, class papers, and formal documents, Jim uses Dragon Naturally Speaking, a voice recognition program. However, he says it often 'acts up,' failing to recognize his speech and becoming frustrating to him. Sometimes fatigue or medications alter his voice and make speech recognition problematic. He also says that it is tiresome to put

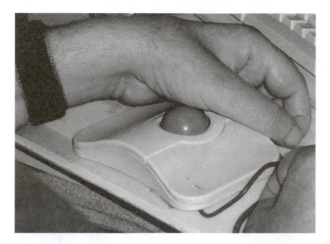

Figure 14.14 *Jim's hand upon his Stingray trackball.*

on and take off his microphone headset whenever he wants to use speech recognition, especially for writing quick replies to emails. Furthermore, Jim works in a lab where others sit nearby, and speaking aloud can disturb them. Finally, Jim says that certain computer-related tasks don't work well with voice recognition, like filling out web forms, writing search queries, naming or renaming files, entering email addresses, editing spreadsheet formulae, working with command-line interfaces, and retrieving contacts in an address book. Thus, Jim has always relied on a secondary method of text entry: point-and-dwell with a mouse cursor on an on-screen keyboard. He has tried numerous on-screen keyboards but has found the Microsoft Accessibility Keyboard to be his favorite. He uses it with the minimum hover-time setting of 0.5 seconds. This means that after his mouse cursor remains over a virtual key for half a second, the key is 'pressed' and the letter is sent to the active application.

Jim has three main complaints about on-screen keyboards. The first is that they are extremely visually intense and therefore fatiguing. He finds himself constantly looking back and forth between the on-screen keyboard and his document. He also must locate each letter on the on-screen keyboard in a visually taxing 'hunt and peck' manner. Jim's second complaint is that the on-screen keyboard is slow. He must have the dwell time set long enough that he does not trigger unwanted keys as he moves over them, but short enough that once he arrives at his target key, it does not take forever to actuate. This inherent trade-off makes typing with point-and-dwell laborious, but point-and-click is not viable for Jim. Jim's third complaint is that performing repeated letter-by-letter selections is, in his words, 'mind numbing.'

Jim says that word prediction can reduce the letter-by-letter doldrums, but that he feels it often slows him down by adding more visual elements to inspect. This sentiment is consistent with the findings of some word prediction studies (e.g. Koester and Levine, 1996).

14.8.2 **Procedure**

We met with Jim nine times from May to November 2005. Meetings consisted of two objectives. The first was to receive Jim's feedback from using the latest version of trackball EdgeWrite. This feedback consisted of improvements to the writing mechanics and the overall application design. The second objective was to measure Jim's speed and accuracy in short 'checkpoint studies' that compared his performance with his on-screen keyboard to that of EdgeWrite in a series of five test phrases with each. This was to ensure that the design changes we were making were beneficial, and also to collect detailed data about Jim's performance.

Jim permitted us to log his use of EdgeWrite at all times, providing us with valuable information on which to base our changes. Over the course of the study, Jim used EdgeWrite sporadically, mainly for short text entry tasks. His weekly usage varied from a few minutes to a few hours. Over time, he became proficient with EdgeWrite and began to use it more. By the end of the study, Jim no longer used his on-screen keyboard, but preferred to use EdgeWrite instead. After 15 years, he said he once again could feel himself 'writing.'

14.8.3 **Results**

Jim's mean speeds over the weekly checkpoints are shown in Figure 14.15. After the first week, Jim's EdgeWrite speed (mean = 5.61, σ = 1.40, max = 8.25) remains consistently higher than his on-screen keyboard speed (mean = 4.86, σ = 1.17, max = 6.90). A Wilcoxon sign test shows that his EdgeWrite speeds were significantly faster than his on-screen keyboard speeds ($z = -19.5$, $p < 0.02$).

Jim's uncorrected errors varied but were generally low for both methods. Uncorrected errors for EdgeWrite were 1.12% (1.39) and for the on-screen keyboard were 2.03% (2.45). These are shown over sessions in Figure 14.16. Although EdgeWrite was lower on average, a Wilcoxon sign test is not quite significant ($z = 8.0$, $p = 0.22$).

Jim's learning curves are shown extended to week 50 in Figure 14.17. Although such an extension is speculative, it gives us an idea of the possible trends for Jim's data. As in the second study, we see that the use of on-screen keyboards, particularly by those familiar with them, is not as well-modeled by the power law of learning as EdgeWrite is.

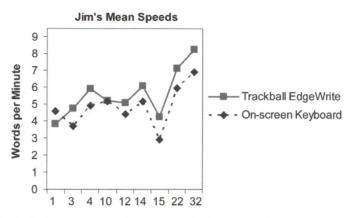

Figure 14.15 *Jim's average speeds over nine checkpoint studies spread over 32 weeks.*

The power law equations and R^2 values for Jim's curves are:

$y = 3.713x^{0.1850}$	$R^2 = 0.5274$	Trackball EdgeWrite
$y = 3.796x^{0.1127}$	$R^2 = 0.2144$	On-screen Keyboard

Jim no longer uses an on-screen keyboard with his trackball, but keeps trackball EdgeWrite running at all times, able to be called up at a moment's notice. To begin writing, Jim simply places the mouse cursor in the top-left corner of his screen, waits a

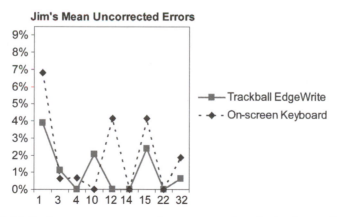

Figure 14.16 *Jim's average uncorrected errors over nine checkpoint studies spread over 32 weeks.*

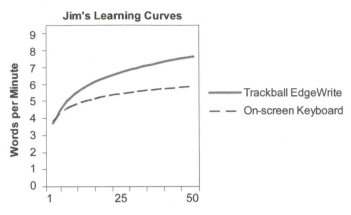

Figure 14.17 *Jim's learning curves as wpm extended to week 50.*

moment, and then watches as the cursor is 'captured' automatically within the EdgeWrite square for writing. When he is done writing, he makes a dedicated stroke to 'release' his mouse cursor and dismiss the EdgeWrite window. Thus, he can operate trackball EdgeWrite without ever clicking a mouse button. The idea for this button-less design was a contribution Jim himself made during our participatory design sessions. He also helped us improve the 'look and feel' of the software with suggestions for altering the on-screen depiction and stroke feedback while writing.

Jim's main reasons for preferring trackball EdgeWrite over an on-screen keyboard are, in his words:

• 'The on-screen keyboard is so terribly boring. EdgeWrite is fun, like a video game. The on-screen keyboard is not fun. I don't care which is faster.'
• 'With EdgeWrite, you can keep your eyes on your document and just write as you would holding a pencil. I don't feel disabled when I'm using EdgeWrite.'
• 'The on-screen keyboard requires too much visual scanning and concentration. In EdgeWrite, if you know the letter, you can just bang it out by feel.'
• 'I feel like I can write again.'

When Jim began working with trackball EdgeWrite, he had trouble using a PDA because he could not enter text. A neat benefit for Jim was that his trackball EdgeWrite knowledge transferred directly to the PDA for use with stylus EdgeWrite (Wobbrock *et al.*, 2003b). We compared his stylus EdgeWrite accuracy to his accuracy with Graffiti 2, the built-in Palm OS alphabet, and found that Jim was 99.0% accurate with

EdgeWrite compared to just 54.8% accurate with Graffiti 2. This comparison did not require Jim to recall strokes from memory, but was simply a comparison of motor performance while Jim looked at a character chart.

14.9 Implications for Stakeholders

The current work has implications for a variety of stakeholders. This section describes some of those implications, highlighting areas of importance for future work.

14.9.1 Users

People with motor impairments who wish to access computers are faced with a variety of challenges in acquiring, configuring, and maintaining access technologies (Dawe, 2006). Accordingly, less than 60% of people who indicate they need adaptations to use computers actually use them (Fichten *et al.*, 2000). The current work attempts to lower the barriers to access for users by providing text entry solutions for use with devices that are readily available, inexpensive, robust, and easy to configure and maintain. So-called 'commodity' devices can be purchased at everyday electronics and computer stores, and do not require a therapist or specialist to configure. This is particularly true of our touchpad and trackball EdgeWrite solutions. Our joystick solution, on the other hand, was prototyped specifically for use with the Everest & Jennings 1706–5020 power wheelchair joystick. In order for joystick EdgeWrite to become widely available, wheelchair manufacturers would have to make wheelchair joystick inputs available to third-party software. One can imagine future wheelchairs equipped with USB or serial ports, making it possible for users to benefit from add-on software solutions like joystick EdgeWrite.

All of the software discussed in this chapter is available for free download at http://www.edgewrite.com.

14.9.2 Developers

This work brought to light issues relevant to developers of both software and hardware. One issue is that access technologies must achieve a high level of robustness in order to be genuinely useful. Our trackball version, for example, was not 'academicware,' but commercial-grade software capable of running stably in a user's System Tray for weeks or even months. This level of robustness and reliability was necessary for the software to become adopted into actual daily use. Furthermore, if prototypes are successful, disabled users may come to rely heavily on them. The developer therefore has an additional responsibility to his subjects to provide them with stable software that will support their real-world needs.

Another consideration for developers is to prioritize their application's interoperability with other software. Too often, research software is engineered to run in a stand-alone test bed where its integration with other software, if appropriate, is left for later (or never). High fidelity prototypes, in particular, should strive to integrate well into users' actual computing environments. For example, joystick, touchpad, and trackball EdgeWrite could have been built as stand-alone applications where the text destination was contained within the prototype software itself. Instead, extra care was taken to make these versions able to send text to any other Windows application, allowing them to support real-world text entry.

Developers can download an EdgeWrite library (a Windows DLL) and create their own versions in any .NET language (C#, J#, VB .NET) in under 10 lines of code. The library is fully documented with examples and code snippets. Visit http://www.edgewrite.com to obtain the developer's library.

14.9.3 **Researchers**

As assistive technology researchers, we learned three important lessons from conducting this work:

- *Small changes can make big differences*. The success of input systems depends on a tight perceptual-motor loop that is quite fickle. Small adjustments, from beveling edges to adjusting timeouts by milliseconds, can have a large effect on the resulting user experience of such systems. Similar sentiments were expressed by Ted Selker in his development of the Trackpoint isometric joystick found on many IBM laptops (Ehrlich, 1997).
- *Logging is essential*. When designing input systems, 'intuition' is generally not reliable for making quantitative adjustments like segmentation timeouts or the size of input regions. Input systems must be outfitted with log-writing capabilities so that adjustments can be made based on quantitative data of actual user performance. Similarly, log data can capture extended field use over days, weeks, or months, and yield insights not available in laboratory settings.
- *Real users are invaluable*. All of this work relied heavily upon multiple sessions with real power wheelchair and trackball users. Our best attempts at designing apart from them produced solutions that were lacking in many ways. Early deployment, continual testing, and rapid iteration are keys to successful input technique development. Designers and engineers should sit with users during

these sessions and not completely offload this work onto usability specialists. Only then will they see how their innovations fare. In assistive technology and human–computer interaction, if a design does not succeed with real users, it does not succeed.

14.9.4 Policymakers

Those who make policy concerning assistive technologies may be able to contribute in meaningful ways to the spirit motivating this work. Policies that help reduce the cost of specialized assistive technologies and make it easier for special populations to acquire computer access devices will help lower barriers to access. Standards committees also can influence the interoperability of hardware and software devices. Certainly our work on joystick EdgeWrite would have been made much easier, and potentially much more successful, if wheelchair joysticks had standardized ports from which computers could receive data. Then subjects would have been able to use their own wheelchair joysticks instead of the one in our prototype.

In addition, American and European populations are aging rapidly. By 2030, over 20% of the population in the United States will be 65 or over; in Europe this number will exceed 23.5% (Kinsella and Phillips, 2005). Many more people will have motor impairments of some kind, particularly those associated with aging (e.g. arthritis). These users must have adequate computer access technologies if they are to continue to participate in an information society. Policies must be upheld or enacted that put real emphasis on the need for handheld and desktop computing technologies to become more accessible, lest we risk creating another digital divide.

14.10 Conclusion

In this chapter, we described three means of integrating text entry into pre-existing input devices for power wheelchair and trackball users. All three devices – joysticks, touchpads, and trackballs – are small, light, inexpensive, and require minimal configuration, giving them significant practical advantages as integrated control systems over dedicated computer access technologies. We described our design and implementation of EdgeWrite and the participatory role real power wheelchair and trackball users played in our development process. We presented results from three separate studies of real-world users in which EdgeWrite was compared to various on-screen keyboards. Although these techniques still have much room for improvement, this work has opened the way for their future refinement, and ultimately, better computer access.

Acknowledgments

The authors thank the following people for their input and contributions: Edmund F. LoPresti, Htet Htet Aung, Janis Thoma-Negley, Steve Hayashi, John A. Kembel, Ryan S. Baker, Richard Simpson, Elaine Wherry, and John SanGiovanni.

This work was supported in part by grants from the NEC Foundation of America, NISH, General Motors, Microsoft Corporation, and the National Science Foundation under Grant No. UA-0308065. Any opinions, findings and conclusions, or recommendations expressed in this material are those of the authors and do not necessarily reflect those of any supporting person or institution.

References

Accot, J. and Zhai, S. (1999) Performance evaluation of input devices in trajectory-based tasks: an application of the Steering Law. *Proceedings of the ACM Conference on Human Factors in Computing Systems (CHI '99),* ACM Press, New York, pp. 466–472.

Accot, J. and Zhai, S. (2002) More than dotting the I's: foundations for crossing-based interfaces. *Proceedings of the ACM Conference on Human Factors in Computing Systems (CHI '02),* ACM Press, New York, pp. 73–80.

Anson, D.K. (1997) *Alternative Computer Access.* F.A. Davis, Philadelphia.

Buxton, W., Hill, R. and Rowley, P. (1985) Issues and techniques in touch-sensitive tablet input. *Proceedings of the ACM Conference on Computer Graphics and Interactive Techniques (SIGGRAPH '85),* ACM Press, New York, pp. 215–224.

Card, S.K., English, W.K. and Burr, B.J. (1978) Evaluation of mouse, rate-controlled isometric joystick, step keys, and text keys for text selection on a CRT. *Ergonomics,* **21,** 601–613.

Card, S.K., Mackinlay, J.D. and Robertson, G. (1990) The design space of input devices. *Proceedings of the ACM Conference on Human Factors in Computing Systems (CHI '90),* ACM Press, New York, pp. 117–124.

Coleman, M. (2001) *Weegie.* `http://weegie.sourceforge.net/`.

Cook, A.M. and Hussey, S.M. (1995) *Assistive Technologies: Principles and Practice.* Mosby Press, St. Louis, MO.

Co-operwrite Ltd. (1997) *myText.* `http://www.my-text.com/`.

Dawe, M. (2006) Desperately seeking simplicity: how young adults with cognitive disabilities and their families adopt assistive technologies. *Proceedings of the ACM Conference on Human Factors in Computing Systems (CHI '06)*, ACM Press, New York, pp. 1143–1152.

Ehrlich, K. (1997) A conversation with Ted Selker. *Interactions*, **4**(5), 34–47.

Enns, N.R.N. and MacKenzie, I.S. (1998) Touchpad-based remote control devices. CHI 1998 Conference Summary, ACM Press, New York, pp. 229–230.

Farris, J.S., Jones, K.S. and Anders, B.A. (2001) Acquisition speed with targets on the edge of the screen: an application of Fitts' Law to commonly used web browser controls. *Proceedings of the Human Factors and Ergonomics Society 45th Annual Meeting*, Santa Monica, CA, Human Factors and Ergonomics Society, pp. 1205–1209.

Fichten, C.S., Barile, M., Asuncion, J.V. and Fossey, M.E. (2000) What government, agencies, and organizations can do to improve access to computers for postsecondary students with disabilities: recommendations based on Canadian empirical data. *International Journal of Rehabilitation Research*, **23**(3), 191–199.

Fuhrer, C.S. and Fridie, S.E. There's a mouse out there for everyone. *Proceedings of CSUN's 16th Annual Conference on Technology and Persons with Disabilities*, California State University Northridge, available at `http://www.csun.edu/cod/conf/2001/proceedings/0014fuhrer.htm`

Goldberg, D. and Richardson, C. (1993) Touch-typing with a stylus. *Proceedings of the ACM Conference on Human Factors in Computing Systems (CHI '93)*, ACM Press, New York, pp. 80–87.

Guerette, P. and Sumi, E. (1994) Integrating control of multiple assistive devices: a retrospective review. *Assistive Technology*, **6**(1), 67–76.

Guiard, Y., Blanch, R. and Beaudouin-Lafon, M. (2004) Object pointing: a complement to bitmap pointing in GUIs. *Proceedings of Graphics Interface 2004*, Waterloo, Ontario, Canadian Human-Computer Communications Society, pp. 9–16.

Hinckley, K., Czerwinski, M. and Sinclair, M. (1998) Interaction and modeling techniques for desktop two-handed input. *Proceedings of the ACM Symposium on User Interface Software and Technology (UIST '98)*, ACM Press, New York, pp. 49–58.

Isokoski, P. and Kaki, M. (2002) Comparison of two touchpad-based methods for numeric entry. *Proceedings of the ACM Conference on Human Factors in Computing Systems (CHI '02)*, ACM Press, New York, pp. 25–32.

Kinsella, K. and Phillips, D.R. (2005) Global aging: the challenge of success. Population Bulletin, Washington, DC, Population Reference Bureau, **60**(1).

Koester, H.H. and Levine, S.P. (1996) Effect of a word prediction feature on user performance. *Augmentive and Alternative Communications,* **12**(3), 155–168.

Költringer, T. and Grechenig, T. (2004) Comparing the immediate usability of Graffiti 2 and virtual keyboard. Extended Abstracts of the ACM Conference on Human Factors in Computing Systems (CHI '04), ACM Press, New York, 1175–1178.

Kraus, L.E., Stoddard, S. and Gilmartin, D. (1996) *Chartbook on Disability in the United States,* Washington, DC, National Institute on Disability and Rehabilitation Research.

LoPresti, E.F., Romich, B.A., Hill, K.J. and Spaeth, D.M. (2004) Evaluation of mouse emulation using the wheelchair joystick. *Proceedings of the 27th Annual Conference of the Rehabilitation Engineering and Assistive Technology Society of North America (RESNA '04),* RESNA Press, Washington, DC.

Ludolph, F. and Perkins, R. (1998) The Lisa user interface. CHI 1998 Conference Summary, ACM Press, New York, 18–19.

MacKenzie, I.S. and Oniszczak, A. (1998) A comparison of three selection techniques for touchpads. *Proceedings of the ACM Conference on Human Factors in Computing Systems (CHI '98),* ACM Press, New York, pp. 336–343.

MacKenzie, I.S. and Soukoreff, R.W. (2002) Text entry for mobile computing: models and methods, theory and practice. *Human Computer Interaction,* **17**(2), 147–198.

MacKenzie, I.S. and Soukoreff, R.W. (2003) Phrase sets for evaluating text entry techniques. Extended Abstracts of the ACM Conference on Human Factors in Computing Systems (CHI '03), ACM Press, New York, 754–755.

MacKenzie, I.S. and Zhang, S.X. (1997) The immediate usability of Graffiti. *Proceedings of Graphics Interface 1997,* Toronto, Canadian Information Processing Society, pp. 129–137

MacKenzie, I.S. and Zhang, S.X. (1999) The design and evaluation of a high-performance soft keyboard. *Proceedings of the ACM Conference on Human Factors in Computing Systems (CHI '99),* ACM Press, New York, pp. 25–31.

MacKenzie, I.S., Sellen, A. and Buxton, W. (1991) A comparison of input devices in elemental pointing and dragging tasks. *Proceedings of the ACM Conference on Human Factors in Computing Systems (CHI '91),* ACM Press, New York, pp. 161–166.

MacKenzie, I.S., Kauppinen, T., and Silfverberg, M. (2001) Accuracy measures for evaluating computer pointing devices. *Proceedings of the ACM Conference on Human Factors in Computing Systems (CHI '01),* ACM Press, New York, pp. 9–16.

Myers, B.A. (2001) Using hand-held devices and PCs together. Communications of the ACM, **44**(11), 34–41.

Myers, B.A., Wobbrock, J.O., Yang, S. et al. (2002) Using handhelds to help people with motor impairments. *Proceedings of the ACM SIGCAPH Conference on Assistive Technologies (ASSETS '02),* ACM Press, New York, pp. 89–96.

Palm Inc. (1996) Graffiti text input system. `http://www.palm.com/us/prod-ucts/input/ Palm_Graffiti.pdf`.

Rekimoto, J. (2003) ThumbSense: automatic input mode sensing for touchpad-based interactions. Extended Abstracts of the ACM Conference on Human Factors in Computing Systems (CHI '03), ACM Press, New York, 852–853.

Romich, B.A., LoPresti, E.F. and Hill, K.J. (2002) Mouse emulation using the wheel-chair joystick: preliminary performance comparison using four modes of control. *Proceedings of the 25th Annual Conference of the Rehabilitation Engineering and Assistive Technology Society of North America (RESNA '02),* RESNA Press, Washington, DC, pp. 106–108.

Sears, A. and Young, M. (2003) *Physical disabilities and computing technologies: an analysis of impairments.* In Jacko, J. & Sears, A. (**Eds.**). *The Human-Computer Interaction Handbook,* Lawrence Erlbaum Associates, Mahwah, NJ, 482–503.

Shein, F., Hamann, G. and Brownlow, N. (1991) WiViK: a visual keyboard for Windows 3.0. *Proceedings of the 14th Annual Conference of the Rehabilitation Engineering and Assistive Technology Society of North America (RESNA '91),* RESNA Press, Washington, DC, pp. 160–162.

Soukoreff, R.W. and MacKenzie, I.S. (2003) Metrics for text entry research: an eval-uation of MSD and KSPC, and a new unified error metric. *Proceedings of the ACM Conference on Human Factors in Computing Systems (CHI '03),* ACM Press, New York, pp. 113–120.

Spaeth, D.M., Jones, D.K., and Cooper, R.A. (1998) Universal control interface for people with disabilities. *Saudi Journal of Disability Rehabilitation,* **4**(3), 207–214.

Sperling, B.B. and Tullis, T.S. (1988) Are you a better 'mouser' or 'trackballer'? A comparison of cursor-positioning performance. *SIGCHI Bulletin,* **19**(3), 77–81.

Switch-It Inc. (2005a) Mouse driver. `http://www.switchit-inc.com/mouse_driver.htm`.

Switch-It Inc. (2005b) Touch drive. `http://www.switchit-inc.com/touch_drive.htm`.

Wobbrock, J.O. (2003) The benefits of physical edges in gesture-making: empirical support for an edge-based unistroke alphabet. Extended Abstracts of the ACM Conference on Human Factors in Computing Systems (CHI '03), ACM Press, New York, 942–943.

Wobbrock, J.O., Aung, H.H., Rothrock, B. and Myers, B.A. (2005a) Maximizing the guessability of symbolic input. Extended Abstracts of the ACM Conference on Human Factors in Computing Systems (CHI '05), ACM Press, New York, 1869–1872.

Wobbrock, J.O. and Myers, B.A. (2005) Gestural text entry on multiple devices. *Proceedings of the ACM SIGACCESS Conference on Computers and Accessibility (ASSETS '05)*, ACM Press, New York, pp. 184–185.

Wobbrock, J.O. and Myers, B.A. (2006) Analyzing the input stream for character-level errors in unconstrained text entry evaluations. *ACM Transactions on Computer-Human Interaction (TOCHI)*, **13**(4), 458–489.

Wobbrock, J.O., Myers, B.A. and Hudson, S.E. (2003a) Exploring edge-based input techniques for handheld text entry. *Proceedings of the 23rd IEEE Conference on Distributed Computing Systems Workshops (ICDCSW '03)*, Los Alamitos, CA, IEEE Computer Society, pp. 280–282.

Wobbrock, J.O., Myers, B.A. and Kembel, J.A. (2003b) EdgeWrite: a stylus-based text entry method designed for high accuracy and stability of motion. *Proceedings of the ACM Symposium on User Interface Software and Technology (UIST '03)*, ACM Press, New York, pp. 61–70.

Wobbrock, J.O., Myers, B.A. and Aung, H.H. (2004) Writing with a joystick: a comparison of date stamp, selection keyboard, and EdgeWrite. *Proceedings of Graphics Interface 2004*, Waterloo, Ontario, Canadian Human-Computer Communications Society, pp. 1–8.

The Creating Community Connections Project: Social and Cultural Approaches for Engaging Low-Income Communities

15

Randal D. Pinkett

Chairman and CEO, BCT Partners, 105 Lock Street, Suite 207, Newark, NJ 07103, USA

15.1 Introduction

The 'digital divide' (US Department of Commerce, 1995, 1998, 1999, 2000) is a modern-day reflection of historical social and economic divides that have plagued our society for years. Over the past decade, the community technology movement (Morino, 1994; Beamish, 1999; Schön *et al.*, 1999) – 'using the technology to support and meet the goals of a community' (Beamish, 1999, p. 366) – has gathered momentum toward closing the gap with programs targeted at access, training, content, technological fluency, and more. Over the past century, the community building movement (Kretzmann and McKnight, 1993; Naparstek *et al.*, 1997; Schorr, 1997; The Aspen Institute, 1997; Kingsley *et al.*, 1999) – an approach to community revitalization that is focused on 'strengthening the capacity of residents, associations, and organizations to work, individually and collectively, to foster and sustain positive neighborhood change' (The Aspen Institute, 1997, p. 2) – has wrestled with complimentary issues in its efforts to alleviate poverty by instituting programs aimed at education, health care, employment, economic development, and the like.

The intersection between these domains holds tremendous possibilities, as both efforts seek to empower individuals and families, and improve their overall community. Ironically, approaches that combine these areas have received very little attention in theory and practice. From among the three models of community engagement with technology – community technology centers (CTCs), community networks, and community content (Beamish, 1999) – there is a limited number of projects that have engaged community residents as active participants in using technology to define processes and design tools for neighborhood revitalization. Conversely, from among the multitude of models for community engagement with revitalization – such as community organizing, community development, community building, and comprehensive community initiatives (CCIs) (Hess, 1999) – we are only beginning to witness the benefits that are afforded by incorporating socially and culturally appropriate design methodologies and technologies into these approaches in a way that truly leverages their potential.

The best practices of community technology see community members as active producers of community information and content. Similarly, the best practices of community building see community members as active agents of change. As community technology and community building initiatives move toward greater synergy, there is a great deal to be learned regarding how community technology, community building, and community design can be mutually supportive, rather than mutually exclusive. The Camfield Estates–MIT Creating Community Connections Project provides the basis for this chapter, which endeavors to shed light on the possibilities inhered at this nexus.

Started in January 2000, the Camfield Estates–MIT project has the goal of establishing Camfield Estates as a model for other low-income housing developments as to how individuals, families, and a community can make use of information and communications technology to support their interests and needs. To achieve this goal, the Camfield Tenants Association (CTA) and the Massachusetts Institute of Technology (MIT) have formed a unique partnership with support from various organizations in the public, private, and nonprofit sectors. This multisector collaboration (Robinson, 2000) has joined to create an infrastructure at Camfield Estates that combines the three primary models for *community technology* (Morino, 1994; Beamish, 1999) – a *community network* where state-of-the-art desktop computers, software, and high-speed Internet connectivity have been offered to every family, a *community technology center (CTC)* located on the premises in the community center, and *community content* delivered through a community-based web system, the Creating Community Connections (C3) system – along with a *community building* agenda (Mattessich and Monsey, 1997; The Aspen Institute, 1997; Kingsley *et al.*, 1999). Note that there is a parallel, and related initiative being conducted at Camfield to build empowerment and self-sufficiency amongst residents that is beyond the scope of this chapter.

This chapter is a case study of the Camfield Estates–MIT project to-date, including the history and background of the project, the theoretical frameworks guiding the initiative, the methodology that has been employed, early results, as well as a set of recommendations for future community–university partnerships involving technology.

15.2 History of the Camfield Estates–MIT Project

Camfield Estates, formerly Camfield Gardens, is a predominantly African-American, low-income housing development in the Roxbury section of Boston, Massachusetts. Camfield is a participant in the US Department of Housing and Urban Development's (HUD) demolition-disposition or 'demo-dispo' program. Demo-dispo was implemented by HUD in 1993, as a strategy to deal with its growing inventory of foreclosed multifamily housing, much of which was in poor physical and financial condition (MHFA, 2001). Through this national demonstration program, approved only in the City of Boston, the Massachusetts Housing Finance Agency (MHFA) was designated to oversee the renovation and sale of HUD properties to resident-owned organizations. As a result, the 136 low- to medium-rise apartments of Camfield Gardens were demolished in 1997 and residents were relocated throughout the greater Boston area. Reconstruction of the property was completed in 2000 as residents returned to Camfield Estates – 102 units of newly built town houses. The renovated property also includes the Camfield community center which houses meeting space, management offices, and the Neighborhood Technology Center (NTC) – a CTC and HUD Neighborhood Networks site, managed by Williams Consulting Services, and supported by MHFA. Finally, in 2001, HUD disposed (transferred ownership) of the property to the nonprofit Camfield Tenants Association, Inc. (CTA), making Camfield the first of several participants in the demo-dispo program to successfully complete the process.

The Camfield Estates–MIT Creating Community Connections project was initiated in January 2000, by graduate students and faculty from the MIT Media Laboratory, MIT Department of Urban Studies and Planning, MIT Center for Reflective Community Practice, and MIT Laboratory for Computer Science. These researchers shared an interest in the role of technology for the purpose of building community, empowerment, and self-sufficiency in a low-income community. Camfield was identified as an excellent site to examine these issues and conduct a longitudinal study for numerous reasons, including the strong leadership exemplified by CTA, the cable-modem Internet capabilities in each unit, and the presence of NTC, along with its associated course offering and ongoing technical support. However, what made Camfield particularly attractive were the prospects to sustain the initiative as a result of their leading role in the demo-dispo program and impending ownership of the property.

The W.K. Kellogg Foundation provided primary support for the project in the form of a monetary grant, followed by in-kind donations from Hewlett-Packard Company (computers), RCN Telecom Services (cable-modem Internet service), Microsoft Corporation (software), and ArsDigita Corporation (software and technical support), with additional support from MHFA, Williams Consulting Services, Lucent Technologies, HUD, the Institute for African-American eCulture (iAAEC), YouthBuild of Boston, and the William Monroe Trotter Institute at the University of Massachusetts at Boston.

Exploratory meetings between CTA, MIT, Kellogg, and Williams Consulting took place during the winter of 2000, culminating in final approval of the project by CTA. Under CTA's leadership, in spring 2000 a nine-person committee was established to oversee the project's implementation, which consisted of three Camfield residents, two representatives of CTA, two members of Williams Consulting staff, and two researchers at MIT. The project officially began in June 2000.

15.3 Background: Community Technology and Community Building

One of the project's goals is to explore the synergy between *community technology* (Morino, 1994; Beamish, 1999) and *community building* (Mattessich and Monsey, 1997; The Aspen Institute, 1997; Kingsley *et al.*, 1999). *Community technology* has been referred to as 'a process to serve the local geographic community – to respond to the needs of that community and build solutions to its problems' (Morino, 1994), and defined as 'using the technology to support and meet the goals of a community' (Beamish, 1999). *Community building* is an approach to community revitalization that is focused on 'strengthening the capacity of residents, associations, and organizations to work, individually and collectively, to foster and sustain positive neighborhood change' (The Aspen Institute, 1997).

To date, three primary models have emerged for community technology– *community networks, community technology centers,* and *community content* – all of which have been deployed at Camfield and combined with a *community building* agenda:

- *Community networks* are community-based electronic network services, provided at little or no cost to users. Every family at Camfield has been offered a state-of-the-art computer, software, and high-speed Internet connectivity via cable-modem.
- *Community technology centers*, or community computing centers, are publicly accessible facilities that provide computer access for people who cannot afford a

computer, as well as technical instruction and support. As mentioned earlier, the Camfield Estates Neighborhood Technology Center (NTC) has been established in the Camfield community centers where comprehensive courses as well as technical support are provided.

- *Community content* refers to the availability of material that is relevant and interesting to a specific target audience (e.g. low-income residents) to encourage and motivate the use of technology (Lazarus and Mora, 2000). The Creating Community Connections (C3) System, a community-based web system, has been co-designed between MIT students and Camfield residents using the application service provider (ASP) model – Camfield residents create and maintain the content, while MIT administers and maintains the associated hardware and software.

To promote *community building*, Camfield residents and MIT researchers have been actively involved in 'mapping' and 'mobilizing' community assets and resources to create connections among residents, local organizations, and institutions (e.g. libraries, schools, etc.), and neighborhood businesses.

15.4 Theoretical Framework: Sociocultural Constructionism and an Asset-Based Approach to Community Technology and Community Building

Since the project's inception, a heavy emphasis has been placed on engaging the residents at Camfield as active agents of change, as well as active producers of community information and content. This orientation is grounded in the theories of *asset-based community development (ABCD)* (Kretzmann and McKnight, 1993) and *sociocultural constructionism* (Pinkett, 2000) which, in concert, constitute an asset-based approach to community technology and community building (Turner and Pinkett, 2000). These theoretical frameworks have proven extremely useful for conceptualizing how a community–university partnership involving technology can foster community empowerment, rather than dependency.

15.4.1 Asset-Based Community Development

Asset-based community development – a particular model, or technique, for community building – assumes that social and economic revitalization starts with what is already present in the community, not only the capacities of residents as individuals, but also the existing commercial, associational and institutional foundation (Turner and Pinkett, 2000). Asset-based community development seeks to leverage the resources within a community by 'mapping' these assets and then 'mobilizing' them to facilitate productive and meaningful connections.

Kretzmann and McKnight (1993) have identified three characteristics of asset-based community development:

- *Asset-based.* Asset-based community development begins with what is present in the community, as opposed to what is absent or problematic in the community. It is focused on indigenous assets as opposed to perceived needs. An asset-based approach involves community residents, organizations, institutions (e.g. libraries, schools, etc.), and businesses.
- *Internally focused.* Asset-based community development calls upon community members to identify their interests and build upon their capacity to solve problems. One of the distinguishing characteristics of the ABCD approach is its heavy emphasis on leveraging that which is in the community first, before looking to (but not excluding) outside entities and/or resources.
- *Relationship driven.* Community building has also been defined as 'any identifiable set of activities pursued by a community in order to increase the social capacity of its members' (Mattessich and Monsey, 1997). Consequently, asset-based community development encourages the ongoing establishment of productive relationships among community members, as well as the associated trust and norms necessary to maintain and strengthen these relationships.

Asset-based community development is an approach to community building that sees community members as active agents of change, rather than passive beneficiaries or clients.

15.4.2 **Sociocultural Constructionism**

Sociocultural constructionism, here applied to community technology, is a synthesis of the theories of *social constructionism* (Shaw, 1995; Shaw and Shaw, 1998) and *cultural constructionism* (Hooper, 1998), both extensions of the theory of *constructionism* (Papert, 1993). *Constructionism* is a design-based approach to learning, drawing on research showing that people learn best when they are active participants in design activities (Papert, 1993), and that these activities give them a greater sense of control over (and personal involvement in) the learning process (Resnick *et al.*, 1996). There are two extensions to constructionism that demonstrate its relevance to the social and cultural context that surrounds engagement with technology, as well as the role of community technology for the purpose of community building:

- *Cultural constructionism* argues that individuals learn particularly well through creating objects in the world that express their cultural identity and have shared meaning within their home cultures (Hooper, 1998). A cultural construction could be a personal web site, electronic community newsletter, or any other project that is an expression of cultural identity, and at the same time facilitates an engagement with new knowledge. Cultural constructionism is a useful framework for identifying ways that technology can advance the interests and needs of an individual learner.

- *Social constructionism* states that individual developmental cycles are enhanced by shared constructive activity in the social setting, and the social setting is also enhanced by the developmental activity of the individual (Shaw, 1995). Shared constructive activity refers to the creation of 'social constructions,' of which there are five types: (1) social relationships, (2) social events, (3) shared physical artifacts, (4) shared social goals and projects, and (5) shared cultural norms and traditions. Social constructionism is a useful framework for identifying ways in which technology can advance the interests and needs of a community of learners.

- *Sociocultural constructionism* argues that 'individual and community development are reciprocally enhanced by independent and shared constructive activity that is resonant with both the social setting that encompasses a community of learners, as well as the cultural identity of the learners themselves' (Pinkett, 2000). Sociocultural constructionism yields an approach to community technology that regards community members as the active producers of community information and content, rather than passive consumers or recipients.

15.4.3 Community Social Capital and Community Cultural Capital

In theory, the asset-based community development and sociocultural constructionist frameworks foster positive changes in *community social capital* and *community cultural capital*, as a result of promoting residents as active, rather passive participants in the process.

I define *community social capital* as the extent to which members of a community can work and learn together effectively. Community social capital is based on the concept of *social capital* first introduced by Coleman (1988) and extended by Putnam (1993, 1995). This definition of community social capital is similar to Mattessich and Monsey's (1997) definition of social capacity. I define *community cultural capital* as various forms of knowledge, skills, abilities, and interests, which have particular relevance or value within a community. Community cultural capital is based on the concept of *cultural capital* first introduced by Bourdieu and Passeron (1977) and extended by Lamont and Lareau (1988). This definition of community cultural capital is similar to Zweigenhaft's (1993) definition of cultural capital.

In practice, the asset-based community development and sociocultural constructionist frameworks help operationalize a methodology for integrating community technology and community building.

15.5 Camfield Estates–MIT Project Methodology

The project officially started in June 2000, by outlining the following goals and objectives:

- *To promote a stronger, healthier community at Camfield Estates.*
- *To establish greater levels of empowerment and self-sufficiency among residents at Camfield Estates.*
- *To create connections between residents at Camfield Estates, local organizations, neighborhood businesses, and other community members.*
- *To enable residents at Camfield Estates to be the creators and producers of their own information and content on the Internet.*
- *To establish Camfield Estates as a model for other housing developments across the country as to how individuals, families, and a community can make productive use of information and communications technology.*

Based on these goals and objectives, we subsequently outlined a methodology and timeline to integrate community technology and community building, consisting of five interrelated, cyclical, and at times parallel phases, as shown in Figures 15.1 and 15.2. An overview of each phase is presented below.

15.5.1 Phase I: Pre-Assessment and Awareness

During summer 2000, the project team developed a preliminary assessment survey instrument for two related, yet distinctly different purposes. First, to obtain formative data that would guide the project's implementation. With community building identified as an agreed-upon goal at the project's inception, both Camfield residents and MIT researchers were able to provide specific input to the survey's design in this regard. This ensured the results not only benchmarked certain outcomes, but also advanced the initiative toward achieving these outcomes. Second, to obtain baseline data for the research study.

During that same period, an awareness campaign was conducted to inform residents about the initiative. A series of mailings were distributed describing the project's goals

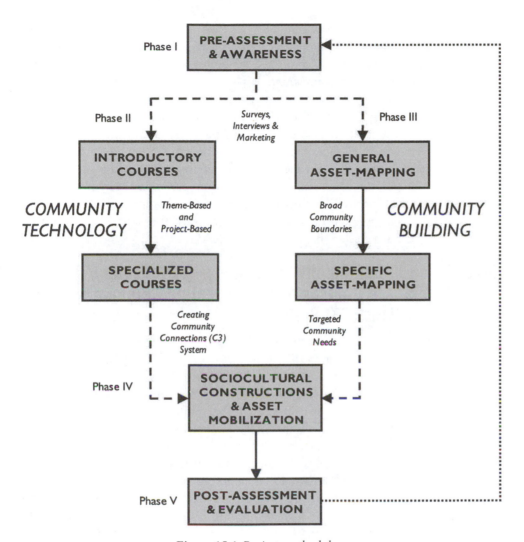

Figure 15.1 *Project methodology.*

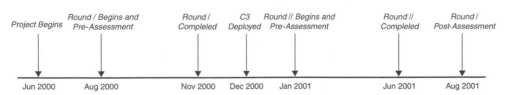

Figure 15.2 *Project timeline.*

and objectives, and offering a new computer, software, high-speed Internet connection (pre-paid for two years) and comprehensive courses at NTC for adults 18 years and older who completed the courses, completed the preliminary and post-interviews, and signed an informed consent form granting permission to track the web-traffic at Camfield through a proxy server (aggregate patterns of use only, and not individually attributable). An open forum was also held in the community center for questions and answers. While families were encouraged to attend the training, at least one adult from each household had to fulfill these requirements in order to receive the computer, software, and Internet access. Given the fact that NTC was primarily used by youth at this time (O'Bryant, 2001), the committee decided to restrict participation to adults only, as we believed it would motivate parents to attend the training for the benefit of their children. August 2000 marked the deadline to sign up for the project, and 32 of the 66 families at Camfield elected to participate in Round I.

15.5.2 Phase II: Community Technology – Introductory/ Specialized Courses and The Creating Community Connections (C3) System

The Creating Community Connections (C3) System is a web-based, community building system designed to establish and strengthen relationships between community residents, local businesses, and neighborhood institutions (e.g. libraries, schools, etc.) and organizations, as shown in Figure 15.3. C3 is built using the ArsDigita Community System (ACS), an open-source software platform.

From June to August 2000, the project team held weekly meetings to discuss design considerations for the Camfield web site, including the site-map, graphics, layout, and user interface. An important component of these discussions was also determining which of the C3 modules would be incorporated into the first release of the Camfield site, given the community building objectives for the project. Eventually, the following modules were selected: *resident profiles, business and organization database, geographic information system (GIS) maps, calendar of events, discussion forums, news and announcements, email lists, chat rooms, file storage,* and *site-wide search*. Scheduled for possible later introduction were the *job and volunteer opportunity postings,* and possibly the *personalized web portals* and *web-based email,* pending use of the system.

From September to October 2000, introductory courses were offered at NTC to Round I participants. For the introductory courses, we employed an activity-based curriculum as a way to combine a variety of learning objectives, rather than focusing on narrow skill development such as how to use a mouse or a keyboard. For example, to

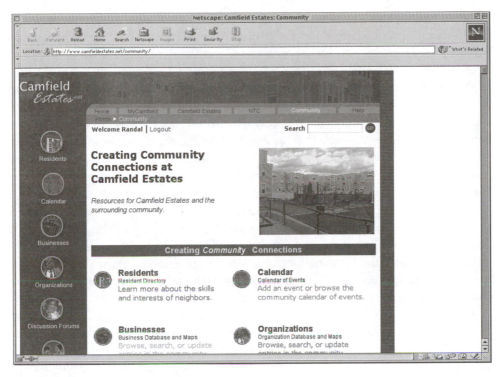

Figure 15.3 The Creating Community Connections (C3) System.

teach participants how to use a browser and the printer, they were instructed to use a search engine to locate information on a topic of interest to them, print out each of their results, and summarize which search terms and associated results they found to be useful.

Designed by Williams Consulting Services (2000), the curriculum lasted 10 weeks (two sessions per week, two hours per session), and covered a variety of areas related to computer and Internet use. In November 2000, two additional specialized courses were offered on how to use the C3 System, made available through the Camfield Estates web site (http://www.camfieldestates.net). The C3 curriculum was co-designed by Williams Consulting and MIT.

In November 2000, 26 families completed the courses and received a computer, software, and subsequent high-speed Internet access, having fulfilled the aforementioned requirements (six heads-of-household were unable to complete the courses due to health-related concerns or scheduling conflicts and were deferred to the next cohort of participants). In January 2001, a second awareness campaign was aimed at the 48 families still eligible for the project (the number of occupied units had increased from 66 to 80), including another round of mailings and meetings. In preparation for this campaign, residents from Round I were asked to speak with neighbors about their experience during the courses. During the holiday season, there were a number of events such as a seniors holiday dinner where elderly participants were asked to give testimonials as a way of encouraging their peers to sign up for Round II. Furthermore, with close to one-third of the development up-and-running with a new computer, software, and high-speed Internet access in their homes, we expected general word-of-mouth to spawn significant interest in Round II from residents who decided to pass on the program during the first awareness campaign.

To our complete surprise, after the second deadline passed for Round II, only 8 out of a possible 48 families elected to participate in the project, the majority of whom were Spanish-speaking, as we were late distributing the flyers in their native-language during Round I. In other words, even the families that elected to participate in Round II were likely to have been Round I participants if the marketing materials had been distributed in Spanish on time.

Unwilling to accept these numbers as being representative of residents' interest, we embarked on a grassroots, door-to-door, outreach campaign to make sure people were fully aware of this special opportunity. As a result, we were able to increase Round II numbers from 8 to 27 families, raising the total number of families participating in the project to 59 out of 80 eligible families.

To clearly demonstrate the relevance of technology to potential participants' lives, we emphasized outcomes instead of access. For example, an elderly, sick-and-shut-in woman at Camfield was one of the project's staunchest opponents. Upon initial contact, she flatly refused being involved. Rather than focusing on the computer and Internet service (access) as a selling point, one of the instructors helped her discover the information she could obtain online in areas such as health care and wellness as well as the people with whom she could communicate to improve her quality-of-life (outcomes). A few weeks later, she commented, 'This computer is better than all of my medication combined!' Other initiatives have made similar observations (Cohill and Kavanaugh, 1997).

For the 19 families that did not participate in Round I and initially did not sign up for Round II, but decided to participate after subsequent outreach, the most commonly cited reasons were:

- *Miscommunication/misunderstanding ('I never received any of the flyers').*
- *Skepticism ('It sounded too good to be true').*

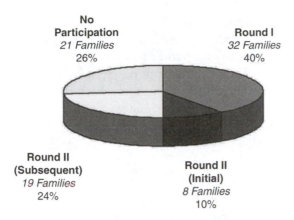

No Participation
21 Families
26%

Round I
32 Families
40%

Round II (Subsequent)
19 Families
24%

Round II (Initial)
8 Families
10%

Figure 15.4 Resident participation and nonparticipation breakdown.

- *They already owned a computer and weren't as quick as others to move on the opportunity.*

For the 21 families that did not participate in either Round I or Round II, the most commonly cited reasons were:

- *Lack of relevance ('I just don't want to be involved').*
- *Too many responsibilities, including a few single mothers juggling multiple jobs.*
- *Health-related conditions preventing involvement, such as pregnancy.*

Figure 15.4 shows the breakdown for resident participation and nonparticipation in Round I and Round II.

In January 2001, Round II courses began. These courses lasted approximately 16 weeks (one session per week, one-and-a-half hours per session), and covered roughly the same material as the Round I courses. One of the areas we improved upon between the Round I and the Round II courses was linking the curriculum to our desired outcomes. The Round I curriculum was more generic when compared with the Round II curriculum which achieved greater depth with respect to how technology can support community building. First, we dedicated more time to learning the C3 modules. For example, after participants learned how to use a browser, they were required to post subsequent technical questions to the C3 'Help' discussion forum as a way of establishing this habit and acclimating them to the system. We believed the 'Help' forum was a natural entry point due to the inevitability of technical problems. This facilitated a natural transition from a familiar context into other contexts such as the 'News and Announcements' or calendar of events modules. Second, we explored how the various modules could improve communication at the development inside the actual class sessions, as opposed to solely relying on residents to do so outside the classroom. For example, as part of the introductory courses, each class created an email list so they could stay in touch, and each participant added their email address to their class email list and the residents' email list. Third, we encouraged more resident interaction during classes. For example, in classes where we observed a marked skill-differential amongst participants we facilitated peer mentoring to build relationships.

In the fall of 2001, the 27 families from Round II received their computers, software, and high-speed Internet access.

15.5.3 Phase III: Community Building – General and Specific Asset-Mapping

Per the asset-based community development approach, a resident-led, general asset-mapping took place during the summer of 2000 with technical assistance from me and my co-principal investigator and doctoral student, Richard O'Bryant in the MIT Department of Urban Studies and Planning. Our efforts were heavily informed by the work being conducted at the ABCD Institute at Northwestern University pertaining to asset-mapping and asset-mobilization.

We conducted our asset-mapping in two steps: general and specific. General asset-mapping began in June 2000, and consisted of identifying all the associations, institutions (e.g. libraries, schools, etc.), and businesses within a specified radius of Camfield, and gathering basic information about these entities. We gathered the following information for associations and institutions: name, address, contact, telephone number, fax number, email address, web site address, mission, and up to four program/service descriptions according to a predefined typology (e.g. religious, social service, etc.). For businesses, we gathered the following information: name, address, district, hours of operation, telephone number, fax number, email address, web site address, and primary and secondary product/service descriptions according to a predefined typology (e.g. market/grocery, restaurant, etc.).

This broad attempt to identify community resources was done to obtain local information of potential benefit to residents that would eventually be made available through C3, and as a preparatory step for asset-mobilization to be conducted after analyzing the results of the preliminary assessment. Not surprisingly, the process of gathering this information served to heighten residents' awareness of assets in their own neighborhood. For example, the first-pass general asset map was conducted within a few square blocks of the property. Residents soon discovered there were very few

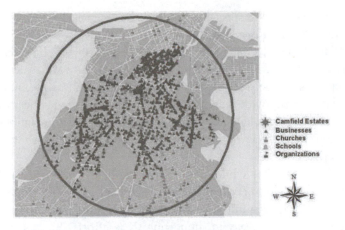

Figure 15.5 *Camfield Estates catchment area.*

organizations and institutions and only a small cluster of businesses in this catchment area. The decision was then made to expand the radius of the asset map to 1.5 miles, which captured approximately 757 businesses, 178 organizations, 67 churches, and 29 schools, as shown in Figure 15.5.

Recognizing that much of the information we needed to gather was likely to exist already, we made every effort to avoid reinventing the wheel. Consequently, we conducted our general asset-mapping by gathering as many relevant and up-to-date publications, directories, listings, and databases as possible, with a particular focus on gathering these items in electronic format to avoid unnecessary data entry. Despite these efforts, the process did involve a limited amount of data entry, as well as occasional outreach via telephone to verify certain pieces of information.

Once gathered, this information was formatted and entered into an Excel spreadsheet that could easily be uploaded to C3. This was not necessarily the best approach to gathering community information in terms of keeping it up-to-date, especially since it is likely to be subject to change and rendered obsolete. Nonetheless, we have found both the process of residents exploring the assets in their community and the product of the resulting database to be very useful. Alternatively, many municipalities and cities are known to maintain and offer similar databases to the public. This is an option we have yet to explore.

Specific asset-mapping began in November 2000, and consisted of mapping the formal and informal skills of residents as well as a more detailed mapping of a targeted sample of the organizations, institutions, and businesses previously identified during general asset-mapping, to be conducted after compiling the results of the preliminary assessment. As mentioned earlier, the former activity took place during the final two weeks of the introductory and specialized courses. Using an early release of C3, residents entered their formal and informal skills and interests online, by selecting from an inventory of more than 150 items, including plumbing, babysitting, web design, etc., according to those skills they 'can perform' and those skills they 'want to learn.' Given this information, as well as the data gathered during the general asset-mapping, residents could now use the C3 site-wide search module to perform a single query and identify all of the individual gifts and talents, as well as local businesses and neighborhood institutions and organizations, relevant to a particular search term such as photography, sewing, or computer repair.

We also recognized that while many of the publications furnished by the Asset-Based Community Development Institute were excellent guides for understanding how to conduct an asset-mapping initiative and identify relevant tools, they made little reference to the role of technology in supporting these efforts. Because technology can dramatically improve the efficiency with which asset-oriented data is gathered and disseminated (Turner and Pinkett, 2000), one must take into consideration the means by which this information is obtained. Stated differently, there is a tension that often arises between 'process,' or capacity-building activities that build relationships, and 'product,' or tangible outcomes such as a completed database of resources (The Aspen Institute, 1997). For example, residents' skills and interests were entered directly into C3 as part of the introductory courses at NTC. We found this method to be extremely efficient as it bypassed the need for paper-based records and data entry. The disadvantage to this approach is the lost opportunity and effectiveness of residents interviewing other residents to obtain this information, which can heighten their awareness and appreciation of their neighbors' abilities. In a previous research project conducted at Northwest Tower in Chicago, Illinois (Turner and Pinkett, 2000), in collaboration with Nicol Turner from the Asset-Based Community Development Institute, we found the process of resident-to-resident interviewing with subsequent data entry to be slightly less efficient with respect to time, but much more effective in fostering relationships. As a general rule, one should attempt to find as much balance as possible between process and product given the available human resources, money, and time.

15.5.4 Phase IV: Sociocultural Constructions and Asset-Mobilization Online and Offline

Sociocultural constructions are physical, virtual, and cognitive artifacts that are resonant with a given social environment and its culture as mediated by technological fluency. Asset-mobilization involves the establishment of productive and meaningful connections between residents, organizations, institutions, and businesses, which previously did not exist, toward achieving specific outcomes, as facilitated by asset-mapping. The nature of sociocultural constructions and strategies for asset-mobilization are heavily informed by the preliminary assessment and involve outreach and the formation of new community partnerships.

In April, the results of the preliminary assessment were compiled, and suggested the following strategies: (1) offer more activities for youth, (2) improve community communication and social interaction at the development, (3) augment current safety and security measures, and (4) expand employment opportunities for residents. Although seniors' concerns were not visibly represented in the results of the assessment, another recommended strategy was to offer more activities for seniors in addition to youth. With this information, a series of meetings took place among members of the project committee to discuss these findings and address the issues raised by residents. Because sociocultural constructions and asset-mobilization manifest themselves online and offline in the context of an integrated community technology and community building initiative, these discussions focused on ways to effect change in both physical and virtual settings. A number of strategies were undertaken in response to these findings, including use of the C3 system to improve communication and information flow at the development, activities during Black Family Technology Week that paired youth with seniors to create PowerPoint presentations, the establishment of a newsletter in both paper-based and electronic formats, thematic workshops for adults on the topics of 'Online Educational Services,' 'Online Banking Services,' 'Online Shopping Services,' 'Online Government Services,' and 'Online Housing Services,' and the establishment of a Cisco Networking Academy at NTC, a program that teaches students how to design, build, and maintain computer networks toward becoming certified as a Cisco Certified Network Associate (CCNA). Note that an in-depth discussion of these strategies is beyond the scope of this chapter.

15.5.5 Phase V: Post-Assessment and Evaluation

During summer 2000, we developed a post-assessment survey instrument that included many of the same questions from the pre-assessment survey as well as additional questions pertaining to computer use. The post-assessment survey instrument was designed to obtain comparative data relative to the preliminary assessment and summative data to evaluate the overall initiative to-date. For comparative purposes, it included the following areas (that were also included on the preliminary assessment): *demographics, community interests and satisfaction, social networks, neighboring, awareness of community resources, community impressions,* and *community involvement and attachment.* For summative purposes, the following areas were also included: *Camfield Estates–MIT project, training experience,* and *computer and Internet use.*

In August 2001, the post-assessment was conducted and consisted of face-to-face interviews with the head-of-household from the 26 out of 32 families that completed Round I of the project (only the data for 19 of these 26 families was available at the time of this publication). The early results from the post-assessment and evaluation are presented below.

15.6 **Early Results**

Demographic information for the participants in the post-assessment is presented first. This is followed by a discussion of the early results in relation to community social capital and community cultural capital.

15.6.1 **Demographics**

The 26 participants who completed the program represent a subset of the 32 participants who initially agreed to participate in Round I. Consequently, the demographics for these 26 participants are almost identical to the demographics of the larger superset that was represented in the preliminary assessment sample (note that complete data was only available for 19 of these 26 participants at the time of this publication). Again, the average participant could be described as a single, Black/African-American female, head-of-household. Figure 15.6 shows the race of participants, Figure 15.7 shows the gender of participants, Figure 15.8 shows the age of participants, Figure 15.9 shows the marital status of participants, Figure 15.10 shows the education of participants, Figure 15.11 shows the family size of participants, and Figure 15.12 shows the annual income of participants. Here, 14 participants (74%)

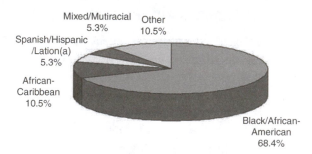

Figure 15.6 *Race of participants.*

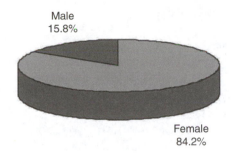

Figure 15.7 *Gender of participants.*

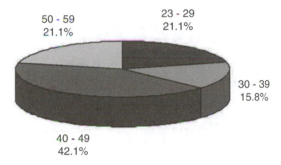

Figure 15.8 *Age of participants.*

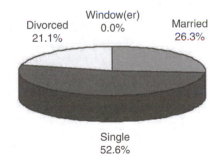

Figure 15.9 *Marital status of participants.*

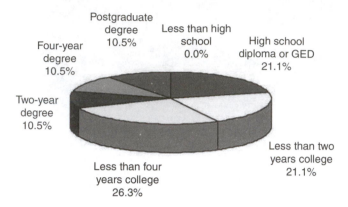

Figure 15.10 *Education of participants.*

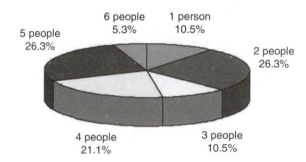

Figure 15.11 *Family size of participants.*

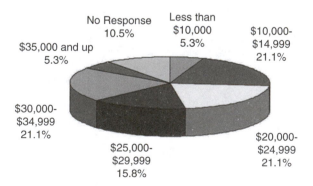

Figure 15.12 *Annual income of participants.*

were parents with an average of 1.5 children, while 5 participants (24%) were either single, married, or divorced without children.

15.6.2 Community Social Capital

I define community social capital as the extent to which members of a community can work and learn together effectively. Increased community social capital includes: (1) reconfigured (Bishop *et al.*, 1999) social networks (e.g. broader extent, proximity, and value inhered in strong and weak social ties as opposed to reinforcing existing ties), (2) increased obligations and expectations of trustworthiness (e.g. increased reliance on neighbors for advice or help and other social support measures), (3) expanded access to information channels (e.g. heightened awareness of community resources), and (4) strengthened norms and effective sanctions (e.g. increased interaction among residents that inhibits negative behaviors). The following is a summary of the early results from the post-assessment in the context of community social capital:

1. *Social Networks: Participants have expanded their local ties.* The number of residents that were recognizable by name increased from 30 to 40 out of a possible 137 adults; the number of residents contacted via telephone and email doubled ($t = -1.978$; $p = 0.063$); 53% of participants reported that they were more connected to family and friends in the local area as shown in Table 15.1.
2. *Access to Information Channels: Participants have a heightened awareness of community resources.* The number of City of Boston services, programs, and/or departments that participants had heard of or used increased from 34 to 43; a paired-samples t-test of residents' awareness and utilization of community resources in nine categories resulted in a statistically significant increase in four of those categories (a fifth was nearly significant) including: residents' skills and abilities ($t = 3.284$; $p = 0.004$), volunteer opportunities in the neighborhood ($t = 3.684$; $p = 0.002$), social services and programs provided for the community ($t = 3.240$; $p = 0.005$), community projects, activities, and events ($t = 4.371$; $p = 0.000$), and employment opportunities in the community ($t = 1.924$; $p = 0.070$) as shown in Table 15.2. The Camfield Estates web site and the C3 system received high marks from participants when asked to rate its usefulness in this regard.

15.6.3 Community Cultural Capital

I define community cultural capital as various forms of knowledge, skills, abilities, and interests, which have particular relevance or value within a community. Activated community cultural capital constitutes: (1) exchanging knowledge and resources (e.g. formal

Table 15.1 Residents' social networks at Camfield Estates

Question	Mean		Paired-samples *t*-test	
	August 2000	August 2001	*t*	*p*
Please identify those residents whom you recognize *by name*?	29.7	39.5	−1.108	0.283
Please identify those residents whom you *talk to* on what you would consider to be la regular basis?	10.2	9.2	0.604	0.553
Please identify those residents whom you have invited into *your home* in the last six months?	4.4	4.5	−0.043	0.966
Please identify those residents whom have invited you into *their home* in the last six months?	3.4	4.2	−0.790	0.440
Please identify those residents whom you have called on the *phone* in the last six months?	2.4	4.6	−1.542	0.141
Please identify those residents whom you have contacted using *email* in the last six months?	1.3	3.0	−1.978[a]	0.063

[a]Denotes statistical significance ($t > 1.96$; $p < 0.05$).

or informal sharing of information, products, services, etc.), (2) improving technological fluency (Papert and Resnick, 1995[S2]; Resnick *et al.*, 1998) and the ability of community members to express themselves via technology (e.g. the ability to create a personal web site that portrays a particular interest such as books), (3) coalescing around shared interests (e.g. a group of mothers discussing effective child rearing practices), and (4)

Table 15.2 *Residents' awareness and utilization of community resources*

Resource	Very well/well informed		Paired-samples *t*-test	
	August 2000	August 2001	*t*	*p*
Skills and abilities of other residents at Camfield Estates	11%	32%	3.284[a]	0.004[a]
Associations and organizations that serve the community	26%	58%	1.278	0.217
Volunteer opportunities in the community	0%	42%	3.684[a]	0.002[a]
Institutions located in the community (e.g. schools)	74%	84%	0.809	0.429
Social services and programs provided for the community	26%	63%	3.240[a]	0.005[a]
Community projects, activities, and events	11%	58%	4.371[a]	0.000[a]
Businesses located in the community	53%	63%	0.224	0.826
Products and services sold by local businesses	32%	32%	0.357	0.725
Employment opportunities in the community	5%	37%	1.924	0.070

[a]Denotes statistical significance ($t > 1.96$; $p < 0.05$).

shifting individuals' attitudes and perceptions of themselves and the world (e.g. renewed confidence in their abilities, their capacity to learn, and their appreciation of assets in their community). The following is a summary of the early results from the post-assessment in the context of community cultural capital, two of which represent observations pertaining to technological fluency:

(1) *Knowledge and Resources: Participants are better informed about local issues and there is an improved communication and information flow at the development.* Almost half of participants (47%) reported that they are more aware of what is

going on at Camfield when compared with before the project was started; this was partly due to the fact that a core group of residents and staff have taken the lead in actively contributing to the Camfield Estates web site and the C3 system; the most popular C3 modules were the resident profiles (31% of traffic), calendar of events (18% of traffic), and discussion forums (13% of traffic) on the Camfield Estates web site, and while these modules experienced moderate use, their traffic has steadily increased since the site went live.

(2) *Technological Fluency: Participants desired to use technology in a variety of creative ways but were often too busy to do so* or their schedule was not amenable to attending follow-up courses. From among the top-ranked uses of their computer and Internet access, participants' ranked several creative activities low such as contributing content to the Camfield Estates web site (#18), designing a flyer, poster, or newsletter (#19), and contributing content to another web site (#19), designing a web page (#26), and creating an online photo album (#27). One possible explanation why some residents have not chosen to make time for such activities is that creative uses of technology were sometimes relegated to the category of leisure activities and often subordinated to more immediate, pressing concerns in their midst. In other words, for adults at Camfield, with multiple, competing demands on their time such as their jobs and their children, time is a scarce resource. Similarly, a 'lack of time' was one of the most commonly cited reasons for residents' nonparticipation during assessment and awareness (Phase I).

(3) *Technological Fluency: Participants' making the greatest strides toward technological fluency were those receiving some form of ongoing support for continuous learning.* This was not surprising, however, the interviews clearly demonstrated the difference between users who had structures to support their learning and those who did not. Those who did not have readily accessible or convenient means of support made only moderate progress toward becoming more technologically fluent since completing the introductory course, despite their desire to do so. For those that had support it came in various forms. In some cases, a family member, typically a son or a daughter, or a close friend provided technical assistance after they completed the introductory course. In other cases, participants relied on the staff at NTC, to the extent that they were home during the center's hours of operation.

(4) *Attitude and Perception: Participants have cultivated the meta-competence of a renewed confidence in themselves and their ability to learn.* Qualitative responses from the one-on-one interviews revealed a shift in participants' attitudes and perceptions of themselves as learners. Several participants described their personal transition of moving from a reticence toward technology to envisioning

themselves as (or taking actual steps to becoming) web designers, network administrators, and programmers. In particular, their participation in the training has given them a greater appreciation of their strengths, and it has given the community a greater appreciation of its most basic assets, the skills and abilities of its residents.

15.7 **Project Status**

The Camfield Estates–MIT project has continued to progress along a number of lines. Eventually, ownership of the property was transferred from HUD to the residents, giving them certain control over the financial and operational management of the property. In 2003, the term of the subsidized cable-modem Internet connection serving each of the units expired. In order to continue providing affordable Internet access, the Internet connection that serviced NTC was also made available wirelessly using antennas atop the development's main buildings. This service was offered at no cost to residents, notwithstanding the need to purchase a wireless card. Depending on their circumstances, residents were able to buy wireless cards at full price, at a discount, or for free.

MIT continued its relationship with Camfield through the Center for Reflective Community Practice (CRCP) under the direction of Professor Ceasar McDowell. CRCP is housed in the Department of Urban Studies and Planning, a department with expertise in teaching, learning, research, and training of professionals in the field of urban planning and development. Through a range of long-term relationships, CRCP offers the opportunity to link students and faculty at MIT with community partners for mutual benefit, and to help develop the resource and leadership capacity of low-income communities and communities of color. It also allows community- and university-based partners to engage in community practice and in strategies for change in more thoughtful and deliberative ways, leading to a new and shared knowledge base of resources and approaches that include the best practices of both community-based and academic teaching and learning. CRCP identified Camfield as one of its core communities, which constituted a multiyear relationship. As part of this effort, Camfield residents were selected for the 'CRCP Reflective Practitioner Fellowship,' which is designed to provide the opportunity and space for frontline practitioners to examine their current practice and to begin to plan for how that practice can be informed through thoughtful consideration of some of the major issues facing our society and world. With this commitment in place, Camfield and MIT will continue to explore the mutual benefits associated with a long-term, institutional, community-wide partnership.

15.8 **Implications for Researchers, Practitioners, and Policymakers**

The following three recommendations are offered for researchers, practitioners, and policymakers seeking to deploy information and communications technology in low-income communities. They are not presented as strict rules to follow, but rather lessons learned as a result of our experience with the Camfield Estates–MIT project thus far.

(1) *Conduct ongoing assessment to establish a baseline and guide implementation.* Good survey instruments are designed with outcomes in mind, and if done properly, the information gleaned can be very useful. The Camfield Estates–MIT preliminary survey data has been invaluable. It has provided tremendous insight into how technology can be made relevant to people's lives. It is important to note that the survey was designed for two related, yet distinctly different purposes. First, to obtain baseline data for later comparative analysis, and second, to obtain formative data that would guide the project's implementation. With community building identified as an agreed upon goal (among others) at the project's inception, both Camfield residents and MIT researchers were able to provide specific input to the survey's design in this regard. This ensured the results not only benchmarked certain outcomes, but also advanced the initiative toward achieving these outcomes.

(2) *Recognize that 'process' is just as important as 'product.'* In this context, process refers to maintaining a 'commitment to community building, capacity building, empowerment, [and] participation' (The Aspen Institute, 1997). Product refers to more concrete outcomes such as a training curriculum, software product, or a research report. The distinction between product and process has also been characterized as the difference between short-term, 'intermediate outcomes,' such as collective goal setting and relationship building, that are building blocks for longer-term, 'final outcomes,' such as an increase in the number of students engaged in community projects, or markers of neighborhood improvement (Dewar, 1997). In community–university partnerships, trust, clarification of roles, responsibilities and expectations, and mutual understanding must all be developed and cannot be taken for granted. Despite the fact that process-related activities are often time- and resource-consuming, they should be valued as being supportive of, rather than subordinated to, product-related outcomes.

(3) *Establish multisector collaborations to build capacity and promote sustainability.* CTA has established relationships with universities, government agencies, corporations, foundations, nonprofit organizations, and neighboring tenant associations.

HUD and MHFA have played a critical role with respect to the demo-dispo program, which will ensure NTC remains operational. Support from Kellogg, Hewlett-Packard, Microsoft, and others, has been instrumental in establishing a state-of-the-art technological infrastructure. MIT's strength in areas such as research, education, and technology positioned the institute to provide useful technical assistance, evaluation, software development, and more. Similarly, each of the remaining entities, which span the public, private, and nonprofit sectors, has contributed something different, yet valuable to sustaining this initiative. However, it is CTA's demonstrated commitment to internal capacity-building, which is strengthened by their ability to cultivate and leverage these relationships, that ultimately bodes well for these efforts to be sustained.

15.9 Implications for Users

The following three recommendations are offered for users and residents of low- to moderate-income communities seeking to undertake similar or related initiatives. Once again, this information represents lessons learned from our experience working with the tenants of Camfield Estates.

(1) *Demonstrate relevance clearly.* At times, it has required nothing short of going door-to-door to demonstrate the relevance of technology, as evidenced by the grassroots mobilization required to solicit Round II participants. We have endeavored to demonstrate relevance in two particular ways. First, by providing a curriculum that is project-based and combines a variety of learning objectives, rather than focusing on narrow skill development such as how to use a mouse or a keyboard. For example, to teach participants how to use a browser and the printer, they are instructed to use a search engine to locate information on a topic of interest to them, print out each of their results, and summarize which search terms and associated results they found to be useful. Second, by emphasizing outcomes instead of access. For example, an elderly woman at Camfield was one of the project's staunchest opponents. Upon initial contact, she flatly refused being involved. Rather than focusing on the computer and Internet service (access) as a selling point, one of the instructors introduced her to the information she could obtain online and the people with whom she could communicate to improve her quality-of-life (outcomes). A few weeks later, she commented, 'This computer is better than all of medication combined!' Other initiatives have expressed a similar observation (Cohill and Kavanaugh, 1997).

(2) *Link curriculum to outcomes.* One of the areas we improved upon between the Round I courses and the Round II courses, was linking the curriculum to our desired outcomes. The Round I curriculum was more generic when compared with the Round II curriculum, which achieved greater depth with respect to how technology could support community building. We dedicated more time to learning the C3 modules, and exploring how these modules could improve communication at the development. Furthermore, once the results of the pre-assessment were compiled, we were able to follow up the project-based curriculum, and couple it with a theme-based curriculum. These thematic workshops (e.g. using online educational resources) were designed around the areas deemed important by residents, as articulated during the preliminary interviews.

(3) *Engage residents as active participants in the process.* Although the Camfield Estates–MIT project was initially proposed by MIT to CTA, MIT researchers did not approach this initiative as if we had all the answers. Instead, we have worked hard to create an atmosphere of trust and mutual respect with CTA and the broader community at Camfield. The process has not been easy, rather, it has required relationship building, commitment, patience, and empathic listening on both sides. From the beginning, CTA and MIT recognized that these foundational elements were fundamental to the project's success. Collectively, we acknowledged that for residents to feel a sense of ownership and empowerment, they must be actively involved in the process.

15.10 Conclusion

Since its inception, the Camfield Estates–MIT Creating Community Connections Project has sought to integrate community technology and community building by drawing upon the theories of sociocultural constructionism and asset-based community development. However, the community technology movement, primarily in the form of community technology centers (CTCs), and the community building movement, primarily in the form of community-based organizations (CBOs), have historically existed in separate, rather than holistic spheres of practice. In *Bridging the Organizational Divide: Toward a Comprehensive Approach to the Digital Divide,* Kirschenbaum and Kunamneni (2001)[S3] coin this disconnect as the 'organizational divide.' They write, 'As we develop policies and programs to bridge the Digital Divide we must insure that these are linked to broader strategies for social change in two ways. First, we must allow the wisdom and experience of existing community infrastructure to inform our work. Second, we must focus our efforts on emerging technologies as a tool to strengthen and support the community infrastructure' (p. 3).

Leaders in both fields must devise strategies to connect these two movements toward unleashing their collective transformative power. For this to occur, the following things must happen:

- *Theories must be developed.* This chapter offers the theoretical framework of sociocultural constructionism and an asset-based approach to community technology and community building, which represents just one of a growing number of theories dealing with these issues. There is both a need to further develop this perspective by applying it in different contexts toward different outcomes, and a need to establish new perspectives that suggest alternate approaches which can also be explored. Such a strategy can simultaneously serve to broaden and deepen our understanding of these issues.
- *Research must be advanced.* The Camfield Estates–MIT project is one of a growing number of initiatives seeking to demonstrate the role of technology for community revitalization (Kirschenbaum and Kunamneni, 2001). These other examples fall into the categories of advocacy and online organizing, community information clearinghouses, networking and online communities, innovations in service delivery, interactive database development, and community mapping (Kirschenbaum and Kunamneni, 2001), and are beginning to grow in number, size, and scope. We must continue to study and highlight examples of community technology and community building projects as a means to disseminate lessons learned and advance our understanding.
- *Practices must be changed.* Community technology practitioners must connect their activities to more traditional, outcome-driven program areas such as youth, workforce development, and health care – as these areas also represent more established and stable sources of funding. Community building practitioners must closely examine the role of technology in improving their organizational effectiveness and supporting their efforts to reach out to the community – as such an examination also holds the greatest promise for identifying new innovations in the work they perform.
- *Funding must be shifted.* There are a number of grant programs that will provide money for hardware or software only, without associated funds for the necessary courses and training required to make productive use of these tools. Conversely, there are a number of grant programs that will provide money for specific programs, such as youth development or improved delivery of health care, without simultaneous support for technology development and infrastructure. Community technology and community building initiative requires funding that allows them to pursue an integrated and comprehensive agenda. Although both movements combined would benefit from additional resources, an easier 'win' could be achieved by simply leveraging existing resources more synergistically.

- *Policies must be altered.* For example, the federal E-rate program that provides subsidized telecommunications services to schools and libraries should be extended to nonprofit organizations. In short, government must acknowledge the inherent synergy between programs aimed at bridging the digital divide and those aimed at alleviating poverty.

At Camfield, we have been fortunate that through the combined support of the W.K. Kellogg Foundation, MIT, Hewlett-Packard Company, Microsoft Corporation, RCN Telecom Services, US Department of Housing and Urban Development (HUD), Massachusetts Housing Finance Agency (MHFA), Williams Consulting Services (WCS) and others, we have been able to pursue a combined agenda. Accordingly, for the existing pool of community technology and community building practitioners to unite their efforts, it will require the coordinated activities of presently disjoint foundations, policymakers, government agencies and nonprofit organizations, as well as technical assistance providers, researchers, industry representatives, and circuit riders, in order to be successful.

Our goal to establish Camfield as a model for other communities manifests itself in two ways. First, as a methodology that can inform the work being done in other communities to strengthen the capacity of residents, organizations, and businesses in their neighborhood. Second, as an example that demonstrates the limitless possibilities when community members are engaged as active agents of change and active producers of information and content. Years from now I expect to see new realities at Camfield Estates, and new areas within cyberspace by Camfield residents, that continue to inspire other communities across the globe.

Acknowledgments

The Camfield Estates–MIT Creating Community Connections project has been a true team effort. Leadership at Camfield Estates consists of Paulette Ford, CTA President, and Nakia Keizer, Project Leader and MIT Reflective Community Practitioner, along with the following board members and advisors: Constance Terrell, Malissa Evans, Luon Williams, Edward Harding, Susan Terrell, Marzella Hightower-Hunt, Cora Scott, Alberta Willis, Minnie Clark, and Daniel Violi. At MIT, Randal Pinkett, PhD candidate, MIT Media Laboratory, and Richard O'Bryant, PhD candidate, MIT Department of Urban Studies and Planning (DUSP) are the co-principal investigators, under the supervision of Professor Mitchel Resnick, MIT Media Laboratory, Professor Joseph

Ferreira, Jr., DUSP, Professor Ceasar McDowell, DUSP and Director of the Center for Reflective Community Practice (CRCP), Professor Brian Smith, MIT Media Laboratory, and Professor David Gifford, MIT Laboratory for Computer Science (LCS), with assistance from undergraduate students Megan Henry and Wei-An Yu. Without support from the following individuals and organizations, as well as countless others, the project would not have been possible: Dr Gail McClure and Caroline Carpenter, Kellogg Foundation, Thaddeus Miles, Massachusetts Housing Finance Agency (MHFA), Wayne Williams, Jackie Williams, Garfield Williams, and Luis Herrera, Williams Consulting Services, Donna Fisher, Cornu Management, Bess Stephens, Catherine Gowen, Camilla Nelson and Robert Bouzon, Hewlett-Packard Company, Dave Mitchell, Microsoft Corporation, John McGeough and Ken Rahaman, RCN Telecom Services, and Philip Greenspun, ArsDigita Corporation. I would particularly like to thank Mitchel Resnick, Richard O'Bryant, and Ceasar McDowell for their guidance and support. Above all, I would like to thank all of the residents at Camfield Estates for the wonderful opportunity to work together with them. For more information about the Camfield Estates–MIT project, visit http://www.camfieldestates.net.

References

Beamish, A. (1999) Approaches to community computing: bringing technology to low-income groups. In Schön, D., Sanyal, B., & Mitchell W.J. (Eds.). *High Technology in Low-Income Communities: Prospects for the Positive Use of Information Technology,* MIT Press, Cambridge, MA, 349–368.

Bishop, A.P., Tidline, T.J., Shoemaker, S. and Salela, P. (1999) *Public Libraries and Networked Information Services in Low-Income Communities*. Graduate School of Library and Information Science, University of Illinois at Urbana-Champaign, Urbana-Champaign, IL.

Bourdieu, P. and Passeron, J.C. (1997) *Reproduction in Education, Society and Culture. Translated by Richard Nice*. Sage, Beverly Hills, CA.

Cohill, A.M. and Kavanaugh, A.L. (1997) *Community Networks: Lessons from Blacksburg, Virginia*. Artech House Telecommunications Library, Blacksburg, VA.

Coleman, J.S. (1998) Social capital in the creation of human capital. *American Journal of Sociology,* **94**, S95–S120.

Dewar, T. (1997) *A Guide to Evaluating Asset-Based Community Development: Lessons, Challenges and Opportunities*. ACTA Publications, Chicago, IL.

Hess, D.R. (1999) *Community Organizing, Building and Developing: Their Relationship to Comprehensive Community Initiatives.* Working paper series for COMM-ORG: The On-Line Conference on Community Organizing and Development, June. `http://comm-org.utoledo.edu/papers99/hess.html`.

Hooper, P. (1998) They have their own thoughts: children's learning of computational ideas from a cultural constructionist perspective. Unpublished PhD Dissertation, MIT Media Laboratory, Cambridge, MA.

Kingsley, G.T., McNeely, J.B. and Gibson, J.O. (1999) *Community Building Coming of Age.* The Urban Institute. `http://www.urban.org/comminity/combuild.htm`

Kretzmann, J.P. and McKnight, J.L. (1993) *Building Communities from the Inside Out: A Path Toward Finding and Mobilizing a Community's Assets.* ACTA Publications, Chicago, IL.

Lamont, M. and Lareau, A. (1988) Cultural capital: allusions gaps and glissandos in recent theoretical developments. *Sociological Theory,* **6**(2), 153–168.

Lazarus, W. and Mora, F. (2000) *On-line Content for Low-Income and Underserved Americans: The Digital Divide's New Frontier.* The Children's Partnership, Santa Monica, CA, `http://www.childrenpartnership.org`.

Mark, J., Cornebise, J. and Wahl, E. (1997) *Community Technology Centers: Impact on Individual Participants and their Communities.* Educational Development Center, Inc., Newton, MA. `http://www.ctcnetorg/eval.html`

Mattessich, P. and Monsey, B. (1997) *Community Building: What Makes It Work: A Review of Factors Influencing Successful Community Building.* Amherst H. Wilder Foundation, Saint Paul, MN.

Morino, M. (1994) *Assessment and Evolution of Community Networking.* Paper presented at Ties That Bind, at Apple Computer, Cupertino, CA.

Naparstek, A.J., Dooley, D. and Smith, R. (1997) *Community Building in Public Housing: Ties That Bind People and Their Communities.* The Urban Institute/Aspen Systems Corporation `http://www.cpn.org/sections/tools/manuals/cb_in_public_housing.html`.

O'Bryant, R. (2001). Establishing neighborhood technology centers in low-income communities: a crossroads for social science and computer information technology. *Projections: The MIT Student Journal of Planning - Making Places through Information Technology,* 2, 2.

Papert, S.A. (1993) Instructionism vs. constructionism. In Papert S., *The Children's Machine,* Basic Books, New York, NY.

Pinkett, R.D. (2000) Bridging the Digital Divide: Sociocultural Constructionism and an Asset-Based Approach to Community Technology and Community Building. Paper presented at the 81st Annual Meeting of the American Educational Research Association (AERA), New Orleans, LA, April 24–28. (`http://www.media.mit.edu/&sim;rpinkett/papers/aera2000.pdf`).

Putnam, R. (1993) The prosperous community - social capital and public life. American Prospect, **26**, 18–21.

Putnam, R. Tuning in, tuning out: the strange disappearance of social capital in America. *Political Science and Politics,* December 1995.

Resnick, M., Bruckman, A. and Martin, F. (1996) Pianos not stereos: creating computational construction kits. *Interactions,* 3, September/October, 6, `http://el.www.media.mit.edu/el/Papers/mres/chi-98/digital-manip.html`.

Resnick, M., Rusk, N. and Cooke, S. (1998) The computer clubhouse: technological fluency in the inner city. In Schön D., Sanyal B., & Mitchell W.J. (Eds.) *High Technology in Low-Income Communities: Prospects for the Positive Use of Information Technology,* MIT Press, Cambridge, MA, 263–286.

Robinson, J. (2000) The role of information technology in economic development of the inner city. *Proceedings of the 2000 Inner City Business Leadership Conference,* Boston, MA, November.

Schön, D.A., Sanyal, V. and Mitchell, W.J. (1999) *High Technology and Low-Income Communities: Prospects for the Positive Use of Advanced Information Technology.* MIT Press, Cambridge, MA.

Schorr L. (1997) *Common Purpose: Strengthening Families and Neighborhoods to Rebuild America,* Anchor Books, New York, NY.

Shaw, A.C. (1995) Social constructionism and the inner city: designing environments for social development and urban renewal. Unpublished PhD Dissertation, MIT Media Laboratory, Cambridge, MA.

Shaw A. and Shaw M. (1998) *Social empowerment through community networks.* In Schön D., Sanyal B., & Mitchell W.J. (Eds.) *High Technology in Low-Income Communities: Prospects for the Positive Use of Information Technology,* MIT Press, Cambridge, MA, 316–335.

The Aspen Institute (1997) *Voices from the Field: Learning from the Early Work of Comprehensive Community Initiatives.* The Aspen Institute: Washington, DC (`http://www.aspenroundtable.org/voices/index.htm`).

Turner N.E. and Pinkett R.D. (2000) An asset-based approach to community technology and community building. *Proceedings of Shaping the Network Society: The Future of the Public Sphere in Cyberspace,* Directions and Implications of Advanced Computing Symposium 2000 (DIAC-2000), Seattle, WA, May 20–23. `http://www.media.mit.edu/&sim;rpinkett/papers/diac2000.pdf`.

US Department of Commerce (1995) *Falling Through the Net: A Survey of the 'Have Nots' in Rural and Urban America.* Full Report, July (`http://www.ntia.doc.gov/ntiahome/digitaldivide/`).

US Department of Commerce (1998) *Falling Through the Net II: New Data on the Digital Divide.* Full Report, July (`http://www.ntia.doc.gov/ntiahome/digitaldivide/`).

US Department of Commerce (1999). *Falling Through the Net III: Defining the Digital Divide.* Full Report, July (`http://www.ntia.doc.gov/ntiahome/digitaldivide/`).

US Department of Commerce (2000) *Falling Through the Net IV: Toward Digital Inclusion.* Full Report, October (`http://www.ntia.doc.gov/ntiahome/digitaldivide/`).

Williams Consulting Services, (2000) Course syllabus: Introduction to Windows and Internet Explorer. *Prepared and delivered by Williams Consulting Services (WCS) for the Camfield Estates Neighborhood Technology Center (NTC),* Williams Consulting Services, Roxbury, MA.

Zweigenhaft, R. (1993) Prep school and public school graduates of Harvard: a longitudinal study of the accumulation of social and cultural capital. *Journal of Higher Education,* **64**(2), 211–225.

Implementing Community-Based Participatory Research to Reduce Health and Technology Disparities Among Low-Income African-American Women

16

Diane Maloney-Krichmar, Eleanor Walker, David Bushnell, and Sadanand Sirvastava

Bowie State University, MD, USA

16.1 Introduction

This chapter describes an exploratory research study designed to develop online health informatics and social support systems to assist low-income African-American women in changing their health-related behavior. The research team was comprised of researchers from the disciplines of nursing, computer science, information science, human factors, and the social sciences. This project will provide the foundation for the development of a more detailed study to evaluate the effectiveness of the model under development. Commonly used approaches to designing intervention strategies often do not adequately involve all stakeholders in the decision-making process. New approaches are needed to engage stakeholders in developing and sustaining effective interventions for health behavior change. This community-based participatory designed project actively involves stakeholders at every stage of the study.

Despite major technological and medical advances, and subsequent improvements in the overall health of the nation, the health status of African Americans continues to lag behind that of the majority race (USDHHS, 2000). The Institute of Medicine Report *Unequal treatment confronting racial and ethnic disparities in healthcare* (Smedley *et al.*, 2002) clearly documented the existence of institutional barriers to health care for African Americans and other minorities and the ongoing disparity in health status among minorities. Morbidity and mortality among African Americans for the diseases of cancer, heart disease, diabetes, HIV and AIDS, and infant mortality are disproportionately higher than the majority population. Reasons for this disparity include lack of access to care, lack of health insurance, lack of knowledge, distrust of the health care system, inability to purchase health care, discrimination, and language barriers. The uninsured are less likely to seek health care until a crisis occurs. This behavior results in increased health care costs because the initial problem has progressed to a state requiring more intense and costly intervention. There is a need to shift the paradigm from studying the problem to identifying effective interventions.

African Americans are the victims of serious health disparities, defined as differences in the incidence, prevalence, mortality, and burden of diseases and disorders (NIH, 2000). Health disparities have existed since the beginnings of slavery and were documented in the United States as early as 1904 when W.E.B. DuBois authored *The Health and Physique of the Negro American*. In 1914, Booker T. Washington also wrote about the poor health status of African Americans (Thomas, 2001).

Health disparities occur due to a complex interaction among several factors including social and economic variables, personal lifestyle choices, environmental factors, and limitations of the health care system (Wisconsin Department of Health and Family Services, 2001). Social and economic factors include cultural values, language, attitudes toward health and wellness, educational attainment, and income levels. Personal lifestyle choices may involve lack of preventive care, an unhealthy diet, and lack of exercise. Environmental conditions such as exposure to toxins, unhealthy living and working conditions, and poor water quality may also contribute to the existence of health disparities.

Studies have shown that African Americans are less likely than the majority population to receive a wide range of medical services including life-saving surgical procedures (Peterson *et al.*, 1997; Smedley *et al.*, 2002). African Americans have an average life span that is 6 years shorter than whites, with little change in that disparity over the last 30 years (USDHHS, 2000). The incidence of heart disease is 27% higher in African-American men and 55% higher in African-American women than whites; one in every 10 African Americans has diabetes and the prevalence of diabetes among African Americans is 70% higher than whites (USDHHS, 1999, 2001a); African Americans experience higher rates of HIV and AIDS, the leading cause of death among African Americans 25 to 44 years of age (USDHHS, 2001b); African-American babies are more than twice as likely as white babies to die before their first birthday (The Henry and Kaiser Family Foundation, 1999; USDHHS, 1999); African Americans are diagnosed with cancer 10% more often than the general population; and African-American children and older adults are less likely to receive recommended immunizations against preventable diseases (USDHHS, 1999). Figure 16.1 displays age-adjusted deaths per 100 000 for selected causes of death by race.

Federal efforts to reduce health disparities began in 1979 with Healthy People: The Surgeon General's Report on Health Promotion and Disease Prevention. In 1980,

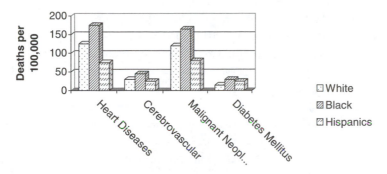

Age-Adjusted Death Rates for Selected Causes of Death by Race 1950-1998

Figure 16.1 Health, United States 2000. From National Institutes of Health. (2000). Trans-NIH initiative: Addressing health disparities, definition of health disparities.

Promoting Health/Preventing Disease: Objectives for the Nation identified 226 national health objectives to be accomplished over the next 10 years. In 1986, The Report of the Secretary's Task Force on Black and Minority Health described the existing knowledge about health disparities. Healthy People 2000: National Health Promotion and Disease Prevention Objectives was published in 1990. The next national strategy was the United States Department of Health and Human Services (USDHHS) Initiative to Eliminate Racial and Ethnic Disparities in Health which began in 1998. This program committed the United States to the elimination of racial and ethnic health disparities by the year 2010. The newest initiative, Healthy People 2010, identifies 10-year health objectives for the nation to be accomplished by the year 2010 (USDHHS, 2000).

If we are to achieve the health objectives for the nation, new strategies must be implemented to change the health behaviors of individuals, reduce barriers to care within the health care system, and focus on prevention. The cost of prevention is generally less than the cost of treatment (Coffield *et al.*, 2001). For example, the cost for mammography screening is far less than that associated with intensive treatment of breast cancer with chemotherapy, radiation, and surgery. According to the Agency for Healthcare Research and Quality (AHRQ, 2002), the cost of care for patients with Acquired Immune Deficiency Syndrome can be reduced by the administration of prophylactic antibiotics to prevent the development of *pneumocistis carinii* pneumonia. Researchers at Johns Hopkins University School of Medicine conducted an AHRQ-funded study of patients admitted to hospitals diagnosed with *pneumocistis carinii* pneumonia who were not treated with prophylactic antibiotics. The findings indicated that these patients accounted for 85% of hospital days, 100% of the intensive care unit days, and 89% of inpatient hospital charges. They estimated that not administering prophylactic antibiotics resulted in the deaths of 62 patients and cost the State of Maryland $4.7 million (Gallant *et al.*, 1995).

Taking a somewhat different approach to assessing the impact of effectiveness research, AHRQ published a paper in 2001 (AHRQ, 2001) on the outcomes of its first 10 years of effort to strengthen the overall effectiveness of outcomes research. They reported the results of a survey of 91 principal investigators, 64% of whom responded to the survey. A four-level model for describing the potential levels of impact was developed. Level 1 represented basic studies that 'identify problems, generate hypotheses, establish the effectiveness of interventions, and develop new tools to explore these problems (p. 984).' Level 2 describes those policies or programs that were created as a result of the research being conducted. 'Potential conduits of level 2 impacts include what we have termed "change agents" in today's health care delivery environment . . . (p. 985).' Level 3 impacts are those studies in which a documented change in what clinicians or patients do are reported, and level 4 impacts describe those research efforts that result in changes in health outcomes, including clinical, economic, quality of life, and satisfaction. It is to this last category of research effort that the effort being reported here aspires.

16.2 **How was this Project Developed**

The proposed project builds on an ongoing intervention funded by the United States Department of Housing and Urban Development (HUD). In 2001, funding from HUD was provided to establish a Nurse Managed Health Center in a Section Eight housing complex inside the beltway in Prince George's County, Maryland. Prince George's County is the second largest jurisdiction in the State of Maryland. According to the 2000 Census, the population of Prince George's County is 801 515. Over the past 10 years, the county has evolved from a stable rural population to a Washington, DC suburb. More than 8%, an estimated 64 120 residents, live in poverty. The county has a diverse population: 65% of the population is African American and the foreign born population increased 90.8% from 1980 to 1990. Moreover, the health care needs of county residents as a whole are substantial. Health disparities exist in several areas. A recent report by the Prince George's County Health department revealed a high level of breast cancer, prostate cancer, diabetes, and high blood pressure among county residents. There is also a high rate of asthma among children. According to the County's Consolidated Plan, the top health care problem in the county is infant mortality, which has increased gradually in recent years and is significantly higher among African Americans compared with Caucasians.

The apartment complex in this study is an enclosed village-like community located in Lanham, Maryland adjacent to what has been a high crime area in the

Prince George's County. There is an estimated population of 1502 residents, 14.8% are children between 2 and 5 years old ($n = 222$). A single female headed the majority of the families in this community. The income characteristics indicate that 28.4% of the households earn less than $25 000.

16.3 The User Population

The participants in this study included 11 women and 1 man residing in the apartment complex, most of whom participated in the *Dinner and Health Discussion* seminars sponsored by the Nurse Managed Health Center. These seminars or workshops were held twice each month between 2003 and 2004. The purpose of the workshops was to increase the knowledge of residents of the apartment complex about their risk for developing various health problems and strategies to decrease their risk. A healthy meal was provided using the National Institutes of Health *Heart Healthy Cookbook* and information was provided about a variety of diseases and disorders, particularly the six priority areas for the United States Department of Health and Human Services: cancer, heart disease, diabetes, infant mortality, HIV and AIDS, and adult immunizations. At the end of one year, participants demonstrated increased knowledge about and interest in their health. In addition, small changes in health behavior were observed, including self-reports of more participation in exercise such as walking and nutritional changes resulting in weight loss.

Upon completion of the *Dinner and Health Discussion* workshops, an Exercise and Nutrition Program funded by Kaiser Permanente and the Consumer Health Foundation was implemented. This series of 6-week programs was designed to introduce residents to appropriate exercise techniques and nutritional information. Residents signed a consent form, completed several assessment instruments including endurance and balance, identified their goals and were expected to continue exercising at home at least one other day during the week. A resident advisory committee met regularly with staff to assist with process evaluation.

16.4 Background Research Literature on the Targeted User Population

This study sought to determine if computer-based health information could support a decision to adopt desired health behaviors among those residents who had participated in the previous health-related outreach programs at the apartment complex. Identifying strategies that support continuation of healthy lifestyles may contribute to the reduction in health disparities among this population and contribute to a subsequent reduction in overall health care costs. The innovative features of this study include the participation of community members in identifying and adapting online health information to support changes in health behaviors. Online health information and social support groups are becoming an important resource for women who want to better manage their own health and the health of their families. Fox and Fallows (2003) pointed out that the Internet could be a significant resource in the health education process. Research shows that of all Americans who go online, whites are more likely than African Americans to search for health-related information. Differences in education levels largely explain why some people are more likely than others to look for health care information online. Those with higher educational levels are more likely to seek online heath information than the less educated (Fox and Fallows, 2003). In addition, Americans living in households with less than $30 000 annual income are less likely to be online and, when they go online, are less likely to search for health information than those with higher incomes. Further, the Fox and Fallows (2003) study shows that lower levels of exposure to health-related information and lack of computer literacy skills limits the ability of low-income members of marginalized groups to understand and make use of online health information.

In addition to online health information resources, online social support groups are changing the way individuals communicate and learn about health-related issues. Lamberg (1997) noted that health chat rooms and discussion groups were among the most widely visited sites on the Internet: 48% of those who sought health information online reported that the advice they found improved the way they cared for themselves and 55% said that having access to the Internet improved the way they obtained health information (Rainie and Packel, 2001). In a study by Turner *et al.* (2001), participants in illness-related online communities reported that they were able to develop a close match between their support needs and the needs of others, who often provided more support for them than their 'real world' friends and families. A key to the success of this study was the participation of community members in the review and evaluation of Internet health information sites. We were particularly interested in determining if online health information and social support activities adapted and designed by community members for their own community would affect the decisions to make healthier lifestyle choices and help sustain health-enhancing behavioral changes.

16.5 How this Project Helps the Targeted User Population

Little is known about the variables related to health decision-making among African Americans and other minorities despite the fact that disparities in health status among African Americans have been well documented. Elimination of health disparities has been the focus of Federal health policy for the past 30 years with minimal success. An appropriate next step is to identify strategies for decreasing health disparities and increasing the use of health-promoting lifestyles among African Americans. There is a need to identify cost-effective interventions that work.

Very little research exists about the effectiveness of online health informatics and support communities for low-income African-American women. Conversely, there is a great deal of research on the lack of culturally relevant information and social support on the Internet for low-income and marginalized groups. Current research on this disparity, often referred to as the Digital Divide, indicates that it is no longer so much an issue of access to the Internet, as it is an issue of technology fluency (the ability to find, understand, and use informational resources on the Internet). One solution that has been proposed to reduce the technology disparity is community designed and developed online information and social support systems. This project addresses disparities in both health and technology fluency. The community-based participatory approach is being implemented to develop online health information and determine its effectiveness in supporting changes in health behavior. The project will contribute to the knowledge base regarding the use of computers to disseminate health information and encourage behavior change.

Identification of the variables associated with decision-making for health-related behavior change may have a major impact on health care costs. Health care costs associated with cancer detected in the later stages, renal failure, and severe cardiovascular disease can be astronomical. The economic value of early detection and prevention are well documented. In addition to decreased health care costs, this project has the potential to improve the quality of life of African Americans and other minorities, improve the health of Americans, and expand the health-related uses of technology. It is anticipated that the model that will be developed through this project will be applicable to other groups with customization to address ethnic, racial, and geographic variables.

The Internet increasingly provides information about issues related to health and health care, especially for women who are often managing the health of their entire family. Forty-six percent of white households in the United States have Internet access, while the percentage of African-American households with Internet access is only 23%. This disparity in access is the result of a number of factors: lower average incomes and education rates, lower assets and savings, lower literacy rates, and fewer personal connections with others who know how to use computers (Warschauer, 2003).

In addition, the United States, the world leader in web site production, has significant content gaps in areas that affect low-income/marginalized communities. A study (Lazarus and Mora, 2000) of Internet content and diversity in the USA identified the primary problem for low-income communities as a total lack of practical and relevant online information that affects their daily lives. When desired information is available online, it is generally presented in ways that do not reflect the resources, education and income levels, cultural practices and heritages of underserved communities.

Research has shown that marginalized and low-income communities can use Internet communication tools and resources to pursue goals related to community-based initiatives. This is best accomplished when they are actively involved in defining their informational and social support needs and authoring and publishing informational resources for their own communities. In this project, technology serves as the focal point and organizing tool in creating social capital and support networks to strengthen community members' decisions to engage in behavioral changes related to their health. This project will lead to the creation of a community-based and designed health informatics Internet site with health-related information and online social support group opportunities where members may discuss their specific goals, barriers to reaching their goals, and possible solutions. Studies have shown that online health information and support groups can play an important role in helping people manage their health (Dimond, 1979; Bloom, 1982; Turner *et al.*, 2001; Maloney-Krichmar and Preece, 2005). The goals of the project include bringing health-related Internet resources to low-income African-American woman through the design and development of a culturally relevant web site and to share this model with others seeking to serve low-income and marginalized communities.

As the project unfolds, our evaluation strategy is to employ *empowerment evaluation*. As defined by the American Evaluation Association (2005) 'empowerment evaluation is the use of evaluation concepts, techniques, and findings to foster improvement and self-determination. It employs both qualitative and quantitative methodologies. Although it can be applied to individuals, organizations, communities, and societies or cultures, the focus is usually on programs. Empowerment evaluation has an unambiguous value orientation – it is designed to help people help themselves and improve their programs using a form of self-evaluation and reflection. Program participants – including clients – conduct their own evaluations; an outside evaluator often serves as a coach or additional facilitator depending on internal program capabilities.'

Three steps are involved. The first step is to establish a purpose and a timetable. The expected results of the project are articulated, and, based on the expected outcomes of the implemented project, specific activities required to achieve those outcomes are identified. The second step, taking stock, involves identifying and prioritizing the most significant program activities. Project staff members and participants are asked to rate how well the program is doing in each of those activities, typically on a 1 (low) to 10 (high) scale, and discuss the ratings. This helps to determine where the program stands, including strengths and weaknesses. The third step involves charting a course for the future. The group states goals and strategies to achieve their dreams. Goals help program staff members and participants determine where they want to go in the future with an explicit emphasis on program improvement. Strategies help them accomplish project goals. These efforts are monitored using credible documentation. The empowerment evaluator helps program staff members and participants identify the type of evidence required to document progress toward their goals. Evaluation becomes a part of the normal planning and management of the program, and serves as a means of institutionalizing and internalizing evaluation.

16.5.1 **The Study**

This project was developed to continue the health-related outreach activities of the Nurse Managed Health Center. Residents who had participated in previous outreach activities of the Health Center were contacted by phone and invited to a meeting with the researchers to learn about this study. Those who expressed interest in participating in the study met with two of the researchers at the Nurse Managed Health Center. Following introductions, a light meal was served family style and the study was explained. Participants asked questions to clarify their understanding of the study. When they indicated their understanding, each person signed a consent form. A schedule of meetings was developed and participants agreed to meet on the university's campus for the orientation session.

16.6 **The Computer, Email, and Web Fluency Scale**

During the orientation session, additional individuals who were unable to attend the first meeting attended. The study was explained again and consent forms were signed. Following dinner, the participants in the study completed a modified version of Bunz's computer–email–web (CEW) fluency scale (Bunz, 2004). Bunz developed the instrument to assess people's fluency with the computer, email, and the web while at the University of Kansas. It was her feeling that such an instrument was needed to fill the void that existed 'between previously developed computer literacy or experience scales and the ever faster development of Internet technology' (Bunz, 2004, p. 479). Using factor analysis, she was able to reduce 52 Internet fluency items to 21. These fell into four constructs: computer fluency, email fluency, web navigation, and web editing. The resulting CEW fluency scale was then tested for its reliability and validity by correlating it with other scales. Regression analysis revealed that the duration of Internet usage and level of expertise as defined by the Georgia Tech WWW survey were the strongest predictors of CEW fluency. Bunz concluded that her CEW fluency scale 'differs from the existing scales because it incorporates e-mail and Web items.' With her permission, we adapted her scale to fit our needs.

In our study, all of the participants except one are female. Two of the participants are under the age of 25. Two are between 26 and 35; seven are 36 to 55 years of age; and one is over 56. Responses to the CEW fluency scale instrument revealed that all but two of the participants own a computer; and, all but one said that they have access to a computer either at home, at work, or at the library. When asked how long they have been using the computer, seven of the participants indicated one or more years, one responded one to five months, and four indicated 'not at all' or did not respond to the question. Of the eight respondents who said they use computers, six indicated that they are 'very' comfortable with the use of a computer and two responded that they are 'somewhat' or 'not too' comfortable. The most prominent reason for using a computer is for playing games, sending or receiving emails, and word processing.

When asked how familiar they were with using the Internet, all eight respondents who said they had used computers frequently indicated that they are able to surf the net and six indicated that they have accessed health information. Correspondingly, of those who are not familiar with the use of the Internet, none had been able to access web-based health information.

A final set of questions on the CEW asked where the participants obtained their health-related information. Talking with family members or friends ranked first on the list, with 92% of the participants indicating that they did this 'often;' magazines, news-papers, or newsletters ranked second (83% checked 'often'). A little over half of the group said they often talk with a doctor, nurse, or pharmacist. And last on the list was the Internet, with only 42% indicating that they tapped into this information source often (two said 'not too often' and four 'not at all'). Other sources of information mentioned were medical books and pamphlets, nutritionists, and health care providers.

Following the administration of the CEW, participants were assigned computers and provided with the evaluation instrument (adapted from WebMac Junior by Arnone and Small, 1999) to be used for each Internet site. An evaluation instrument (see Appendix A) was reviewed and participants who were not comfortable using a computer were paired with those who were. As the group evaluated the first health-related web site, the research team circulated in the room to assist with questions and navigation of the site. Following exploration of the site the group was reconvened to discuss their evaluations and impressions of the site.

The first web site the group evaluated was the American Heart Association Delicious Decisions web site (Figure 16.2.) Three-quarters of that group found the web site simple, clear, and understandable. Most found that it was easy to locate the

Figure 16.2 *Delicious Decisions web site. www.deliciousdecisions.org*

information they needed and that there were links to other sites when needed. Half of the group said that they learned something new while exploring this site. A little over a third of the group indicated that the lettering was too small. When asked for comments, one respondent said that 'eating a well balanced diet with plenty (of) fruits and vegetables is just the beginning to living a healthy life.' Another said that she learned that 'there are (different) types of diabetics' and that she could get more information by going to the American Diabetes Association web site. Still another observed 'you can never get enough information on health matters. I want and continue to need more information on heart failure, diabetes, asthma and losing weight.' All of the respondents felt that the web site would be very useful to others in their community. Table 16.1 summarizes their evaluations of the site.

A week later, in the second evaluation session, the group explored the American Diabetes Association web site. Several persons indicated while viewing the site that they learned the difference between Type I and Type II diabetes. Other group members said that they had not realized how important foot care was for diabetics until they read the information provided at the site. Several persons in the group are diabetic or have family members who are diabetic. One group member was going to print the material and give it to a friend. Another member commented that while he was not a diabetic himself, 'it helped me understand what they experience and have to go through.' The consensus was that this site 'provided lots of useful information.'

Table 16.1 *Summary of the evaluations of the American Heart Association's Delicious Decisions web site by per cent of responses (N = 8; scale of 0–3 with 0 lowest and 3 highest)*

Questions	0	1	2	3	NR
1. Were the directions for using this information site simple and clear?		12.5%	12.5%	75%	
2. Could you read and understand most of the words that were used?		12.5%	25%	62.5%	
3. Was it easy to find your way around the site without getting lost?		12.5%	25%	62.5%	
4. Did the pictures, sounds, or videos make the site more interesting?		12.5%	12.5%	62.5%	12.5%
5. Was it easy to find what you needed at this site?			25%	75%	
6. Did this site have links to other interesting or useful sites?			25%	75%	
7. Did all the parts of this site work the way they should?			25%	75%	
8. Were there any activities to do at this information site?	12.5%	25%		50%	12.5%
9. Did you lean anything new at this site?			50%	50%	
10. Would you be likely to use this information site again?			25%	75%	
	Yes	No			
11. Do you think this site would be useful to others who might be looking for similar information?	100%				

The group discussed the need to get the information about diabetes to the community. They observed that often doctors are too busy to educate patients about a specific problem or condition. Doctors, they said, give them pamphlets; but as one group member explained 'there is a difference between being informed and being educated' about a health problem. Group members noted that what they liked about having access to health information on the Internet was that it allowed them to move through the information at their own speed, get the information in several different ways (text, photos, diagrams, multimedia), and that they could go back over information when needed. The

Figure 16.3 Fun and Games section of the American Diabetes Association web site.
www.diabetes.org

group suggested that technical and medical terms should be hyperlinked to their definitions for the sake of clarity. Several persons found the 'Youth Zone' Fun and Games interaction section (Figure 16.3) enjoyable and informative. The group thought that an expansion of this section of the site to include more health-related games for kids, adults, and families would make the site more attractive to their community.

Over 50% of the group found the directions for using the site simple and clear. A majority (89%) could read and understand most of the words used on the site. 78%

Table 16.2 Summary of the evaluations of the American Diabetes Association web site by per cent of responses (N = 12; scale of 0–3 with 0 lowest and 3 highest)

Questions	0	1	2	3	NR
1. Were the directions for using this information site simple and clear?			44%	56%	
2. Could you read and understand most of the words that were used?			11%	89%	
3. Was it easy to find your way around the site without getting lost?		11%	11%	78%	
4. Did the pictures, sounds, or videos make the site more interesting?			22%	78%	
5. Was it easy to find what you needed at this site?			44%	56%	
6. Did this site have links to other interesting or useful sites?			22%	78%	
7. Did all the pats of this site work way they should?			22%	78%	
8. Were there any activities to do at this information site?	22%		22%	33%	22%
9. Did you lean anything new at this site?			22%	78%	
10. Would you be likely to use this information site again?			11%	89%	

	Yes	No
11. Do you think this site would be useful to others who might be looking for similar information?	100%	

of the participants learned something new at this site and 100% thought the site would be useful to others. Table 16.2 summarizes their evaluations of the site.

In the next evaluation session, the group was asked to locate and evaluate a number of other web sites such as www.healthfinder.gov, www.aarp.org/health, and *Bob's ACL WWWBoard*. Participants in the study were surprised by the amount of health information available online. After evaluating an online health support community for persons with knee injuries, one participant said: 'For any individual who had a knee injury the information gathering is great.' Another participant stated: 'I have a very long history of chronic knee pain and if this site can get me information to help me better understand, I definitely would use it again.' Another individual wrote in at the end of the evaluation form for the American Heart Association web site: '. . . this is indeed new for me and not only do I find this to be of benefit and a blessing . . . so too the American Heart Association Learn and Live – I give a tremendous heartfelt appreciation.'

In each session, we found that once participants had finished the evaluation of the assigned web sites, they surfed the Internet for other sites. They completed evaluations on these sites as well. A record of all group discussion was taken and a written summary provided to the participants at subsequent sessions. Researchers asked the participants for corrections to the discussion summary and if they felt that their discussion was accurately reflected in the written summary. In addition, the web site evaluation forms completed by participants on each of the web sites they viewed were collected. This additional data will be analyzed and presented in the study's final report.

We are now at the midpoint in the pilot study and several themes have already emerged. Trust between the researchers and the community is critical to the successful implementation of this project. The prevalence of computers at home contributed to the computer literacy skills of many of the study's participants. Participants in the study expressed that they believe that, for their community, access to computers and the Internet is far more important than making online health information 'more culturally relevant.' The research team continues to adapt the original research plan to adjust to the specific characteristics of the participants and to their suggestion, comments, and recommendations.

16.7 Lessons Learned

An unanticipated finding of this study concerned the levels of computer literacy that existed within the study's participants. Based upon current research on the digital divide and computer literacy, we had anticipated that we would have to spend a great deal of time developing the computer and Internet navigation skills of the participants. However, we actually had to spend very little time on this aspect of the project. Ten of the 12 participants had computers at home. Eight of the participants indicated that they were capable of surfing the Internet and six of the eight said they were able to access health-related sites and navigate them with relative ease. Six of the participants, however, indicated that accessing health information was not easy because they were not sure how to find it on the Internet, but when teamed up with others with more experience, they were able to do so. By the middle of the study, everyone could log on and find an Internet site with ease. In the discussions that followed each evaluation session participants who did not have computers or Internet access at home indicated that they had a general idea about the Internet because they have been exposed to it at the homes of friends and relatives or that their children had access school. Therefore, there was a basic familiarity with the Internet even among those who did not have any or much experience using it. When these persons teamed up with participants who had greater experience searching the Internet, they quickly learned how to search and find health-related sites.

Another surprise for the research team was that in spite of the emphasis in the literature on the digital divide and the need for culturally relevant Internet information for minorities (Warschauer, 2003; van Dijk, 2005), participants in this study at no time indicated that culturally relevant information was a major issue for them. There are a number of health sites that target African Americans, such as BlackWomensHealth (www.blackwomenshealth.com) and African American Health Collation (www.aahc-portland.org). These sites have photos of African Americans and address health needs of the target audience. However, the participants in this study expressed the opinion that health-related information would not have to be adapted or presented in a particular way to meet the needs of their community. This may have been related to the fact that the Federal government or national health associations sponsored the majority of sites evaluated by this group.

However, we did find that it is important, when seeking to apply technological solutions to needs of minority communities, to attend to issues related to *technology within the context of community*; the cultural and social environment of the target group (Pinkett, 2000). Our preliminary findings agree with those of Shaw (1995), Hooper (1998), and Pinkett (2000) that note how a community makes use of technology and the level of engagement is significantly influenced by the culture and social setting in which the technology is introduced and used. A major strength of this project, which was culturally relevant, was the scheduling of discussions about Internet health sites and self-reports of exercise, diet, and weight loss during family style meals at the beginning of each meeting and coming back together at the end of each evaluation session to discuss their findings. These are examples of ways to embed technological solutions within the context of community where social and cultural considerations were taken into account within the framework of the project.

Participants reported that the major issue in their community is **access** to computers and the Internet. In the United States there has been a great deal of effort to provide Internet access through the Schools and Libraries Universal Service support mechanism established in the Telecommunications Act of 1996. The express purpose of this act was to provide affordable access to telecommunications services for all eligible schools and libraries, particularly those in rural and economically disadvantaged areas. According to Bertot and McClure (2002), as of June 2002, 98.7% of public libraries in the United States had at least one Internet connection and 95.3% provided free Internet access to patrons. However, the participants in our study indicated that it is not always possible to use the public libraries because you might have to wait for a computer and your time on the computer is limited. Many of the participants in the study do not own a car and depend on public transportation or friends. In addition, the majority of the participants in the study work and have family commitments, making it difficulty to get to the library during operating hours to gain access to the Internet. The participants in the study indicated that making computers and Internet access available to a larger number of community members, preferably in their homes, would have a major impact on their ability to access and use online health information. One of the things they said was that having a computer and Internet access in their homes permitted them to take as long as necessary to review and understand the online information.

The researchers observed that the diagnoses of specific health problems among the participants and their families were strong motivators for seeking information. Those who were diagnosed with diabetes or had a family member with diabetes were particularly interested in the *American Diabetes Association* site and spent considerable time reading and discussing the information they found.

This pilot study demonstrates the importance of trust in conducting a study of this nature. The prior history of the Department of Nursing with the community involved was a key factor in being able to move so quickly with the pilot study. The fact that one of the researchers had been involved with them in previous community health-related programs made it easier for the research team to implement the community-based participatory research model since there was an established track record of genuine interest in their community and one member of the research team was recognized as an authentic voice in the community. Community members do not want persons from outside the community coming in and providing capacity-building programs top down. Many of these programs end when the funding runs out and the benefits to the community are small. The research team made it clear that community members who participated in the study were, in effect, co-researchers. They received a stipend for participating in the evaluation and web site development sessions. They will serve as trainers and facilitators in the next phase of the study in which other nearby communities will be recruited to join in the project.

The goals of the study were important to the community and answered real community needs. This study is a natural extension of the involvement of the university in maintaining the community health center and its outreach programs. In addition, several participants in the study were leaders of the tenants association and had participated in previous health-related programs. One of the activities of the Health

Center had been to survey the community to assess health needs; the community-based participatory design model requires that researchers continuously adjust the study to adapt to the characteristics, suggestions, and recommendations of the participants. This is critical to the development of trust and the commitment of the participants to the project as a whole. Participants were willing to invest their time and money to drive (30 minutes) to the university for evening sessions to evaluate online health-related informational sites. The interest level remained high throughout the first half of the study because, in part, they felt that they were co-researchers working for the betterment of their community. This is a powerful model for community development.

16.8 Implications for Designers

The primary lesson that this study provides for designers is that the target population must be involved in the design process. The use of community-based participatory design models is critical to the success of a project. Our experience with this group did not reflect the current research in the field on the difficulty that minority populations encounter because of a lack of culturally relevant material on the Internet. We had to adjust the study's design to adapt to this discovery. For example, a community web site is being developed that will contain links to online health-related sites that participants indicated are useful. After discussing the format for the information page, we decided to list online sites (with their links) that community members thought were most useful with reviews and comments from participants in the study. Participants felt that with this type of recommender system on the front end of the health information page, they could explain what will be found on the site, point others in the direction of the most useful portion of the site, and include helpful comments and suggestions for making use of the information. In addition, the major suggestion for improvement of health-related web sites was that they should contain a list of medical terms and their definitions or, better yet, medical and technical terms should be hyperlinked to their definitions.

16.9 Implications for Users

Within the context of our study, we feel that members of minority communities should insist on being part of capacity-building projects because research has shown that sustainability is dependent on the social and culture environment within the community. Community members need to guide the implementation of technological solutions to meet needs identified by the community. Preliminary findings of our study show the value of having community members to teach and assist each other in learning how to use the computer to search the Internet and to evaluate online health information sites. Users can find resources within their own communities to build capacity. In addition, we found that through careful evaluation of online sites, users can gain a better understanding of how to develop community-based online information and support to inform their decisions to adapt health lifestyles.

16.10 Implications for Researchers

Because community-based participatory research requires the inclusion of participants from the inception of the project, participants in this study were involved in all decision-making after the consent forms were signed. Researchers shared the findings from the assessment instruments and requested feedback and verification of findings. Convening the group to discuss their evaluation of web sites with researchers proved to be a valuable experience for the participants and researchers. Participants were able to discuss their observations and reflect on their experiences with the health care system. Researchers were able to learn how the participants used the Internet and gained insight as to how to tailor the evaluation instruments. Researchers can benefit from recognizing and valuing the contributions of participants and recognizing the need to be flexible in implementing their projects.

In addition, we gained valuable information during the discussion sessions related to the study's design and implementation that served to strengthen triangulation of data. We also found that the participatory design model engendered strong commitment to the study and a desire to attend each group session and complete evaluations of Internet health-related sites.

16.11 Implications for Policymakers

Preliminary findings from this study indicate a need for policymakers to increase access to the Internet for all individuals. Libraries should receive funding to increase the number of computers and extend the time available to search the Internet. Programs to assist low-income individuals to purchase computers and obtain Internet access should be considered. The Internet may be a valuable vehicle for providing access to health information for minority and underserved individuals. When individuals have access to health information that they can process in their own time with additional information available to clarify their questions, there may be a change in health behavior. We certainly found that the participants of this study expressed that one of the most empowering aspects of the project was their new-found ability to locate, use, and share online health information. Those individuals who prefer a support group can find one and those who prefer to work alone can do so.

16.12 **Conclusion**

Our research team discovered the importance of keeping an open mind about the needs of a specific community and to use a research model that allows for flexibility and adaptation as the project progresses. In the second part of our pilot study (January–June 2006), participants will be given a laptop computer and Internet connection in their homes. Their activity on the Internet will be monitored and they will continue to evaluate online health-related sites with the goal of creating an online health support resource for their community (June–August 2006). The research team will refine the community-based participatory model for this specific group. Our study suggests that minority communities can benefit from Internet health-related information and support and that access is a critical need in these communities.

Appendix A

Health Information Evaluation Adapted from WebMac Junior (Arnone and Small, 1999)

A.1 **Instructions**

As a Health Information Evaluator, you are being asked to check out various health information web sites for clues on whether or not a selected site is interesting and/or useful. A good health information site will have information you can use. You should also look for clues as to who wrote the information, how easy it is to understand, and whether it points out other places to go for additional information. There are no right or wrong answers to the questions that follow. It is up to you as to whether you find the information helpful or useful.

       0   1   2   3

    If you circle the sad face, it means that this information site is really poor. It didn't provide you with anything of interest. So you give it your lowest score, which is zero points. If you circle the face with no expression, it means that this information site is OK but there's nothing special that interests you and you give it one point. If you circle the face with a small smile, it means that this information site is not the best but it is helpful so you give it two points. If you circle the face with a big smile, it means that this information site is excellent – definitely one of the best information sites you have seen and you give it three points, the highest score.

So here we go. Please turn to page 2.

Health Information Questions

Name(s) of Evaluator(s): _____

Name of the Site being Evaluated: _____

1. Were the directions for using this information site simple and clear?

0   1   2   3

Comments:

2.   Could you read and understand most of the words that were used?

0   1   2   3

Comments:

3. Was it easy to find your way around the site without getting lost?

0   1   2   3

Comments:

4. Did the pictures, sounds, or videos make the site more interesting?

0   1   2   3

Comments:

5. Was it easy to find what you needed at this site?

Comments:

6. Did this site have links to other interesting or useful sites?

Comments:

7. Did all the parts of this site work the way they should?

Comments:

8. Were there any activities to do at this information site?

Comments:

9. Did you learn anything new at this site?

Comments:

10. Would you be likely to use this information site again?
    Comments:

    0   1   2   3

11. Do you think this site would be useful to others who might be looking for simi-
    lar information?

    ___ Yes ___ No

If you answered 'no' to this last question, please explain why.

    If you care to add any comments to the previous questions or about your answers, please do so here.

Thank you for helping us evaluate health information sites.

References

AHRQ (2001) Report on the Outcomes of Outcomes and Effectiveness Research: Impacts and Lessons from the First Decade. AHRQ Publication No. 01-R027, January 2001. *Agency for Healthcare Research and Quality,* Rockville, MD. Available at: `http://www.ahrq.gov/research/htm`.

AHRQ (2002) Research to Reduce Cost and Improve the Quality of Health Care. AHRQ Publication No. 02-P024, April 2002. *Agency for Healthcare Research and Quality,* Rockville, MD. Available at: `http://www.ahrq.gov/research/costqual.htm`.

Arnone, M.P. and Small, R.V. (1999) *WWW Motivational Mining: Finding Treasures for Teaching Evaluation Skills,* Linworth Publishing, Worthington, Ohio.

Bertot, J.C. and McClure, C.R. (2002) Public Libraries and the Internet 2002: Internet Connectivity and Networked Services. *Information Use Management and Policy*

Institute, Tallahassee, FL. Available at: `http://www.ii.fsu.edu/publications/2002.plinternet.study.pdf`.

Bloom, J. (1982) Social support, accommodation to stress and adjustment to breast cancer. *Social Science and Medicine,* **16**, 13290–1338.

Bunz, U. (2004) The computer-email-web (CEW) fluency scale development and validation. *International Journal of Human Computer Interaction,* **17**(4), 477–504.

Coffield, A.B., Maciosek M.V., McGinnis J.M. et al. (2001) Priorities among recommended clinical preventive services. *American Journal of Preventive Medicine,* **21**(1), 1–9.

Dimond, M. (1979) Social support and adaptation to chronic illness: the case of maintenance hemodialysis. *Research in Nursing Health,* **2**, 101–108.

Fox, S. and Fallows, D. (2003) *Internet Health Resources: Health searches and email have become more commonplace, but there is room for improvement in searches and overall.* Pew Internet & American Life Project. `www.pewinternet.org`.

Gallant, J.E., McAvinue, S.M. and Moore, R.D. (1995) The impact of prophylaxis on outcome and resource utilization in Pneumocystis carinii pneumonia. *Chest,* **107**(4), 1018–1023.

Hooper, P. (1998) *They have their own thoughts: children's learning of computational ideas from cultural constructionist perspective.* Unpublished PhD Dissertation, MIT Media Laboratory, Cambridge, MA.

Lamberg, L. (1997) Computers enter mainstream psychiatry. *Journal of the American Medical Association,* **278**, 799–801.

Lazarus, W. and Mora, F. (2000) *Online content for low-income and underserved Americans: the digital divide's new frontier.* Children's Partnership, Santa Monica, CA.

Maloney-Krichmar, D. and Preece, J. (2005) A multilevel analysis of sociability, usability and community dynamics in an online health community. *Transactions on Computer Human Interaction* (Special Issue on Social Issues and HCI).

National Institutes of Health (NIH) (2000) *Trans-NIH intiative: Addressing health disparities, definition of health disparities.* Available at: `http://www.niaid.nih.gov/director/slide7.htm`.

Peterson, E.D., Shaw, L.K., DeLong, E.R. et al. (1997) Racial variation in the use of coronary-revascularization procedures. Are the differences real? Do they matter?. *New England Journal of Medicine,* **336**(7), 480–486.

Pinkett, R. (2000) Bridging the Digital Divide: Sociocultural constructionism and an asset-based approach to community technology and community building. *Paper presented at the 81st Annual Meeting of the American education Research Association (ERA),* New Orleans, LA, April, 24–28.

Rainie, L. and Packel, D. (2001) More Online, Doing More: 16 million newcomers gain Internet access in the last half of 2000 as women, minorities, and families with modest incomes continue to surge online. *Pew Internet & American Life Project.* www.pewinternet.org.

Shaw, A. (1995) *Social constructionism and the inner city: designing environments for social development and urban renewal.* Unpublished PhD Dissertation, MIT Media Laboratory, Cambridge, MA.

Smedley, B.D., Stith, A.Y. and Nelson, A.R. (2002) *Unequal treatment confronting racial and ethnic disparities in health care.* National Academies Press, Washington, DC.

The Henry and Kaiser Family Foundation (1999) *The faces of Medicare - Minority Americans.* Menlo Park, CA.

Thomas, S.B. (2001) The color line: race matters in the elimination of health disparities. *American Journal of Public Health,* **91,** 1047–1048.

Turner, J., Grube, J. and Meyers, J. (2001) Developing an optimal match within online communities: an exploration of CMC support communities and traditional support. *Journal of Communication,* **51(2),** 231–251.

United States Department of Health and Human Services (USDHHS) (1979) Healthy People: The Surgeon General's Report on Health Promotion and Disease Prevention.

United States Department of Health and Human Services (USDHHS) (1980) Promoting Health/Preventing Disease: Objectives for the Nation.

United States Department of Health and Human Services (USDHHS) (1986) Report of the Secretary's Task Force on Black and Minority Health.

United States Department of Health and Human Services (USDHHS) (1990) Healthy People 2000: National Health Promotion and Disease Prevention Objectives.

United States Department of Health and Human Services (USDHHS) (1999) Race and health: Diabetes: How to reach the goals. Available at: http://www.raceamd-jea;tj.omhrc.gov/3rdpgBlue/Diabetes/3pgGoalsDiabetes.htm.

United States Department of Health and Human Services (USDHHS) (2000) Healthy people 2010 healthy people in healthy communities. Information Sheet.

United States Department of Health and Human Services (USDHHS) (2001a) Healthy people 2000 fact sheet. Available at: `http://www.hhs.gov/news/press/2001pres/011sminorityhealth.html`.

United States Department of Health and Human Services (USDHHS) (2001b) Healthy people 2010 healthy people in healthy communities. Information Sheet.

van Dijk, J.A.G.M. (2005) *The Deepening Divide: Inequality in the Information Society*. Sage Publications, Thousand Oaks, CA.

Warschauer, M. (2003) *Technology and Social Inclusions: Rethinking the Digital Divide*. MIT Press, Cambridge, MA.

Wisconsin Department of Health and Family Services (2001) *Eliminating health disparities*. Madison, WI.

Evaluating the Usability and Accessibility of an Online Form for Census Data Collection

Elizabeth D. Murphy, Lawrence A. Malakhoff, and David A. Coon

US Census Bureau, Washington, DC 22033-9100, USA

Summary

Through design and evaluation activities, the Census Internet form has been evolving toward a user-interface design for potential use in the 2010 Census of population and housing. This chapter examines several key design challenges presented by offering an online option within a national data-collection effort. It illustrates ways in which user interfaces to online surveys can pose usability and accessibility obstacles to users despite designers' best intentions; and it uses examples from two rounds of usability and accessibility testing to show that at least some of these obstacles can be overcome by design.

17.1 Introduction

Some online surveys ask about personal opinions, attitudes, or intentions to purchase products. Such surveys are often sponsored by corporations or other nongovernmental organizations. Such surveys are not the focus of this chapter. Here we are concerned with official, government-sponsored surveys, primarily surveys of population and housing. The online questionnaires used to collect this kind of survey data are typically based upon pre-existing paper questionnaires. The questions, instructions, and techniques for laying out the paper questionnaire have undergone thorough research and testing, often conducted over decades, with research findings fed into successive iterations of the questionnaire. Issues of usability and accessibility are being addressed as paper forms transition to the online environment. Making such online forms usable and accessible involves much more than simply coding the paper form for presentation on the World Wide Web.

In the interest of encouraging high response rates to paper forms, the US Census Bureau follows a rigorous process of questionnaire development and evaluation. This process is meant to ensure that all respondents will understand and readily be able to follow the content and layout of the paper questionnaire. All new surveys and all new questions to old surveys must go through cognitive pretesting to identify any difficulties potential respondents might have with the content of questions or instructions (US Census Bureau, 2003). In some cases, respondents are given the choice of providing their data on paper or online. For surveys with an electronic option, usability testing is strongly recommended but not required. Electronic forms developed by or for the Census Bureau must comply with Federal regulations for accessibility by persons with disabilities (US Access Board, 2000); therefore, testing for compliance with those regulations is required.

17.1.1 Overview of the Literature on Web-Based Surveys

Collecting data on the Internet may seem to be a fairly straightforward proposition, but it is fraught with pitfalls for the unwary (see e.g. Ramos *et al.*, 1998; Tedesco *et al.*, 1999; Couper, 2000; Dillman, 2000; Tourangeau *et al.*, 2000; Lazar and Preece, 2001; Solomon, 2001; Lozar Manfreda *et al.*, 2002; Schonlau *et al.*, 2002; Andrews *et al.*, 2003; Vu and Proctor, 2006). Major issues in web surveys include coverage and sampling error, which apply when a sample of the population of interest is selected for participation in the survey (Couper, 2000). Coverage error occurs when people are missing from the sampling frame, that is the list of members of the target population who can be identified to some extent before a probability-based sample is selected (Groves, 1989). In a probability-based sample, the chances of any one person or household being selected into the sample are known (Couper, 2000). Online sample surveys suffer from a lack of representativeness, that is some respondents are not members of the target population and some members of the sample do not respond. Since this chapter deals with online collection of census data, coverage and sampling issues are minimized because everyone who receives a paper questionnaire has the option of responding online. The target population for the Census is every person in the USA on Census Day, not a sample of persons. Of course, those who choose to respond online cannot be considered representative of the general population (Ramos *et al.*, 1998), but their data are merged with the data collected from others who return their paper forms.

A major motivation for offering an option to respond by means of the Internet is the potential for increasing survey participation (Contrino *et al.*, 2005). Research indicates, however, that offering a choice of mode sometimes increases overall response rates (e.g. Westat, 2002) and sometimes decreases response rates (e.g. Griffin *et al.*, 2001). The reasons for this effect are the subject of ongoing debate.

An issue of general concern in the design of web-based surveys is the target population's access to the Internet (Ramos *et al.*, 1998; Couper, 2000). A major concern is that survey results will be skewed because the Internet is available to some subset of the population. This issue is less of a concern for an online Census, again because responding online is optional. If someone really wants to respond online but does not have Internet access at home, the neighborhood library generally provides access. Alternatively, the person can complete and submit the paper form. Providing the online option meets the requirements of the Paperwork Reduction Act of 1995 (chapter 35 of title 44, United States Code).

Web-based technology offers design possibilities not available to designers of paper forms. For example, it is possible for the automation to evaluate respondents' answers and provide dynamic feedback in the form of error messages. In a census context, for example, dates of birth and ages can be checked for consistency; and messages can be displayed to the respondent when inconsistencies are found. Design issues include how to word such messages and how to present them. To be effective, such messages should indicate clearly what needs to be changed and how it needs to be changed. Error messages should not prevent the respondent from continuing with the form if they do not know the answer or have given their best answer. It must be remembered that what appears to be an 'error' from the perspective of the data-checking rules may be the respondent's best answer. For this reason, we prefer to refer to error messages as 'edit' messages. In no case should the word 'error' be used in presenting data-checking results to users.

The issue of communicating with non-native speakers of English arises both in the design of basic questionnaire content as well as in the design of edit messages. A risk is that non-native speakers, as compared with native speakers, may be more likely not to complete an online form because of problems understanding pop-up dialog boxes (Pyle and Giff, 2003). Edit messages are typically presented in pop-up dialog boxes. It is open to question whether non-native speakers who have problems interacting with an online census form will then go and fill out the paper form.

Designers of web-based surveys need to be concerned with the issue of measurement error, the difference between the truth and the answers given by respondents (Couper, 2000). Dynamic checking of data entries and presentation of edit messages is one approach to bringing the respondents' answers in line with truth. To foster a successful experience for everyone who attempts to provide census data online, the web-based questionnaire must be designed for ease of understanding and ease of completion; it must motivate respondents to provide their best answers, and it must 'reassure respondents regarding the confidentiality of their responses' (Couper, 2000, p. 475). Indeed, the confidentiality of their personal information is a key concern of respondents.

Of utmost importance in the census context is the need for the security and confidentiality of data that are protected by Federal law (Title 13, US Code). Web-based surveys conducted by government agencies carry the added burden of ensuring the security of the data not only after collection, but also during collection (General Services Administration, 2003). Authentication requirements present user-interface designers with the challenge of guiding users through the process as quickly and painlessly as possible. In the US census context, authentication involves automated matching of a unique numeric code for the housing unit (i.e. the code printed on the package mailed to that housing unit) with the number entered at the log-in screen. The authentication process raises several potential usability and accessibility obstacles for respondents, such as the need to locate a particular number on the paper form and then key it into data-entry fields in the online form. We examine the authentication process in detail later in this chapter.

Issues of usability and accessibility are gaining attention in the context of web-based surveys developed for the Census Bureau (e.g. Tedesco *et al.*, 1999; Norman *et al.*, 2000; Murphy *et al.*, 2001). For guidelines on developing usable and accessible web surveys, see Online Survey Design Guidelines at http://lap.umd.edu/survey_design/index.html. For a detailed bibliography of the literature on web surveys, see web SM (web Survey Methodology) at http://www.websm.org/. Many other resources on the design of official and unofficial web-based surveys are available on the Internet.

17.1.2 Target Population

As mentioned earlier, for the US Census of population and housing, which is conducted every 10 years, everyone residing within the United States on the designated Census Day is part of the target population. Census forms are mailed or otherwise distributed to every known housing unit in the country (i.e. every house, apartment, or mobile home). A resident over 15 who owns, rents, occupies, or is purchasing a housing unit is responsible for answering the Census questions for all persons in the household. Thus, Census respondents can be male or female, young or old, highly educated or barely literate, and so forth. They may be homeless. They may be persons with one or more disabilities.

In 2002, 18% of Americans reported having a disability, and 12% reported having a severe disability (Steinmetz, 2006). That is 50 million people across all age levels in the United States. The following information further describes the US population with disabilities (Steinmetz, 2006):

- About 7.9 million people age 15 and older had difficulty seeing the text in ordinary newspaper print, including 1.8 million who were unable to see.
- Some 7.8 million people age 15 and older had difficulty hearing a normal conversation, including 1 million who were unable to hear.
- About 14.3 million people age 15 and older had limitations in cognitive functioning or a mental or a disabling emotional condition, such as Alzheimer's disease, depression, or mental retardation.
- Of those ages 15 to 64, 36% with a severe disability used a computer and 29% used the Internet at home.

Target users with visual disabilities occupy a range from low vision to blindness, and they use a variety of assistive devices, ranging from magnification software to screen readers. They may have other disabilities as well, such as hearing loss, which makes it difficult for them to use a screen reader.

Target users with or without disabilities may be native speakers of English or native speakers of any other language; they may be native born or foreign born. They may be of any race and ethnicity. The broad diversity of the target population poses a tremendous challenge to designers of paper and online forms.

17.1.3 Improved Usability and Accessibility Through Testing

Usability testing and accessibility testing have become integral to the testing of a series of prototypes leading toward an eventual Census Internet form. Through testing with demographically diverse and visually challenged participants, researchers in the Census Bureau's usability laboratory have identified design 'features' that foster respondent error and frustration. These researchers have made many recommendations to improve usability (i.e. reduce error, improve efficiency, and increase user satisfaction); they have also provided numerous recommendations on improving accessibility for respondents with disabilities.

In the spirit of universal usability, testing of prototypes has included testing for visual clarity, readability, and navigability with a variety of screen resolutions, fonts, and font sizes (Murphy *et al.*, 2005a). We have tested with JavaScript enabled and disabled, as recommended by the Census Bureau's Information Technology (IT) Standard 20 (2002). In most cases, if a function did not work without JavaScript, the software contractor was required to provide an alternative with equal functionality, as mandated by the Federal regulations.

When possible, implemented recommendations have been retested to ensure that they actually correct the observed problems and to identify any new issues traceable to the changes. Automated tests for compliance with Federal accessibility regulations identify violations pertaining to all the disability categories covered by those regulations (visual, auditory, psychomotor, and cognitive). The specific regulations are documented in the Rehabilitation Act of 1973 as amended, Section 508, 29 United States Code 794d, and they can be examined at http://www.section508.gov. Later sections of the chapter deal with specific usability and accessibility issues.

17.1.4 Evolution of an Online Census Form

In 2000, for the first time, respondents had the option of filling out the paper census form or responding online. Over 65000 respondents were successful in providing their Census 2000 data over the Internet (Whitworth, 2001), but this represented a small percentage of total responses across all modes. The Internet mode was not advertised widely during Census 2000 because it was considered experimental. The Census 2000 Internet form was designed as a long, scrollable page that mimicked the paper form, for example, in layout and use of foreground and background colors. There was minimal use of JavaScript and no dynamic cross-checking of responses for inconsistencies.

In the 2003 National Census Test, 10% of responses were obtained by Internet from those who had a choice of paper or Internet (Brady *et al.*, 2004). In the 2005 National Census Test, the Internet response rate was slightly over 7% (Zajac *et al.*, 2006). The reasons for the low uptake of the Internet form are unknown; but speculation has suggested that security concerns are among them. Another hypothesis is that people form an intention to respond online but then forget to do so and lose track of their paper forms in piles of other mail that they have set aside.

Since Census 2000, the Census Internet form has evolved in several design dimensions, and it continues to evolve toward the version that may be used in the 2010 Census. This chapter looks back over the series of usability and accessibility tests that contributed to this evolution. After discussing obstacles to usability and accessibility, the remainder of the chapter focuses on several key design challenges of the Census Internet form and illustrates ways in which user interfaces to online surveys can seem inscrutable to users despite designers' best intentions. Eliminating such obstacles to usability and accessibility is a continuing design goal.

17.2 Obstacles to Usability and Accessibility

When user-interface design raises obstacles to usability and accessibility, users often respond by becoming frustrated. Other researchers who have investigated frustration with computers have defined frustration as the user's emotional response to being unable to meet their goals (e.g. Lazar *et al.*, 2006b). A frustrated user is likely to be an unsuccessful and dissatisfied user. Frustration with the authentication process, for example, is likely to cause a prospective respondent to quit trying to access the online form.

17.2.1 **Sources of Frustration**

In a survey or census context, the user's goal is to finish the questionnaire as quickly as possible and get back to his or her real work. Thus, frustration arises if progress through an online form seems slower than expected. Anything that slows forward progress can cause frustration, as well as related impacts on successful completion of the form and respondent satisfaction with the experience of using the online form. Since online surveys are often 'sold' to respondents as time savers, it becomes counterproductive if it takes longer to complete an online survey than it takes to complete a paper form.

Aside from the high incidence of frustration due to hardware problems, observations in the Census Bureau's Usability Laboratory indicate that frustration arises when software does not behave in the way users expect. Previous researchers have listed several specific causes of user frustration that can be traced to the user interface, for example unpredictable behavior, hard-to-find or missing features, inscrutable error messages (Ceaparu *et al.*, 2004; Lazar *et al.*, 2006a); insufficient information provided to the user (Preece *et al.*, 2002); confusing menus (Bessiere *et al.*, 2004); and deceptive use of standard interface controls (Lazar *et al.*, 2003). Most, if not all, of these design flaws have negative effects on user success and satisfaction. Such design flaws may disproportionately affect the ability of respondents with disabilities to access and complete the online form.

For users with visual impairments, frustration results when they are unable to figure out why the design provides particular input elements or how to interact with the input elements provided (Thatcher, 2003). Input elements may include pushbuttons, image buttons, text-entry fields, radio buttons, check boxes, drop-down boxes, and menus. Under Federal accessibility regulations in the United States, all such elements must support the accessibility of electronic forms (Rehabilitation Act, as amended, Section 508, § 1194.22 (n)):

When electronic forms are designed to be completed online, the form shall allow people using assistive technology to access the information, field elements, and functionality required for completion and submission of the form, including all directions and cues.

Users who are unable to interact with input elements will have degraded accuracy and efficiency even if they report fairly high levels of satisfaction. Compliance with the formal regulations is meant to ensure accessibility, but it does not guarantee usability for persons with disabilities (Theofanos and Redish, 2003).

For example, in usability testing with a blind respondent who was an employee of the Census Bureau, it became clear that he had expectations for the design of forms that one of the early online Census form could not fulfill. He could not believe that the first question on the form was asking, 'How many persons were living in this house . . . ?' Based on his previous experience with online forms, he was sure that there had to be some preliminary questions asking for his name and address somewhere before the question about the number of residents. This gentleman relied completely on a screen reader as an assistive device, and he kept sending the screen reader back to the beginning of the form looking for data-entry fields for his name and address. Although he was advised that he could stop at any time, he chose to spend over an hour working with the prototype form. He never got beyond the first few questions even though the form had passed automated tests for compliance with the Federal accessibility regulations. By observation, however, this participant did not exhibit any signs of frustration. He was enormously patient and wanted to keep trying.

The form was technically accessible but unusable for this participant. Respondents who have similar disabilities need some way to verify that they are beginning in the right place. The consequence of not providing such a capability is the potential loss of these nonrespondents from the population count. It could be helpful for such users if a short introduction to the form and a summary of the questions were provided at the beginning of the form and read by the screen reader.

17.2.2 **Other Sources of Error, Inefficiency, and Dissatisfaction**

The negative effects of design flaws are well documented in the literature on computer–human interaction (e.g. Lewis and Norman, 1986; Mayhew, 1992; Hix and Hartson, 1993; Shneiderman, 1998; Shneiderman and Plaisant, 2005). A design that violates one or more usability principles is likely to generate user error, inefficiency, and dissatisfaction. For example, an inconsistently designed user interface will make it difficult for users to build up expectations about screen layout and the location of pushbuttons and other controls/input elements. A design that imposes heavy demands for remembering information from one screen to another will quickly overload the user's working memory capacity and lead to forgetting or misremembering. An insidious effect of such designs is that the blame is then placed on the user for committing 'human error,' when the error is really in the design.

17.3 Identifying and Resolving Usability and Accessibility Issues

The Census Bureau tests prototype Census Internet forms for usability and accessibility by persons with disabilities. The purpose of usability testing is to identify problems that actual respondents are likely to have as they attempt to access the site, complete the form with their household data, and submit the form. Actual respondents include all possible respondents, that is those with disabilities and those currently without disabilities. Usability-testing methods typically include collection of think-aloud protocols from demographically diverse test participants as each participant attempts to access, complete, and submit the prototype form. Thinking aloud entails providing a running commentary on one's thought process and expectations for system behavior. Participants are also asked to complete a tailored version of the Questionnaire for User Interaction Satisfaction (e.g. Chin *et al.*, 1988; Harper and Norman, 1993; for further information, see http://lap.umd. edu/QUIS/). Recent rounds of usability testing have included four individuals with some degree of visual impairment, including tunnel vision and blindness. One of the four also had auditory impairments, which made it difficult for him to hear the screen reader.

Accessibility testing methods used at the Census Bureau have included automated diagnosis of accessibility violations by InSight/InFocus (SSB Technologies, 2004) and reading of the pages with several versions of a popular screen reader, Job Access with Speech (JAWS) (Freedom Scientific, 2004). When violations are identified, an accessibility specialist checks the screens manually to verify the findings.

17.3.1 Evaluating and Enhancing the User's Experience

The respondent to an official online survey or census has four basic tasks to complete:

- Satisfy the authentication requirements.
- Provide data to complete the form.
- Resolve dynamically generated edit messages, if any.
- Submit the completed form.

In the prototype evaluations conducted thus far, usability and accessibility evaluations of successive iterations of the Census Internet form have identified obstacles to the completion of the first three tasks. The following sections provide an overview of the methods used in first-round testing to evaluate the most recent prototype applications, those developed for the 2005 National Census Test (NCT). All usability and accessibility testing at the Census Bureau is authorized by the US White House Office of Management and Budget (OMB).

Usability Testing Methods

Staff of the Census Bureau's Usability Laboratory used established methods for identifying obstacles to respondents' successful completion of the online data-collection form. Our methods are modeled on those recommended by Dumas and Redish (1999).

Recruiting participants

The recruiter screened prospective participants by phone using a standard set of questions on, for example, age, sex, race, education, and family composition. To be qualified, participants for usability testing were required to report a minimum of one year's experience using the Internet on a regular basis (three to four times per week). For the 2005 National Census Test, we recruited 22 sighted adult men and women from outside the Census Bureau. Outside participants received a small stipend to compensate them for travel expenses.

In addition to the 22 sighted participants, we recruited two visually impaired participants to help us evaluate software usability for persons with visual disabilities. A highly productive computer programmer, the female participant with no vision, was a regular user of screen-reading software; the other visually impaired, male participant was a low-vision user who typically enlarges his font to 14-point and uses yellow or white text on a black background. Both of these participants were Census employees and, therefore, did not receive any special compensation for their participation.

Facilities and equipment

First-round usability testing took place in the Census Bureau's Usability Laboratory, which includes three testing rooms and three observation and recording consoles (Figure 17.1). These consoles are located in a combined observation-and-control room adjacent to the testing rooms. Screen-reading software is installed on the computers in the testing rooms. As shown in Figure 17.1, one-way glass allows test administrators and observers to view the test participants. The test participant sits in one of the three testing rooms, facing the one-way glass and a wall-mounted camera, under a ceiling-mounted camera, and in front of a Liquid Crystal Display (LCD) monitor placed on a table at standard desktop height. Two microphones pick up sound in each testing room.

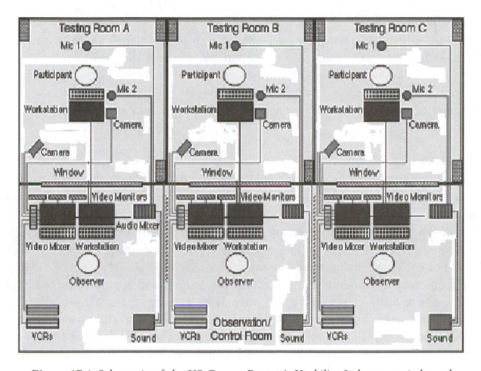

Figure 17.1 Schematic of the US Census Bureau's Usability Laboratory (adapted from Norman, 1998, figure 1).

The observation/control room has microphones and headsets for the test personnel as well as logging equipment and software, video cameras, scan converters, and digital recording equipment. This area has monitors at each console, which allow test administrators and observers a clear view of the participant's screen. The test administrator may sit in the observation/control room and communicate by speaker with the participant; or the test administrator may sit in the test room with the participant, as decided ahead of time by the test team.

Automated accessibility testing is conducted in an adjunct area, the Accessibility Laboratory, where the hardware for the automated testing tools occupies dedicated space. When we bring in test participants with disabilities from the local area, they come to the Usability Laboratory and assist us in evaluating software user interfaces using whatever assistive technologies they are used to. A screen reader is available, along with various tools for screen customization.

Materials

Video recording began when the participant had read and signed a standard consent form. Other materials included a questionnaire on computer and Internet experience, a general introduction to a testing session, a mailing package containing the paper form, and a tailored satisfaction questionnaire. The test administrator gave information orally and read the log-in code aloud for the participants with visual impairments.

User-interface prototypes

The online form tested in the first round consisted of a set of screens with the questions from the Census short form. The respondent was asked to supply information about the number of people in the household; contact information for the person filling out the form (Person 1); the name, sex, date of birth, and age for everyone in the household; as well as ethnic origin, race, and ancestry for each person in the household. For each participant, these questions were asked in one of two ways: a person-based manner or a topic-based manner. In the person-based approach, responses for all items (e.g. name, date of birth, sex, race) were collected for one household member (person), after which the same task was repeated for each successive household member. In the topic-based approach, the participant provided data for a given item (e.g. name) for all persons in the household, and then completed the same task for each successive item (e.g. date of birth, sex, race).

In testing prototypes of both the person-based application and the topic-based application for usability and accessibility, we found various issues from the respondent's perspective. In this chapter, we give examples mainly from the testing of the topic-based application. If there is an online form in the 2010 US Census, it is likely to be topic based because this approach allows respondents to use known answers to help them figure out less-well-known information. For example, we observed that remembering birth dates for members of a large household appears to be easier when the participant can work on all the birth dates at the same time, instead of having to retrieve each date separately as required by the person-based approach (Murphy *et al.*, 2005b). Many accessibility findings applied to both the topic-based and person-based versions of the application. Screen shots from the topic-based application are provided in later sections of the chapter.

Procedure

The test administrator greeted the participant and provided a general introduction to the session. All sighted participants and one with visual impairments came to the usability lab to help us test user interfaces. One participant with visual disabilities preferred that we come to his office because he has his equipment customized for his own needs. When we went to his office, we took a portable video camera to record the session.

Procedures for the visually impaired test participants were similar to those used for sighted participants, but they were tailored for the needs of those with visual disabilities. For participants with visual disabilities, we covered some steps verbally. For example, we asked the nonsighted participant where, in the mailing package, she would expect to find the URL for the site and where she would expect to find her Census Identification Number (CIN); but the test administrator supplied this information to her. The test administrator read the CIN aloud to facilitate the process of getting started on the form itself.

Automated Accessibility Testing Methods

Automated accessibility testing of both the person-based and the topic-based prototype applications took place in the Census Bureau's Accessibility Laboratory. Testing tools available in the Accessibility Laboratory included a screen reader and automated evaluation software. A report detailing the accessibility violations identified in first-round testing included recommendations for resolving the identified issues. At the direction of the design team, the contractor corrected all accessibility violations prior to the launch of the 2005 National Census Test in August of 2005.

Diagnosis of compliance with Federal Regulations

Conducted by an accessibility specialist, the automated testing evaluated the prototype Internet applications for compliance with the Section 508 regulations (paragraphs (a) through (p)). For example, this testing identified missing label elements for radio buttons, checkboxes, and entry fields. The testing software looked for tags wherever it found JavaScript. In addition to identifying any instances where color was used by itself to convey information, the software tool tested color combinations (foreground on background) for possible problems for colorblind/color-deficient users. It looked for any use of embedded tables for page layout. The software tool provided descriptive statistics on the accessibility violations it identified.

Some of the automated test findings needed to be checked manually to verify the following conditions:

- Hypertext Markup Language (HTML) tables used in both applications contained proper markup and complied with Section 508.
- HTML markup for all images had appropriate alternative text (ALT or Longdesc tags).

- Navigation tabs that were inactive in the early stages of form completion contained appropriate ALT text indicating that the tabs were disabled.
- HTML ALT tags accurately described the content of the images with which they were associated.

A manual verification was performed with JavaScript turned on and off (enabled/disabled) to ensure that each application could be navigated both with and without JavaScript enabled.

Testing with a screen reader

In testing the applications with a screen reader, the accessibility specialist listened to each version using JAWS, version 5.1, with the default settings enabled. He selected the instructions and question text for reading by using the up and down arrow keys. He tabbed to each field and listened for the label, then pressed and entered some data. He verified that the forward and backward tab order for text and data matched the visual presentation. The interaction between the screen reader and form controls was evaluated for accuracy, and inconsistencies were documented. This testing also verified that the screen reader properly vocalized each button control or label element.

17.3.2 **Selected Results and Recommendations**

The end-to-end process of accessing and completing the online Census form presented various usability issues to users with and without disabilities.

Authenticating the Housing Unit (logging on)

To ensure the security of their household data and to protect the confidentiality of their data, respondents were required to complete a housing-unit identification process before gaining access to the Census 2005 Internet form. This is comparable to a log-on requirement for a secure site. The authentication process presented a set of potentially frustrating obstacles to test participants: they had to find and enter a unique identifier, an 18-digit number that identified their housing unit (e.g. house, apartment, mobile home). This Census Identification Number (CIN) was printed on the back of the paper short form (i.e. the form mailed originally to the housing unit) underneath a bar code. Users with visual disabilities would have needed a special text-from-paper-reading device (e.g. a Kurzweil reader), a scanner hooked to a screen reader, and/or the help of a sighted person to find their CINs.

Figure 17.2 shows the screen for entering the 18-digit CIN in the 2005 National Census Test. Based on our experience with authentication issues in Census 2000 and

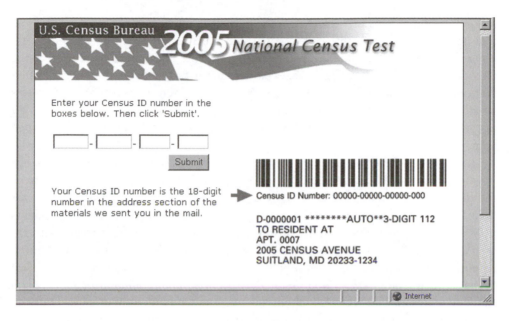

Figure 17.2 *Prototype screen for entry of the Census Identification Number (CIN) in the 2005 National Census Test: 18 digits grouped into four chunks; instructions on left integrated with graphic on right.*

later Census tests, the screen included a graphic on the right side. This graphic was intended to show participants where to find their CINs. However, once they saw the blank data-entry fields, many sighted participants tended to look away from the screen. They began looking through the paper form for their CINs and typically needed to be told where to look. Sighted participants also needed to be told which of the numbers was the CIN, because there were two long strings of numbers under the bar code on the paper form.

In a previous Census test, in which the CIN had been parsed into three data-entry fields, some test participants made the assumption that they were to enter their Social Security Number (e.g. xxx-xx-xxxx). The screen shown in Figure 17.2, however, parses the CIN into four data-entry fields instead of three. Thus, in testing with this screen, we did not anticipate that any test participants would assume that the form wanted their Social Security Number (SSN). Even so, a couple of participants thought it might be their Social Security Number, but they reasoned against this because there were four fields for digits and the SSN only needs three.

Since many sighted participants did not read the instructions about where to find their CIN, we moved the instructions from their original position above the bar code to the location shown in Figure 17.2. The participant with tunnel vision commented that he never looks at anything on the right side of the screen because he assumes that it is not important. We added a red arrow to direct the respondent's attention to the CIN. The screen shown in Figure 17.2 was used in the production version of the 2005 National Census Test. We have since retested it in a laboratory situation to assess whether it helps with the authentication (log-in) process. In the retesting, about half of the 18 able participants found their CINs, but the other half struggled and needed help.

Based on usability findings, many actual respondents, with or without disabilities, are likely to be unsuccessful in getting past the log-in procedure because of the difficulty of finding the CIN. This is likely to be a frustrating experience for them. The consequence of user frustration for an official survey is that respondents may decide not to fulfill their legal obligation to provide the data to the government. For the decennial Census, this lack of participation will lower the initial response rate and tend to decrease the quality of the data, on which many critical decisions are based (e.g. Congressional reapportionment, allocation of Federal funds to states and localities). Helping the user get past the authentication portion of the survey is a key design challenge that requires knowledge of user expectations as well as input from user testing. The authentication process may work as designed but still be inscrutable and frustrating to potential respondents, especially those with disabilities. As the authentication process is currently designed, many respondents with visual impairments will need a Kurzweil reader (Kurzweil Educational Systems, 2005) or the help of a sighted person to find their CINs on the back of the paper form.

The Census operation includes visits to households that do not respond by mail or Internet. Visits by Census workers add greatly to the cost of taking the Census. These costs could be reduced if it were easier for respondents to go online and provide their information. The cost of transferring data from paper to a digital format could also be reduced by widespread use of an online form. As discussed by Bias and Karat (2005), a modest investment in usable and accessible design can produce impressive returns in cost savings and efficiencies. To achieve these savings, barriers to access need to be removed for all respondents.

Problems in Completing the Online Form

As they made their way through the online form, test participants encountered design features that sometimes violated their expectations or did not provide enough information for them to feel confident in proceeding. Once they reached the submission page, all test participants succeeded in submitting their data.

Cognitive issues at the start

Once they had been given access to the form, participants were directed to start with the first question, which asks, 'How many people were living or staying in this house, apartment, or mobile home on September 15, 2005?' Some participants were confused by the 'Exclude' and 'Include' links on the form above the data-entry field for entering the number of people in the household (Figure 17.3). The content of these links is the set of residence rules that the Census Bureau wants respondents to use in deciding which persons to include in the household count. For those who clicked on these links, the residence rules presented some cognitive challenges. For example, the respondent must decide whether or not to count a college student who attends school away from home, but who is home on school vacations and over the summer. Along with other instructions and the questions themselves, these rules have been tested for comprehension in the Census Bureau's cognitive laboratory. According to a Census Bureau standard (2003), all new content material and major changes must be tested for comprehension. This standard recommends, but does not require, usability testing.

In usability testing, one participant, who grew up with computers, thought that clicking on the 'Exclude' or 'Include' link would cause the computer to take an action of excluding or including people. Like him, others did not recognize those as help links, but we think that was because they were not expecting a help link to be positioned there. If they did think these links were help, they were not sure how the help would function. Those who had read the residency instructions on the paper form recognized the 'exclude' and 'include' as referring to those lists of people. Others knew right away that they were help links.

The usability team recommended merging the two links into one and calling it 'More Guidelines (Help).' This change was suggested to give the respondent cues that clicking on this link would bring up a continuation of the guidelines started in the

---

Before you answer the first question, count the people living at your house, apartment, or mobile home using our guidelines.

- We want to count people where they usually live and sleep.
- For people with more than one place to live, this is the place where they sleep most of the time.

EXCLUDE these people   INCLUDE these people
We will count them at the other place.

Figure 17.3 *'Exclude' and 'Include' links preceding the question on number of people in the household.*

two bullet points. It would reinforce the inference that the two bullet points ARE guidelines and clarify what the respondent will get by clicking on the link. Including the word Help in parentheses verifies that it is information and that respondents should expect the link to behave as a help link usually behaves. Although the design team was supportive of this recommendation and tried to obtain approval from subject-matter stakeholders, time was too short. This design went into the 2005 National Census Test as shown. The wording and layout of this information will continue as open issues until we are able to conduct further testing.

Accessibility issues in navigation tabs

Below the banner on each screen, a set of navigation tabs allows the respondent to move to previously visited pages within the form. As shown in Figure 17.4, automated accessibility testing found that there was no skip link to bypass the tab navigation. The absence of such a link is a violation of Section 508. The screen reader attempted to pronounce 'Date of Birth' as one word. When the accessibility specialist examined

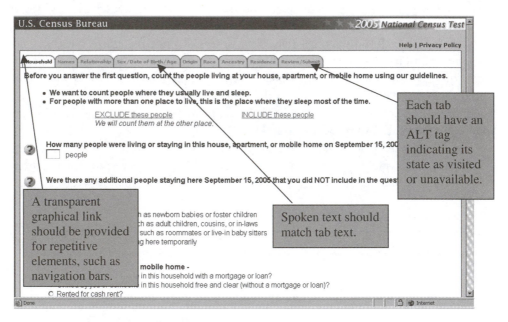

Figure 17.4 *Accessibility issues for navigation tabs: there was no skip link to allow the respondent to bypass tab navigation. The text spoken for the fourth tab, Sex/DateofBirth/Age, did not match the tab text and was not understandable. Visited and unavailable tabs did not have ALT tags indicating the state of the tabs.*

the source code, he found that the entry was keyed in as 'dateofbirth' without any spaces between the words. The accessibility specialist recommended placing a transparent graphical link in front of the Household tab and the insertion of spaces in 'dateofbirth' so that a screen reader would read it correctly. Both problems were corrected.

To comply with the Section-508 regulations, the visited navigation tabs must have ALT text indicating the state of the tabs, that is they are 'visited' tabs. Similarly, the unavailable navigation tabs must have ALT tags indicating the state of the tabs, that is they are 'unavailable' tabs. All issues were corrected.

Inaccessibility due to lack of explicit labels

Under paragraph (n) of Section 508, all form controls (radio buttons, check boxes, and text entry fields) must have an explicit label in the hypertext markup code. This means that the HTML label for a form control must be clearly associated with that control. As shown in Figure 17.5, the data-entry fields for each person's full name were inaccessible in the person-based application. The recommendation was to label those fields appropriately in the code so that the screen reader would read each label in association with the appropriate data-entry field. The same recommendation applied to the data-entry field for the number of people in Figure 17.4.

On other pages in the topic-based application, the same issue applied to the data-entry fields for other personal characteristics. For example, the date-of-birth and age

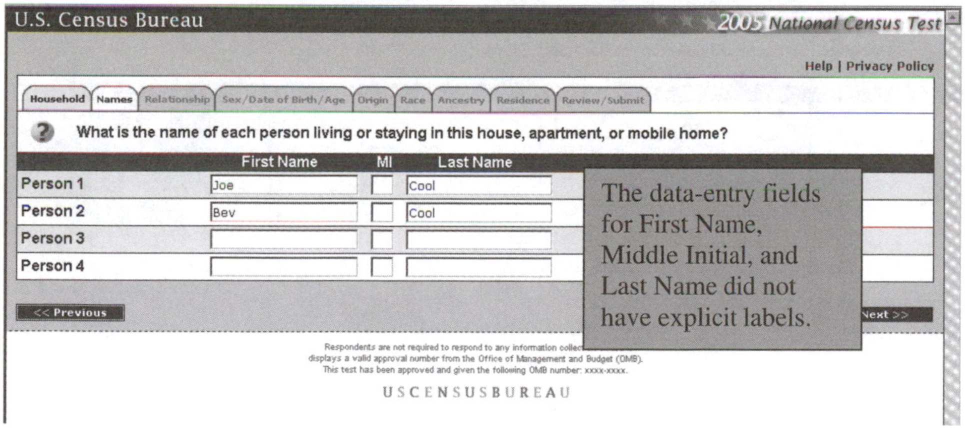

Figure 17.5 *Because labels for name fields are not associated with their corresponding data-entry fields, the screen reader cannot distinguish which field is for First Name versus Middle Initial (MI) versus Last Name (Section 508, paragraph (n) rule).*

fields were inaccessible because the labels were not associated with the data-entry fields. In usability testing, the user with no vision commented quite negatively on the labeling issue. Even so, this user was so careful that she never triggered an edit message. This user tested both the person-based and topic-based applications.

The recommendation was to associate each person's month of birth, day of birth, year of birth, and age with the corresponding data-entry fields. The same issue of labels not associated with data-entry fields was identified on the pages containing data-entry fields for ethnic origin, race, and ancestry. The identical issues were identified in the person-based application. This problem was corrected in all cases.

Mismatch in tab order

In the topic-based application, as shown in Figure 17.6, the visual order of the race link examples did not match the tab order. As the user tabbed through the checkbox table, the links for the examples were not read until after the last checkbox. To correct this, the example link should be read immediately after the name of each racial group.

In the person-based version of the race question (Figure 17.7), example links were read after each racial label, but the race checkboxes were not associated with explicit labels, as required by Section 508 (paragraph (n)).

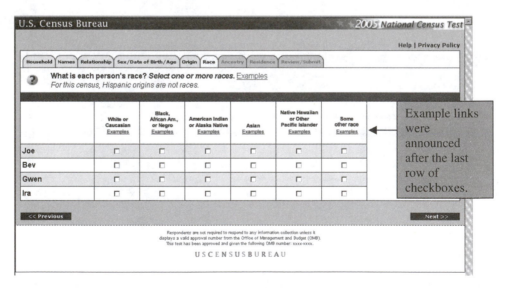

Figure 17.6 *In the topic-based application for the 2005 National Census Test, JAWS read the 'Examples' links for each racial category after announcing the last row of checkboxes.*

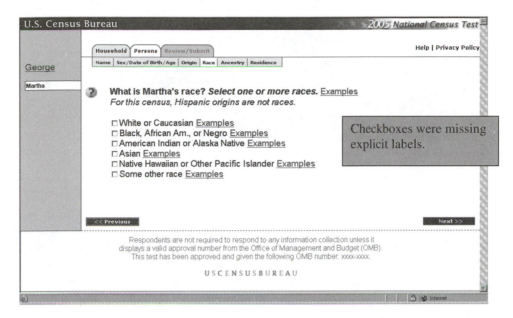

Figure 17.7 *The example links were read correctly in the person-based version of the Internet form for the 2005 National Census Test, but checkboxes did not have explicit labels.*

Further, a user without vision who tested the application discovered that the race category was being associated with the wrong column of checkboxes. After going back and forth several times on this screen, she discovered that the columns of checkboxes were associated with the wrong header category for race and corrected her entries. A similar user who was less experienced with online forms might have provided incorrect data for this question.

The development contractor made the recommended changes; and retesting after the explicit labels were included showed that navigation was less awkward for users of screen readers.

Missing alternative text (ALT tags)
The Federal regulations require an ALT tag to be associated with any graphic or image map (paragraph (a)). In both the opening screen and the confirmation screen (Figure 17.8), the banner and the seal were missing ALT tags. This issue was corrected in all cases.

The recommendation was to add descriptive ALT text for all images; and this recommendation was implemented.

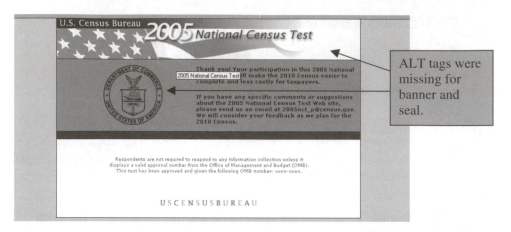

Figure 17.8 In both versions of the prototype form for the 2005 Internet option, the screen reader did not describe the seal of the Department of Commerce or the banner above the seal because of missing ALT tags.

Confusion induced by edit messages

Electronic technology affords designers the opportunity to introduce capabilities not possible with paper forms. For example, the computer can check a respondent's data, determine whether the data fall within valid ranges, and display an edit message if the data are out of range. Many other kinds of dynamic edit checks are possible. In Census 2000, it was decided not to perform any automated edit checking because of the relatively short time available for development and because using edit messages was fraught with accessibility and browser-compatibility issues. Census 2000 results showed that the quality of the data reported on the Internet form was no worse than the quality of the data reported on the paper form; and there were fewer questions left blank on the Internet form, even though there were no edits (Whitworth, 2001). In later prototyping efforts, for example, for the 2005 National Census Test, automated edit checking was prototyped and evaluated by user testing.

In the preliminary design for the 2004 Overseas Enumeration Test, users were given edit messages if fields were left blank or if the entered data did not pass an edit test on the first click of the Next button (a link to go to another screen). In exercising the site prior to usability testing, the test administrators found it difficult to browse screens that were not complete. It was necessary to click twice on the Next button to escape an edit message. Not knowing this, some test participants developed elaborate, circuitous methods to get past the edit messages, or they simply came to a stop and said they could not proceed. Thus, such edit messages became a source of frustration for test participants: They were not going to be able to complete the survey if they could not respond effectively to these edit messages.

In debriefings after the first round of 2004 testing, participants commented that they expect to have to correct the problems identified by edit messages before they can continue. Thus, their tendency to stop without trying to proceed was presumably based on prior experience. Usability testing has helped to reveal such user expectations so that screen designs can be revised to avoid violating them.

Members of the design team who observed the first round of 2004 usability-test sessions recognized the need to do something to overcome the obstacle presented by the edit messages. As shown in Figure 17.9, wording was added to encourage respondents to continue if they had given their best answer or did not know the answer. This solved the problem of test participants coming to a standstill, and this approach was used again in the edit messages composed for the 2005 National Census Test (e.g. Figure 17.10).

The screen reader read the edit messages in the same order in which they were displayed to sighted users. It did not matter what font or color was used. To the screen reader, the edit messages were just more text. If multiple edit messages were delivered, the screen reader read them one after another, placing a burden on the user's working memory. In contrast, a sighted user can deal with each message separately, then

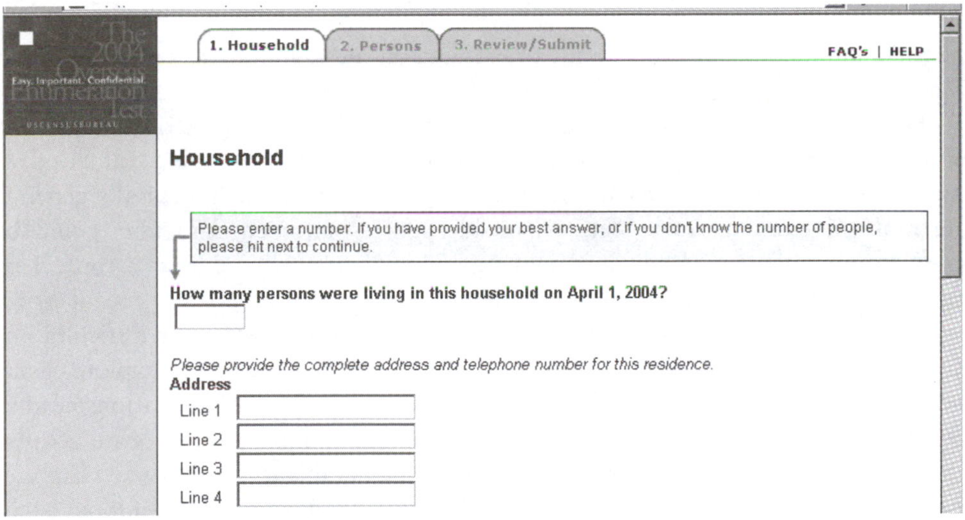

Figure 17.9 *For the 2004 Overseas Enumeration Test, wording of edit messages was revised to encourage respondents to continue if they had provided their best answer or did not know the answer.*

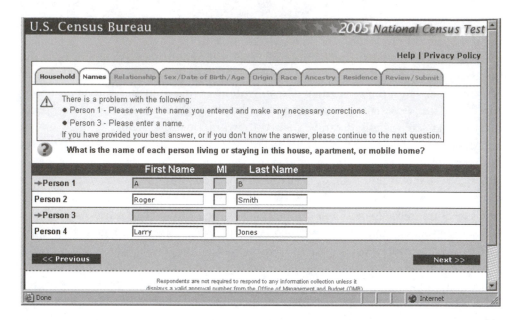

Figure 17.10 Edit messages in the Internet form for the 2005 National Census Test told respondents to continue even if they were not able to answer a question.

go back and read the next one. How to present edit messages to users without vision is an issue for investigation.

Up until the time of this writing, the prototype designs have used only server-side processing. In an edit-checking situation, with server-side processing, all the data entered on a particular screen are checked at the same time, thus potentially generating multiple edit messages. With client-side processing, each data item could be checked upon entry and edit messages generated if necessary, one at a time. This approach could also resolve many violations of the Federal accessibility regulations, which arose because of the exclusive server-side processing. Given the difficulties of the test participants with visual disabilities, the design team decided to explore client-side processing in future prototypes. However, potential security implications need to be addressed before adopting a client-side approach. Such implications arise because client-side processing would make the data more vulnerable to unauthorized capture.

Text of the edit message is displayed in dark blue on a pale salmon-colored background. Red arrows point to the persons for whom corrections are suggested. The affected data-entry fields are highlighted in a pale pink. These colors appear as shades of gray for the respondent with a color deficit.

Success in submitting the data

In our various iterations of the Census Internet form, test participants have rarely had any problem intentionally submitting their data. All versions of the form display a large, labeled button for submitting, and its function seems clear to test participants. What some participants have had trouble with is the unintentional submission of their data. This was a problem in the Census 2000 Internet form: when a test participant using Internet Explorer hit the Enter key out of habit, the data were submitted and the form cleared. This behavior did not occur in Netscape. In 2000, there were no User Agent Accessibility Guidelines (e.g. W3C, 2002) to instruct browser manufacturers in developing accessible form controls that would behave consistently across different browsers. The initial candidate recommendation for such standards was approved by the World Wide Web Consortium (W3C) in 2001.

Pressing the browser's Back button also submitted the data and cleared the form. The solution for the Census 2000 Internet form was to disable the Enter key and to tell respondents not to use their back buttons. The Federal regulations prohibit disabling browser controls, such as back buttons. Even when respondents are told not to use their back buttons, however, the force of habit often takes over. When a respondent loses his or her data upon hitting the back button, that person is not likely to want to re-enter everything from the beginning.

In prototyping the Internet form for the 2005 National Census Test, and in the actual test, respondents were told to use the 'Next' and 'Previous' buttons to navigate and not to use the 'Back' button. If JavaScript was turned on, the Enter key was trapped and nothing happened if the user pressed Enter. We plan to revisit the issues surrounding use of the Enter key in a later iteration of design, development, and testing. We think it may be possible to assign a different function to the Enter key (S. Ciochetto, personal communication, November 15, 2005). For the back-button issue, we need a better solution than an instruction not to use it.

17.4 Methods and Findings from Second-Round Usability and Accessibility Testing

While the 2005 NCT operation was in progress, we made use of the time back at the Census Bureau by evaluating several alternative design features in the usability and accessibility laboratories. Obtaining research data to inform future decision-making on design issues was the goal of this second round of usability testing. We also conducted appropriate accessibility testing to ensure the application complies with Section 508 requirements.

17.4.1 **Usability Testing Methods**

Two versions of the topic-based application were developed for this round of testing. Each version incorporated a set of design alternatives, which were to be assessed for observable effects on participants' success and satisfaction. Seventeen recruited participants and one new Census employee completed one or the other version of the online application. Participant testing took place in the Census Bureau's Usability Laboratory.

The following figures provide examples of design alternatives that we evaluated in this round of testing. The design that was in the production version, which was tested in the 2005 NCT, is provided in Figure 17.3. The next figure (Figure 17.11) shows one of the alternative designs that we tested in the second round. In this alternative, we placed the emphasis on counting, and we changed the link wording. We combined the 'Exclude' and 'Include' links into one link, which we labeled 'Additional Guidelines.'

On their first pass through the form, participants used their own household data to respond to the Census short-form questions, while thinking aloud. On their second pass, participants completed the form using scripted household data. The Test Administrator provided the data to the participants in the course of playing the role of a fictitious friend named 'Ethel,' who needed help in submitting her data online. Ethel's family included her husband, their six-month-old baby, her husband's college-age son from a previous marriage, her husband's mother, and a nanny. The college-age son was actually attending college but living at home.

This scenario we constructed for a complex household was designed to exercise options in the form that might not have been necessary for participants' own household situations. It was also designed to prod participants into using the online help functions. During the scenario-based portion of the testing, a dialog took place between the participant and the Ethel persona adopted by the Test Administrator.

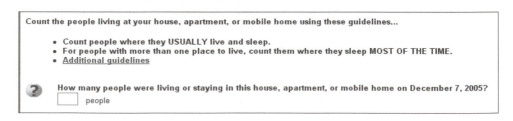

Count the people living at your house, apartment, or mobile home using these guidelines...

- **Count people where they USUALLY live and sleep.**
- **For people with more than one place to live, count them where they sleep MOST OF THE TIME.**
- **Additional guidelines**

How many people were living or staying in this house, apartment, or mobile home on December 7, 2005?
people

Figure 17.11 First alternative to providing the residence rules; compare with Figure 17.3.

User satisfaction ratings were collected at the end of each testing session, and a short debriefing followed.

Selected Observations from Second-Round Usability Testing

The two figures in this section represent alternative designs that we tested while the 2005 NCT production design was out in the field (Figures 17.10 and 17.11). Both of these figures show alternative approaches to presenting the residence rules, as compared with the approach used in the production version (Figure 17.2). In the first alternative, we placed the emphasis on counting and combined the 'Exclude' and 'Include' links into one link, labeled 'Additional Guidelines.' In the second alternative (Figure 17.11), the residence rules are presented in full on the screen; but the exclude and include wording has been replaced by wording that emphasizes counting.

In the group of participants who saw Figure 17.11, only one clicked on the 'Additional Guidelines' link when filling out her own data. When interviewing the Test Administrator for the scenario, two participants used the link to see how college students should be counted. One participant asked the Test Administrator/Ethel if she needed additional guidelines and clicked on the link when she said yes. Combining the 'Exclude' and 'Include' links into one link and changing the link label to 'Additional Guidelines' appeared to improve participants' understanding of what they would find behind the link.

A second alternative to displaying the residence rules appears in Figure 17.12. This version presented the detailed residence rules on the screen. Although some

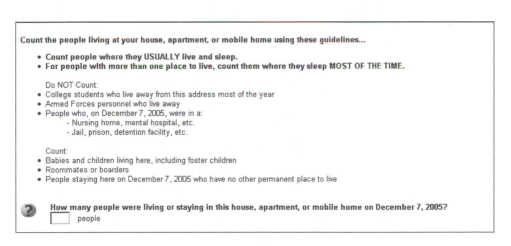

Figure 17.12 *Second alternative design for presenting the residence rules; compare with Figure 17.3.*

participants read or scanned through all of the detailed residence rules, a couple went straight to the first question without even reading the introductory sentence or even the first two bulleted guidelines. These actions are not totally unexpected because people are known to scan quickly or skip text when completing an online form (Nielsen, 1997).

A benefit of both alternative designs was that the question was now perceivable above the bottom edge of the viewing space (above the fold). In the production version, seeing the question required the user to scroll down because the residence rules occupied all the space on the screen.

This is just one example of the many alternative designs that we tested in this second round of usability testing.

Summary of Second-Round Usability Results

All participants completed the online form successfully, both for their own household and for the scenario-based household. Finding the Census ID number continued to be problematic for some participants, as it has been in all previous rounds of usability testing that have required participants to find and enter a housing unit identification number. We believe that many respondents will quit before they get into the form if the log-in process is not streamlined.

We found most participants reluctant to click on links for examples or other help. When they did click on help links, however, participants were better served by the revised, streamlined, context-sensitive help content, as compared with one, long, scrolling help page. Based on our observations, we are convinced that the long, scrolling help file is not particularly helpful to users in a self-administered mode. They are likely not to find what they are looking for. In the revised, more usable help, each topic opens in its own window, the content is presented in a more easily grasped outline format, and links to other topics remain stable (i.e. they do not scroll off the page).

Almost all participants had trouble deciding how to answer the question on race for a person from Argentina (the nanny) who was identified as Hispanic. We found an absolute higher number of errors when the detailed residence rules were displayed on the screen as opposed to being available behind a hyperlink.

Ratings for user satisfaction were extremely high, with just a few, scattered low ratings. General success and satisfaction indicate that this form has been tested and revised to the point where few usability problems remain; however, the occasional low ratings indicate there is some room for improvement. The biggest remaining problem is helping the respondent do what is necessary to access the form, that is to complete the authentication (log-in) process.

Summary of Second-Round Usability Recommendations

A major, high-priority recommendation is that the log-in process should be *designed* from start to finish. Respondents trying to access the Internet form have no way of knowing that they will need their Census ID number. Respondents do not know that they have a Census ID number, which is essentially hidden from view on the back of the paper form. A concern is that some people may discard their paper form without realizing that it has the number they need. The contents of the mailing package, including the letter from the Director of the Census Bureau, should call attention to the Internet address for the online Census form and the Census ID number, not leave these essential pieces of information in limbo. To avoid the user confusion observed in testing, finding the Census ID number and logging in need to be designed as an easy, logical process.

Other high-priority recommendations follow:

- Inform respondents about the residence rules that apply to them.
- Shorten edit messages so that the user gets the point immediately.
- When an edit message is displayed on the household screen, anchor the page where the message appears so that the user is not confused about returning to the same screen.
- Redesign help content and presentation to make the content easier to scan and more context specific.
- Allow the respondent to go back to the previous page without triggering edit messages for unanswered questions on the current page.
- To foster reading of the questions, use a more subdued separator between the question and the response options.

A medium-to-high-priority recommendation is to emphasize to respondents that they are permitted to continue even without resolving edit messages. The report includes other recommendations rated as low or medium in priority. If most of the usability recommendations are implemented and the form is retested, the resulting Internet form for Census data collection can be expected to serve its purpose well, assuming that security obstacles are overcome.

17.4.2 Methods and Findings from Second-Round Accessibility Testing

In the second round of accessibility testing, we used primarily automated methods with manual checking by the accessibility specialist. These methods identified several violations of the Federal accessibility regulations. We recommended changes to bring the code into compliance with the regulations.

Methods of Second-Round Accessibility Testing

Automated testing methods were used to check the prototypes for compliance with the Federal regulations. These were the same tools as used in the first round of testing, Insight/Infocus and the JAWS screen reader. For the purposes of this evaluation, an item was judged to be accessible (compliant with regulations) if its screen text was read aloud by the screen reader.

Selected Findings from Second-Round Accessibility Testing

Testing with the screen reader identified an accessibility issue with the design of the Next and Previous buttons in the online Census form. When the screen reader encountered the Next and Previous buttons, it also vocalized the characters used to symbolize left and right arrows. As shown in Figure 17.13, the word 'Previous' was preceded by two left-pointing arrows to indicate a backwards movement to sighted participants. Similarly, the word 'Next' was followed by two right-pointing arrows to indicate forward movement.

The screen reader read the left-pointing arrows as 'less than less than.' As a result, the label for the Previous button was read as, 'less than less than Previous.' The label for the Next button was read as 'Next greater than greater than.' The recommendation was to make images of these buttons and to define the ALT text for them as 'Previous' and 'Next.'

This is one example of the deviations found by the automated accessibility tools.

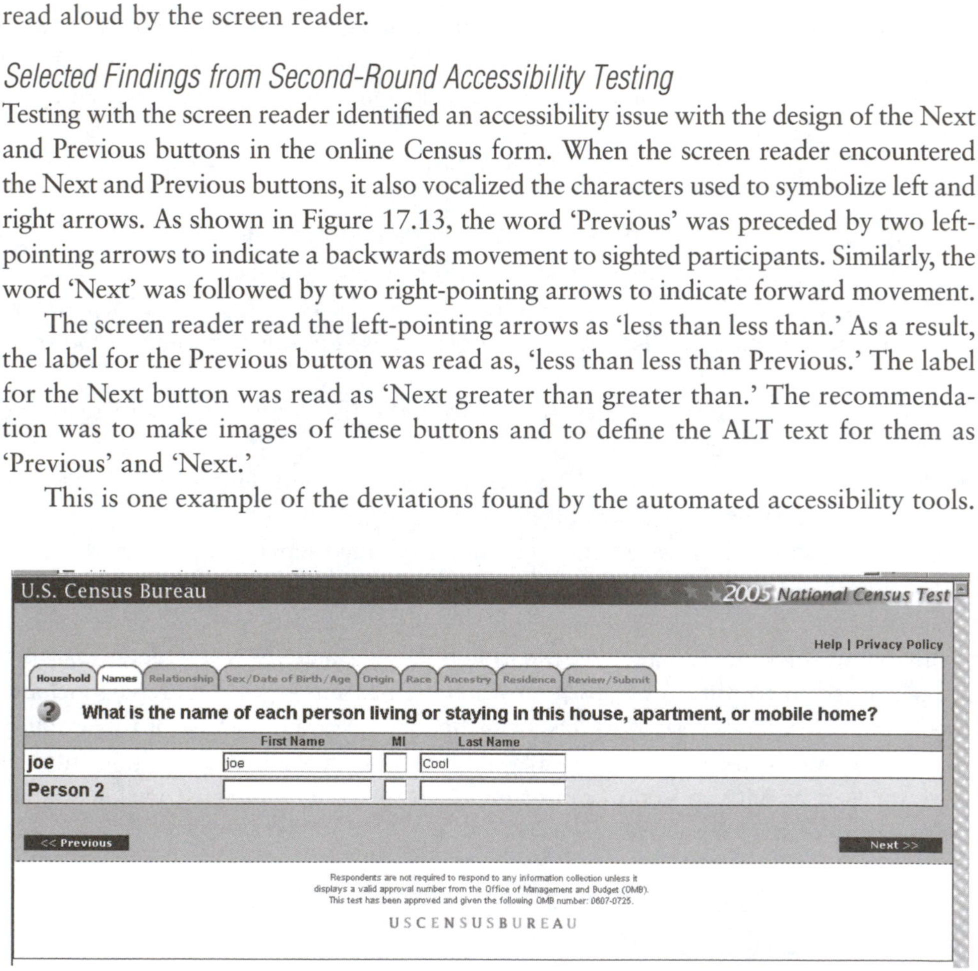

Figure 17.13 Design of Previous and Next button labels caused the screen reader to vocalize the 'less than' and 'greater than' symbols.

Summary of Second-Round Accessibility Results

In general, the automated accessibility evaluation found that ALT text was sometimes less than informative; some checkboxes were not labeled; and certain terms were mis-associated with others. Mathematical symbols were used to create arrows. A utility that counted down remaining spaces available for text entry was not accessible during text entry. Help windows were cumbersome because of the order in which topics were vocalized: the specific help topic of interest was read after a list of other help topics.

Summary of Second-Round Accessibility Recommendations

We recommended providing a separate help window for every help topic, instead of a long, scrolling help page. This would benefit sighted users also because they were sometimes confused about where they were in the help file. The recommendation to make images for the Next and Previous buttons was intended to eliminate the confusion created by using mathematical symbols to indicate direction.

We recommended providing clearer ALT text. For example, the abbreviation for middle initial, 'MI,' was read simply as 'MI.' We recommended making the ALT text 'Middle Initial' so that it would be more readily understood. We also recommended associating names of persons in the household with the correct sets of checkboxes. In all cases, checkboxes should be labeled correctly. For the utility that counts down the spaces remaining for text entry, we recommended placing a notice about the space available before the open text-entry field and sounding a chime when the space was used up.

This application had elements that were technically accessible, but were not really usable, such as the scrolling help window, navigation arrows, and alternate text for middle initial. While these items met the letter of the Section 508 regulation, they did not meet the spirit of creating an accessible application. If an application is unusable it is also inaccessible. Abbreviations need to be spelled out completely for the screen reader to vocalize them properly. Response options must be properly associated with the primary variable, such as person name, to be accessible. Row and column names in checkbox tables must be detected as labels for each checkbox.

At this writing, the 2005 National Census Test has ended its data-collection phase, and analysis of results is progressing. A preliminary finding is that only 7.2% of respondents in the national sample opted to respond via the Internet (Zajac *et al.*, 2006). This is consistent with the Internet response rate that the Census Bureau has found for other electronic surveys when a paper form is also offered. When close to 60% of US households have Internet access (Pew, 2005), there is a vast potential for increasing the Internet response rate by designing an easier, yet still secure, end-to-end process for online respondents.

17.5 **Lessons Learned**

As we have seen at the Census Bureau, iterative usability and accessibility testing can identify issues and prompt design changes that foster effective and efficient performance for a wide spectrum of respondents. Including participants with disabilities in usability testing goes a long way in supplementing knowledge gained from the automated accessibility evaluation tools. It is important to include persons with disabilities in usability testing because satisfying the letter of the Federal accessibility regulations does not ensure a truly usable experience for respondents with disabilities. Compliance with Section 508 is just the beginning (Theofanos and Redish, 2003; Murphy, 2005).

As a result of testing early prototypes of the Census Internet form with visually and hearing-impaired participants, the Census Bureau's usability analysts inferred that usability is not the same thing as accessibility. A prototype may have passed the tests for formal accessibility, but not be fully usable by people with these kinds of disabilities. Our inference is strongly supported by authorities in the fields of accessibility and usability (e.g. Theofanos and Redish, 2003, p. 38):

> "Meeting the required accessibility standards does not . . . necessarily mean that a web site is *usable* for people with disabilities. And if a web site is not usable, it is not really accessible, even if it has all the elements required by law."

The goal is to make electronic Census forms both accessible and usable for all potential respondents. Toward this goal, the Census Bureau's IT standards group has sponsored the development and revision of standards and guidelines for the development of web-based user interfaces (US Census Bureau, 2002). Although this document is limited to distribution within Federal agencies, it incorporates the Section 508 regulations as requirements and recommends adherence to the W3C Accessibility Initiative guidelines (Web Accessibility Initiative, 2006). The Census Bureau's standard also incorporates policy and guidance provided by its parent agency, the US Department of Commerce (2005). These guidelines are readily available on the Internet. Interested readers are encouraged to contact the first author and request Appendix A to the Census standard, which provides research-based guidelines and rationales for user-centered web design and development.

17.6 **Future Plans**

The findings from testing of alternative designs will inform the design of future web-based surveys developed by the Census Bureau. They will be applied not only to the Internet form for a future Census, but also to the design of other web-based data-collection forms, such as the user interface to the coverage follow-up questionnaire.

This questionnaire is to be administered by interviewers in telephone call centers who will be using laptop computers to capture data that will help improve the accuracy of the 2010 Census. We plan to continue evaluating alternative designs for usability and accessibility, as time and other resources permit.

Looking toward the 2010 Census, it is not entirely certain that there will be an Internet form. If support is found for the Internet option, we will evaluate prototyped designs for usability and accessibility. For future testing, we plan to recruit participants with motor and cognitive disabilities. We have found that each person with a disability has a different level of severity and often a combination of disabilities. We want to include more participants with disabilities in usability testing.

17.7 Implications

The results of the usability and accessibility testing described in this chapter contain messages for various groups: users, designers, researchers, and policymakers.

17.7.1 Implications for Users

If the US Census Bureau offers an optional online form in the 2010 Census, users will have a choice of paper or electronic modes. A user who chooses to respond online must first accomplish the task of finding the Census Identification Number (CIN) for his or her household. The difficulties experienced by usability test participants suggest that this is the most demanding aspect of responding online, for users with and without disabilities. Unless an alternative method of logging-in is developed, users with visual disabilities will not be able to find the Census ID Number on their own. If the necessary number is still located on the back of the paper form, these potential respondents will need the help of a sighted person or of an assistive device that can read from paper. There is no guarantee that such an assistive device will be able to locate the number if it is on the back of the paper form.

Those respondents who make it past the authentication process, by entering their CIN correctly, can be expected to proceed with little or no trouble and to submit their data successfully, assuming that usability and accessibility recommendations have been implemented. Online respondents will be able to complete their forms at their convenience and submit without having to mail a paper form. They will be notified immediately that the Census Bureau has received their information. People who send back the paper form will not receive a confirmation notice, but they will be called upon for a personal interview if the paper form is not received.

Implementation of the recommendations from usability and accessibility testing can be expected to reduce the burden on respondents. Cognitive burden is lessened by simplifying the wording of instructions and by providing context-sensitive help. Cognitive burden is further reduced by ease of navigation and ease of making corrections to data entries. Users are well served by a consistent design that allows them to build up expectations for what's coming next and for the behavior of the user interface. A consistent design fosters efficient data entry. Users can complete the task quickly and get back to their lives.

17.7.2 **Implications for Designers**

Our experience testifies to the need to consider accessibility from the earliest possible moment, early in development of the system architecture. Developing for users without disabilities and then going back to retrofit is probably not the best way to provide usability for persons with disabilities. Going back to retrofit will add to the cost of development by extending the time spent in marking up the code (Marcus, 2005). The accommodations need to be built in early to achieve development efficiency and to allow for earlier user testing of the overall solution.

Content development must be guided by knowledge of users' reading behavior on the Internet: users with average and above literacy tend to scan written content, looking for keywords and promising links (Nielsen, 1997). They do not read complete sentences and dense paragraphs of text. Textual content should be relatively brief and highly structured, for example, in bulleted lists instead of sentences (Price and Price, 2002). White space should be integrated with the content to provide visual relief and enhance grouping of related items.

Designers need to make sure that all informative content on the Internet questionnaire is available in text for respondents who use screen-reading software (Brinck, 2005). It is not advisable, however, to provide a text-only alternative to the site provided for users without disabilities (Theofanos and Redish, 2003; Brinck, 2005). For flexibility and ease of making changes, the design of the user interface should be kept separate from the functional design (Vanderheiden and Zimmermann, 2002). This can be accomplished by using Cascading Style Sheets (CSS), as recommended in the Census Bureau's IT standard on web-based user interfaces (2002) and other resources on user-centered web site development (e.g. Redish, 2004; Lazar, 2005; Lie and Bos, 2005). We recommend a lifecycle approach that integrates usability-and-accessibility engineering processes with software engineering processes (O'Connell and Murphy, 2007).

17.7.3 **Implications for Researchers**

There is plenty of work remaining for researchers (e.g. Stepanidis, 2000; LaPlant, 2001; Vanderheiden and Zimmermann, 2002). Practitioners need baselines on the capabilities of people with one or more disabilities, including age-related decrements in perception and performance. As people live longer, they are expected to work longer, but the technology is made for people with high manual dexterity and high spatial ability, both of which decline with age. Research is needed on ways to adapt user interfaces for successful use by people with hand tremors, low spatial ability, and other borderline disabilities, as well as for use by people with major disabilities.

To be applicable beyond the research context, research to develop baselines and to evaluate proposed technologies must be conducted with random samples, not with convenience samples. The results of research with recruited participants or with volunteers do not generalize to the general population (Keppel and Zedeck, 1989). Although selection of a random sample presents difficulties to researchers, the use of nonrandomly-selected samples violates the underlying assumptions of statistical tests used to assess the significance of findings.

Random assignment of volunteers to treatment conditions and counterbalancing of treatment conditions are standard practices in well-designed experimental research (Kirk, 1994). To distribute the possible effects of learning, each participant should receive the treatment conditions in a randomized order. For example, if three designs are being evaluated (that is, A, B, and C), some participants should experience the designs in the following orders: B, A, C; C, B, A; and A, C, B. Without counterbalancing, the effects of learning cannot be separated from the effects of the alternative design features.

Researchers and their managers must remember that usability testing is not an experiment in the technical sense. Its purpose is to identify problems caused by flaws in user-interface design, not to compare alternatives or to find statistically significant differences between one user group and another. Usability testing can evaluate alternative designs, but it does not provide a valid basis for determining a 'best' design. That is a job for research designs that incorporate random sampling, sufficient sample sizes, and random assignment of participants to alternatives. In developing alternative designs, researchers must be careful not to introduce so many manipulations (independent variables) that analysis is unable to sort out the effects. Design changes must be systematic across alternative user interfaces if the human-performance results are to be reliable.

17.7.4 Implications for Policymakers

The usability and accessibility of online data-collection forms need to be improved if Federal agencies want to increase the participation of people with disabilities. In the case of the online census form, a major barrier to accessibility is created by the requirement to find the household's Census Identification Number on the paper form and copy it into a set of data-entry fields. A respondent with low or no vision will find this task next to impossible without help. An alternative method for logging in is needed to support access to the online form by individuals with low or no vision; and the acceptability of this alternative needs to be promulgated by regulation or legislation.

A requirement to design and test for universal accessibility needs to be stated clearly in requests for proposals from outside contractors; and submitted proposals need to be evaluated in terms of their understanding of and provision for achieving universal accessibility. Design contractors should be expected to test their software on multiple platforms using various browsers as well as older versions of browsers (Brinck, 2005). Software should be routinely tested for compatibility with assistive devices used by people with disabilities, for example, screen readers, screen magnification software, and text browsers (Brinck, 2005). Government agencies should not permit contractors to control the timing and supervision of testing for usability and accessibility. Agencies should require independent user testing with participants who have visual, cognitive, auditory, and motor disabilities as well as clusters of disabilities. Software development schedules must have time built in to allow for changes to be made to resolve usability and accessibility issues identified in independent testing.

Low usability can be expected to discourage people with disabilities from participating in the online Census. Low participation by nearly 20% of the US population can only increase the already high cost of the manual follow-up operation in which Census personnel make personal visits to nonresponding households. Improving the accessibility and usability of online forms can be expected to reduce the long-term costs of the Decennial Census and to increase public participation in E-government initiatives. Complaints about discrimination on the basis of disability can be expected to increase if official web sites are inaccessible (Waddell and ten Veen, 2003). Making the online Census form both usable and accessible requires resources that allow project managers to direct designers and developers to comply not only with the letter of the law, but also with its spirit. The goal is not optimal design for everyone, which is impossible (Brinck, 2005), but a design that provides a mostly positive and successful experience to anyone who chooses the Internet option.

17.8 **Disclaimer**

This material is released to inform interested parties of ongoing research and to encourage discussion of work in progress. The views expressed are those of the authors and not necessarily those of the US Census Bureau.

Acknowledgments

The authors extend thanks to the anonymous reviewer and the reviewers at the US Census Bureau (Manuel de la Puente, Suzanne Fratino, and Tommy Wright) for their helpful and constructive comments. Thanks to Theresa O'Connell for useful suggestions and encouragement. Special thanks to all members of the various Census Internet design teams and to the test participants who showed up for usability and accessibility testing with enthusiasm for improving the eventual respondent's experience.

References

Andrews, D., Nonnecke, B. and Preece, J. (2003) Electronic survey methodology: a case study in reaching hard to involve Internet users. *International Journal of Human-Computer Interaction* 16(2): 185-210. Retrieved May 4, 2006 from http://www.clis.umd.edu/people/preece/papers/Online_survey_design_IJHCI04.pdf.

Bessiere, K. *et al.* (2004) Social and psychological influences on computer user frustration. In Bucy, E. & Newhagen, J. (Eds.) *Media access: social and psychological dimensions of new technology,* Erlbaum, Mahwah, NJ, 169–192.

Bias, R. and Karat, C.-M. (2005) Justifying cost-justifying usability. In Bias, R.G. & Mayhew, D.J. (Eds.) *Cost-Justifying Usability,* Elsevier/Morgan Kaufmann, New York, 1–16.

Brady, S., Bouffard, J. and Stapleton C. (2004) *2003 National Census Test: Response mode analysis.* Washington, DC, US Census Bureau.

Brinck, T. (2005) Return on goodwill: return on investment for accessibility. In Bias, R.G. & Mayhew, D.J. (Eds.) *Cost-Justifying Usability: An update for the Internet age,* Elsevier/Morgan Kaufmann, New York, 385–414.

Ceaparu, I. *et al.* (2004) Determining causes and severity of end-user frustration. International Journal of Human-Computer Interaction, 17, 333–356.

Chin, J.P., Diehl, V.A. and Norman K.L. (1988) Development of an instrument measuring user satisfaction of the human-computer interface. *Proceedings of SIGCHI '88,* New York, ACM/SIGCHI, 213–218.

Contrino, H., Echevarria-Cruz, S. and Shleymovich, J. (2005) Potential utility of web based data collection options. Retrieved May 22, 2006 from http://www.fcsm.gov/events/papers05.html.

Couper, M.P. (2000) Web surveys: A review of issues and approaches. *Public Opinion Quarterly,* **64,** 464–494.

Dillman, D.A. (2000) *Mail and Internet Surveys: The tailored design method.* 2nd edn, John Wiley & Sons, New York.

Dumas, J.S. and Redish J. (1999) *A Practical Guide to Usability Testing,* revised edition, Portland, OR, Intellect.

Griffin, D.H., Fischer, D.P. and Morgan, M.T. (2001) Testing an Internet response option for the American Community Survey. Paper presented at the annual meeting of the American Association for Public Opinion Research, Montreal, Canada, May 17–20. Retrieved May 21, 2006 from `http://www.census.gov/acs/www/Downloads/ACS/Paper29.pdf`.

General Services Administration (2003) Authentication policy for federal agencies (Draft E). Federal Register, 68(133), pp. 41371–41374. Retrieved June 9, 2006 from `http://a257.g.akamaitech.net/7/257/2422/14mar20010800/edocket.access.gpo.gov/2003/pdf/03-17634.pdf`.

Groves, R.M. (1989) *Survey Errors and Survey Costs,* John Wiley & Sons, New York.

Harper, B.D. and Norman, K.L. (1993) Improving user satisfaction: the Questionnaire for User Interaction Satisfaction Version 5.5. *Proceedings of the 1st Annual Mid-Atlantic Human Factors Conference,* Virginia Beach, VA, pp. 224–228.

Hix, D. and Hartson, H.R. (1993) *Developing User Interfaces: Ensuring Through Product & Process.* John Wiley & Sons, New York.

Keppel, G. and Zedeck, S. (1989) *Data Analysis for Research Designs,* W.H. Freeman, New York.

Kirk, R.E. (1994) *Experimental Design: Procedures for Behavioral Sciences,* 3rd edn, Boston, MA, Wadsworth.

Kurzweil Educational Systems (2005) Believe you can. Retrieved November 21, 2005 from `http://www.kurzweiledu.com/`.

LaPlant, W.P., Jr. (2001) A proposal for a research agenda in computer human interaction. Retrieved May 14, 2006 from `http://www.icdri.org/technology/indexbp.htm`.

Lazar, J. (2005) *Web Usability,* Addison-Wesley, Boston, MA.

Lazar, J. and Preece, J. (2001) Using electronic surveys to evaluate networked resources: from idea to implementation. In McClure, C.R. & Bertot, J.C. (Eds.)

Evaluating Networked Information Services: Techniques, policy, and issues, Medford, NJ, Information Today, 137–154.

Lazar, J., Bessiere, K. and Ceaparu, I. (2003) *Help!* I'm lost: user frustration in web navigation. *IT&Society,* **1**(3), 18–26.

Lazar, J., Jones, A. and Shneiderman, B. (2006a) Workplace user frustration with computers: an exploratory investigation of the causes and severity. *Behavior and Information Technology,* **25**(3), 239–251.

Lazar, J., Jones, A., Hackley, M. and Shneiderman, B. (2006b) Severity and impact of computer user frustration: a comparison of student and workplace users. *Interacting with Computers,* **18**(2) 187–207.

Lewis, C. and Norman D.A. (1986) Designing for error. In Norman, D.A. & Draper, S.W. (Eds.) *User Centered System Design: New Perspectives on Human-Computer Interaction,* Erlbaum, Hillsdale, NJ, 411–432.

Lie, H.W. and Bos, B. (2005) *Cascading Style Sheets: Designing for the Web.* 3rd edn, Addison-Wesley, Boston, MA.

Lozar Manfreda, K., Batagelj, Z. and Vehovar, V. (2002) Design of web survey questionnaires: three basic experiments. Journal of Computing and Media Communication 7(3). Retrieved May 14, 2006 from `http://www.websm.org/upload/editor/Lozar_2002_Design.da`.

Marcus, A. (2005) User interface design's return on investment: examples and statistics. In Bias, R.G. & Mayhew, D.J. (Eds.) *Cost-Justifying Usability: An update for the Internet age,* Elsevier/Morgan Kaufmann, New York, 17–39.

Mayhew, D.J. (1992) *Principles and Guidelines in Software User Interface Design.* Prentice-Hall, Englewood Cliffs, NJ.

Murphy, B., Ciochetto, S., Malakhoff, L. et al. (2005a) *2005 Census Internet prototype applications: Usability and accessibility testing* (Human–Computer Interaction Memorandum #81). US Census Bureau, Statistical Research Division, Washington, DC.

Murphy, B., Conrad, F., Couper, M. and Steinberg, C. (2005b) *Web-based data collection at the U. S. Census Bureau: Usability test of a topic-based, Census short-form prototype* (Human–Computer Interaction Memorandum #74). US Census Bureau, Usability Laboratory, Washington, DC.

Murphy, E.D. (2005) Steps toward integrating accessibility into development of an Internet option for the 2010 U. S. Census (Research Report Series: Survey Methodology #2005-11). US Census Bureau, Washington, DC. Retrieved June 9, 2006 from `http://www.census.gov/srd/papers/pdf/rsm2005-11.pdf`.

Murphy, E., Marquis, K. and Nichols, E. (2001) Refining electronic data-collection instruments and data-dissemination tools through usability testing. *Research on Official Statistics,* **4**(2), 23–33.

Nielsen, J. (1997) How users read on the web. Retrieved May 10, 2006 from `http://www.useit.com/alertbox/9710a.html`.

Norman, K.L. (1998) *Requirements document for usability laboratories* (report prepared for the US Census Bureau). Laboratory for Automation Psychology and the Human/Computer Interaction Laboratory, College Park, MD.

Norman, K.L., Friedman, Z., Norman, K.D. and Stevenson, R. (2000) Navigational issues in the design of online self administered questionnaires. *Behavioral Information Technology,* **20**, 37–45.

O'Connell, T.A. and Murphy, E.D. (2007) The usability engineering behind user-centered processes for web site development lifecycles. In *Human Computer Interaction Research in Web Design and Evaluation,* P. Zaphiris and S. Kurniawan (eds). Idea Group: Hershey, PA, 1–21.

Pew Internet and American Life Project (2005) Both coasts lead the nation in Internet use. Retrieved November 21, 2005 from `http://www.perinternet.org/PPF /r/65/press_release.asp`.

Preece, J., Rogers, Y. and Sharp, H. (2002) *Interaction Design: Beyond Human–Computer Interaction.* John Wiley & Sons, New York.

Price, J. and Price, L. (2002) *Hot Text: Web Writing that Works.* New Riders Press, Berkeley, CA.

Pyle, D.M. and Giff, S. (2003) Nonresponse bias of non-native speakers in web-based research. In *Universal access in HCI: Inclusive design in the information society,* C. Stephanidis (ed.) (Vol. 4, *Proceedings of HCI International 2003,* pp. 1193–1197). Erlbaum, Mahwah, NJ.

Ramos, M., Sedivi, B.M. and Sweet, E.M. (1998) Computerized self-administered questionnaires. In Couper, M.P., Baker, R.P., Bethlehem, J., Clark, C.Z.F., Martin, J., Nicholls, W.L.II, & O'Reilly, J.M. (Eds.) *Computer Assisted Survey Information Collection,* John Wiley & Sons, New York, 389–408.

Redish J. (2004) User-centered website development: a human-computer interaction approach. *Technical Communications,* **51**(3), 553–556.

Schonlau, M., Fricker, R.D.Jr. and Elliott, M.N. (2002) *Conducting Research Surveys via e-mail and the Web.* RAND, Santa Monica, CA.

Shneiderman, B. (1998) *Designing the User Interface*. 3rd edn, Addison Wesley Longman, Reading, MA.

Shneiderman, B. and Plaisant, C. (2005) *Designing the User Interface*. 4th edn, Pearson/Addison, Wesley New York.

Solomon, D.J. (2001) Conducting web-based surveys. *Practical Assessment, Research & Evaluation 7(19)*. Retrieved May 4, 2006 from `http://pareonline.net/getvn.asp?v=7&n=19`.

Steinmetz, E. (2006) Americans with disabilities: 2002. (US Census Bureau Current Population Report P70-107). Retrieved May 15, 2006 from `http://www.census.gov/prod/2006pubs/p70-107.pdf`.

Stepanidis, C. (2000) Challenges towards universal access in the information age. Retrieved May 14, 2006 from `http://www.ercim.org/publication/Ercim_News/enw40.stephanidis.html`.

Tedesco, H., Zuckerberg, R.L. and Nichols E. (1999) Designing surveys for the next millennium: web-based questionnaire design issues. *Proceedings of the Third International Conference on Survey and Statistical Computing,* Edinburgh, Scotland, pp. 103–112.

Thatcher, J. (2003) Accessible forms. Retrieved January 20, 2005 from `http://jimthatcher.com/webcourse8.htm`.

Theofanos, M.F. and Redish, J. (2003) Guidelines for accessible - and usable - web sites: observing users who work with screenreaders. *Interactions,* 10(6), 38–51.

Tourangeau, R., Rips, L.J. and Rasinski K. (2000) *The Psychology of Survey Response*. Cambridge University Press, New York.

US Access Board (Architectural and Transportation Barriers Compliance Board) (2000). Electronic and information technology accessibility standards. Federal Register (December 21), Washington, DC. Retrieved January 15, 2005 from `http://www.access.board.gov/secton508/508standards.htm`.

US Census Bureau (2002) Information Technology (IT) standard 20.0.0: Design requirements and guidelines for web-based user interfaces. Systems Support Division, Software and Standards Management Branch, Washington, DC.

US Census Bureau (2003) *Census Bureau standard: Pretesting questionnaires and related materials for surveys and censuses* (SRD/03-PQRMSC). US Department of Commerce, Washington, DC (available at `http://www.census.gov/srd/pretest-standards.pdf`).

US Department of Commerce (2005) Electronic and information technology accessibility policy. Retrieved June 9, 2006 from `http://www.osec.doc.gov/cio/oipr/eitpolicy.htm`.

Vanderheiden, G.C. and Zimmermann G. (2002) State of the science: access to information technologies. In Winters, J.M., Robinson, C., Simpson, R., & Vanderheiden, G. (Eds.) *Emerging and Accessible Telecommunications, Information and Healthcare Technologies,* RESNA Press, Arlington, VA, 152–184.

Vu, K.-P.L. and Proctor, R.W. (2006) Web site design and evaluation. In Salvendy, G. (Eds.) *Handbook of Human Factors and Ergonomics,* 3rd edn, John Wiley & Sons, New York, 1317–1343.

Waddell, C.D. and ten Veen, R.C. (2003) ICDRI update on global accessible web policy and law. In *Proceedings of Technology and Persons with Disabilities Conference,* California State University, Northridge (CSUN). Retrieved May 14, 2006 from `http://www.csun.edu/cod/conf/2003/proceedings/136.htm`.

Web Accessibility Initiative (2006) WAI guidelines and techniques. Retrieved June 9, 2006 from `http://www.w3.org/WAI/guid-tech.html`.

Westat (2002) *Response mode and incentive experiment for Census 2000* (Final report). US Census Bureau, Census 2000 Testing and Experimentation Program, Washington, DC.

Whitworth, E.M. (2001) Implementation and results of the Internet response mode for Census 2000. *Proceedings of the American Association for Public Opinion Research Conference,* Montreal, Quebec.

World Wide Web Consortium (W3C) (2002) User agent accessibility guidelines 1.0. Retrieved November 21, 2005 from `http://www.w3c.org/TR/2002/REC-UAAG10-20021217/cover.html#toc`.

Zajac, K.J., Allmang, K. and Barth, J. (2006) *2005 National Census Test: Response mode analysis.* US Census Bureau, Decennial Statistical Studies Division, Washington, DC.

Internationalizing Greenstone: A Multilingual Tool for Building Digital Libraries

18

David M. Nichols, Te Taka Keegan, David Bainbridge, Sally Jo Cunningham, Michael Dewsnip, and Ian H. Witten
Department of Computer Science, University of Waikato, Hamilton, New Zealand

18.1 Introduction

This chapter describes how the digital library creation tool Greenstone addresses the problem of internationalization. Digital collections served by Greenstone involve several different groups of users:

- Readers – who consult the multimedia documents in the collections to support their personal tasks.
- Anthologists – who gather documents together and establish collections.
- Librarians – who monitor and update collections as they are used by readers.
- Technicians – who respond to user feedback and implement new functionality.

In practice, although the other boundaries are clear, there is little difference between the anthologists who create collections and the librarians who maintain them and in this chapter we call both groups 'librarians.'

These groups of users are common to all digital library applications. However, Greenstone aims to be a multilingual solution for building digital libraries and therefore needs to accommodate documents and interfaces in any language. While it is most common to browse collections in their native language, this is not always the case (and cannot be the case for multilingual collections). Therefore, Greenstone strives to support arbitrary combinations of languages. In other words, one might employ an English interface to Chinese text documents, or an Arabic interface to Spanish documents.

Multilingual software typically breaks the problem of language support down into two parts: internationalization and localization. Internationalization involves using a software architecture that can easily be localized, while localization refers to the process of adapting an application for a *particular* culture or market (Yeo, 2001; Aykin, 2005). As an open source project, Greenstone does not have the linguistic resources to achieve localization itself. Consequently, a further set of users is identified:

• Translators – who translate the interface into their own language.

Greenstone allows end-user communities to both adapt the software and add their language contributions into a central repository from which all users can benefit. In this chapter we describe how the software infrastructure manages the relationships between the various user groups to enable the improvement and localization of the Greenstone interface.

We first outline the challenges in building global digital libraries and how the Greenstone software has evolved over the past decade. We describe the problems of serving multilingual content with multilingual interfaces and then explain the approach that the Greenstone developers have adopted. The chapter concludes with a summary of the lessons learnt during the development of the toolset and their relevance for the different user groups.

18.2 **Global Digital Libraries**

Libraries have been an important element in the development of modern societies, providing low-cost access to diverse information sources for their patrons. Digital libraries increase the accessibility of information sources, lowering costs, extending access via networking, and adding new access mechanisms such as full-text searching. As the Internet spreads over the world, digital libraries, along with other software applications, face the three *universal usability* challenges: technological variety, user diversity, and gaps in user knowledge (Shneiderman, 2000). These challenges become apparent when we consider how to spread the benefits of universal information access in developing countries: hardware and software from a decade ago are common, networking may be unreliable or absent, languages and cultures of users differ from those of the software developers and the fundamental concepts involved in digital libraries may not be widely understood by library users or by potential digital library creators (Witten *et al.*, 2002).

In addressing the global challenges of producing tools to build digital libraries it is useful to briefly consider the context of use. Although it is undeniably useful to disseminate information collections built in the developed world, as present digital libraries tend to do, a better strategy for sustained long-term development is to disseminate the capability to *create* information collections rather than the collections themselves. Effective human development blossoms from empowerment rather than gifting. Digital libraries enable indigenous people to participate actively in preserving and disseminating their own culture (Nichols *et al.*, 2005). In accepting this rationale of *tool* distribution we also implicitly accept the technical challenges of designing software to work on older computer systems and without the assumption of fast reliable network access (Witten *et al.*, 2002; Witten and Bainbridge, 2003).

The universal usability challenge of user diversity has several aspects, including the capacity to support differences in age, gender, language, culture, literacy, disability, etc. (Shneiderman, 2000). In this chapter we concentrate on language; other work in this volume addresses other aspects of the challenge. The use of language, for a reader, in a digital library occurs in two different ways: the language of the documents and the language of the interface. As documents may be any multimedia resource (e.g. images, audio, video, etc.) then it is the *interface* that is the only ever-present element. The librarians, however, also interact with the software tools needed to construct the collection and its interface for the readers. The translators may experience a different subset of the software as their specialized task can usually be isolated from more general maintenance issues. Finally, the technicians have to create tools and documentation that can function in diverse multilingual environments on, potentially, less sophisticated computer systems. In the following sections we describe how Greenstone has responded to these challenges.

18.3 Conception and Birth of Greenstone

The project that grew into Greenstone began in 1995 with the construction of a New Zealand digital library for computer science research (Witten *et al.*, 1995), one of many early technology-based projects that build searchable collections of papers in computer science. A few years later we worked with a Belgium-based humanitarian organization, the Human Info NGO, to build stand-alone CD-ROM collections of practical information on topics such as agriculture, building, energy, health, nutrition, sanitation, and water. This work forced us to consider the essential but mundane business of making the software work reliably on low-end Windows systems, for all our research work had been done on Linux, and to build installers that allowed end-users to install the collections on their computer. This work produced an end-user system for working with information collections that we refer to as the 'reader's' interface to Greenstone.

Human Info's connections led to discussions with UNESCO, who encouraged us to consider distributing the *capability* for building digital libraries, rather than the collections themselves, for all the reasons discussed above. An international cooperative effort with UNESCO and Human Info was formally initiated in 2000 and led to the production of the first of a series of CD-ROM distributions of the Greenstone software itself, not collections that had been built with it. This involved an extensive effort in documentation and multilingual computing, for UNESCO wanted to issue an English, Spanish, French, and Russian version of the Greenstone CD-ROM as the second of the series. In parallel, we had been working to make it possible for volunteers to translate the reader's interface into their own language, and – importantly – update it when changes were made to the software. It also involved the design and production of an end-user system for building collections that we call the 'librarian's' interface to Greenstone.

Greenstone's original design philosophy emphasized the following points:

- Trivial to install (for individuals without any institutional computer support).
- Easy for end-users to build collections with existing documents and metadata.
- Open approach to document and metadata formats: anything can be accommodated.
- End-users can wrap individual collections into a package (e.g. on CD-ROM or DVD) for use on non-networked machines.
- Exactly the same interface will be provided for networked and non-networked Greenstone installations.
- Librarian's interface runs on all machines.
- Reader's interface runs all machines right down to very low-end ones (Windows 3.1).
- Multilingual, with the capability of easily adding new languages and maintaining existing ones.

Only when these basic requirements were satisfied did we turn to more sophisticated facilities, such as distributed use of the librarian's interface and interoperation with standard protocols and other digital library systems. While others were doing research on interoperability, our internal motto was 'first operability, then interoperability.'

18.4 **Related Work**

There are many examples – hundreds if not thousands – of digital libraries on the web. With only a few exceptions, these are done with custom software. One-offs! The pattern such projects tend to follow is that the organization (typically an institution of some form) that is responsible for the source material (typically empowered to be the guardian of the material) decides to make the material available over the web to make it more accessible. In other words, they need to build a digital library. The size of the organization is such that it is within their resources to either commit IT staff to develop the necessary software or to outsource the work to a company who then, more often than not, writes custom software. In the case of documents starting in physical form, digitization – a considerable undertaking – is factored in as part of the process.

At the top end of the scale in terms of investment, the American Memory project by the Library of Congress (www.memory.loc.gov) is testimony to what can be achieved with this approach. With the aim of providing 'a digital record of American history and creativity,' the digital library embodies dozens of collections providing open access over the web to over 5 million items. Artifacts include video, maps, sheet music in addition to the written and spoken word. In its peak period of development (1996–2000) it received over US$45 million of funding.

Despite the wide array of end-result digital libraries, there are only a few digital library systems that are frameworks, like Greenstone, to target the abstract concepts and constructs of digital libraries, thereby enabling others to accomplish their online delivery aims with minimal IT investment. Of note are *DSpace* (Tansley *et al.*, 2005) and *Fedora* (Lagoze *et al.*, 2006). Both are open source, like Greenstone.

DSpace (www.dspace.org) facilitates the building of institutional repositories that capture, distribute, and preserve intellectual output at an institutional level. It is produced by Hewlett-Packard and designed in partnership with MIT. Its designers note that much of the intellectual output of professors and researchers is in digital form, and unless their home institution has an aggressive policy for collecting and preserving it, this information is potentially ephemeral. DSpace is designed to help capture and organize everything produced by faculty and staff – digitized versions of lecture notes, videos, papers, and data sets – into an 'institutional repository' that will make it available to future generations in its original digital form.

Fedora (www.fedora.info) is a general purpose repository service developed jointly by the University of Virginia Library and Cornell University. The Fedora project is devoted to the goal of providing open-source repository software that can serve as the foundation for many types of information management systems. The software demonstrates how distributed digital information management can be deployed using web-based technologies, including XML and web services. At its core is a powerful digital object model that supports multiple representations or views of each digital object. Relationships among digital objects can be stored and queried, providing the foundation for expressing rich information networks. These objects exist within a repository architecture that supports a variety of management functions such as fine granularity access control, version control, and ingest and export of information in standard XML formats.

Unlike Greenstone, which evolved, both these projects were conceived and implemented as general frameworks. The abstraction in DSpace is tightly focused on an institutional repository model and has seen significant uptake in universities. To stray beyond these bounds and repurpose the software, however, requires significant programming effort, although this is clearly possible given the open source nature of the code. Born out of digital library work, Fedora is at the other end of the spectrum in terms of levels of abstraction, with the broad remit of information management systems, of which digital libraries is just one example. This comes at a price, however. For instance, it is assumed that the XML-based document object model used by Fedora is the starting point. It is up to a project using Fedora to develop software that converts source documents into this format. Also, in response to the difficult issue of the end-user interface, Fedora essentially leaves this unspecified, as it is not possible to design something in the realm of information management that is all things to all people. Again, it is up to a particular project to design and implement this.

In terms of internationalization, DSpace has work underway with the user interface being translated into several languages (nine European languages as well as Chinese, Japanese, and Indonesian at the time of writing) in various stages of completion. The underlying mechanism used for this is based on the Java Standard Tag Library, with a property file for each language storing the language strings akin to the language-specific macro files used by Greenstone (see below). Of course, the reader's interface is merely one component to full internationalization (again see below) and the developers list some technical areas of DSpace that need attention, such as indexing. In Fedora there is no evidence of internationalization work, however it should be noted that they make use of the same Java Standard Tag Library, and therefore the same technical solution is available to them, should they pursue this.

18.5 Greenstone: A Tool for Creating Digital Libraries

Greenstone is a suite of software for building and distributing digital library collections (Witten and Bainbridge, 2003). It is not a digital library but a *tool* for building digital libraries. It provides a new way of organizing information and publishing it on the Internet in the form of a fully-searchable, metadata-driven collection. It is open source, multilingual software, issued under the terms of the GNU General Public License. Collections built with Greenstone automatically include effective full-text searching and metadata-based browsing facilities that are attractive and easy to use. They are easily maintainable and can be rebuilt entirely automatically.

Table 18.1 A representative cross-section of Greenstone-based public digital libraries from around the world

Association of Indian Labour Historians, Delhi	New York Botanical Garden
California University at Riverside	Peking University Digital Library
Chicago University Library	Philippine Research Education and Government Information Network
Detroit Public Library	
Gresham College, London	Secretary of Human Rights of Argentina
Illinois Wesleyan University	Slavonski Brod Public Library, Slovenia
Kyrgyz Republic National Library	State Library of Tasmania
Lehigh University, Pennsylvania	Stuttgart University of Applied Sciences
Mari El Republic, Russia	Vietnam National University
National Centre for Science Information, Bangalore, India	Vimercate Public Library, Milan, Italy
	Washington Research Library Consortium
Netherlands Institute for Scientific Information Services	Welsh Books Council

Greenstone runs on all versions of Windows, Unix, and Mac OS X. It is easy to install. For the default Windows installation absolutely no configuration is necessary, and end-users routinely install Greenstone on their personal laptops or workstations. Institutional users run it on their main web server, where it interoperates with standard web server software (such as Apache).

In common with many other open-source projects the precise user base for Greenstone is unknown. It is distributed on SourceForge, a leading distribution center for open-source software. Since 2003 the average number of downloads per month has been over 4500, with 40% of those being the software and the remaining 60%, documentation. 80% of the software downloads are for Windows binaries, with the next biggest category being 15% for Linux, also binaries. Although we do not have detailed information on Greenstone's users, we are aware of many public digital libraries that use the software around the world (Table 18.1).

Greenstone allows users to create digital library collections using a wide variety of source documents: text, web pages, images, audio, video, etc. An inevitable consequence of this broad approach is that the collections contain documents in more than one language.

Figure 18.1 shows typical images from interacting with a Greenstone collection: in this case the Niupepa (2005) collection of Māori newspapers (Apperley *et al.*, 2002). A user has accessed the home page of the Niupepa collection where three

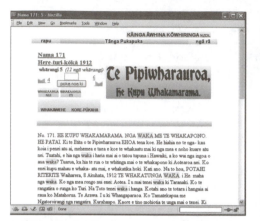 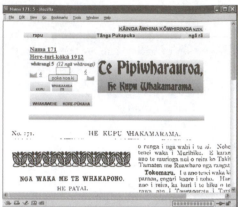

(a) Viewing a document: extracted text   (b) Viewing a document: scanned text

Figure 18.1 *The Niupepa collection of Māori newspapers displayed via Greenstone.*

options are available to access the Māori language newspapers: rapu (Search), Tānga Pukapuka (Series Listings), and Ngā Rā (Date). The user has selected the full-text search option and has undertaken a search for the word 'waka' (canoe). This has returned a list of results and the user has selected the first one. The Greenstone software then displays a textual representation of the newspaper page with the search term highlighted as in Figure 18.1(a). This feature allows the user to easily find an inconspicuous search term on a large page of text. To view the original image the user clicks on the 'Whakaahua Nui' (Large Image) button and it is displayed as in Figure 18.1(b).

This example illustrates three aspects of international digital library work:

- Access to a textual representation (thereby allowing textual searching and other access mechanisms).
- Access to an original image of a document.
- The interface through which access is provided.

In the case described above the interface language is Māori and the documents themselves are also in Māori. However, universal usability mandates that access to original material should be possible in any language: the interface should be capable of being translated. It makes little sense (and is sometimes distasteful) to have a collection whose content is in Chinese or Hindi, but whose supporting text –

instructions, navigation buttons, labels, images, help text, and so on – can only be seen in English.

Automated translation of the original content is a much more difficult problem and is beyond the scope of this chapter. However, the textual elements of interfaces are usually simpler, smaller (in terms of number of words), and more easily separated into manageable fragments (Purvis *et al.*, 2001; Bainbridge *et al.*, 2003). Although the text of an interface is important there are also other characteristics of interfaces that influence usability, such as interactivity, position, color, sound, fonts, etc. A general solution to creating international digital libraries has to cope with the potential variability of all these interface elements (Savarimuthu and Purvis, 2004). In other words, translation is necessary, but not sufficient, for localization.

18.6 Internationalizing Greenstone

A distinction is often made between the *internationalization* of software architecture and the specific *localization* work necessary to adapt software to a specific language and culture (Crystal, 2000; Purvis *et al.*, 2001; Hogan *et al.*, 2004). Using this framework we can divide up the work required to create multilingual interfaces.

Technicians:
- Internationalize the software architecture of Greenstone to permit the textual strings of interfaces to be used in more than one language.
- Provide a mechanism for nontextual interface elements to be customized.

Translators:
- Translate the textual strings for the interface.

Librarians:
- Localize the interface based on the translated textual strings.

This division of labor is a natural consequence of the expertise of the respective groups: technicians are not necessarily good at translation and translators should not need to learn a programming language in order for the project to benefit from their skills.

Technically, Greenstone uses the international standard Unicode (Unicode Consortium, 2000) to represent text and builds on the display capabilities of web browsers for displaying documents to users. Documents in any language and character encoding can be imported and example collections in Arabic, Chinese, Cyrillic,

```
package Global

_header_   { The New Zealand Digital Library Project }
_content_  { Oops. If you are reading this then an error
             has occurred in the runtime system. }
_footer_   { Powered by <a href="www.greenstone.org">Greenstone</a>. }

package query

_content_  { _If_(_cgiargqb_ eq "large",_largequerybox_,_normalquerybox_)
   ... }

# ... the macro descriptions for _largequerybox_, _normalquerybox_,
#  and other nested macros are omitted for brevity

_header_ [l=en] {Begin search }
_header_ [l=fr] {Démarrer la recherche }
_header_ [l=es] {Iniciar la búsqueda}

# ... and so on

# Images containing language-dependent text

## "HELP" ## top_nav_button ## chelp ##
_httpiconchelp_ [l=en,v=1] {_httpimg_/en/chelp.gif}
_httpiconchelp_ [l=en,v=0] {HELP}

# ... and so on
```

Figure 18.2 *Excerpt of Greenstone macro file syntax to illustrate some of the internationalization features.*

French, Spanish, German, Hindi, and Māori can be examined at the New Zealand Digital Library website (www.nzdl.org).

However, internationalization is not just about translating or displaying text fragments. Technology-centric issues such as nontextual elements and user-driven ones such as cultural differences need to be considered.

The software developers had to create a mechanism for more detailed customization that could be used by the librarians. This task involved generalizing the output architecture of Greenstone so that interface components could be selected contextually by language or manually customized. The mechanism to achieve this internationalization of the Greenstone software architecture is a macro language facility.

Figure 18.2 shows an artificially constructed excerpt that illustrates the syntax through which macros are defined and used. Macro definitions comprise a name, flanked by underscores, and the corresponding content, placed within braces {···}.

They are grouped together into *packages*, with lexical scoping, and an inheritance scheme is used to determine which definitions are in effect at any given time. This allows global formatting styles to be embedded with the particular content that is generated for a page.

Figure 18.2 shows a baseline page defined in the 'Global' package, which, in fact, is never intended to be seen. It is overridden in the 'query' package below to generate a page that invites the user to enter search terms and perform a query. Like other pages, it comprises a _header_ ⋯ _content_ ⋯ _footer_ sequence.

Macros can include parameters interposed in square brackets between name and content. Such parameters are known as 'page parameters' because they control the overall generation of a page. They are expressed as $[x = y]$, which gives parameter x the value y. Two parameters of particular interest are l, which determines what language is used, and v, which controls whether or not images are used in the interface.

Figure 18.2 shows the definition of three versions of the macro _header_ within the 'query' package, corresponding to the languages English, French, and Spanish. They set the language parameter l to the appropriate two-letter international standard abbreviation (ISO 639), enabling the system to present the appropriate version when the page is generated. If a macro has no definition for a given language, it will resolve to the version given without any language parameter – which, in the current implementation, is English (though another language could be chosen as the default).

Greenstone uses many images that contain language-dependent text. These are created by an open-source utility using scripting to automate image generation. Macro files use a specially constructed form of comment (signified by a double hash, ##) to convey additional information for a progressing program – in this case the image generation script. Near the end of Figure 18.2 an icon with the text *HELP* is generated and placed in the file *chelp.gif* in subdirectory *en* (for 'English'). The image generation script parses the comment to determine the type of image to generate, the text to be placed on it, and where to put the result. Then it automatically generates the image and stores it in the language-specific directory appropriate to the l page parameter.

A precedence ordering for evaluating page parameters is built into the macro language to resolve conflicting definitions. Also included are conditional statements. An example can be seen in Figure 18.2's _content_ macro, which uses an *If* statement, conditioned by the macro _cgiargqb_, to determine whether the query box that appears on the search page should be the normal one or a large one. The value of _cgiargqb_ is set at runtime by the Greenstone system (the user can change it on a *Preferences* page). Many other system-defined macros have values that are determined at runtime: examples include the URL prefix where Greenstone is installed on the system, and the number of documents returned by a search.

Figure 18.2 is artificial in both content (to demonstration the salient features of the macro language) and layout (for expository convenience). In reality, all English text phrases are stored together in the file *english.dm*, with French phrases in *french.dm* and so on (the suffix *.dm* denotes a macro file). Package names serve to lexically scope the phrase definitions. There are two files for each language, for example *english.dm* and *english2.dm*. The first contains the core Greenstone phrases and the second those used in auxiliary subsystems. This allows the translation facility to differentiate between these two classes.

The internationalization support systems described in this chapter fulfill the same goal as those in the *Firstsearch* interface case study (Perlman, 2000). However, features such as lexical scoping, inheritance, integration with the release system, and translation support system (described below) provide a more general solution to the localization challenge. It is interesting to note that Greenstone has independently evolved a similar community solution to the translation problem as that used by the CITIDEL project (Perugini *et al.*, 2004). CITIDEL's evaluation showed that their community translation was of significantly better quality than a machine translation of the same content. In contrast to the *International Children's Digital Library* (Hutchinson *et al.*, 2005), Greenstone does not face the issues of managing metadata in multiple languages as we provide an infrastructure for *others* to publish content, rather than becoming a content publisher ourselves.

The detail of the macro facility outlined above illustrates some of the work that was required to provide an internationalized architecture for Greenstone. The goal of the technicians in performing this work is to provide an abstraction for the librarians – to enable customization without coding. Tennant (2002) outlines a similar level of abstraction:

> . . . all librarians need not know how to code software. But they should know what software is capable of doing, when a program could be easily written to accomplish a task, and what skills someone needs to write one.

18.7 Supporting Localization: The Translator's Interface

The deployment of a localized digital library collection can be viewed as a long-term collaboration between technicians, librarians, and translators. Each of these groups lacks the expertise to succeed on its own, and the role of the Greenstone translator's interface is to provide the infrastructure for the deployment and maintenance of the collection. It allows users to:

- Translate the interface into a new language.
- Update an existing language interface to reflect new Greenstone facilities.
- Refine an existing language interface by correcting errors.

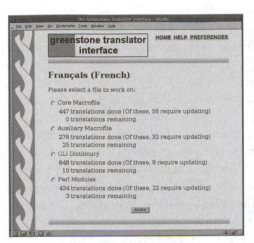

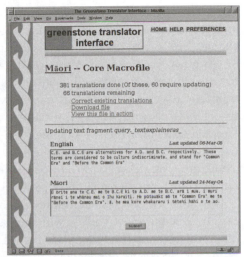

(a) The status page for French   *(b) Updating a section of the Māori interface*

Figure 18.3 *Using the translator's interface.*

On entry the user selects the target language that they are translating into. The base language is always English, because this is what is used to develop Greenstone and is guaranteed to be the most up-to-date representation of the interface. Originally we planned to allow users to select other base languages, but we removed this facility for practical reasons: we did not want to compound errors by using a base language that was incomplete or included incorrect translations.

Having selected the target language, the user is shown a status page for that language (Figure 18.3(a)). Greenstone distinguishes between phrases that are used in the main system – for instance, search, browsing, and help pages – and phrases in less-frequently-used subsystems – for instance, the site administration pages through which usage statistics and logs are viewed, and the translator service itself – for this too needs translating! The phrases are divided into a few sections that reflect this distinction; currently there are four. For each one, the status page shows the number of translations that have been done and the number remaining to do.

In Figure 18.3(b) the user has begun to update the core macro file for the Māori language interface. A single language fragment is shown, and when this string was last updated. Also included is a progress indicator: how many fragments remain to be done. The English phrase appears at the top; below it is the box into which the translated version can be entered. Two kinds of phrase appear: ones that are missing from the Māori version, and ones whose Māori translation is outdated because the English version has been edited more recently. In the latter case the outdated translation appears as a visual cue (as in Figure 18.3(b)). After completing the translation the changes are committed back to the translation server.

Another feature of the translator, not shown in the figures, is the ability to search for a language fragment and then, on choosing a particular occurrence, enter into a translation window similar to that shown in Figure 18.3(b). The sort of situation where this is useful is when a translator is checking the text *in situ* in the reader's interface and spots an error, say a typing mistake. Using the search feature they can quickly locate the macro with the mistake in it, and correct it. Internally, the language fragments are managed as a private collection to Greenstone (which means it does not normally appear to a regular user), and therefore the ability to search it comes for free.

Hogan *et al.* (2004) note the importance of the 'ability to incorporate the context of each translation' when working with internationalized software applications. Changes to the translator's interface take place immediately: users can see their new translations in context by accessing (or reloading) the appropriate pages in Greenstone. However, these changes are not made automatically to the public Greenstone site, nor are they automatically committed to the master software repository. Instead, to guard against error and misuse, they take effect in a special replica of the Greenstone site used for translation. When satisfied with the entire translation, users notify the central Greenstone repository's administrator of the change through email. Then, issuing a single command fully integrates the changes into the officially released version of the software.

Because each translated text string is saved when it is submitted, a user need not translate all phrases in one sitting. Moreover, when they return to the service the system regenerates everything from scratch, which means that only the outstanding phrases are shown. For well-maintained language interfaces such as Spanish, French, and Russian, only a few new translation requests are generated when new features are added. However, some less-used language interfaces contain translations only for the core phrases that appear in the main system.

New languages are added in the same way that existing ones are updated, except that no existing translations appear in the right-hand column. A would-be translator emails the system administrator and the administrator manually adds the new language to the list. There are a total of about 750 phrases in the entire interface. Of these about 60% (450 phrases) pertain to the core Greenstone system, which every language interface covers; the remainder are for the less-used 'auxiliary' parts of the interface. Of the existing language interfaces, 15 are for the complete interface and the remaining 23 cover just the core parts.

Sometimes phrases in an existing language interface need to be refined. For example, a typographical error may have been overlooked when entering a phrase, or seeing a phrase in its actual interface context may suggest a better form of expression. To accommodate this requirement, users need to be able to locate an existing phrase and update its translation. Consequently each page of the interface contains a link to a search facility that allows you to find all fragments that contain the specified search terms.

As with the macro language, the Translator's Interface provides a simplified view of the complex internals of Greenstone. The textual fragments are separated from other elements so that translators only see relevant content. The ability to perform this separation, and provide this service, is an effective operational test of the internationalization of a software application.

18.7.1 A Localization Example

The localization process involves adapting the textual elements of the digital library interface and customizing other elements of the interface. For example, the collections at *Ulukau: The Hawaiian Electronic Library* (Ulukau, 2005) use a customized version of Greenstone that provides a graphical aid for creating queries containing specific Hawaiian characters, allowing users to create an accurate query without having to remember sequences of keystrokes.

The localization shown in Figure 18.4 goes beyond that shown in Figure 18.1. In the case of *Ulukau* the local Hawaiian language community had sufficient technical knowledge to be able to add more extensive customization. This customization was possible because Greenstone is released as open source software; the community had permission to look inside and change the program. The librarians who made these changes were aware that their reader community had difficulty using standard keyboards to construct their Hawaiian language queries. Local contexts such as this are

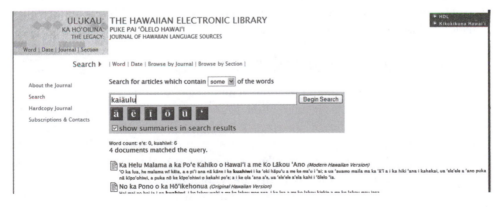

Figure 18.4 Ulukau: the Hawaiian Electronic Library.

Context: Training

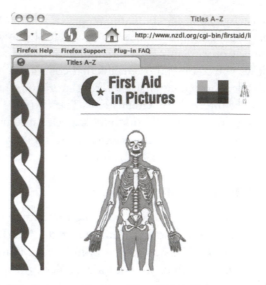

Figure 18.5 *The Greenstone collection First Aid in Pictures.*

difficult to predict for the technicians developing the Greenstone software. Although the internationalization of the architecture meets many localization needs, it is unlikely to ever be complete: in many circumstances the flexibility of the open source model provides the final localization step.

The flexibility of the localization possible in Greenstone is also evident in the creation of a collection aimed at illiterate users (Deo *et al.*, 2004). The collection *First Aid in Pictures* derives from an internationalized book that describes medical procedures without a textual interface. Figure 18.5 shows searching and browsing structures provided by nontextual means.

18.8 **The Effects of Localization**

As multilingual collections are created and achieve significant usage levels, it becomes possible to study the effects of internationalization on the user experience, to tease out insights into the effect of interface language on user information behavior. Research is no longer limited to small-scale experiments over artificial tasks and collections – it suddenly becomes feasible to learn what real users do in multilingual digital libraries, as they attempt to satisfy authentic information needs.

Log analysis is a particularly promising tool, as it allows the researcher to summarize large amounts of user activity over extended periods. Analysis of a year's usage of the *Niupepa* collection of Māori newspapers (Figure 18.1), for example, has identified patterns of behavior with implications for interface and interaction design (Keegan and Cunningham, 2005a,b). The *Niupepa* collection allows users to choose between an English and a Māori interface to the predominantly Māori language document collection. Three patterns of usage emerged from the log data: usage sessions conducted primarily via the English language interface (surprisingly, two-thirds of sessions), sessions conducted via the Māori interface, and 'bilingual' sessions in which the user switched between the two languages. Users in 'bilingual' sessions presumably changed interface to access a retrieval strategy in a language that they were more comfortable with, or perhaps to access a certain text that was only stored in one language in a multi-language collection – further (qualitative) research is needed to come to a deeper understanding of the 'why' behind the patterns located in the logs. Information retrieval strategies differed between sessions conducted under the Māori or the English language interface; the Māori interface users tended to rely more heavily on browsing methods to access pages of interest in the collection rather than search, and the English language interface sessions included considerably more searching than browsing. Historically, Māori has been an oral rather than a written language, and so it is likely that the proportion of *Niupepa* users who are fluent in written Māori is small – and so browsing is a more effective information-seeking mechanism for these users. The implications for interface design are clear: to provide more, and more flexible, browsing tools through the Māori language.

Experiments with alternating the default interface language between English and Māori indicate that, as perhaps might be expected, users tend to accept the default – no matter which of the two languages it is (Keegan and Cunningham, 2005a,b). Given that users appear to have weak preferences as shown by their disinclination to switch languages, it seems more natural to make Māori the default. Digital library developers who have more than one interface language available have the opportunity, perhaps obligation, to ensure that the default language best matches the language of content of the collection and thus provides the user of the collection a smoother and more comfortable information retrieval experience.

18.9 **Understanding Localization in Context: Training**

Training is a serious barrier to the adoption of advanced information systems in public institutions – particularly in poorer parts of the world where commercial courses are infeasible. UNESCO's Communication and Information program has mounted courses on the use of Greenstone for building collections, in Bangalore (India), Almaty (Kazakhstan), Dakar (Senegal), and Suva (Fiji). Courses sponsored by other sources have been mounted in Colima (Mexico), Puna and Kohzikode (India), Havana, Cape Town, Shanghai, Singapore, and Arusha (Tanzania). There have also been many courses in the USA and Europe.

These workshops promote the development and sharing of digital library collections using Greenstone. The aim of the UNESCO workshops is to train trainers, and participants are expected to promote digital library collection development by conducting similar programs in their countries. Attendees are supplied with a full set of teaching material, in printed form and also on CD-ROM, that they can use for local courses back home.

To give a specific early example, the first Fiji workshop took place in November 2003, sponsored jointly by the University of the South Pacific Library. It was attended by 15 participants from 7 countries in the Pacific region: Fiji, Marshall Islands, Papua New Guinea, Samoa, Solomon Islands, Tonga, and Vanuatu. Most of the participants were librarians and library systems personnel from national and educational institutions in these countries. The workshop was designed and conducted by members of the New Zealand Digital Library project. The content was based on an earlier workshop at NCSI, Indian Institute of Science, Bangalore.

The workshop covered the following aspects: overview of Greenstone's features, capabilities, and applications; platforms, installation, and configuration; using the Librarian Interface to build collections and add and use metadata; advanced features of the Interface; sample collections; multilingual support; new interface languages. Most of the presentation and demonstration sessions were followed by laboratory sessions where the participants experimented with Greenstone through carefully designed exercises. Each participant had a dedicated workstation with the Windows XP operating system. Apart from the printed course material, Greenstone and associated software were distributed to the participants on CD-ROM.

During the lab sessions, each participant built (among other things) a small Greenstone collection of images about tourism in their home country, downloaded from the web, with manually assigned metadata. At the end of the workshop these were all placed on a self-installing Greenstone CD-ROM entitled 'Pacific Tourism,' and copies were made for participants to take away as a memento. The collections were charming: all had striking images, some had maps, and one included an underwater video.

Course evaluation forms were used to assess the effectiveness of presentations and lab exercises. Based on formal and informal feedback from participants, the workshop was successful in imparting a conceptual and practical understanding of the development of digital collections and the use of Greenstone. There was a consensus that further time was needed to cover all the features of the software that participants wanted to learn about, and many expressed interest in a more advanced follow-up workshop. However, opinion was split as to whether additional time would be better spent in presenting new information or reinforcing existing material through more lab exercises. In fact, it would be useful in future to divide attendees on the basis of their prior knowledge and experience and run parallel sessions.

All course material (slightly revised to correct minor errors that were discovered during the workshop) has been made freely available on the Greenstone web site (www.greenstone.org) for others to use in future workshops. Face-to-face training sessions have been especially useful for connecting the technicians and the librarians; who usually only communicate electronically.

18.10 Implications for users

18.10.1 Shift the User Mindset: Users are Part of the Team

Greenstone has many of the attributes of a 'real' piece of software: its releases have version numbers indicating that it has been in existence a respectable amount of time, regular updates are released, documentation is available, and so forth. 'Proper' software should be accompanied by extensive user support services: help lines, dedicated user support personnel, guaranteed response times for queries. This level of user support is simply not possible for a product created in a university research lab.

So as we make it easy for users to contribute, we must also try to shift the mindset of users: to let users see that they *do* have something to contribute to Greenstone. One part of this shift comes from literally allowing users to join the Greenstone family: a donation allows an individual or a group to become a 'Friend of Greenstone,' the advantages of which include additional support and time from a project member to explore that individual's particular requirements.

We also seek to engage users in dialog, to have our users tell us what features of Greenstone they find frustrating or difficult to understand. The aim is to move users from seeing themselves as powerless end-users, to participants in an ongoing usability evaluation and interface design refinement process. To this end, we have created a software framework for this 'participatory usability' approach that allows users to easily report the context of a Greenstone interaction that they find problematic (Nichols *et al.*, 2003).

18.10.2 Make it Easy for Users to Contribute

Most of our users are end-users, typically readers and librarians, rather than programmers. In many ways this has been a disadvantage. We feel that we have not been able to benefit as much as other open source systems do from others helping us develop the system and fix bugs. Many of the responses on our mailing lists come from our own software developers, rather than being contributed by the wider community.

However, we have found users very eager to collaborate and contribute. One way we have benefited from this is in translation of the interface into different languages – an area which the software developers could not possibly tackle by themselves. The sheer magnitude of effort involved in translating a substantial user interface into different languages is staggering. In the case of Greenstone, there are about 700 separate language strings in the reader's interface alone, which has been translated into nearly 40 languages. (There are almost twice as many strings in the librarian's interface, but this has been rendered in only five languages.)

18.11 Implications for Designers

18.11.1 Adapt the Infrastructure to the Strengths of the Respective User Groups

Examining the infrastructure that has evolved with Greenstone, it appears as if we have converged on an arrangement called 'central oversight with local empowerment' (COLE) (Woods, 2005). This COLE organization is regarded as best practice in global enterprises for playing to the strengths of the various stakeholders whilst retaining sufficient coordination to benefit from the advantages of consistency. The localization work is pushed away from the core of developers to those places where it can be performed most efficiently: the language communities themselves. The strengths of the COLE approach mean that locale-specific issues are dealt with by local experts, but as this work is performed within a global standard structure then it can easily be reused by other groups (Woods, 2005). For example, although a language interface for use in Brazil needs to be tailored to represent differences from Portuguese, the work is incremental rather than starting from a blank slate.

The COLE structure of Greenstone leaves the technicians free to concentrate on their speciality – designing and coding software – whilst hiding the complexity from other groups. The librarians see a tool that abstracts away from code and represents familiar concepts such as collections and metadata. The translators see language fragments (and their contexts of use) and can effectively ignore many other aspects of the application. The readers see their locale-specific content presented with an appropriate interface that facilitates their access to information.

It is easy for designers and developers to regard universal usability as a challenge for *their* skill set. The experience of the localization of Greenstone is that involving the users as partners in development can be an effective approach that can spread the workload.

18.11.2 **Don't be a Linguistic Perfectionist**

Despite our exhortation to cultivate attention to detail in the interface itself, we have been remarkably simplistic in our approach to linguistic support of different languages. For example, stemming is implemented only for English and, in a rather simple form, for French. Alphabetization of browsing lists has not been examined carefully in different languages. It probably does not work well for many languages, and certainly not for idiographic ones from which the very notion of alphabetic ordering is absent. For example, in Chinese we need a Pinyin browser and a stroke-based browser for those older readers who are more comfortable with this representation of character ordering. Greenstone presently has neither. Alphabetical lists of titles in English follow the convention that initial articles (*A* and *The*) are ignored in the ordering; this is not extended to other languages.

In fact, we are surprised that we have been able to get away with this sloppiness. Users submit countless many questions and requests for further features to the mailing list, but rarely comment on linguistic issues like this. Despite the attention paid to stemming in information retrieval, most users do not really seem to care – and many do not even know whether their favorite search engines stem query terms or not. As far as non-English languages are concerned, we believe that most users are surprised and grateful to find that the interface is available at all in their own language, and do not worry too much about linguistic deficiencies. It would have been easy for us to get bogged down in trying to cope properly with different languages, to the extent that the software was never released or used. Fortunately, we have avoided this optimality trap.

18.12 **Implications for Policymakers**

18.12.1 **Reap the Benefits of Open Source Software**

The elements of localization that extend beyond translating the text are hard for a software development to predict. A global user base means that there will always be requests for types of customization that the software does not currently provide. However, an open source application, such as Greenstone, allows unlimited customization by technically competent users. The *Ulukau* digital library shows that localization can be facilitated by an appropriate licensing scheme; it is instructive to contrast *Ulukau* with previous localization experiences in Hawaii. Warschauer (1998) describes how the Hawaiian language community developed their own software systems because they could not find localized versions appropriate to their needs. In Greenstone's case, the licensing facilitated developers to *incrementally* localize, rather than develop appropriate software from scratch.

Although the philosophy behind Greenstone's development has been one of tool empowerment, it is clear that constructing a completely generic digital library tool is very difficult. Although Greenstone, as distributed, is a very flexible tool, the open source licensing model provides local communities with the potential for fine-grained localization for their specific needs.

Greenstone has received funding from the New Zealand government to aid its development. It is common for funded projects to be asked to justify their economic impact and, of course, Greenstone can be freely downloaded and used. However, a spin-off company, DL Consulting, is now providing support, consulting, and custom collection-building services based around Greenstone software. Policymakers need to recognize that the impact of open source projects can be more indirect and diffuse than that of clearly commercially relevant projects. For example, given Greenstone's work in developing countries it could almost be considered part of New Zealand's overseas development aid.

18.12.2 Provide Support for Development as Well as Research

Greenstone has been created within a research group. While some aspects of Greenstone are in themselves research, the majority of the Greenstone effort has been straightforward software development. But having created Greenstone, it is a research tool: it supports experimentation by ourselves and researchers worldwide in digital library user interfaces, novel approaches to searching and browsing, facilities for multimedia documents, and so forth. The benefits to us as researchers are incalculable, but at times the costs to the group have seemed high, and the path precarious.

Recognition by funding agencies and policymakers of the dual development/ research roles that a group must take on for a project such as Greenstone would ease the pain of producing both solid software and solid research. Researchers typically do not have the experience, expertise, or energy to distribute and market their work; it would be invaluable if infrastructure were available for these portions of the software creation cycle that are so far outside normal research activities.

18.12.3 Do not Neglect Training

As we have noted above, training courses are an important part of the overall program of getting Greenstone widely used, particularly in developing countries. It is easy for software developers to neglect this because they are used to dealing with other software specialists. In our case the principal users are librarians, and they often need to be gently introduced to the system in a carefully designed training program.

We should probably have identified trainers as a further class of user, with their own requirements. In fact, most training courses have been run by the system developers, or by self-taught users. In future, as we expand our training program, we will probably have to identify the needs of trainers and cater for them as a separate user group.

Our holistic view of software distribution that includes training end-users has been immensely valuable. It has enabled face-to-face contact between developers and users which affords the developers new insights into how people sometimes struggle valiantly with the software – problems that may not be discussed in other fora, such as mailing lists. Running training courses has also given us an immense amount of personal satisfaction.

18.13 Implications for Researchers
18.13.1 Partner with Global Organizations

Partnering with global organizations can provide an invaluable source of expertise and resources. In August 2000 the Greenstone project entered into a partnership with UNESCO (and also with the Belgium-based *Human Info* NGO). Through its *Information for all* program, UNESCO recognizes that digital libraries are radically reforming how information is acquired and disseminated in its partner communities and institutions in the fields of education, science, and culture around the world, and particularly in developing countries. UNESCO distributes the Greenstone software widely in developing countries with the aim of empowering users, particularly in universities, libraries, and other public service institutions, to build their own digital collections. Their hope is that this software will encourage the effective deployment of digital libraries to share information and place it in the public domain.

The partnership with UNESCO has been a crucial feature of the development and internationalization of Greenstone. They give universal credibility to the international branding of Greenstone. They have strongly encouraged us to take a global outlook (particularly in developing countries). They have provided us with contacts, with multilingual resources, and (though to a far lesser extent) a limited amount of seed funding.

For example, all of the Greenstone documentation has, with the aid of UNESCO, been translated into Spanish, French, and Russian. This includes not just the end-user reader's interface, but the full documentation for building collections, all buttons, menu items, and online help in the Greenstone Librarian Interface which is used for building collections, and all error and warning messages. For example, some of the output from our Perl scripts is fed to the user to indicate the status of the collection-building operations, or warning messages, and these have also been translated. To produce a comprehensive piece of interactive software, with full documentation, in four languages is something far beyond our own resources.

The global outlook of Greenstone has been facilitated through UNESCO cooperation and has provided momentum to ensure that the software can be successfully localized. The readers and librarians have benefited from the multilingual focus that a large organization such as UNESCO has brought to the software development. In effect, UNESCO has acted as a user champion to ensure the thorough internationalization of the software.

18.14 **Future Directions**

The Greenstone project is negotiating a delicate tightrope between producing and promulgating socially useful software on the one hand and undertaking cutting edge computer science research on the other. The current 'production' version of the system, which we call Greenstone2, was designed over five years ago and has reached a stage where it is comprehensive, mature, and reliable. Nevertheless, new requirements continue to emerge. For example, as we write we are extending a new facility for incorporating CDS/ISIS databases into Greenstone collections, a format that is unknown in the West but widely used in developing countries for storing bibliographic records, even in major libraries. To debug this facility we must collaborate closely with users in developing countries: at home there are no CDS/ISIS users.

We are also striving to improve the software engineering methodology used to develop the system. Refactoring is the process of restructuring code to improve its design in a way that does not alter its observable behavior (Fowler *et al.*, 1999). The improved design is intended to ensure that further enhancements to the software are easier to make, and reduce the possibility of introducing new bugs or unintended side-effects. Backwards compatibility has become a watchword for Greenstone2 development, and is motivating the design of a refactoring tool that leverages off aspects peculiar to digital library software. Creating a digital library collection involves generating many static files such as indexes and database tables that encapsulate much of the external behavior of the digital library. Spotting differences between files generated by original and refactored code allows developers to identify potential errors in the revised version. This provides a kind of regression testing facility.

Alongside the production version of Greenstone we are working on a radical redesign and complete reimplementation, called Greenstone3, informed by end-users' and collection developers' experience over the last decade. This provides flexible ways of dynamically configuring the run-time system and adding new services. It modularizes the internal structure and simplifies the addition of new modules. It is written in

Java to promote portability, dynamic loading of objects, and internationalization. Modules communicate by streaming XML messages between each other. Using SOAP this communication can be distributed across a network. All modules have the ability to describe themselves in a machine readable form, and to apply an XSLT to transform messages. This is instrumental in providing different levels of configurability, an important ability given the different types of people involved in the lifecycle of a digital library.

In keeping with our original philosophy of laying the basic groundwork first, Greenstone3 already provides full backwards compatibility to collections built with Greenstone2. It can serve collections built under the old regime without any modification at all, and present them in a way that looks indistinguishable to readers. At present we recommend librarian-level users to work with Greenstone2, secure in the knowledge that their collections will continue to operate when they eventually upgrade to the new system. We recommend computer science-level users who wish to develop new services that correspond to new ways of accessing and presenting information to work with Greenstone3.

This twin approach is intended to satisfy users in developing countries who want reliable, easy-to-use software that runs on low-level hardware (Greenstone2), as well as high-end research-level users who enjoy sophisticated computer environments (Greenstone3). Our long-term research aim is to encourage digital library researchers, including ourselves, to make their new facilities available to real end-users. Our long-term service aim is to do this in a way that will eventually allow people in all corners of the world to benefit from the advances.

18.15 **Conclusion**

Providing truly international digital library collections requires a collaboration infrastructure that connects the librarians, technicians, and translators. Greenstone can provide end-users (the readers) with multilingual documents using different interface languages. However, in terms of universal usability the software developers have to consider the librarians as a separate set of users, whose goal is to produce collections for the readers. A current goal of research on Greenstone is to address the needs of this group of users to make it easier to adapt and localize collections without being overwhelmed by the technical details of server-side collection customization. The recent results (Keegan and Cunningham, 2005a,b) that collection interfaces translated into indigenous languages are actually *used* in those languages provides the Greenstone development team with additional rationale for easing the process of collection customization.

Greenstone has adapted its multilingual support to accommodate many languages, in doing so it has simplified usage for technicians, translators, and librarians. As the user base has become more diversified the range of contexts of use has become greater and consequently the software has had to adapt to these diverse conditions. As a result of coping with these 'edge' conditions, the software is now increasingly robust in normal usage. This experience supports Shneiderman's (2000) belief that a 'broader spectrum of usage situations forces researchers to consider a wider range of designs and often leads to innovations that benefit all users.' In fact, the multilingual nature of Greenstone has encouraged a more diverse user population than an English-only application; the effects of this diversity of use are felt throughout the application and are not constrained to the language components. In this way the benefits arising from addressing the universal usability challenge are distributed to all the user groups: the translators, the technicians, the readers and the librarians.

References

Apperley, M., Keegan, T.T., Cunningham, S.J. and Witten, I.H. (2002) Delivering the Māori-language newspapers on the Internet. In Curnow, J., Hopa N. & McRae, J. (Eds.) *Rere atu, taku manu! Discovering History, Language and Politics in the Māori-Language Newspapers,* Auckland University Press, Auckland, New Zealand, 211–232.

Aykin, N. (2005) Overview: where to start and what to consider. In Aykin, N. (Ed.) *Usability and Internationalization of Information Technology,* Lawrence Erlbaum Associates, Mahwah, NJ, 3–20.

Bainbridge, D., Edgar, K.D., McPherson, J.R. and Witten, I.H. (2003) Managing change in a digital library system with many interface languages. *Proceedings of the 7th European Conference on Research and Advanced Technology for Digital Libraries (ECDL 2003),* Springer-Verlag, Berlin, Germany, LNCS 2769, pp. 350–361.

Crystal, D. (2000) *Language Death.* Cambridge University Press, Cambridge.

Deo, S., Nichols D.M., Cunningham, S.J. et al. (2004) Digital library access for illiterate users. *Proceedings of the International Research Conference on Innovations in Information Technology (IIT 2004),* UAE University, Dubai, UAE, pp. 506–516.

Fowler, M., Beck, K., Brant, J. et al. (1999) *Refactoring: Improving the Design of Existing Code.* Addison-Wesley, Reading, MA.

Hogan, J.M., Ho-Stuart, C. and Pham, B. (2004) Key challenges in software internationalisation. *Proceedings of the Australasian Workshop on Software*

Internationalisation (AWSI 2004). ACSW Frontiers 2004: Conferences on Research and Practice in Information Technology, Volume 32, Australian Computer Society, Inc., Sydney, Australia, 187–194.

Hutchinson, H.B., Rose, A., Bederson, B. et al. (2005) The International Children's Digital Library: a case study in designing for a multi-lingual, multi-cultural, multi-generational audience, *Information Technology and Libraries,* **24**(1), 4–12.

Keegan, T.T. and Cunningham, S.J. (2005a) Language preference in a bi-language digital library. *Proceedings of the Joint Conference on Digital Libraries (JCDL '05),* ACM Press, New York, pp. 174–175.

Keegan, T.T. and Cunningham, S.J. (2005b) What happens if we switch the default language of a website? *Proceedings of the 1st International Conference on Web Information Systems and Technologies (WEBIST '05),* INSTICC, Setúbal, Portugal, pp. 263–269.

Lagoze, C., Payette, S., Shin, E. and Wilper, C. (2006) Fedora: an architecture for complex objects and their relationships. *International Journal on Digital Libraries,* **6**(2), 124–138.

Nichols, D.M., McKay, D. and Twidale, M.B. (2003) Participatory usability: empowering proactive users, *Proceedings of the 4th Annual Conference of the ACM Special Interest Group on Computer Human Interaction – New Zealand Chapter (CHINZ'03),* ACM SIGCHI New Zealand, Dunedin, New Zealand, pp. 63–68.

Nichols, D.M., Witten, I.H., Keegan, T.T. et al. (2005) Digital libraries and minority languages. *New Review of Hypermedia Multimedia,* **11**(2), 139–155.

Niupepa: Māori newspapers (2005) Available online at: http://nzdl.org/niupepa (accessed 25 October 2005).

Perugini, S., McDevitt, K., Richardson, R. et al. (2004) Enhancing usability in CITIDEL: multimodal, multilingual and interactive visualization interfaces. *Proceedings of the Joint Conference on Digital Libraries (JCDL' 04),* ACM Press, New York, pp. 315–324.

Perlman, G. (2000) The FirstSearch user interface architecture: universal access for any user, in many languages, on any platform. *Proceedings of the Conference on Universal Usability (CUU '00),* ACM Press, New York, pp. 1–8.

Purvis, M., Hwang, P., Purvis, M. et al. (2001) A practical look at software internationalisation. *Journal of Integrated Design Processes in Science,* **5**(3), 79–90.

Savarimuthu, B.T.R. and Purvis, M. (2004) Towards a multi-lingual workflow system – a practical outlook. *Proceedings of the Australasian Workshop on Software*

Internationalisation (AWSI 2004). ACSW Frontiers 2004: Conferences on Research and Practice in Information Technology, Volume 32, Australian Computer Society, Inc., Sydney, Australia, pp. 205–210.

Shneiderman, B. (2000) Universal usability. *Communications of the ACM,* **43**(5), 85–91.

Tansley, R., Smith, M. and Walker, J.H. (2005) The DSpace open source digital asset management system: challenges and opportunities. *Proceedings of the 9th European Conference on Research and Advanced Technology for Digital Libraries (ECDL 2005),* Springer-Verlag, Berlin, Germany, LNCS 3652, pp. 242–253.

Tennant, R. (2002) The digital librarian shortage. *Library Journal,* **127**(5), 32.

Ulukau: the Hawaiian Electronic Library (2005) Available online at: http://ulukau.org (accessed 25 October 2005).

The Unicode Consortium (2000) *The Unicode Standard, Version 4.0.* Addison-Wesley, Boston, MA.

Warschauer, M. (1998) Technology and indigenous language revitalization: analyzing the experience of Hawai'i. *Canadian Modern Language Review,* 55(1), 140–161.

Witten, I.H. and Bainbridge, D. (2003) *How to Build a Digital Library.* Morgan Kaufmann, San Francisco, CA.

Witten, I.H., Cunningham, S.J., Vallabh, M. and Bell, T.C. (1995) A New Zealand digital library for computer science research. *Proceedings of the Second Annual Conference on the Theory and Practice of Digital Libraries (DL'95),* Texas A&M University, Austin, TX, pp. 25–30.

Witten, I.H., Loots, M., Trujillo, M.F. and Bainbridge, D. (2002) The promise of digital libraries in developing countries. *The Electronic Library,* **20**(1), 7–13.

Woods, J. (2005) Managing multicultural content in the global enterprise. In Aykin, N. (Ed.) *Usability and Internationalization of Information Technology,* Lawrence Erlbaum Associates, Mahwah, NJ, 123–154.

Yeo, A.W. (2001) Global-software development lifecycle: an exploratory study. Proceedings of the Conference on Human Factors in Computing Systems (CHI' 01), ACM Press, New York, 104–111.

Making Universal Access Truly Universal: Looking Toward the Future

19

Jennifer Preece

College of Information Studies, University of Maryland, MD, USA

19.1 Introduction

During the last 20 years digital technologies have shrunk in size and cost, while growing in power. Cell phones and small digital devices enable those who cannot afford laptops and big screens to join the communications and information revolution. Those who are continually moving from place to place, or who live or work in remote areas are gaining access to the Internet through various digital devices, though access is still limited and nonexistent in remote areas. Political barriers, though severe, are less formidable as those who seek to control information flow gradually lose the battle to the ingenuity of freedom-hungry people. Digital technology is a powerful device against repression; it enables the human spirit to speak to the world about the injustices imposed by dictators. Email and blogs unite soldiers in Iraq with their families and friends, bringing comfort and a sense of connection across the miles. Of course, there is a dark side too, technology makes it easier for terrorists to carry out their dastardly deeds.

Authors in this book speak eloquently about how technology improves everyone's quality of life by helping them to overcome physical and cognitive constraints and disabilities so that they can participate more fully in the world around them. Well-designed technologies enable people with disabilities to get both the care and companionship that they need. More importantly, they can help themselves and retain some of the dignity that is challenged by being dependent upon others. In addition, technology offers respite to carers and loved ones who dedicate themselves day and night to sick family members and friends. Bulletin boards, wikis, web sites, online journals, and digital libraries can be accessed for information, while email, chat, instant messaging, phone texting, and voice-over-IP (VOIP) support more personal, informal communication. Supported by powerful search facilities, such as those of Google, information can be found in seconds that would otherwise take weeks, months, and years of a librarian's time. Of course, the quality of information varies and this is an issue that those researching universal usability (Shneiderman, 2000) could address. If people put in effort to finding information, then they want high quality information to be returned. How can we ensure that? This is all the more important if a person with a disability expends a huge amount of time and energy. Participants at a recent workshop identified the following three aspects that must be addressed to ensure that information is usable by the general public (Internet Credibility and the User, 2006):

- Skills, including information literacy and related literacies that users must possess to be effective in an information environment.
- Tools and technologies that are designed to allow users to navigate information.
- Institutions such as libraries and schools that transfer these skills and prepare individuals to be critical thinkers and consumers of information.

Search engines are providing increasingly powerful support tools for language translation, geographical positioning, scholarly support, and other services that offer steps toward improving universal usability but more can be done. For example, researchers working on the Semantic Web want to bring more meaning to information on the web. Another approach is taken by B.J. Fogg and his colleagues; they are exploring the potency of prominence interpretation theory for identifying components of a web site that users find prominent, how users interpret them and thus, how credible the web site is (Fogg, 2003). Such things as the user's involvement, the topic, the user's task, the user's experience, and the user's individual differences determine prominence. The interpretation component includes assumptions that the user is likely to make. These are influenced by the user's skills and knowledge, and the context in which the user is using the web site. For any approach to impact universal usability it must take account of the contexts and environments of use, and needs of the broad population of users, including those with disabilities.

The authors of chapters of this book speak of special applications for young children, older adults, people with disabilities, underserved communities, cross-cultural communication, and more. But as many of these authors point out, technology alone is not enough to bring universal usability, a deep knowledge of cognitive and social psychology, sociology, psychotherapy, anthropology, and culture are necessary partners for a marriage in which technology serves the universal needs of all the world's peoples. Without these, technology will never become universally accessible and usable.

In this chapter, I briefly examine the concept of universal usability in relation to individuals, communities, and society at large and modestly suggest a few things that HCI specialists, interaction designers, and community and technology advocates can do to make technology more universal and more usable and to encourage research on universal usability. Next I discuss a range of communications and information technologies from list servers and phone texting to YouTube, Wikipedia, Flickr, and Del.icio.us. Then I explore some trends in the way these technologies are currently used and speculate about future directions. Finally, I draw a few conclusions and discuss my personal hopes for the future. Since my passion is community communication and empowerment, this provides a focus for the chapter. I believe that *three working together will achieve as much as six working singly* (unaccredited Spanish Proverb).

19.2 Individuals, Communities, and Technology

Much has been written about technology for individual communication and for small groups. For example, in 1991 Ellis, Gibbs, and Rein proposed the time/space matrix (Ellis *et al.*, 1991) – same vs. different time, same vs. different space – for classifying communications technologies. Even though the range of communications software has increased dramatically since 1991, this simple matrix is still applicable. Furthermore, some of the oldest, lightweight technologies and their more recent ancestors have the greatest penetration in terms of reaching underprivileged minority groups. Why? Because of accessibility and usability. For example, email and list servers remain the *killer aps* in parts of the world (e.g. USA), particularly among older users. Cell phone and instant messaging replace them with younger users in the USA, but in Europe, the Philippines, and throughout Asia, texting via cell phones is the most popular mode of communication. These preferences remind us that choices involve more than just usability, they are based on other things; in this case low-cost business models win the day. Ease of mobility is important too.

	Same time	Different times
Same place	Synchronous local (face to face). For example, control rooms, local meetings, traditional classes.	Asynchronous local. For example, messages left on message boards, logs of equipment usage, group calendars on paper.
Different places	Synchronous distributed. For example, phone, chat, texting, instant messaging (IM), voice-over-IP (VOIP), audio/video conferencing.	Asynchronous distributed. For example, email, list servers, newsgroup, discussion boards, wikis, blogs, photo & video galleries, annotations, online and networked community platforms.

So what has changed since Ellis *et al.*'s time/space matrix of 1991? The answer is *many* things. Some of these are social and some are technical; they include the following four big changes, which are interdependent to a greater or lesser extent:

- *Broader range of users using technology.* There are millions more people using an increasingly wide range of information and communications technologies (ICTs) across the world. In addition, the demography of these users is much broader. People of all ages now access the web for information and communication. Age, income, education, though still impediments to technology use in some parts of the world, are declining in influence. The Internet, web and cell phone technology have opened up accessibility across the world, with different patterns of usage depending on prevailing business models, software penetration, political influences, cultural and personal preferences. For many living in the western world bandwidth is no longer a big issue, but for even more people in poor, remote parts of the world it is still a limitation. Therefore, software developers still need to provide low-bandwidth, reliable technology. This means that the option to access text is needed despite advances in graphics, photography, and video computer-mediated communication.

- *Open source software development.* Open source software development makes it easier for technology developers to build seamless software platforms in which users can move from synchronous to asynchronous communication modes, to rating/personal preference systems, to blogs, the web and back again without needing to learn completely new interfaces; look and feel is carried across applications within a single platform.

- *A flat world.* Communication across the world is easier, and more fun than even five years ago. As Thomas Friedman points out, *the world is flat* or at least flatter (Friedman, 2005). Time and space are no longer barriers to global business and communications practices. Instead, time differences and cultural differences are the key challenges to smooth communication and productive, harmonious collaboration. Other factors also come into play, such as serendipitous meetings for those in close enough proximity and it is often an advantage to know the personal behavior patterns of one's colleagues. As Olson and Olson (2000) pointed out from the findings of a large number of collaborative projects, distance does matter. Other factors too come into play; certain locations are attractive, and communes of like-minded people tend to come together, such as artists in New York, Paris and London, and technology entrepreneurs in Silicon Valley, Taipei and Tokyo. In this respect, there are creative peaks in the flat world (Florida, 2005).

- *Users become producers and organizers.* The collective power of users to produce and organize themselves should never be overlooked. Jimmy Wales set out with a band of followers to make all the knowledge in the world available to all the world's people by creating Wikipedia (Wales, 2006). Less than five years later almost 1.4 million entries exist in English with growth in many different languages, supported by an annual conference in the USA known as Wikimania, that was attended by some 400 people in August 2006. Almost all these participants paid for themselves and are ardent Wikipedia contributors and users. This is perhaps the single biggest and most surprising trend in the social use of the Internet. Who would have imagined 10 years ago, or even five years ago that large numbers of people would spend hours creating and editing entries for an encyclopedia without receiving payment. Today's Internet and software applications are fueling and being fueled by the *power of the people.* Not surprisingly this trend is coupled with a move in which hierarchical governance structures, professional publishing, and media control, are being replaced by flatter, less hierarchical structures that emerge from within participant groups rather than being created and validated externally by professional bodies. Anyone can try to be a star on American Idol, or to make and show a film on YouTube. You don't have to be a *New York Times* journalist to write a political blog, or an acknowledged literary figure to write a critique on Amazon. Fame is there to be seized if you are prepared to work for it, and have talent and a little luck. Even models of government are starting to change. For example, at a recent meeting of the Aspen Institute, members of that think-tank recognized that *hard power* diplomacy is giving way to *soft power* diplomacy (Kalathil, 2005). In other words, hierarchical, controlled forms of diplomacy are being replaced by flat, networked structures. In summary these changes are marked by an increased emphasis on dialog and relationship building that pays greater attention to the needs and cultures of others, by being networked and responsive to the majority of people. The table below summarizes these changes.

Hard power old diplomacy	Soft power new diplomacy
Monolog	Dialog
Mission driven	Mission driven, market-savvy
About us	About them
Bilateral	Bi- & multilateral
Managing images	Building relationships
Stove-piped	Coordinated and networked
Reactive	Proactive

With these new trends in mind, and paying particular attention to the notion of users as producers and organizers, in the next section I provide a brief survey of some of the ways that today's Internet software is being designed and used to support universal usability and access.

19.3 **Applications and Examples**

In our recent text (Preece *et al.*, 2007) we define usability in terms of how useful, how efficient, how effective and how safe a software application is to use; how easy it is to learn and remember; and how satisfying the experience of using it is for users. I have also pointed out the importance of taking sociability into account as well as usability when developing software for communities or for general social usage (Preece, 2000). Sociability is concerned with the social interactions among people via information and communications technology. More specifically, it focuses on:

- *People's* individual and social characteristics, particularly those of social psychology, such as the need for empathy, trust, identity, and reputation; and social dynamics, such as the way people network, develop and show reciprocity, and how social capital is built (Preece, 1999).
- The *purposes* for which people come together and communicate, which may include: getting and giving information and support, connecting with others; collaborating to produce something, and coordinating activities.
- The *policies* that guide social behavior can be broad, ranging from cultural norms to rules established by a community or formal policies backed by law.

As I look toward the future, I am sure that software designers will pay even more attention to sociability. The HCI community has a good grasp of usability; we have been discussing it for over 30 years and it has been clearly documented (e.g. Shneiderman, 1986), but less is understood about the relationship of sociability to design (Preece, 2000). This is a problem that those working on universal usability may wish to address; particularly as many new applications provide opportunities for social interactions. For example, YouTube allows people across the world to share their videos. Flickr, though quite different in design, look, and feel, provides a similar opportunity for those wanting to display and exchange photographs, and Del.icio.us enables people to add annotations to text and video.

Technology alone is not enough, community thrives on empathy and trust, supporting new and old friendships, and communicating personal information. The developers of Myspace, a social space for students, understood how to engage college students. Using this software, students can provide information about themselves that signals their presence to old friends and attracts new ones. Each person then decides with whom they will communicate.

Getting and giving information and support can be done via combinations of technologies depending on the kind of experience users want. For example, in an online community for older adult users three types of communications technology were available: voice chat, bulletin board, and instant messaging (Xie, 2007). An ethnographic study revealed that technology choice was closely associated with the kind of communication experience the users sought. Voice chat became the medium for entertainment, which frequently took the form of karaoke with much singing and laughing. The bulletin board mostly supported serious, thoughtful, information exchange about health issues, social services, and other topics of interest to the older adults. When communication became intimate instant messaging was the medium of choice.

Thomas Jefferson's famous comment: *I cannot live without books* speaks to many of us. Yet there are millions of people in the world who do not have access to books. Digital libraries such as the Greenstone digital library (described in Chapter 18) and the International Children's Digital Library (Chapter 2) are examples of how digital technology can be harnessed to bring books to underprivileged people. These technologies provide translation facilities so that users can read the books in their chosen language. Communities, like the International Children's Digital Library community (Komlodi *et al.*, in press) develop around the collection. Of course, in the case of children's communities, safety online is an issue, so the communities tend not to be open, and instead are used as part of a school activity or under parental supervision. Personal blogs also provide a focus for community.

Collaborating to produce something requires expertise and time. Increasingly, people who don't know each other and probably will never meet are getting together online to create software and to help others. This behavior is not typical in online communities (Nonnecke and Preece, 2000; Preece *et al.*, 2004). It seems to mark a new trend, defying the notion of social dilemma (Axelrod, 1984) associated with the Internet (Smith and Kollock, 1999). This change in behavior seems to result from people's desire for fame and community participation.

Even unsophisticated ways of acknowledging participants' contributions provide incentives. Slashdot.com simply reports the names of the people who contribute the largest number of messages. Amazon.com recognizes its super reviewers, people who contribute many reviews. Other communities have more sophisticated systems for rating contributions; e-Bay uses a star system to allow purchasers to rate vendors' services. People appear to want to interact with others and to contribute to a community of people who are building something.

The birth of Wikipedia demonstrated the power of collective action to produce an artifact, follow a dream, and develop a community. Founded in 2003 by entrepreneur Jimmy Wales, this passionate community has developed an online encyclopedia with over 1.4 million articles in English. Spin-off encyclopedias and communities also exist in nine other languages, the next biggest being the German encyclopedia with just fewer than half a million articles. Even though the efficacy of some of the entries is questioned and compared with Britannica, Wikipedia is prominent on the Internet and regularly returned by Google searches. So what motivates participants to spend hours working on their entries, editing, re-editing, and arguing a point, all without payment and for only modest recognition? Is it passion about a particular topic? Is it simply being part of a large world-movement that challenges traditional social structures and dares to create its own encyclopedia? These reasons may draw in some people. Others revel in the spirit of community. Looking beneath the surface reveals that the majority of work is done by a few thousand people, most of whom know or know of each other. They know who is reliable, who writes well, who knows what, and through this grass-roots knowledge their community has developed social norms that guide its behavior.

A different kind of social interaction is provided by Second Life, a 3-D world created in 2003 that has over 1.2 million participants from around the world. Participants in Second World are creating all kinds of things, from avatars to represent themselves, to buildings, to wild and weird fantasy objects that they own and can sell for lindens (Second Life's currency) or for real money on e-Bay.

These examples seem to signal a new era among some Internet participants, one that is more concerned with contributing and collaborating than taking. For sure, there is still a dark side, identity theft, pornography, hate-groups, breaches in privacy and security are realities, but social interaction supported by creative social software developers is here, and it can and does go hand-in-hand with a desire for universal usability.

19.4 Looking to the Future: Encouraging Universal Usability by Empowering Communities

Anthropologist Margaret Mead (1901–1978) commented that we should *never doubt that a small group of thoughtful, committed citizens can change the world. Indeed, it is the only thing that ever has*. The Internet provides the power for a small group of committed citizens to engage millions of others in ways that were not previously possible. So as we look toward the future we can imagine more commitment for universal usability. The same people who so honorably want to make information available to all or design open source software will likely, with a little provocation, start to question what needs to be done to make that information and software universally usable rather than just universally available. What is needed to cause this momentum? In this age of technology billionaires perhaps one of them will make this his or her dream.

Another possibility is that powerful legislation could help to make software more accessible, perhaps by extending laws such as Section 508 of the Rehabilitation Act and the Americans with Disabilities Act (ADA) in the United States so that their coverage is broader. The former Act requires government web sites to be accessible to those with hearing, sight, or physical disabilities, while the latter applies to private companies, groups, and nonprofit organizations, but it is not clear if it applies to the web. Both Acts need to cover access issues as well as other aspects of universal usability. For example, could we have a universal usability act that addresses the needs of older adults, children, those with limited education and low resources? As the Internet 'shrinks our world' imagine the impact of such thinking worldwide. Already search engines support language translation. What they do not do is support cross-cultural differences. Shouldn't universal usability be sensitive to culture? American culture tends to be individualistic; it encourages individuals to seek reward for themselves rather than for their company or community. In contrast, Japanese culture is traditionally collectivist, in that the success of the corporation or group is of paramount importance (Hall, 1981; Hofstede, 1991). Other cultural differences include how people use body language and represent their identity on- and offline. Recent work in which children in Mexico and the USA used the Internet to communicate about the books they read revealed, for example, that each group had strong preconceived notions about the other and that these stereotypes were often not accurate (Komlodi *et al.*, in press).

As technology use increases across the human lifecycle, more attention to older adults, children, and people with disabilities is needed. Older adults are using technology more (e.g. Xie, 2007), particularly those in their 50s and 60s. Technology for children is also receiving more attention from developers to meet the market's demand for new kinds of computerized toys. However, as Clarke and Lazar (2005) and Evers *et al.* (2005) point out, universal usability is not a widely applied concept; particularly for children with disabilities. Children with Down Syndrome, for example, can benefit from applications that stimulate their creativity, while those with diabetes can learn more about their disease and how to stay healthy by playing online games (Clarke and Lazar, 2005). Designers of technology for partially sighted children sometimes fail to realize that these children can use them more effectively if animation is kept to a minimum. Displays with things that jump around are more difficult for these children to use (Evers *et al.*, 2005).

This discussion has only touched upon some of the many steps that can be taken to make systems more universally usable. The first step in promoting universal usability is to raise people's consciousness about the issues. It is well known that software designs that take account of universal usability help everyone not just the group of people for whom they were designed. Universal usability can be thought of as a form of social capital. More usable software will unite families, communities, and society. The elegant, minimalist design of the Google search engine demonstrates that simplicity and usability can go hand-in-hand with developing popular software that makes billions of dollars for its developers.

19.5 **Some Conclusions**

As a wise British politician once said: *It is a mistake to look too far ahead. The chain of destiny can only be grasped one link at a time* (Sir Winston Churchill, 1874–1965). It is an even bigger mistake to predict the future of technology, though there is one thing we can be sure about – the future holds many surprises, just as the past did. Who would ever have imagined that millions of people would work for free connected by an invisible digital network or that generations would be marked as much by their technology use as by their dress and choice of music; or that people would propose medical solutions to their doctors thus changing the power balance in doctor–patient relationships; or that diplomacy as we know it would come under question. Just as our ancestors could not conceive of a horseless carriage, or light being available 24 hours a day, there will be inventions that go beyond the imagination of today's citizens. These may be as radical socially as they are technologically brilliant. Howard, Rheingold was quick to observe and predict the growing impact of cell phone technology for smart mobs (Rheingold, 2002). He saw political activists in Thailand marshal and direct supporters, and fisherman in India decide where to land their catch to get the day's best price. Shneiderman (2003) predicts a worldwide med in which doctors, anywhere in the world, can obtain a patient's record in a matter of seconds, and a 'data-needle' can be found in a vast 'data-haystack' using powerful visualization tools that may help us to spot terrorist plots, identify gene defects, and improve the market performance of companies.

Universal usability requires that both hardware and software are universally accessible and that the population at large, regardless of income, education, cognitive and physical characteristics can use it. In today's world of social interaction software designers must strive to go beyond universal usability for individuals to build software that is universally usable by communities and societies. This means that they must understand how to design to support empathy, trust, reciprocity, and social capital development. It is often not enough to provide a language translation, culture must also be understood, so that concepts are communicated in culturally and socially meaningful and acceptable ways. As the authors in this book demonstrate, universal usability has come a long way, but there is still more to do. The road ahead leads beyond universal usability, our next goal must be to use technology to support universal sociability.

Acknowledgments

I warmly thank Jonathan Lazar for offering me the opportunity to contribute this chapter and for his insightful comments on drafts. My colleague and partner, Ben Shneiderman, has broadened my intellectual horizons by sharing his vision and passion for universal usability over the years. Ben is a tireless advocate for universal usability. I thank him for his support and encouragement.

References

Axelrod, R. (1984) *The Evolution of Cooperation,* Basic Books, New York.

Clarke, J. and Lazar, J. (2005) Website usability issues in children and children with disabilities. *Proceedings of HCI International,* Las Vegas, USA.

Ellis, C.A., Gibbs, S.J. and Rein, G.L. (1991) Groupware: some issues and experiences. *Communications of the ACM,* **34**(1), 680–689.

Evers, V., Luteijn, C., Damsma, P. and Norgaard, J. (2005) Beyond W3C guidelines: building a virtual community for blind and seeing children. *Proceedings of HCI International,* Las Vegas, USA.

Florida, R. (2005) *Flight of the Creative Class.* Harvard Business Press, New York.

Fogg, B.J. (2003) Prominence-interpretation theory: explaining how people assess credibility online. *Conference on Human Factors in Computing Systems, CHI '03 extended abstracts on human factors in computing systems,* Fort Lauderdale, FL, pp. 722–723.

Friedman, T. (2005) *The World is Flat: A Brief History of the Twenty-First Century.* Farrar, Straus and Giroux, New York.

Hall, E.T. (1981) *The Silent Language.* Anchor Books, New York.

Hofstede, G. (1991) *Cultures and Organizations: Software of the Mind.* McGraw-Hill, London.

Internet Credibility and the User (2006) `http://projects.ischool. washington.edu/credibility/` (accessed November 24, 2006).

Kalathil, S. (2005) *Soft Power, Hard Issues*. Report of the Aspen Institute Forum on Communications and Society and the Roundtable on Public Diplomacy and the Middle East.

Komlodi, A. *et al.* (in press). Evaluating a cross-cultural children's online book community: lessons learned for sociability, usability and cultural exchange. *Interactive Computers*.

Nonnecke, B. and Preece, J. (2000) Lurker demographics: counting the silent. *Proceedings of CHI'2000,* Hague, The Netherlands, pp. 73–80.

Olson, J. and Olson, G. (2000) Distance matters. *Human–Computer Interaction,* Lawrence Erlbaum Associates, **15**, pp. 139–178.

Preece, J. (1999) Empathic communities: balancing emotional and factual communication. *Interactive Computers,* **12**(1), 63–77.

Preece, J. (2000) *Online Communities: Designing Usability, Supporting Sociability*. John Wiley & Sons, Chichester, UK.

Preece, J., Nonnecke, B. and Andrews, D. (2004) The top 5 reasons for lurking: improving community experiences for everyone. *Computers and Human Behavior,* **20**(2), 201–223.

Preece, J., Rogers, Y. and Sharp, H. (2007) *Interaction Design: Beyond Human-Computer Interaction*. John Wiley & Sons, New York.

Rheingold, H. (2002) *Smart Mobs: The Next Social Revolution*. Perseus Publishing, New Year.

Shneiderman, B. (1986) *Designing the User Interface: Strategies for Effective Human-Computer Interaction* (2nd edn (1992), 3rd edn (1998), 4th edn (2005)). Addison-Wesley, Reading, MA.

Shneiderman, B. (2000) Universal usability: pushing human-computer interaction research to empower every citizen. *Communications of the ACM,* **43**(5), 84–91.

Shneiderman, B. (2003) *Leonardo's Laptop: Human Needs and the New Computing Technologies* MIT Press, Cambridge, MA.

Smith, M.A. and Kollock, P. (1999) *Communities in Cyberspace*. London, Routledge.

Wales, J. (2006) `http://en.wikipedia.org/wiki/Jimbo_Wales` (accessed November 24, 2006).

Xie, B. (2006) *Growing Older in the Information Age: Civic Engagement, Social Relationships, and Well-being of Older Internet Users in China and the United States*. Unpublished dissertation, Rensselaer Polytechnic Institute, Troy, New York.

Index